T0191640

Lecture Notes in Computer Science   12938

Zhe Liu · Fan Wu · Sajal K. Das (Eds.)

Wireless Algorithms, Systems, and Applications

16th International Conference, WASA 2021
Nanjing, China, June 25–27, 2021
Proceedings, Part II

 Springer

Editors
Zhe Liu
Nanjing University of Aeronautics
and Astronautics
Nanjing, China

Fan Wu
Shanghai Jiao Tong University
Shanghai, China

Sajal K. Das
Missouri University of Science
and Technology
Rolla, MO, USA

ISSN 0302-9743   ISSN 1611-3349   (electronic)
Lecture Notes in Computer Science
ISBN 978-3-030-86129-2   ISBN 978-3-030-86130-8   (eBook)
https://doi.org/10.1007/978-3-030-86130-8

LNCS Sublibrary: SL1 – Theoretical Computer Science and General Issues

This Springer imprint is published by the registered company Springer Nature Switzerland AG
The registered company address is: Gewerbestrasse 11, 6330 Cham, Switzerland

Preface

The 16th International Conference on Wireless Algorithms, Systems, and Applications WASA 2021 and its workshops was held in Nanjing Dongjiao State Guest House during June 25–27, 2021. The conference was hosted by the Nanjing University of Aeronautics and Astronautics and co-organized by the Beijing University of Posts and Telecommunications, Tsinghua University, Southeast University, Nanjing University, Hohai University, Shandong University, and the Collaborative Innovation Center of Novel Software Technology and Industrialization. WASA is an international conference on algorithms, systems, and applications of wireless networks. WASA is designed to be a forum for theoreticians, system and application designers, protocol developers, and practitioners to discuss and express their views on the current trends, challenges, and state-of-the-art solutions related to various issues in wireless networks. Topics of interests include, but are not limited to, effective and efficient state-of-the-art algorithm design and analysis, reliable and secure system development and implementations, experimental study and testbed validation, and new application exploration in wireless networks.

The conference received 315 submissions. Each submission was reviewed by at least three Program Committee members or external reviewers. The Program Committee accepted 97 full papers and 63 workshop papers which were included in the conference program. The Program Committee also selected the three best papers: "Deep Reinforcement Learning Based Intelligent Job Batching in Industrial Internet of Things" by Chengling Jiang, Zihui Luo, Liang Liu, and Xiaolong Zheng, "A Robust IoT Device Identification Method with Unknown Traffic Detection" by Xiao Hu, Hong Li, Zhiqiang Shi, Nan Yu, Hongsong Zhu, and Limin Sun, and "TS-Net: Device-free Action Recognition with Cross-modal Learning" by Biyun Sheng, Linqing Gui, and Fu Xiao.

We thank the Program Committee members and the external reviewers for their hard work in reviewing the submissions. We thank the Organizing Committee and all volunteers from the Nanjing University of Aeronautics and Astronautics for their time and effort dedicated to arranging the conference.

July 2021

Zhe Liu
Fan Wu
Sajal K. Das

Organization

General Co-chairs

Bing Chen   Nanjing University of Aeronautics and Astronautics, China
Huadong Ma   Beijing University of Posts and Telecommunications, China
Junzhou Luo   Southeast University, China
Ke Xu   Tsinghua University, China

Program Co-chairs

Zhe Liu   Nanjing University of Aeronautics and Astronautics, China
Fan Wu   Shanghai Jiao Tong University, China
Sajal K. Das   Missouri University of Science and Technology, USA

Local Co-chairs

Baoliu Ye   Nanjing University, China
Fu Xiao   Nanjing University of Posts and Telecommunications, China
Shuai Wang   Southeast University, China
Kun Zhu   Nanjing University of Aeronautics and Astronautics, China

Web Co-chairs

Yanchao Zhao   Nanjing University of Aeronautics and Astronautics, China
Bin Tang   Hohai University, China

Organizing Co-chairs

Lei Xie   Nanjing University, China
Liming Fang   Nanjing University of Aeronautics and Astronautics, China

Publicity Co-chairs

Haipeng Dai   Nanjing University, China
Chi (Harold) Liu   Beijing Institute of Technology, China

| Zhibo Wang | Zhejiang University, China |
| Chenren Xu | Peking University, China |

Publication Co-chairs

| Weizhi Meng | Technical University of Denmark, Denmark |
| Junlong Zhou | Nanjing University of Science and Technology, China |

Steering Committee

Xiuzhen Cheng	American University of Sharjah, UAE
Zhipeng Cai	Georgia State University, USA
Jiannong Cao	Hong Kong Polytechnic University, Hong Kong, China
Ness Shroff	Ohio State University, USA
Wei Zhao	University of Macau, China
PengJun Wan	Illinois Institute of Technology, USA
Ty Znati	University of Pittsburgh, USA
Xinbing Wang	Shanghai Jiao Tong University, China

Technical Program Committee

Ran Bi	Dalian University of Technology, China
Edoardo Biagioni	University of Hawaii at Manoa, USA
Salim Bitam	University of Biskra, Algeria
Azzedine Boukerche	University of Ottawa, Canada
Zhipeng Cai	Georgia State University, USA
Srinivas Chakravarthi Thandu	Amazon, USA
Sriram Chellappan	University of South Florida, USA
Quan Chen	Guangdong University of Technology, China
Xianfu Chen	VTT Technical Research Centre of Finland, Finland
Xu Chen	Sun Yat-sen University, China
Songqing Chen	George Mason University, USA
Soufiene Djahel	Manchester Metropolitan University, UK
Yingfei Dong	University of Hawaii, USA
Zhuojun Duan	James Madison University, USA
Luca Foschini	University of Bologna, Italy
Jing Gao	Dalian University of Technology, China
Xiaofeng Gao	Shanghai Jiao Tong University, China
Jidong Ge	Nanjing University, China
Chunpeng Ge	Nanjing University of Aeronautics and Astronautics, China
Daniel Graham	University of Virginia, USA
Ning Gu	Fudan University, China
Deke Guo	National University of Defense Technology, China
Bin Guo	Northwestern Polytechnical University, China

Meng Han	Kennesaw State University, USA
Suining He	University of Connecticut, USA
Zaobo He	Miami University, USA
Pengfei Hu	Shandong University, China
Yan Huang	Kennesaw State University, USA
Yan Huo	Beijing Jiaotong University, China
Holger Karl	University of Paderborn, Germany
Donghyun Kim	Kennesaw State University, USA
Hwangnam Kim	Korea University, South Korea
Bharath Kumar Samanthula	Montclair State University, USA
Abderrahmane Lakas	UAE University, UAE
Sanghwan Lee	Kookmin University, South Korea
Feng Li	Shandong University, China
Feng Li	Indiana University-Purdue University Indianapolis, USA
Ruinian Li	Bowling Green State University, USA
Wei Li	Georgia State University, USA
Zhenhua Li	Tsinghua University, China
Zhetao Li	Xiangtan University, China
Peng Li	University of Aizu, Japan
Qi Li	Tsinghua University, China
Yaguang Lin	Shaanxi Normal University, China
Zhen Ling	Southeast University, China
Weimo Liu	George Washington University, USA
Jia Liu	Nanjing University, China
Fangming Liu	Huazhong University of Science and Technology, China
Liang Liu	Beijing University of Posts and Telecommunications, China
Hongbin Luo	Beihang University, China
Jun Luo	Nanyang Technological University, Singapore
Liran Ma	Texas Christian University, USA
Jian Mao	Beihang University, China
Bo Mei	Texas Christian University, USA
Hung Nguyen	Carnegie Mellon University, USA
Pasquale Pace	University of Calabria, Italy
Claudio Palazzi	University of Padova, Italy
Junjie Pang	Qingdao University, China
Javier Parra-Arnau	University of Ottawa, Canada
Tie Qiu	Tianjin University, China
Ruben Rios	University of Malaga, Spain
Kazuya Sakai	Tokyo Metropolitan University, Japan
Omar Sami Oubbati	University of Laghouat, Algeria
Kewei Sha	University of Houston - Clear Lake, USA
Hao Sheng	Beihang University, China
Bo Sheng	University of Massachusetts Boston, USA

Contents – Part II

Data Center Networks and Cloud Computing

Privacy-Aware Computing

Internet of Vehicles

Visual Computing for IoT

Mobile Ad-Hoc Networks

Scheduling and Optimization II

Scheduling of Mobile Charger with Multiple Antennas

Lanlan Li[1,2]([✉]), Yue Zhao[1], Haipeng Dai[1], Xiaoyu Wang[1], and Guihai Chen[1]

[1] State Key Laboratory for Novel Software Technology, Nanjing University, Nanjing, Jiangsu, China
{lanlanli,zhaoyue1996,xiaoyuwang}@smail.nju.edu.cn,
{haipengdai,gchen}@nju.edu.cn
[2] Department of Information Engineering, Nanhang Jincheng College, Nanjing, Jiangsu, China

Abstract. Wireless Power Transfer (WPT) technology has been developed rapidly and widely applied to numerous applications for its convenience and reliability. In this paper, we study the issue of Scheduling mobIle charGer with Mutiple Antennas (SIGMA), *i.e.*, determining the stopping positions and orientations of antennas for mobile charger (MC) in a charging tour to maximize the overall received energy of sensors while guaranteeing that the energy capacity of MC is not exhausted. To address the SIGMA problem, we first partition charging field into many subareas by drawing some concentric sectors with different radiuses for each sensors. Second, we propose a greedy method named stopping strategy extraction algorithm to determine the orientations of antennas for MC at a randomly selected stopping point in each subarea. Third, we prove the submodularity of our objective function, and propose an efficient cost-benefit approximation algorithm to obtain the final result from all the candidate stopping positions and orientations of MC. Finally, we conduct simulations to appraise the performance of our proposed algorithm. The results show that our algorithm outperforms comparison algorithms by at least 23.1%.

Keywords: Wireless power transfer · Wireless rechargeable sensor networks · Directional charging · Multiple antennas

1 Introduction

Due to its notable characteristics of convenience and reliability, Wireless Power Transfer (WPT) technology has flourished in recent years and has already been applied to a wide range of applications, including wireless identification and sensing platform (WISP), mobile phones and portable smart devices, wireless rechargeable sensor networks, electric/hybrid vehicles, medical apparatuses, *etc.*. According to a report, the global wireless charging market is expected to reach a value of US\$15 billion in 2024 with a compound annual growth rate of 12% [1].

© Springer Nature Switzerland AG 2021
Z. Liu et al. (Eds.): WASA 2021, LNCS 12938, pp. 3–17, 2021.
https://doi.org/10.1007/978-3-030-86130-8_1

In order to achieve efficient transmission of power, high-gain directional antennas are often adopted in wireless charging networks. Omni-directional antennas broadcast power towards all directions and lead to power attenuating rapidly with distance, by contrast, the usage of directional antenna at the power transmitter/receiver can make the transmission power focus on a narrow beam to prevent great waste of energy, thus enhance the capacity and performance of network as well as reduce the interference from unwanted sources [2,3]. Additionally, more than one antennas are equipped at the power transmitter/receiver, the network would have better performance in terms of transmission efficiency or link reliability. When charger with multiple antennas are deployed in wireless charging network, it has the possibility to transmit power simultaneously towards more directions and the flexibility to select what receivers to schedule for reception in the network [4].

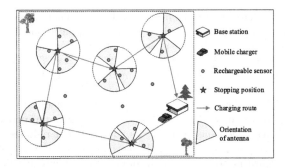

Fig. 1. A diagram of scheduling mobile charger with multiple antennas

In this paper, we investigate the problem of Scheduling mobIle charGer with Mutiple Antennas (SIGMA) with the optimization objective of maximizing the overall energy received by sensors through devising a closed charging tour of mobile charger (MC). As shown in Fig. 1, a MC travels and stops at some stopping positions to replenish energy for its surrounding rechargeable sensors to sustain network perpetual operations. Our aim is to determine all the stopping positions and orientations of antennas for MC to maximize the overall received energy of sensors in a charging tour, meanwhile guarantee that the energy consumption of MC for completing the tour does not exceed the energy capacity of MC. Although there exist lots of works [9–12] focusing on the problem of scheduling mobile charger, none of them explore the scheduling of mobile charger with multiple antennas, *i.e.*, consider the stopping positions and orientations of multiple antennas for MC simultaneously. Therefore, no study can be adapted to address our problem.

There are two main technical challenges when addressing our SIGMA problem. The first challenge is that both the stopping positions and antennas' orientations of MC are continuous, thus there exists an infinite search space in our problem. The second challenge is that scheduling the charging tour of MC with limited capacity budget is a variant of the classic Traveling Salesman Problem (TSP), which is NP-hard.

To address the first challenge, we discretize the charging field into many subareas by drawing some concentric sectors with different radiuses in each sensor's power receiving sector, thus the charging power from any stopping points for omnidirectional charger in a subarea to its surrounding sensors is constant after approximating actual charging power with piecewise constant function. Further, considering the infinity of orientations for MC with multiple antennas, we propose a greedy method named stopping strategy extraction algorithm to determine the antennas' orientation of MC at a randomly selected stopping point in each subarea. To address the second challenge, we prove the submodularity of our objective function, then propose an efficient cost-benefit approximation algorithm, joint with using the nearest neighbour rule to approximate the charging tour, to obtain the final result from all the candidate stopping positions and orientations of MC.

We conduct extensive simulations to evaluate the performance of our proposed algorithm. Our simulation results show that in terms of overall received energy of sensors, our algorithm outperforms comparison algorithms by at least 23.1%.

2   Related Work

Wireless Charger Placement Problem. There exist many research works [5–8] studying on wireless charger placement problem. However, most existing works consider the placement problem for stationary charger which is fixed at a position to replenish energy for sensors. It is not applicable for our mobile charging problem. For example, Dai et al. [6] studied the wireless placement problem to maximize the overall expected charging utility for all points. Yu et al. [8] explored the issue of maximizing the overall charging utility by determining the placement position and orientation angle for each charger under connectivity constraint for wireless charger.

Mobile Charger Scheduling Problem. A lot of research works [9–12] explore scheduling problem of mobile charger, but none of them take into consideration the scheduling of mobile charger with multiple antennas. Chen et al. [10] focused on charging path planing to maximize the number of nodes charged within a fixed time horizon and designed a quasi-polynomial time algorithm that achieved poly-logarithmic approximation to the optimal charging path. Lin et al. [11] proposed a pragmatic energy transfer model and investigated minimizing charging delay by developing a method of charging power discretization and adopting the K-means clustering algorithm.

3   Problem Statement

3.1   Network Model and Charging Model

Suppose there are N stationary rechargeable sensors $O = \{o_1, ..., o_N\}$ located in a 2D plane Ω, and the required charging energy of sensor o_j is $E_j(E_j \geq 0)$. The locations and orientation of each sensor in the network can be known beforehand using techniques such as [13]. A mobile charger (MC), with limited energy capacity E_{mc}, starts from the service station v_0, travels and stops at some positions to charge its surrounding sensors, and finally returns to the depot v_0 after finishing the charging tour. The MC is outfitted with multiple directional antennas to launch electromagnetic waves towards different directions, thus charging more sensors. Suppose that the relative orientations of multiple directional antennas of the MC is unfixed, namely, the angle between any two antennas' orientations $< \theta^{l_1}, \theta^{l_2} >$ for the MC is a variable where $l_1, l_2 \in \{1, 2, ..., L\}$ and L is the number of directional antennas for the MC.

The MC with L directional antennas can be regarded as L single directional antenna chargers located at the same position. For each antenna's orientation of MC, we adopt the practical directional charging model proposed in [6,14], whose power transferring area of MC and power receiving area of rechargeable sensor are both modeled as sectors, further, one sensor receives nonnegligible power from MC if and only if they are just located in the coverage area of each other. For brevity, we use s_i to denote the i-th stopping position of MC during a charging tour. The charging power received by sensor o_j from the l-th orientation of MC at the i-th stopping position during charging tour can be given by

$$P(s_i, \theta_i^l, o_j, \phi_j) = \begin{cases} \frac{\alpha}{(\|s_i o_j\| + \beta)^2}, & 0 \leq \|s_i o_j\| \leq D, \\ & \overrightarrow{o_j s_i} \cdot \overrightarrow{r_{\phi_j}} - \|o_j s_i\| \cos(A_o/2) \geq 0, \\ & \text{and } \overrightarrow{s_i o_j} \cdot \overrightarrow{r_{\theta_i^l}} - \|s_i o_j\| \cos(A_s/2) \geq 0. \\ 0, & \text{otherwise,} \end{cases} \tag{1}$$

where α and β are two constants determined by hardware parameters as well as the surrounding environment, $\|s_i o_j\|$ is the distance between s_i and o_j, D is the charging radius of MC, A_s is the charging angle for each antenna of MC, A_o is the receiving angle of sensor, $\overrightarrow{r_{\phi_j}}$ is the unit vector denoting the orientation of sensor o_j, and $\overrightarrow{r_{\theta_i^l}}$ is for the l-th antenna's orientation of MC at the i-th stopping position. We list main notations in Table 1.

3.2   Energy Consumption Model

The energy consumed by MC in completing a charging tour consists of two parts: the traveling energy cost and charging energy cost. For the stopping points set S, the traveling energy cost of MC is

$$E_{travel} = \sum_{d \in C^{TSP}(S)} (q \cdot d), \tag{2}$$

where q is the energy consumption rate per unit length and $C^{TSP}(S)$ is a closed traveling tour that starts and ends at the depot v_0, meanwhile goes through all the stopping points in S.

Table 1. Notations

Symbol	Meaning	Symbol	Meaning
MC	Mobile Charger	E_{mc}	Battery capacity of MC
BS	Base Station	L	Number of MC's directional antennas
N	Number of sensors	E_j	Required charging energy of sensor j
o_j	Sensor j	s_i	The i-th stopping position for MC
S	Stopping positions set of MC during charging tour	O_i	Set of sensors covered by MC at the i-th stopping position
q	Energy consumption rate of MC per unit length for traveling	λ	Energy consumption rate of MC per unit time for charging
A_o	Receiving angle of sensor	E_{travel}	Traveling energy consumption of MC
A_s	Charging angle for each antenna of MC	E_{charge}	Charging energy consumption of MC
ϕ_j	Orientation of sensor o_j	E_{cost}	Overall energy consumption of MC
t_i	Stay time of MC at the i-th stopping position	θ_i^l	Orientation of the l-th antenna of MC at the i-th stopping position

For the i-th stopping point of MC, the stay time is determined by replenishing the required power for all the covered sensors at the point. Suppose O_i and t_i denote the covered sensors set and the stay time of MC at the i-th stopping point, respectively, we have

$$t_i = \underset{o_j \in O_i}{Max}(E_j / \sum_{k=1}^{L} P(s_i, \theta_i^k, o_j, \phi_j)). \qquad (3)$$

Then the charging cost of MC is

$$E_{charge} = \sum_{i=1}^{|S|} (\lambda \cdot t_i), \qquad (4)$$

where λ is the energy consumption rate per unit time and $|S|$ is the number of stopping points during the whole tour.

Combining the consumed energy on traveling and charging during the whole closed tour, the total energy cost of MC can be expressed as

$$E_{cost} = E_{travel} + E_{charge} = \sum_{d \in C^{TSP}(S)} (q \cdot d) + \sum_{i=1}^{|S|} (\lambda \cdot t_i). \qquad (5)$$

3.3   Problem Formulation

Based on the aforementioned definitions and models, Our objective is to determine the MC's stopping positions and corresponding orientations of antennas at each position to maximize the overall energy received by sensors while guaranteeing that the energy capacity of MC is not exhausted during the whole charging tour. Therefore we can formulate the problem of Scheduling mobIle charGer with Mutiple Antennas (SIGMA) problem as

$$\textbf{(SIGMA)} \quad \max \quad \sum_{i=1}^{|S|} \sum_{o_j \in O_i} (E_j \cdot h_j) \tag{6}$$

$$s.t. \quad E_{cost} \leq E_{mc} \tag{7}$$

$$h_j \in \{0, 1\}, \quad (j = 1, \dots, N). \tag{8}$$

In the above formulation, binary variable h_j is used to denote whether sensor o_j is covered by MC repetitively at different stopping positions or not. Variable h_j is initialized to value 1. When sensor o_j, which has been charged by MC at one stopping position, is covered by MC again at another different stopping position, h_j would be set to 0. It means that duplicated covering a sensor is useless. Note that S is a variable that should be optimized to find all the stopping positions of MC during a charging tour and corresponding orientations of antennas at each stopping point. Constraint (7) guarantees that the total energy consumption during a closed charging tour will not exceed the MC's capacity.

4   Solution

In this section, we present our algorithm to address the SIGMA problem. Generally, the SIGMA algorithm consists of three processes: *Area discretization*, *Stopping strategy extraction*, and *Cost-benefit approximation algorithm*. For *Area discretization* process, the 2D area is partitioned into many subareas by drawing K concentric sectors with different radiuses for each sensor and the charging power received by sensors are approximated by using piecewise constant function. For *Stopping strategy extraction* process, we randomly select a point as MC's stopping position in each subarea, then determine the orientations for all the antennas of MC one by one using greedy method. For *Cost-benefit approximation algorithm* process, only part of stopping positions and corresponding orientations of MC are selected using a heuristic method from all the obtained ones to maximize the overall energy received by sensors under capacity constraint of MC.

4.1   Area Discretization

In this subsection, our goal is to limit the number of stopping positions of MC. Let $P(d)$ denote the power received by a sensor from a position where MC stays with distance d, $P(d) = \frac{\alpha}{(d+\beta)^2}$ if sensor and MC are just located in the coverage area of each other, otherwise $P(d) = 0$.

We use a piecewise constant function $\widetilde{P}(d)$ to approximate the charging power function $P(d)$. $\widetilde{P}(d)$ is defined as

$$\widetilde{P}(d) = \begin{cases} P(\ell(1)), & d = \ell(0), \\ P(\ell(k)), & \ell(k-1) < d \le \ell(k) \ (k = 1, ...K), \\ 0, & d > \ell(K), \end{cases}$$

where $\ell(0) = 0$, $\ell(K) = D$. To bound the approximation error, we set $\ell(k) = \beta((1+\epsilon)^{k/2} - 1)(k = 1, ..., K-1)$, where ϵ is a pre-specified tiny positive number. Then we have the following theorem.

Theorem 1. *The approximation error satisfies*

$$1 \le \frac{P(d)}{\widetilde{P}(d)} \le 1 + \epsilon . \tag{9}$$

To save space, we omit most proofs of theorems in this paper.

Figure 2 shows an instance of power approximation with $K = 3$. In the figure, the red curve stands for the actual charging power received by sensor, while the three blue lines stand for the approximated value of charging power. Then, area discretization is executed based on piecewise constant approximation of charging power. We draw K concentric sectors with radius $\ell(1), \ell(2), ..., \ell(K)$ centered at each sensor, respectively. If a stopping position of MC is located between two successive arcs with radius $\ell(k)$ and $\ell(k+1)$ centered at a sensor, then the sensor must also lie between two arcs with radius $\ell(k)$ and $\ell(k+1)$ centered at the stopping point, then the approximation power of the charging power received by the sensor is $\widetilde{P}(\ell(k))$ if the MC and sensor cover each other. Through the area discretization process, the whole plane is partitioned into a number of subareas, and we have the following theorem.

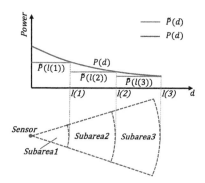

Fig. 2. Power approximation

Theorem 2. *The number of subareas partitioned by N sensors is at most* $O(N^2\epsilon^{-2})$.

4.2   Stopping Strategy Extraction

After the area discretization process, the power from MC at any point in one subarea to its surrounding sensors is constant. Therefore, the only thing we need to consider is the coverage relationship between MC and sensors in each subarea, which is determined by stopping positions and orientations of MC. In this subsection, we will pick one MC's stopping point and corresponding orientations for each subarea. In each subarea, we first randomly select a point as the stopping position of MC, then determine orientations of L antennas to maximize the total charging power of all the sensors covered by these L antennas. To begin with, we introduce the following definitions.

Definition 1 *(**Stopping Strategy**). One stoping position and corresponding orientations of MC are briefly named one Stopping Strategy, and marked as $< s_i, \Theta_i >$, where $\Theta_i = \{\theta_i^1, \theta_i^2, ..., \theta_i^L\}$ denotes the orientations set of L antennas for MC.*

Definition 2 *([6] **Key Coverage Set (KCS)**). For one stopping strategy $< s_i, \Theta_i >$ and its corresponding covered sensors set O_i, if there doesn't exist covered sensors set O_j corresponding to another stopping strategy $< s_j, \Theta_j >$, such that $O_i \subset O_j$, then O_i is a key coverage set.*

Definition 3 *(**Candidate Coverage Set**). The candidate coverage set $\hat{O}_{f_i}$ of the subarea F_i contains the sensors that can be covered by a MC's stopping strategy in F_i.*

The algorithm described in this subsection contains two steps. At the first step, we consider a special case where MC only has one antenna. In each subarea, we randomly select a point as the stopping position of the single-antenna MC. Then, we will extract all the KCSs of the single-antenna MC at the stoping point. Inspired by the method of extracting dominant task sets [15], we adopt the similar method to deal with the extraction of KCSs. The detail of extracting all the KCSs of single-antenna MC at one point is presented in Algorithm 1. The algorithm rotates the single-antenna MC at one point by 360° counterclockwise. During the process of rotating, it identifies and records all the KCSs satisfying the definition above. Let G_{f_i} be the set of all obtained KCSs for single-antenna MC at the selected point in subarea F_i and $\widetilde{O}_i$ be the i-th KCS in G_{f_i}. For convenience, the total received energy by all the sensors in $\widetilde{O}_i$ is denoted as $ET(\widetilde{O}_i)$ in short, then we have $ET(\widetilde{O}_i) = \sum_{o_k \in \widetilde{O}_i} E_k$. Moreover, $ET(G_{f_i})$ denotes the total received energy of sensors in G_{f_i}.

At the second step, we will use a greedy method to extract a stop strategy for MC with L antennas in each subarea from the obtained KCSs set of single-antenna MC, which are the output of Algorithm 1. Algorithm 2 presents the detail of extracting one stopping strategy of MC in each subarea. We first obtain a series of KCSs of single antenna at a point in a subarea by performing Algorithm 1, then compute the total received energy $ET(\widetilde{O})$ for each KCS

Algorithm 1: Key Coverage Sets Extraction for Single-antenna MC

Input: The stopping point s_i in the subarea F_i, the candidate coverage set $\hat{O}_{f_i}$

Output: All KCSs of single-antenna MC at s_i in F_i

1   Initialize the orientation of the single-antenna MC to 0.

2   **while** *the rotated angle is not larger than* 2π **do**

3   Rotate the MC counterclockwise to cover the sensors in $\hat{O}_{f_i}$ until some covered sensor lies rightly on the coverage area's clockwise boundary.

4   Add the current covered set of sensors to the collection of KCSs.

$\widetilde{O}$ and sort these KCSs by $ET(\widetilde{O})$ in descending order. Finally, we determine orientations for L antennas of MC one by one through a greedy method, that is, selecting L KCSs from the ordered KCSs set to maximize the total received energy of these selected L KCSs.

4.3   Cost-Benefit Approximation Algorithm

Through the processes of *Area discretization* and *Stopping Strategy Extraction*, we obtain all stopping strategies for MC. In this subsection, we need to select part of stopping strategies from the obtained ones to maximize the overall energy received by sensors under capacity constraint of MC. For the sake of brevity, the i-th stopping strategy of MC in Γ, *i.e.* $< s_i, \Theta_i >$, is also denoted by v_i. Then, we reformulate the SIGMA problem as

$$(\textbf{SIGMA}) \quad \max f(X) = \sum_{v_i \in X} \sum_{o_j \in O_i} (E_j \cdot h_j) \tag{10}$$

$$s.t. \quad X \subseteq \Gamma, \tag{11}$$

$$E_{cost} \leq E_{mc}, \tag{12}$$

where X is undetermined subset of Γ and denotes the selected stopping strategies set that need to be optimized to maximize the overall energy received by all the sensors under cost constraint of MC.

Before addressing our problem, we prove that our objective function has three properties: nonnegativity, monotonicity, and submodularity.

Definition 4 ([16] Nonnegativity, Monotonicity, and Submodularity). *Let S be a finite ground set. A real-valued set function $f : 2^S \rightarrow \mathbb{R}$ is nonnegative, monotone (nondecreasing), and submodular if and only if it satisfies the following conditions, respectively:*

(1) $f(\varnothing) = 0$ and $f(A) \geq 0$ for any $A \subseteq S$ (nonnegative);

(2) $f(A) \leq f(B)$ for all $A \subseteq B \subseteq S$ or equivalently: $f(A \cup \{e\}) - f(A) \geq 0$ for any $A \subseteq S$ and $e \in S \backslash A$ (monotone);

(3) $f(A \cup \{e\}) - f(A) \geq f(B \cup \{e\}) - f(B)$ for any $A \subseteq B \subseteq S$ and $e \in S \backslash B$ (submodular).

Algorithm 2: Stopping Strategy Extraction Algorithm

Input: MC with L antennas
Output: The stopping strategies set Γ of the MC

1 **foreach** *subarea* F_i **do**
2   Computing the candidate coverage set $\hat{O}_{f_i}$ for F_i.
3   Randomly select a point s_i as the stopping position of the MC in F_i.
4   Extract the KCSs set G_{f_i} for single antenna at s_i in F_i by executing algorithm 1.
5   Compute $ET(\widetilde{O})$ for each KCS $\widetilde{O} \in G_{f_i}$.
6   Sort all the obtained KCSs by their $ET(\widetilde{O})$ in descending order and get the ordered KCSs set $G_{f_i} = \{\widetilde{O}_1, \widetilde{O}_2, ..., \widetilde{O}_{|G_{f_i}|}\}$.
7   Set $j = 2, G'_{f_i} = \{\widetilde{O}_1\}, G_{f_i} = G_{f_i} \setminus \widetilde{O}_1$.
8   **while** $j \leq L$ **do**
9   **foreach** $\widetilde{O} \in G_{f_i}$ **do**
10   Compute $ET(G'_{f_i} \bigcup \{\widetilde{O}\})$.
11          $\widetilde{O}'_j = \underset{\widetilde{O} \in G_{f_i}}{argmax}\, ET(G'_{f_i} \bigcup \{\widetilde{O}\})$.
12          $G'_{f_i} = G'_{f_i} \bigcup \{\widetilde{O}'_j\}, G_{f_i} = G_{f_i} \setminus \widetilde{O}'_j$.
13          $j = j + 1$.
14   Record the stopping strategy $< s_i, \Theta_i >$ for the MC in F_i, where $\Theta_i = \{\theta_i^1, \theta_i^2, ..., \theta_i^L\}$ is the orientations set corresponding to the obtain KCSs set $G'_{f_i} = \{\widetilde{O}_1, \widetilde{O}'_2, ..., \widetilde{O}'_L\}$.
15 Finally obtain the stopping strategies set Γ of the MC for all subareas.

Based on the definition, we have the following theorem:

Theorem 3. *The objective function in the SIGMA problem is nonnegative, monotone, and submodular.*

Proof. According to the Definition 4, we check whether our objective function $f(X)$ has the three properties.

First, As $E_j \geq 0$, $f(X) = \sum_{v_i \in X} \sum_{o_j \in O_i} (E_j \cdot h_j) \geq 0$, then it is nonnegative.

Second, set $A \subseteq B \subseteq \Gamma$, and suppose O_A denotes the covered sensors set of A, O_B denotes the covered sensors set of B, then we have $O_A \subseteq O_B$ and $f(A) = \sum_{o_j \in O_A} (E_j \cdot h_j) \leq f(B) = \sum_{o_j \in O_B} (E_j \cdot h_j)$, then it is monotone.

Third, set $A \subseteq B \subseteq \Gamma$, $v_i \in \Gamma \backslash B$ and $C = \{x | x \in B, x \notin A\} = B - A$, suppose O_i denotes the covered sensors set of v_i and O_C denotes the covered sensors set of C, and we know $O_A \subseteq O_B$ and $O_C \subseteq O_B$.

We present four cases to give the proof of submodularity.

(Case 1) If $O_B \bigcap O_i = \varnothing$, thus $O_A \bigcap O_i = \varnothing$, and we have
$f(A \cup \{v_i\}) - f(A) = \sum_{o_j \in O_i} (E_j) = f(B \cup \{v_i\}) - f(B)$.

(Case 2) If $O_C \bigcap O_i = \varnothing$ and $O_A \bigcap O_i = O_D$, thus $O_B \bigcap O_i = O_D$, then we have
$f(A \cup \{v_i\}) - f(A) = \sum_{o_j \in O_i \backslash O_D} (E_j) = f(B \cup \{v_i\}) - f(B)$.

(**Case 3**) If $O_C \bigcap O_i = O_E$ and $O_A \bigcap O_i = \varnothing$, we have
$f(A \cup \{v_i\}) - f(A) = \sum_{o_j \in O_i} (E_j)$,
$f(B \cup \{v_i\}) - f(B) = \sum_{o_j \in O_i \setminus O_E} (E_j)$.
Then $f(A \cup \{v_i\}) - f(A) > f(B \cup \{v_i\}) - f(B)$.

(**Case 4**) If $O_C \bigcap O_i = O_F$ and $O_A \bigcap O_i = O_G$, we have
$f(A \cup \{v_i\}) - f(A) = \sum_{o_j \in O_i \setminus O_G} (E_j)$,
$f(B \cup \{v_i\}) - f(B) = \sum_{o_j \in O_i \setminus (O_F \bigcup O_G)} (E_j)$.
Then $f(A \cup \{v_i\}) - f(A) > f(B \cup \{v_i\}) - f(B)$.
Therefore, we prove that $f(X)$ is submodular.

The objective of SIGMA problem is to maximize a submodular function, which is NP-hard [17]. While the energy cost constraint in the SIGMA problem involves tour scheduling for the selected stopping positions of MC, *i.e.* computing a shortest tour through all the selected stopping positions of MC on a graph, which belongs to a variant of the traveling salesman problem (TSP) and is also NP-hard. Moreover, the two NP-hard problems are not independent, but directly impact each other. Through considering the two-fold hard optimization jointly, we propose the cost-benefit approximation algorithm referring to the idea of [18]. Since optimal cost can not be computable in polynomial time for its complexity, we make use of approximate cost function $\hat{E}_{cost}$, which can be computed in polynomial time, to replace the optimal cost E_{cost}. The approximate cost function $\hat{E}_{cost}$ adopted in our proposed algorithm is a general and fast algorithm, *i.e. nearest neighbour rule*, to compute the TSP tour, which is $\log m$-approximation [19].

The core idea of our proposed cost-benefit approximation algorithm is to use a heuristic method to iteratively add a stopping strategy which has the largest cost-benefit ratio to set X until violating the energy capacity constraint of MC. In the i-th iteration, add to set X a stopping strategy v_i such that

$$v_i = \underset{v \in \Gamma \setminus X_{i-1}}{argmax} \frac{f(X_{i-1} \cup \{v\}) - f(X_{i-1})}{\hat{E}_{cost}(X_{i-1} \cup \{v\}) - \hat{E}_{cost}(X_{i-1})}. \tag{13}$$

Initially, $X_0 = \emptyset$ and $X_i = \{v_1, v_2, \cdots, v_i\}$.

Algorithm 3 demonstrates the detailed process of our proposed cost-benefit approximation algorithm. Note that the solution A at Step 1 contains only a single stopping strategy. During the iterative process, we can add more stopping strategies until violating the capacity constraint of MC. At the end of the iteration, we can obtain the stopping strategy X_i, where $\hat{E}_{cost}(X_{i-1}) \leq E_{mc}$ and $\hat{E}_{cost}(X_i) \geq E_{mc}$. Then, we would compare $f(A)$ with $f(X_{i-1})$ to choose the larger one and get the final solution.

5   Simulation Results

In this section, we conduct extensive simulations to verify the performance of our proposed algorithm, named SIGMA algorithm in short, by comparing it with two other algorithms in terms of number of sensors N, MC capacity E_{mc}, charging radius D and error threshold ϵ.

5.1   Evaluation and Baseline Setup

In our simulation, stationary rechargeable sensors are randomly distributed in a $40\,\mathrm{m} \times 40\,\mathrm{m}^2$ area. If no otherwise stated, we set $\alpha = 100, \beta = 50, A_s = \pi/3, A_o = 2\pi/3, N = 6, E_{mc} = 40, D = 10, q = 0.1, \lambda = 0.1, \epsilon = 0.2$, and $L = 3$, respectively. Besides, we suppose that the required charging energy of each sensor is 1. As there are no available algorithms concerning the scheduling problem of mobile charger with multiple antennas, we design two algorithms for comparison, that is, Uniformly Distributed Orientation Algorithm (UDOA) and Random Stopping strategies Algorithm (RSA). For UDOA, the orientations of antennas are uniformly distributed at the randomly selected stopping point of MC in each subarea, it means that the angles between any two adjacent antennas' orientations are equal. After determining the stopping strategy of MC in each subarea, the cost-benefit approximation algorithm presented in Sect. 4.3 is executed. For RSA, area discretization presented in Sect. 4.1 and stopping strategy extraction presented in Sect. 4.2 are executed by turn, then the final stopping strategies of MC are selected from all the obtain stopping strategies randomly under the capacity constraint of MC. Moreover, each data point in the following figures is obtained by averaging results for 100 topologies generated randomly.

Algorithm 3: Cost-Benefit Approximation Algorithm

Input: Starting point v_0, stopping strategies set Γ, objective function $f(X)$, battery capacity of MC E_{mc}

Output: Stopping strategies set X

1 Initailization. $\Gamma' = \Gamma$, $i = 1$, $X_0 = \emptyset$ and $\hat{E}_{cost}(X_0) = 0$;

   $A = argmax\{f(v)|v \in \Gamma, \hat{E}_{cost}(v) \le E_{mc}\}$.

2 **while** $\Gamma' \neq null$ **do**

3   **foreach** $v \in \Gamma'$ **do**

4   Computing objective function $f(X_{i-1} \cup \{v\})$ and $f(X_{i-1})$

5   Computing the approximate TSP energy cost $\hat{E}_{cost}(X_{i-1} \cup \{v\})$ and $\hat{E}_{cost}(X_{i-1})$.

6      $v_i = \underset{v \in \Gamma \setminus X_{i-1}}{argmax} \; \frac{f(X_{i-1} \cup \{v\}) - f(X_{i-1})}{\hat{E}_{cost}(X_{i-1} \cup \{v\}) - \hat{E}_{cost}(X_{i-1})}$.

7   **if** $\hat{E}_{cost}(X_{i-1} \cup \{v_i\}) \le E_{mc}$ **then**

8          $X_i = X_{i-1} \bigcup \{v_i\}$

9          $i = i + 1$.

10      $\Gamma' = \Gamma' \setminus v_i$

11 **if** $f(A) \ge f(X_{i-1})$ **then**

12      $X = A$

13 **else**

14      $X = X_{i-1}$.

15 Output $X \subset \Gamma$.

5.2   Performance Comparison

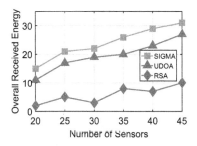

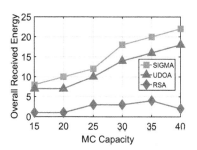

Fig. 3. Overall received energy vs. sensor number

Fig. 4. Overall received energy vs. MC capacity

Impact of Number of Sensors. *Our simulation results show that on average, SIGMA outperforms UDOA and RSA by* 23.1% *and* 311.4%, *respectively, as the number of sensors increases from* 25 *to* 45. As shown in Fig. 3, the overall received energy of three algorithms is monotonically increasing with the growth of the sensor number. The reason is that more sensors are covered by MC at most stopping positions as distribution density of sensors increases, and the overall received energy becomes larger accordingly.

Impact of MC Capacity. *Our simulation results show that on average, SIGMA outperforms UDOA and RSA by* 25.0% *and* 542.9%, *respectively, as the MC capacity increases from* 15 *to* 40. As illustrated in Fig. 4, the overall received energy of SIGMA and UDOA are rising with the MC capacity increasing, while the overall received energy of RSA just fluctuates in a certain range. This is because larger MC capacity makes MC visit more charging positions in SIGMA and UDOA, thus improves the overall received energy of sensors. However, in RSA, the number of charging positions is relatively stable regardless of the variation of MC capacity.

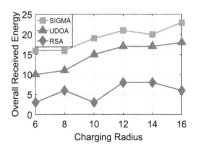

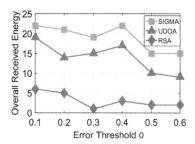

Fig. 5. Overall received energy vs. charging radius

Fig. 6. Overall received energy vs. error threshold

Impact of Charging Radius. *Our simulation results show that on average, SIGMA outperforms UDOA and RSA by* 30.7% *and* 238.2%, *respectively, as the charging radius increases from* 6 *to* 16. The variation tendencies of overall received energy for three algorithms in terms of charging radius are illuminated in Fig. 5. We can see that overall received energy of SIGMA and UDOA increases monotonically with charging radius. This is because longer charging radius makes more sensors covered by MC at charging positions, thus leads to larger overall received energy.

Impact of Error Threshold. *Our simulation results show that on average, SIGMA outperforms UDOA and RSA by* 35.7% *and* 500.0%, *respectively, as the error threshold ϵ increases from* 0.1 *to* 0.6. As shown in Fig. 6, overall received energy of three algorithms decreases on the whole as error threshold ϵ becomes larger. When higher error threshold ϵ is set, the gap between these algorithms and optimal solution becomes larger, thus the overall received energy of sensors declines accordingly.

6   Conclusion

The key novelty of this paper is that we are the first to explore the issue of scheduling of mobile charger with multiple antennas in wireless rechargeable sensor networks. The key contribution of this paper is proposing stopping strategy extraction and cost-benefit approximation algorithms as well as carrying out simulations for evaluation. The key technical depth of this paper is in transforming the optimization problem with infinite search space into limited candidate solutions by presenting the methods of area discretization and stopping strategy extraction, and making the charging tour planning problem with NP-hard complexity solvable in a polynomial time by proposing cost-benefit approximation algorithms. Our simulation results show that our proposed algorithm outperforms comparison algorithms by at least 23.1%.

Acknowledgment. This work was supported in part by the National Natural Science Foundation of China under Grant 61872178, in part by the Natural Science Foundation of Jiangsu Province under Grant No. BK20181251, in part by the open research fund of Key Lab of Broadband Wireless Communication and Sensor Network Technology (Nanjing University of Posts and Telecommunications), Ministry of Education, in part by the Key Research and Development Project of Jiangsu Province under Grant No. BE2015154 and BE2016120, in part by the National Natural Science Foundation of China under Grant 61832005, and 61672276, in part by the Collaborative Innovation Center of Novel Software Technology and Industrialization, Nanjing University, and in part by the Jiangsu High-level Innovation and Entrepreneurship (Shuangchuang) Program.

References

1. https://www.chyxx.com/research/202006/873045.html
2. Schlub, R., Lu, J., Ohira, T.: Seven-element ground skirt monopole ESPAR antenna design from a genetic algorithm and the finite element method. IEEE Trans. Antennas Propag. **51**(11), 3033–3039 (2003)
3. Ramanathan, R.: On the performance of ad hoc networks with beamforming antennas. In: MobiHoc, pp. 95–105 (2001)
4. Rusek, F., et al.: Scaling up MIMO: opportunities and challenges with very large arrays. IEEE Signal Process. Mag. **30**(1), 40–60 (2013)
5. Chiu, T.-C., Shih, Y.-Y., Pang, A.-C., Jeng, J.-Y., Hsiu, P.-C.: Mobility-aware charger deployment for wireless rechargeable sensor networks. In: IEEE APNOMS (2012)
6. Dai, H., Wang, X., Liu, A.X., Ma, H., Chen, G.: Optimizing wireless charger placement for directional charging. In: IEEE INFOCOM (2017)
7. Wang, X., et al.: Heterogeneous wireless charger placement with obstacles. In: ICPP, pp. 1–10 (2018)
8. Yu, N., Dai, H., Liu, A.X., Tian, B.: Placement of connected wireless chargers. In: IEEE INFOCOM, pp. 387–395 (2018)
9. Fu, L., Cheng, P., Gu, Y., Chen, J., He, T.: Minimizing charging delay in wireless rechargeable sensor networks. In: IEEE INFOCOM (2013)
10. Chen, L., Lin, S., Huang, H.: Charge me if you can: charging path optimization and scheduling in mobile networks. In: ACM MobiHoc, pp. 101–110 (2016)
11. Lin, C., Zhou, Y., Ma, F., Deng, J.: Minimizing charging delay for directional charging in wireless rechargeable sensor networks. In: IEEE INFOCOM (2019)
12. Wu, T., Yang, P., Dai, H., Xu, W., Xu, M.: Collaborated tasks-driven mobile charging and scheduling: a near optimal result. In: IEEE INFOCOM (2019)
13. Ssu, K.-F., Ou, C.-H., Jiau, H.C.: Localization with mobile anchor points in wireless sensor networks. IEEE Trans. Veh. Technol. **54**, 1187–1197 (2005)
14. Dai, H., Wang, X., Liu, A.X., Zhang, F.: Omnidirectional chargability with directional antennas. In: IEEE ICNP (2016)
15. Dai, H., Sun, K., Liu, A.X., Zhang, L., Zheng, J., Chen, G.: Charging task scheduling for directional wireless charger networks. In: ICPP (2018)
16. Fujishige, S.: Submodular Functions and Optimization, vol. 58. Elsevier, Amsterdam (2005)
17. Khuller, S., Moss, A., Naor, J.S.: The budgeted maximum coverage problem. Inf. Process. Lett. **70**(1), 39–45 (1999)
18. Zhang, H., Vorobeychik, Y.: Submodular optimization with routing constraints. In: Association for the Advancement of Artificial Intelligence 2016, pp. 819–826 (2016)
19. Rosenkrantz, D.J., Stearns, R.E., Lewis II, P.M.: An analysis of several heuristics for the traveling salesman problem. SIAM J. Comput. **6**(3), 39–45 (1977)

Sequential Recommendation via Temporal Self-Attention and Multi-Preference Learning

Wenchao Wang, Jinghua Zhu$^{(\boxtimes)}$, and Heran Xi$^{(\boxtimes)}$

School of Computer Science and Technology, Heilongjiang University,
Harbin 150080, China
{zhujinghua,2003071}@hlju.edu.cn

Abstract. The sequential recommendation selects and recommends next items for users by modeling their historical interaction sequences, where the chronological order of interactions plays an important role. Most sequential recommendation methods only pay attention to the order information among the interactions and ignore the time intervals information, which leads to the limitations of capturing dynamic user interests. And previous work neglects diversity in order to improve recommendation accuracy. The model Temporal Self-Attention and Multi-Preference Learning (TSAMPL) is proposed to improve sequential recommendation, which learns dynamic and general user interests separately. The proposed temporal gate self-attention network is introduced to learn dynamic user interests, which takes both contextual information and temporal dynamics into account. To model general user interests, we employ a multi-preference matrix to learn users' multiple types of preferences for improving recommendation diversity. Finally, the interest fusion module combines dynamic user interests (accuracy) and general user interests (diversity) adaptively. The experiments in sequential recommendation confirm our method is superior to all comparison methods, we also study the impact of each component in the model.

Keywords: Temporal gate self-attention · Multi-Preference Learning · Sequential recommendation

1 Introduction

In the Internet, each user can interact with various items easily, it is difficult to recommend the next suitable items for users by modeling their historical interaction sequences. To solve this problem, people propose the sequential recommendation systems.

Although existing methods can model the dependence between the interactions in sequences, they ignore an important information: the time intervals between interactions. Intuitively, two interactions with a short time interval are often more related than those with a long time interval. Similarly, user interests

Z. Liu et al. (Eds.): WASA 2021, LNCS 12938, pp. 18–30, 2021.
https://doi.org/10.1007/978-3-030-86130-8_2

have strong similarities in a small time interval and user interests may change and drift in a large time interval. The focus of modeling is different for sequences with different time spans, so the time intervals should be taken into consideration when modeling sequential data. Previous work [22] added a time gate to Long Short-Term Memory (LSTM) for capturing the temporal information of sequences. Recent method [11] improved the self-attention mechanism by introducing relative time intervals, which added the interval vectors and item embeddings to calculate the attention weight matrix. There are still some problems in modeling the temporal patterns of sequences for learning user interests.

To learn dynamic user interests better, the temporal gate self-attention network is proposed to consider the time intervals between interactions when modeling. We first denote the time intervals as a time function and then combine the encoded intervals with contextual information to construct a temporal gate that filters the important factors in sequence attention matrix according to the time intervals. Before the temporal gate self-attention network, we capture the sequential context information from user interaction sequences through Gated Recurrent Unit (GRU) [3]. Then we adopt the temporal gate self-attention network to learn the dynamic user interests accurately, which can model the drifting process of user interests. To improve the recommendation accuracy, recommender systems may recommend similar items for users, which causes the singleness and homogeneity of recommendation. For improving the diversity of recommendation, we employ the user multi-preference matrix to model general user interests, which can reflect users' multiple types of preferences. We classify the items in sequences according to the user multi-preference matrix and each category corresponds to a certain latent user preference. We get general user interests by combining different types of user preferences. Finally, the interest fusion module combines dynamic and general interests adaptively.

In summary, we have made these contributions to enhance sequential recommender systems:

- A novel sequential recommendation method called TSAMPL is proposed, which learns user interest representations by modeling dynamic and general user interests.
- To model dynamic user interests, we use the proposed temporal gate self-attention network to capture the dynamic changes of user interests and improve the recommendation accuracy. In modeling general user interests, we introduce a multi-preference matrix to learn the users' multiple types of preferences, which aims to improve the recommendation diversity.
- Experiments on two datasets prove our method is more advanced than several comparison methods in sequential recommendation. Similarly, we present that key components have positive effects on final predictions by conducting ablation studies.

2   Related Work

Recommendation systems [10,14,20] and other tasks [1,4] have introduced and applied deep neural networks because they have excellent advantages in modeling data. The sequential recommendation systems take the interaction sequences of users as inputs, the purpose is to learn user interests and recommend items for users. Fossil [5] was a sequential recommendation method with item similarity which used Markov chains to model. Benefiting from the success of Recurrent Neural Network (RNN) in modeling sequential data [12,15], many researchers proposed to use RNN-based models for sequential recommender systems. Hidasi et al. proposed the model GRU4Rec [7] for session-based recommendation, they divided user behaviors into several short sessions and adopted GRU to learn user preferences. They proposed an more advanced version [6] on this basis, which used advanced loss function and different sampling strategies. The method [22] used a time gate to improve LSTM unit, it could capture the temporal information of sequences by a time and content controller. Computer visions applies Convolutional Neural Network (CNN) to various tasks widely [9], it can capture local important features. Caser [18] stacked the item embeddings into a matrix and treated the matrix as an "image" in latent space, then it applied convolution filters to capture short-term user interests.

The attention mechanism can assist recommendation systems to extract the more critical information for next predictions from the input sequences [2,21]. The self-attention mechanism was primarily proposed in Transformer [19], which has been used in sequential recommendation. Kang et al. [8] and Zhang et al. [23] suggested applying the original self-attention to adaptively learn the relations between items in sequence, Sun et al. [17] suggested using bidirectional self-attention. TiSASRec [11] was an extension to self-attention, which added time interval vectors when calculating the attention weights.

3   Problem Statement

Let $U = \{u_1, u_2, ..., u_M\}$ represent the user set and $I = \{i_1, i_2, ..., i_N\}$ represent the item set. For user u, we obtain his/her sequence S^u by sorting the interactions in chronological order, $S^u = \{(i_1^u, t_1^u), (i_2^u, t_2^u), ..., (i_{|S^u|}^u, t_{|S^u|}^u)\}$. We denote (i_s^u, t_s^u) as the s-th interaction in S^u, which means that user $u \in U$ interacted with item $i_s^u \in I$ at time t_s^u. By modeling the sequence S^u, we calculate the probability that user u will interact with item i_c at time $t_{|S^u|+1}^u$ and recommend candidate items to u based on the probability.

4   The Proposed Method

We will introduce our model TSAMPL in detail, Fig. 1 shows the model diagram.

First, we extract the lastest n interactions of each user as his/her input sequence, it is denoted as $S^u = \{(i_1^u, t_1^u), (i_2^u, t_2^u), ..., (i_n^u, t_n^u)\}$, where n is the maximum of $|S^u|$. If $|S^u| < n$, we will add padding items (indicated by 0) and time stamps (the time of user's first interaction) at the beginning of $|S^u|$.

To capture the temporal correlations in S^u, we construct a time interval matrix $\Delta T_S^u \in \mathbb{R}^{n \times n}$ according to the sequence S^u, which records the time intervals between any two interactions in sequence. We denote the time interval between interaction i and j as $\Delta t_{ij}^u = \Delta t_{ji}^u = |t_j - t_i|$. The diagonal element of

$\Delta \boldsymbol{T}_S^u$ is 0 and it is a symmetric matrix. The $\Delta \boldsymbol{T}_S^u$ corresponding to S^u (length n) is defined as follows:

$$
\Delta \boldsymbol{T}_S^u = \begin{bmatrix} \Delta t_{11}^u & \Delta t_{12}^u & \cdots & \Delta t_{1n}^u \\ \Delta t_{21}^u & \Delta t_{22}^u & \cdots & \Delta t_{2n}^u \\ \vdots & \vdots & \cdots & \vdots \\ \Delta t_{n1}^u & \Delta t_{n2}^u & \cdots & \Delta t_{nn}^u \end{bmatrix}, \quad \boldsymbol{R}_S^u = \begin{bmatrix} r_{11}^u & r_{12}^u & \cdots & r_{1n}^u \\ r_{21}^u & r_{22}^u & \cdots & r_{2n}^u \\ \vdots & \vdots & \vdots & \vdots \\ r_{n1}^u & r_{n2}^u & \cdots & r_{nn}^u \end{bmatrix}. \tag{1}
$$

Inspired by [11], in order to discrete the time interval Δt_{ij}^u better, we scale it to $\Delta t_{ij}^u = \lfloor \frac{\Delta t_{ij}^u}{\Delta t_{min}^u} \rfloor$, where $\Delta t_{min}^u = min(\Delta \boldsymbol{T}_S^u \neq 0)$. We believe that there is no temporal correlation between two interactions when their relative time interval exceeds the maximum k. To avoid arbitrarily large values, we use cropping operation to limit the maximum relative time intervals, that is $r_{ij}^u = min(\Delta t_{ij}^u, k)$. The cropped $\Delta \boldsymbol{T}_S^u$ is represented as $\boldsymbol{R}_S^u \in \mathbb{R}^{n \times n}$.

4.1 Embedding Layer

In the embedding layer, using the entire user embedding look-up matrix $\boldsymbol{U} \in \mathbb{R}^{M \times d}$, we can embed each user into a d-dimensional unique vector. Using the entire item embedding look-up matrix $\boldsymbol{I} \in \mathbb{R}^{N \times d}$, we can embed each item in S^u into an item embedding $\boldsymbol{x}_i^u \in \mathbb{R}^{1 \times d}$(the padding items are mapped into zero vector). Stack the embeddings of n items to get the embedding matrix $\boldsymbol{X}_S^u = [\boldsymbol{x}_1^u, \boldsymbol{x}_2^u, ..., \boldsymbol{x}_n^u] \in \mathbb{R}^{n \times d}$.

4.2 Dynamic User Interest Modeling

In fact, the user interests are dynamic and will change over time. In modeling dynamic user interests, we first obtain multiple intentions of user u by using GRU network to model the sequence S^u. Then we capture the correlations between the various intentions by adopting the temporal gate self-attention network, which takes both context and time information into account. Finally, we get dynamic user interests through aggregation network.

Gated Recurrent Unit. GRU network is capable of modeling sequential patterns, so we use it to handle the sequence S^u. The embedding matrix $\boldsymbol{X}_S^u$ is the input of GRU network, the output is the intention representations $\{\boldsymbol{h}_1, \boldsymbol{h}_2, ..., \boldsymbol{h}_n\}$ of u at each time step, where $\boldsymbol{h} \in \mathbb{R}^{1 \times d}$. We stack these representations into a matrix $\boldsymbol{H}_S^u \in \mathbb{R}^{n \times d}$.

Temporal Gate Self-attention. The hidden states of GRU only capture the sequential relations between items and do not learn the drift process of user interests well, so that it cannot capture dynamic user interests accurately. To solve this problem, the temporal gate self-attention network is introduced to further capture the complex correlations between the multiple intentions of u.

The self-attention mechanism maps the entire sequence embeddings into the query matrix $\boldsymbol{Q}$, key matrix $\boldsymbol{K}$ and value matrix $\boldsymbol{V}$. The weights are obtained

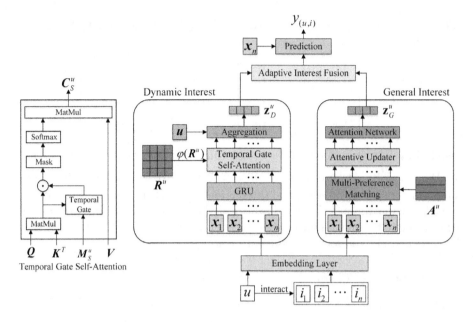

Fig. 1. The overall architecture of TSAMPL model.

by calculating the similarity between the query q and key k, which represent the contextual relationships between items. We use the 'Scaled Dot-Product Attention (SDPA)' to calculate the attention matrix:

$$SDPA(\boldsymbol{Q}, \boldsymbol{K}, \boldsymbol{V}) = softmax(\frac{\boldsymbol{Q}\boldsymbol{K}^T}{\sqrt{d}})\boldsymbol{V}, \tag{2}$$

where $\sqrt{d}$ is the scale factor to avoid excessive inner product value. The influence of time interval between query q and key k is not considered by the conventional self-attention mechanism in the calculation process. We find user intentions with long time intervals will change and the correlations between them will decrease, user intentions with relatively short time intervals have strong sequential correlations, which is called user interest drift. To simulate this process, we use a time function to handle the intervals:

$$\boldsymbol{M}_S^u = \varphi(\boldsymbol{R}^u) = -\beta log(1 + \boldsymbol{R}^u), \tag{3}$$

where $\boldsymbol{M}_S^u \in \mathbb{R}^{n \times n}$ encodes the time intervals between each pair of intentions in $\boldsymbol{H}_S^u$, β is a coefficient. To take both contextual and temporal information into account when learning dynamic user interests, we design a gate as follows:

$$\boldsymbol{G}_{QK} = \sigma(\boldsymbol{W}_{g1} \cdot (\boldsymbol{Q}\boldsymbol{K}^T) + \boldsymbol{W}_{g2} \cdot \boldsymbol{M}_S^u + \boldsymbol{B}_g), \tag{4}$$

where $\boldsymbol{G}_{QK} \in \mathbb{R}^{n \times n}$ is the gate matrix, $\boldsymbol{W}_{g1}, \boldsymbol{W}_{g2}, \boldsymbol{B}_g \in \mathbb{R}^{n \times n}$ are the weight and bias matrix respectively, $\sigma(\cdot)$ is the sigmoid function. We define the proposed temporal gate self-attention (TGSA) based on the gate, it is as follows:

$$TGSA(\boldsymbol{Q}, \boldsymbol{K}, \boldsymbol{V}, \boldsymbol{M}_S^u) = softmax(\frac{\boldsymbol{Q}\boldsymbol{K}^T \odot \boldsymbol{G}_{QK}}{\sqrt{d}})\boldsymbol{V}, \tag{5}$$

where $\boldsymbol{Q} = \boldsymbol{H}_S^u\boldsymbol{W}_Q, \boldsymbol{K} = \boldsymbol{H}_S^u\boldsymbol{W}_K, \boldsymbol{V} = \boldsymbol{H}_S^u\boldsymbol{W}_V$ and $\boldsymbol{W}_Q, \boldsymbol{W}_K, \boldsymbol{W}_V \in \mathbb{R}^{d \times d}$ are the projection matrices. $\boldsymbol{H}_S^u$ is the input of $TGSA$ and $\boldsymbol{C}_S^u \in \mathbb{R}^{n \times d}$ is the output. $TGSA$ can learn the drift process of user interests well and capture dynamic user interests accurately.

We make dynamic user interest into a latent vector $\boldsymbol{z}_D^u \in \mathbb{R}^{1 \times d}$:

$$\begin{aligned} score(\boldsymbol{C}_S^u, \boldsymbol{u}) &= \sigma(\boldsymbol{C}_S^u \cdot \boldsymbol{w}_C + \boldsymbol{W}_u \cdot \boldsymbol{u}^T), \\ \boldsymbol{z}_D^u &= sum(\boldsymbol{C}_S^u \odot score(\boldsymbol{C}_S^u, \boldsymbol{u})), \end{aligned} \tag{6}$$

where $score(\cdot)$ represents the attention scores of user u for different intentions, $sum(\cdot)$ is a sum function. $\boldsymbol{u} \in \mathbb{R}^{1 \times d}$ is the user embedding of u, $\boldsymbol{w}_C \in \mathbb{R}^{d \times 1}$ and $\boldsymbol{W}_u \in \mathbb{R}^{n \times d}$ are learnable parameters.

4.3   General User Interest Modeling

In this section, we model general user interests without considering the order of interactions. After analyzing the user interaction sequences, we find that the items in sequences can be roughly divided into several categories and each category corresponds to a certain type of latent user preference, which indicates that each user has multiple types of latent preferences. In modeling general user interest, our purpose is to learn the combination of user's different types of preferences from S^u.

We use a matrix to represent different types of user latent preferences, where each row of the matrix represents a certain type of user latent preference. Let $\boldsymbol{A}^u = [\boldsymbol{a}_1^u, \boldsymbol{a}_2^u, ..., \boldsymbol{a}_L^u] \in \mathbb{R}^{L \times d}$ denotes the multi-preference matrix of user u, where the number of types is L, $\boldsymbol{a}_l^u$ represents the l-th type of user preference. First, the attention scores between each item in S^u and each type of user preference in $\boldsymbol{A}^u$ are calculated as follows:

$$e_{lj}^u = \frac{exp((\boldsymbol{a}_l^u\boldsymbol{W}_A) \cdot (\boldsymbol{x}_j^u\boldsymbol{W}_X)^T)}{\sum_{k=1}^n exp((\boldsymbol{a}_l^u\boldsymbol{W}_A) \cdot (\boldsymbol{x}_k^u\boldsymbol{W}_X)^T)}, \tag{7}$$

where e_{lj}^u measures how likely the item j belongs to the l-th type of user preference. $\boldsymbol{W}_A, \boldsymbol{W}_X \in \mathbb{R}^{d \times d}$ are projection matrices. Then we update $\boldsymbol{a}_l^u$ to:

$$\boldsymbol{a}_l^u = \sum_{j=1}^n e_{lj}^u(\boldsymbol{x}_j^u\boldsymbol{W}_X), \tag{8}$$

it means that we use the weighted sum of item embeddings belonging to l-th type of preference to represent $\boldsymbol{a}_l^u$. Through the above calculation, we can update the multi-preference matrix $\boldsymbol{A}^u$ of user u. To learn a combination of different types of preferences to reflect the general user interest $\boldsymbol{z}_G^u \in \mathbb{R}^{1 \times d}$, it is as follows:

$$\boldsymbol{z}_G^u = softmax(\boldsymbol{m}_A(\boldsymbol{A}^u)^T)\boldsymbol{A}^u, \tag{9}$$

where $\boldsymbol{m}_A \in \mathbb{R}^{1 \times d}$ represents a learnable vector.

4.4 Adaptive Interest Fusion

The dynamic and general user interests have different contributions to the final recommendation, so we apply an adaptive interest fusion module to combine them, it can adjust the importance of dynamic and general user interest adaptively. The interest combination is calculated as follows:

$$
\begin{aligned}
\boldsymbol{g} &= \sigma([\boldsymbol{z}_D^u, \boldsymbol{z}_G^u] \cdot \boldsymbol{W}_g^1 + \boldsymbol{u} \cdot \boldsymbol{W}_g^2 + bg), \\
\boldsymbol{z}^u &= \boldsymbol{z}_D^u \odot \boldsymbol{g} + \boldsymbol{z}_G^u \odot (1 - \boldsymbol{g}),
\end{aligned}
\tag{10}
$$

where $[\cdot, \cdot]$ represents a concatenation of vectors. $\boldsymbol{W}_g^1 \in \mathbb{R}^{2d \times d}$, $\boldsymbol{W}_g^2 \in \mathbb{R}^{d \times d}$, $\boldsymbol{b}_g \in \mathbb{R}^{1 \times d}$ are learnable parameters, $\boldsymbol{g} \in \mathbb{R}^{1 \times d}$ is a learnable gate. $\boldsymbol{z}^u \in \mathbb{R}^{1 \times d}$ is the hybrid interest representation of user u.

4.5 Objective Function

We find the closely related items may appear one after another in the interaction sequence such as mobile phone and its case, so we consider the relations between the last item i_n^u in S^u and the candidate items in final prediction. Next we use $\boldsymbol{z}^u$ and i_n^u to calculate the probability that candidate item i will be interacted by user u, which determines whether we choose to recommend this item to user, it is as follows:

$$
y_{u,i} = \boldsymbol{z}^u \cdot \boldsymbol{v}_i^T + \boldsymbol{x}_n^u \cdot \boldsymbol{v}_i^T,
\tag{11}
$$

where $\boldsymbol{x}_n^u$, $\boldsymbol{v}_i \in \mathbb{R}^{1 \times d}$ is the embedding vector of item i_n^u and i respectively.

We train TSAMPL by minimizing the binary cross-entropy loss and Adam optimizer. The loss function is :

$$
\mathcal{L} = -\sum_{u \in U} \sum_{i \in I} (log(\sigma(y_{u,i})) + log(1 - \sigma(y_{u,j}))) + \lambda ||\boldsymbol{\Theta}||^2,
\tag{12}
$$

where j denotes the negative item we sample from candidate set, λ is the regularization parameter, $\boldsymbol{\Theta}$ contains all the model parameters that need to be learned.

5 Experiments

In this section, we will introduce the experimental setups, results and analysis in detail.

5.1 Experimental Setup

Datasets. MovieLens-1M[1](ML1M) is a dataset including user ids, movie ids, ratings and timestamps. We eliminate those users with fewer than 10 ratings

---

[1] https://grouplens.org/datasets/movielens/.

and those movies with fewer than 5 ratings for filtering noisy data. Gowalla[2] is a check-in dataset including user ids, location ids and check-in time, we remove users whose check-in locations are less than 10 and those locations with fewer than 10 users for filtering noisy data.

The detailed statistics of the pre-processed data are shown in Table 1. For each user, we use 70% of interaction data as the train set, the next 10% is the validation set for hyperparameter adjustment, the remaining 20% is the test set to evaluate the model performance.

Table 1. Statistics of the two datasets.

Dataset	#users	#items	#feedbacks	Avg. actions	Sparsity (%)
MovieLens-1M	6040	3416	1000209	165	95.22
Gowalla	18737	32510	1278275	60	99.76

Baselines. The proposed method is compared with the following baselines:

- **BPRMF**: it is a non-sequential method, which models implicit feedback through matrix factorization and makes recommendations through Bayesian Personalized Ranking [16].
- **GRU4Rec+**: it improves GRU-based session recommendation GRU4Rec by adopting an advanced loss function and sampling strategy.
- **Caser**: a sequential recommender based on CNN, it divides short-term user interests into point-level, union-level and adopts horizontal and vertical convolution filters to learn.
- **SASRec**: a sequential recommendation method based on self-attention mechanism, which models the user interaction sequences for predicting with the help of multi-head self-attention.
- **TiSASRec**: it considers the time intervals on the basis of SASRec. It maps the intervals to vectors and calculates the attention scores between items by adding the item embeddings and interval vectors.
- **HGN** [13]: it is a recently proposed approach which adopts feature gating and instance gating to learn short-term interests hierarchically and captures long-term interests with matrix factorization.
- **TSAMPL**: the proposed model, it combines the temporal gate self-attention network with multi-preference learing for learning dynamic and general user interests.

Evaluation Metrics. We choose the $HR@K$ and $NDCG@K$ metrics to compare our model with the baseline methods, K is the length of recommended item list for each user. $HR@K$ is hit rate, it measures whether the method accurately recommends the target items. NDCG@K is short for normalized discounted cumulative gain, which measures whether items with high recommended scores appear at the front of the list. We set K to 10 or 20 in this paper.

---

[2] http://snap.stanford.edu/data/loc-gowalla.html.

Parameter Settings. We use PyTorch[3] to implement proposed model and baselines. All hyperparameters are set following the suggestions from the original papers. In our experiment, the maximum sequence length n is set to 50, the batch size to 128, the embedding dimension d to 50, the learning rate to 0.001, the dropout rate to 0.2 and the number of preference types L to 10. The time intervals of MovieLens-1M and Gowalla are set to 128 and 256 respectively.

5.2 Experimental Results

We show the final performances of our method and all baselines in Table 2. By analyzing the data in Table 2, we can find:

The final results of GRU4Rec+ are better than BPRMF, it proves that considering sequential information contributes to learning user preferences better and improving the recommendation accuracy. Caser performs better than GRU4Rec+ because Caser adopts a sliding window strategy to capture the changes of short-term user interests, but matrix factorization cannot really capture the long-term interest of users. Because HGN models the dependence between closely relevant items by using the feature gating and instance gating network hierarchically, it performs better than Caser. SASRec applies the self-attention mechanism to model interaction sequences and outperforms GRU4Rec+ and Caser. This proves that the self-attention network is capable of modeling sequential data and performs well. TiSASRec introduces relative time intervals on the basis of SASRec, which models different time intervals as relations between any two interactions. Experiments prove that TiSASRec is better than SASRec and time information is helpful to improve recommendation performance.

Our method TSAMPL performs best on two datasets and all metrics. Because TSAMPL introduces the temporal information and multi-preference learning to model user interests, the temporal gate self-attention network can capture the dynamic changes of user interests according to the time intervals and it can improve the recommendation accuracy. The multi-preference martix can learn users' multiple types of preferences, which helps to increase diversity.

5.3 Effect of Components

We conduct ablation experiments to prove that each component of model helps to improve recommendation performance. To study the influence of temporal information, we replace temporal gate self-attention with ordinary self-attention to obtain a variant TSAMPL-R. The variants TSAMPL-D and TSAMPL-G remove the general user interest module and dynamic user interest module respectively. We use average operation instead of the adaptive fusion operation to get a variant TSAMPL-F. We conduct experiments on the above four variants, the comparison results are shown in Table 3.

By comparison, we find that the performance of TSAMPL is better than TSAMPL-R, which proves that the temporal gate self-attention helps to capture

---

[3] https://pytorch.org/.

Table 2. Recommendation performance comparison of different methods on two datasets. The best performance is denoted in bold.

Method	MovieLens-1M				Gowalla			
	HR@K		NDCG@K		HR@K		NDCG@K	
	10	20	10	20	10	20	10	20
BPRMF	0.3545	0.3813	0.2516	0.2570	0.3903	0.4071	0.3316	0.3482
GRU4Rec+	0.4022	0.4380	0.2811	0.2918	0.4615	0.4829	0.3966	0.4034
Caser	0.4094	0.4522	0.2898	0.3033	0.4872	0.5125	0.4139	0.4305
HGN	0.4359	0.4833	0.3094	0.3276	0.5028	0.5351	0.4259	0.4439
SASRec	0.4312	0.4755	0.3073	0.3192	0.5155	0.5547	0.4363	0.4577
TiSASRec	0.4387	0.4801	0.3147	0.3223	0.5306	0.5730	0.4544	0.4692
TSAMPL	**0.4558**	**0.4989**	**0.3291**	**0.3378**	**0.5831**	**0.6444**	**0.4833**	**0.4903**
Improv.	3.90%	3.22%	4.58%	3.11%	9.89%	12.40%	6.36%	4.50%

dynamic user interests. TSAMPL-D performs better than TSAMPL-G, which shows that dynamic user interests reflect user real interests better than general user interests. The fusion module can adaptively adjust the contribution of dynamic and general user interests to the final prediction because TSAMPL-F is worse than TSAMPL. In summary, each component has an effect on improving recommendation performance.

Table 3. Performance in ablation studies with different components.

Variant	MovieLens-1M		Gowalla	
	HR@10	NDCG@10	HR@10	NDCG@10
TSAMPL-R	0.4515	0.3249	0.5744	0.4789
TSAMPL-D	0.4476	0.3195	0.5732	0.4766
TSAMPL-G	0.3984	0.2735	0.4241	0.3767
TSAMPL-F	0.4529	0.3274	0.5790	0.4824
TSAMPL	0.4558	0.3291	0.5831	0.4833

5.4 Influence of Hyper-parameters

In this section, we study the impacts of two hyperparameters: user preference types L and item embedding dimension d. Figure 2 shows the effects of two parameters respectively. We only show the results on $HR@10$ because the space is limited. Figure 2(a) shows that the model performance improves as L increases, it means the multi-preference learning can learn users' multiple types of preferences and is beneficial to model general user interests. However, if L is too large, the model may classify items belonging to the same user preference into different types. Figure 2(b) shows that the model performance improves significantly as d increases. Because the long-dimensional item embedding can represent the complex latent item features more comprehensively, some important information will be discarded by the small dimension. And the performance of model begins to stabilize when d increases to a certain value, we set d to 50 for balancing performance and computational expense.

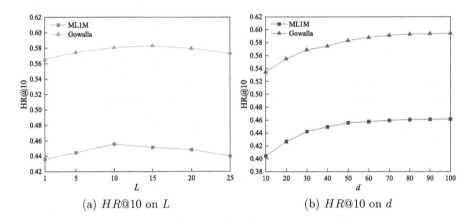

(a) $HR@10$ on L (b) $HR@10$ on d

Fig. 2. The effects of types L and embedding dimension d.

6   Conclusion

We propose a novel sequential recommender method called TSAMPL, which learns user interest representations by modeling dynamic and general user interests. In modeling dynamic user interests, we propose the new temporal gate self-attention network for learning the dynamic changes of user interests, which aims to improve the recommendation accuracy. In modeling general user interests, we introduce a multi-preference matrix to learn the user' multiple types of preferences, which aims to improve the diversity of recommendations. Compared with other methods, our proposed method can achieve more accurate recommendation results, it can be competent for sequential recommendation tasks.

References

1. Cai, Z., Duan, Z., Li, W.: Exploiting multi-dimensional task diversity in distributed auctions for mobile crowdsensing. IEEE Trans. Mob. Comput. (2020)
2. Chen, J., Zhang, H., He, X., Nie, L., Liu, W., Chua, T.S.: Attentive collaborative filtering: multimedia recommendation with item-and component-level attention. In: Proceedings of the 40th International ACM SIGIR Conference on Research and Development in Information Retrieval, pp. 335–344 (2017)

3. Chung, J., Gulcehre, C., Cho, K.H., Bengio, Y.: Empirical evaluation of gated recurrent neural networks on sequence modeling. Eprint Arxiv (2014)
4. Duan, Z., Li, W., Zheng, X., Cai, Z.: Mutual-preference driven truthful auction mechanism in mobile crowdsensing. In: 2019 IEEE 39th International Conference on Distributed Computing Systems (ICDCS), pp. 1233–1242. IEEE (2019)
5. He, R., McAuley, J.: Fusing similarity models with Markov chains for sparse sequential recommendation. In: 2016 IEEE 16th International Conference on Data Mining (ICDM), pp. 191–200. IEEE (2016)
6. Hidasi, B., Karatzoglou, A.: Recurrent neural networks with top-k gains for session-based recommendations. In: Proceedings of the 27th ACM International Conference on Information and Knowledge Management, pp. 843–852 (2018)
7. Hidasi, B., Karatzoglou, A., Baltrunas, L., Tikk, D.: Session-based recommendations with recurrent neural networks. arXiv preprint arXiv:1511.06939 (2015)
8. Kang, W.C., McAuley, J.: Self-attentive sequential recommendation. In: 2018 IEEE International Conference on Data Mining (ICDM), pp. 197–206. IEEE (2018)
9. Krizhevsky, A., Sutskever, I., Hinton, G.E.: Imagenet classification with deep convolutional neural networks. Commun. ACM 60(6), 84–90 (2017)
10. Li, G., Cai, Z., Yin, G., He, Z., Siddula, M.: Differentially private recommendation system based on community detection in social network applications. Secur. Commun. Netw. 2018 (2018)
11. Li, J., Wang, Y., McAuley, J.: Time interval aware self-attention for sequential recommendation. In: Proceedings of the 13th International Conference on Web Search and Data Mining, pp. 322–330 (2020)
12. Liu, Q., Wu, S., Wang, L.: Multi-behavioral sequential prediction with recurrent log-bilinear model. IEEE Trans. Knowl. Data Eng. 29(6), 1254–1267 (2017)
13. Ma, C., Kang, P., Liu, X.: Hierarchical gating networks for sequential recommendation. In: Proceedings of the 25th ACM SIGKDD International Conference on Knowledge Discovery & Data Mining, pp. 825–833 (2019)
14. Pan, Q., Dong, H., Wang, Y., Cai, Z., Zhang, L.: Recommendation of crowdsourcing tasks based on word2vec semantic tags. Wirele. Commun. Mob. Comput. 2019 (2019)
15. Quadrana, M., Karatzoglou, A., Hidasi, B., Cremonesi, P.: Personalizing session-based recommendations with hierarchical recurrent neural networks. In: Proceedings of the Eleventh ACM Conference on Recommender Systems, pp. 130–137 (2017)
16. Rendle, S., Freudenthaler, C., Gantner, Z., Schmidt-Thieme, L.: BPR: Bayesian personalized ranking from implicit feedback. arXiv preprint arXiv:1205.2618 (2012)
17. Sun, F., et al.: Bert4rec: sequential recommendation with bidirectional encoder representations from transformer. In: Proceedings of the 28th ACM International Conference on Information and Knowledge Management, pp. 1441–1450 (2019)
18. Tang, J., Wang, K.: Personalized top-n sequential recommendation via convolutional sequence embedding. In: Proceedings of the Eleventh ACM International Conference on Web Search and Data Mining, pp. 565–573 (2018)
19. Vaswani, A., et al.: Attention is all you need. In: Advances in Neural Information Processing Systems, pp. 5998–6008 (2017)
20. Wang, Y., Yin, G., Cai, Z., Dong, Y., Dong, H.: A trust-based probabilistic recommendation model for social networks. J. Netw. Comput. Appl. 55, 59–67 (2015)
21. Xiao, J., Ye, H., He, X., Zhang, H., Wu, F., Chua, T.S.: Attentional factorization machines: Learning the weight of feature interactions via attention networks. arXiv preprint arXiv:1708.04617 (2017)

22. Yu, Z., Lian, J., Mahmoody, A., Liu, G., Xie, X.: Adaptive user modeling with long and short-term preferences for personalized recommendation. In: IJCAI, pp. 4213–4219 (2019)
23. Zhang, S., Tay, Y., Yao, L., Sun, A.: Next item recommendation with self-attention. arXiv preprint arXiv:1808.06414 (2018)

Multi-connection Based Scalable Video Streaming in UDNs: A Multi-armed Bandit Approach

Yuanyuan Xu[1]([✉]), Chen Dai[2], and Lujiu Li[2]

[1] School of Computer and Information, Hohai University, Nanjing, China
yuanyuan_xu@hhu.edu.cn
[2] College of Computer Science and Technology, Nanjing University of Aeronautics and Astronautics, Nanjing, China
{daichen,lilujiu_69}@nuaa.edu.cn

Abstract. Scalable video coding (SVC) has been proposed as a promising paradigm for video transmission over wireless communications due to its flexibility. In this paper, we study the SVC-based video streaming in ultra-dense networks (UDNs), which allows each user to download different layers of its demanded video block from different base stations (BSs), rather than a single one in most existing work. Specifically, an optimization problem is formulated aiming to maximize the quality of experience (QoE) for each user. To this end, we first formulate a subproblem of choosing the optimal connection strategy as a multi-armed bandit (MAB) problem with no information exchange among users. In addition, each user is enabled to adapt its connection strategy in a self-learning process. For obtaining the optimal arm for the MAB problem, a best-arm-selecting upper confidence bound (UCB) algorithm is proposed. Based on this, we further develop an SVC-based video downloading scheme which provides an approximately optimal solution to the original optimization problem. Finally, simulations and comparisons are conducted to show the feasibility and superiority of our proposed schemes.

Keywords: SVC video streaming · Ultra-dense network · Multiple connections · Multi-armed bandit

1 Introduction

In recent years, video applications are increasing rapidly. However, the current network capacity cannot adapt to dynamically increasing users' demands, especially in wireless networks. According to Cisco's report [1], global mobile data traffic has grown dramatically over the past few years and mobile video traffic accounts for more than half of all mobile data traffic. In increasingly crowded

This work is supported by National Natural Science Foundation of China under Grant No. 61801167, and the Fundamental Research Funds for the Central Universities under Grant No. B200202189.

wireless networks, smooth and high-quality video streaming may not be guaranteed, which results in a low quality of experience (QoE) for mobile video users. Therefore, it is necessary while challenging to improve video streaming efficiency and quality as much as possible under limited wireless network resources.

Scalable video coding (SVC) as an extension of H.264/AVC standard can provide video users with a variety of video qualities. Because of such flexibility, SVC video streaming has attracted a lot of interests in the literature, and some research studies have been dedicated in improving its performance by applying device-to-device communications, content caching, and video scheduling [2,3]. However, most of existing work considered that users were connected to a single base station (BS) only. Currently, wireless networks are evolving towards heterogeneity and density with the deployment of small cell base stations (SCBSs), and the concept of ultra-dense network (UDN) has emerged. In a UDN, the density of SCBSs is close to or even higher than that of mobile users, and it is possible for a mobile user to connect to multiple BSs [4].

In [5], the authors proposed a framework of scalable video streaming over a dense small-cell network with the aid of software-defined networking (SDN). In the system model of [5], all SVC-based videos requested by users are stored in the video server, and SDN controls SCBSs to distribute SVC videos to users by multiple connections. However, with the increasing number of users and SCBSs, the server load of SDN will be exploded, which could restrict the system performance. Compared to [5], we consider utilizing the computing resources of user equipment to determine the connection strategy rather than pushing this work to servers. Besides, our proposed solution enables the capability of caching video files in BSs, which can improve the downloading rate.

In this paper, we study the SVC video streaming in a UDN. Specifically, an optimization problem is formulated aiming to maximize the QoE for each user. Considering that this optimization problem is hard to solve without the prior knowledge, we split the problem into multiple ones, each of which corresponds to the download of individual video block. In particular, we consider a combination of connecting BSs for a video block as a connection strategy, and its determination is regarded as the subproblem of video block downloading. For the first video block, a video block downloading strategy is proposed to decide the maximum number of downloading layers, and the connection strategy is selected to minimize the downloading delay when the layer number is fixed. For the remaining video blocks, we adopt the same connection strategy to avoid repeated calculations, but the layer numbers are adaptively adjusted according to the dynamic network condition. Since the video streaming rate is affected by the connection strategy and current connection states of other users, which may vary randomly over the time and are hard to predict, we formulate the subproblem of choosing the optimal connection strategy as an MAB problem. Based on the solution of this subproblem, we then develop an SVC-based video downloading scheme to obtain the approximate optimal solution to the original optimization problem. Finally, we show the feasibility and superiority of proposed schemes by simulations.

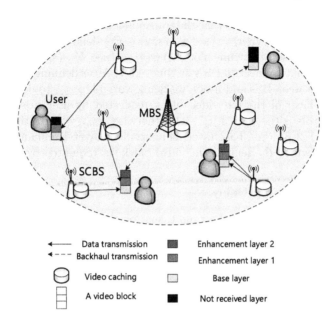

Fig. 1. SVC-based video streaming in a UDN

2 System Model and Problem Formulation

2.1 Network Model

We consider the SVC-based video streaming in a UDN, with a macro base station (MBS), z SCBSs and y users as shown in Fig. 1. $\mathcal{S} = \{s_1, s_2, ..., s_{z+1}\}$ and $\mathcal{U} = \{u_1, u_2, ..., u_y\}$ are used to denote the set of BSs (including the MBS and all SCBSs) and users. BSs and users are randomly distributed, and both SCBSs and MBS could cache SVC-based video contents. For simplicity, the bandwidth of each BS is set to the same. Eacg video block is assumed to contain three video layers at most. According to the characteristics of SVC and multi-connection UDNs, we assume that each user can connect to multiple BSs for downloading one video (consisting of multiple blocks), and each layer of a video block can only be downloaded from one BS [4].

2.2 Wireless Connection Model

For a requested video block with multiple layers, the user can choose to download it from a combination of BSs. The combination of connecting BSs selected by a user is viewed as a connection strategy, and hereafter we term such selection process as the connection strategy selection.

We adopt a graph specified as $G_t = (U_t, S; E_t)$ to describe the connection status of BSs and users, where t represents the time slot, U_t and S denote the user set and the BS set respectively. The edge set E_t consists of all pairs

$(s, u) \in S \times U_t$, which indicates that the transmission connection between s and u varies with time slot t. $\mathcal{N}_t(u) = \{s \in S : (s, u) \in E_t\}$ denotes the set of BSs that are connected by user u at time slot t. $\mathcal{M}_t(s) = \{u \in U : (s, u) \in E_t\}$ denotes the set of users that connect to BS s at time slot t. After defining the connection relationships between BSs and users, we define variable x_{ubjs} to denote whether the jth video layer of the bth video block requested by user u is downloaded from BS s. If this is the case, $x_{ubjs} = 1$; otherwise, $x_{ubjs} = 0$. In this paper, we consider $j \in \{1, 2, 3\}$ (i.e., base layer, enhancement layer 1, enhancement layer 2) and $b \in \mathcal{B}_u$, where $\mathcal{B}_u$ denotes the video block set requested by user u.

2.3   Video Streaming Delay

The video streaming delay is the time taken for all connected BSs to complete downloading the whole video block:

$$D_{X_t}(t) = max(\frac{\sum_{j \in \{1,2,3\}} \eta_j x_{ubjs}}{R_{usX_t}}), s \in \mathcal{N}(u), \tag{1}$$

where $X_t = \{x_{ubjs}, u \in \mathcal{U}, b \in \mathcal{B}_u, j \in \{1, 2, 3\}, s \in \mathcal{S}\}$ denotes the decision of which video layer is downloaded from which BS at time slot t for bth video block of user u. $D_{X_t}(t)$ denotes the downloading delay of a video block for a user at time slot t. η_j denotes the size of the jth video layer. $max()$ denotes taking the maximum of given values, aiming to calculate the maximum downloading delay of all the connected BS(s).

In (1), R_{us} denotes the downloading rate of user u from BS s. The rate can be calculated by the *Shannon-Hartley Theorem* as follows:

$$R_{usX} = B_{usX} \log_2(1 + p_s \cdot \frac{G_{us}}{I_{s'uX} + \sigma^2}), \tag{2}$$

where $B_{usX} = \frac{B}{|\mathcal{M}(s)|}$ denotes the bandwidth occupied by user u connecting to BS s when the status of the network connection is X, and p_s denotes the power level of BS s. $G_{us} = |h_{u,s}|^2 d_{s,u}^{-\xi}$ is the channel gain between user u and BS s, where $|h_{u,s}|^2$ denotes the integrated channel power gain, $d_{s,u}$ denotes the distance between them and ξ denotes the path-loss exponent [6]. σ^2 is the additive white Gaussian noise (AWGN). $I_{s'uX}$ denotes the interferences caused by any other BS s' except s when the status of the network connection is X, which is defined as follows:

$$I_{s'uX} = \sum_{s' \in \mathcal{S} \setminus \{s\}} p_{s'} G_{s'u}(1 - x'_{us'}) \sum_{u'=1}^{\mathcal{U}} x'_{u's'}, \tag{3}$$

x'_{us} is a connection binary variable to indicate whether user u is connected to BS s, and u' denotes any other user except user u. $x'_{us} = 1$ if user u connects to BS s, otherwise, $x'_{us} = 0$. Note that both B_{usX} and $I_{s'uX}$ depends on all users' connection status, and the video downloading rate depends on the connection strategy selection and the connection status of other users.

2.4 Maximum Delay to Ensure Video Fluency

In order to avoid any interruption in video streaming, it is necessary to define the maximum tolerable delay to guarantee video fluency. For the bth video block, the maximum delay to ensure its fluency is the time interval between the current time and the ending time of the last video block playback, which can be defined as:

$$MD_b(t) = \begin{cases} \theta, & b = 1, \\ (b-1)\tau - t, & b \geq 2, \end{cases} \tag{4}$$

where τ is the playing time of a video block, which is a constant, and $(b-1)\tau$ denotes the ending time of playing the last video block. t is the time that the bth video block starts being downloaded. Because the video has not started playing yet when the first video block is downloaded, the delay requirement for the first video block is different from those of the others. Here we set the delay θ as two seconds to ensure the first video block fluency.

2.5 Utility of QoE

Similar to [7], we adopt the Mean Opinion Score (MOS) to measure the quality of video services. In the considered model, the video quality of a user only fluctuates occasionally during the process of viewing videos. Therefore, we only focus on the impact of video quality on QoE of a user. We consider three levels of the MOS. Let $q_u(t)$ denote the MOS level of user u at time slot t and let $l_u(t) \in \{1, 2, 3\}$ be the number of video layers viewed by user u at time slot t. $q_u(t)$ is a function of $l_u(t)$, which is expressed as:

$$q_u(t) = f[l_u(t)] = 2l_u(t) - 1. \tag{5}$$

We consider that the utility of QoE depends on the MOS level of each viewed video block. Based on the above analysis, the utility of user u (reflected by its QoE) in playback time period $[0, T]$ can be defined as:

$$Q(T) = \sum_{b=1}^{B_u} q_u(b\tau), \tag{6}$$

where T denotes the time when the video request is played completely. B_u denotes amount of video blocks that is requested by user u.

2.6 Problem Formulation

When the connection strategy and the number of video layers are determined, a video block starts being downloaded. Then this process is repeated until all the played video blocks in $[0, T]$ (i.e., a video sequence) are downloaded completely. Therefore, the utility of user u in $[0, T]$ can be further written as:

$$Q(T) = \sum_{b=1}^{B_u} q_u(t_b), \quad t_b \in [0, T'], \tag{7}$$

where t_b denotes the time of starting downloading the bth video block, and T' denotes the time for downloading all video blocks in sequence. Correspondingly, the utility maximization problem for each individual user u within $[0, T]$ is formulated as:

$$\underset{X_{ut}}{maximize}\ Q(T),$$

$$subject\ to\ \ C1: l_u(t_b) = \sum_{s \in \mathcal{N}_{t_b}(u)} \sum_{j \in \{1,2,3\}} x_{ubjs}(t_b),$$

$$C2: D_{X_{ut_b}}(t_b) \le MD_b(t_b),$$

$$C3: t_b = D_{X_{t_{b-1}}}(t_{b-1}) + t_{b-1},$$

$$C4: \sum_{s \in \mathcal{S}} x_{ubjs} \ge \sum_{s \in \mathcal{S}} x_{ub(j+1)s}, 1 \le j \le 2,$$

$$C5: s \in \mathcal{S}, b \in \mathcal{B}_u, j \in \{1,2,3\},$$

$$C6: t_b \in [0, T'].$$

(8)

Constraint $C1$ states that the number of video layers downloaded from each video block is equal to the number of video layers viewed by the user. Constraint $C2$ is imposed for avoiding the interruption of the bth video block. Constraint $C3$ denotes the next video block that should start to be downloaded when the current block has been downloaded completely. Constraint $C4$ avoids receiving only the higher layer without the lower layer. $X_{ut} = \{x_{ubjs}, b \in \mathcal{B}_u, j \in \{1,2,3\}, s \in \mathcal{S}\}$ denotes the decision of which video layer is downloaded from which BS at time slot t for bth video block of user u. The goal of the problem is to choose a set of optimal connection strategies and optimal layer numbers for a video sequence so that the utility of a video viewer is maximized.

The formulated optimization problem is an integer programming problem which is hard to solve due to the random downloading rate. Therefore, we consider splitting the problem into multiple ones, each of which corresponds to individual video block. For each video block, when its number of layers is fixed, we focus on minimizing the downloading delay of the first video block of user u. However, for each user, the current state of the network is unknown, and the connection states of other users are unpredictable. Each user has no prior information about other users. Therefore, to circumvent this difficulty, we consider the connection strategy selection as an MAB problem. After solving the MAB problem and obtaining the video block downloading strategy, the number of downloading layers and the connection strategy are calculated for each video block. Then we obtain the approximate optimal solution of optimization problem (8) by SVC-based video downloading scheme. The specific solution process will be introduced in Sect. 3.

3 SVC-Based Video Downloading Scheme Based on MAB Problem

3.1 Base Station Connection Strategy Selection as Multi-armed Bandit

We first consider the BS connection strategy selection problem for a fixed layer number of a video block. To this end, we formulate the problem as an MAB problem, in which a user is viewed as a gambler and a BS connection combination of downloading a video block is viewed as an arm. We expect to obtain an approximately optimal connection strategy by solving the MAB problem. The reward R_{MAB} in the MAB problem can be expressed as:

$$R_{MAB} = -D_{X_{ut_b}}(t_b). \tag{9}$$

For a general MAB problem, the goal is to maximize the accumulated reward after a limited number of trials. However, for our problem, the final goal is to obtain an optimal connection strategy to download the video block. In other words, we expect to acquire a unique exploitation strategy after a limited number of trials. Correspondingly, we propose a modified UCB algorithm to solve the formulated MAB problem.

3.2 Best-arm-selecting Upper Confidence Bound Algorithm

For above considerations, we develop a best-arm-selecting UCB algorithm for our problem. Similar to the conventional UCB algorithm [8], the best-arm-selecting UCB algorithm also selects an arm based on the upper confidence indices. The upper confidence index includes the current average reward and the bonus of each arm, which is expressed as:

$$I_j = \widehat{\mu}_j + \alpha \sqrt{\frac{2ln(m)}{G_j(m)}}, \tag{10}$$

where $\widehat{\mu}_j$ denotes the average reward of selecting strategy j. $G_j(m)$ denotes the number of selecting the strategy j in m pulling times. $\alpha\sqrt{\frac{2ln(m)}{G_j(m)}}$ denotes the bonus of selecting strategy j. α is a scaling parameter and its impact to the performance of the algorithm will be analyzed in Sect. 4.

The proposed best-arm-selecting UCB algorithm is shown in Algorithm 1. At first, all strategies are tried once and the reward from trying each strategy is recorded in variable $\widehat{\mu}_j$. Then $M - J$ times of attempts are executed, where M denotes the total number of attempts and J denotes the total number of strategies. The strategy is selected based on the upper confidence index in each attempt. Finally, the strategy with the most selections is considered as the best strategy. And the average reward of the best strategy is considered as the maximum reward. Due to the short running time and fast learning rate of UCB algorithm, it is suitable for real-time video streaming.

Algorithm 1. Best-arm-selected UCB Algorithm

Input:
>   The number of strategies J;The number of attempts M;
>   The coefficient for adjusting the exploration α;
>   The current time t.

Output:
>   The best strategy number j_{best};
>   The average reward of the best strategy $\widehat{\mu}_{j_{best}}$.
> $\forall i = 1$ to $J : \widehat{\mu}_i = 0, count(i) = 0$
> $flag = 1$
>   **for** $j = 1$ to J **do**
> $\widehat{\mu}_j = R_{MAB}$
> $count(j) = count(j) + 1$
>   **end for**
>   **for** $t = J + 1$ to M **do**
> $k = \arg\max_i(\widehat{\mu}_i + \alpha\sqrt{\frac{2ln(t)}{count(i)}})$
> $count(k) = count(k) + 1$
> $\widehat{\mu}_k = \frac{1}{count(k)}((count(k) - 1)\widehat{\mu}_k + R_{MAB})$
>   **end for**
> $j_{best} = \arg\max_i count(i)$

Algorithm 2. Video Block Downloading Strategy

Input:
>   The maximum delay of ensure video fluency MD;
>   The strategy number selected by the first video block j_{first}.

Output:
>   The download strategy of the video block X_{ut}.
>   **for** $v = 3$ to 1 **do**
>   **if** $j_{first} == -1$ **then**
>   Obtain j_{best} when downloading v layer(s)' video in Algorithm 1.
>   Calculate the delay D according to j_{best} and v.
>   **else**
> $j_{best} = j_{first}$.
>   Calculate the delay D according to j_{best} and v.
>   **end if**
>   **if** $MD > D$ **then**
>   Convert v and j_{best} into X_{ut}.
>   Return X_{ut}.
>   **end if**
>   **end for**

Besides, in Algorithm 1, we can apply the regret to denote the accumulative differences between the current reward and the maximum reward. The regret can be used to prove the convergence of this algorithm. Since there is a proof of the maximum expected regret in [9], which is also applicable to our algorithm, such proof is omitted for conciseness.

3.3   SVC-Based Video Streaming Scheme

In Sect. 3.2, we have considered the process of BS connection strategy selection for a video block given that its number of layers is fixed. Next, our remaining problem is how to download a video block with uncertain size and how to download a video sequence.

The video block downloading strategy is summarized in Algorithm 2. At first, the three layers of the video block are tried to be obtained. Then the current approximate optimal BS connection strategy is calculated by Algorithm 1. If the connection strategy can ensure the video fluency, it will be used as the downloading method for the video block. Otherwise two layers and one layer of the video block would be tried to be obtained in turn. Because there are three layers of a video block at most, it is easy to assign the selected video layers to the selected BS(s) to download. For example, when two BSs are selected to download three video layers, two layers are downloaded from the BS whose downloading rate is faster and one layer is downloaded from the BS whose downloading rate is slower.

Finally, we present an SVC-based video downloading scheme. The first video block needs to be downloaded in two seconds according to the analysis in Sect. 2.4. Subsequent video blocks are downloaded from the same BS combination or its subset. In order to ensure the video fluency, the next video block needs to be downloaded before the current video block has been played completely, otherwise the video would be stuck. By analogy, similar process continues until all video blocks are completely downloaded. This eventually provides an approximate optimal solution to the original optimization problem (8).

4   Simulation Results and Analysis

For simulations, the area that we consider is a 200 m × 200 m square UDN, which includes 7 SCBSs, 1 MBS and 4 users according to the definition of the UDN [10]. BSs (including the MBS and all SCBSs) and users are randomly within this area. The power of BSs and the power of user equipment are set to be 5 W and 1 W, respectively. For simplicity, the size of all video layers is assumed to be 200 kb, and each BS caches all the popular video contents. The noise level is set as −121 dBw, and the path-loss exponent is 2. Besides, the bandwidth of BSs is chosen to be 20. In the following simulations, we focus on a particular user in the considered network. Other users are also connected to the network in a multi-connection manner, and their connection strategies randomly change over the time.

4.1   Performance Analysis

We first verify the effectiveness of the best-arm-selected UCB algorithm for solving the problem of video block downloading, and analyze the impact of adjusting the coefficient parameter α on the performance of the algorithm.

At first, we analyze the feasibility of the algorithm. Figure 2 shows the percentage of the times that the optimal strategy was selected after each iteration. The reason for the initial fluctuation is that the algorithm mainly tends to exploration, and the reason for the later stability is that the optimal strategy for exploitation is constantly selected. We regard the downloading delay of a video block as the cost of the MAB problem. By selecting the optimal strategy many times, we obtain the average cost of the optimal strategy, which is shown in Fig. 3. As shown in Fig. 2 and Fig. 3, the algorithm can eventually converge, and an approximately optimal strategy can be obtained. Specifically, it only takes about 0.22 seconds for the algorithm to iterate 2,000 times. Before the video starts playing, spending the time in choosing the optimal BS connection strategy would hardly affect the user's QoE.

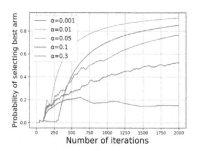

Fig. 2. Accuracy of the algorithm in the case of different α values.

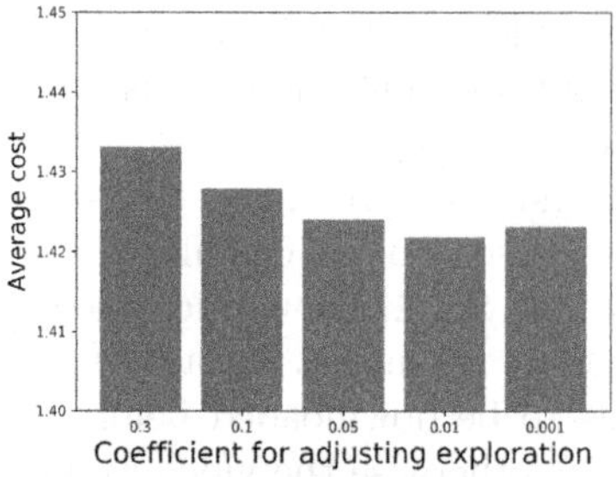

Fig. 3. Average cost of the optimal strategy in the case of different α values.

Next, we analyze the impact of α on the performance of the algorithm. As shown in Fig. 2, decreasing α from 0.3 to 0.01 makes the algorithm converge quickly. However, when α decreases from 0.01 to 0.001, the convergence speed of the algorithm becomes slower. The reason is that the algorithm excessively tends to exploitation and the suboptimal strategy is frequently selected in the first 300 iterations, which leads to smaller convergence speed of the algorithm. When α decreases from 0.01 to 0.001, the average cost becomes higher in Fig. 3. The reason is that the convergence speed of the algorithm is slower and the convergence value is smaller when α equals 0.001. This result confirms our analyses in Fig. 2.

4.2 Performance Comparison

The proposed algorithm is compared with epsilon-Greedy and Softmax algorithms, which are common solutions of MAB problem. The epsilon-Greedy algorithm [8] tries to balance the two opposite goals of exploration and exploitation by a certain probability of exploration. The Softmax algorithm [8] compromises exploration and exploitation based on the currently known average reward of arms. However, it is worth noting that these two algorithms did not consider

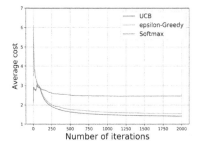

Fig. 4. Performance of different algorithms.

how much they know about the reward distribution of each arm. Maybe the reward of a certain arm is not representative at the certain time, in other words, this arm is not enough to be understood. The best-arm-selecting UCB algorithm avoids such problems. We replace the best-arm-selecting UCB algorithm with the two algorithms mentioned above. The experimental results in Fig. 4 illustrate that the proposed UCB algorithm outperforms the existing epsilon-Greedy and Softmax algorithms. This is because the best-arm-selecting UCB algorithm can find the optimal strategy quickly and obtains very low average cost.

4.3   SVC-based Video Downloading Scheme

We verify the feasibility of the SVC-based video downloading scheme based on the best-arm-selected UCB algorithm. The experimental video contains 10 video blocks and the playback time of each video block is 1.2 seconds. The time of starting playing and downloading completely of each video block is shown in Fig. 5. The number of layers downloaded per video block is shown in Fig. 6. According to these two pictures, an approximate optimal solution to the original optimization problem can be obtained by the proposed downloading scheme. In

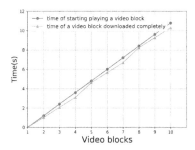

Fig. 5. Time of starting playing and downloading completely for each video block.

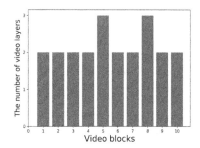

Fig. 6. The number of video layers for each video block downloaded.

addition, through our proposed scheme, video interruption is well avoided and the video quality well adapt to the current network and playing status.

5   Conclusion

In this paper, we have investigated the SVC-based video streaming problem in UDNs, which allows each user to download different layers of its demanded video block from different BSs. Specifically, we have formulated the problem as an optimization problem to maximize the QoE for each user. To this end, we have split the problem into multiple problems of downloading individual video block. For downloading individual video block, we have presented a best-arm-selecting UCB algorithm and a video block downloading strategy. Furthermore, we have presented an SVC-based video downloading scheme which provides an approximately optimal solution to the original optimization problem. Finally, the superiority of proposed solution has been demonstrated by simulations.

References

1. Global mobile data traffic forecast update 2016–2021 white paper. https://www.cisco.com/c/en/us/solutions/collateral/service-provider/visual-networking-index-vni/mobile-white-paper-c11-520862.html. Accessed 15 Apr 2017
2. Zhan, C., Yao, G.: SVC video delivery in cache-enabled wireless HetNet. IEEE Syst. J. **12**(4), 3885–3888 (2018)
3. Otwani, J., Agarwal, A., Jagannatham, A.K.: Optimal scalable video scheduling policies for real-time single- and multiuser wireless video networks. IEEE Trans. Veh. Technol. **64**(6), 2424–2435 (2015)
4. Kamel, M., Hamouda, W., Youssef, A.: Performance analysis of multiple association in ultra-dense networks. IEEE Trans. Commun. **65**(9), 3818–3831 (2017)
5. Yang, J., Yang, B., Chen, S., Zhang, Y., Zhang, Y., Hanzo, L.: Dynamic resource allocation for streaming scalable videos in SDN-aided dense small-cell networks. IEEE Trans. Commun. **67**(3), 2114–2129 (2019)
6. Elshaer, H., Boccardi, F., Dohler, M., Irmer, R.: Downlink and uplink decoupling: a disruptive architectural design for 5G networks. In: Proceedings IEEE GLOBE-COM, pp. 1798–1803, December 2014
7. Moldovan, A., Ghergulescu, I., Muntean, C.H.: VQAMap: a novel mechanism for mapping objective video quality metrics to subjective MOS scale. IEEE Trans. Broadcast. **62**(3), 610–627 (2016)
8. White, J.M.: Bandit Algorithms for Website Optimization. O'Reilly Media Inc., Sebastopol (2013)
9. Auer, P., Cesa-Bianchi, N., Fischer, P.: Finite-time analysis of the multiarmed bandit problem. IEEE Trans. Broadcast. **47**(2–3), 235–256 (2002)
10. Kamel, M., Hamouda, W., Youssef, A.: Ultra-dense networks: a survey. IEEE Trans. Commun. Surveys Tutorials **18**(4), 2522–2545 (2016)

Security

FIUD: A Framework to Identify Users of Devices

Yimo Ren[1,2], Hong Li[1,2(✉)], Hongsong Zhu[1,2], and Limin Sun[1,2]

[1] School of Cyber Security, University of Chinese Academy of Sciences, Beijing, China
[2] Institute of Information Engineering, Chinese Academy of Sciences, Beijing, China
{renyimo,lihong,zhuhongsong,sunlimin}@iie.ac.cn

Abstract. The device detected from the public network usually associates with an IP as the unique identity generally. The problem is that many registrants of devices are always different from their true users, which make it difficult for operators to discover whether the IPs are used normally. The research on users of IPs plays an important role to help us for network security and protection. In this paper, we are seeking the users of devices and investigating why they are exposed to the public from five aspects: SSL certificates, protocol banners, address, topology and location. We presented FIUD: A Framework to Identify Users of Devices to extract users automatically. FIUD is based on Seed Extension so as to ensure both accuracy and coverage of user identification. We evaluated our methodology in laboratory and in the real-world. Compared with the mature results in the industry, the experiment shows that our methodology has achieved higher performances to discover the true users of IPs. At the same time, we did the network measurement in Beijing based on our methodology.

Keywords: Users of devices · Seed extension · Network measurement · Data fusion

1 Introduction

On November 26, 2019, the approximately 4.3 billion IPv4 have already been used up world-wide. In order to meet the demands of connecting to the Internet, on one hand, IPv6 is gradually used to expand the number of IPs on the basis of IPv4. On the other hand, cloud services, dynamic allocation and other mechanisms are deployed to use the limited IP resources more effectively. For example, after Internet Service Providers (ISPs) obtain the addresses from the national Internet Registry, they further assign it to the intermediate agents (Clouds, etc.) or assign it to the true users dynamically. The problem is that: who truly uses the IPs in the Internet?

Supported by National Key Research and Development Projects (No. Y950201104) and National Natural Science Foundation of China (No. U1766215).

Z. Liu et al. (Eds.): WASA 2021, LNCS 12938, pp. 45–57, 2021.
https://doi.org/10.1007/978-3-030-86130-8_4

Users of IPs has very important and interesting applications. For example, [1,6] used IPs with high confidence users as landmarks to improve the accuracy of IP geolocation. Through the user identification of IPs, it can be more accurate and meaningful for us to carry out network measurement in cyber-physical space. Also, it can be more effective to understand and well-directly protect the devices used by lots of users on their own side for security regulators.

A very straight forward idea is to send an online query to existed databases, such as WHOIS, to search the related information of IPs. Some researches [2] obtain the registration information of devices through querying the WHOIS, while we could only get the registers of IPs, not who truly use them. There are also a few researches about getting the users of IPs sideways. Jia Y [3] automatically extracted users by rule-based regexes from the response data of IoT devices. Researchers [4,5] found locations could lead to the discovery of detailed information about the devices, including the user. And AIWEN TECH, an industrial company, mined the users of IPs through their official domains, so as to get the pairs of IPs and users [6]. However, the methods described above did not realize the fusion of multi-sources data of IPs to achieve better performance. At the same time, the methods only consider the single IP, without considering the relations or similarities between IPs. And what's more, the performance of existing methods is not yet satisfactory.

In this paper, we designed the Seed Extension Based framework for user identification of IPs in Internet, which improves both the accuracy and coverage compared with the existing methods. It is important to note that we use the data exposed to the public Internet by the devices, so there is no risk of violating the privacy of users. Overall, our contributions are summarized as follows:

(a) We first gave the Seed Extension Based model and proposed a complete framework to identify the users of IPs in Internet.
(b) We used Neutral Network enhanced Seeds Mining to ensure the accuracy and Bayesian improved User Extension to expand coverage of user identification.
(c) We evaluated our methodology and found our methodology have achieved a higher performance: 75.41% precision, 76.12% recall in a specific dataset and 74.70% coverage of all IPs in Beijing.

2   Methodology

The paper processes a Seed Extension Based methodology to ensure the accuracy and coverage of user identification both. Seed Extension methods concludes: Mining the high-confidence results and considering them as labels to expand the coverage of the results by supervision.

Therefore, our methodology contains three steps: Seeds Mining, Users Extension and Results United. First, we extracted high-confidence users as seeds with subtle methods based on heterogeneous data of IPs. Second, we focused on the research of similarities of two IPs to infer the users of other IPs. Finally, because of multi methods, Results United should fuse different results to provide a united and unique user for each IP. Figure 1 shows the description of our methodology.

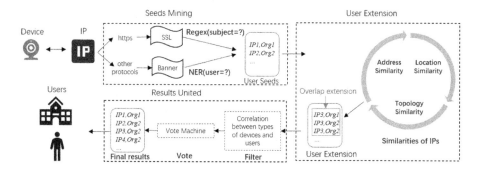

Fig. 1. Overview of our methodology.

2.1 Seeds Mining

Active Detection is a common method to realize active network measurement. We send packets to online devices to get their interactive information to know how the devices are performing. Taft [7] introduces how the active detection works. Rüth [8] and Holz [9] uses Internet-wide scans to study security properties or protocol adoption on the Internet.

Here, we use active detection to get information of IPs such as: SSL certificates and protocol banners. The target users in SSL and Protocol banners as Fig. 2 shows.

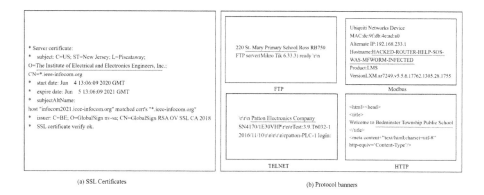

Fig. 2. Users in SSL certificates and protocol banners of IPs.

SSL. SSL are digital certificates serving as the backbone of Internet security. Weinstein [10] introduced how the SSL certificates work and Clark [11] discussed the mechanism and security of issuing certificates.

For the protocols using SSL certificates, such as HTTPS, we can extract users from the content of SSL certificates, which we call as SSL Orgs. We used curl to download all the response data of each IP and used regexes to extract possible users of IPs. For SSL certificates, the regexes and keywords we used are (subject: (.*?)) and (O = (.*?);).

We found lots of obvious error of certificates, so we did some filterings: we drop the self-signed certificates, the expired certificates and the certificates with risk issuers or risk subjects.

NER. Protocol banners are the public response data when we send queries to IPs. Because of the various formats of the returned information caused by multiple protocols, it is hard to use single regexes or keywords to extract possible users, therefore we used Named Entity Recognition (NER) methods. NER is often used to extract information from natural languages. Goyal [12] presents a survey of developments and progresses made in NER and Georgescu [13] enhances the process of diagnosing and detecting possible vulnerabilities within an Internet of Things (IoT) system by using a NER-based solution.

BiLSTM-CRF is one of common and mature methods of NER [14]. We choose to build a BiLSTM-CRF to extract users from protocol banners, which we call as NER Orgs. We put protocol banners into BiLSTM-CRF by words, and the BiLSTM-CRF judge whether a group of words are a name of possible users according to the relation between the words. For example, "Welcome to Bedminster Township Public School" will be tagged as "O O B-USER I-USER I-USER I-USER", which means "Bedminster Township Public School" is the possible user of the IP.

2.2 Users Extension

When a small set of nodes have been preidentified, the common way to infer the identification of other nodes is to find similarities between them and their neighbors. In this section, we used three kinds similarities of IPs to extend the users identification of IPs except seeds from Sect. 2.1.

Address. There are two forms of IP address: IPv4 and IPv6. For IPv4, the first 24-bit groups identify Network ID, and the remaining 8 bits represent Host ID [15]. For IPv6, the address is more standardized, which could be more easily solved. To calculate address similarity, we can compare the digits of two addresses of IPv4, the result indicates whether IPs is in the same subnet. Therefore, the similarity of IP_i and IP_j can be calculated as follows:

$$sim_{addr}(i,j) = 1 - \left| \frac{host_{id}(i) - host_{id}(j)}{255} \right| \tag{1}$$

where $host_{id}$ is the last 8 bits of IP address.

After defining the similarity of IP address, we use it to get similar users by sending an IP queries to search in the IP seeds. We call this kind of users as Addr Orgs.

Topology. Topology is commonly used in network measured, and we can get the topology from the BGP [16]. Katz-Bassett [17] presented topology-based geolocation to estimating the geographic location of IPs. We can assume that the more similar the topology of IPs are, in other words, the more similar the nearest neighbor routers of IPs are, the more likely the IPs are to have the same users. Edit distance is an effective method to matching the similarity of two strings or lists [18], so that we use it to calculate the similarity of topology. The topology similarity is defined as:

$$sim_{topo}(i,j) = 1 - \left| \frac{edit\_distance(nrr(i), nrr(j))}{max(len(nrr(i)), len(nrr(j)))} \right| \tag{2}$$

Where $nrr(i)$ represents the nearest reachable routes of the IP_i, $len(nrr(i))$ is the number of $nrr(i)$.

After defining the similarity of IP topology, we use it to get users of other IPs by sending an IP query to search in the IP seeds and we call this kind of users as Topo Orgs.

Location. Geohash [19] is a commonly used algorithm that encodes the longitude and latitude into a string to reduce the complexity to calculate the proximity of two locations. For example, WX4ERQR represents a 4.9 km × 4.9 km size area. So, we selected the IPs locating in the same districts which have same geohash. Therefore, the similarity of IP locations can be calculated as follows:

$$sim_{loc}(i,j) = \begin{cases} 1 & if \quad geohash(i) = geohash(j) \\ 0 & if \quad geohash(i) \neq geohash(j) \end{cases} \tag{3}$$

Using IP location to seek similarity between IP seeds and other IPs is to check whether the two IPs are located in the same area. We call this kind of users as LOC Orgs.

2.3 Results United

The results of user identification in Sect. 2.1 and Sect. 2.2 are probably inaccurate and overlapped. Therefore, we need to build a filter and vote machine, which can improve the accuracy and make a unique user for each IP.

Filter. We built models to represent the correlations between devices' types and the users' types based on the preidentified IPs. We enumerated 6 kinds of devices: **Server, Security, Personal, Industrial, Routing and Other** with 5 kinds of users: **Company, Factory, Government, School and Other**.

We used $Corr(T_d, T_o)$ to represent the correlations between devices' types T_d and the users' types T_o. A higher value indicates that T_o tends to use the T_d. We chose to build a Bayesian model to calculate the correlations. Thanks to the prior work, we know the type of IPs and we need to infer the type of users, therefore the model is defined as:

$$Corr(T_d, T_o) = P(T_o \mid T_d, IPs) = \frac{P(T_d \mid T_o) P(T_o)}{P(T_d)} \tag{4}$$

where $P(T_o)$ and $P(T_d)$ are prior probabilities, $P(T_d \mid T_o)$ is posterior probability. At the same time, the probabilities could be calculated by the preidentified IPs. Then, the purpose of the filter is to select the most relevant users from the results of different methods according to the correlation and delete irrelevant ones.

Vote. The users obtained from multi-sources data may be different. As Fig. 1 shows, the infer users of IP_3 are org_1, org_2, org_2 based on the similarities between it and seeds. So, it is very necessary to unite the different users results for each IP. In this case, we built a vote machine to select the most probably in User Extension. Then the user we get of IP_3 is org_2.

2.4 Summary

In the section, we collated the key points of the methodology as below:

(a) For various formats of banners from devices, we used NER to enhance the ability to extract high confidences users of IPs.
(b) We used similarities of IPs to extend the coverage of user identification, and we used the Bayesian correlations between devices' types and users' types to build a filter to ensure the performance.
(c) Because of heterogeneous data of IPs, we used a vote machine to disambiguate the outputs results.

3 Datasets

3.1 Real World

We deployed our methodology in Beijing network block, which has 2,533,046 IPv4 addresses. Table 1 shows the protocols distribution of IPs in Beijing. One IP may use multiple protocols at the same time.

For the IPs with the various protocols listed in the table, seeds mining is used to extract SSL orgs for HTTS, and NER focuses on protocols with banners, especially HTTP. Similarities of IPs are used to get transfer users of those IPs, with protocols not having obvious content about users, such as ICMP [20].

Table 1. Top protocols distribution.

Protocol	Num/ratio	Protocol	Num/ratio
ICMP	1642233/64.91%	TELNET	115930/4.58%
HTTP	1016876/40.19%	RTSP	73043/2.89%
HTTPS	453333/17.92%	EthernetIP	65735/2.60%
SSH	384390/15.19%	Modbus	65441/2.59%
FTP	343911/13.59%	⋯	⋯

3.2 A Specific Dataset

We also built an evaluation dataset called Stock's network block(snb) with 4284 IPs, which are obtained from the stock exchanges, including Shanghai Stock Exchange, Shenzhen Stock Exchange, etc. We could get the official websites of the listed company according to the stock exchanges, and query the corresponding IP according to the official websites, so as to get the relation between the users and IPs.

4 Experiments

4.1 Settings

NER Orgs. In Sect. 2.1, the content of protocol banners mainly includes two languages: Chinese and English. So, we build a Chinese NER model and an English NER model, both based on BiLSTM-CRF. Each of NER models has 2 LSTM layers with 300 units and 1 CRF layer.

We trained the models with 30,000 labeled samples and test the models with 1000 labeled samples relatively. In order to simplify the training process, it is regarded as correct as long as the relevant information of the user is extracted. At this time, the accuracy of Chinese NER model on test dataset is 90.1% and accuracy of English NER model is 93.8%.

Topology. Some researchers provide services for the connections between IPs in the Internet, such as CAIDA [21]. We downloaded the about 20 million IPs within China from 2018/12/01 to 2019/12/01 as the topology for our methodology.

Similarity Orgs. To ensure the feasibility of the filter and vote in Sect. 2.3, we choose the top 3 of each kind of Similarity Orgs. Therefore, we could get total 9 extension users for each IP from Sect. 2.2.

Correlations. In Sect. 2.3, we built a Bayesian model $P(T_o \mid T_d)$ to represent the correlations between the devices' types and users' types based on SSL Orgs and NER Orgs. The correlations calculated as Fig. 3 shows.

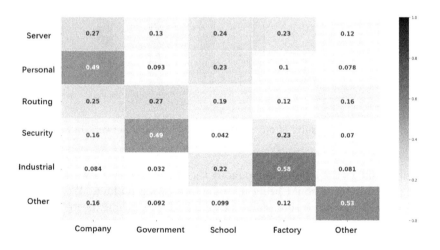

Fig. 3. The correlations calculated by Bayesian model.

As can be seen from the Fig. 3, most of the devices' types and users' types have obvious correlation. For example, if the device type of IP is Security Device, the most possible user type of IP is Government. Also, if the device type of IP is Industrial Device, the most possible user type of IP is Factory. At the same time, we find that the distribution of user types is relatively uniform, when the device type of IP is Routing Device.

Since the correlations are used to filter the results, we keep the most 3 similar users' types from the results of Seeds Mining and User Extension based on the device type of the IP. In this way, the performance of our methodology will be improved as the experiment says.

4.2   Real World Evaluation

To get results of network measurement, we deployed and evaluated our methodology in real-world environment: Beijing network block.

Results. The user results of each method in our methodology are showed in Fig. 4. It should be noted that the results of each method could possibly overlap. We can find that similarities could benefit the coverage of user identification a lot, two times than seeds.

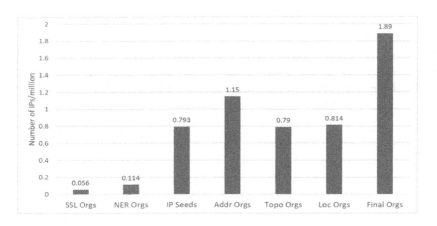

Fig. 4. The results of our methodology in Beijing network block.

Figure 5 shows the top 10 users among the IPs in Beijing network block. The network measurement could bring us some interesting findings. We have found that HUAWEI has more than 80,000 exposed IPs. And unexpectedly, Xueersi also in the top 10, as an education company.

Comparison. We compared our methodology with existing methods. AIWEN [6] extracted IPs with users through the domain of organizations from yellow pages. Also, the method sending queries to existed databases, such as Whois [2], is a comparison. For Whois, we only select the possible users in query results.

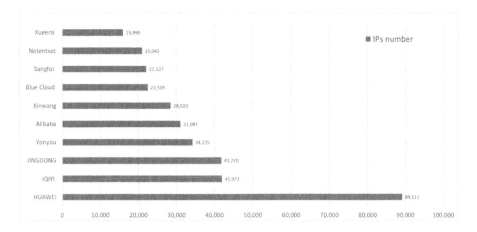

Fig. 5. The top 10 users in Beijing network block.

Table 2. Contrasted with other methods in real world.

Data	Method	Results	Coverage
Beijing network block	WHOIS	0.653M	25.81%
	AIWEN TECH	0.08M	3.30%
	Our methodology	1.89M	74.70%

We can see that the coverage of our methods is much more than AIWEN TECH and Whois, as Table 2 shows.

Because the number of IPs with users is unknown in the real world, we could only calculate how many IPs are correctly identified. We gave the users results of IPs with five mainstream protocols and tagged some random sampling IPs to measure the performance of our methodology in the real world, as Table 3 shows. It should be noted that: Coverage is the ratio of identified IPs of the corresponding protocol. Randomly Selected Num is the number of randomly and proportionally selected IPs.

Table 3. Accuracy of users identification.

Protocols	Coverage	Randomly Selected Num	Accuracy
HTTP	79.52%	2900	80.48%
HTTPS	70.81%	1160	88.53%
SSH	50.42%	700	59.71%
FTP	60.24%	740	63.64%
TELNET	47.82%	200	78.5%
Total	65.82%	5700	77.31%

As Table 3 shows, due to the seeds mining, HTTP and HTTPs could be well covered and have better user identification results. While SSH, FTP, TELNET have so few protocol contents that we are more dependent on IPs similarities to identify users and the performance is relatively poor.

Parameters. The number of IP seeds is an important parameter of our methodology. To verify the relation between the number of IP seeds and accuracy, coverage of our methodology, we built a line chart of their relationship in real world, as Fig. 6 shows.

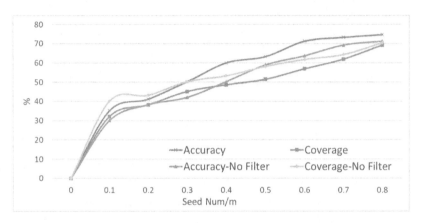

Fig. 6. The relation between seeds number and accuracy, coverage of our methodology.

It can be seen from the figure above that: with the increase of IP seeds, the accuracy and coverage are improved both. At the same time, if we continue to increase the number of IP seeds, there should be a significantly slower improving process of performance. Also, the filter based on the relation between devices' types and users' types could easily improve accuracy of our methodology at the cost of coverage.

4.3   Specific Dataset Evaluation

Metric. In this section, we calculate the precision and recall to evaluate our methodology. The definitions are as follows:

$$Precision = \frac{TP}{TP+FP}$$

$$Recall = \frac{TP}{TP+FN}$$

(5)

where TP presents the number of the true positive, FP presents the number of the false positive, and FN is the number of the false negative. For those IPs that could not be identified, we treat the users results as None.

Performance. Figure 7 gives the comparisons of our methodology on snb. We can see that both the precision and recall of our methodology (75.41% precision, 76.12% recall) is better than AIWEN TECH and Whois. Because we constructed the evaluation dataset from domains, NER-based model plays an important role in our methodology at this time. Also, we can see that Seeds Mining have better performance at precision and User Extension could benefit the coverage (95.86 %) of our methodology. But we found the similarities of IPs are probably too weak to be high-confidence results of user identification and need to be improved.

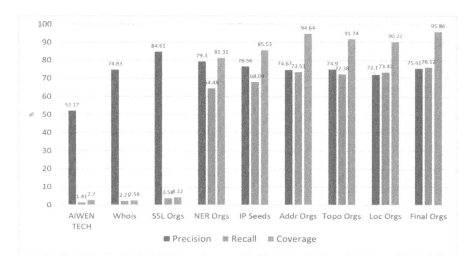

Fig. 7. Contrasted with other methods based on dataset snb.

5   Conclusion

In this paper, we are seeking the users of IPs and investigating why they are exposed to the public Internet from five aspects. We used Active Detection, NER, and three kinds of IP similarities to fully use heterogeneous data of IPs and extract users automatically. Compared with the mature results in the industry, we have greatly expanded the coverage of identification with further improving accuracy. We did network measurement of users based on our methodology and proposed an Evaluation dataset based on listed companies in China. The evaluation results show that our approaches have achieved 75.41% precision, 76.12% recall in a specific dataset and 74.70% coverage of all IPs in Beijing. At the same time, we found HUAWEI have most devices exposed to the public in Beijing at present.

User identification of devices is very interesting and meaningful. In the future, we will apply users of devices to common IoT applications to better protect connected devices. However, it is obvious that the accuracy of similarity is not so much high. Therefore, continuing to improve the performance based on more seeds and similarities of IPs is our next direction of work.

References

1. Chen, J.: Towards IP location estimation using the nearest common router. J. Internet Technol. **19**(7), 2097–2110 (2018)
2. Daigle, L.: WHOIS protocol specification. RFC **49**(8), 756–757 (2004)
3. Jia, Y., Han, B., Li, Q., et al.: Who owns Internet of Thing devices? Int. J. Distrib. Sens. Netw. **14**(11), 155014771881109 (2018)
4. Zheng, X., Cai, Z., Yu, J.: Follow but no track: privacy preserved profile publishing in cyber-physical social systems. IEEE Internet Things J. **6**, 1868–1878 (2017)
5. Pingley, A., Yu, W., Zhang, N., et al.: CAP: a context-aware privacy protection system for location-based services. In: IEEE International Conference on Distributed Computing Systems. IEEE (2009)
6. Wang, Y., Burgener, D., Flores, M., Kuzmanovic, A., Huang, C.: Towards street-level client-independent IP geolocation. In: Proceedings of the 8th USENIX Conference on Networked Systems Design and Implementation (NSDI 2011), pp. 365–379. USENIX Association, USA (2011)
7. Roughan, M., Chang, R. (eds.): PAM 2013. LNCS, vol. 7799. Springer, Heidelberg (2013). https://doi.org/10.1007/978-3-642-36516-4
8. Rüth, J., Zimmermann, T., Hohlfeld, O.: Hidden treasures – recycling large-scale Internet measurements to study the Internet's control plane. In: Choffnes, D., Barcellos, M. (eds.) PAM 2019. LNCS, vol. 11419, pp. 51–67. Springer, Cham (2019). https://doi.org/10.1007/978-3-030-15986-3_4
9. Holz, R.: The SSL landscape: a thorough analysis of the x.509 PKI using active and passive measurements. In: Proceedings of the 2011 ACM SIGCOMM Conference on Internet Measurement Conference, pp. 427–444 (2011)
10. Weinstein, J., Weinstein, T., Elgamal, T.: SSL step-up (2000)
11. Clark, J., Oorschot, P.C.V.: SoK: SSL and HTTPS: revisiting past challenges and evaluating certificate trust model enhancements. In: 2013 IEEE Symposium on Security and Privacy (SP). IEEE (2013)
12. Goyal, A., Gupta, V., Kumar, M.: Recent named entity recognition and classification techniques: a systematic review. Comput. Sci. Rev. **29**, 21–43 (2018)
13. Georgescu, T.M., Iancu, B., Zurini, M.: Named-entity-recognition-based automated system for diagnosing cybersecurity situations in IoT networks. Sensors **19**(15), 3380 (2019)
14. Ling, L., Zhihao, Y., Pei, Y., et al.: An attention-based BiLSTM-CRF approach to document-level chemical named entity recognition. Bioinformatics **34**(8), 1381–1388 (2019)
15. Meng, X., Xu, Z., Zhang, B., et al.: IPv4 address allocation and the BGP routing table evolution. ACM SIGCOMM Comput. Commun. Rev. **35**(1), 71–80 (2005)
16. Bakker, N., Jasinska, E., Raszuk, R., et al.: Internet exchange BGP route server (2016)
17. Katz-Bassett, E., John, J.P., Krishnamurthy, A., et al.: Towards IP geolocation using delay and topology measurements. In: ACM SIGCOMM Conference on Internet Measurement. ACM (2006)

18. Cohen, W.W.: A comparison of string distance metrics for name-matching tasks. In: IIWEB 2003 Proceedings of the 2003 International Conference on Information Integration on the Web, pp. 73–78 (2003)
19. Miller, F.P., Agnes, F., et al.: Geohash. Alphascript Publishing, USA (2010)
20. Taylor, T., Leech, M., Bellovin, S.: ICMP traceback messages Internet draft (2003)
21. Claffy, K.C.: CAIDA: visualizing the Internet. IEEE Internet Comput. 5(1), 88 (2011)

SAPN: Spatial Attention Pyramid Network for Cross-Domain Person Re-Identification

Zhaoqian Jia⬤, Wenchao Wang⬤, Shaoqi Hou⬤, Ye Li⬤, and Guangqiang Yin$^{(\boxtimes)}$⬤

University of Electronic Science and Technology of China, Chengdu, China
{zqjia,wenchao_wang,sqhou,liye}@std.uestc.edu.cn, yingq@uestc.edu.cn

Abstract. The background differences between domains poses a huge challenge for cross-domain person re-identification (Re-ID). And the attention mechanism is usually used to select regions of interest and suppress irrelevant background noises. However, many realizations of the attention mechanism do not deeply dig the relevance of the internal information of the features, and the attention information at different stages in the model is independent of each other. In response to the above problems, we propose the Spatial Attention Pyramid Network (SAPN), which can fuse the saliency information at different stages, thereby enhancing the model's adaptability to cross-domain Re-ID. First, the Instance Normalization (IN) layer is inserted in the backbone to eliminate the style differences of images by normalizing the data distribution. Secondly, a novel Spatial Attention Block (SAB) is designed to accurately locate the salient features of pedestrains and suppress background noises. Finally, we draw on the idea of Feature Pyramid Network (FPN) to design the Attention Embedded Pyramid Module (AEPM), which combines high-level semantic information with low-level location information, improves the cross-domain generalization capability of the model. We validate our SAPN through extensive experiments on three datasets which usually used in person Re-ID, the experiments show consistent improvements in a variety of cross-domain scenarios.

Keywords: Attention · Salient features · Background noises · Cross-domain person re-identification

1 Introduction

Re-ID refers to the deployment of non-overlapping cameras in a wide area space, and using computer vision technology to search for specific person in the collected images or videos. At present, person Re-ID on single domain has made considerable progress [1]. However, it is difficult to obtain satisfactory results when transferring models trained in the source domain to other target domains. The main factor leading to the performance decline of cross-domain Re-ID is the sample differences between the source domain and the target domain [2]. In cross-domain

© Springer Nature Switzerland AG 2021
Z. Liu et al. (Eds.): WASA 2021, LNCS 12938, pp. 58–69, 2021.
https://doi.org/10.1007/978-3-030-86130-8_5

scenes, the appearance information of the same person changes drastically, which greatly interferes with the extraction of the salient features of pedestrains. In addition, the trained model cannot distinguish person well with completely different background styles, which leads to the sharp performance decline in cross-domain person Re-ID [3]. Therefore, enhancing the model's ability to extract salient features of pedestrains is essential for cross-domain person Re-ID.

Suppressing background noise can effectively improve the generalization ability of the model and improve the accuracy of cross-domain person Re-ID [4]. On the one hand, the segmentation of pedestrain and background can effectively suppress background interference. Kalayeh et al. [5] proposed the SPReID, which includes a backbone and a human segmentation branch. The branch outputs a partial region mask of the human body, which is regarded as an activation map. The activation map and the backbone's output are multiplied to obtain the saliency region of the human body. Based on the framework of [5], Quispe et al. [4] combined the saliency features and semantic features of pedestrains, and proposed the SSPReID, but it cannot deal with the occlusion. Song et al. [6] used the person foreground mask as an aid, combined with the triplet loss and the contrast loss, making the model pay more attention to the human body so as to separate the pedestrain and the background. However, a large number of high-quality person images are required for network training to obtain high-quality segmentation results. On the other hand, some methods use attention mechanism to obtain salient features of person. Jian et al. [7] proposed a new strategy to fuse the salient features in visual attention mechanism. By building the saliency maps according to background information and getting the supplement saliency maps from salient features, they fuse various saliency cues effectively to get better results. Quan et al. [8] proposed a novel attribute-identity and visual attention model, which combines an attribute-identity and visual attention network with a vision-based person Re-ID network. In addition, a MIL-based image saliency detection method is designed to further suppress background interference and highlight pedestrian features in the foreground.

Aiming at the decline of cross-domain person Re-ID performance caused by background interference, we propose a novel Spatial Attention Pyramid Network to eliminate background information and retain pedestrian salient features which is similar to the idea proposed in [9,10]. Specially, we introduces the IN layer to normalize the style of images in different datasets, so as to eliminate the style differences of person images. Then, use the attention mechanism to locate pedestrian features, and the attention information at different stages is connected by a spatial attention pyramid to obtain the attention weights that focus more on the salient features. We summarize the main contributions as follows:

(1) The simple and efficient SAB is proposed, which is plug-and-play and can be combined with many backbones to improve their feature positioning ability.
(2) We propose the attention information fusion module AEPM, which merges the spatial attention weights of different stages to enhance the model's ability to extract salient features of pedestrains.

(3) Based on the above-mentioned SAB and AEPM, a novel SAPN is built. Suppressing the background interference and extracting saliency features by fusing the spatial attention information of different stages, thereby enhancing the performance of cross-domain person Re-ID. Compared with the baseline, SAPN's cross-domain generalization ability has been greatly improved.

2   Related Work

2.1   Style Differences Suppression

Recently, many studies about cross-domain person Re-ID focus on how to reduce the differences in image style between different datasets. Liu et al. [11] proposed the ATNet, which decomposes the overall style transfer of images into multiple style transfers for specific imaging factors. Liu et al. [12] designed a GAN-based model to suppress the deviation between the source domain and the target domain. Wei et al. [13] proposed PTGAN, which transforms the labeled source domain images to generate images with the target domain style and retain the original label, which reduces the sample difference between domains. Lv et al. [14] proposed a similarity-preserving generative adversarial network SimPGAN, which uses similarity consistency loss to preserve the similarity of the transformed images of the same person. We do not use the complex GAN, but normalize the style of images in all domains to suppress style differences.

2.2   Attention Mechanism

At present, there are many researches on attention mechanism in the field of person Re-ID. Liu et al. [15] proposed a network HydraPlus-Net (HPNet) that is conducive to extracting fine-grained features based on the attention network. It feeds the multi-layer attention map to different layers to enhance the recognition. Li et al. [16] proposed a new spatiotemporal attention model, which can automatically locate special parts of the pedestrian's body. It uses multiple spatial attention models to extract the useful part information of each image, and integrates the output through the temporal attention model to deal with occlusion and misalignment. We use the spatial attention mechanism to help the model accurately locate pedestrians.

2.3   Attention Pyramid

The proposal of FPN [18] is based on the fact that the low-level features contain poor semantic information and the location information, and the high-level features contain rich semantic information and rough location information. There are many works that draw on the idea of FPN. Hu et al. [19] proposed a new neural network combines the advantages of the attention mechanism and FPN, which can effectively solve the scale problem. Li et al. [20] combined attention mechanism and spatial pyramid to extract fine-grained features of the image.

Guo et al. [21] considered both structural regularization and structural information, and three SPANet structures are proposed based on different attention path
topologies. Wang et al. [22] proposed a novel attention module, which contains
a bottom-up and top-down feedforward structure.

3   Method

We first introduced the overall structure of SAPN in detail in Subsect. 3.1,
and then introduced SAB and AEPM in detail in Subsect. 3.2 and Subsect. 3.3
respectively.

3.1   Spatial Attention Pyramid Network

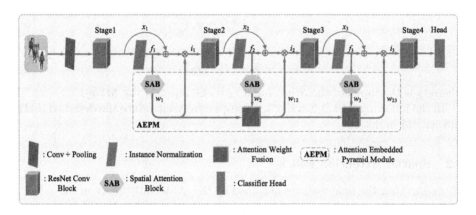

Fig. 1. Spatial Attention Pyramid Network. $Conv + pooling$ stands for the operations
before layer1 in ResNet50. $Stage1$, $Stage2$, $Stage3$, and $Stage4$ represent layer1, layer2,
layer3, and layer4 of the ResNet50, respectively. $Classifier Head$ represents a classifier
after a batch normalization layer.

In order to extract the salient features of pedestrians and suppress the influence
of background noise, we designed the SAPN based on the ResNet50. First, we
insert the IN layer after $Stage1$, $Stage2$ and $Stage3$ to normalize the features of
different stages, and get $f_i, i \in 1, 2, 3$ to eliminate the style differences of images
in different domains. Specifically:

$$f_i = \gamma \times \frac{(x_i - \mu(x_i))}{\sigma(x_i)} + \beta \tag{1}$$

among them, $x_i, i \in 1, 2, 3$ are the output features of $Stage1$, $Stage2$ and $Stage3$,
respectively. For each sample, $\mu(\cdot)$ and $\sigma(\cdot)$ respectively represent the mean
and standard-deviation calculated in each channel, γ and β are the learnable
parameters.

Then, the AEPM is built to merge the attention weights of different stages, and the fused weights are used to improve the model's ability to extract the salient features of pedestrians. Specifically, the normalized features $f_i, i \in 1, 2, 3$ in different stages are the input of the AEPM, which are used to obtain the corresponding spatial attention weights by SAB, and then merge them to obtain the fused spatial attention weights w_{12} and w_{23} respectively.

Finally, considering that the IN will cause the loss of some discriminative information, we use residual connection to compensate for the loss. And the added feature is filtered by the attention weight w_1 to suppress the background noise.

$$i_1 = w_1 \times (f_1 + x_1) \tag{2}$$

where i_1 is the input of the $Stage2$.

Similarly, w_{12} and w_{23} is used to filter the added features respectively to suppress background interference.

$$i_2 = w_{12} \times (f_2 + x_2) \tag{3}$$

$$i_3 = w_{23} \times (f_3 + x_3) \tag{4}$$

where i_2 is the input of the $Stage3$ and i_3 is the input of the $Stage4$.

In the following Sect. 3.2 and 3.3, we respectively introduce the designed SAB and AEPM in detail.

3.2 Spatial Attention Block

We expect that the final features obtained by the model only focus on the salient information of pedestrians and do not contain background noise. Therefore, we designed the spatial attention block, which uses the spatial relationship between features to generate spatial attention weights to locate the information of interest. The structure is shown in Fig. 2.

First, given the input feature $F \in R^{c \times h \times w}$, maximize and average operations are performed along the channel dimensions to generate two 2D feature maps. The feature map obtained by average operations focus more on global information, and the feature map obtained by maximize operation pays more attention to the salient information. Then maximize and average operations is performed on the two generated 2D feature maps along the H and W dimensions respectively to obtain a total of 8 feature vectors, which are focused on certain rows or columns in the original feature map. Then, we combined the 8 feature vectors in pairs by matrix multiplication and scaled by softmax to obtain 4 spatial attention masks. The softmax makes the sum of the internal values of each mask 1, which increases the attention difference between the pedestrain and the background. Finally, the spatial attention masks are concatenated in the channel dimension, and merged by convolution and sigmoid to obtain the final spatial attention weight, which only focuses on the pedestrian.

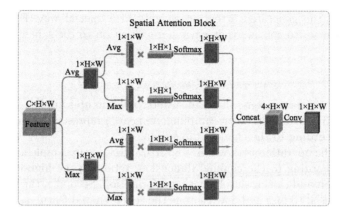

Fig. 2. The diagram of the SAB.

3.3 Attention Embedded Pyramid Module

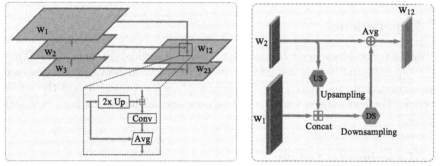

(a) The schematic diagram of the attention pyramid.

(b) The schematic diagram of the *Attention Weight Fusion*.

Fig. 3. $2 \times Up$ and US represents 2 times upsampling, $Conv$ and DS represents downsampling through convolution, and Avg represents averaging.

In order to make full use of the semantic and location information in the different level features, we designed a pyramid structure to fuse attention information at different stages. Figure 3(a) is a schematic diagram of it. As shown in Fig. 1, the attention weight of each stage is obtained from the corresponding normalized feature by the SAB.

$$w_i = sa_i(f_i) \tag{5}$$

among them, $sa_i, i \in 1, 2, 3$ are three independent SAB, $w_i, i \in 1, 2, 3$ represent the attention weights.

We fused the generated attention weights in a special way. For example, fusing w_1 and w_2 to get w_{12} that pays more attention to the salient features of pedestrians:

$$w_{12} = (ds(cat(us(w_2), w_1)) + w_2)/2 \tag{6}$$

among them, $us(\cdot)$ represents the bilinear interpolation up-sampling, $ds(\cdot)$ represents the 3×3 convolution down-sampling, and $cat(\cdot)$ represents the concatenate operation according to the channel dimension.

The specific operation is shown in Fig. 3(b). First, we upsample w_2 and splice it and w_1 according to the channel dimension, retaining the high-level semantic information and the low-level location information. Secondly, the convolution operation is used to fuse and downsample the concatenated features. Finally, the downsampled feature and w_2 are added in element-wise to ensure the integrity of the feature information while avoiding the disappearance of the gradient. And then w_3 is fused with w_{12} in the same way to obtain w_{23} that can effectively suppress background noise. In particular, we don't apply spatial attention to high-level features after the *stage*4, because the features contain high abstract semantics and the resolution is too small, there is no need to filter spatial information.

4   Experiments

In Sect. 4.1, we introduced the datasets and the evaluation indicators. Then some experimental details are introduced in Sect. 4.2. In Sect. 4.3, we designed some experiments to verify the effectiveness of each component and the whole network. The comparison between our scheme and advanced methods is shown in Sect. 4.4.

4.1   Experimental Details

Datasets Market1501 [23]: A total of 1,501 pedestrian and 32,668 detected pedestrians rectangle were captured in the dataset. These pedestrian IDs are divided into 751 (containing 12,936 images) for training and 750 for querying.

DukeMTMC-reID [24]: This dataset contains 36,411 images from 1,812 pedestrians captured by 8 high-definition cameras. 16,522 images with 702 IDs were randomly selected from the dataset as the training set. 2,228 images with 702 IDs are used as the query set.

MSMT17 [13]: In this dataset, 32,621 bounding boxes with 1,041 pedestrian IDs are the training set, and 93,820 bounding boxes with 3,060 pedestrian IDs are the test set. 11,659 images were randomly selected from the test set as the query set, and the remaining 82,161 images were used as the gallery set.

Evaluation Protocols We adopt the cumulative matching characteristics (CMC) at rank-1 and the mean average precision (mAP) as the evaluation indicators to measure the performance of different Re-ID methods.

4.2   Implementation Details

In the training phase, we randomly select 4 IDs from the training set, and randomly sample 6 images for each ID to meet the requirements of the triplet loss. We scale the images to 256×128, and adopt some commonly used data augment operations, such as horizontal flip and random rotation. We caculate the cross entropy classification loss and the triplet metric loss, and use the adam optimizer to update the model's parameters. We train the model for 130 epochs without pre-training. During our experiment, in order to ensure the transmission efficiency and security of the datasets between different devices, we use the novel mechanism for uploading data proposed in [25].

4.3   Ablation Experiments

We adopt the ResNet50 as the backbone and use the settings mentioned in the experimental details. Baseline: ResNet50. Baseline-IN: Insert the IN layer after layer1, layer2 and layer3 of the ResNet50. Baseline-IN-A: Add SAB on the basis of the Baseline-IN. SPAN: Build a pyramid network on the basis of the Baseline-IN-A.

Table 1. The results of the ablation experiment. Market1501 is abbreviated as M, DukeMTMC-reID is abbreviated as D, and MSMT17 is abbreviated as MS. As an example, M-D represents that we train the model on Market1501 and test it on DukeMTMC-reID.

Method	M-D (%)		D-M (%)		MS-D (%)		MS-M (%)	
	mAP	Rank-1	mAP	Rank-1	mAP	Rank-1	mAP	Rank-1
Baseline	24.6	43.4	26.6	55.2	39.6	59.2	31.7	60.5
Baseline-IN	25.9	45.5	30.5	61.8	41.7	61.8	34.0	63.9
Baseline-IN-A	27.8	48.5	32.5	63.6	41.9	62.1	36.7	66.2
SAPN	29.9	50.6	33.1	64.0	43.6	63.6	36.8	66.7

It can be seen from Table 1 that the SAPN which includes all components obtains the best performance of cross-domain person Re-ID. By adding components in turn, we evaluated the performance of each component and found that each one effectively improved the cross-domain generalization ability of the model. For different cross-domain scenarios, adding the IN residual connections to the baseline can improves the performance of cross-domain person Re-ID. Then, on the basis of Baseline-IN, we added the SAB. The overall gain from the MS to the M is the largest, with the mAP and the Rank-1 increasing by 2.7% and 2.3%, respectively. This is because the model has learned how to accurately locate pedestrians by the SAB from the MS with a large amount of data. Applying the learned knowledge to the M with better data quality has naturally achieved a better cross-domain person Re-ID effect. Experiments show that the SAPN has further improved the performance of cross-domain person Re-ID compared to the Baseline-IN-A. It can be proved that the AEPM can effectively integrate high-level and low-level attention information, enabling the SAPN to effectively extract the salient features of pedestrians, and suppress background noises, thereby enhancing the domain generalization ability.

4.4 The Effectiveness of Different Attention Realizations

We choose the Baseline-IN as the backbone and design a comparative experiment. NL: Embed the Non-local [26] structure to the backbone. SE: Embed the Squeeze-and-Excitation [27] structure to the backbone. CBAM: Insert the spatial sub-module of the CBAM [28] to the backbone.

Table 2. The comparision between different attention realizations.

Method	M-D (%)		D-M (%)		MS-D (%)		MS-M (%)	
	mAP	Rank-1	mAP	Rank-1	mAP	Rank-1	mAP	Rank-1
NL	25.7	46.0	31.0	61.9	41.3	61.6	35.8	65.3
SE	25.2	44.2	30.7	61.2	42.8	63.2	35.1	65.1
CBAM	26.3	46.0	31.2	61.8	41.8	61.9	35.9	66.1
SAPN	29.9	50.6	33.1	64.0	43.6	63.6	36.8	66.7

The Non-local structure, the Squeeze-and-Excitation structure and the CBAM are three commonly used attention realization methods in the field of computer vision. It can be seen from Table 2 that under the condition of cross-domain, compared with other attentions, the SAPN proposed in this paper has achieved significant advantages. Proving that the SAPN can more accurately locate the salient features of pedestrians and suppress the influence of background on the performance of cross-domain person Re-ID (Table 3).

5 Comparisons with State-of-the-Arts

We compared the SAPN with some advanced methods, including unsupervised domain adaptation(UDA) and domain generalization(DG) methods. UDA methods use unlabeled target domain information and benefit from information obtained from target domain. It can be seen that our method still performs well without using target domain information by comparing with various UDA methods. In addition, our method also has advantages compared with some GAN-based methods, not only the effect is better, but the model's structure is simpler. Compared with the OSNet-IBN, which also belongs to the DG method, our method improves the mAP by 3.2% and 7.0% in the M-D and D-M processes, respectively. It can be proved that our method is advanced and can effectively improve the cross-domain generalization ability of the model without any target domain data.

Table 3. Comparison with state-of-the-art methods.

Method	M-D (%)		D-M (%)	
	mAP	Rank-1	mAP	Rank-1
HHL [29]	27.2	46.9	31.4	62.2
BUC [30]	27.5	47.4	38.3	66.2
CamStyle [31]	27.7	51.7	30.4	64.7
FSRM-STS [32]	29.1	51.5	30.2	61.3
IPGAN [12]	27.0	47.0	28.0	57.2
SPGAN+LMP [33]	26.2	46.4	26.7	57.7
CSGLP [34]	36.0	56.1	33.9	63.7
AF3 [35]	37.4	56.8	36.3	67.2
OSNet-IBN [36]	26.7	48.5	26.1	57.7
Ours (SAPN)	**29.9**	**50.6**	**33.1**	**64.0**

6   Conclusion

In this paper, we designed a novel spatial attention pyramid network (SAPN) to suppress background interference and enhance cross-domain person Re-ID performance. We designed an effective spatial attention block (SAB), which generates attention masks and merges them to obtain the final spatial attention weights to accurately locate the salient features of pedestrians. On this basis, Attention Embedded Pyramid Module (AEPM) is designed to fuse spatial attention information at different stages to enhance the extraction of pedestrian salient features and suppress background interference. We verify the various components and the overall network proposed in this paper through ablation experiments and comparison experiments, and the results show that our scheme has achieved good performance of cross-domain person Re-ID.

References

1. Ye, M., Shen, J., Lin, G., Xiang, T., Shao, L., Hoi, S.C.H.: Deep learning for person re-identification: a survey and outlook. IEEE Trans. Pattern Anal. Mach. Intell., 1 (2021)
2. Kumar, D., Siva, P., Marchwica, P., Wong, A.: Fairest of them all: establishing a strong baseline for cross-domain person ReID (2019)
3. Jia, J., Ruan, Q., Hospedales, T.M.: Frustratingly easy person re-identification: generalizing person Re-ID in practice (2019)
4. Quispe, R., Pedrini, H.: Improved person re-identification based on saliency and semantic parsing with deep neural network models. Image Vis. Comput. **92**, 09 (2019)
5. Kalayeh, M.M., Basaran, E., Gökmen, M., Kamasak, M.E., Shah, M.: Human semantic parsing for person re-identification. In: 2018 IEEE/CVF Conference on Computer Vision and Pattern Recognition, pp. 1062–1071 (2018)

6. Song, C., Huang, Y., Ouyang, W., Wang, L.: Mask-guided contrastive attention model for person re-identification. In: 2018 IEEE/CVF Conference on Computer Vision and Pattern Recognition, pp. 1179–1188 (2018)
7. Jian, M., et al.: Assessment of feature fusion strategies in visual attention mechanism for saliency detection. Pattern Recogn. Lett. **127**, 08 (2018)
8. Quan, H., Feng, S., Lang, C., Chen, B.: Improving person re-identification via attribute-identity representation and visual attention mechanism. Multimedia Tools Appl., 1–20 (2019)
9. Xiong, Z., Cai, Z., Han, Q., Alrawais, A.: ADGAN: protect your location privacy in camera data of auto-driving vehicles. IEEE Trans. Ind. Inf. 1 (2020)
10. Xiong, Z., Li, W., Han, Q., Cai, Z.: Privacy-preserving auto-driving: a GAN-based approach to protect vehicular camera data. In: 2019 IEEE International Conference on Data Mining (ICDM), pp. 668–677. IEEE (2019)
11. Liu, J., Zha, Z.-J., Chen, D., Hong, R., Wang, M.: Adaptive transfer network for cross-domain person re-identification. In: Proceedings of the IEEE/CVF Conference on Computer Vision and Pattern Recognition, pp. 7202–7211 (2019)
12. LiuLiu, J., et al.: Identity preserving generative adversarial network for cross-domain person re-identification. IEEE Access **7**, 114021–114032 (2019)
13. Wei, L., Zhang, S., Gao, W., Tian, Q.: Person transfer GAN to bridge domain gap for person re-identification. In: 2018 IEEE/CVF Conference on Computer Vision and Pattern Recognition, pp. 79–88 (2018)
14. Lv, J., Wang, X.: Cross-dataset person re-identification using similarity preserved generative adversarial networks. In: Liu, W., Giunchiglia, F., Yang, B. (eds.) KSEM 2018. LNCS (LNAI), vol. 11062, pp. 171–183. Springer, Cham (2018). https://doi.org/10.1007/978-3-319-99247-1_15
15. Liu, X., et al.: HydraPlus-Net: attentive deep features for pedestrian analysis. In: 2017 IEEE International Conference on Computer Vision (ICCV), pp. 350–359 (2017)
16. Li, S., Bak, S., Carr, P., Wang, X.: Diversity regularized spatiotemporal attention for video-based person re-identification. In: 2018 IEEE/CVF Conference on Computer Vision and Pattern Recognition, pp. 369–378 (2018)
17. Chen, D., Li, H., Xiao, T., Yi, S., Wang, X.: Video person re-identification with competitive snippet-similarity aggregation and co-attentive snippet embedding. In: 2018 IEEE/CVF Conference on Computer Vision and Pattern Recognition, pp. 1169–1178 (2018)
18. Lin, T., Dollár, P., Girshick, R., He, K., Hariharan, B., Belongie, S.: Feature pyramid networks for object detection. In: 2017 IEEE Conference on Computer Vision and Pattern Recognition (CVPR), pp. 936–944 (2017)
19. Hu, X., Zhang, Z., Jiang, Z., Chaudhuri, S., Yang, Z., Nevatia, R.: SPAN: spatial pyramid attention network for image manipulation localization. In: Vedaldi, A., Bischof, H., Brox, T., Frahm, J.-M. (eds.) ECCV 2020. LNCS, vol. 12366, pp. 312–328. Springer, Cham (2020). https://doi.org/10.1007/978-3-030-58589-1_19
20. Li, H., Xiong, P., An, J., Wang, L.: Pyramid attention network for semantic segmentation (2018)
21. Jingda Guo, et al.: SPANet: spatial pyramid attention network for enhanced image recognition. In: 2020 IEEE International Conference on Multimedia and Expo (ICME), pp. 1–6. IEEE (2020)
22. Wang, F.: Residual attention network for image classification. In: 2017 IEEE Conference on Computer Vision and Pattern Recognition (CVPR), pp. 6450–6458 (2017)

23. Zheng, L., Shen, L., Tian, L., Wang, S., Wang, J., Tian, Q.: Scalable person re-identification: a benchmark. In: Proceedings of the 2015 IEEE International Conference on Computer Vision (ICCV), ICCV 2015, pp. 1116–1124. IEEE Computer Society (2015)

24. Ristani, E., Solera, F., Zou, R., Cucchiara, R., Tomasi, C.: Performance measures and a data set for multi-target, multi-camera tracking. In: Hua, G., Jégou, H. (eds.) ECCV 2016. LNCS, vol. 9914, pp. 17–35. Springer, Cham (2016). https://doi.org/10.1007/978-3-319-48881-3_2

25. Cai, Z., Zheng, X.: A private and efficient mechanism for data uploading in smart cyber-physical systems. IEEE Trans. Netw. Sci. Eng. **7**(2), 766–775 (2020)

26. Wang, X., Girshick, R., Gupta, A., He, K.: Non-local neural networks. In: 2018 IEEE/CVF Conference on Computer Vision and Pattern Recognition, pp. 7794–7803 (2018)

27. Hu, J., Shen, L., Albanie, S., Sun, G., Wu, E.: Squeeze-and-excitation networks. IEEE Trans. Pattern Anal. Mach. Intell. **42**(8), 2011–2023 (2020)

28. Wang, X., Girshick, R., Gupta, A., He, K.: Non-local neural networks. In: Proceedings of the IEEE Conference on Computer Vision and Pattern Recognition (CVPR), June 2018

29. Zhong, Z., Zheng, L., Li, S., Yang, Y.: Generalizing a person retrieval model hetero- and homogeneously. In: Ferrari, V., Hebert, M., Sminchisescu, C., Weiss, Y. (eds.) ECCV 2018. LNCS, vol. 11217, pp. 176–192. Springer, Cham (2018). https://doi.org/10.1007/978-3-030-01261-8_11

30. Lin, Y., Dong, X., Zheng, L., Yan, Y., Yang, Y.: A bottom-up clustering approach to unsupervised person re-identification. In: Proceedings of the AAAI Conference on Artificial Intelligence, vol. 33, pp. 8738–8745 (2019)

31. Zhong, Z., Zheng, L., Zheng, Z., Li, S., Yang, Y.: CamStyle: a novel data augmentation method for person re-identification. IEEE Trans. Image Process. **28**(3), 1176–1190 (2019)

32. Daifeng Li, L., Huang, B.Y., Wan, F., Madden, A., Liang, X.: FSRM-STS: cross-dataset pedestrian retrieval based on a four-stage retrieval model with selection-translation-selection. Futur. Gener. Comput. Syst. **107**, 601–619 (2020)

33. Deng, W., Zheng, L., Ye, Q., Kang, G., Yang, Y., Jiao, J.: Image-image domain adaptation with preserved self-similarity and domain-dissimilarity for person re-identification. In: 2018 IEEE/CVF Conference on Computer Vision and Pattern Recognition, pp. 994–1003 (2018)

34. Ren, C., Liang, B., Ge, P., Zhai, Y., Lei, Z.: Domain adaptive person re-identification via camera style generation and label propagation. IEEE Trans. Inf. Forensics Secur. **15**, 1290–1302 (2020)

35. Haijun Liu, J.C., S.,Wang, Wang, W.: Attention: a big surprise for cross-domain person re-identification. ArXiv, abs/1905.12830 (2019)

36. Zhou, K., Yang, Y., Cavallaro, A., Xiang, T.: Omni-scale feature learning for person re-identification. In: 2019 IEEE/CVF International Conference on Computer Vision (ICCV), pp. 3701–3711 (2019)

A Lattice-Based Ring Signature Scheme to Secure Automated Valet Parking

Shiyuan Xu, Xue Chen, Chao Wang$^{(\boxtimes)}$, Yunhua He, Ke Xiao, and Yibo Cao

North China University of Technology, Beijing 100144, China

Abstract. Automated Valet Parking (AVP) systems have great potential to mitigate parking pressure. The core of AVP is parking space reservation which users send relevant information to parking lot providers to complete the parking reservation and automatic parking. However, that reveals the drivers' identity information and the reservation messages might be forged. In addition, with quantum computers developing rapidly, existing systems also suffer from privacy and security issues under quantum attacks. These become the major obstacles to the development of the AVP system. To deal with the above challenges, our paper proposes a lattice-based ring signature scheme for autonomous vehicles which is the first AVP privacy preservation system capable of resisting quantum attacks. More significantly, our system applies lattice-based ring signatures to ensure the correctness, anonymity and unforgeability of messages. Finally, security analyses are conducted to compare our system with others in terms of security and privacy, and also the efficiency analysis shows that the performance of our system is superior to others.

Keywords: Automated Valet Parking · Lattice · Ring signature · Message unforgeability · Security · Privacy preservation · Anonymity

1 Introduction

Automotive technology is one of the most significant applications which targets at the promotion of traffic situations enhancement to achieve self-driving. Autonomous driving technology is also one of the most promising directions in the Internet of Vehicles (IoV) [1–3]. However, individuals lives have been huge affected by the lack of guiding parking system. Thus, AVP is highly-esteemed since advanced sensors help steering vehicular parking. Drivers need to submit their expected time, which these process may be the risk of privacy disclosure. Moreover, it has possibility that malicious users try to falsify the parking reservation. For this respect, it is important to guarantee the message transmitted to PSP not to be forged in any case. Furthermore, the emergence of quantum

S. Xu and X. Chen—This work is supported in part by the National Natural Science Foundation of China under Grant 61802004 and Grant 61802005, and the Scientific Research Project of Beijing Educational Committee under Grant KM202010009008.

Z. Liu et al. (Eds.): WASA 2021, LNCS 12938, pp. 70–83, 2021.
https://doi.org/10.1007/978-3-030-86130-8_6

computers has threatened the security of AVP system again. Malicious users utilize the Shor algorithm [4] or Grover algorithm [5] to extract users secret keys to produce various unauthorized transactions. Thus, the importance of security is essential and profound in terms of stronger demand of privacy protection as well as message unforgeability.

Previous research works have conducted research on the privacy and security issues [6–9] in the IoV. Furthermore, none of these methods can withstand quantum attacks. So far, researchers basically use classical encryption methods such as ECC, RSA to protect user message security. However, research of AVP system security should consider not only traditional cryptography but also quantum computer attacks. Thus, many researchers have focused on anti-quantum methodologies. Specifically, the research of lattice cryptography [10] has been widely used to against quantum attacks especially for the signature schemes. In 2010, Cash et al. [12] proved other beneficial characteristics of lattice trapdoors, defined as bonsai tree technology. Then, some researchers proposed lattice-based construction of Preimage Sampleable trapdoor Function (PSF) in 2012 [13], with a signature scenario which is dependable security in the random oracle model based on the Small Integer Solution (SIS) problems.

For the problems mentioned above, our paper proposes a lattice-based ring signature scheme for autonomous vehicles which guarantees the anonymity of users. The contributions of this article are as listed follows.

1) User's real identity is loosely coupled with the vehicle to realize the anonymity in the reservation process to ensure the privacy while obtaining the service.
2) This paper is the first one that proposes an AVP privacy protection system which can resist quantum attacks while utilizing a novel lattice-based ring signature scheme. The request message is unforgeability and tamper-proof modification. In addition, the attacker cannot obtain any information through statistical analysis.
3) We conduct security and comparative analysis, showing that our system guarantees correctness, anonymity and unforgeability, and also communication cost, signature length and system security are superior to existing solutions.

2   Models and Design Goal

2.1   System Model and Threat Model

The AVP architecture in our proposed system is shown in Fig. 1. Parking Lot Terminal (PLT) is the terminal deployed by the parking lot owner. The real-time status of parking spaces is provided by PLT. Parking Service Provider (PSP) provides users with automatic parking registration, reservation, parking, and other services.

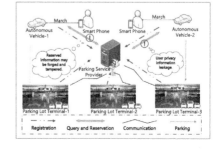

Fig. 1. The system model and threat model of Automatic Valet Parking.

Autonomous Vehicle (AV) possesses self-driving mode for autonomous parking. Smart Phone (SP) is utilized to communicate with AV.

There are two security issues in AVP systems. First and foremost one is user identity and location information. When users search parking spaces and book parking spaces, their identity information will be disclosed. Attackers may infer user's daily behavior. The second one is reserved information tampering attack. A malicious adversary may tamper with the message and modify the user's real reservation information, which causes him/her unable to find parking space on time.

2.2 Design Goal

There are four goals in our paper: The first one is Anonymity, in order to protect the privacy of users, PSP is unable to know the true identity of users except registration. The second one is Authenticity, PSP authenticates user requesting the service. After that, PSP provides parking space queries, parking space reservations and others. The third one is Unlinkability, different request information of the same user is designed to avoid being linked. The last one is unforgeability, attackers can not modify the parking space query and reservation information.

3   Preliminary

The main notations are shown in Table 1.

Table 1. Notations

Notation	Description	Notation	Description
U_i	i-th user	L	Lattice
ID_i^{Real}	i-th user's real identity	m	$3 + (2c/3n^c)logn$
ID_i^{Cred}	i-th user's anonymous credential	u	Vector
Tok_{bk}	Token for parking reservation	X, Y	Random variables
Tok_{pk}	Token for check-in	$\Delta(X, Y)$	Statistical distance
α, β	Token pool of Tok_{bk}, Tok_{pk}	v	Shortest vector
Req_{que}	Parking query message	A, B	Matrix
Req_{res}	Parking reservation message	r	Standard deviation
ϑ_q	Signature of query message	n	Security parameter
ϑ_r	Signature of reservation message	l	Ring member
(sk_i, pk_i)	i-th user's secret-public key	a_i	Public polynomial
(sk_{PSP}, pk_{PSP})	PSP's privacy-public key	$[i]$	Set $\{1, 2, \cdots, i\}$
$Timestamp$	Current timestamp	$x \leftarrow S$	Uniformly random sample
$b_1, b_2, \cdots, b_n$	Linearly independent vectors	Random oracle H	$\{0, 1\}^* \rightarrow D_{S,c}$

3.1 Lattice

Definition 1 (Lattice) [10]:

Given n liearly independent vectors $b_1, b_2, \cdots, b_n \in \mathbb{R}^m$, the resulting lattice L is $L(b_1, b_2, \cdots, b_n) = \{\Sigma x_i \cdot b_i | x_i \in \mathbb{Z}\}$, where $b_1, b_2, \cdots, b_n$ is a set of basis of lattice L, n is the rank of lattice L, and m is the dimension of lattice L, $m \geq n$.

Definition 2 (Statistical distance):

Let X and Y be two random variables on a finite set Ω. The statistical distance $\Delta(X, Y)$ between X and Y is defined as:

$$\Delta(X, Y) = \frac{1}{2}\Sigma_{s \in \Omega}|Pr[X = s] - Pr[Y = s]|. \tag{1}$$

Definition 3 (Minimum integer solution problem $(SIS_{n,q,\beta,m})$):

The most eminent computational problem based on lattice is named as Trapdoors and basis delegation functions SIS, which is as follows: Given dimensions m, n and modulus q, matrix $B \in \mathbb{Z}_q^{m \times n}$ and real β, seeks non-zero vector $t \in \mathbb{Z}^m$ such that $B \cdot t = 0 mod q$ with the condition $\|t\| \leq \beta$. The SIS problem, which is defined by Ajtai [10], shows that solving the random instances of $(SIS_{n,q,\beta,m})$ problem can be reduced to settle down worst-case problems in lattices. Without reducing the security level, Micciancio and Peikert [23] optimized the modulus q of the SIS from $q \geq \beta n^\delta$ to $q \geq \beta \sqrt{n log q}$.

Theorem 1: For any $m = poly(n)$, $\beta > 0$, a sufficiently large modulus $q \geq \beta \cdot poly(n)$, in the case of n-dimensional lattice L, the difficulty of $SIS_{n,q,\beta,m}$ is the worst case. The performance is similar with the decision-type approximate shortest vector problem $GapSVP_\gamma$ and the approximate shortest independent vector problem $SIVP_\gamma$, where $\gamma = \beta \cdot poly(n)$.

3.2 Trapdoors and Basis Delegation Functions

In this part, we introduce a set of one-way preimage functions defined as [11]:

TrapGen(1^n):

Let $q = poly(n)$, m be a positive integer such that $q \geq 2, m \geq 5n \; log \; q$. By using the $TrapGen(1^n)$ algorithm, it outputs the matrix $A \in \mathbb{Z}_q^{n \times m}$ and $B_A \in \mathbb{Z}_{n \times m}$ where B_A is a good basis of $L^\perp(B) = \{x \in \mathbb{Z}^m : Bx = 0 \; mod \; q\}$, such that $\|\tilde{B}_A\| \leq O(\sqrt{n \; log \; q})$.

SampleD(B, r, c):

Having input a m-dimensional basis B of lattice L, a center vector c which $c \in \mathbb{R}^m$ and a parameter r, the algorithm $SampleD(B, r, c)$ samples from a discrete Gaussian distribution over the lattice L with the standard deviation r around the center vector c.

SamplePre(A, B, y, σ):

Inputs matrix $A \in \mathbb{Z}_q^{n \times m}$ and $B_A \in \mathbb{Z}^{n \times m}$, a vector $y \in \mathbb{Z}_q^n$ and σ. Then, output e is within negligible statistical distance of $D_{L_y^\perp(A),\sigma}$ and $e \in \{e \in \mathbb{Z}^m : \|e\| \leq \sigma\sqrt{m}\}$ such that $Ae = y(mod \; q)$ with overwhelming probability.

3.3   Gaussian Distribution and Rejection Sample

Gaussian Distribution. Utilize Gaussian Distribution to randomly choose elements in $\mathbb{Z}_q^n$ is associated with difficult problems on lattice.

Definition 4 (Gaussian function):
   Suppose $L \in \mathbb{R}^m$ is a m-dimensional lattice. Take any vector $c \in \mathbb{R}^m$ and a positive number $\sigma > 0$, then the Gaussian function is defined as $\forall x \in \mathbb{R}^n, \rho_{\sigma,c}(x) = exp(\frac{-\pi\|x-c\|^2}{2\sigma^2})$. Among them, c represents the center of L, and σ represents the standard deviation. If $c = 0$, we simplify $\rho_{\sigma,c}(x)$ to $\rho_\sigma(x)$.

Definition 5 (Discrete Gaussian distribution):
   Let $\rho_{v,\sigma}(\mathbb{Z}^m)$ denoting the discrete integral of $\rho_{v,\sigma}$ over $\mathbb{Z}^m$, then the discrete Gaussian distribution over $\mathbb{Z}^m$ is defined as $D_{v,\sigma}^m(x) = \frac{\rho_{v,\sigma}^m(x)}{\rho_\sigma^m(\mathbb{Z}^m)}$. According to the paper proposed by Lyubashevsky[13], We have the following Lemmas.

Lemma 1: For $j \geq 1$, it follows that: $Pr[\| z \| > j\sigma\sqrt{m} : z \leftarrow D_\sigma^m] < j^m exp(\frac{m}{2}(1 - k^2))$. Moreover, for any vector $v \in \mathbb{R}^m$, and $\sigma, r > 0$, we have $Pr[| \langle z, v \rangle | > r : z \leftarrow D_\sigma^m] \leq 2 \cdot exp(-\frac{r^2}{2\|v\|^2\sigma^2})$.

Lemma 2: For any $v \in \mathbb{Z}^m$, if $\sigma = \delta \| v \|$, where $\delta > 0$, then

$$Pr[\frac{D_\sigma^m(z)}{D_{v,\sigma}^m(z)} < exp(\frac{12}{\delta} + \frac{1}{2\delta^2}) : z \leftarrow D_\sigma^m] = 1 - 2^{-100}. \tag{2}$$

Rejection Sampling. There is an aborting method for rejection sampling, one could stop the interactive protocol if his secret key(sk) has been leaked. For nearly all x, having given a probability distribution $f(x)$, we have to find other probability distribution $g(x)$ to certify $f(x) \leq Mg(x)$, which M is the excepted number of times to output the sample. Then, $x \leftarrow g$ will be rejected if $\frac{f(x)}{Mg(x)} \neq f$.

Lemma 3: Let V be a set of $\mathbb{Z}^m$, $\sigma \in R$ and h: $V \to R$ be a probability distribution. If $\sigma = \omega(T\sqrt{log\ m})$, then it will exist a constant M as the following algorithm: 1. $v \leftarrow h$; 2. $z \leftarrow D_{v,\sigma}^m$; 3. outputs (z, v) with probability $min(\frac{D_\sigma^m(z)}{MD_{\sigma,v}^m(z)}, 1)$ which is within statistical distance $\frac{2^{-\omega(logm)}}{M}$ of the distribution illustrated as below: 1. $v \leftarrow h$; 2. $z \leftarrow D_\sigma^m$; 3. outputs (z, v) with probability $\frac{1}{M}$.
   Therefore, the probability of output is at least $\frac{1-2^{-\omega(logm)}}{M}$.

4   Our Proposed Lattice-Based Ring Signature Scheme

4.1   Our Proposed Scheme

In this section, we present our privacy protection scheme. Lattice-based ring signature [14] guarantees the authenticity and unforgeability of user messages. Besides, we also use cuckoo filters [15] to add and delete parking service items.

(1) Registration Setup

PLT creates an account and submits relevant certificates to PSP. Then, PSP verifies the validity and issues a public-secret key to PLT. Each user U_i creates his/her account and submits identity information ID_i^{Real} to PSP. PSP verifies and chooses sk_i as its secret key and compute $pk_i = a \cdot sk_i$ as its public key. Selects t_i to computes verification information $S_i = H(a \cdot t_i || ID_i^{Real})$ and $c_i = t_i + pk_i \cdot S_i$. Then user sends $(pk_i, ID_i^{Real}, S_i, c_i)$ to PSP, and PSP checks whether equation $S_i = H(a(c_i - pk_i \cdot H(a \cdot t_i || ID_i^{Real})) || ID_i^{Real})$ holds. If it holds, PSP will store (pk_i, ID_i^{Real}) and create $ID_i^{Cred} = sig(pk_i, S_i, Timestamp; sk_{PSP})$ for user U_i with PSP's secret key sk_{PSP}. During the following process, ID_i^{Cred} is used as a certificate so as to show the real identity which he/she registered.

(2) Service Phase

User Authentication: A user has to submit an anonymous certificate ID_i^{Cred} to PSP. PSP verifies credential and issues booking tokens Tok_{bk}, then stores it in the token pool α.

Parking Query: User sends his/her required information $Req_{que} = (Information || Timestamp || Tok_{bk})$ to PSP to query empty parking spaces. Besides, we ask user to Ring-Sign the message Req_{que}. According to Sign-Gen procedure in Section V, user generates a signature ϑ_q of the message Req_{que}. A ring R which contains members with a set of public keys $L = pk_i$ where $i \epsilon[l]$, $\vartheta_q = (z_i : i \epsilon[l], c)$, $c \leftarrow H(\sum_{i \epsilon[l]} pk_i \cdot y_i, L, Req_{que})$. Then, user sends the $(Req_{que} || \vartheta_q)$ to PSP to verifies signature and timestamp. After that, PSP examines the token pool α for the presence of token Tok_{bk}. If validation passed, PSP withdraw the booking token Tok_{bk}. Then, PSP filters free parking space and return results.

Parking Reservation: A user selects one parking space and sends the reservation request Req_{res} (including reserved parking space, parking time and pick-up time) to PSP. To prevent tampering, the user has to Ring-Sign the sent message Req_{res} and the signature of the message is ϑ_r. During PSP verification, if the signature ϑ_r is valid, PSP will notify the PLT to retain its corresponding parking space within the corresponding time. Then, it will issue a token Tok_{pk} to the user as a parking voucher and store Tok_{pk} in the token pool β.

(3) Parking Phase

Parking Request: After own parking token, user operates SP to autopilot parking mode, and user has to relay information $(Tok_{pk} || Timestamp || \vartheta_r)$ to AV.

Check-in: AV sends relevant information to the PLT. Then PLT verifies it and searches the token Tok_{pk} in the token pool β. If token exists, it will verify the timestamp; otherwise, it will reject the token. If both token Tok_{pk} and the timestamp are valid, PLT will allow the vehicle to park on the corresponding parking space, while it takes back the corresponding token Tok_{pk}.

User Payment: Users pay for it by anonymous payment.

4.2 Lattice-Based Ring Signature Scheme Under the Random Oracle Model

In this section, we show the lattice-based ring signature scheme in Fig. 2, which includes four $Probabilistic Polynominal - Time(PPT)$ algorithms:

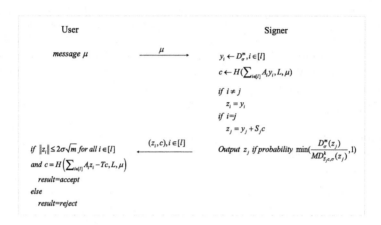

Fig. 2. Our lattice-based ring signature protocol.

(1) $Setup(U, S, pk, sk, M)$

Let $q \geq 3$ be a prime member, a positive integer n which larger than 64, and a positive integer m such that $m \geq 5n\ log\ q$. Moreover, the user sets a hash function $H : \{0,1\}^* \rightarrow \{v \in \{-1,0,1\}^k, \|v\|_1 \leq \kappa\}$, where k and κ are positive integers. Also, there is a matrix T which is chosen at random from $Z_q^{n \times k}$.

(2) $Key - Extract(pk, sk)$

In a ring R which contains l members, for all $i \in [l]$, we compute $A_i \in Z_q^{n \times m}, B_i \in Z_q^{n \times m} \leftarrow TrapGen(1^n)$, which B_i is a basis of $\Lambda_q^{\perp}(A_i) = \{v \in Z^m : A_i\ v = 0(mod\ q)\}$ as well as $\| \tilde{B_i} \| \leq L$ which $L = O(\sqrt{nlogq})$ and $r = L \cdot \omega(\sqrt{logn})$. For all $i \in [l], t_j \in Z_q^n(j \in [k])$, we utilize the algorithm $SamplePre(A_i, B_i, t_j, \omega)$ k times with a positive integer $d \geq max_{i \in [l]}\{\|B_i\| \cdot \omega\sqrt{logn}\}$. Then, it outputs vector $s_{i,j} \in Z_m, A_iS_i = T$ and $S_i = (s_{i,l}, \cdots, s_{i,k}) \in \{-d, \cdots, 0, \cdots, d\}^{m \times k}$. Thus, we let $A_i \in Z_q^{n \times m}$ be the public key pk, and $S_i \in \{-d, \cdots, 0, \cdots, d\}^{m \times k}$ be the secret key sk which is relevant to the pk.

Algorithm 1. $Key - Extract(1^n, a_i, l)$

Input: Security parameter n, Public polynomial a_i, Ring members l
Output: Secret key sk_i, Public key pk_i

1: **for** $i \leftarrow 1$ to l **do**   6: $t_i \leftarrow a_i s_i + e_i \pmod{q}$
2:     $s_i, e_i \leftarrow Z_q^{n \times m}$ 7: $sk_i \leftarrow (s_i, e_i)$
3:     **if** $TrapGen(1^n)$ **then**   8: $pk_i \leftarrow t_i$
4:         Restart   9: **end for**
5:     **end if**   10: Return sk_i, pk_i

---

(3) $Sign - Gen(sk, S, U)$

We take the input message μ, a ring R which contains l members with a set of public keys $L = A_i$ where $i \in [l]$, and a secret key S_j of the signer j. To begin with, we sample random vector $y_j \leftarrow D_\sigma^m$, which D_σ^m is a discrete Normal distribution of Z^m with standard deviation σ. After that, we compute $c \leftarrow H(\sum_{i \in [l]} A_i y_i, L, \mu)$. Furthermore, for all $i \in [l]$, we have $z_i = y_i, if \ i \neq j$ and $z_j = S_j c + y_j, if \ i = j$ with probability $min(\frac{D_\sigma^m(z_j)}{MD_{S_j,c,\sigma}^m(z_j)}, 1)$. Last but not least, it will output $(z_i : i \subset [l], c)$ as the signature of message μ.

Algorithm 2. $Sign - Gen(S_\gamma, R, a_i, \mu, l)$

Input: Signer's secret key S_γ(part of sk_i), Set of public keys R, Public polynomials a_i, Message μ, Ring members l
Output: Signature $(z_1, z_2, \cdots, z_n, c)$

1: **for** $i \leftarrow 1$ to l **do**   12: $z_i \leftarrow a_i y_i + t_i c$
2:     $y_i \leftarrow R_q, [B]$ 13:   **end if**
3:     $v_i \leftarrow a_i y_i + e_i \pmod{q}$ 14: **end for**
4: **end for**   15: **for** $i \leftarrow 1$ to l **do**
5: $v \leftarrow v_1 + v_2 + \cdots + v_N$ 16: $e' \leftarrow D_\sigma^m$
6: $c' \leftarrow hash(\lfloor v \rfloor_{d,q}, \|\mu)$ 17: $w_i \leftarrow v_i - e'c \pmod{q}$
7: $c \leftarrow F(c')$ 18:   **if** $[W_i]_{2^d} \notin R_{2^d} - L \lor z_i \notin R_{B-U}$
8: **for** $i \leftarrow 1$ to l **do**   **then**
9:     **if** $i = \gamma$ **then**   19:   Restart
10:         $z_\gamma \leftarrow (y_\gamma + s_\gamma c) a_\gamma$ 20:   **end if**
11:     **else**   21: **end for**
    22: Return $(z_1, z_2, \cdots, z_n, c)$

---

(4) $Sign - Veri(A, B, M, z, c, t)$

We take the input message μ as well as a ring R of l members with public keys $L = A_i$ where $i \in [l]$ and the signature $(z_i : i \in [l], c)$. We consider it will be accept for the verifiers only if $\|z_i\| \leq 2\sigma\sqrt{m}$ *for all* $i \in [l]$ and $c = H(\sum_{i\in[l]} A_iz_i - Tc, L, \mu)$.

Algorithm 3. $Sign - Veri(z_1, z_2, \cdots, z_n, c', \mu, l)$

Input: Signature $z_1, z_2, \cdots, z_n, c'$, Set of public keys message μ, Ring members l
Output: True 1 or False 0

1: $c \leftarrow F(c')$	7: $c'' \leftarrow hash(\lfloor w \rceil_{d,q}, \|\mu)$
2: $w \leftarrow 0$	8: **if** $c' = c''$ **then**
3: **for** $i \leftarrow 1$ to l **do**	9: Return 1
4: $w_i' \leftarrow z_i - t_ic \pmod{q}$	10: **else**
5: $w \leftarrow w + w_i'$	11: Return 0
6: **end for**	12: **end if**

---

5 Security Analysis

In this section, we give the proof of our scheme user anonymity, message correctness and unforgeability is greatly guaranteed.

5.1 Correctness

In our scheme, correctness is inherited by the properties of trapdoor functions [16]. We take $(z_i : i \in [l], c)$ as the signature which generated by user j. We let S_jc in our signature algorithm and consider it as equivalent as the random vector v shown in Lemma 3. From Lemma 3, we know that the distribution of $z_j = S_jc + y_j$ is with statistically distance $\frac{2^{-\omega(logm)}}{M}$ of Gaussian distribution D_σ^m. Therefore, the distribution of $z_j = S_jc + y_j$ is statistically closed to Gaussian distribution D_σ^m and $z_i(i \in [l]\backslash\{j\})$ will come from Gaussian distribution in addition to index user j. Thus, according to Lemma 1 and Lemma 2, we have $Pr[|z| > 2\sigma\sqrt{m}; z \leftarrow D_\sigma^m] < 2^{-m}$ for all $z_i(i \in [l])$.

Moreover, we calculate $\sum_{i\in[l]} A_iz_i - Tc = A_jz_j - Tc + \sum_{i\in[l]\backslash\{j\}} A_iz_i = A_jS_jc + A_jy_j - Tc + \sum_{i\in[l]\backslash\{j\}} A_iy_i = \sum_{i\in[l]} A_iy_i$. So, we can consider our scheme is correct.

5.2 Anonymity

Theorem 2 (Anonymity): Assume n is the security parameter, and other parameters m, s, β, α, q are functions of n. It is negligible for an adversary with the polynomial time to win the anonymity game. Thus, our scheme is anomymous.

5.3   Unforgeability

To achieve message unforgeability, we compute the vector s, s' with certain probability to make $As = As'$, and $A \in Z_q^{n \times m}$.

Theorem 3: Given $n > 64$, and $m > 5n\ log\ q$, chosen $s \leftarrow \{-d, \cdots, 0, \cdots, d\}^m$ randomly, there is another $s \leftarrow \{-d, \cdots, 0, \cdots, d\}^m$ such that $As = As'$ with probability $1 - 2^{-100}$.

Theorem 4: Given a polynomial-time forger, it succeed to forge the ring signature with probability δ which is non-negligible when the forger makes s queries to signing oracle and h queries to the random oracle H. After that, there is a polynomial-time algorithm, which can figure out the $SIS_{q,n,ml,\beta}$ problem with non-negligible probability $= \frac{\delta^2}{2(h+s)}$ when $\beta = (4\sigma + 2dk)\sqrt{ml}$.

Theorem 5: Given D be a distinguisher, the advantage of D at most $(2^{-nl+1} \cdot (s+h) + \frac{2^{-\omega(logm)}}{M}) \cdot s$ in differentiating the real ring signing algorithm from Algorithm 2.

Theorem 6: There is a forger who makes s queries to the signing oracle and h queries to the random oracle, and given $A = [A_1 \| A_2 \| \cdots \| A_l] \leftarrow Z_q^{n \times ml}$. Existing an algorithm which can compute a non-zero vector $v \in Z^{ml}$, such that $Av = 0$ and $\|v\| \leq (4\sigma + 2dk)\sqrt{ml}$ with minimum probability is $(\frac{1}{2} - 2^{-100})(\delta - \frac{1}{|D_H|})(\frac{\delta - \frac{1}{|D_H|}}{t} - \frac{1}{|D_H|})$.

6   Efficiency Analysis

In this section, we evaluate the performance of our proposed scheme in terms of communication overhead, system security, and signature length.

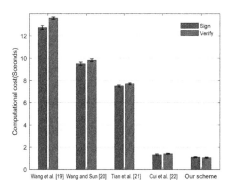

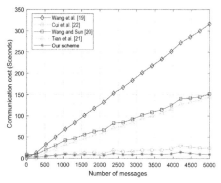

Fig. 3. Comparison of sign and verify cost.

Fig. 4. Comparison of system communication cost.

In the existing research [17,18], no researcher has proposed an AVP system that can resist quantum attacks. Therefore, we compare with systems that utilized lattice-based ring signatures. As shown in Fig. 3, the scheme [19] expands the mother lattice under the bonsai tree model. This increases the dimension of lattice in ring signature. Wang and Sun [20] achieved more powerful security models and less expensive signatures, but there is still places for promotion. Tian et al. [21] proposed scheme was proved strongly unforgeable for selection subring and adaptive selection message attack, and the signature and verification overhead are lower than the previous scheme. The scheme proposed by Cui et al. [22], then cost is much lower than previous scheme. We have proposed a scheme to protect the unforgeability of messages in AVP systems, and proved its strongly unforgeable security in random prophecy models. As can be seen from Fig. 3, the cost of signature and verification of our scheme is lower than that of the other four schemes. Therefore, our scheme guarantees the efficiency of the AVP privacy preservation system while ensuring that it can resist quantum attacks.

We assume that the size of the group is l, k is the safety parameter, T_m is the time cost for n point multiplications, T_e, T_s, and T_z represents the time cost on the *ExtBasis* algorithm, *SamplePre* algorithm and zero-knowledge proof, respectively. m can be expressed as $3 + (2c/3n^c) \log n$, where n is a power of 2. In Table 2, we list the calculation methods in terms of signature cost, verification cost and signature length. Our scheme achieves higher efficiency without paying heavy price on the length of the signature. In Fig. 4, we set the interval between the sum of all user message numbers in the AVP system from 0 to 5000 as well as simulate and compare the communication overhead when system received a different number of messages. The scheme proposed by Wang et al. [19], which extends the dimension of signature lattice when signing, has to pay heavy price in communication. The communication cost proposed by Wang and Sun [20] is slightly higher than that proposed by Tian et al. [21]. However, the scheme proposed by Cui et al. [22] which improves this problem, has lower communication overhead and more stable growth. As can be seen from Fig. 4, our proposed scheme applied to the privacy protection of AVP system is better than that of Cui et al. [22]. With the increase of the number of messages, the communication overhead of our proposed scheme is lower than that of other schemes, and it will not lead to system overload or heavy price.

Table 2. Comparison of signature cost, verification cost and signature length.

Scheme	Signature cost	Verification cost	Signature length
Wang et al. [19]	$m(l+d)T_e + m(l+d+1)T_s$	$m(l+d+1)T_m$	$((l+d+1)m$
Wang and Sun [20]	$mT_s + (l+k-1)T_m$	$m(l+k)T_m$	$(l+k)m+l$
Tian et al. [21]	$mT_s + m(l+1)T_m$	$m(l+2)T_m$	$(l+2)m$
Cui et al. [22]	$5lT_m$	$T_n + 5lT_m$	$2(l+1)m$
Our scheme	$m(l+1)T_m$	$m(l+1)T_m$	$lm+k$

In addition, we also compare our proposed scheme with others for AVP system privacy protection [17,18]. In the scheme proposed by Huang et al. [18], the methods of signatures, geo-indistinguishable mechanism and one-time token solve exist question. But they did not mention the correctness and unforgeability of the messages. The scheme proposed by Ni et al. [19] mainly solves the traceability of vehicles and mobile phones. The above two papers have proposed solutions for the privacy protection of the AVP system, but neither of them consider that the messages sent by users may be tampered with or forged. Furthermore, none of AVP privacy protection systems can resist quantum attacks. In this paper, we issue tokens to ensure user privacy and anonymity, and require users to reapply for tokens every time they apply for parking services to ensure unlinkability. After that, we propose an efficient lattice-based ring signature to ensure the correctness and unforgeability of the message. As shown in Table 3, our scheme has higher security and is capable of resisting quantum attacks.

Table 3. Security requirements.

Security requirement	Ni et al. [18]	Huang et al. [17]	Our scheme
Privacy	✓	✓	✓
Anonymity	✓	✓	✓
Unlinkability	×	✓	✓
Correctness	×	×	✓
Unforgeablity	×	×	✓
Quantum	×	×	✓

7   Conclusion

In this paper, we discuss a lattice-based ring signature scheme for autonomous vehicles. Our scheme is the first AVP privacy preservation system that is able to resist quantum attacks. First, we propose the system model and threat model of AVP system. After that, we design the privacy preservation scheme. In our scheme, users need to send relevant information to parking service provider to complete parking reservation and automatic parking. We remain anonymous during the parking services, which ensures that parking service provider only provides services without knowing the real identity of the user, hence ensuring privacy. The lattice-based ring signature guarantees the correctness and unforgeability of the message, so as to resist quantum attacks. Finally, we analyze the security and efficiency. The results show that our scheme effectually achieves our design goal and is superior to the existing system.

References

1. Wang, J., Cai, Z., Yu, J.: Achieving personalized k-anonymity-based content privacy for autonomous vehicles in CPS. IEEE Trans. Industr. Inf. **16**(6), 4242–4251 (2020)
2. Xiong, Z., Xu, H., Li, W., Cai, Z.: Multi-source adversarial sample attack on autonomous vehicles. IEEE Trans. Veh. Technol. **70**(3), 2822–2835 (2021)
3. Xiong, Z., Cai, Z., Han, Q., Alrawais, A., Li, W.: ADGAN: protect your location privacy in camera data of auto-driving vehicles. IEEE Trans. Ind. Inform. **17**(9), 6200–6210 (2021)
4. Shor, P.W.: Polynomial-time algorithms for prime factorization and discrete logarithms on a quantum computer. SIAM Rev. **41**(2), 303–332 (1999)
5. Grover, L.K.: A fast quantum mechanical algorithm for database search. In: Proceedings of the Twenty-Eighth Annual ACM Symposium on Theory of Computing, vol. 8, pp. 212–219 (1996)
6. Cai, Z., Zheng, X., Yu, J.: A differential-private framework for urban traffic flows estimation via taxi companies. IEEE Trans. Industr. Inf. **15**(12), 6492–6499 (2019)
7. Wang, C., Cheng, X., Li, J., He, Y., Xiao, K.: A survey: applications of blockchain in the internet of vehicles. EURASIP J. Wirel. Commun. Netw. **2021**(1), 1–16 (2021)
8. Hu, C., Cheng, X., Tian, Z., Yu, J., Lv, W.: Achieving privacy preservation and billing via delayed information release. IEEE-ACM Trans. Netw. **29**(3), 1376–1390 (2021)
9. Xu, S., Chen, X., He, Y.: EVchain: an anonymous blockchain based-system for charging-connected electric vehicles. Tsinghua Sci. Technol. **26**(6), 845–856 (2021)
10. Ajtai, M.: Generating hard instances of lattice problems. In: Proceedings of the Twenty-Eighth Annual ACM Symposium on Theory of Computing, pp. 99–108 (1996)
11. Gentry, C., Peikert, C., Vaikuntanathan, V.: Trapdoors for hard lattices and new cryptographic constructions. In: Proceedings of the Fortieth Annual ACM Symposium on Theory of Computing, vol. 10, pp. 197–206 (2008)
12. Cash, D., Hofheinz, D., Kiltz, E., Peikert, C.: Bonsai trees, or how to delegate a lattice basis. In: Gilbert, H. (ed.) EUROCRYPT 2010. LNCS, vol. 6110, pp. 523–552. Springer, Heidelberg (2010). https://doi.org/10.1007/978-3-642-13190-5_27
13. Lyubashevsky, V.: Lattice signatures without trapdoors. In: Pointcheval, D., Johansson, T. (eds.) EUROCRYPT 2012. LNCS, vol. 7237, pp. 738–755. Springer, Heidelberg (2012). https://doi.org/10.1007/978-3-642-29011-4_43
14. Cayrel, P.-L., Lindner, R., Rückert, M., Silva, R.: A lattice-based threshold ring signature scheme. In: Abdalla, M., Barreto, P.S.L.M. (eds.) LATINCRYPT 2010. LNCS, vol. 6212, pp. 255–272. Springer, Heidelberg (2010). https://doi.org/10.1007/978-3-642-14712-8_16
15. Fan, B., Andersen, D.G., Kaminsky, M., Mitzenmacher, M.D.: Cuckoo filter: practically better than bloom. In: Proceedings of the 10th ACM International on Conference on emerging Networking Experiments and Technologies, no. 14, pp. 75–88 (2014)
16. Yang, J.H., Chang, C.C.: An ID-based remote mutual authentication with key agreement scheme for mobile devices on elliptic curve cryptosystem. Comput. Secur. **28**(3–4), 138–143 (2009)
17. Huang, C., Lu, R., Lin, X., Shen, X.: Secure automated valet parking: a privacy-preserving reservation scheme for autonomous vehicles. IEEE Trans. Veh. Technol. **67**(11), 11169–11180 (2018)

18. Ni, J., Lin, X., Shen, X.: Toward privacy-preserving valet parking in autonomous driving era. IEEE Trans. Veh. Technol. **68**(3), 2893–2905 (2019)
19. Wang, F.H., Hu, Y.P., Wang, C.X.: A lattice-based ring signature scheme from bonsai trees. J. Electron. Inf. Technol. **32**(2), 2400–2403 (2010)
20. Wang, J., Sun, B.: Ring signature schemes from lattice basis delegation. In: Qing, S., Susilo, W., Wang, G., Liu, D. (eds.) ICICS 2011. LNCS, vol. 7043, pp. 15–28. Springer, Heidelberg (2011). https://doi.org/10.1007/978-3-642-25243-3_2
21. Tian, M.M., Huang, L.S., Yang, W.: Efficient lattice-based ring signature scheme. Chin. J. Comput. **35**(4), 713–717 (2012)
22. Cui, Y., Cao, L., Zhang, X., Zeng, G.: Ring signature based on lattice and VANET privacy preservation. Chin. J. Comput. **40**(169), 1–14 (2017)
23. Micciancio, D., Peikert, C.: Trapdoors for lattices: Simpler, Tighter, Faster, Smaller. In: Annual International Conference on the Theory and Applications of Cryptographic Techniques (EUROCRYPT), pp. 700–718, Springer, Heidelberg, Apr. 2012

AOPL: Attention Enhanced Oversampling and Parallel Deep Learning Model for Attack Detection in Imbalanced Network Traffic

Leiqi Wang[1,2], Weiqing Huang[1], Qiujian Lv[1(✉)], Yan Wang[1], and HaiYan Chen[3]

[1] Institute of Information Engineering, Chinese Academy of Science, Beijing, China
{wangleiqi,huangweiqing,lvqiujian,wangyan}@iie.ac.cn
[2] School of Cyber Security, University of Chinese Academy of Science, Beijing, China
[3] Chinese Research Academy of Environmental Sciences, Beijing, China
chenhy@craes.org.cn

Abstract. Machine learning-based approaches have been widely used in network attack detection. Existing solutions typically train the model on a balanced dataset and get a superior detection result. However, the actual network traffic data is imbalanced due to the less frequent network attacks than the normal, which decreases the models' performance. To reduce the impact of imbalanced data, an AOPL model is proposed in this paper, consisting of Attention Mechanism Enhanced Oversampling (AMEO) and Parallel Deep Learning (PDL). AMEO uses the attention mechanism to reduce redundancy when generating attack traffic samples. By forming data pairs as the input, PDL models each network traffic separately and requires less data than Deep Neural Network. Extensive comparison experiments on four real network traffic datasets show that AOPL has better Accuracy, Precision, and F1-score performances. Significantly, AMEO can help models perform better attack detection on the imbalanced data.

Keywords: Imbalanced traffic · Attack detection · Attention mechanism enhanced oversampling · Parallel deep learning · Machine learning

1 Introduction

The number of network attacks is increasing along with the continuous expansion of the networks scale [1]. The CNCERT/CC sampling monitoring results in 2019 show that the total number of IP addresses of control servers was 102,554, an increase of 32.5% compared with 2018 [2]. However, detecting attacks makes it feasible to discover attacks and prevent further destruction. Therefore, experts in the industry and academia put forward measures to detect network attacks and hope to reduce the loss as far as possible. It has become a significant concern that which method of detecting network attacks is the best.

Z. Liu et al. (Eds.): WASA 2021, LNCS 12938, pp. 84–95, 2021.
https://doi.org/10.1007/978-3-030-86130-8_7

Network attack detection studies based on machine learning have been proposed, like Linear regression (LR) [3], Supported Vector Machine (SVM) [4] and Decision Tree (DT) [5]. Recently, Deep Learning (DL) techniques have also been developed for identifying network attacks [9]. The distribution characteristics of data have a large influence on performance [10]. Models provide accurate classification results on balanced data. However, the actual network traffic data is imbalanced due to fewer network attacks. Dealing with imbalanced datasets is challenged because a classifier can not always recognize the minority class. The imbalanced distribution may lead to biased or inaccurate models and the decrease of the performance of the model trained on balanced data [1]. Therefore, it is essential to construct an attack detection model for imbalanced datasets.

At present, combining a classifier with a sampling method that rebalances the distribution of data is common to solve the imbalance problem [3,11]. Undersampling removes the majority class samples, which may cause the classifier to miss important information carried by the majority class samples. It is not suitable when the dataset is small. On the contrary, oversampling generates samples similar to original minority class samples while does not need to consider the dataset's size. Therefore, oversampling makes up for the lack of undersampling. Unfortunately, oversampling causes overfitting due to the repetition of the minority samples. To eliminate the redundancy of oversampling, a solution needs to be found.

To tackle the above challenges, this study develops attention enhanced oversampling and parallel deep learning (AOPL) for attack detection, the combination of the attention mechanism enhanced oversampling (AMEO) and parallel Deep Learning (PDL) method. It aims at network attack detection on imbalanced data. Experiments show that AOPL performs better than compared models on four real datasets. Besides, AMEO can help the models achieve better attack detection on the imbalanced data. PDL reduces the data amount requirements. Overall, the contributions of this study can be summarized as follows:

- AMEO is an innovative oversampling method combined with the attention mechanism. AMEO can interchange the information carried by features to solve the redundancy problem of oversampling on imbalanced data. Meanwhile, AMEO helps attack detection models perform better on the imbalanced data.
- AOPL is proposed in this paper to detect network attacks based on imbalanced network traffic data. The results demonstrate that AOPL has better scores in Accuracy, Precision and F1-score on the imbalanced data. Moreover, PDL requires less data than Deep Neural Network by forming data pairs as the input.
- Extensive experiments are conducted on four real datasets. The conclusions are drawn based on the solid experimental foundation.

The rest of the paper is organized as follows. Section 2 reviews the related work. Section 3 presents the details of the proposed model. Section 4 describes the detailed setup of the experiments. The results and analysis are described in Sect. 5. Finally, Sect. 6 concludes this paper.

2 Related Work

This section first reviews network attack detection models based on machine learning. Methods of resolving the imbalance problem are the second. Finally, the migration use of the attention mechanism is described.

With the continuous growth of computing capability, machine learning methods have been widely used for network attack detection [3–5]. Dada [6] proposed a hybrid approach for combining Support Vector Machine (SVM), K Nearest Neighbor and Primal-Dual Particle Swarm Optimization to achieve high accuracy. Yuan [7] used the C5.0 method and the Naive Bayes algorithm for adaptive network intrusion detection. Meng [8] compared the performance of neural networks, SVM and decision trees in a uniform environment to detect abnormal behaviours. However, most previous studies usually assumed that their training datasets were well-balanced. Their works are conducted on balanced data, and ignore the effect of network traffic's imbalanced distribution on the performance of a detection model.

People have been paying attention to the imbalance problem and have proposed many methods to offset its impact [1,12–15]. It is a common way to resolve the imbalance problem that a detection model is combined with a sampling method [3,11]. Generally, oversampling and undersampling are two techniques to rebalance data distribution. The random undersampling method and NearMiss-1 are two commonly used undersampling algorithms to rebalance the data distribution [12]. However, undersampling tends to remove the majority class samples and miss important information carried by original data. Especially when data size is small, the performance of the model may be weakened. Liu [16] proposed two ensemble algorithms, EasyEnsemble and BalanceCascade. EasyEnsemble isolates subsets from the majority class, while BalanceCascade uses trained classifiers to guide the sampling process for subsequent classifiers. These two algorithms divide majority class samples to form multiple balanced subsets with minority class samples. The problem still exists that information carried by other subsets can be missed. In contrast, oversampling appends similar data to the original dataset. SMOTE and ADASYN are two classic algorithms of oversampling algorithms to generate minority class samples [17,18]. Unfortunately, oversampling may lead to overfitting because of adding too many similar samples to minority samples. To address the redundancy problem of oversampling, an Attention Mechanism Enhanced Oversampling (AMEO) method is proposed to avoid adding duplicate data.

The attention mechanism is widely used in the processing of data feature characteristics. Its primary function is to redistribute the weights for all the inputs by calculating the deviation between the input features [19]. It was first proposed to explain the cognition of human. Then, it was widely applied to Natural Language Process (NLP) and computer vision later to automatically learn to find core vocabulary or fix its gaze on salient objects [20]. Tehrani [21] introduced the attention mechanism into fault detection to address the feature characteristics problem. Inspired by this study, the attention mechanism is applied to oversampling to resolve sample generation's redundancy.

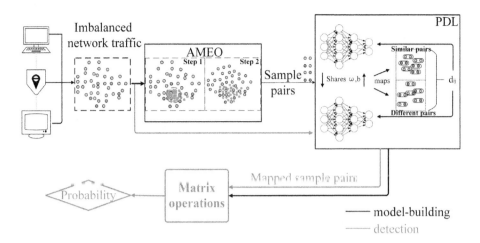

Fig. 1. AMEO, PDL, and matrix operations are the main parts of AOPL. In the model-building phase, AMEO rebalances the data distribution and reduces the redundant samples. PDL synchronously classifies network traffic sample pairs and maps them to the new feature space. In the detection phase, matrix operations determine the sample label.

3 Model Architecture

This section describes the model architecture and the technical details behind the AOPL. The architecture of AOPL is depicted in Fig. 1. It consists of three parts:

- Attention mechanism enhanced oversampling (AMEO) first rebalances the distribution of data and reduces the redundant network traffic samples.
- Parallel Deep Learning (PDL) synchronously trains two DNNs to maximize the distance from similar traffic sample pairs, minimize the distance from different traffic sample pairs, and map sample pairs to the new feature space.
- Matrix operations determine the network traffic sample label based on the similar distances calculated between sample pairs mapped by PDL.

The detailed process of AOPL model training and attack detection is as followed.

3.1 Attention Mechanism Enhanced Oversampling

In the model-building phase, AMEO is the first step. There are two parts of AMEO: SMOTE and attention mechanism. Firstly, AMEO generates new attack traffic samples with SMOTE to rebalance the data distribution and then reduces redundancy with the attention mechanism.

Network traffic sample x $(x \in X)$ describes the packet's context. y $(y \in Y)$ is the label of x. First, the data X is fed into SMOTE to generate attack data.

SMOTE method creates artificial data based on the feature space similarities between existing attack samples until X is balanced. For the subset $X_{attack} \in X$, the K-nearest neighbours for each attack traffic sample $x_i \in X_{attack}$ is chosen, for some specified integer k. K-nearest neighbours are defined as the k elements of S_{attack} whose Euclidean distance between itself and x_i under consideration exhibits the smallest magnitude along the N-dimensions of feature space. To create a synthetic sample, one of the K-nearest neighbours is randomly selected. The formula (1) is used to generate a new attack traffic sample x_{new} [17].

$$x_{new} = x_i + (\hat{x}_i - x_i) \times \delta \tag{1}$$

where $\hat{x}_i$ is the k nearest neighbor of x_i. δ is a random number that $\delta \in [0, 1]$. vector x_{new} is added to X and X is balanced.

Then, attention mechanism redistributes the data X by interchanging the information carried by features. Attention function computes on a set of traffic samples packed together into a matrix Q. The keys are also packed together into matrices K. Matrix of outputs [19] is computed as:

$$Attention(Q, K) = softmax(\frac{QK^T}{\sqrt[2]{d_k}})Q \tag{2}$$

where Q, K are two adjacent traffic samples, and d_k is the dimension of Q. At this point, network traffic data X is balanced and with less redundancy.

3.2   Parallel Deep Learning

PDL, a classifier made up of two synchronously trained DNNs, is the second step of the model-building phase. The operation process consists of two steps: classifying data pairs and mapping data. PDL distinguishes similar and different network traffic sample pairs of samples and maps them to the new space. Similar network traffic pairs consist of two network traffic samples with the same label. Different network traffic pairs are composed of two network traffic samples with different labels.

Sometimes samples are not adequate enough, but fed in pairs can increase the sample size. To prove that data pairs can increase the sample size, it's assumed that there are n samples in the sample set. When Two samples are randomly selected into pairs, the amount of samples increases from n to n_{new}. n_{new} is calculated according to the following formula:

$$n_{new} = C_n^2 = \frac{n \times (n-1)}{2} \tag{3}$$

Firstly, Network traffic samples in X are randomly combined to construct a pair $(x_i, x_j)_{i \neq j}$ $(\forall i, j = 1, 2, 3, ...n)$ after AMEO. The value of its label F_{ij} is:

$$F_{ij} = \begin{cases} 1, & \text{if } Y_i = Y_j \\ 0, & \text{if } Y_i \neq Y_j \end{cases} \tag{4}$$

Then, with sharing the same parameters ω and b, two DNNs of PDL distinguishes similar and different pairs of samples and maps them to the new space. Network traffic sample pairs (x_i, x_j) are fed and mapped to (z_i, z_j) $(z \in Z)$ in PDL. The similar distance d_{ij} between z_i and z_j is calculated. The similar distance d_{ij} can be defined as:

$$d_{ij} = ||z_i - z_j|| \tag{5}$$

The goal is that the distance from similar samples is minimized, and from different samples is maximized. To achieve this, $Loss$ is used to constantly corrects the PDL by adjusting ω and b. $Loss(\omega, b)$ is defined as:

$$Loss(\omega, b) = \sum_{i,j_{i \neq j}} \alpha \times F_{ij} \times d_{ij}^2 + \beta \times (1 - F_{ij})$$
$$\times max\left(0, (C - d_{ij})^2\right) + C_{L2} \times ||W||^2 \tag{6}$$

where α and β represent the weights of similar inputs and heterogeneous inputs. C_{L2} is the weights of L2 regularization.

In the end, parameters (ω, b) are confirmed, and the model-building phase is over.

3.3 Matrix Operations and Detection

In the detection phase, matrix operations are calculated to determine the labels of new traffic samples. When there are network traffic data X_{detect} unknown labels, X and X_{detect} are first fed into PDL, and then D_{detect} is calculated through Z, Z_{detect} and Y. Finally, the sample label is confirmed by calculating the P_{detect}, representing the probability that the sample belongs to the attack category. D_{detect} and P_{detect} are defined as:

$$D_{detect} = Z_{detect} \times Z^T \times Y \tag{7}$$

$$P_{detect} = -\ln D_{detect} \tag{8}$$

The closer P_{detect} is to 1, the more likely it is to be an attack.

4 Experiments Setup

4.1 Datasets

Experiments are set on public and real datasets: IoT Botnet Attacks Dataset [22] and Kitsune Network Attack Dataset [23]. IoT Botnet Attacks Dataset collects real traffic data, which gathers traffic data from 9 commercial IoT devices authentically infected by Mirai and BASHLITE. Three kinds of attack traffic data (COMBO, TCP, Junk) from the Ennio doorbell are used in the experiments.

Kitsune Network Attack Dataset contains 10 different network attacks on a Wi-Fi network populated with 9 IoT devices and three PCs. The dataset collects 10 kinds of attack network traffic in total: OS Scan, Fuzzing, Video Injection, ARP MitM, Active Wiretap, SSDP Flood, SYN DoS, SSL Renegotiation and Mirai. Experiments are conducted on the OS Scan attack dataset. The experiments are finished on the four attack datasets separately.

4.2   Data Preprocessing

To evaluate the effectiveness of proposed model AOPL, datasets are built with different severity of the imbalance. To indicate the severity of the imbalance, imbalance Ratio IR [11] is defined as the ratio between the normal class and attack class samples. Normal and attack are separately set as the majority class and the minority class. Formula (9) and (10) represent the method to calculate IR of the attack class:

$$LC(D) = \frac{1}{|D|} \sum_{i=1}^{|D|} |X_i| \tag{9}$$

$$IR = \frac{|X_i|}{LC(D) - |X_i|} \tag{10}$$

Label cardinality of D $(LC(D))$ is the average number of labels of the samples in D. In this paper, D stands for the attack class.

To build imbalanced datasets, we change the number of attack class samples and form distinct datasets with different IR. The normal class samples size is set as 1000, and the number of attack class samples is increased from 100 to 700 with the step as 100. IRs of datasets are calculated as 0.22, 0.5, 0.85, 1.3, 2, 3, 4.67, separately. The smaller IR is, the more serious imbalanced the dataset is. The network attack detection experiments are carried on these imbalanced datasets. Moreover, experiments are also conducted on the original datasets to evaluate the model's performance in the real attack scenario. Therefore, the results can fully show whether the AOPL model addresses the imbalance problem.

4.3   Experimental Design and Evaluation Metrics

As shown in Table 1, experiments are divided into three parts. The first part verifies the effectiveness of AOPL to detect network attacks on imbalanced traffic data and compares the results with three machine learning models in the contrast experiments. The second part verifies whether AMEO is better than other rebalance methods by comparing detection results of DT combined with different rebalance methods. The third part explores and proves whether AMEO can help models perform better attack detection in the imbalance problem.

All the experiments of this paper are implemented with Python 3.7. Experiment results are measured by confused matrix: Precision, Accuracy and F1.

Table 1. Experimental purpose and compared models

Experiments	Purpose	Algorithm	
I	Whether the model AOPL is effective for attack detection on imbalanced traffic data	SVM	
		DT	
		DNN	
		AOPL	
II	Whether the AMEO can solve the imbalance problem and be better than general rebalance methods	Oversample	SMOTE
			ADASYN
		Under-sample	Random Under-Sampler
			Near Miss-1
		Ensemble	Easy Ensemble
			Balance Cascade
		AOPL	AMEO
III	Whether AMEO is portable and helps models achieve better attack detection	SVM	AMEO-SVM
		DT	AMEO-DT
		DNN	AMEO-DNN

5 Evaluation

The results are summarized and plotted in the tables and figures. The results verify whether AOPL can detect network attacks on imbalanced traffic data. Meanwhile, they verify whether the model can solve the general imbalance problem and contribute to other models.

Table 2. Attack detection results of models on four imbalanced datasets

Dataset	Indicator	SVM	DT	DNN	AOPL
COMBO	Precision	0.436	0.081	0.384	**0.659**
	Accuracy	0.629	0.402	0.654	**0.722**
	F1 score	0.498	0.074	0.352	**0.769**
Junk	Precision	0.419	0.091	0.428	**0.661**
	Accuracy	0.605	0.445	0.618	**0.73**
	F1 score	0.435	**0.079**	0.469	**0.777**
TCP	Precision	0	0	0.08	**0.501**
	Accuracy	0.648	**0.688**	0.132	0.501
	F1 score	0	0	0.007	**0.435**
Kitsune	Precision	0.991	1	0.998	0.993
	Accuracy	**0.997**	0.992	0.994	0.988
	F1 score	**0.995**	0.989	0.993	0.988

AOPL is Effective in Imbalanced Data. Table 2 shows the attack detection results among AOPL, SVM, DT and DNN on four different original datasets. AOPL has advantages in COMBO, Junk and TCP datasets, and its evaluation metrics scores are mostly higher than other models. About the Kitsune, AOPL and others almost show the same performance. Results claim that AOPL can successfully detect network attacks on imbalanced traffic data. However, it cannot be denied that all models' performances on the TCP dataset are poor. Because the samples belonging to the TCP are frequently repeated, the models' scores are low except for AOPL. It partly evidences that the AOPL model has strong robustness.

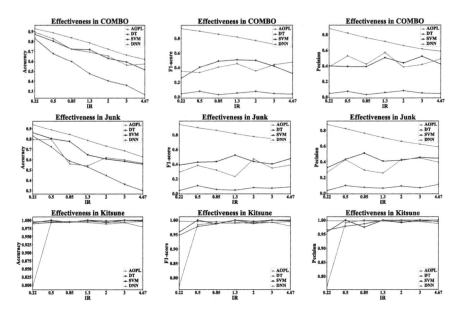

Fig. 2. Experiment I: Results of network attack detection under different IRs. AOPL performs almost the same as the other models on Kitsune but behaves better on COMBO and Junk. It is proved that AOPL is suitable for the imbalanced problem.

Figure 2 shows that models' attack detection performances are under the different IRs on the COMBO, Junk and Kitsune. Considering that the TCP dataset's negative impact on the models makes the results not credible, the experiment on the TCP is cancelled. The red line represents the results of the AOPL. The advantage of AOPL is more evident than other models under each IR on COMBO and Junk. Results indicate that AOPL can achieve better performance in almost every imbalanced scenario. That means AOPL is a good way to solve imbalance problems.

However, when IR increases, the detection performance of models declines to some extent, evaluation metrics of models going down. Feature characteristic is the influencing factor. The downward trend of results is nonexistent when the experiment is on the Kitsune but is apparent on the COMBO and Junk. In the kitsune dataset, the characteristic similarity between the samples is low. The characteristics of COMBO and Junk samples have obvious similarities, such as in mean value and variance. Models could be overfitting on the dataset with too many similar samples. Therefore, the overfitting caused by too many similar original samples leads to the downward trend.

AMEO is Better Than the General Rebalance Methods. Figure 3 presents the ability to solve the imbalance problem of AMEO and other rebalance methods. DT is chosen as the classifier combined with rebalance methods to detect the network attacks under different IRs. Experiments are on the COMBO and Junk. The broken red line represents the results of AMEO. The performance of AMEO is better than others, and scores are higher, especially in F1 score and

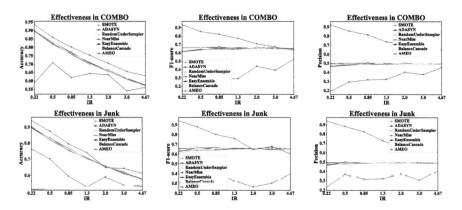

Fig. 3. Experiment II: Attack detection results from the DT model combined with rebalance methods. AMEO gets higher scores in Accuracy, Precision and F1 score on both COMBO and Junk. It is proved that AMEO is a better method than other rebalance methods

Precision. The experimental results are sufficient to prove that AMEO is efficient in solving the imbalance problem and better than other rebalance methods.

Table 3. Enhancement effect of AMEO on the models

Dataset	Indicator	AMEO-SVM	AMEO-DT	AMEO-DNN
COMBO	△Precision	0.24	0.636	0.252
	△Accuracy	0.11	0.303	0.01
	△F1 score	0.288	0.632	0.341
Junk	△Precision	0.239	0.565	0.206
	△Accuracy	0.117	0.203	0.036
	△F1 score	0.34	0.566	0.199
Average		**0.22**	**0.484**	**0.174**

AMEO Can Help Models Achieve Better Attack Detection. Table 3 shows the enhanced effectiveness of AMEO. Experiment III combines AMEO with the models in Experiment I and carries out the detection experiments under the same IR as Experiment I on the COMBO and Junk. $\triangle$ represents the difference between results of twice experiments. After being combined with AMEO, the three performance evaluation metrics of SVM, DT and DNN are improved in average 0.222, 0.484 and 0.174, respectively. It claims that AMEO helps enhance the performance of models in network attack detection on imbalanced traffic data. Because AMEO helps capture more information between samples. Therefore, AMEO can be regarded as a portable method to solve the imbalance problem.

PDL Reduces the Need for the Amount of Data Than DNN. Both AOPL and AMEO-DNN are based on DNN and use AMEO to rebalance the data distribution. However, the AOPL performs better than AMEO-DNN on the same

Table 4. Results of AOPL and AMEO-DNN on Kitsune

	Model	IR							Average	Standard deviation
		0.22	0.5	0.85	1.3	2	3	4.67		
Precision	AOPL	0.998	0.998	0.997	0.997	0.993	0.995	0.987	**0.995**	**0.004**
	AMEO-DNN	0.948	0.876	0.894	0.882	0.91	0.894	0.944	0.907	0.027
Accuracy	AOPL	0.9965	0.995	0.995	0.993	0.988	0.993	0.98	**0.992**	**0.005**
	AMEO-DNN	0.944	0.894	0.9	0.892	0.884	0.896	0.912	0.903	0.018
F1 score	AOPL	0.996	0.995	0.994	0.993	0.988	0.993	0.993	**0.993**	**0.002**
	AMEO-DNN	0.948	0.9	0.904	0.9	0.883	0.901	0.906	0.906	0.018

amount of data. The comparison of the experimental results is shown in Table 4. The average performance evaluation metrics of AOPL is higher than AMEO-DNN. The standard deviation of AOPL is lower than AMEO-DNN. These show that AOPL is not only better but also more robust. As mentioned in the model architecture Sect. 3.2, PDL adopts the method of forming sample pair to increase the amount of data so that more data are available to train, acquire more information about sample pairs, and achieve better results. Thus PDL reduces the need for the amount of data instead of requiring plenty of data like DNN.

6 Conclusion

This paper proposes an AOPL model to detect network attacks in imbalanced traffic, and a series of experiments are conducted on real datasets. As a result, AOPL can successfully detect attacks and solve the imbalance problem as a general model. AMEO behaves better than the common rebalance methods. Especially, AMEO could be a portable method to solve the imbalance problem and help models perform better attack detection. Instead of requiring plenty of data like DNN, PDL reduces the need for data by forming data pairs.

In future, it is hoped that this method can be validated in imbalance problems from various domains. AOPL has been tested on real datasets with a series of *IR*s, which lays a foundation for application to imbalance problems in other domains. The efforts here may motivate the necessity and encourage further research into network attack detection and imbalance problem.

References

1. Okutan, A., Werner, G., et al.: Forecasting cyberattacks with incomplete, imbalanced, and insignificant data. Cybersecurity **1**(1), 1–16 (2018)
2. The National Internet Emergency Response Center (CNCERT): China's Internet Network Security Report 2019 (2020)
3. Wheelus, C., Bou-Harb, E., Zhu, X.: Tackling class imbalance in cyber security datasets. 2018 IEEE International Conference on Information Reuse and Integration (IRI), pp. 229–232 (2018)

4. Zhang, H., Li, Y., et al.: A real-time and ubiquitous network attack detection based on deep belief network and support vector machine. IEEE/CAA J. Automatica Sin. **7**(3), 790–799 (2020)
5. Ferrag, M.A., et al.: RDTIDS: rules and decision tree-based intrusion detection system for internet-of-things networks. Future Internet **12**(3), 44 (2020)
6. Dada, EG.: A hybridized SVM-kNN-pdAPSO approach to intrusion detection system. Proceedings of the Faculty Seminar Series, pp. 14–21 (2017)
7. Yuan, Y., Huo, L., Hogrefe, D.: Two layers multi-class detection method for network intrusion detection system. 2017 IEEE Symposium on Computers and Communications (ISCC), pp. 767–772 (2017)
8. Meng, Y.X.: The practice on using machine learning for network anomaly intrusion detection. In: 2011 International Conference on Machine Learning and Cybernetics, vol. 2, pp. 576–581 (2011). https://doi.org/10.1109/ICMLC.2011.6016798
9. Zheng, W.F.: Intrusion detection based on convolutional neural network. In: 2020 International Conference on Computer Engineering and Application (ICCEA), pp. 273–277 (2020)
10. Kwon, O., Sim, J.M.: Effects of data set features on the performances of classification algorithms. Expert Syst. Appl. **40**(5), 1847–1857 (2013)
11. Seo, J.H., Kim, Y.H.: Machine-learning approach to optimize SMOTE ratio in class imbalance dataset for intrusion detection. Comput. Intell. Neurosci. (2018)
12. Mani, I., Zhang, I.: kNN approach to unbalanced data distributions: a case study involving information extraction. In: Proceedings of Workshop on Learning from Imbalanced Datasets, vol. 126 (2003)
13. He, H., Garcia, E.A.: Learning from imbalanced data. IEEE Trans. Knowl. Data Eng. **21**(9), 1263–1284 (2009)
14. Liu, S., Lin, G.: DeepBalance: deep-learning and fuzzy oversampling for vulnerability detection. IEEE Trans. Fuzzy Syst. **28**(7), 1329–1343 (2019)
15. Sun, D., Wu, Z. et al.: Risk prediction for imbalanced data in cyber security : a Siamese network-based deep learning classification framework. In: 2019 International Joint Conference on Neural Networks (IJCNN) (2019)
16. Liu, X.Y., Wu, J., Zhou, Z.H.: Exploratory undersampling for class-imbalance learning. IEEE Trans. Syst. Man Cybern. Part B (Cybern.) **39**(2), 539–550 (2008)
17. Chawla, N.V., et al.: SMOTE: synthetic minority over-sampling technique. J. Artif. Intell. Res. **16**, 321–357 (2002)
18. He, H., Bai, Y., et al.: ADASYN: adaptive synthetic sampling approach for imbalanced learning. In: 2008 IEEE International Joint Conference on Neural Networks (IEEE World Congress on Computational Intelligence), pp. 1322–1328 (2008)
19. Vaswani, A., Shazeer, N., Parmar, N., et al.:: Attention is all you need. In: Advances in Neural Information Processing Systems, pp. 5998–6008 (2017)
20. Xu, K., Ba, J., et al.: Show, attend and tell: neural image caption generation with visual attention. In: International Conference on Machine Learning, pp. 2048–2057 (2015)
21. Tehrani, P., Levorato, M.: Frequency-based multi task learning with attention mechanism for fault detection in power systems (2020)
22. Meidan, Y., Bohadana, M., Mathov, Y., et al.: N-BaIoT: network-based detection of IoT Botnet attacks using deep autoencoders. IEEE Pervasive Comput. **17**(3), 12–22 (2018). Special Issue - Securing the IoT
23. Mirsky, Y., Doitshman, T., et al.: Kitsune: an ensemble of autoencoders for online network intrusion detection. In: Network and Distributed System Security Symposium (2018)

Greedy-Based Black-Box Adversarial Attack Scheme on Graph Structure

Shushu Shao[1], Hui Xia[2(✉)], Rui Zhang[2], and Xiangguo Cheng[1(✉)]

[1] College of Computer Science and Technology,
Qingdao University, Qingdao 266100, China
[2] College of Information Science and Engineering, Ocean University of China,
Qingdao 266101, China
xiahui@ouc.edu.cn

Abstract. Effective attack schemes that simulate adversarial attack behavior in graph network is the key to exploring potential threats in practical scenarios. However, most attack schemes are not accurate in locating target nodes and lock unnoticeable perturbations from the perspective of graph embedding space, leading to a low success rate of attack and high perturbation on node classification tasks. To overcome these problems, we propose a greedy-based black-box adversarial attack scheme on graph structure, which named GB-Attack. Firstly, we use local betweenness centrality to accurately locate target node set to modify graph structure data with high importance. Secondly, we combine the similarity of graph in latent space and theorems in graph theory to obtain adversarial samples with low perturbation. Finally, we apply greedy strategy to get adversarial samples with higher score function to maximize the probability of target nodes being misclassified. Experimental results show that the attack accuracy of GB-Attack on *GCN* models is significantly improved compared with other four attack schemes. Notably, the attack accuracy under multilateral perturbations of GB-Attack is 9.73% higher than that of RL-S2V.

Keywords: Black-box adversarial attack · Graph network · Node classification

1 Introduction

Deep graph learning models can implement various knowledge inference and prediction tasks on the modeling ability of local structure and the common node dependency on graph, and have been successfully applied to semi-supervised node classification [1], graph classification [2] and recommender system [3], etc.

Supported by the National Natural Science Foundation of China (NSFC) under Grant No. 61872205, the Shandong Provincial Natural Science Foundation under Grant No. ZR2019MF018, and the Source Innovation Program of Qingdao under Grant No. 18-2-2-56-jch.

Z. Liu et al. (Eds.): WASA 2021, LNCS 12938, pp. 96–106, 2021.
https://doi.org/10.1007/978-3-030-86130-8_8

Although deep graph learning models have excellent performance in many practical tasks, they are vulnerable to the threat of hostile adversarial samples, as a slight adversarial perturbation can lead to a serious degradation of model performance [4,5]. For instance, in social networks, hackers could steal users' private information by adding abnormal relation links [6,7]; and unlawful users might cheat on the recommendation system of commercial websites by manipulating online reviews or product websites [8,9]. As a kind of non-European structure data, the structure and node features of graph are all discrete, so it is difficult to design an effective attack algorithm to generate adversarial samples. In particular, there is no uniform principle to ensure that the perturbations on the original graph are unnoticeable. In brief, the graph data with discrete features has brought unique challenges to the research of adversarial attack in graph field.

Based on the attackers' knowledge about the target model, current attack schemes mainly focus on white-box attack and black-box attack. In white-box attack [10], attackers can access the complete knowledge of target model, including the internal structure, training parameters, prediction and gradient information, etc. However, it is hard for attackers to obtain the parameter information of target model in most practical scenarios, and the detection of the vulnerability of target model is only based on certain assumptions. Black-box attack is applicable to a wider range of physical scenarios and it depends on the returned results of queries to generate adversarial samples. For example, Chang et al. [11] studied the theoretical relationship between graph signal processing and graph embedded models, and constructed attackers by graph filter and feature matrix to attack graph embedded models. To further query the target classifier, reinforcement learning is applied to black-box attack algorithm. For example, Dai et al. [12] introduced RL-S2V scheme, which uses reinforcement learning to model the attack process as a finite $Markov$ $Decision$ $Process$ (MDP). Ma et al. [13] proposed a rewiring operation on target graph network. However, the above attack schemes show low success rate of attacking on nodes in large dense graph, as it does not include accurate positioning of target nodes with high importance in graph. Moreover, current attack schemes do not set the unnoticeable perturbations from the perspective of graph embedded space, which makes it difficult for the attackers to evade the detection of target model.

To overcome the above shortcomings of black-box attack scheme, we propose a greedy-based black-box adversarial attack scheme on graph structure. The main contributions are as follows:

(1) To improve the success rate of the attack, an accurate locating method is developed in this paper. Firstly, we use local betweenness centrality to obtain the attackable target nodes. Then, with the Jaccard similarity calculated between each node in the target node set and its first-order neighbors, we get the more important edges to construct an attackable edge set.
(2) To avoid the detection of target model, firstly, we use $Graph$ $Neural$ $Network$ (GNN) to set the similarity criteria in the latent space of graph set. Secondly, we use the Weak Regularity Lemma in graph theory to guarantee the structural similarity of graphs. Finally, a score function is set for

adversarial samples according to the unnoticeable perturbations. With the greedy strategy, the adversarial samples with larger score function value are selected and put into the target classifier for black-box query to maximize the probability of nodes being misclassified.

(3) Experimental results show that the GB-Attack has higher attack accuracy than Random Sampling, DICE, RL-S2V and ReWatt schemes in *Graph Convolutional Network* (*GCN*) models. Strict unnoticeable perturbation conditions reduce the perturbations of the adversarial samples.

2 Attack Model

2.1 Accurately Locate the Target Nodes

We first calculate the local betweenness centrality of nodes to accurately locate the attackable target node set. Then, the Jaccard similarity is used to calculate the correlation degree between the target node and the nodes in its first-order neighborhood, and the edges between nodes with higher correlation degree are selected as the set of attackable edges.

Since it is extremely complex to calculate the betweenness centrality of all nodes in a large-scale graph, we select nodes randomly and use the local betweenness centrality, which considers the longest path constraint M in the traditional calculation of betweenness centrality. The local betweenness centrality of node v is represented as follows:

$$C_B^M(v) = \sum_{s \neq v \neq t \in V} \frac{\sigma(s, t \,|v)}{\sigma(s, t)} = \sum_{s \neq v \neq t \in V} \delta_{st}^M(v) \tag{1}$$

where $\sigma(s, t \,|v)$ is the number of shortest paths from the source node s through node v to node t. $\sigma(s, t)$ is the number of all shortest paths from source node s to node t. M is the longest path constraint, which meets the distance $D_G(s, t) \leq M$ between node s and node t.

In this paper, nodes in graph are randomly selected to construct a node set $S = \{s_1, s_2, ..., s_u\}$. The s_i in S is taken randomly as the source node, and we search the shortest path between the node pairs centered on s_i and within the range of the longest path distance constraint M through *Breadth-First Search* (*BFS*) algorithm. Then we calculate the betweenness centrality of node v. By accumulating the betweenness centrality of each node as the source node in S, we get the betweenness centrality of important nodes in graph. That is:

$$\delta_{s\cdot}^M(v) = \sum_{w, v \in P_s(w)} \frac{\sigma(s, v)}{\sigma(s, w)} \left(1 + \delta_{s\cdot}^M(w)\right) \tag{2}$$

where node v is the precursor node of w and $P_s(w)$ is the direct precursor node set of node w.

Finally, we use the principle of approaching sampling as an approximate method to obtain betweenness centrality. With the source node selected in S as the center and given the range of the longest path distance constraint M, the node set N_c is selected, and each node of N_c is searched to obtain $\delta_s.(v)$. After adding up, the betweenness centrality is amplified by the sampling ratio, and the approximate betweenness centrality of each node on the entire graph network is obtained:

$$\hat{C}_B^M(v) = (n/d) \sum_{s \in N_c} \delta_s.(v) \tag{3}$$

where n is the number of all nodes in graph, and d is the number of nodes in N_c. If the shortest path set with the source node in N_c has the same distribution as the shortest path set in the whole graph, the approximate betweenness centrality will fit well with the actual value.

With the above calculation method of betweenness centrality, nodes with larger betweenness centrality within the longest path constraint M can be obtained, and then the attackable target node set $V_{attack} = \{v_1, v_2, ..., v_m\}$ is formed.

In graph networks, graph structure features reflect the interdependence between network instances. In this paper, the Jaccard similarity is used to measure the similarity between two nodes by calculating the overlap of their features. By selecting edges with higher Jaccard similarity value between each attackable node and its neighbors, we form the set of attackable edges $E_{attack} = \{e_1, e_2, ..., e_m\}$.

2.2 Unnoticeable Perturbations

To avoid the detection of target model, the attackers need to ensure that the original graph is similar to the attack graph as much as possible to reduce the perturbation of adversarial samples. Considering both the similarity in the embedded space and the similarity in the graph structure, we set strict unnoticeable perturbation conditions.

Similarity Measure of Graph Embedded Space. We use *GNN* model to process the embedding of graph data. Each hidden layer contains information exchange between adjacent nodes on the graph through several layers of calculation. The goal is to learn the embedded representation h_v of each node v, and aggregate the embedded information of all nodes to generate the overall embedding of the graph.

GNN encodes the features of each node and each edge on the graph in the process of neural network transmission, where the node features are represented as $x(v) \in \mathbb{R}^{D_{node}}$ and the edge features are represented as $w(u, v) \in \mathbb{R}^{D_{edge}}$. The encoder of *GNN* is a simple neural network with hidden layers. The embedding of any node and edge is represented as:

$$h_{v_i}^{(0)} = MLP_{node}(x(v_i)), \ \forall v_i \in V \tag{4}$$

$$e(v_i, v_j) = MLP_{edge}(w(v_i, v_j)), \ \forall e(v_i, v_j) \in E \tag{5}$$

Each node integrates the relevant information of others through rounds of information transmission. To reduce the computational complexity, we calculate the correlation information between nodes and nodes in its first-order neighbors, so as to form new node representations. Thus, the vector of node v_i in the layer k network which aggregates its neighbors' information is represented as:

$$h_{v_i}^{(k)} = MLP_{node} \left(\left\{ w\left(v_i, v_j\right), x\left(v_j\right), h_{v_j}^{(k-1)} \right\}_{v_j \in N(v_i)}, x\left(v_i\right), h_{v_i}^{(k-1)} \right) \quad (6)$$

where $k \in \{1, 2, ..., K\}$, K is the total number layers of GNN. The vector representation of node v in the hidden layer network of layer k includes its own feature $x\left(v_i\right)$, neighbor feature $x\left(v_j\right)$, edge feature $w\left(v_i, v_j\right)$, and node embedded information $h_{v_i}^{(k-1)}$ and $h_{v_j}^{(k-1)}$ in layer k-1. $N\left(v_i\right)$ represents the neighbor node set of node v_i. The node embedding $h_v^{(0)} \in \mathbb{R}^{D_{node}}$ is initialized to all zeros, and through the transmission of K-layer network, the final node embedding is represented as $h_{v_i} = h_{v_i}^{(K)}$. Thus, the graph level is represented as:

$$h_G = f_G \left(\left\{ h_{v_i}^{(K)} \right\} \right) \quad (7)$$

Based on the above steps, the representation information of all nodes is aggregated to form the embedded representation h_G of the whole graph. The aggregation function is as follow:

$$h_G = MLP_G \left(\sum_{v_i \in V} \sigma \left(MLP_{gate} \left(h_{v_i}^{(K)} \right) \right) \odot MLP \left(h_{v_i}^{(K)} \right) \right) \quad (8)$$

where $\odot$ is element-by-element multiplication. The aggregation process uses the weighted sum with the gating vector, and the features are aggregated through cross-node method. This manner is to capture the correlation of dispersion features for more accurate overall results.

Based on the GNN embedded model, the embedded representations $h_{G_{old}}$ and $h_{G_{attack}}$ of the original graph and the attack graph can be obtained. Next, we use Euclidean distance to calculate the similarity of graph pair (G_{old}, G_{attack}) in the embedded space. The formula is as follow:

$$d\left(G_{old}, G_{attack}\right) = \left\| h_{G_{old}} - h_{G_{attack}} \right\|^2 \quad (9)$$

Based on the Euclidean similarity measure of graph, we define the margin-based pairwise loss function as the optimization method of the GNN model, the formula is as follow:

$$L_{embedding} = E_{(G_{old}, G_{attack})} [\max \{0, \lambda - r\left(1 - d\left(G_{old}, G_{attack}\right)\right)\}] \quad (10)$$

where $r \in \{-1, 1\}$ is the label to judge whether the original graph is similar to the attack graph, and λ is the parameter of margin. When $d\left(G_{old}, G_{attack}\right) < 1 - \lambda$, it can be said that the original graph is similar to the attack graph pair, i.e., $r = 1$. On the contrary, when $d\left(G_{old}, G_{attack}\right) > 1 - \lambda$, graph pairs are not similar, i.e., $r = -1$.

Similarity Measure on Graph Structure. We utilize the cutting norm of matrix to measure the distance between two graphs and apply Weak Regularity Lemma to guarantee the similarity between the attack graph and the original graph. Let G_{old} and G_{attack} be two graphs with common node sets. For an unweighted graph $G = (V, E)$ and set $S, T \subseteq V$ (select two subsets S, T randomly in the node set V), with one endpoint in the set S, the other in the set T. The cut distance of graph G_{old} and G_{attack} is defined as follow:

$$d_{cut}(G_{old}, G_{attack}) = \max_{S,T \subseteq V(G_{old})} \frac{|e_{G_{old}}(S,T) - e_{G_{attack}}(S,T)|}{n^2} \tag{11}$$

where $e_{G_{old}}(S,T)$ and $e_{G_{attack}}(S,T)$ represent the number of edges that meet the requirements of the above nodes in the original graph and the attack graph respectively. If the endpoint belongs to $S \cap T$, then $e_G(S,S) = 2e_G(S)$.

Then, based on the Weak Regularity Lemma in graph theory, the node set V in the original graph $G = (V, E)$ can be divided into a subset of w categories, i.e., $P = \{v_1, v_2, ..., v_w\}$, $(1 < w < n)$, then:

$$d_{cut}(G_{old}, G_P) \leqslant \frac{2}{\sqrt{\log w}} \tag{12}$$

where P is not required to be divided fairly. We only need to add the error boundary between graph G and the subgraph consisting of nodes of a certain class in P, that is $d_{cut}(G_{old}, G_P) \leqslant 4/\sqrt{\log w}$.

Inspired by the above idea, we introduce the Weak Regularity Lemma to the similarity measure between the original graph G_{old} and the attack graph G_{attack}. The node set V_{attack} in the attack graph is divided into w subsets of nodes, $P_{attack} = \{v_1, v_2, ..., v_w\}$, $(1 < w < n)$. To make the original graph and the attack graph as similar as possible, the unnoticeable perturbation conditions are set as follows:

$$d_{cut}(G_{old}, G_{attackP}) \leqslant 4/\sqrt{\log w} \tag{13}$$

Based on the above steps, we obtain the unnoticeable perturbation conditions that meet the similarity in graph embedding space and the similarity of graph structure at the same time.

2.3   Greedy-Based Black-Box Attack

In black-box untargeted attack on the target model, the goal is to increase the probability of target nodes being misclassified. Under the black-box setting, as the attackers do not have the parameters and gradient information of the target model, the optimal perturbations can only be found through continuous queries. To ensure the accuracy of attack and query efficiency, the greedy strategy is adopted to select the adversarial samples. The score function is set according to the unnoticeable perturbations, and the adversarial samples with larger score function value are selected by the greedy strategy and sent to the target model for black-box query, aiming to select the best set of adversarial samples to improve

---

Algorithm 1: The overall attack framework

Input: Graph $G_{old}^{(0)} = (A, X)$, target node v_i, modification
  budget Δ: the maximum number of perturbations
Output: Modified graph $G_{attack} = (A', X')$
01:**Procedure** Attack ()
02:    Select target attack nodes by betweenness centrality
03:    Select attackable edges $E = \{e_1, e_2, ..., e_m\}$
04:    A black box query on target classifier using the original
       graph to obtain the original label of target node v_i
05:    Time $t=1$
06:    **while** $d(G_{old}, G_{attack}) < 1 - \lambda$ **do**
07:        **if** $d_{cut}(G_{old}, G_{attackP}) \leqslant 4/\sqrt{\log k}$ **then**
08:            edges sort by score function
09:            select the maximal sore function value then
10:    $G^{(t+1)} = G^{(t)} \pm e^*$
11:    $t=t+1$
12: return $G(t)$

---

the success rate of attack on the target model. The definition of the score function is given as follows:

$$S_{greedy} = L_{embedding} + d_{cut}(G_{old}, G_{attackP})$$
$$= E_G[\max\{0, \lambda - r(1 - d(G_{old}, G_{attack}))\}] + d_{cut}(G_{old}, G_{attackP}) \quad (14)$$

With the above score function, we are able to select and delete the perturbable edges and obtain different attack graphs. Update the graph without exceeding the attack budget and query the predictive value of the target node classification until the iterative query stops after exceeding the budget Δ.

We use the original graph to perform black-box query on a trained target model, and obtain the label y of target node classification. Then, according to the principles in Sect. 2.1, we select target nodes and the perturbable edges, and remove edges that meets unnoticeable perturbation conditions based on Sect. 2.2, so as to get adversarial samples of graph after attack. Finally, the attacked sample input into target model for black-box query, and the overall framework of GB-attack is shown in Algorithm 1.

3   Experiment

3.1   Relevant Settings

We utilize three widely applied citation network datasets from the real world, i.e., Cora, Citeseer and Pubmed, each node in the citation network is a document with corresponding bag-of-word features, and the edges represent the relationship between documents. We apply GB-Attack to attack *GCN* [14] and *Deep Walk* [15] models which can be used for node classification tasks. In the experiment, we verify the attack performance of GB-Attack by comparing the other four benchmark schemes: Random Sampling [12], DICE [16], RL-S2V [12] and ReWatt [13]. In each attack scenario, we use the change in the accuracy of node classification to show the success rate of attack after fully querying the target model, and analyze the experimental results in detail.

3.2   Attack Assessment

Evaluation on Different Attack Schemes. We use transductive learning to perform black-box query on the trained *GCN* model. In the experiment, we randomly select 50 nodes in a given graph, and use the local betweenness centrality (setting the longest path distance constraint M as 5) to obtain the attackable target node set. As the adversarial examples are limited to the modification of the graph structure, we modify the single edge in the first-order neighborhood of the target node.

Under the condition when the unnoticeable perturbations and perturbation budget Δ are met, we set the maximum number of perturbable edges to no more than 5% of the total number of existing edges in the original graph. Based on the above settings, we select 10–15 nodes with high betweenness centrality under each category of each dataset as our target nodes for subsequent detection. To evaluate the attack performance of GB-Attack strategy, we compare our attack scheme with four benchmark schemes. Under the attack settings of each scheme, the classification accuracy of nodes is shown in Table 1.

Table 1. Accuracy comparison of node classification schemes.

Attack method	CORA		Citeseer		Pubmed	
	GCN	*DeepWalk*	*GCN*	*DeepWalk*	*GCN*	*DeepWalk*
Original graph	80.14%	77.23%	72.30%	69.68%	80.30%	78.02%
RandSampling	77.86%	75.37%	69.44%	63.06%	78.56%	77.10%
DICE	76.55%	73.93%	68.12%	60.05%	76.44%	76.24%
RL-S2V	72.03%	71.02%	63.18%	57.28%	73.71%	72.05%
ReWatt	72.45%	71.04%	62.64%	60.61%	72.90%	72.53%
GB-Attack	69.79%	68.64%	62.40%	57.04%	69.52%	70.28%

Table 1 summarizes the comparison of node classification accuracy of different attack schemes on well-trained *GCN* model and *Deepwalk* model. As expected, GB-Attack scheme shows the best attack performance in all benchmark schemes and proves to be effective. In the experiment, although deleting an edge is the minimum perturbation to the graph, the attack rate still reaches about 10%. As shown in the table, the attack rate of GB-Attack algorithm on *GCN* model under CORA dataset reaches 9.35%, 10.9% on Citeseer and 10.78% on Pubmed.

Next, we will explain why GB-Attack has a better attack success rate than the other four algorithms: 1) The target nodes with high importance are chosen through the betweenness centrality, and attacking these nodes will cause maximum damage to graph network. 2) The adversarial samples satisfying the unnoticeable perturbation conditions are searched by greedy strategy and put into the trained black-box classification model for iterative query, which ensures the accuracy and query efficiency of the attack to a certain degree.

Multilateral Perturbation Assessment. In this section, with CORA dataset, we focus on the node classification after deleting edges in the first-order neighbors of the target node in GB-Attack, with the number of deleted edges as one, two and three respectively. Other schemes delete the same number of edges according to their respective attack methods. The node misclassification rate of each attack scheme under the above attack settings is shown in Fig. 1.

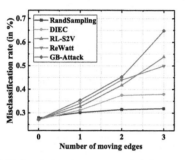 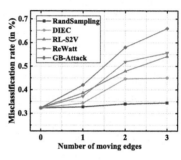

(a) Node misclassification rate of *GCN* model   (b) Node misclassification rate of *DeepWalk* model

Fig. 1. Node misclassification rate of attack methods under.

Figure 1 shows the misclassification rate of GB-Attack scheme compared with other four schemes under multilateral modification. We can infer that the misclassification rate of the target classifier increases greatly when two or more edges in the graph are allowed to be modified. This shows that under the slight perturbations, the more the number of edges in the graph are allowed to be modified, the higher the success rate of the attack algorithm on the model is. As shown in Fig. 1(a), deleting one and three edges in the first-order neighbors of the target node makes the misclassification rate of *GCN* model in the node classification task 35.4% and 64.8% respectively. In addition, we can see that the attack accuracy of GB-Attack algorithm has obvious advantages compared with other schemes. As shown in Fig. 1(b), when one, two and three target nodes are modified, the attack accuracy of GB-Attack on *DeepWalk* is 3.9%, 10.56% and 12.04% higher than that of RL-S2V, respectively. The above results verify the effectiveness of the GB-Attack proposed in this paper.

Evaluation on the Node Degree and *GCN* Layers. We use Citeseer dataset to study the attack accuracy of nodes with different degree ranges on the *GCN* model, and observe the classification accuracy of nodes with different degree ranges. The results are shown in Fig. 2. In addition, in order to test the migration ability of the attack, we select the same dataset to study the node classification ability of *GCN* model at different levels when facing adversarial samples. The detailed results are shown in Fig. 3.

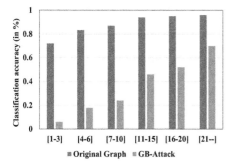

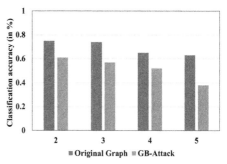

Fig. 2. Different degree ranges.   **Fig. 3.** Different *GCN* layers.

From Fig. 2, we can see that the classification accuracy of nodes increases with nodes degree, which indicates that attackers have higher attack success rate on nodes with lower degree. Figure 3 shows the node classification accuracy of *GCN* model under different layer structures of the original graph and the attack graph. We can see that *GCN* model in the two-tier structure has a higher node classification accuracy. In addition, we present the attack results of *GCN* in 2, 3, 4, 5 layers respectively, from which we see that the 5-layer *GCN* model has the lowest node classification accuracy when facing attack. This shows that high-order information has a positive impact on the attackers.

4   Conclusion

This paper proposes a greedy-based black-box adversarial attack scheme on graph structure. To improve the success rate of attack, betweenness centrality is applied to accurately locate the target nodes. To avoid the detection of target model, the scheme combines the similarity of graphs in the embedding space and the important properties of graph theory to construct adversarial samples with low perturbation. To ensure the accuracy of attack, greedy strategy is used to select adversarial samples to maximize the probability of the target node being misclassified. The experiment verifies that the scheme has high attack accuracy on graph data. For future studies, we will focus on dual perturbations of node features and graph structure in graph networks, and design effective attack algorithm which can be applied to more complex graph data.

References

1. Yao, L., Mao, C., Luo, Y.: Graph convolutional networks for text classification. In: 33rd AAAI Conference on Artificial Intelligence, Honolulu, pp. 7370–7377. AAAI (2019)
2. Li, J., Rong, Y., Cheng, H., Meng, H., Huang, W., Huang, J.: Semi-supervised graph classification: a hierarchical graph perspective. In: Proceedings of the World Wide Web, San Francisco, pp. 972–982. ACM (2019)
3. Cai, H., Zheng, V., Chang, K.: A comprehensive survey of graph embedding: problems, techniques, and applications. IEEE Trans. Knowl. Data Eng. **30**(9), 1616–1637 (2018)
4. Zügner, D., Akbarnejad, A., Günnemann, S.: Adversarial attacks on neural networks for graph data. In: 24th International Conference on Knowledge Discovery and Data Mining, London, pp. 2847–2856. ACM (2018)
5. Cai, Z., Xiong, Z., Xu, H., Wang, P., Li, W., Pan, Y.: Generative adversarial networks: a survey towards private and secure applications. ACM Comput. Surv. **37**(4), 1–37 (2020)
6. Cai, Z., He, Z., Guan, X., Li, Y.: Collective data-sanitization for preventing sensitive information inference attacks in social networks. IEEE Trans. Dependable Secure Comput. **15**(4), 577–590 (2018)
7. Zheng, X., Cai, Z.: Privacy-preserved data sharing towards multiple parties in industrial IoTs. IEEE J. Sel. Areas Commun. **38**(5), 968–979 (2020)
8. Cai, Z., He, Z.: Trading private range counting over big IoT data. In: 39th IEEE International Conference on Distributed Computing Systems, Dallas, pp. 144–153. IEEE (2019)
9. Cai, Z., Zheng, X.: A private and efficient mechanism for data uploading in smart cyber-physical systems. IEEE Trans. Netw. Sci. Eng. **7**(2), 766–775 (2020)
10. Wu, H., Wang, C., Tyshetskiy, Y., Docherty, A., Lu, K., Zhu, L.: Adversarial examples for graph data: deep insights into attack and defense. In: 28th International Joint Conference on Artificial Intelligence, Macao, pp. 4816–4823. IJCAI (2019)
11. Chang, H., et al.: A restricted black-box adversarial framework towards attacking graph embedding models. In: 34th AAAI Conference on Artificial Intelligence, New York, pp. 3389–3396. AAAI (2020)
12. Dai, H., et al.: Adversarial attack on graph structured data. In: 35th International Conference on Machine Learning, Stockholm, pp. 1115–1124. IMLS (2018)
13. Ma, Y., Wang, S., Wu, L., Tang, J.: Attacking graph convolutional networks via rewiring. arXiv preprint arXiv:1906.03750 (2019)
14. Kipf, T.N., Welling, M.: Semi-supervised classification with graph convolutional networks. In: 5th International Conference on Learning Representations, ICLR, Toulon (2017)
15. Perozzi, B., Al-Rfou, R., Skiena, S.: DeepWalk: online learning of social representations. In: 20th International Conference on Knowledge Discovery and Data Mining, New York, pp. 701–710. ACM (2014)
16. Waniek, M., Michalak, T., Wooldridge, M., Rahwan, T.: Hiding individuals and communities in a social network. Nat. Hum. Behav. **2**(2), 139–147 (2018)

SECCEG: A Secure and Efficient Cryptographic Co-processor Based on Embedded GPU System

Guang Fan[1,2,3], Fangyu Zheng[1,3](✉), Jiankuo Dong[4], Jingqiang Lin[5],
Lili Gao[1,2,3], Rong Wei[1,2,3], and Lipeng Wan[1,2,3]

[1] State Key Laboratory of Information Security, Institute of Information
Engineering, Chinese Academy of Sciences, Beijing, China
[2] School of Cyber Security, University of Chinese Academy of Sciences,
Beijing, China
[3] Data Assurance and Communication Security Research Center,
Chinese Academy of Sciences, Beijing, China
zhengfangyu@iie.ac.cn
[4] School of Computer Science, Nanjing University of Posts and Telecommunications,
Nanjing, China
[5] School of Cyber Security, University of Science and Technology of China,
Hefei, China

Abstract. With the rise of IoT, e-commerce, and 5G, the demands
of secure communications and identity authentications dramatically
increase, which largely rely on high-volume cryptographic computing.
Meanwhile, driven by deep learning, the embedded GPU system is rapidly
evolving. In this paper, we discuss the feasibility of turning the lightweight
and energy efficient system into a cryptographic co-processor, where security and performance are two daunting challenges. From the aspect of security, we leverage the available resources in the embedded GPU system to
achieve on-chip uninterrupted cryptographic computing, secure key storage, and trusted system bootstrapping. From the aspect of performance,
targeting the prevailing digital signature algorithm Ed25519, we develop
an entire framework to make full use of the system's cryptographic computing power, including the Ed25519 implementation with embedded GPU
acceleration and a high-performance network processing architecture. In
Jetson Xavier and Jetson Xavier NX, we implement a prototype called
SECCEG and conduct comprehensive experiments to evaluate its performance. SECCEG can serve as a network cryptographic accelerator via
TCP/IP stack with 3.6×10^6 ops signature generation and 1.0×10^6 ops for
signature verification. At the performance-power ratio, SECCEG achieves
122 kops/W and 35.6 kops/W for signature generation and verification,
respectively, which is 1 to 2 multitude higher than ARM CPU, FPGA and
discrete GPU implementations.

Keywords: Cryptographic co-processor · Embedded GPU system ·
Security · ECC · Energy-efficiency

This work was partially supported by National Key R&D Program of China under
Award 2018YFB0804401 and National Natural Science Foundation of China under
Award No. 61902392.

© Springer Nature Switzerland AG 2021
Z. Liu et al. (Eds.): WASA 2021, LNCS 12938, pp. 107–122, 2021.
https://doi.org/10.1007/978-3-030-86130-8_9

1   Introduction

In recent years, the demand for network communication rising rapidly. With the development of emerging technologies such as IoT, e-commerce, edge computing, and 5G, mobile devices have taken on more roles in our daily life [19,25]. Wearable devices, cars, and also mobile phones have become more intelligent with more and more functions. At the same time, in order to achieve high deployability and modifiability, cloud services are undergoing a transformation from monolithic applications to multiple loosely-coupled microservices, leading to an further increase in network communication demand [1,24]. All the above have led to a surge in the number of both device-to-device, device-to-server, and even server-to-server interactions, as well as an increasing proportion of large-size data such as high-definition pictures and videos.

For security and privacy considerations, the interchange of information through networks should be protected by means of encryption and authentication technologies based on cryptographic algorithms. Some of the algorithms involved have high computing requirements, especially those related to public-key cryptography. The increase in the number of network transactions also means an increase in the amount of processing overhead. The hardware co-processor is a general solution to offload CPU's expensive cryptographic computation and secure the cryptographic keys during their lifecycle. Hardware Security Modules (HSMs) [4,12,21] are widely used in industry. However, dedicated hardware always has a long development cycle , which make it difficult to keep up with the huge demand growth. There are recent studies that evaluate the cryptographic computing abilities of discrete GPUs (i.e., GPU cards) [2,7,17]. Those solutions can achieve even much higher throughput than general HSMs [4,12,21], yet those devices have to cooperate with CPU, motherboard and memory, resulting in greater power consumption and costs and lower flexibility. As a PCIE slave device, discrete GPUs are under full control of CPUs, and lack security mechanisms, which leads to some security vulnerabilities, e.g., the disclosure of confidential information [20,26]. The hardware cryptographic accelerator based on FPGAs were reported in numerous previous works [13,18,22]. Those devices have the advantage of being compact and low power-consumption, but their throughput is limited.

For cryptographic computing, the embedded GPU systems happen to have the advantages of discrete GPUs and FPGAs–sufficient performance, lightweight architecture and high energy efficiency. To accelerate compute-intensive workload in embedded projects, NVIDIA proposed a series of mobile processors named Tegra, which are equipped with embedded GPUs with their most advanced GPU architecture and have been widely used in the field of computer vision, deep neural networks, etc. Their flagship product, Jetson Xavier NX, takes 10 W to provide a throughput of 20 TOPS (10^{12} operations per second) for 8-bit integer arithmetic. Meanwhile, compared with discrete GPUs, embedded GPUs are integrated into the system on chip (SoC), along with CPU, northbridge, southbridge, and memory controller, which enables more security mechanism deployment to secure the GPU computing and decreases the risk of attacks [20,26] from operational environments.

Based on the above observations, we made an attempt to explore embedded GPUs as secure and efficient cryptographic accelerators. Nevertheless, few researches on cryptographic implementation contribute to mobile and embedded GPUs, which are faced with many technical challenges. Firstly, although embedded GPUs have security advantages over discrete GPUs, embedded GPU systems do not natively equip with hardware protections. For example, it is vulnerable to hardware-specific attacks like cold-boot attack and hard drive tampering. Secondly, as a parallel platform, an embedded GPU only runs at full utilization only when a large number of equally-shaped tasks are processed simultaneously regarding respective inputs, which implies that IO architecture in the embedded system has to support a large number of connections and "feed" enough workload to embedded GPUs.

Our Contributions. In this paper, we propose an overall architecture for a secure and efficient embedded-GPU-based cryptographic co-processor and implement a prototype called SECCEG based on NVIDIA Jetson embedded GPU systems. Our contributions are three-fold:

- Firstly, we discuss the feasibility and challenges of using embedded GPU systems as high-performance cryptographic co-processors, and propose an overall architecture to address the performance and security issues.
- Secondly, under the overall architecture, we modify and optimize an uninterrupted GPU execution model according to embedded GPU characteristics, for key protection. At the same time, we leverage the available resources on embedded GPU, including TrustZone and fuse devices, to build a complete security mechanism.
- Thirdly, we implement a prototype system that uses Jetson Xavier and Jetson Xavier NX as cryptographic co-processors, including high-throughput Ed25519 and network IO interfaces. Our experimental results show that our performance-power ratio sets a record in all devices. Our throughput also outperforms contemporaneous ARM CPU, FPGA and HSM, even comparable with discrete GPU.

2   Preliminaries

2.1   NVIDIA Jetson Systems

NVIDIA Jetson is a series of embedded computing systems from NVIDIA. Compared to other common embedded GPU products, Jetson systems are more friendly for general-purposed computing and also have a high computing power, so we mainly focus on the platform.

Our experiments are performed on 2 different kinds of NVIDIA Jetson systems, Jetson Xavier and Jetson Xavier NX. The former is most powerful in the

Jetson family, while the latter focuses more on compactness and low power consumption. They are both armed with a powerful Tegra SoC that integrates an embedded Volta GPU and an ARM CPU. Surrounding the SoC, there are also LPDDR4x memory, eMMC storage chip on the boards.

Besides, there are also various IO interfaces on embedded GPU systems, for example, PCIE interface and Ethernet port. They even have the ability to be a PCIE endpoint. With those characteristics, those devices are very flexible for use. They can be plugged directly into the main processor's motherboard of the to provide cyptographic service, like a cryptographic card, or serve through network for a large number of clients, like a cryptographic server.

2.2   ARM Security Extensions

Modern ARM processors support a security extension known as TrustZone, which can separate the system into two environments – Trusted Execution Environment (TEE) and Rich Execution Environment (REE). TEE is a secure area inside the CPU. It guarantees that the trusted applications (TAs) and data loaded in the TEE are protected concerning confidentiality and integrity. Some ARM manufacturers also provide write-once-read-multiple fuse devices for key storing. They are accessible in the TEE only.

Jetson Xavier and Jetson Xavier NX both have a full implementation of ARMv8.2 ISA compliant architecture, including TrustZone and Trusted memory. They also support fuse devices. Users can generate user-defined keys and flush them into the Jetson device's Encrypted Key Blob (EKB) partition. In EKB, the content is protected by the EKB Encryption Key (EKB_EK) derived from a fuse key and is only visible to the secure world.

Jetson systems also provide a Secureboot package based on TEE and Public Key Cryptography (PKC) keys in fuse device. It prevents Jetson systems from execution of unauthorized boot codes through chain of trust based on PKC keys.

3   Overall Design

3.1   Design Goals

A cryptographic processor is only available when it can store keys securely. The embedded systems do not provide hardware protections as HSMs. Thus, an adversary may temper the data on the hard drive or duplicate secrets on DRAM through the cold-boot attack. In this situation, a security mechanism is necessary to protect the integrity and confidentiality of the code and data on embedded GPU systems. For this goal, We assume that the adversary can not temper or snoop the on-chip area, including registers and fuse devices, and can not get the administrator privileges of the operating system.

Besides the goal in security consideration, the system should also easy-to-use. Therefore, SECCEG is also designed with the following goals:

- It should work on the off-the-shelf Jetson modules without hardware modifications.
- The common cryptographic algorithms can be easily ported to work under the SECCEG framework.
- It should be able to serve plenty of main processors simultaneously.
- Despite the overhead of security mechanisms and IO interface, SECCEG should still achieve high performance outclass CPU and FPGA implementations, even comparable with discrete GPU implementations.

3.2 Overall Architecture

The Overall Architecture of SECCEG is shown in Fig. 1. In SECCEG, GPU is in charge of cryptographic computing. We use a set of Key Management, including an uninterrupted GPU execution model to keep the secret only appear in on-chip area. We choose the network as the interface to provide cryptographic computing service. Through network, SECCEG can connect to any number of clients or tenants, namely heavily loaded application servers. In this way, it is easier for the embedded GPU to get more requests to make full use of its computing capability. A network handler is required for network packages processing, which should also cooperate with the GPU kernel. Besides, there is also a secure launch supported by the ARM TrustZone to ensure the system's integrity.

Next, we introduce the design of key management and secure launch. Other details are described in Sect. 4.

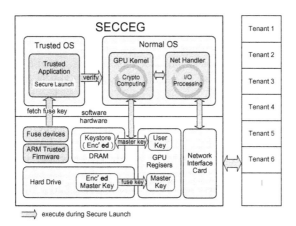

Fig. 1. The architecture of SECCEG

Key Management. In SECCEG, we deal with the key storage in an unusual way to avoid cold-boot attack. In the unified memory model of embedded GPU system, the GPU memory is no longer isolated from the CPU memory. Therefore, a better approach is to store the secret in on-chip storage, providing it with additional physical isolation to protect against attacks that break the operating system's memory isolation. For the non-addressable characteristic, we choose the GPU registers to store the master key.

In a typical execution model of CUDA program, the kernel can be invoked many times but only last shortly for each time. The registers will be cleared after the kernel ends, for the register storage is unsustainable. Consequently, the values are transferred to registers over and over through insecure channel.

To address the problem, Previous works [11,23] adopted an uninterrupted GPU execution model to store sensitive data in registers permanently. Instead of spawning a GPU kernel execution every time a new task needs to be performed, the system uses an autonomous GPU kernel that runs indefinitely. The GPU kernel continuously monitors predefined host memory regions (shared with the CPU) for new requests. After performing necessary computations, it informs the CPU thread within the shared memory too. The registers are available during the entire process.

Unfortunately, this approach can not perform on embedded GPUs directly. It encounters segment fault or severe delay on different unified memory type. As detailed in Sect. 4.2, we modify and optimize the approach. The modified model can execute even faster than the traditional execution model because it save the time of kernel launch and only have low synchronization overhead.

SECCEG also manages users' keys which will not appear in memory as plain text too. We generate those keys in the GPU kernel within registers. After generation, we use the master key to encrypt users' keys with symmetrical cryptography and store the encrypted keys in a DRAM buffer called Keystore. When we need a user key, we decrypted it into GPU registers and do calculations within the GPU kernel.

Secure Launch. Before the service of SECCEG starts, a secure launch is needed to ensure the system's integrity. An extra symmetric key is introduced in this part. It should be burned into fuse devices. We use the key to encapsulate the master key and make an HMAC of the critical data on hard drive, including the execution files of SECCEG and the vital part of the operating system. The result is still stored on it. During the device boot, the TA fetches the key in fuse devices and use it to do the HMAC again to verify the data has not been tampered with.

Then, the TA decrypt and verify the encrypted master key and transfer it to GPU registers. Since there is not GPU driver in the trusted OS, TA can not invoke GPU kernel. Therefore, it can not copy the key to GPU registers from the trusted memory directly. We need to store the key in DRAM briefly. The operation should be performed before launching any user process or connecting to the Internet. During this process, the GPU kernel is launched, and the key is transferred to GPU registers by the client application corresponding to the TA.

To avoid sensitive data disclosure, the intermediate data that appears in memory should be cleared immediately. Thanks to the uninterrupted execution model, the key is transferred to on-chip registers only once, then permanently loaded in there. This approach exposes any sensitive information on the DRAM only for a minimal amount of time.

4   Implementation

Based on the architecture, we implemented a key-secure cryptographic co-processor on NVIDIA Jetson Xavier and Jetson Xavier NX to provide high-performance Ed25519 signature generation and verification service through a network interface. This section details the implementations of Ed25519, uninterrupted GPU execution model, Keystore, secure launch, and network processing.

4.1   Ed25519

Ed25519 [9] is an EdDSA signature scheme using SHA-512 and Edwards25519, deployed in many prevailing cryptographic applications and network protocols, such as TLS 1.3 and SSH, deployed Ed25519. Our Ed25519 implementation can be generally decomposed into three levels: finite field arithmetic, point arithmetic, and signature implementation.

Finite Field Arithmetic. Overall, the finite arithmetic is implemented with 32-bit integers (radix 2^{32}) based on CUDA assembly. The large integer addition/subtraction of p_{25519} are operated with only 8 $addc/subc$ instructions. For multiplication(-add) and square, these algorithms are all accomplished with fused multiply-add instructions $mad.low/hi$. We carefully design the well-structured reduction method, which is accomplished with only one round addition for p_{25519} as the method in [2].

Point Arithmetic. The point arithmetic consists of two layers. The upper layer includes fixed-point and unknown-point scalar multiplication. Fixed-point Scalar Multiplication is implemented with the offline pre-computing technique described in [17]. With the method, the pre-table is loaded into GPU global memory from file system. The size of pre-table is 160 MB.

Unknown-point Scalar Multiplication is implemented with the traditional fixed-windows technique [10]. The table for each thread has 2^w points. To avoid the expensive inverse operations, the online generating and storage of table employ the *extended twisted Edwards* coordinates (X, Y, Z, T). The table size is 768 MB, which could fit in the Jetson devices' global memory.

The lower layer serves the upper layer, including point addition, point doubling, and mixed point addition. We implement the lower layer in the same way as previous work [7] did with the efficient method proposed by Hisil et al., the *extended twisted Edwards* coordinates (X, Y, Z, T), with $x = \frac{X}{Z}$, $y = \frac{Y}{Z}$ and $xy = \frac{T}{Z}$ [8, §3.1], to remove the expensive modular inversion.

Ed25519. The scalar multiplication over the Edwards25519 is the most time-consuming workload of Ed25519. The signature generation requires one fixed-point scalar multiplication, while the signature verification requires one fixed-point and one unknown-point scalar multiplication.

Besides the scalar multiplications, point decoding and SHA-512 were also implemented. We implement the most costly workload of the decoding function, i.e., modular exponentiation, using Fermat's little theorem [9]. For SHA-512, we implement a 64-bit right rotate operation with logic and shift instructions in CUDA assembly. In order to improve the efficiency of operation, we initialize the array of SHA-512 round constants in constant memory.

4.2   Uninterrupted GPU Execution Model

For a unified memory architecture, which most embedded GPU systems use, off-chip memory is shared between the CPU and the GPU. In this way, we can allocate unified memory as a high bandwidth communication channel, which is faster than transferring information with PCIE interface as traditional discrete GPU does. In theory, the uninterrupted GPU execution model can achieve better results than it on discrete GPUs. However, in reality the naive model does not work on Jetson modules. Cache consistency issue is the main problem. On Jetson modules, the GPU is allowed to snoop CPU cache but not vice versa.

The CUDA toolkit provides two sets of APIs for memory sharing between the CPU and the GPU, *unified memory* and *pinned memory* [14]. The caching behavior of the two types of memory is different. On the Jetson Xavier and Xavier NX, the *Unified memory* is cached on both CPU and GPU, while the *Pinned memory* is cached only on CPU.

In our execution mode, *unified memory* could lead to segment fault for cache consistency issues. So we must use *pinned memory* for real-time communication between CPU and GPU. Nevertheless, the synchronization still encounter delays and even deadlocks. We try to use memory barriers at both ends. It turns out that the *__threadfence()* function of cuda API can solve the problem. The function can prevent the reordering of the nvcc compiler from interfering with the GPU kernel to get the updated value. In this way, the synchronization between the CPU and the GPU can proceed smoothly.

Also, we optimize the communication between CPU and GPU in this execution model. In the embedded GPU system, the GPU can access DRAM directly to communicate with CPU threads using worker threads for faster communication and a greater parallelism degree. So each GPU thread communicate with CPU thread themselves without relying on a dedicated communication thread.

4.3   Keystore

In order to protect users' keys, we encrypt and store them in Keystore, a buffer in DRAM, and use AES-KW (AES Key Wrap) algorithm [3] to provide both privacy and integrity protection. Those keys are generated and encrypted by the embedded GPU within registers. During the Ed25519 calculating, AES-KW decryption is involved in signature generation. To accelerate the algorithm, four T-lookup tables, containing 256 entries of 32 bits each, are introduced. Those tables occupy 4 KB of storage space and are copied into shared memory before the service start for faster accessing speed.

We derive the round key of AES at each round to reduce register consumption. So, we need 128 bits for the key and 128 bits for the round key. The decryption result, that is the 256-bit Ed25519 private key also needs to be stored in registers. Totally, we need 20 32-bit registers for AES-KW decryption.

To avoid secret disclosure, we must ensure that the data stored in registers will not appear in DRAM during the computing. In a CUDA program, arrays of small and determined size and local variables are assigned to registers [15]. Nevertheless, when the number of registers required in a kernel exceeds the maximum number of registers that each thread can use, the extra variables will be spilled into the local memory, which actually is DRAM. By supplying the --ptxas-options=-v flag to the nvcc compiler, we are explicitly notified of how many registers were used in the kernel. To ensure that secret variables are all stored in registers, we should make the number of registers used less than the maximum number of registers available for each thread.

In GPUs of Volta architecture, the number of registers available for each block is 65536, while the maximum number of registers available for each thread is 255. When the threads number of each block is greater than 256, the more threads in the block, the fewer registers each thread can use. Therefore, we need to strictly control the number of local variables and small arrays, especially when the number of Threads/Block is relatively large. Under such circumstances, we allocate many of such variables in global memory or shared memory with the keyword __device__ or __shared__, so that the number of registers used in the kernel is less than the upper limit.

We also retrieve the physical memory (address 0x0080000000-0x0400000000 [16]) with the Linux device file /dev/mem while the GPU kernel is running to verify the value in registers are not spilled into DRAM.

4.4 Network Handler

One of the great challenges for SECCEG is to reduce the performance loss caused by network transmission. Different from regular network service programs, in SECCEG, requests are handled by the embedded GPU ultimately. Therefore, the data to be processed in network packages needs to be collected together for GPU threads' accessing. In order to make full use of the embedded GPU, we need to use a large batch size in each round of cryptographic calculation and minimize the wait time of GPU.

The architecture of the network handler is shown in Fig. 2. We use two types of threads to implement the network handler. Network requests processing can be multi-threaded to increase throughput, while the tasks related to GPU kernel dispatching requires a dedicated thread to handle. Optimizing the collaboration between two kinds of threads and GPU kernel is the key to reducing performance loss. Next, we describe the above two types of threads as well as the synchronization between them.

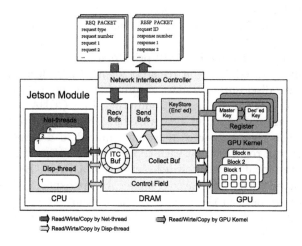

Fig. 2. The architecture of the network handler

Network-Threads (Net-Threads). Net-threads are responsible for handling network transactions, including requests receiving, requests classifying, responses building and sending. We introduce several network server techniques, such as Linux epoll API and socket option–SO_REUSEPORT to monitor thousands of connections simultaneously.

A communication protocol between the SECCEG and tenants is also proposed. As for embedded GPU systems, the computing power of GPU outshines the network handling ability. The maximum speed of packets processing is limited. Therefore, we use a single-packet-multiple-requests (SPMR) model, in which each packet contains tens of requests to reduce the network overhead. The amount is flexible but less than the number of CUDA threads in a block, otherwise, it is difficult to dispatch effectively. Actually, it is easy for tenants (heavily loaded servers) to generate tens of requests at one time.

For our implementation with epoll API and SPMR communication protocol, two or three net-threads are enough to deliver the full workload to the embedded GPU. With an additional disp-thread, there are only three or four active threads, ensuring that, with hyper-threading, the system could function well even when the energy-saving mode is set, at which there are only two or four CPU cores online.

Dispatch-Thread (Disp-Thread). In our implementation, the disp-thread serves as a bridge between the net-threads and the GPU kernel. It collects the data of the same request type together, namely, duplicate it from the receive buffers into the collect buffer, and dispatch the GPU kernel to do the calculation.

The disp-thread communicates with the uninterrupted kernel using the control field, a block of *unified memory*, similar to the way we describe in Sect. 4.2.

The uninterrupted GPU kernel can handle different types of requests. For one round of GPU calculation, the data corresponding requests are all the same type. The default policy is to take turns processing different types of requests, so that different kinds of requests can be processed in time.

On Jetson systems, the GPU kernel can not communicate with multiple CPU threads simultaneously and correctly. So we can not use multiple threads to cover the delay of data transfer, but, thanks to unified memory, the overhead is actually insignificant. A single disp-thread can make good use of the GPU kernel.

Inter-threads Synchronization. While the SECCEG is running, net-threads store the requests to receive buffers. They notify the disp-thread through the inter-threads communication buffer (ITC buffer) which receive buffers are filled with data and what request type they are. Once the GPU kernel calculation is completed, the disp-thread copies the result from the collect buffer to receive buffers and notifies the network-threads through the ITC buffer.

In such a communication model, multiple threads read and write a shared data structure, leading to a severe penalty for performance. To lower the synchronization overhead, we build several ring buffers as the ITC buffer.

The ring buffer is actually an integer array storing the ID of receiving and sending buffer pairs, with three integer values as pointers to indicate the state of the buffers' data, including received, processed, and sent. The array can be recycled after it is filled, and the three integer pointers point back to the beginning after it is beyond the array's size. So there is no need to allocate memory dynamically, which could lead to extra time consuming and err handling.

Lock-free is the most amazing feature of our ITC mechanism. We use multiple ring buffers to build single-producer and single-consumer scenarios. Each net-thread has two such data structures for signature generation requests and verification requests. All data is updated and read by only one thread, respectively. On the one hand, the array, the sent pointer, and the received pointer are updated by a net-thread and read by the disp-thread. On the other hand, the processed pointer is updated by the disp-thread and read by a net-thread. It will not cause data missing or reprocessing even without a lock.

5   Performance Evaluation

We now evaluate the performance of our implementation of SECCEG. In this section, we give the setup of our experiments, discuss the implementation performance and compare the results with related works.

5.1   Experiment Settings and Results

We use off-the-shelf Jetson Xavier and Jetson Xavier NX boards with NVIDIA L4T as the operating system. Different power modes are used on two Jetson boards. We set the Jetson Xavier board to MAXN_MODE, the maximum power mode, to unlock it's maximum performance and set the Jetson Xavier NX board to 10W_2CORE_MODE, the energy-saving mode with 2 CPU cores online, to inspect it's best energy efficiency. Random keys and messages are generated as the test vectors for the Ed25519 signature generation and verification. We also generate a random AES-KW key for the Keystore implementation. The results are verified against OpenSSL version 1.1.0.

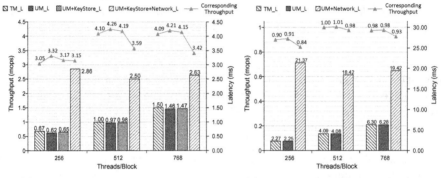

(a) Signature Generation of Ed25519   (b) Signature Verification of Ed25519

Fig. 3. Throughput and Latency of Experiments on Jetson Xavier (The Number of Blocks is 8.)

Figure 3 shows the throughput and latency of SECCEG tested on the Jetson Xavier board. In the figure, "L" denotes Latency. "TM" means the traditional execution model. "UM" means the uninterrupted execution model. First, we test the performance of our Ed25519 implementation with the traditional execution model. The throughputs of Ed25519 signature generation and verification peak high points at 4.10M ops and 1.00M ops when the batch size is 8 × 512. The corresponding latencies are 1.00 ms and 4.09 ms. We also counted the time spent on data transmission. For signature generation and verification, the values are both about 0.03 ms. Thanks to the unified memory architecture, the time accounts for a very low proportion of the total.

Then we test the performance of Ed25519 with the uninterrupted execution module. For saving the overhead of the launch and synchronize functions, it can reach an even higher peak performance than the traditional execution module, which is 4.26M ops for signature generation and 1.01M ops for signature verification on Jetson Xavier boards. Enabling the Keystore on the basis of the uninterrupted execution model adds a small overhead, less than 3%.

To test the output performance of SECCEG, we also write a client program running on an Intel i7-8700 CPU, which use hundreds of thread to simulate the same amount of tenants. Each thread generates 80–100 sets of data as the test vector randomly for a single request. It sends the requests to SECCEG and waits for the reply, which is repeated 200 times. When taking network handler into account, the network bandwidth will be the main limitation of performance, so we use an Intel Ethernet server adapter X520-SR2 to enhance the network process capability for Jetson Xavier.

In this case, serving 100 tenants, the throughput can reach 3.59M ops for signature generation and 0.98M ops for signature verification. The corresponding latencies are 2.50 ms and 18.42 ms. To get the best throughput of SECCEG, we provide it with a large computational load, so the network testing latency is relatively high to local tests, but still acceptable.

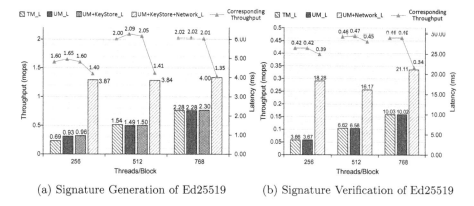

(a) Signature Generation of Ed25519   (b) Signature Verification of Ed25519

Fig. 4. Throughput and Latency of Experiments on Jetson Xavier NX (The Number of Blocks is 6.)

Figure 4 presents the result tested on the Jetson Xavier NX board. The peak performances of Ed25519 with the traditional execution model are 2.02M ops for signature generation and 0.46M ops for signature verification. The measured latencies are 1.54 ms and 6.62 ms. In comparison, the throughput results of the uninterrupted execution model are 2.09M ops and 0.47M ops with latencies of 1.49 ms and 6.58 ms. We use the built-in Ethernet port to transfer network data. The highest network output throughputs of signature generation and verification are 1.41M ops and 0.45M ops. Though Jetson Xavier NX's performance is not as powerful as Jetson Xavier, it is more energy efficient with the running power of 11.52 W. Compared with the test result of Jetson Xavier, the Jetson Xavier NX achieve nearly half the performance with just 29% power consumption.

5.2   Related Work Comparison

In Table 1, we list implementation results for the various platforms, including ARM CPU, discrete GPU and FPGA.

- **_vs. CPU:_** Our performance and power consumption are both much better than the AVX2-based work [5], even running with 8 cores. We also evaluate the ARM v8.2 CPU's performance on Jetson Xavier by OpenSSL console command `openssl speed`. It can be found that compared with the ARM CPU in the same platform, we achieve 18 to 29 times speedup.

- **vs. FPGA:** The advantage of FPGA is energy-saving, yet as for power efficiency, our implementation has an order of magnitude advantage over FPGA implementations.
- **vs. HSM:** To the best of our knowledge, the fastest Hardware security module specifically optimized for ECC available on the market as of January 2020 is the Nitrox V XL NHB Adapter. It achieves 300K ops for ECC-256, which is with similar numbers of security bits as Ed25519. The average power of HSMs is in the tens to hundreds of watts. So, obviously, our implementation have much better performance and and power efficiency to the off-the-shelf HSMs that we know.
- **vs. discrete GPU:** Pan's work is one of the few that implemented complete Ed25519 signature generation and verification on discrete GPU. The system-wise power consumption of the Server reached approximately 400 W (the thermal design power of E5-2697 v2 and GTX 780Ti respectively reach 130 and 250 W), which is an order of magnitude higher than our implementation. However, the network output throughput of our Ed25519 signature verification implementation on Jetson Xavier is higher than their implementation. The throughput of our Ed25519 signature generation is also comparable with Pan's. Moreover, the energy efficiency of our implementation on Xavier is about 416% and 1063% compared to [17], for signature generation and verification, respectively. Moreover, the ratio rises to 561% and 1534% for our implementation on Jetson Xavier NX.

Table 1. Comparison with related works

	Platform	Ed25519 SigGen. (kops)	Ed25519 SigVer. (kops)	Power (w)	Energy Effic. of SigGen.(kops/w)	Energy Effic. of SigVer.(kops/w)
Faz-Hernández et al. [5]	i7-7820X@3.6 GHz (Single-core)	91.14	29.20	140[1]	0.65	0.21
OpenSSL [6]	ARM v8.2 CPU in Xavier (8-core)	126.23	53.42	35.7	3.53	1.50
Turan et al. [22]	Zynq-7020	0.62	0.27	0.41[2]	1.51	0.66
Pan et al. [17]	E5-2697 v2 + GTX 780Ti	8,710	929	400[3]	21.78	2.32
SECCEG Network Output	Embedded GPU in Xavier	3,593	977	39.6	90.73	24.67
SECCEG Network Output	Embedded GPU in Xavier NX	1,407	410	11.52	122.14	35.59

[1] TDP; [2] Estimation using Xilinx Power Estimator tool [13]; [3] Our estimation.

To sum up, the energy efficiency of SECCEG has significant advantages over the Ed25519 implementation above any other platform. The throughput of our implementation is comparable to the server based on discrete GPU GTX 780Ti. Our computation latency on Jetson boards is weaker than CPU and FPGA implementations, but SECCEG can achieve a much better throughput than them.

6   Conclusion

In this contribution, making full use of the embedded GPU system's resources, we propose an efficient cryptographic co-processor with security mechanisms to provide secure key storage. Our results demonstrate that the embedded GPU system is a more competitive candidate for implementing hardware cryptographic co-processor. In Jetson Xavier and Jetson Xavier NX boards, our performance-power ratio sets a record in all devices on performance-power ratio. Our throughput also outperforms contemporaneous ARM CPU, FPGA, and HSM, even comparable with discrete GPUs.

Our future work will focus on more cryptographic algorithm implementations on embedded GPU systems, including high quantum-safe cryptographic algorithms.

References

1. Chen, L.: Microservices: architecting for continuous delivery and devOps. In: 2018 IEEE International Conference on Software Architecture (ICSA), pp. 39–397. IEEE (2018)
2. Dong, J., Zheng, F., Cheng, J., Lin, J., Pan, W., Wang, Z.: Towards high-performance X25519/448 key agreement in general purpose GPUs. In: IEEE Conference on Communications and Network Security (2018)
3. Dworkin, M.: Recommendation for block cipher modes of operation: methods for key wrapping. NIST Spec. Publ. **800**, 38F (2012)
4. ENTRUST: nShield connect HSMs. https://www.entrust.com/digital-security/hsm/products/nshield-hsms/nshield-connect. Accessed 1 Apr 2021
5. Faz-Hernández, A., López, J., Dahab, R.: High-performance implementation of elliptic curve cryptography using vector instructions. ACM Trans. Math. Softw. (TOMS) **45**(3), 1–35 (2019)
6. Foundation, O.S.: OpenSSL cryptography and SSL/TLS toolkit (2016). http://www.openssl.org/
7. Gao, L., Zheng, F., Emmart, N., Dong, J., Lin, J., Weems, C.: DPF-ECC: accelerating elliptic curve cryptography with floating-point computing power of GPUs. In: 2020 IEEE International Parallel and Distributed Processing Symposium (IPDPS), pp. 494–504. IEEE (2020)
8. Hisil, H., Wong, K.K.-H., Carter, G., Dawson, E.: Twisted Edwards curves revisited. In: Pieprzyk, J. (ed.) ASIACRYPT 2008. LNCS, vol. 5350, pp. 326–343. Springer, Heidelberg (2008). https://doi.org/10.1007/978-3-540-89255-7_20
9. Josefsson, S., Liusvaara, I.: Edwards-curve digital signature algorithm (EdDSA). In: Internet Research Task Force, Crypto Forum Research Group, RFC, vol. 8032 (2017)
10. Koç, C.K.: Analysis of sliding window techniques for exponentiation. Comput. Math. Appl. **30**(10), 17–24 (1995)
11. Kwon, O., Kim, Y., Huh, J., Yoon, H.: ZeroKernel: secure context-isolated execution on commodity GPUs. IEEE Trans. Dependable Secure Comput. (2019)
12. Marvell: Nitrox security processors - nitrox v. https://www.marvell.com/products/security-solutions/nitrox-v.html. Accessed 30 Dec 2020

13. Mehrabi, M.A., Doche, C.: Low-cost, low-power FPGA implementation of ed25519 and curve25519 point multiplication. Information **10**(9), 285 (2019)
14. NVIDIA: CUDA for Tegra: CUDA toolkit documentation (2020). https://docs. nvidia.com/cuda/cuda-for-tegra-appnote/index.html. Accessed 1 July 2021
15. NVIDIA: Programming guide: CUDA toolkit documentation (2020). https://docs. nvidia.com/cuda/cuda-c-programming-guide/index.html. Accessed 31 Dec 2020
16. NVIDIA: Xavier series SoC technical reference manual (2020). https://developer. nvidia.com/embedded/dlc/xavier-series-soc-technical-reference-manual. Accessed 1 Jan 2021
17. Pan, W., Zheng, F., Zhu, W., Jing, J.: An efficient elliptic curve cryptography signature server with GPU acceleration. IEEE Trans. Inf. Forensics Secur. **12**(1), 111–22 (2017)
18. Parrilla, L., Álvarez-Bermejo, J.A., Castillo, E., López-Ramos, J.A., Morales-Santos, D.P., García, A.: Elliptic curve cryptography hardware accelerator for high-performance secure servers. J. Supercomput. **75**(3), 1107–1122 (2019)
19. Pham, Q.V., et al.: A survey of multi-access edge computing in 5G and beyond: fundamentals, technology integration, and state-of-the-art. IEEE Access **8**, 116974–117017 (2020)
20. Pietro, R.D., Lombardi, F., Villani, A.: CUDA leaks: a detailed hack for CUDA and a (partial) fix. ACM Trans. Embed. Comput. Syst. (TECS) **15**(1), 1–25 (2016)
21. Thales: Luna network hardware security modules (HSMs). https://cpl.thalesgroup. com/encryption/hardware-security-modules/network-hsms. Accessed 14 Jan 2021
22. Turan, F., Verbauwhede, I.: Compact and flexible FPGA implementation of Ed25519 and X25519. ACM Trans. Embed. Comput. Syst. (TECS) **18**(3), 1–21 (2019)
23. Vasiliadis, G., Athanasopoulos, E., Polychronakis, M., Ioannidis, S.: PixelVault: using GPUs for securing cryptographic operations. In: Proceedings of the 2014 ACM SIGSAC Conference on Computer and Communications Security, pp. 1131–1142 (2014)
24. Yu, D., Jin, Y., Zhang, Y., Zheng, X.: A survey on security issues in services communication of microservices-enabled fog applications. Concurr. Comput. Pract. Exp. **31**(22), e4436 (2019)
25. Zhou, Z., Chen, X., Li, E., Zeng, L., Luo, K., Zhang, J.: Edge intelligence: paving the last mile of artificial intelligence with edge computing. Proc. IEEE **107**(8), 1738–1762 (2019)
26. Zhu, Z., Kim, S., Rozhanski, Y., Hu, Y., Witchel, E., Silberstein, M.: Understanding the security of discrete GPUs. In: Proceedings of the General Purpose GPUs, pp. 1–11, February 2017

Understanding and Mitigating Security Risks of Network on Medical Cyber Physical System

Zhangtan Li[1,2]([✉]), Liang Cheng[2], Yang Zhang[2], and Dengguo Feng[2]

[1] University of Chinese Academy of Sciences, Beijing, China
[2] TCA Lab, Institute of Software, Chinese Academy of Sciences, Beijing, China
{zhangtan2015,chengliang,zhangyang}@iscas.ac.cn, fengdg@263.net

Abstract. The Medical Cyber-Physical System (MCPS) holds the promise of reducing human errors and optimizing healthcare by integrating medical devices, applications and network. MCPS utilizes high-level supervisory and low-level communication middleware to enable medical devices to interoperate efficiently. Despite the benefits provided by MCPS, the integration of clinical information also brings new threats for the clinical data. In this paper, we performed a study on security and safety risks in MCPS's networks. We systematically analyzed different attack surfaces on MCPS's networks based on misuse and abuse of clinical data. We successfully performed end-to-end attacks based on OpenICE, a popular MCPS prototype, and demonstrated the clinical risks of these attacks and the design flaws in OpenICE. We further proposed a Topic-based access control model with Break-The-Glass feature to provide fine-grained access control for clinical data. We implemented the model in two MCPS prototypes, and evaluated its effectiveness and efficiency.

Keywords: Medical Cyber Physical System · Publish-subscribe · Network security · Access control

1 Introduction

A cyber physical system (CPS) is an integration of physical processes, communication and computation. Embedded computers and networks are involved to monitor and control physical processes, which interact with the human through various modalities. The applications of these modalities vary from power grid, smart home, and intelligent transportation to smart health care and many more. Among these CPS infrastructures, the Medical Cyber-Physical System (MCPS) indicates a promising future for healthcare domain. Compared to the traditional medical practices that rely upon disconnected, standalone devices, the interoperability of MCPS can reduce medical errors and improve the productivity of medical care. Meanwhile, the MCPS design faces numerous challenges, including interoperability, security/privacy, and high assurance in the system software [8]. One noticeable effort for the design of MCPS is the ASTM F2761 standard [2],

Z. Liu et al. (Eds.): WASA 2021, LNCS 12938, pp. 123–134, 2021.
https://doi.org/10.1007/978-3-030-86130-8_10

which defines a standardized framework for MCPS, called Integrated Clinical Environment (ICE). The ICE framework integrates medical devices, applications and clinicians into an interoperable system for monitoring and treating patients with embedded computers and networking capabilities. Since ICE standard was published, many stakeholders, such as Massachusetts General Hospital and Kansas State University, developed MCPS prototypes (e.g., OpenICE [10] and MDCF [7]).

In the meantime, various threats and attacks could be newly introduced by MCPS [6]. Actually, due to the popular publish-subscribe mechanism used by MCPS, medical devices and applications are exposed to a myriad of sensitive data and control commands. Adversary could utilize compromised device to intercept or tamper medical data and control command, which would induce security or even safety risks. As a recent example, in September 2020, a ransomware attack affecting a German hospital caused the death of a patient who had to be moved to another hospital 20 miles away [15].

Since ICE standard was proposed, many research approaches focused on high-level security threats and requirements for MCPS [8,11,16]. These works only theoretically analyzed the attack patterns and risks in MCPS, and could not give practical attacks and corresponding consequences in the clinical scenarios.

The integration of clinical information in MCPS enables the interoperability of medical devices and apps, and also brings new threats for the clinical data. The malicious excessive access to sensitive data and misuse or abuse of them will be highly damaging to security and safety in MCPS. Generally, the key to protect sensitive data is a fine-grained access control. As for the access control in MCPS, previous works mainly focused on the protection of electronic health record [17] and medical device [13]. Few works established fine-grained access control for different kinds of clinical data in MCPS's networks. Although the network middleware utilized by MCPS prototypes may provide basic access control mechanism, it could not provide out-of-the-box access control for satisfying abundant clinical tasks due to the lack of knowledge about clinical scenarios.

Based on the aforementioned motivations, in this paper, we perform a systematic study on misuse and abuse of sensitive data in MCPS's networks. We propose practical attacks and analyzed corresponding clinical consequences based on OpenICE, a popular open-source instantiation of MCPS. To mitigate the unauthorized access to clinical data, we propose a Topic-based access control model to provide fine-grained authorization polices, and evaluate the efficacy of our model. The contributions of our research are summarized as follows:

- We systematically analyze different attack surfaces on MCPS's networks based on misuse and abuse of clinical data. We find design flaws and propose various kinds of practical attacks on a prototype of MCPS (i.e., OpenICE), and show the detailed attack results in the clinical scenarios.
- We propose a Topic-based access control model, which provides fine-grained and context-sensitive access control for clinical data. It also supports Break-The-Glass feature for the emergency situation.
- We implement the model on OpenICE and MDCF, and the evaluation demonstrates the efficacy and applicability of this model.

2 Background

2.1 ICE and OpenICE

The ICE framework defines a set of elements that compose the clinical environment. 1) Equipment Interfaces, which interact with medical devices to enable their hardware and software capabilities (e.g., network connection); 2) Medical Devices, which are connected to the system dynamically in a plug and play manner; 3) Medical Apps, which are software applications installed in Supervisor to support the completion of clinical procedures; 4) Supervisor, which orchestrates medical devices and apps, and provides the portal of interaction for clinicians to monitor and control patients' vital signs; 5) Network Controller (i.e., network middleware), which is in charge of managing the communication between devices, apps and Supervisor.

Several instantiations of ICE framework have been proposed by the academia and industry, e.g., OpenICE and MDCF. Among these instantiations, the most prominent example is the open-source OpenICE system developed by the MD PnP group. OpenICE provides abundant simulated devices and applications for simulating clinical tasks. Meanwhile, it has detailed documentations and is always up-to-date. Therefore we choose OpenICE as the experiment environment.

2.2 Publish-Subscribe Communication in MCPS

OpenICE adopts Data Distribution Service (DDS) [4] as its network controller. This section introduces DDS as a typical interoperable communication mechanism in MCPS.

DDS is an Object Management Group (OMG) middleware standard that aims to enable scalable, real-time and interoperable data exchanges. DDS utilizes a data-centric publish-subscribe model to handle the data distribution. This model builds on a "global data space" concept, which is accessible to all interested participants. Participants that want to publish or subscribe data declare their intent to become "Publishers" or "Subscribers". Everytime a publisher posts new data into "global data space", DDS propagates the data to all interested subscribers. DDS mainly involves the following concepts:

– Global Data Space: the abstraction of DDS storing all the data of domains.
– Domain: a data space that links all entities to communicate with each other. Only publishers and subscribers attached to the same domain could interact.
– Domain Participant: a fundamental entity that represents the local membership of the application in a domain.
– Publisher: sends data into topic through DataWriter.
– DataWriter: writes data into the topic sent by Publisher.
– Subscriber: receives data from topic through DataReader.
– DataReader: declares the data it wishes to receive and accesses the data received by Subscriber.
– Topic: a single data type, and the distribution and availability of sample. Topic is the most basic description of the data to be published/subscribed and is identified by its unique name.

3 Related Work

3.1 Security Threats in MCPS

MCPS indicates a promising future of healthcare, and establishing security challenges and threats for MCPS attracted much attentions. Insup et al. [8] discussed the challenges and open research issues in developing MCPS. Hatcliff et al. [5] proposed reasonable high-level security requirements for MCPS. Vasserman et al. [16] enumerated five typical categories of attacks for MCPS including destroy, reprogram, disturb, denial of service and eavesdrop. Raju et al. [11] presented a security analysis of MCPS based on the perception layer, network layer and application layer, and proposed attack patterns on different layers. These works only theoretically discussed attack patterns and threats in MCPS. In contrast to these works, we analyzed the misuse and abuse of sensitive clinical data, and proposed realistic attacks in the clinical scenarios.

3.2 Access Control in MCPS

Recently, establishing access control for integrated clinician environment attracted more attentions. Salazar [12] implemented a role-based access control model in MDCF. Tasali et al. [13] introduced attribute inheritance for a flexible authorization in interoperable medical systems. They also talked about a controlled emergency access model for access control overriding during Break The Glass state [14]. None of these models provides fine-grained access control for real-time data generated by medical devices/apps within an interoperable environment. In contrast to these works, we proposed an enhanced access control model for sensitive data within an ICE standard-compliant middleware. Our model provided fine-grained authorization for real-time data generated by interoperable devices/apps and also supported Break-The-Glass feature.

4 Security Analysis of MCPS's Networks

4.1 Threat Model

In this paper, we consider malicious insiders or attackers who are capable of exploiting the vulnerabilities of medical devices or the design flaws in MCPS prototypes to perform misuse and abuse attacks on sensitive data. OpenICE provides abundant topics for clinical data. We classified all topics into four groups based on their types: 1) Medication Data, which includes the name, dosage and other parameters of drug. 2) Control Command, which indicates the clinical instruction. 3) Device Information, which includes the device name, identifier, state, etc. 4) Patient Information, which describes the data of patient. The message of clinical data usually contains content and identity. For the content, we analyzed the misuse attacks based on topics. For the identity, we analyzed the abuse attacks based on the identity (i.e., Id) in topics. The attack patterns include overprivileged access to clinical data, and performing spoofing, tampering or guessing to obtain sensitive data and alter clinical procedures. The Supervisor and its apps are assumed to be trusted, and we do not consider the attacks towards them.

4.2 Clinical Scenario

Figure 1 displays typical clinical scenarios in OpenICE: 1) InfusionPump and Pulse Oximeter publish HeartBeat topic containing **DeviceId** to Supervisor to keep alive. 2) Infusion Safety app subscribes InfusionStatus topic from Infusion-Pump for monitoring its status. 3) Simulation Control app publishes Spo2 topic to Pulse Oximeter to control its operation. 4) Supervisor publishes PatientData topic containing **PatientId** to establish simulated patients in Patient Id app.

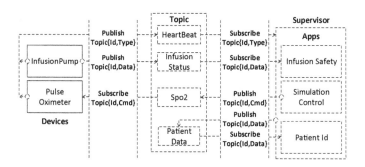

Fig. 1. Clinical scenarios of OpenICE

4.3 Misuse of Topic

OpenICE lacks fine-grained authorization for clinical topics. Actually, misuse of sensitive topics will be highly damaging to security, privacy and even safety. Following we present the attack surfaces and risks in the clinical scenarios of OpenICE due to the insecure management of topics.

Unauthorized Medication Data. Medication data are used by different devices for simulating clinical tasks. For example, InfusionPump is a device that delivers medication or nutrient into patient's body through InfusionStatus topic. The malicious device created a new participant and subscribed to InfusionStatus topic. Through this way, when Pump sent medication data to Supervisor, the malicious device could intercept and tamper the medication data.

Result: Supervisor originally showed Pump's drug name and complete percent. After adversary intercepted and forged data through InfusionStatus, Supervisor showed tampered drug name and the complete percent stopped at 0.

Unauthorized Control Command. Control command is used by OpenICE applications to control vital signs data emitted from medical devices. For example, Simulation Control app controls the value of Spo2 emitted from Pulse Oximeter through Spo2 topic. The adversary could forge fake control command to tamper Spo2 value through unauthorized access to Spo2 topic. Generally, a normal Spo2 value is between 95 and 100%. The modified Spo2 value could induce medical incidents and cause safety risks.

Result: We used the adversary device to set Spo2 value to 1000% and published the data to Spo2 topic. The result showed that the Spo2 value on Supervisor increased from 98% to 1000% and caused the alarm of Infusion Safety app once the value exceeded 100%.

4.4 Abuse of Identity

Clinical environment has many subjects including Device, Application, Supervisor and Patient. Different subjects have their own identities, i.e., Ids. These unique Ids are used to distinguish different subjects and the topics published by them. This section will discuss the attack surfaces and risks based on the abuse of identity.

DeviceId Hijack. To maintain connection, Supervisor and every connected device continuously publish and subscribe the HeartBeat topic. As the name implies, HeartBeat topic is used for transmitting signals that indicate the sender is alive in the network. Supervisor distinguishes HeartBeat messages from different devices through the DeviceId in HeartBeat topic. Based on this mechanism, the adversary could utilize a compromised device to intercept the DeviceId from a normal device's HeartBeat. Then adversary set the compromised device's DeviceId to the same Id and published HeartBeat containing this intercepted Id.

Result: We used the Pulse Oximeter as adversary, which intercepted an InfusionPump's DeviceId and published the fake HeartBeat containing the intercepted Id to Supervisor. The result demonstrated that Supervisor could not distinguish between the HeartBeats from InfusionPump and Pulse Oximeter, and surprisingly displayed them on the same panel. Moreover, after InfusionPump was shut down, Pulse Oximeter could communicate with Supervisor on behalf of InfusionPump.

PatientId Guess. PatientId is used to identify different patients. During the initialization phase, Supervisor establishes five simulated patients among which two PatientIds are 14c89b52fb7 and 14cd923b336. These two numbers seem to have some relationship. To figure out this issue, we examined the source code and found that OpenICE generated PatientId based on system clock. Specifically, OpenICE got the current time in milliseconds through $System.currentTimeMillis$ function, and then converted the time to PatientId through $Long.toHexString$ function. This mechanism only makes PatientId be unique but never makes it be random and secure. Adversary could guess PatientId based on the system clock or obtain the creation time of PatientIds that have been created.

Summary. For the four kinds of clinical data in MCPS (i.e., medication data, control command, device information and patient information), we have discussed the misuse of medication data and control command. Similar attack patterns could misuse device and patient information to tamper device's name and establish fake patients. We also discussed the abuse of device and patient identity. Similar attack surfaces could exist for the identity of Supervisor and applications. Note that all the attack patterns and risks are also applicable to other MCPS instantiations that adopt the publish-subscribe paradigm in their communication mechanisms.

5 Mitigation

In this section, we discuss the protection for clinical data. To mitigate the abuse of identity, the key principle is to authenticate the protocol-layer identity and the design flaws of identity (e.g., Id hijack and Id guess) should be avoided. As for the unauthorized topics, we propose an enhanced access control model.

5.1 Access Control Model

Topic-Based UCON Model. The key to protect sensitive data in MCPS is the fine-grained authorization for accessing sensitive data in MCPS's interoperable environment. However, related works of access control for MCPS [12,13] mainly focused on the authorization between clinician, medical app and medical device. How to establish an access control model for real-time data generated by medical device/app within an interoperable environment remains an unsolved problem. To bridge this gap, we propose a Topic-based Usage Control (UCON) [9] model for MCPS. We choose UCON model because it goes beyond traditional access control, and supports mutable attributes and transaction-based decision-making, which are suitable for highly dynamic and distributed environment. The key idea of our model builds on the following concepts from UCON, and we improved these concepts and designed new rules to adapt to MCPS prototypes:

- Subject(S): Subject is an entity (e.g., devices and applications in OpenICE) associated with attributes, and holds or exercises certain rights on objects.
- Subject Attributes $(ATT(S))$: Subject attributes are properties of a subject that can be used for the usage decision process. The subject's attributes in our model are specified as Eq. 1.

$$ATT(S) = \{Id, Type, Topic\_publish, Topic\_subscribe\} \tag{1}$$

  Id includes identity information of subject (e.g., DeviceId). $Type$ indicates the model name of subject (e.g., InfusionPump). $Topic\_publish$ includes the set of topics permitted to send messages to. $Topic\_subscribe$ includes the set of topics permitted to read messages from.
- Object(O): Object is the entity that subjects hold rights on (i.e., the topic).
- Object Attributes $(ATT(O))$: Object attributes include certain properties that can be used for access decisions. The Object's attributes in our model are specified as Eq. 2.

$$ATT(O) = \{Topic\{Name, Type\}, Content, Source\} \tag{2}$$

  $Content$ is the topic-layer information (e.g., drug name and dosage). $Source$ represents the subject that created the topic. $Topic$ includes the topic's $name$ and $type$. Note that both of topic's name and type can be utilized for access control depending on the corresponding strategy.
- Rights(R): Rights are privileges that a subject can hold and exercise on an object. Our model has two general classes of rights, $Publish$ (write a message into a topic) and $Subscribe$ (read a message from a topic).

– Authorization: Authorization is the predicate for usage decision and returns whether the subject is allowed to perform the requested rights on the object. Specifically, authorization functions evaluate $ATT(S)$, $ATT(O)$ and requested $Right$ together with a set of policies for access decision. We designed two authorization rules based on different contexts in MCPS.

Rule1: The authorization rule against subject's request for topic publishing or subscribing should check the attributes of both subject and object as follows:

$$Allow(s, o, Publish) \Rightarrow o.Topic \in s.Topic\_publish \tag{3}$$

$$Allow(s, o, Subscribe) \Rightarrow o.Topic \in s.Topic\_subscribe \tag{4}$$

In Eq. 3, $Allow(s, o, Publish)$ indicates that subject s is allowed right $Publish$ to object o (e.g., an InfusionPump is allowed to Publish InfusionStatus). This access decision is made by checking the condition at the right of the arrow. The rule checks whether $subject$ is allowed to publish o by checking if this topic is in the allowed topic set $s.Topic\_publish$.

Similarly, in Eq. 4, the rule of $Allow(s, o, Subscribe)$ checks whether the subject is allowed to subscribe to the requested object (i.e., topic).

Rule2: The authorization rule against topic receiving should check the attributes of both the current subject and the topic's source as follows:

$$Allow(s, o, Subscribe) \Rightarrow o.Topic \in s.Topic\_sub \land o.Topic \in o.source.Topic\_pub \tag{5}$$

This rule checks whether the subject (i.e., the topic subscriber) is allowed to subscribe to the topic, and whether the topic's source (i.e., the topic sender) still owns the privilege to publish this topic. This rule ensures that if a topic's source has lost permissions for accessing this topic, then the messages in this topic should be rejected by the subscribers. Based on this rule, we can prevent subscribers from receiving an "expired" topic, which could perform replay attacks.

– Condition: Condition predicates evaluate current environmental or system status to check whether relevant requirements are satisfied or not. Subject attributes or object attributes can be used to select which condition requirement has to be used for a request. Our model utilizes condition predicates to restrict the writing value of topic's field as Eq. 6.

$$getCON(s, o, Publish) = curValue \in o.Topic\_name.ValueLimit \tag{6}$$

In Eq. 6, predicate $getCON(s, o, Publish)$ indicates the function for evaluating condition restriction of request $Allow(s, o, Publish)$. Based on topic's name, this function queries the topic's restriction on its value $ValueLimit$ and compares it with the requested value $curValue$. If the requested value is in the range of restriction, then $getCON(s, o, Publish)$ returns true. The condition predicate restricts the value of requested writing to avoid malicious writing on the safety-critical topics in MCPS.

Break-The-Glass. CPSs do not necessarily operate in a stable environment [1]. Ideally, the policy defined for the UCON system of MCPS prevents apps/devices from acting maliciously. However, in emergency situations, enforcing least privilege through defined access control polices can result in situations in which clinicians could be prevented from delivering potential care to patients. In these situations, the need for a clinician to be able to administer care to a patient outweighs the risks associated with unauthorized access to sensitive data. Therefore, we add Break-The-Glass (the name is BTG because it is a similar process to breaking the glass on a fire alarm) feature into our model.

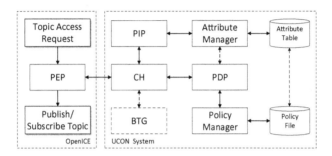

Fig. 2. Implementation of access control model

5.2   Implementation

We implemented our access control model in OpenICE as shown in Fig. 2. The main components are introduced as follows:

1) Policy Enforcement Point (PEP) is the point where policy is enforced. It intercepts the invocation and communicates with the authorization system. As for OpenICE, PEP is the location where devices or apps request to access topics.
2) Context Handler (CH) is the front-end of authorization system. It converts and forwards messages for communicating with PEP, PIP and PDP.
3) Policy Information Point (PIP) provides an interface for retrieving mutable attributes needed by the authorization system to produce access decisions. The PIP obtains required attributes from Attribute Manager (AM) which provides facilities for storing and updating attributes.
4) Policy Decision Point (PDP) is the component that evaluates access requests and performs access decisions. PDP communicates with Attribute Manager for attributes acquisition and evaluates access requests by means of existing policies in Policy Manager's policy database, which includes authorization, condition and obligation policies.
5) Policy Manager stores and manages authorization policies configured in the policy files. The policies would be reconfigured while the attributes changed.
6) BTG are state variables related to emergency cases.

We manually implemented the components of CH, PIP and AM in Java. And we implemented the PDP model and authorization policy based on an open-source project called Casbin [3]. Casbin is a popular access control library and provides various access control models for different programming languages. Casbin implements models and policies through configuration files based on PERM metamodel (Policy, Effect, Request, Matchers). Switching or upgrading the authorization mechanism is just as simple as modifying a configuration.

We established basic access control policies which should be designed by the OpenICE developers. As shown in Table 1, we listed several basic strategies containing device/application (Subject), topic (Object) and corresponding operation (Right). By means of these strategies, more complex policies would be developed, such as restricting the writing range of value for the topic publisher.

Table 1. Access control policy

Policy	Device/application	Topic	Operation	BTG
Basic strategy	InfusionPump	InfusionStatus	Read&write	–
Basic strategy	Infusion Safety	InfusionStatus	Read	–
Basic strategy	Simulation Control	Spo2	Read&write	–
Basic strategy	Pulse Oximeter	Spo2	Read	–
Basic strategy	Patient Id	PatientData	Read& write	–
BTG-based strategy	Infusion Safety	Spo2/Pulse	Read	BTG1

We introduced BTG, a state variable related to emergency case, into the access control policy as shown in Table 1. This BTG-based strategy is performed as follows. During an emergency, a BTG interface will appear and require the clinician to log in to protect the privacy of patients' information and avoid abuse of break-glass. After the clinician has successfully been authenticated, the BTG1 variable is set as True by Supervisor. When Infusion Safety requests to access the topics (Spo2/Pulse) which should not be accessed by this app in the normal case, the UCON system checks the related BTG variable and policy, grants the request and returns the obligation. When the access is accomplished, Infusion Safety will notify Supervisor to set the BTG1 variable back to False.

5.3   Evaluation

We deployed our access control model in OpenICE and evaluated its effectiveness and performance. All the experiments were performed using the same settings: a laptop with an Intel i7-4600U CPU and 8 GB memories running OpenICE.

To evaluate the effectiveness of our access control model, we launched all the attacks by the adversary (a malicious Pulse Oximeter) in Sect. 4.3. Our access control model denied all the unauthorized operations (i.e., reading and writing InfusionStatus, and writing Spo2) and defeated the corresponding attacks. When the emergency case occurred, e.g., Spo2 value was abnormal, the BTG function launched and successfully displayed the requested topics as shown in Fig. 3.

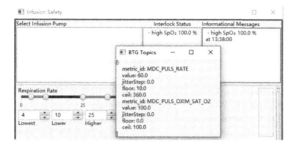

Fig. 3. Case of Break-The-Glass

To evaluate the performance overhead brought by our model, we recorded the average invocation latency, and average CPU/memory usage. We tested the InfusionStatus, Spo2 and PatientData topic in OpenICE. In addition, we also added the access control model into MDCF and tested three kinds of topics including Spo2, InfusionDrug and TickTock. As shown in Table 2, Baseline indicates the performance of original system without protection and Defense indicates the performance of system within our protection. The results show that our access control model incurred negligible invocation latency (from 0.864 ms to 5.060 ms). The CPU overheads in OpenICE and MDCF were at most 6.33% and 2.21% respectively. The memory overheads were at most 6.08% and 7.04%.

Table 2. Access control model's overhead

Topic	Latency(ms)			CPU(%)			Memory(MB)		
OpenICE	Baseline	Defense	↑	Baseline	Defense	↑	Baseline	Defense	↑
Status	0.075	5.135	5.060	10.57	11.03	4.35%	31.27	33.17	6.08%
Spo2	0.054	3.276	3.222	17.38	18.48	6.33%	41.77	42.31	1.29%
Patient	0.832	4.828	3.996	15.70	16.54	5.35%	31.94	33.38	4.51%
MDCF	Baseline	Defense	↑	Baseline	Defense	↑	Baseline	Defense	↑
Spo2	0.002	1.321	1.319	42.04	42.97	2.21%	29.13	30.42	4.43%
Drug	0.001	0.905	0.904	34.08	34.49	1.20%	26.74	28.40	6.21%
TickTock	0.001	0.865	0.864	37.10	37.62	1.40%	25.84	27.66	7.04%

6   Conclusion

In this paper, we performed a study on security and safety risks in the network of publish-subscribe based MCPS. We revealed different attack surfaces based on the misuse and abuse of clinical data, and demonstrated the clinical errors and risks brought by these attacks in a popular prototype of MCPS. To mitigate the threats, we proposed a Topic-based access control model with Break-The-Glass feature, and evaluated its effectiveness and efficiency on MCPS prototypes.

Acknowledgments. This work was supported by National Key R&D Program of China (Y9YFB26511).

References

1. Akhuseyinoglu, N.B., Joshi, J.: A constraint and risk-aware approach to attribute-based access control for cyber-physical systems. Comput. Secur. **96**(1), 101802 (2020)
2. ASTM: Astm f2761(09) (2018). https://www.astm.org/Standards/F2761.htm
3. Casbin: Casbin project (2021). https://casbin.org/
4. Group, O.M.: DDS specification v1.4 (2015). https://www.omg.org/spec/DDS
5. Hatcliff, J., et al.: Rationale and architecture principles for medical application platforms. In: Proceedings of the 2012 IEEE/ACM Third International Conference on Cyber-Physical Systems, pp. 3–12. IEEE Computer Society (2012)
6. Jiang, Y., Song, H., Wang, R., Gu, M., Sun, J., Sha, L.: Data-centered runtime verification of wireless medical cyber-physical system. IEEE Trans. Ind. Inform. **13**(4), 1900–1909 (2016)
7. King, A., Arney, D., Lee, I., Sokolsky, O., Hatcliff, J., Procter, S.: Prototyping closed loop physiologic control with the medical device coordination framework. In: Proceedings of the 2010 ICSE Workshop on Software Engineering in Health Care, pp. 1–11. ACM (2010)
8. Lee, I., et al.: Challenges and research directions in medical cyber-physical systems. Proc. IEEE **100**(1), 75–90 (2012)
9. Park, J., Sandhu, R.: THE UCON ABC usage control model. ACM Trans. Inf. Syst. Secur. (TISSEC) **7**(1), 128–174 (2004)
10. Plourde, J., Arney, D., Goldman, J.M.: OpenICE: an open, interoperable platform for medical cyber-physical systems. In: Proceedings of the 2014 ACM/IEEE International Conference on Cyber-Physical Systems, p. 221. IEEE (2014)
11. Raju, M.H., Ahmed, M.U., Atiqur Rahman Ahad, M.: Security analysis and a potential layer to layer security solution of medical cyber-physical systems. In: Balas, V.E., Solanki, V.K., Kumar, R., Ahad, M.A.R. (eds.) A Handbook of Internet of Things in Biomedical and Cyber Physical System. ISRL, vol. 165, pp. 61–86. Springer, Cham (2020). https://doi.org/10.1007/978-3-030-23983-1_3
12. Salazar, C.: A security architecture for medical application platforms. Ph.D. thesis, Kansas State University (2014)
13. Tasali, Q., Chowdhury, C., Vasserman, E.Y.: A flexible authorization architecture for systems of interoperable medical devices. In: Proceedings of the 22nd ACM on Symposium on Access Control Models and Technologies, pp. 9–20. ACM (2017)
14. Tasali, Q., Sublett, C., Vasserman, E.Y.: Controlled BTG: toward flexible emergency override in interoperable medical systems. EAI Endorsed Trans. Secur. Saf. **6**(22), e2 (2020)
15. Theverge: Woman dies during a ransomware attack on a German hospital (2020). https://www.theverge.com/2020/9/17/21443851/
16. Venkatasubramanian, K.K., Vasserman, E.Y., Sokolsky, O., Lee, I.: Security and interoperable-medical-device systems, part 1. IEEE Secur. Priv. **10**(5), 61–63 (2012)
17. Zhang, Y., Zheng, D., Deng, R.H.: Security and privacy in smart health: efficient policy-hiding attribute-based access control. IEEE Internet Things J. **5**(3), 2130–2145 (2018)

RF-Ubia: User Biometric Information Authentication Based on RFID

Ningwei Peng[1], Xuan Liu[1,2(✉)], and Shigeng Zhang[3]

[1] College of Computer Science and Electronic Engineering, Hunan University, Changsha 410000, China
{pengnw,xuan_liu}@hnu.edu.cn
[2] State Key Laboratory for Novel Software Technology, Nanjing University, Nanjing 210023, China
[3] School of Computer Science, Central South University, Changsha 410000, China
sgzhang@csu.edu.cn

Abstract. Traditional authentication technologies usually perform identity authentication based on user information verification (e.g., inputting the password) or biometric information (e.g., fingerprints) for identity authentication. However, there are security risks when these authentication methods are applied solely. For example, if the password is compromised, it is unlikely to determine whether the user is legitimate based on the password. In this paper, we propose RF-Ubia, which combines user information and biometric features to double guarantee the security of identity authentication. The RF-Ubia is a user identification system composed of an array of nine passive tags and a commercial RFID reader, which firstly verifies the user's password, and then identifies the biometric characteristics of the legitimate user. Due to the coupling effect among tags, any tag signal change caused by the user's touch operation will affect other tag signals at the same time. Since each user has different fingertip impedance, their touch will cause a unique change of tag signal. Therefore, by combining biometric information, the tag array will uniquely identify users. Evaluations results show that RF-Ubia achieves excellent authentication performance with an average recognition rate of 92.8%.

Keywords: RFID · Authentication · Biometric information

1 Introduction

With the rapid development of modern technology, new automatic identification technologies emerge endlessly, among which Radio Frequency Identification (RFID) technology has become the core technology of the Internet of Things with its excellent advantages.

With the commercialization of RFID, the application scope of RFID is more and more extensive, including item tracking, motion detection [8,21], goods security and so on [2,4,11,13,14]. As the demand on protection for security industry and personal privacy increasingly grows, user authentication technology becomes

© Springer Nature Switzerland AG 2021
Z. Liu et al. (Eds.): WASA 2021, LNCS 12938, pp. 135–146, 2021.
https://doi.org/10.1007/978-3-030-86130-8_11

Fig. 1. Illustration of RF-Ubia design. The user touches the surface of the tag array to enter the password, and the signal integrating the user's biometric characteristics is captured by the reader.

particularly important. The purpose of user authentication is to verify whether a user is indeed a legitimate user registered in the system, which is a vital task in many applications, such as area or event access control, electronic payment, *etc.*.

We get inspired from existing work [11,15,22], where many access control systems gain access to an area by entering the correct password. However, it's easy to get their accounts stolen when users make their passwords too short and simple, or use the same passwords in other systems such as bank accounts. If the use of complex passwords composed of numbers and letters alternately, although it can increase the security strength of the password, it is not appropriate in the access control system. It will increase the complexity of the use of the system, which is not friendly to the user. Above all, ensuring the security of the account with a simple and friendly password has become the focus of this paper.

As the passive tags can not use encryption algorithms under the constraints of energy, many classic security solutions can not be applied in commercial passive tags. Therefore, we creatively propose to form a password array with nine tags, each one of which is used as a password button, as illustrated in Fig. 1. Users will only need to touch the surface of the tag once to enter a password number. When the user touches multiple tags continuously, the sequence of numbers will be obtained to play the role of the user authentication password.

In the process of touching, we have also skillfully incorporate our biometric information into the tag signal. When different users touch the RFID tag, different phase changes of the tags will occur as a result of users' different body impedance, which is distinctive for every user. The closer these tags in the array are, the stronger the coupling effect among them will become [15,22]. When one tag is touched, not only its signal will change, but also the signals of the other eight tags will change due to the coupling effect. These signal changes are highly correlated with the user's body impedance. Different users have different body impedance. Normally the impedance of the human body is about 300–1000 Ω, which leads to different changes in the phase signal of the tag. Combining user biometric information makes it possible to distinguish between different users who use the same password.

2   Related Work

User authentication methods can be divided into three main categories: information, possessions, physiological or behavioral characteristics.

Information, such as a password or security code. The information-based approach is designed to use traditional cryptographic algorithms to perform authentication and use encryption technology to protect tags from illegal access [7,10,12,16,20]. Most of these methods require modification of commercial communication protocols or tag hardware, so it is difficult to apply them to lightweight passive tags.

Possessions, such as various certificates or ID cards. The method based on the physical layer information is to identify and verify the tag by taking advantage of the difference of the tag circuit characteristics which will be reflected in the backscattering signal. Ding *et al.* proposed a reader authentication solution based on physical layer signals, namely Arbitrator [3], which can effectively prevent unauthorized access to tags. Ma *et al.* proposed a new physical layer recognition system GenePrint [6] based on internal similarity. Yang *et al.* used additional phase offset as a new kind of fingerprint called Tagprint [19] for identifying a pair of readers and tags. Chen *et al.* explored a new fingerprint called Eingerprint [1], which is used to authenticate passive tags in the commodity RFID system. Eingerprint uses the electrical energy stored in the tag circuit as a fingerprint. Wang *et al.* explored a verification method Hu-Fu [15]. The author observed the phenomenon of inductive coupling between two adjacent tags [5,18]. When two tags are placed very close and the coupling effect occurs, Hu-Fu can achieve the purpose of verification.

Physiological or Behavioral Characteristics. In recent years, the mainstream user authentication methods are based on different biological characteristics (such as fingerprint, face and retina, *etc.*) for identity recognition. Compared with traditional authentication technology, the biometric authentication technology (especially fingerprint authentication) achieves more excellent performance owing to its universality, uniqueness, permanence and anti-counterfeiting characteristics. RF-Mehndi [22] uses the physical characteristics of the tag and the biometric characteristics of the holder to verify the user's validity. When the user touches the tag, the physical layer information of the tag and the user's body impedance are combined to achieve verification.

Although RF-Mehndi combines the physical characteristics of tags and the biometric information of users, it still fails to get rid of the influence of personal ID card which will still be lost and bring trouble to users. Therefore, we explore a system that can verify the user by entering a password and combining the user's biometric information without the card.

3   Design Background and Overview

In this section, we will introduce passive tags and how they are coupled, as well as the implementation flow of our system.

3.1 Passive Tag

Passive tags are used in our system, which have no energy source of their own, and rely on reflecting the carrier signals emitted by the reader to obtain the working electric energy [17]. An RF tag consists of an antenna and a chip. The main function of the tag antenna is to receive the radio frequency signal emitted by the reader and transfer it to the tag chip for processing, and send the data of the tag chip to the reader. The antenna is a conductor structure specially designed for coupling radiated electromagnetic energy. In general, the smaller the size of the tag antenna, the smaller the radiation impedance of the antenna and the working efficiency. Taking the above factors into consideration, the tag layout is as small and easy as possible under the condition of satisfying the working efficiency. We use an Alien-9629 model tag with a size of 22.5 mm × 22.5 mm, and working frequency of 840–960 MHz.

3.2 Tag Coupling

Tag coupling is actually the transfer of energy and exchange of information between two devices. There are two ways of tag coupling: Backscatter coupling and Inductive coupling.

Backscatter Coupling. The electromagnetic wave emitted by the antenna activates the tag after touching the target tag and carries back the tag information. This is based on the spatial propagation law of electromagnetic waves. The recognition range is greater than 1 m.

Passive tags require the reader to send electromagnetic waves to provide sustained energy to keep the tags working. We know that changing magnetic fields produce electric fields, and changing electric fields produce magnetic fields. When a section of magnetic flux changes, there will be induced current generated in the closed coil. The current in the signal transmitter radiates radio electromagnetic waves through the antenna, forming the changing electromagnetic field. The changing electromagnetic field is sensed by the antenna coil at the receiving end, and the voltage is generated inside the coil. The tag can be thought of as a closed coil that generates an induced current inside when it senses a signal emitted by the reader. It should be noted that the induced current generated in the tag will also radiate electromagnetic waves back to the reader antenna after being modulated, and generate signals that can be recognized by the reader antenna, also known as backscattered signals. It is considered that the voltage varying with the electric field can generally be converted into the description form of sine wave, and the voltage period equations with respect to frequency ω and amplitude v_0 can be obtained as

$$V(t) = v_0 \cdot \cos(\omega t). \tag{1}$$

The energy is generally expressed in terms of power in the circuit. For a direct current system, according to the current I, voltage V and the load resistance R, the instantaneous power P is calculated as

$$P = I \cdot V = \frac{V^2}{R}. \tag{2}$$

The load resistance R is composed of the resistance of the tag chip and the antenna. The load resistance of each tag is different when it leaves the factory due to the difference in manufacture. According to the sinusoidal variation of the electric field, we can use calculus to calculate the energy produced by the current in a period and then divide it by the time of the period to obtain its average power:

$$P_{av} = \frac{v_0^2}{2R}. \tag{3}$$

Inductive Coupling. The inductive coupling is realized through the tag magnetic field according to the law of electromagnetic induction. Each tag generates a magnetic field around its coil when it is activated. When two tags are placed close to each other, the magnetic field of each other will pass through the coil of the other, resulting in a change in magnetic flux. An induced electromotive force will be generated inside the tag, thus affecting the power and signal of the tag. Figure 2 shows the single tag state and the coupling state of two tags. The power after tag coupling is

$$P_c = \frac{v_0^2 + v_c}{2R}. \tag{4}$$

When the user touches one of the tags in the array, the power of the touched tag changes to

$$P_c' = \frac{v_0^2 + v_c'}{2R + Z}, \tag{5}$$

where Z represents the impedance of the human body, and v_c' represents the induced electromotive force caused by the coupling effect of other tags when the user touches. The power expression of other tags is

$$P_c'' = \frac{v_0^2 + v_c''}{2R}. \tag{6}$$

The position of each tag in the array is different, and the change of the magnetic field around it is also different, which leads to the different induced electromotive force v_c'' caused by coupling.

3.3 System Architecture

In this part, we briefly describe the four steps for implementing the RF-Ubia system.

Hardware Settings. In order to realize the password function of RF-Ubia, we need to first arrange a single RFID tag into the layout of 3×3. The tag array is then fixed to prevent the signal change caused by the relative movement of the tag from affecting the user authentication result.

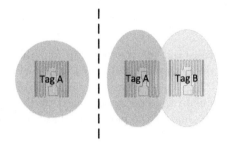

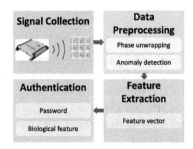

Fig. 2. Left: single tag; right: two tags are coupling.

Fig. 3. The working flow of the RF-Ubia system.

Tag Identification. The reader sends a signal to activate the nine tags in the array, carries out a preliminary identification according to the EPC of the tag [9]. The reader obtains the signal of the legitimate tag and then waits for the user to touch the corresponding tag and collects the signal data of the tag.

Data Processing. The purpose of this step is to process the tag data acquired by the reader, eliminate the inverted π phenomenon and periodic surround (*i.e.* phase unwrapping) of the tag phase. Extract the characteristic information we need, and identify the password sequence entered by the user.

User Authentication. This step first determines whether it is a valid password based on the recognized password sequence. If the password sequence entered by the user is indeed the registered one in the system, then the second stage of verification is performed. The second stage verifies that the user is legitimate to prevent an illegal attacker from stealing the password sequence of the legitimate user.

4   System Design

In order to explain the working flow of our proposed system, this section is composed of four parts, which are signal collection, data preprocessing, feature extraction and authentication. Figure 3 depicts these four key steps.

4.1   Signal Collection

The signal collection of our system is divided into registration stage and verification stage. In the registration stage, each user sets his or her password and touches the tag corresponding to its password in order. Each user collects data many times and collects their identity information. The identity information is related to the user's password and its body impedance. Different user's impedances and passwords result in unique identity information for each person. In the verification stage, the user only needs to touch the tag array once, enter his or her password set in the registration stage. And then the background can obtain the relevant signal data of the tag and complete the authentication.

4.2   Data Preprocessing

Due to the essential characteristics of the tag signal, phase is a periodical function with the period around and inverted π phenomenon. In order to obtain usable phase characteristics, we need to preprocess the data after getting the tag signal. The tag information is phase unwrapping and the inverted π phenomenon is eliminated. As shown in Fig. 4, the figure above shows the wrapped phase, and the figure below shows the inverted π phenomenon of the phase.

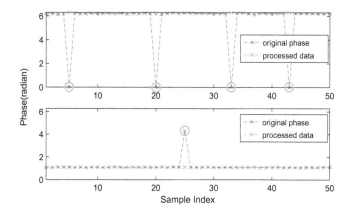

Fig. 4. The data in the red circle is the original phase, and the red symbol '×' is the processed phase. In the figure above is phase wrapped. In the figure below is the inverted π phenomenon. (Color figure online)

When the user touches the tag, we find that some tags in the tag array are unable to feedback the tag signal. In Fig. 5, two adjacent pieces of data are connected by dashed lines. A large amount of signal data is missing between the two pieces of data surrounded by a blue circle. This is because after the user touches the tag, due to the influence of the user's impedance and coupling, the tag power becomes relatively small and cannot reach the threshold value of activating the tag. Therefore, the tag data cannot be read by the reader in this touch stage, and there is no phase signal in this stage of the tag. We will take advantage of this phenomenon as a feature when verifying the user's identity. In order to preserve this feature, interpolation and data smoothing processing will not be carried out.

4.3   Feature Extraction

After data preprocessing, we obtained a continuously available tag phase signal, and we further extracted the phase features related to user identity information. We found that the moment when the user touched the tag and the moment when the user removed the finger, the tag signal changes were relatively complex

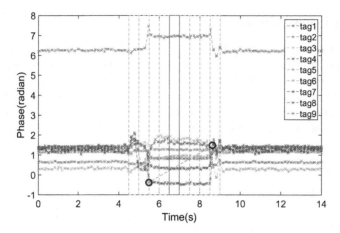

Fig. 5. The dashed rectangle represents the window of abnormal phase signal, and the red rectangle represents the feature window. After phase unwrapping, some phase values will exceed the range from 0 to 2π. (Color figure online)

and chaotic, and the phase characteristics is also unstable. However, during the touch process, the phase signal of the tag tended to be stable. So we propose an anomaly detection algorithm to extract the middle stable part of the tag phase signal. We first empirically set up a fixed-size window to detect the abnormal part. The average amplitude in the k-th window of tag i can be expressed as

$$A_i(k) = \frac{\sum_{j=1}^{l} |x_j - x_m|}{l} \quad and \quad x_m = \frac{\sum_{j=1}^{l} |x_j|}{l}, \tag{7}$$

where l represents the data volume of the phase in the window, x_j represents the phase value, and x_m represents the average phase value of the tag obtained from the stable tag signal in the first window, and is used as a metric to evaluate the anomaly. In Eq. 8, the amplitude function $G(k)$ is obtained by summing the amplitudes of all tags in the same window.

$$G(k) = \sum_{i=1}^{9} A_i(k). \tag{8}$$

After a series of sliding window detection anomalies, and then compared with the set threshold value, we can get an anomaly sequence. The first detected exception window is taken as the left exception window, which is caused when the user just touches the tag. And the last successive exception window is taken as the right exception window, which is caused when the user picks up finger and leaves the tag surface. We take the middle window between the left exception window and the right exception window as our feature window. The purpose is to avoid using the tag signal which is more volatile when the user touches, and to obtain the relatively stable signal when the user touches steadily at the middle moment. Figure 5 shows the feature window portion of the tag phase signal. The mean value of the nine tag phases in this window is

$$V = [A'_1, A'_2, A'_3, A'_4, A'_5, A'_6, A'_7, A'_8, A'_9]. \tag{9}$$

Then the phase difference between two of the nine tags is calculated to form the eigenvalue

$$\Delta A_{ij} = \left| A'_i - A'_j \right|. \tag{10}$$

Since ΔA_{ij} and ΔA_{ji} are equal, and ΔA_{ii} is equal to 0, we can get 36 effective eigenvalues from a feature window to form the eigenvector

$$F = [\Delta A_{12}, \cdots, \Delta A_{19}, \Delta A_{23}, \cdots, \Delta A_{29}, \Delta A_{34}, \cdots, \Delta A_{89}]. \tag{11}$$

4.4 Authentication

For the authentication, we use the classification function in Weka to train the user information collected during the registration stage into the validation model. User data is collected and feature information is extracted, and then the classification model is used to determine whether the user is legitimate.

5 Experiment and Evaluation

In this section, we will initially implement RF-Ubia, and through extensive experiments to verify its performance.

The RF-Ubia consists of a commercial reader, a directional antenna and several passive tags. The RFID reader is the ImpinJ R420 commercial reader, the antenna model is Laird S9028PCR, and the tag is Alien 9629. The software of RF-Ubia runs on a computer with an Intel(R) Core(TM) i5-3230M CPU@2.60 GHz and 12 GB RAM.

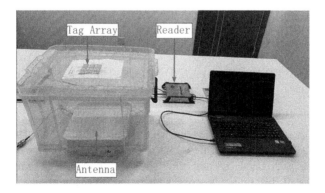

Fig. 6. Experimental environment.

Experimental Setups. We carried out the experiment in a conference room. As shown in the Fig. 6, the tag array formed by 9 Alien-9629 tags was fixed on the top of the box, where the antenna connected to the reader was placed at the bottom to read tags data, and finally the data was processed by the computer.

Metric. In order to describe the performance of RF-Ubia, we used the three major indicators, namely True Positive Rate (TPR), False Positive Rate (FPR) and Accuracy. TPR as shown in Eq. 12 is used to measure the accuracy of a single password identification performance. FPR as shown in Eq. 13 is RF-Ubia passed the illegal user validation of the measurement. Accuracy is refers to the combination of RF-Ubia first stage and second stage of the overall validation results.

$$TPR = \frac{true\ positives}{true\ positives + false\ negatives} \tag{12}$$

$$FPR = \frac{false\ positives}{false\ positives + true\ negatives} \tag{13}$$

First, we evaluate the performance of the system to identify the password, that is, to identify which tag the user has touched. We collected 360 sets of data for evaluation. From password 1 to password 9, the TPR of each password is shown in Fig. 7. The average accuracy of the system to identify the password is more than 96.9%, indicating that RF-Ubia can effectively distinguish which tag the user touches and can realize the function of entering the password.

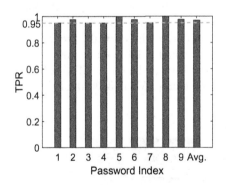
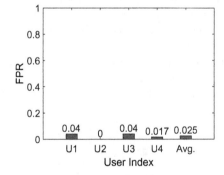

Fig. 7. The TPR of RF-Ubia identification password.

Fig. 8. The FPR of RF-Ubia distinguish user when the password length is 2.

We verify the validity of the system when multiple users use the same password. In Fig. 8, the FPR of the RF-Ubia does not exceed 0.04 when the user's password length is 2. RF-Ubia can effectively distinguish different users. After that, in the case of different password length, we experimented with users who used the same password. When the password length is 3, the user identification accuracy with the same password is 98.75%. When the password length is 4, the accuracy reaches 100%. The longer the password is, the more user features can be utilized, so the higher the authentication accuracy of the user is. Considering the identification of passwords and the distinction of different users, the average accuracy of RF-Ubia system is more than 92.8%.

6   Conclusion

In this paper, we proposed a user biometric information authentication system called RF-Ubia. The system uses the user's impedance information and integrates the user's biometrics into the password entered by the user. RF-Ubia uses two-stage authentication, which first identifies the user's password, and then identifies the legitimate user according to different biometric information. We evaluate RF-Ubia through extensive experiments. The results show that RF-Ubia is effective and has good authentication performance.

Acknowledgement. This work was supported by in part by the National Natural Science Foundation of China (Grant Nos. 61772559, 61602167), the Hunan Provincial Natural Science Foundation of China under grant No. 2020JJ3016. Dr. Xuan Liu's work is partially supported by the National Defense Science and Technology Innovation Special Zone Project of China.

References

1. Chen, X., Liu, J., Wang, X., Liu, H., Jiang, D., Chen, L.: Eingerprint: robust energy-related fingerprinting for passive RFID tags. In: 17th USENIX Symposium on Networked Systems Design and Implementation, NSDI 2020, pp. 1101–1113. USENIX Association (2020)
2. Chen, Z., Yang, P., Xiong, J., Feng, Y., Li, X.: Tagray: contactless sensing and tracking of mobile objects using COTS RFID devices. In: 39th IEEE Conference on Computer Communications, INFOCOM 2020, pp. 307–316. IEEE (2020)
3. Ding, H., et al.: Preventing unauthorized access on passive tags. In: 2018 IEEE Conference on Computer Communications, INFOCOM 2018, pp. 1115–1123. IEEE (2018)
4. Han, J., et al.: CBID: a customer behavior identification system using passive tags. IEEE/ACM Trans. Netw. **24**(5), 2885–2898 (2016)
5. Han, J., et al.: Twins: device-free object tracking using passive tags. IEEE/ACM Trans. Netw. **24**(3), 1605–1617 (2016)
6. Han, J., et al.: Geneprint: generic and accurate physical-layer identification for UHF RFID tags. IEEE/ACM Trans. Netw. **24**(2), 846–858 (2016)
7. Li, T., Luo, W., Mo, Z., Chen, S.: Privacy-preserving RFID authentication based on cryptographical encoding. In: Proceedings of the IEEE INFOCOM 2012, pp. 2174–2182. IEEE (2012)
8. Liu, X., Yin, J., Liu, Y., Zhang, S., Guo, S., Wang, K.: Vital signs monitoring with RFID: opportunities and challenges. IEEE Netw. **33**(4), 126–132 (2019)
9. Liu, X., Zhang, S., Xiao, B., Bu, K.: Flexible and time-efficient tag scanning with handheld readers. IEEE Trans. Mob. Comput. **15**(4), 840–852 (2016)

10. Lu, L., Han, J., Xiao, R., Liu, Y.: ACTION: breaking the privacy barrier for RFID systems. In: 28th IEEE International Conference on Computer Communications, Joint Conference of the IEEE Computer and Communications Societies, INFO-COM 2009, pp. 1953–1961. IEEE (2009)
11. Pradhan, S., Chai, E., Sundaresan, K., Qiu, L., Khojastepour, M.A., Rangarajan, S.: RIO: a pervasive rfid-based touch gesture interface. In: Proceedings of the 23rd Annual International Conference on Mobile Computing and Networking, MobiCom 2017, pp. 261–274. ACM (2017)
12. Sun, M., Sakai, K., Ku, W., Lai, T., Vasilakos, A.V.: Private and secure tag access for large-scale RFID systems. IEEE Trans. Dependable Secur. Comput. **13**(6), 657–671 (2016)
13. Wang, C., Xie, L., Wang, W., Chen, Y., Bu, Y., Lu, S.: RF-ECG: heart rate variability assessment based on COTS RFID tag array. Proc. ACM Interact. Mob. Wearable Ubiquitous Technol. **2**(2), 85:1–85:26 (2018)
14. Wang, C., Xie, L., Zhang, K., Wang, W., Bu, Y., Lu, S.: Spin-antenna: 3D motion tracking for tag array labeled objects via spinning antenna. In: 2019 IEEE Conference on Computer Communications, INFOCOM 2019, pp. 865–873. IEEE (2019)
15. Wang, G., Cai, H., Qian, C., Han, J., Li, X., Ding, H., Zhao, J.: Towards replay-resilient RFID authentication. In: Proceedings of the 24th Annual International Conference on Mobile Computing and Networking, MobiCom 2018, pp. 385–399. ACM (2018)
16. Weis, S.A., Sarma, S.E., Rivest, R.L., Engels, D.W.: Security and privacy aspects of low-cost radio frequency identification systems. In: Hutter, D., Müller, G., Stephan, W., Ullmann, M. (eds.) Security in Pervasive Computing. LNCS, vol. 2802, pp. 201–212. Springer, Heidelberg (2004). https://doi.org/10.1007/978-3-540-39881-3_18
17. Xi, Z., Liu, X., Luo, J., Zhang, S., Guo, S.: Fast and reliable dynamic tag estimation in large-scale RFID systems. IEEE Internet Things J. **8**(3), 1651–1661 (2021)
18. Yang, L., Chen, Y., Li, X., Xiao, C., Li, M., Liu, Y.: Tagoram: real-time tracking of mobile RFID tags to high precision using COTS devices. In: The 20th Annual International Conference on Mobile Computing and Networking, MobiCom 2014, pp. 237–248. ACM (2014)
19. Yang, L., Peng, P., Dang, F., Wang, C., Li, X., Liu, Y.: Anti-counterfeiting via federated RFID tags' fingerprints and geometric relationships. In: 2015 IEEE Conference on Computer Communications, INFOCOM 2015, pp. 1966–1974. IEEE (2015)
20. Yao, Q., Qi, Y., Han, J., Zhao, J., Li, X., Liu, Y.: Randomizing RFID private authentication. In: Seventh Annual IEEE International Conference on Pervasive Computing and Communications, PerCom 2009, pp. 1–10. IEEE Computer Society (2009)
21. Zhang, S., Liu, X., Liu, Y., Ding, B., Guo, S., Wang, J.: Accurate respiration monitoring for mobile users with commercial RFID devices. IEEE J. Sel. Areas Commun. **39**(2), 513–525 (2021)
22. Zhao, C., et al.: RF-mehndi: a fingertip profiled RF identifier. In: 2019 IEEE Conference on Computer Communications, INFOCOM 2019, pp. 1513–1521. IEEE (2019)

NFDD: A Dynamic Malicious Document Detection Method Without Manual Feature Dictionary

Jianguo Jiang[1,2], Chenghao Wang[1,2], Min Yu[1(✉)], Chenggang Jia[1,2], Gang Li[3], Chao Liu[1], and Weiqing Huang[1,2]

[1] Institute of Information Engineering, Chinese Academy of Sciences, Beijing, China
{jiangjianguo,wangchenghao,yumin,jiachenggang,liuchao, huangweiqing}@iie.ac.cn
[2] School of Cyber Security, University of Chinese Academy of Sciences, Beijing, China
[3] School of Information Technology, Deakin University, 221 Burwood Highway Vic 3125, Geelong, Australia
gang.li@deakin.edu.au

Abstract. Machine learning method based on feature dictionary is currently the most popular in the field of malicious document (maldoc) detection. But building and updating the feature dictionary is a complex task that requires a lot of manual work. The detection effect of feature dictionary is limited by expert experience, and it cannot deal with unknown samples. To overcome the above limitations, we propose the no manual feature dictionary detection model (NFDD). We introduce a neural network based on word embedding and combine it with dynamic analysis that can capture behavioral information of unknown samples. Also, we have implemented traditional models based on feature dictionary for comparison. Experiments show that NFDD can effectively improve the accuracy to 99.05% on 27,500 Office compound and open XML documents. NFDD can detect unknown samples that cannot be detected by traditional methods.

Keywords: Malicious document · Dynamic analysis · Feature dictionary · Neural network

1 Introduction

Recent reports pointed out that compared with 2019, the number of malicious Office documents in the first half of 2020 increased by 176%, and accounted for 22% of the 120,910 newly discovered malware [1]. Besides, in 2020, malicious Office documents with the theme of COVID-19 have appeared in large numbers in many countries, challenging the effectiveness of existing detection methods. Since Office compound and Open XML documents are two completely different types, it is more difficult to detect malicious Office than other documents. Therefore, detecting malicious Office documents is still a significant problem.

Z. Liu et al. (Eds.): WASA 2021, LNCS 12938, pp. 147–159, 2021.
https://doi.org/10.1007/978-3-030-86130-8_12

The prior researchers have proposed several methods to detect maldocs. Most existing research work falls into the categories of static analysis and dynamic analysis. In the static detection methods respect, researchers extract the content [2–4], structural [5–7] or statistics [8–11] features of documents. However, this method can not deal with code obfuscation and imitate attack [12]. And in the dynamic detection methods respect, researchers extract and analyze the behavior and status information of the document [13–15] or code [16–21] runtime, and builds a feature dictionary to realize the classification of maldocs. In short, they are the research methods that we focus on. However, the existing dynamic detection methods have the following problems: (1) Rely on the manual feature dictionary constructed by experts. Not only the analysis and construction process of the feature dictionary is complicated, but the upper limit of the model's detection effect is also low. (2) When faced with unknown samples, the accuracy of the feature dictionary-based methods will decrease significantly. In this case, the feature dictionary will be seriously invalid, but the update of the dictionary is difficult. For example, in the experiments of Xu et al. [22] on Hidost [23] and PDFrate [12], new samples generated by changing the structure of existing samples can perfectly escape the detection of feature dictionary.

To deal with the above problems, we propose the NFDD model. NFDD preprocesses the sample report output by Cuckoo [24] to generate a word sequence and then uses CNN to classify the word sequence. This process doesn't require any feature dictionary. In addition, based on the dynamic report capturing sample behavior information and the model updating according to word frequency changes, NFDD can maintain the ability to detect unknown samples. It is worth noting that Zhang et al. [25] have combined deep learning with dynamic analysis to detect malware. But their model structure is complex and the data preprocessing process is cumbersome. The feature dictionary they built for malware is also not suitable for maldocs. As far as we know, in the current field of maldoc detection, we have not seen the combined application of deep learning and dynamic analysis on Office. We also implemented traditional detection models based on feature dictionary to compare with NFDD. By analyzing the experimental results, the contributions of this paper are as follows:

- We propose a maldoc preprocessing method without a feature dictionary. It avoids the process of manually building a feature dictionary, breaking the limitations of expert experience, and improving the detection effect.
- We propose an update mechanism and show that NFDD based on dynamic reports has excellent detection capabilities for unknown samples. NFDD can achieve a 99.87% accuracy on the unknown sample set, while the method based on feature dictionary only has an 82.45% accuracy.
- Based on the above method and CNN, we propose a unified detection model NFDD for Office compound documents and Open XML documents. The results show that NFDD achieves 99.96% accuracy on compound documents and 99.05% accuracy on all documents, while the method based on feature dictionary has an accuracy of only 94.93% on compound documents.

The rest of this paper is organized as follows. Section 2 introduces the related work of dynamic detection methods. Section 3 details the method we used.

Section 4 shows the results of the experiments and analysis. Section 5 explains the conclusions obtained.

2   Related Work

For briefly, we focus on the existing dynamic detection methods and analyze their pros and cons. There are two different types of dynamic detection. Some researchers advocate directly putting the document into a virtual environment for execution and monitoring the internal and external behaviors, instructions, and other information of the reader during running. Willems et al. [26] first designed CWSandbox, which can track all related system calls when the malware is opened. It automatically generates readable reports to describe runtime details of samples. The realization of CWSandbox provides a model for researchers to write monitoring programs. Xu et al. [14] proposed that benign PDF documents behave the same on different platforms, while maldocs behave differently. Therefore, they monitor the internal processing of the reader and the impact on external hosts when samples are opened in different systems. They detect maldocs by comparing the differences in behavior sequences. Yagemann et al. [15] implement a document tracking program based on Intel processors to reduce resource overhead and improve the accuracy of behavior acquisition. Scofield et al. [27] implement an instruction-level behavior monitor, and summarize behaviors of benign documents through feature distillation to build a feature whitelist. Behaviors not on this list are considered malicious. When the behavior score exceeds the threshold set by the model, the sample will be classified as malicious.

On the other hand, some researchers firstly extract the code in documents, then execute them and monitor their behaviors to classify. For example, Schreck et al. [19] use "Pin", a dynamic binary analysis tool, to automatically identify malicious code embedded in Office documents and track its behaviors. When suspicious behaviors are detected, dump their information. Based on the information, the model determines whether the document exploits known vulnerabilities. But it can only detect exploits on the stack. Liu et al. [13] insert a context monitoring program into the PDF reader. When the reader starts to parse Javascript, it records the behaviors. In this way, they solved the problem of Javascript positioning and de-obfuscation, but couldn't deal with attacks without Javascript. Iwamoto et al. [21] locate suspicious byte sequences according to the entropy distribution of documents. They package these byte sequences into an executable file and execute it, monitoring whether there are suspicious behaviors. This method damages the execution logic of code, making it impossible to detect return-oriented attacks. Other studies using similar ideas include MDScan [18], MPScan [20], etc. Since maldocs mainly use script to achieve malicious purposes, behavior sequences obtained by this method are more useful than the method of directly running the document. But it requires researchers to pay attention to the location and extraction technology of code in documents.

As mentioned earlier, Zhang et al. [25] have used deep learning and dynamic analysis to detect malware. They use Cuckoo to obtain the Application Programming Interface (API) logs of Portable Executable (PE) files when they are running. By analyzing logs, they summarize 102-dimensional features in three categories: API name, category, and arguments. They use feature hashes to convert strings into numbers to generate input data that can be processed by the neural network. Because they use a complex combination of multiple Gated-CNNs and Bi-LSTM, the performance is average. In addition, PE files and Office documents have different behavioral patterns. It may not be applicable to directly apply malware detection methods to maldocs.

The above methods all focus on mining richer and finer-grained behavioral features, and most of them independently implemented complex monitoring programs. They all need to analyze the collected behaviors to build a feature dictionary. Compared with NFDD, the cost of manual analysis in these methods is huge. Researchers cannot ensure that the constructed feature dictionary exhausts all the sensitive content of the malicious document, so the detection effect is restricted by experience and the upper limit is low. Also, with the evolution of attack methods, the old behavior patterns may be replaced. However, it is difficult to update the feature dictionary. When faced with an unknown sample, these methods may not be able to extract the feature value, or even if the feature sequence can be extracted, the correct classification cannot be completed.

3   System Framework

In this section, we will introduce the system architecture, preprocessing algorithm, update mechanism, and network design of NFDD.

3.1   Overview

The architecture of NFDD is shown in Fig. 1. The sample is first submitted to Cuckoo for analysis and obtaining the report. Secondly, we preprocess all reports and build a vocabulary. Then match the words that appear in the vocabulary in each report to generate word sequences. A fixed-dimensional vector is used to represent each word to generate a word sequence matrix. Finally, all the matrices are input into the deep learning model for training and testing, and the category of the document is output.

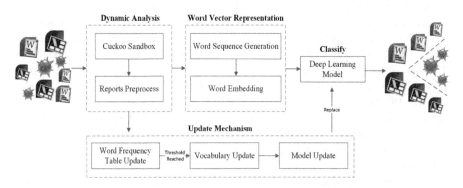

Fig. 1. System architecture

At the same time, the word frequency table will be updated after preprocessing reports. When the change exceeds the threshold, the vocabulary update will be triggered, and the model will be retrained to replace the original one.

3.2   Dynamic Analysis

Cuckoo Sandbox is an open-source malicious file automated analysis tool that supports multiple file-formats including PE, PDF, and Office files. We input the document to be detected into Cuckoo to obtain the analysis report. The specific preprocessing process is shown in Algorithm 1. The report contains 9 parts: info, signatures, target, network, dropped, behavior, debug, screenshots, strings, and metadata. We believe that the four parts: info, target, debug, and screenshots are of little significance to classification, so they are deleted. For example, the info part records information such as the platform and Cuckoo version, but they are the same for all documents. Then delete all empty dictionaries, and replace meaningless characters except numbers and letters with *. Since different attacks have different IP addresses embedded in documents, the number of IPs is used instead of specific content.

Algorithm 1. Analysis reports preprocessing and word vector representation.

Input:
     Analysis reports of Office documents, R_n;
     Vocabulary used in training, V_n;

Output:
     Standard vector data of analysis reports, O_n;

1: **for** each $i \in R_n$ **do**
2:    Delete four parts: info, target, debug, screenshots and empty dictionary in i;
3:    urls = len(urls); //Use len(urls) instead of specific URLs
4:    Replace str $\notin$ [0-9a-zA-Z.] with $*$;
5:    wordsInReport = spilt('*');
6:    voc = update(wordsInReport);
7: **end for**
8: V_n = top5000(voc);
9: word2id = buildWord2id(V_n);
10: **for** each $i \in R_n$ **do**
11:    wordSeq = np.zeros(config.maxSeqLen); //i has been preprocessed
12:    **for** each $word \in i$ **do**
13:      **if** $word \in V_n$ **then**
14:        update(wordSeq);
15:      **end if**
16:    **end for**
17:    O_n.add(wordSeq);
18: **end for**
19: **return** O_n

3.3   Word Vector Representation and Update Mechanism

As shown in Algorithm 1, we will count the frequency of all words in preprocessed reports and build a word frequency table. The top 5,000 words with the highest frequency will be used as the vocabulary list of NFDD. Match the words in the vocabulary in each analysis report to generate the corresponding word sequence. Set the maximum length of the word sequence to 200,000, and use 0 to complete the word sequence with insufficient length. We use a 50-dimensional vector to represent a word. A word sequence is converted into a 200,000*50 vector matrix.

We maintain a word frequency table that contains all the words that have appeared in known samples. Whenever a sample is input into NFDD, we will extract words in the analysis report and update the word frequency table. Set a model update threshold according to the change of the word frequency table. For example, when 100 of the 5,000 most frequent words are replaced, the model will be retrained to ensure the model's ability to detect new samples.

3.4   Network Structure

Classifying the input samples according to the content of reports is actually a classification problem of text sequence. TextCNN [28] can solve this problem well. TextCNN improves the traditional CNN model and uses multiple convolution kernels of different scales to extract multiple n-gram information of the input text. Besides, in all kinds of neural networks, CNN has the least amount of calculation and the fastest calculation speed. So we decide to make improvements based on TextCNN.

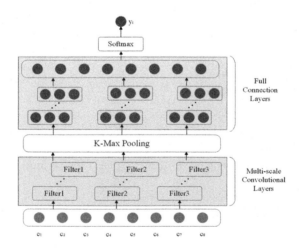

Fig. 2. Network Structure

The network structure is shown in Fig. 2. Through word embedding, each word is converted into a 50-dimensional word vector. Multiple sets of different numbers and scales of convolution kernels are used for comparison and we finally selected 3 convolution kernels with sizes of 2*50, 3*50, 4*50 to extract the 2-gram, 3-gram, and 4-gram semantic information of the input word sequence. Since the input word sequence is long, we use k-max pooling to extract the top k strongest feature values to retain richer information. Then splice all the output vectors of the pooling layer, and use the Softmax function to activate the output results.

4   Experiments and Evaluation

In this section, we will introduce the dataset we used, the indicators, and the settings of the experiments. We will prove the superiority of our method through comparison and analyze the results.

4.1   Dataset

We have collected 17,738 malicious samples and 17,762 benign samples. This dataset mainly includes Office compound documents and Office Open XML documents. Their specific quantity distribution is shown in Table 1. Since there are far fewer cases of using Open XML documents to attack in reality than compound documents, the number of malicious Open XML documents we collected is less than compound documents. The malicious samples in the dataset all come from the Virus Share [29], which is a relatively authoritative malicious file-sharing website that has published multiple authoritative malicious sample datasets. The benign samples are mostly crawled on search engines such as Google, Bing, and Baidu through crawlers, and some samples come from the FUZE, an Excel dataset for academic research. It should be noted that the NFDD model is trained on a computer with Intel(R) Core(TM) i7-7800X CPU 3.50 GHz and NVIDIA Corporation GP102. Accuracy, precision, recall, and F1-Score are used as evaluation indicators for experiments.

Table 1. Data distribution

Label	Malicious				Benign			
Type	Compound		Open XML		Compound		Open XML	
	doc	xls	docx	xlsx	doc	xls	docx	xlsx
Number of files	11150	3269	2468	851	3302	5902	3519	5039
Total	14419		3319		9204		8558	
	17738				17762			

We designed three experiments in this paper. Cuckoo's analysis time for each sample is set to 1 min. In the first experiment, compound documents are used as research targets to compare the detection capabilities of NFDD and feature dictionary. We use 5,000 compound documents totally to train and verify, where the ratio of maldocs to benign documents is 1:1. In all experiments, the ratio of the training set to the validation set is 9:1. In the test set, the number of maldocs is 11,919, and the number of benign documents is 6,704. We train the NFDD, the model based on feature dictionary and machine learning, and the model based on feature dictionary and deep learning respectively. The implementation of the machine learning model is to match feature items in the binary stream of the input sample. If it matches, the vector position corresponding to the feature item is set to 1, otherwise, it is 0. Finally, each sample can form a 139-dimensional feature vector. After processing all samples, input the generated vector-matrix into the classifier for training. We use 9 classifiers, including Nearest Neighbors, Linear SVM, RBF SVM, Decision Tree, Random Forest, AdaBoost, LogisticRegression, GradientBoosting, MLP. Select the one with the highest accuracy as the final model. The method based on CNN adopts the same network structure as NFDD. The difference is that the input of NFDD is a word sequence matrix, while the input of this model is a feature sequence matrix. The feature items are regarded as words, and each feature is also represented as a 50-dimensional vector through word embedding.

The second experiment will verify the detection ability of NFDD for unknown samples. We use 2,500 malicious Office compound documents created between 2012 and 2014 and 2,500 benign documents as training and validation sets, and 4,798 malicious compound documents created in 2020 as the test set. In the case of such a large time span, there must be samples in the test set that are different from the attack methods before 2014. In other words, for the training set, there will be many "0-day" samples in the test set. We will train the model based on feature dictionary and NFDD respectively, and compare their accuracy on the test set to evaluate the ability of different models to deal with unknown samples.

In the third experiment, 1,500 malicious and 1,500 benign Open XML documents were randomly selected to be added to the training and validation sets in the first experiment. All the remaining samples were added to the previous test set, and the number of malicious samples is 13,738, and the number of benign samples is 13,762. Retrain the NFDD model to verify whether it is universal for different types of documents.

4.2   Feature Dictionary Used in the Comparison Experiment

We constructed a 139-dimensional feature dictionary using the most popular features in maldoc detection. The specific categories and the number distribution of feature items are shown in Table 2. "Common keywords in maldocs" mainly including some suspicious APIs, such as CopyFile, and some suspicious keywords, such as Windows. Since most malicious Office documents need to implement the function of auto-executing, APIs related to auto-execution are particularly important, and we classify them as a separate category. "Statistical features" are mainly for obfuscated or encoded strings, calculations or comparison operations in codes, numbers, ordinary strings, etc. We count them in terms of length or quantity. "Network behaviors" detect the URL, IPv4, and email address in the document. The "Executable files" feature is mainly realized by matching the suffix name in the binary stream. There are 32 matching suffixes, such as ".exe", ".dll", etc. Regarding statistical features, network behaviors, and executable files, we not only detect their existence but also classify the sensitivity based on the quantity of them. Based on this feature dictionary, we implemented machine learning and deep learning models respectively.

4.3   Results and Discussion

Experiment on Compound Documents. It can be seen from Table 3 that NFDD is the highest among the four indicators, which is much higher than the other two methods. We repeated the experiment several times and ruled out the possibility that the high accuracy is caused by overfitting. We think the main reasons are as follows. Firstly, the analysis based on the sandbox report won't lead to the failure to parse samples. Secondly, the information in the report has been filtered once, and its effectiveness is stronger. Finally, the large vocabulary based on word frequency maintains words that are common in malicious and benign documents. In addition to the words shared by the two types of documents, their unique words will also be included, avoiding the errors and omissions that may occur in the manual construction of feature dictionaries. Through CNN's backpropagation, the unique words of the two types of documents will be easily separated. And the high-dimensional feature extraction of word sequences of CNN is also helpful for classification.

Table 2. Feature dictionary

Feature	Number
Common keywords in maldocs	103
Statistical features	19
APIs for automatic execution	13
Network behaviors	3
Executable files	1

Table 3. Compared with the detection method based on feature dictionary

Method	Accuracy	Precision	Recall	F1-Score
Feature Dictionary and Machine Learning	0.9469	0.9698	0.9465	0.958
Feature Dictionary and CNN	0.9493	0.9630	0.9576	0.9603
Our Method	**0.9996**	**0.9999**	**0.9994**	**0.9997**

In particular, due to structural abnormalities, for example, the index of some sectors has been changed, some samples can't be resolved by feature dictionary methods. To accurately calculate the indicators, we treat these samples as misclassification. Besides, we found that most of the unresolved samples are malicious. Specifically, in the test set, 166 malicious and 7 benign samples can't be resolved. This proves that changing the structure is a common method in maldocs. We also found that the CNN model has three indicators slightly higher than the machine learning model. In fact, in the k-fold cross-validation, the advantages of CNN are further expanded. We believe that it is because compared with machine learning, CNN can extract high-dimensional information of feature sequence, and the mining of the relationship between features is more sufficient.

Experiment on Unknown Malicious Documents. Since the model based on CNN and feature dictionary is better than machine learning in the first experiment, we choose it for further comparison with NFDD. It can be found from Table 4 that the accuracy of the feature dictionary method is greatly reduced compared with the first experiment, reaching 82.45%. On the other hand, the accuracy of NFDD has hardly changed, maintaining around 99.87%.

Table 4. Experiments with unknown samples

	Accuracy	F1-Score
Feature Dictionary and CNN	0.8245	0.9038
Our Method	**0.9987**	**0.9994**

We analyzed the misclassified samples of the feature dictionary method. Of the 842 samples, 32 samples could not be resolved, 42 samples could not extract feature values, and 768 samples could extract feature values but were still misclassified. This proves that over time, the attack pattern of unknown samples is likely to change, and the feature sequence combination trained based on existing samples can no longer be applied to unknown samples, causing a large number of malicious samples to be underreported. However, NFDD doesn't have this problem. No matter how malicious samples disguise themselves, they will eventually show sensitive behaviors, such as file operation. Cuckoo can capture this information well. Therefore, the update of the attack mode of samples has little impact on the accuracy of NFDD.

Experiment on Open XML Documents. The results are shown in Table 5. We can find that after adding Open XML documents, the scale of the test set became larger, but the four evaluation indicators of the model didn't decrease significantly. For example, F1-Score only dropped by 0.91%. The presumed reason is that even if the types of samples are different, the content of the sandbox report won't change significantly, so the detection effect will not fluctuate significantly. This proves that our method is universal for the detection of different file types.

Table 5. Unified detection of compound documents and Open XML documents

File type	Accuracy	Precision	Recall	F1-Score
Office Compound Document	0.9996	0.9999	0.9994	0.9997
Office Compound Document and Open XML Document	**0.9905**	**0.9848**	**0.9964**	**0.9906**

We found that when the length of word sequence varies from 20,000 to 300,000, the detection effect of NFDD varies little. To obtain the best results, we set the length to 200,000 in the experiments. In terms of performance, we randomly selected 100 samples for testing. The ratio of malicious samples to benign samples was 1:1. When the length of the word sequence changes from 200,000 to 20,000, the data preprocessing speed has changed from 287.43 ms/sample to 146.22 ms/sample, and the detection speed has changed from 37.52 ms/sample to 18.67 ms/sample. The detection accuracy fluctuates between 98% and 100%.

5 Conclusion

In this paper, in view of the limitations of the manual feature dictionary of traditional methods, we propose a method that combines CNN and dynamic analysis to detect maldocs, and designed a corresponding update mechanism. The main process includes obtaining reports, report preprocessing, word embedding, and CNN model training. Finally, we implemented the NFDD model that can detect Office compound documents and Open XML documents. The experimental results show that NFDD achieves good results in all four evaluation indicators, which is better than the traditional methods based on feature dictionary. We designed a simple data preprocessing method, which reduces the research threshold. Any researcher can easily reproduce our experiments for scientific research tasks or comparative experiments.

Acknowledgment. This work is supported by Youth Innovation Promotion Association CAS (No. 2021155).

References

1. SonicWall: 2020 sonicwall cyber threat report (2020). https://www.sonicwall.com/news/sonicwalls-mid-year-cyber-threat-report
2. Laskov, P., Šrndić, N.: Static detection of malicious Javascript-bearing pdf documents. In: Proceedings of the 27th Annual Computer Security Applications Conference, pp. 373–382 (2011)

3. Lin, J.Y., Pao, H.K.: Multi-view malicious document detection. In: 2013 Conference on Technologies and Applications of Artificial Intelligence, pp. 170–175. IEEE (2013)
4. Lu, X., Wang, F., Shu, Z.: Malicious word document detection based on multi-view features learning. In: 2019 28th International Conference on Computer Communication and Networks (ICCCN), pp. 1–6. IEEE (2019)
5. Maiorca, D., Giacinto, G., Corona, I.: A pattern recognition system for malicious pdf files detection. In: Perner, P. (ed.) MLDM 2012. LNCS (LNAI), vol. 7376, pp. 510–524. Springer, Heidelberg (2012). https://doi.org/10.1007/978-3-642-31537-4_40
6. Šrndic, N., Laskov, P.: Detection of malicious pdf files based on hierarchical document structure. In: Proceedings of the 20th Annual Network & Distributed System Security Symposium, pp. 1–16. Citeseer (2013)
7. Nissim, N., Cohen, A., Elovici, Y.: Aldocx: detection of unknown malicious microsoft office documents using designated active learning methods based on new structural feature extraction methodology. IEEE Trans. Inf. Forensics Secur. **12**(3), 631–646 (2016)
8. Shafiq, M.Z., Khayam, S.A., Farooq, M.: Embedded malware detection using Markov n-Grams. In: Zamboni, D. (ed.) DIMVA 2008. LNCS, vol. 5137, pp. 88–107. Springer, Heidelberg (2008). https://doi.org/10.1007/978-3-540-70542-0_5
9. Gao, Y.X., Qi, D.Y.: Analyze and detect malicious code for compound document binary storage format. In: 2011 International Conference on Machine Learning and Cybernetics, vol. 2, pp. 593–596. IEEE (2011)
10. Gu, B., Fang, Y., Jia, P., Liu, L., Zhang, L., Wang, M.: A new static detection method of malicious document based on wavelet package analysis. In: 2015 International Conference on Intelligent Information Hiding and Multimedia Signal Processing (IIH-MSP), pp. 333–336. IEEE (2015)
11. Liu, L., He, X., Liu, L., Qing, L., Fang, Y., Liu, J.: Capturing the symptoms of malicious code in electronic documents by file's entropy signal combined with machine learning. Appl. Soft Comput. **82**, 105598 (2019)
12. Smutz, C., Stavrou, A.: Malicious pdf detection using metadata and structural features. In: Proceedings of the 28th Annual Computer Security Applications Conference, pp. 239–248 (2012)
13. Liu, D., Wang, H., Stavrou, A.: Detecting malicious Javascript in pdf through document instrumentation. In: 2014 44th Annual IEEE/IFIP International Conference on Dependable Systems and Networks, pp. 100–111. IEEE (2014)
14. Xu, M., Kim, T.: Platpal: detecting malicious documents with platform diversity. In: 26th {USENIX} Security Symposium, pp. 271–287 (2017)
15. Yagemann, C., Sultana, S., Chen, L., Lee, W.: *Barnum*: detecting document malware via control flow anomalies in hardware traces. In: Lin, Z., Papamanthou, C., Polychronakis, M. (eds.) ISC 2019. LNCS, vol. 11723, pp. 341–359. Springer, Cham (2019). https://doi.org/10.1007/978-3-030-30215-3_17
16. Polychronakis, M., Anagnostakis, K.G., Markatos, E.P.: Comprehensive shellcode detection using runtime heuristics. In: Proceedings of the 26th Annual Computer Security Applications Conference, pp. 287–296 (2010)
17. Snow, K.Z., Krishnan, S., Monrose, F., Provos, N.: Shellos: enabling fast detection and forensic analysis of code injection attacks. In: USENIX Security Symposium, pp. 183–200 (2011)
18. Tzermias, Z., Sykiotakis, G., Polychronakis, M., Markatos, E.P.: Combining static and dynamic analysis for the detection of malicious documents. In: Proceedings of the Fourth European Workshop on System Security, pp. 1–6 (2011)

19. Schreck, T., Berger, S., Göbel, J.: BISSAM: automatic vulnerability identification of office documents. In: Flegel, U., Markatos, E., Robertson, W. (eds.) DIMVA 2012. LNCS, vol. 7591, pp. 204–213. Springer, Heidelberg (2013). https://doi.org/10.1007/978-3-642-37300-8_12

20. Lu, X., Zhuge, J., Wang, R., Cao, Y., Chen, Y.: De-obfuscation and detection of malicious pdf files with high accuracy. In: 2013 46th Hawaii International Conference on System Sciences, pp. 4890–4899. IEEE (2013)

21. Iwamoto, K., Wasaki, K.: A method for shellcode extractionfrom malicious document files using entropy and emulation. Int. J. Eng. Technol. **8**(2), 101 (2016)

22. Xu, W., Qi, Y., Evans, D.: Automatically evading classifiers: a case study on pdf malware classifiers. In: NDSS (2016)

23. Šrndıć, N., Laskov, P.: Hidost: a static machine-learning-based detector of malicious files. EURASIP J. Inf. Secur. **2016**(1), 22 (2016)

24. Cuckoo: Cuckoo sandbox book (2020). https://cuckoo.sh/docs/index.html

25. Zhang, Z., Qi, P., Wang, W.: Dynamic malware analysis with feature engineering and feature learning. In: Proceedings of the AAAI Conference on Artificial Intelligence, vol. 34, pp. 1210–1217 (2020)

26. Willems, C., Holz, T., Freiling, F.: Toward automated dynamic malware analysis using cwsandbox. IEEE Secur. Priv. **5**(2), 32–39 (2007)

27. Scofield, D., Miles, C., Kuhn, S.: Automated model learning for accurate detection of malicious digital documents. Digital Threats: Res. Pract. **1**(3), 1–21 (2020)

28. Zhang, Y., Wallace, B.: A sensitivity analysis of (and practitioners' guide to) convolutional neural networks for sentence classification. arXiv preprint arXiv:1510.03820 (2015)

29. Virusshare (2019). https://virusshare.com/

Bug Triage Model Considering Cooperative and Sequential Relationship

Xu Yu[1], Fayang Wan[1], Junwei Du[1], Feng Jiang[1], Lantian Guo[2], and Junyu Lin[3(✉)]

[1] College of Information Science and Technology, Qingdao University of Science and Technology, Qingdao 266061, China
[2] College of Automation and Electronic Engineering, Qingdao University of Science and Technology, Qingdao 266061, China
[3] Institute of Information Engineering, CAS, Beijing 100093, China
linjunyu@iie.ac.cn

Abstract. Faced with a large number of bugs in the process of software development and maintenance, the existing bug triage method assigns appropriate fixers to the bug by analyzing the text content of the bug report or relationship network. However, the bug repair is a cooperative process with sequential relationship. The tracking system records bugs successively according to the time, which indicates the dynamic changes of the tracking system. In addition to fixers, reviewers, products and components also play an important role in bug triage. Previous studies have often overlooked the sequential and cooperative relationship in the repair process, and the result of bug triage is not ideal. In this paper, we propose a bug triage model considering cooperative and sequential relationship (BTCSR). Firstly, the similar historical reports are determined by analyzing the text content of the bug report. Secondly, considering the cooperative relationship in the bug tracking system, we construct a heterogeneous bug collaborative network that includes bug reports, fixers, products, components, and reviewers. The time decay function is set up in the network to preserve the sequential connection of nodes. We map different types of nodes to the same space, and generate node representations that retain the cooperative and sequential relationship. Finally, the similarity degree between fixers and bugs are quantified by node representations, and the recommended fixer list is obtained. We conduct extensive comparative experiments on four open source software projects, and the results show that BTCSR has obvious advantages in recall rates, so BTCSR is effective.

Keywords: Collaboration relationship · Sequential relationship · Bug cooperative network · Network embedding

1 Introduction

Due to the increasing complexity and diversity of modern software engineering, a large number of bugs inevitably occur in the process of software development and maintenance. In order to prolong the software life cycle and reduce the maintenance cost, large

© Springer Nature Switzerland AG 2021
Z. Liu et al. (Eds.): WASA 2021, LNCS 12938, pp. 160–172, 2021.
https://doi.org/10.1007/978-3-030-86130-8_13

open source software projects such as Apache, eclipse and Mozilla adopt bug tracking system to manage, supervise, submission, repair and verification.

Bugs are submitted to the tracking system in the form of bug report. The administrator selects the appropriate fixer according to the content of the report and his own historical experience. This process of appointing a professional fixer for bug report is called bug triage. However, in the face of a huge bug tracking system, how to bug triage efficiently is a serious challenge. For Eclipse, about 100 newly submitted bug reports can be received every day; meanwhile, there are about 1800 developers including fixers and reviewers. Faced with such a large number of bugs and developers, it is difficult to allocate human resources.

In order to improve the efficiency of software engineering and reduce the fix time, John et al. [1] proposed an automatic bug triage technology, which allocates bugs to the most skilled fixers by learning historical data. Literatures [1, 2] mapped bug reports to representation space of terms, and calculated the affinity between bugs and fixers according to term features. Literatures [3, 4] uses the topic model to generate the topic distribution of bug reports to express the similarity between the fixer and different bug reports. The literatures [5–8] builds networks based on the relationships existing in the bug tracking system, such as tossing graphs, social networks, etc., to further improve the results of bug triage.

Fig. 1. Example of bug report

However, previous methods often ignore the cooperative and sequential relationship in the bug tracking system. Firstly, this relationship exists between bug reports, fixers, reviewers, products, and components. In addition to the only fixer, there are product and component affected by the bug. Reviewers put forward their personal views on the repair of the bug. Fixers, reviewers, products, and components repeatedly appear in different bug reports, implementing the entire system to form a complex cooperative relationship. Therefore, it is not comprehensive to consider only the fixer for bug triage. Secondly, the system records the bugs in time sequence, which is a dynamic process. Considering the network as a static "snapshot" at a certain point in time, it is impossible to measure the change of tracking system over time. Therefore, it is important to measure the impact of current activity on the results.

414035	PDE	Doc	Michael_Rennie	VERI	FIXE	2013-09-05
410151	PDE	API Tool	Michael_Rennie	VERI	FIXE	2013-09-06
416691	Platform	Debug	Michael_Rennie	RESO	FIXE	2013-09-06
415597	PDE	API Tool	Michael_Rennie	VERI	FIXE	2013-09-11
410069	JSDT	Debug	Michael_Rennie	RESO	FIXE	2013-09-11
329294	JDT	Debug	Michael_Rennie	RESO	FIXE	2013-09-11
414482	Platform	Debug	Michael_Rennie	RESO	WONT	2013-09-11
399318	JDT	Debug	Michael_Rennie	RESO	FIXE	2013-09-12
415596	PDE	API Tool	Michael_Rennie	RESO	FIXE	2013-09-16
414483	JDT	Debug	Michael_Rennie	RESO	WONT	2013-09-16
409428	PDE	API Tool	Michael_Rennie	RESO	FIXE	2013-09-18
414212	Platform	Debug	Michael_Rennie	RESO	FIXE	2013-09-18
389736	Platform	Ant	Michael_Rennie	RESO	FIXE	2013-09-26
170898	Platform	Ant	Michael_Rennie	RESO	FIXE	2013-09-26
215530	Platform	Ant	Michael_Rennie	VERI	FIXE	2013-09-26
248591	PDE	API Tool	Michael_Rennie	RESO	FIXE	2013-10-02
417603	PDE	API Tool	Michael_Rennie	RESO	FIXE	2013-10-10
406990	PDE	API Tool	Michael_Rennie	VERI	FIXE	2013-10-13
419281	JSDT	Debug	Michael_Rennie	RESO	FIXE	2013-10-15
419316	JDT	Debug	Michael_Rennie	RESO	FIXE	2013-10-15
417958	Orion	Doc	Michael_Rennie	RESO	FIXE	2013-10-21
387142	Orion	Client	Michael_Rennie	RESO	FIXE	2013-10-24

437770	Orion	Git	Michael_Rennie	CLOS	DUPL	2014-09-02
441831	Orion	JS Tools	Michael_Rennie	RESO	FIXE	2014-09-05
441478	Orion	Editor	Michael_Rennie	VERI	FIXE	2014-09-05
400232	Orion	Client	Michael_Rennie	RESO	FIXE	2014-09-09
443521	Orion	JS Tools	Michael_Rennie	RESO	FIXE	2014-09-12
444001	Orion	JS Tools	Michael_Rennie	RESO	FIXE	2014-09-15
438432	PDE	API Tool	Michael_Rennie	VERI	FIXE	2014-09-17
442627	JDT	Debug	Michael_Rennie	VERI	FIXE	2014-09-17
443023	Platform	Debug	Michael_Rennie	VERI	FIXE	2014-09-17
418473	JDT	Debug	Michael_Rennie	VERI	FIXE	2014-09-18
444885	Orion	JS Tools	Michael_Rennie	RESO	FIXE	2014-09-30
426733	Orion	JS Tools	Michael_Rennie	RESO	FIXE	2014-09-30
426486	Orion	JS Tools	Michael_Rennie	RESO	FIXE	2014-10-02
445894	Orion	JS Tools	Michael_Rennie	RESO	FIXE	2014-10-03
447189	Orion	JS Tools	Michael_Rennie	RESO	FIXE	2014-10-14
426723	Orion	JS Tools	Michael_Rennie	RESO	FIXE	2014-10-15
447454	Orion	JS Tools	Michael_Rennie	RESO	FIXE	2014-10-15
444973	Platform	Debug	Michael_Rennie	VERI	FIXE	2014-10-16
447595	Orion	Client	Michael_Rennie	RESO	FIXE	2014-10-16
232709	JDT	Debug	Michael_Rennie	RESO	FIXE	2014-10-20
439272	Orion	Client	Michael_Rennie	RESO	FIXE	2014-10-22
448540	Orion	JS Tools	Michael_Rennie	RESO	FIXE	2014-10-23

Fig. 2. Fix records of Michael Rennie at different times

Figure 1 shows an example of a bug report in Eclipse. In the bug report with ID 475576, in addition to the only fixer "Donat Csikos", 5 reviewers submitted 11 comments to express their suggestions for bug repair. After the bug occurred, it has an impact on the product "Buildship" and component "General". This forming a complex cooperative relationship. Figure 2 shows the fix records of Michael Rennie at different times. It can be found that the repair bias of products has changed with time. From September to November 2013, Michael was mainly involved in the bug repair work of PDE and platform. It is different from one year ago, from September to November 2014, Michael is mainly involved in the bug repair work of Orion.

Based on the above analysis, this paper proposes a Bug Triage model considering Cooperation and Sequential Relationship (BTCSR). The model consists of two parts, content based analysis and sequential relationship based cooperative network embedding. In the content based analysis, when faced with a new bug report, this paper extracts term features and topic features from the summary and description in the content, and searches for similar historical bug reports. In the sequential relationship based cooperative network embedding, According to relationship between fixers, reviewers, products, and components in bug tracking system, We establish a heterogeneous bug cooperative network, and set up four different types of meta paths considering sequence. Node representations preserving sequence and cooperation are generated by network embedding. According to the representation similarity between historical similarity reports and fixers, professional fixers are assigned for bugs.

The main contributions of this paper are as follows:

1. Based on the text content, we consider the cooperation among bug reports, fixers, products, components and reviewers to construct heterogeneous bug cooperative network. The combination of them is applied to bug triage to make the result more accurate.
2. For the dynamic bug tracking system, we set the time decay function to preserve the sequential relationship of the nodes in the network, generate a sequence that conforms to the actual repair process, and capture the dynamic changes in the system. We map different types of node representations to the same space.

2   Related Work

Aiming at the problem of automatic bug triage, according to the methods used, the existing research can be divided into text classification and information retrieval, The method of text classification is to treat the fixer as a label, and match the fixer based on the text characteristics in the bug report. The method of information retrieval is to calculate the similarity between bug reports, and then assign the appropriate fixers according to the historical activities participated. According to the use category of information, the existing research can be divided into text content based methods and network based methods. For the text content of bug reports, existing methods quantify term feature from the summary [1, 2] and topic features from description [3, 4]. In addition, more and more researchers begin to pay attention to the relationship in bug tracking system, and constructed network to assign fixers [5–8].

Anvik et al. [1] proposed using a text classification method for bug triage, and tried to use a support representation machine to complete this work. Xi et al. [8] used a bidirectional recurrent neural network to classify bug reports. Cubranic et al. [9] used Naive Bayes to find suitable fixers for bug. Tian et al. [10] proposed an information retrieval method based on the ranking model learning to rank to recommend suitable fixers. Xia et al. [11] proposed a composite method to quantify the affinity between bug report and fixers through the analysis of historical data.

As the main description of the bug, the text content is widely used in previous models. Tamrawi et al. [2] proposed a Bugzie method based on fuzzy sets, which caches the most descriptive terms of each developer to measure. Xia et al. [3] used topic model LDA of supervision to represent the document by a distribution under different topics. Naguib et al. [4] quantified the similarity between bug reports and fixers in the topic space. At present, more and more researchers pay attention to the influence of the network in bug tracking system. Jeong et al. [5] used Markov chains to construct a fixers tossing graph. Based on the work of Jeong, Pamela et al. [6] integrated a multi-feature sorting function into the tossing graph to improve the accuracy of assignment. Xuan et al. [7] constructed a social network based on the interactive activities of the fixer, Combined with classification method to generate prediction list.

3   The BTCSR Model

BTCSR is composed of two parts: content based analysis and sequential relationship-based cooperative network embedding.Firstly, Content based analysis is used to mine term features and topic features to search for similar historical bug reports. Secondly, sequential relationship based cooperative network embedding is constructed a heterogeneous bug cooperative network. Model generate the node representations $X \in R^{|V| \times d}, d \ll |V|$. Finally, according to different types of representation similarity to achieve bug triage. Figure 3 shows the BTCSR model structure.

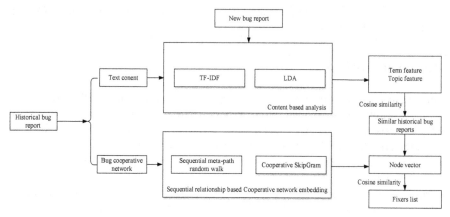

Fig. 3. BTCSR model structure

3.1 Content Based Analysis

In order to search for historical reports that are similar to the new bug report, Content based analysis uses the summary and description in the bug report to generate term features and topic features respectively. The similarity between the new bug report and the historical bug reports is measured according to the cosine similarity.

Bug report. Bug report generally consists of two parts, meta-fields and text content. The specific composition and meaning of the two parts are shown in Table 1.

Table 1. Specific composition and meaning of the bug report

	composition	meaning
Meta-fields	status	Current repair progress of bug
	product	The bug will affect the product when it occurs
	component	The bug will affect the component when it occurs
	fixer	Complete the fix of bug
	submission time	The system records when the bug report is submitted
	fix time	The system records when the fixer submits the solution
Text content	summary	A brief introduction to bug, which is convenient for developers to find bug
	description	The specific introduction of bug, including error prompts, causes and other factors
	reviewer	Participate in bug repair work
	review	Bug repair suggestions filled in by reviewer
	review time	The system records when the reviewer submits review

TF-IDF. The information retrieval model TF-IDF is used to evaluate the importance of words in the corpus. The method consists of term frequency (TF) and inverse document frequency (IDF):

$$TF - IDF(i,j) = TF \cdot IDF = tf(i,j) \cdot \log \frac{|A|}{|A(i)|} \tag{1}$$

$tf(i,j)$ denotes the frequency of a given term i in the bug report j. A is the total number of bug reports in the corpus, and $A(i)$ is the total number of bug reports containing the term i in the corpus.

LDA. Topic model LDA is a generation model with three-layer structure: word, topic and bug report. The probability model shown in the figure above is as follows:

$$p(D|\alpha, \beta) = \prod_{j=1}^{J} \int p(Hj|\alpha)(\prod_{n} \sum_{Zjn} p(Zjn|Hj)p(Wjn|Zjn, \beta))dHj \tag{2}$$

In the topic model, two important parameters are the topic probability distribution H_j of bug and the word probability distribution β under each topic. Parameter estimation can be regarded as the inverse process of the generation process: when the document set is known, the two parameters are learned by Gibbs sampling iteration.

In this paper, we focus on the summary and description in bug report. After stemming and removing stop words, TF-IDF is used to generate the term feature $W_j = (w_1, w_2, w_3, \ldots, w_q)$ for the summary, where w_i represents the TF-IDF value of the i-th term in a bug report; LDA is used to generate the topic feature $H_j = (h_1, h_2, h_3, \ldots, h_p)$ for the description, where h_i represents LDA value of the i-th topic in a bug report. In order to query the historical bug similar to the new bug, we combine the term feature and the topic feature, According to the cosine similarity of features.

$$Sim(Y1, Y2) = \cos(Y1, Y2) = \frac{Y1 \cdot Y2}{||Y1|| ||Y2||} \tag{3}$$

Where Y_1 and Y_2 represent the text features of two different bug reports respectively.

3.2 Sequential Relationship Based Cooperative Network Embedding

Bug Cooperative Network. Heterogeneous network [10] is defined as $G = (V, E, T)$, and each node and edge corresponds to the mapping function $\phi(v):V \to T_V$ and $\varphi(e):E \to T_E$, T_V and T_E respectively represent the node type set and the relationship type set, $|T_V| + |T_E| > 2$. We use a heterogeneous network to represent the relationships that exist in the bug tracking system, and thus constructs a bug cooperative network, as shown in Fig. 4 We defines five node types: B (bug), F (fixer), P (product), C (component), R (reviewer). Four relationship types: Bug-Product (B-P) indicates that the bug affects this product, Bug-Component (B-C) indicates that the bug affects this component, Bug-Fixer (B-F) indicates that the fixer repairs the bug, and Bug-Reviewer (B-R) indicates that the reviewer comments on the bug.

Meta-path composes the relations between different types of nodes to form seman-tics[15]. According to the elements τ_{vi} in node type set T_V and elements τ_{ei} in relation-ship type set T_E, meta-path is defined as: $\rho = \tau v1 \xrightarrow{\tau e1} \tau v2 \xrightarrow{\tau e2} \cdots \xrightarrow{\tau el-1} \tau vl$.According to the relationship existing in the bug cooperation network, four kinds of meta-paths are set up in this paper, bug-reviewer-bug (*BRB*) indicates that the bug is reviewed by the same reviewer, bug-fixer-bug (*BFB*) indicates that the bug is repaired by the same fixer, bug-product-bug (*BPB*) refers to the bug affecting the same product, bug-component-bug (*BCB*) refers to the bug affecting the same component.

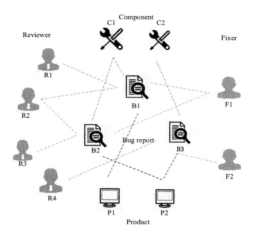

Fig. 4. Bug cooperative network

Sequential Meta-Path Random Walk. In order to realize the generation of network to node representations, it is necessary to realize the transformation from network to sequences [12–18]. In this paper, sequential meta-path random walk is used to generate node sequences preserving connection order and semantic information.

For a given bug cooperative network $G = (V,E,T)$, We use meta-path ρ to distinguish the types of nodes to select adjacent nodes, and then start from this adjacent node to the next node, until the sequence arrives Pre-defined length. We set a total of 4 different meta-paths: *BFB, BCB, BPB, BRB*. Explore the semantics between fixers, products, components, reviewers, and bug reports.

Firstly, it is necessary to integrate the time factor into the edge of the network. The submission time represents the time when the bug affects the product and component, and it is marked the edge between bug report and product and component. The fix time of the bug report represents the time when the fixer submits the solution, and it is marked the edge between bug report and fixer. The review time of the bug report represents the time when the reviewer participated in bug repair, and it is marked on the edge between the bug report and reviewer. The edge of the network can be expressed as (v_i,v_{i+1},t_i).

Secondly, the time factor is used to restrict the walk rule. In any pair of continuous edge pairs (v_i,v_{i+1},t_i) and $(v_{i+1}, v_{i+2},t_{i+1})$ in the sequence, $t_i \leq t_{i+1}$. As much as possible to generate a sequence that is consistent with the actual fix process, the walk rules should also ensure that the time interval t_{i+1}-t_i is as small as possible, In this paper, the monotone decreasing time decay function $\Gamma(t_{i+1}$-$t_i)$ is used to guide the sequence to select adjacent nodes close to the current time t_i, The function is defined as follows:

$$\Gamma(ti + 1 - ti) = \frac{1}{\sigma\sqrt{2\pi}} \exp\left(\frac{-(ti+1 - ti)^2}{2\sigma^2}\right) \tag{4}$$

The selection of adjacent nodes combines the meta-path ρ and the time decay function. Then the transition probability of node v_i at time t_i is defined as follows:

$$P(vi+1|vi, \rho, ti) = \begin{cases} \frac{\Gamma(ti+1-ti)}{\sum_{ti+1' \in Nt(\tau vi+1)} \Gamma(ti+1'-ti)} & (vi,vi+1) \in E, \phi(vi+1) = \tau vi+1, ti \le ti + 1 \\ 0 & (vi,vi+1) \in E, \phi(vi+1) = \tau vi+1, ti \ge ti+1 \\ 0 & (vi,vi+1) \in E, \phi(vi+1) \ne \tau vi+1 \\ 0 & (vi,vi+1) \notin E \end{cases} \tag{5}$$

When the node v_i of the sequence at t_i transfers to the v_{i+1}-th node, The type of current node v_i belongs to τ_{vi}, According to the meta-path, the adjacent node v_{i+1} conforming to the type τ_{vi+1}, $Nt(\tau_{vi+1})$ represents the time set of adjacent nodes of the current node that conforms to the type τ_{vi+1}, and $t_i \le t_{i+1}$.

We generate four types of node sequences that retain connection order of nodes and semantic information in the network. Explore the relationship between bug report and affected product, relationship between bug report and affected component, the relationship between the fixer and bug report, and the relationship between reviewer and bug report. For example, $B1$ and $F1$. There is a relationship between bug reports of the same product, component, fixer, and reviewer, for example: $B1$ and $B2$.

Cooperative SkipGram. In order to convert the connection order and semantic information in the sequence into node representations $X \in R^{|V| \times d}$, $d \ll |V|$ that characterizes the cooperative and sequential relationship. We use cooperative SkipGram to process the node sequences. In order to realize the embedding of the node, the objective function is expressed as maximizing the conditional probability $p(c_\tau|v,\theta)$ of the current node v to generate the neighbor node c_τ on the set of all nodes T_V:

$$O(X) = \arg\max_\theta \sum_{v \in V} \sum_{\tau \in TV} \sum_{c\tau \in N\tau(v)} \log p(c\tau|v, \theta) \tag{6}$$

Where $N\tau(v)$ is the neighbor nodes of type τ of current node v in the sequence.

$$p(c\tau|v,\theta) = \frac{e^{Xc\tau \cdot Xv}}{\sum_{u \in V} e^{Xu \cdot Xv}} \tag{7}$$

Where the probability of nodes becoming neighbors are represented by Softmax, Xv corresponding to representation of the current node v, and Xc_τ corresponding to representation of the neighbor node c_τ.

4 Experiment

4.1 Data Sets

Data sets used is the bug report collection of open source projects in tracking system. In order to obtain the most effective bug reports, we limit the submission time of bug reports to at least four years ago and collection of bug reports with confirmed fix (solution is fixed, the report status is closed, solved or verified). In order to reduce noise, delete fixers who participated less than 10 times and a large number of invalid people (such as Project-inbox, Platform-UI-Inbox, such names may do not represent real fixers). After screening, the bug report data statistics are as follows: (Table 2).

Table 2. Bug report data statistics

project	time	Bug report	Fixer	Product	Component	Reviewer
Eclipse	2014.12.20-2016.1.5	14297	679	159	475	2287
Mozilla	2014.12.20-2016.1.5	10514	551	57	404	1947
Netbeans	2014.12.20-2016.1.5	11047	234	40	346	789
GCC	2014.12.20-2016.1.5	2287	145	2	40	351

4.2 Metrics

In order to evaluate the recommendation accuracy of experimental results, Recall@K is used in this paper This kind of metrics has been widely used in previous related work [1, 3, 4], and the calculation formula is as follows:

$$\text{Recall}@K = \frac{1}{s} \sum_{i=1}^{s} \frac{|Pi \cap Di|}{|Di|} \tag{8}$$

Suppose there are s bug reports to be assigned. For each bug report, D_i is the set of actually fixer, P_i is the set of fixers assigned by the model. K is the size of the assigned fixer set, where $K = 3,5,10$.

4.3 Experimental Setup and Experimental Results

In order to simulate the actual use of the model, the bug reports are sorted in chronological order. 80% of the bug reports are taken as the training set and 20% of the bug reports are taken as the test set.

In this paper, we set up three methods as comparative experiments:

SVM [1] uses support vector machine to complete the classic method of bug report text classification.

MTM [3] updates the proportion of each topic under the current meta-field according to the topic of bug report, so as to obtain better topic distribution by monitoring.

DeepTriage [8] combines the bug report text with the fixer's activity sequence by recurrent neural network to assign fixers.

In the BTCSR, the implementation of content analysis uses the open source Python toolkit gensim. The number of topics m is set to 50, and the LDA hyperparameter α is set to $50/m$, $\beta = 0.01$. In the sequential relationship based cooperative network embedding, the parameter σ in the time decay function is set to 15, the number of walks g of each node is 20, the length of L is 80, the window size n of neighbors is set to 5, the dimension d is 128, and the model iterations are 100 times. Finally, the similar historical defect report k is 15 in the search content.

As shown in Table 3, We verify the effectiveness of the model on 4 different data sets, the model in this paper is better than others.

Table 3. BTCSR and comparative experiment results

	Model	Eclipse	Mozilla	Netbeans	GCC	Average
Recall@3	BTCSR	60.74%	41.78%	56.74%	45.81%	51.26%
	SVM	47.37%	39.74%	47.78%	37.13%	43.01%
	MTM	46.27%	35.32%	42.54%	36.67%	40.20%
	DeepTriage	52.14%	38.14%	49.74%	44.74%	46.19%
Recall@5	BTCSR	71.48%	56.15%	68.24%	57.14%	63.25%
	SVM	59.62%	47.45%	58.45%	45.14%	52.66%
	MTM	54.01%	40.34%	49.64%	41.57%	46.39%
	DeepTriage	62.39%	48.46%	57.79%	52.51%	55.28%
Recall@10	BTCSR	81.31%	65.97%	80.84%	68.47%	74.14%
	SVM	68.62%	53.75%	65.67%	52.78%	60.21%
	MTM	64.34%	51.36%	63.14%	49.57%	57.10%
	DeepTriage	73.63%	57.47%	70.54%	57.17%	64.70%

4.4 Analysis of the Effectiveness of Cooperative and Sequential Relationships

In order to verify the effectiveness of the cooperative and sequential relationship, Split the BTCSR model into two sub-models: BTC (Bug Triage model considering Content), BTCR (Bug Triage model considering cooperative Relationship), the results are shown in Table 4. BTCSR has obvious advantages over BTC and BTCR.

4.5 Parameter Sensitivity Analysis

The parameter settings in the experiment have an important influence on the results, so the model parameters are tested for sensitivity. Including the number of topics m, the

Table 4. BTCSR and sub-models comparative results

	Model	Eclipse	Mozilla	Netbeans	GCC	Average
Recall@3	BTCSR	60.74%	41.78%	56.74%	45.81%	51.26%
	BTC	40.17%	30.11%	38.75%	30.15%	34.79%
	BTCR	54.87%	40.61%	46.99%	38.17%	45.16%
Recall@5	BTCSR	71.48%	56.15%	68.24%	57.14%	63.25%
	BTC	48.14%	35.15%	44.57%	36.24%	41.02%
	BTCR	60.14%	49.14%	55.17%	48.34%	53.19%
Recall@10	BTCSR	81.31%	65.97%	80.84%	68.47%	74.14%
	BTC	58.75%	45.15%	57.94%	45.64%	51.87%
	BTCR	68.15%	58.14%	68.24%	53.14%	61.91%

representation dimension d, the number of node walks g, the window size of neighbors n, the sequence length L, and similar bug Reports number k. We calculates the average recall@K analysis parameter sensitivity. As shown in Fig. 5, the experimental results tend to flatten after a short period of fluctuation with parameter changes.

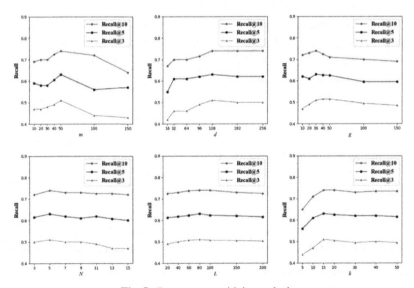

Fig. 5. Parameter sensitivity analysis

5   Conclusion

In this paper, we propose a bug triage model BTCSR, which considers the cooperative and sequential relationship. Firstly, the model analyzes the text content of the bug report.Secondly, it uses heterogeneous network embedding to generate node representations that retain the cooperative and sequential relationship. According to the similarity between representations, the fixers can be recommended. This method, which considers cooperative and sequential relationship. In the future, we will consider the reviewer's comment information, the integration of text and network, and the influence weight of different meta-paths to further improve the performance of the model.

Acknowledgments. This work is sponsored by the National Natural Science Foundation of China (Nos. 61402246, 61872104), and the Natural Science Foundation of Shandong Province (ZR2019MF014).

References

1. John, A., Lyndon, H., Gail C.M.: Who should fix this bug? In: 28th International Conference on Software Engineering, pp. 361–370 (2006)
2. Nguyen, T., Kofahi, J., Nguyen, T.: Fuzzy set and cache-based approach for bug triaging. In: ESEC/FSE (2011)
3. Xia, X., Lo, D., Ding, Y., et al.: Improving automated bug triaging with specialized topic model. IEEE Trans. Softw. Eng. 272–297 (2017)
4. Naguib, H., Narayan, N., Brügge, B., et al.: Bug report assignee recommendation using activity profiles. In: Proc. of the Mining Software Repositories, pp. 22–30(2013)
5. Jeong, G., Kim, S., Zimmermann, T.: Improving bug triage with bug tossing graphs. In: 7th Joint Meeting of the European Software Engineering Conference and the Acm Sigsoft Symposium on the Foundations of Software Engineering, pp. 111–120 (2009)
6. Bhattacharya, P., Neamtiu, I.: Fine-grained incremental learning and multi-feature tossing graphs to improve bug triaging. In: Proceedings of 26th IEEE International Conference on Software Maintenance, Timisoara, pp. 1–10 (2010)
7. Xuan, J., Jiang, H., Ren, Z., et al.: Developer prioritization in bug repositories. In: 34th International Conference on Software Engineering, pp. 25–35 (2012)
8. Xi, S., Yao, Y., Xu, F., et al.: Bug triage based on recurrent neural network. J. Softw. 2322–2335 (2018)
9. Čubranić, D., Murphy, G.C.: Automatic bug triage using text categorization. In: Proceedings of the 16th Int'l Conference on Software Engineering and Knowledge Engineering. DBLP, pp. 92–97 (2004)
10. Tian, Y., Wijedasa, D., Lo, D., et al.: Learning to rank for bug report assignee recommendation. IEEE International Conference on Program Comprehension, pp. 1–10 (2016)
11. Xia, X., Lo, D., Wang, X., et al. Dual analysis for recommending developers to resolve bugs. J. Softw. Evol. Proc. 3–27 (2015)
12. Perozzi, B., Al-Rfou, R., Skiena, S.: Deepwalk: online learning of social representations. In: 20th ACM SIGKDD International Conference on Knowledge Discovery and Data Mining, pp. 701–710 (2014)
13. Jian, T., Meng, Q., Wang, M., et al.: LINE: large-scale information network embedding. In: 24th International World Wide Web Conferences, pp. 978–1–4503 (2015)
14. Aditya, G., Jure, L.: Node2Vec: scalable feature learning for networks. In: 22th ACM SIGKDD International Conference on Knowledge Discovery and Data Mining, pp. 855–864 (2016)
15. Dong, Y., Chawla, N.V., Swami, A.: Metapath2vec: scalable representation learning for heterogeneous networks. In: 23rd ACM SIGKDD International Conference on Knowledge Discovery and Data Mining, pp. 135–144 (2017)

16. Li, Y., Chen, W., Yan, H.F., et al.: Personalized product recommendation based on Web-based representation learning. Chin. J. Comput. **42**(08), 1767–1778 (2019)
17. Chen, T., Sun, Y.: Task-guided and path-augmented heterogeneous network embedding for author identification, In: The 10th ACM International Conference on Web Search and Data Mining. Cambridge, pp. 295-304 (2017)
18. Shi, C., Hu, B., Zhao, W.X., et al.: Heterogeneous information network embedding for recommendation. IEEE Trans. Knowl. Data Eng. 357–370 (2017)

Adaptive Chosen Plaintext Side-Channel Attacks for Higher-Order Masking Schemes

Yanbin Li[1,2], Yuxin Huang[1], Ming Tang[2], Shougang Ren[1(✉)], and Huanliang Xu[1]

[1] Nanjing Agricultural University, Nanjing, JiangSu, China
rensg@njau.edu.cn
[2] The State Key Laboratory of AIS and TC, Wuhan, HuBei, China

Abstract. With the wide use of wireless sensor network (WSN), it is very important to ensure the security of wireless devices, especially for the prevention of side channel attacks. Higher-order masking schemes have been proved in theory to be the secure countermeasures against side-channel attacks. When d th-order masking is involved, the complexity of performing a higher-order SCA grows exponentially with the order d, which can be regarded as the main difficulty for the higher-order analysis. Since the plaintext is random in the traditional analysis process, the attack can be successfully carried out but the efficiency is not high. To reduce the number of traces for higher-order analysis, we combine the measurement setup with selecting plaintexts. We first describe an efficient chosen plaintext strategy for the unprotected design, called Adaptive Chosen Plaintext Power Analysis (ACPPA). Moreover, we apply the adaptive chosen plaintext strategy for different combining functions which is more efficient than the existing higher-order attacks. Finally, we finish the experiments to verify the efficiency of our methods in unmasked and masked contexts by success rate, guessing entropy and the number of traces to recover the secret key.

Keywords: SCA · Higher-order analysis · Chosen plaintext · WSN · Higher-order masking

1 Introduction

With the rapid development of electronic information technology, wireless sensor network technology began to appear in people's daily life. In addition, with the continuous improvement of chip production technology, it provides the best era of wireless sensor network. Routing devices, Internet for things devices, intelligent robots need the support of wireless network to achieve better efficiency. At present, wireless sensor network technology has been widely used in military, aviation, anti-terrorism, explosion-proof, disaster relief, environment and other fields. WSN is recognized as one of the four major technology industries in the world in the future, which will set off a new wave of industry. However,

© Springer Nature Switzerland AG 2021
Z. Liu et al. (Eds.): WASA 2021, LNCS 12938, pp. 173–185, 2021.
https://doi.org/10.1007/978-3-030-86130-8_14

as coin has two sides, we can not ignore the security problems in wireless systems. In order to improve the security of wireless network. In 2020, Chunpeng Ge et al. proposed a ciphertext-policy attribute-based mechanism to conduct a quick search and return the result without losing data confidentiality [1]. The proposed method not only supports attribute-based keyword search, but also enables attribute-based data sharing. The author in [2] considered a new security requirement for encryption schemes based on revocable attributes: integrity. They proposed a specific RABE-DI scheme and proved its confidentiality and integrity under the defined security model. The author in [3] proposed a novel architecture to efficiently detect solar photovoltaic (PV) defects and address the uncertainties of PV cell data. What's more, researchers add AES (Advanced Encryption Standard) to CMAC and CCM mode to ensure the security of data transmission and authentication.

AES algorithm is a generation encryption standard issued by National Institute of standards and Technology (NIST) in 2006. At present, as it is difficult to crack it in mathematics and algorithm, AES has become one of the most popular algorithms in symmetric key encryption. However, the physical method(side channel attacks) is a big threat to AES and its higher-order Masking protection.

There were several works aimed at improving the performance of analysis by biasing measurement [4–6]. Kim et al. tried to change the distribution of power consumption for the improvement of Correlation Power Analysis (CPA) [4]. The selection method increased the Signal to Noise Ratio (SNR) [7] of power traces which would be used for attack. However, it abandoned numerous of power traces. The author in [5] proposed a selection method based on Principal Component Analysis (PCA). The power traces were sorted by the first principle component of the noise matrix. The author in [6] selected electromagnetic traces with high singular value based on Singular Value Decomposition (SVD). It improved the efficiency of Correlation Electromagnetic Analysis (CEMA). All the above methods are needed to select traces from a large number of traces measured. However, the workload and difficulty of measurement can not be ignored in the practical attacks.

Selecting the inputs is a powerful method for adversaries in classical cryptanalysis [8–12]. Werner Schindler performed chosen plaintext timing attack against RSA with the secret exponent using Chinese Remainder Theorem or Montgomerys algorithm [13]. It was the first work applied the selecting plaintexts in the context of side channel attacks. To extend the idea of chosen plaintexts to power analysis, N. V eyrat-Charvillon and F.-X. Standaert proposed an adaptive chosen-message method for Template Attacks (TA) [14]. They selected the plaintext to minimize the entropy of the key candidates and decreased the number of traces in the online attack. This method was generalized to CPA through estimating the probabilities of subkey candidates by Pearson coefficients. However, there exists a gap between probability and Pearson coefficient with the unknown variances of signal and noise. Changhai Ou et al. biased traces through computing the Minkowski distance between the power traces and mean trace, which improved the Pearson coefficient during CPA [15]. However, there was almost no chosen plaintext method considering distinguisher in non-profiled context.

Indeed, the plaintexts chosen under different combining functions should be different in the masked scenarios. The widely used attacks against masked implementations are higher-order power attacks based on combining functions [16]. The attacks depend on the correlation between the combined leakages and the sensitive information. It is well known that using combining function to the leakages inevitably leads to a loss of information [17]. For different plaintexts, the correlation coefficients between the sequence of intermediate values and its combined leakages are also different.

In this paper, we propose an adaptive chosen plaintext power analysis (ACPPA). It exploits the values in distinguisher to bias the distribution of power traces, which reduces the number of traces in both the measurement and analysis. Moreover, we expand the strategy to the higher-order power analysis. After analyzing the characteristics of correlation coefficient in higher-order power analysis under different combining functions, a chosen plaintext method has been proposed for different combining functions which can increase their correlation coefficients. The efficiencies of ACPPA on unmasked and masked implementations are proved and verified in this paper.

This paper is organized as follows. We indicate a distinguisher in non-profiling and recall the relationship between SNR and correlation coefficient in Sect. 2. In Sect. 3, we introduce our adaptive chosen plaintext strategies for unmasked and masked design. Based on this, we propose the algorithms of adaptive chosen plaintext attack on unmasked and masked design. Then, experiments are carried out to compare our schemes with the traditional attacks and verified the efficiency of our method in both unprotected implementation and protected implementation. The last Section is the final conclusion.

2   Distinguishers in Non-profiling

In this Section, we recall the DPA-like distinguishers and introduce the relationship between SNR and correlation coefficient.

In DPA-like distinguishers, let $Q = (q_1, q_2, \ldots, q_m)$ be a sequence containing m input plaintexts to a target cryptographic device. The leakage sequence is denoted as $L = (l_1, l_2, \ldots, l_m)$. Each element l_i corresponds to the encryption of an input q_i under key k. For different subkey candidates k^*, the adversary predicts some intermediate values $f(q_i, k^*)$ and mapping them to hypothetical power consumption $h(f(q_i, k^*))$, where f represents the intermediate function and h represents the leakage model. Then, the hypothetical power consumption sequence for k^* can be denoted as $H_{k^*}^m = (h(f(q_1, k^*)), h(f(q_2, k^*)), \ldots, h(f(q_m, k^*)))$.

The existing distinguishers compute the similarity degree between the hypothetical power consumption and physical leakages. Based on this principle, each candidate k^* can be sorted in descending order $r = (k_1^*, k_2^*, \ldots, k_{|K|}^*)$, where $|K|$

represents the key space. With the number of traces increasing, the sequence is refreshed continuously. An adversary uses distinguisher D to recover key as:

$$k = \arg_{k^* \in K} \max \left[D(L, H_{k^*}^m) \right] \tag{1}$$

In the context of a given attack scenario, the power consumption of each interesting point can be modeled as the sum of exploitable power consumption l_{exp} and the noise component l_{noise} [18].

$$l_{total} = l_{exp} + l_{noise} \tag{2}$$

Considering Pearson coefficient as the distinguisher, the correlation between the hypothetical power consumption and physical power traces can be denoted as [18]:

$$
\begin{aligned}
&\rho\left(h, l_{total}\right) \\
&= \rho\left(h, l_{exp} + l_{noise}\right) \\
&= \frac{E\left(h \cdot \left(l_{exp} + l_{noise}\right)\right) - E\left(h\right) \cdot E\left(l_{exp} + l_{noise}\right)}{\sqrt{Var\left(h\right) \cdot \left(Var\left(l_{exp}\right) + Var\left(l_{noise}\right)\right)}} \\
&= \frac{E\left(h \cdot l_{exp} + h \cdot l_{noise}\right) - E\left(h\right) \cdot \left(E\left(l_{exp}\right) + E\left(l_{noise}\right)\right)}{\sqrt{Var\left(h\right) \cdot Var\left(l_{exp}\right)}\sqrt{1 + \frac{Var(l_{noise})}{Var(l_{exp})}}} \\
&= \frac{\rho\left(h, l_{exp}\right)}{\sqrt{1 + \frac{1}{SNR}}}
\end{aligned}
\tag{3}
$$

where $SNR = \frac{Var(l_{exp})}{Var(l_{noise})}$, $E(\cdot)$ denotes the mean value, $Var(\cdot)$ denotes the variance. From the above formula, we know that when the SNR is higher, the correlation coefficient will be higher.

3 Adaptive Chosen Plaintext Power Analysis

The result of selecting plaintext is to bias power traces for SCAs in profiled or non-profiled scenarios, so that the correct key can be distinguishable more quickly. The profiled allows the adversary to choose plaintext according to the probabilities of subkey hypotheses [14]. By contrast, in the case of non-profiled attacks (e.g. DPA [19] or CPA [20]), the best chosen plaintext is not based on probabilities, but on the value produced by a statistical distinguisher (different-of-means and Pearson correlation coefficient, respectively).

In [14], it considered the Hamming weight or Hamming distance as a Gaussian assumption to calculate the probability. However, as computing the integration of leakage distribution for each guessing subkey, it was of high complexity. In this Section, we propose a non-profiled chosen plaintext strategy in the context of CPA with less complexity. Furthermore, we improved it for masked design. Finally, we introduce the algorithms and detailed process of ACPPA.

3.1   Select the Next Plaintext for Unmasked Design

One of the characteristics of correlation coefficient is that the proximity to 1 is related to the number of data. We denote the number as m. When m is small, the absolute value of the correlation coefficient tends to 1. For the original CPA, with the number of traces increasing, the correlation coefficients of subkey candidates decrease from $1(m = 2)$ to smaller values. In particular, the correlation coefficient of correct subkey decreases more slowly, thus it is distinguishable from other candidates. According to Eq. (3), increasing SNR can improve the efficiency of CPA. The variance of noise is decided by the target device and measurement. We don't focus on the noise reduction technologies and the variance of signals can be changed by the following chosen plaintext strategy. Considering the power traces with larger variance of signals during the attack, the correct subkey can be distinguishable earlier than the traditional attacks.

Since the analysis of different subkey bytes is independent, the analysis of one byte is also applicable to all subkey bytes. We assume that an adversary has analyzed i power traces $L = \{l_1, l_2, \ldots, l_m\}$, corresponding to the plaintexts $q_1, \ldots, q_i$. For each subkey candidates k^*, the adversary calculates the hypothetical power consumption sequence $H_{k^*}^i = (h(f(q_1, k^*)), h(f(q_2, k^*)), \ldots, h(f(q_i, k^*)))$, where f represents the intermediate function and h denotes the leakage model. After analyzing i power traces, the correlation coefficients of subkey candidates can be calculated, denoted as ρ_{k^*}. Based on the principle of maximum variance, we use the following strategy to select the next plaintext q_{i+1}

$$q_{i+1} = \arg\max \sum_{k^*} \rho_{k^*} \cdot \sqrt{Var(\tilde{H}_{k^*}^{i+1})} \tag{4}$$

where $\tilde{H}_{k^*}^{i+1} = H_{k^*}^i \cup h(f(q_{i+1}, k^*))$ represents the joint of the new element and the hypothetical power consumption sequence.

The plaintext sets obtained by using Eq. (4) and random selecting are denoted as Q_1 and Q_2, respectively. After analyzing i power traces, the variances of hypothetical power consumption sequences corresponding to correct subkey k are $Var_1(H_k^i), Var_2(H_k^i)$. The number of trace needed to recover subkey are m_1 and m_2, respectively. When performing correlation coefficient power analysis on the $m(m > max(m_1, m_2))$ power traces using the two above selecting plaintext methods, we have

$$Var_1(H_k^m) > Var_2(H_k^m) \tag{5}$$

and

$$m_1 < m_2 \tag{6}$$

Initially, ρ_{k^*} is same for each subkey candidate, the candidates of q_{i+1} corresponds to the maximum value of $\sum_{k^*} \rho_{k^*} \cdot \sqrt{Var(\tilde{H}_{k^*}^{i+1})}$ are the total space $X = F_2^n$, where n denotes the length of a plaintext byte. With the number of traces increasing, more and more wrong subkey candidates are eliminated. Let X^* be the set of candidates have been eliminated. The probability of selecting q_{i+1} corresponding to the maximum variance for the correct subkey is

$\frac{1}{|X|-|X^*|} > \frac{1}{|X|}$. Moreover, $\lim_{i \to m} \frac{1}{|X|-|X^*|} = 1 > \lim_{i \to m} \frac{1}{|X|} = \frac{1}{|X|}$. The variance of power traces through Eq. (4) is larger than selecting plaintexts randomly, i.e., $Var_1(H_k^m) > Var_2(H_k^m)$. According to Eq. (3), the larger variance of signals leads to higher correlation coefficient. Based on the relationship between the correlation coefficient and the number of traces [18], it can be deduced that $m_1 < m_2$.

The goal of our strategy is to increase the variance of signal in power traces, which can be considered as the variance of hypothetical power consumption. Thus, it is not limited to leakage models. Selecting plaintexts based on Eq. (4) can accelerate the attack. Compared to [14], the plaintext can be selected with lower computational complexity. It is necessary to compute the integration of leakage distribution for each guessing subkey and plaintext. The complexity in [14] is $O(|K| * |X| * n_l)$, where n_l is the interval of distribution. Based on Eq. (4), the complexity is $O(|K| * |X|)$. If the size of subkey and plaintext can be considered as constants, their complexities can be simplified to $O(n)$ and $O(1)$.

3.2   Select the Next Plaintext for Masked Design

Masking scheme uses the idea of secret sharing, its principle is to randomly split every sensitive intermediate variable z into d shares, which satisfy $z_1 \oplus z_2 \oplus \ldots \oplus z_d = z$. The univariate side channel attacks are invalid against masking. However, the result of joint leakage $L(t_1), L(t_2), \ldots, L(t_d)$ in d shares still depends on a sensitive variable, and the leakage is based on intermediate values that appear in multiple positions in the encryption process. Consequently, masking can be broken by higher-order side channel attacks that jointly exhibit a dependency between the d leakages and sensitive variable z.

Several combining functions have been proposed in the literature. Two of them are commonly used: the product combining [17] and the absolute difference combining [21]. Indeed, the application of a combining function to the leakages inevitably leads to a loss of information [17]. Moreover, the loss is not a constant when z is not uniformly distributed. In order to improve the correlation coefficients in higher-order attacks, we propose chosen plaintext strategies for different combining functions and they can be expressed in a unified form.

In general, the attacks start by combining the d leakages $L(t_1), L(t_2), \ldots, L(t_d)$ with a combining function C and by a prediction function h according to some assumptions on leakage model. The adversary can estimate the correlation coefficient:

$$\rho_{k^*} = \rho(C(L(t_1), L(t_2), \ldots, L(t_d)), h(Z)) \qquad (7)$$

where Z denotes the sensitive variable. Due to Corollary 8 in [16], the prediction function is defined as $h(z) = E(C|Z = z)$ to maximize the correlation

$$\rho = \frac{\sqrt{Var(E(C|Z))}}{\sqrt{Var(C)}} \qquad (8)$$

For the sake of simplicity, we start our analysis in the context of second-order attacks, which can be generalized to higher-order. Assume that the two leakages

$L(t_1)$, $L(t_2)$ leak the information of $h(Z \oplus M)$ and $h(M)$, respectively. M represents the mask. Considering the combining function is production combining, for every $z \in F_2^n$, we have

$$E(C|Z = z) = E(h(Z \oplus M) \cdot h(M)|Z = z) \qquad (9)$$

When Z is uniformly distributed, $h(Z \oplus M)$ is independent to $h(M)$. Thus, $Var(C)$ is a constant [16]. Since $E(C|Z = z) = -\frac{1}{2} \cdot h(z) + \frac{n^2+n}{4}$, from Eq. (8), we have that the correlation coefficient is proportional to $Var(h(Z))$.

However, if Z biased, $h(Z \oplus M)$ is not independent to $h(M)$. Thus, $Var(C)$ is not a constant. The variables $z_1, z_2, \ldots, z_{i+1}$ are the unmasked values corresponding to $q_1, q_2, \ldots, q_{i+1}$ and $\tilde{C}_{k^*}^{i+1} = C_{k^*}^i \cup C|z_{i+1} = (C|z_1, \ldots, C|z_{i+1})$ is the combining leakages sequence. The variance of combining leakages sequence can be denoted as

$$Var(\tilde{C}_{k^*}^{i+1}) = \frac{\sum_j^{i+1} Var(C|z_j)}{i + 1} + Var(E(C|z_1), \ldots, E(C|z_{i+1})) \qquad (10)$$

The computational procedure combines variance within classes and variance among classes. Since the masks M can not be controlled, we replace the characteristic of individual with the characteristic of the class. Hence, the variance from the Eq. (10) is an estimated value with few traces. When the number of traces increasing, the estimated value becomes more and more accurate.

The goal of choosing plaintext is to maximize the correlation coefficient between combining leakages and prediction function. Due to Eq. (4) and Eq. (8), we deduce the chosen plaintext strategy for masked design

$$q_{i+1} = \arg\max \sum_{k^*} \rho_{k^*} \cdot \frac{Var(\tilde{H}_{k^*}^{i+1})}{Var(\tilde{C}_{k^*}^{i+1})} \qquad (11)$$

Similarly, the strategy can be generalized to other combining functions, for example the absolute difference combining. $E(C|Z = z)$, $Var(C|Z = z)$ are different for different combining functions. Thus, when analyzing i power traces, the next plaintexts selected for $i+1$ power trace under different combining functions are different. As for unmasked design and masked design in chosen plaintext, we give the chosen plaintext scheme to maximize correlation coefficient of combining functions for the higher-order analysis.

In the experiment, the target device and oscilloscope are directly connected to the PC. The controller sends the instructions to control oscilloscope recording the power traces. The adversary performs SCAs on power traces and sends the results to select the next plaintext. Then, the controller will send the instructions and plaintexts to the device. The attack scenario is shown in Fig. 1. In the practical attack and evaluation, the setting of m is not the only termination condition of SCAs. The adversary or evaluator can terminate the process when the evaluation metrics (success rate, guessing entropy) meet the conditions [23].

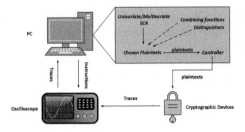

Fig. 1. Measurement setup in the context of ACPPA

4   Experiments

4.1   Simulation Results

We simulated a 128-bit implementation of AES and attacked its output of a S-box in the first round. HD is the HW obtained by calculating the XOR result of two intermediate values. Therefore, we can understand HW as a kind of HD. The next experiment will take the Hamming weight model as an example. We replace the leakages traces with Hamming weight of the S-box outputs, to which is added a normally distribution noise with standard deviation σ_{noise}. Without selecting plaintexts, we utilize the traditional CPA and ACPPA to analyze the simulated traces. We get the success rate and guessing entropy averaged over 100 independent key recoveries shown in Fig. 2 and Fig. 3.

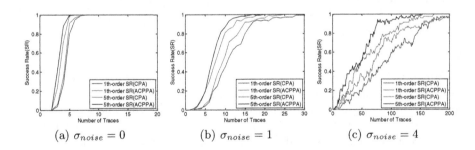

(a) $\sigma_{noise} = 0$ (b) $\sigma_{noise} = 1$ (c) $\sigma_{noise} = 4$

Fig. 2. Success rates by using CPA and ACPPA

The results present in Fig. 2 show the success rate (1th-order, 5th-order) used by ACPPA compared to CPA attack, with respectively noise standard deviations $\sigma_{noise} = 0, \sigma_{noise} = 1$ and $\sigma_{noise} = 4$. The oth-order success rate was defined in [24]. The number of traces required to observe a success rate of 90% in retrieving k for ACPPA is less than CPA. Figure 3 illustrates the guessing entropy of the attacks. As expected, ACPPA performs better for different noise levels.

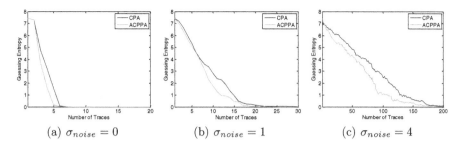

(a) $\sigma_{noise} = 0$ (b) $\sigma_{noise} = 1$ (c) $\sigma_{noise} = 4$

Fig. 3. Guessing entropy by using CPA and ACPPA

4.2   Practical Results

In order to evaluate the efficiency of our methods in a real-world setting, we apply our methods to the practical traces. We perform the experiments against the implementations of the AES in the Atmega-163 chip of smartcard on SASEBO-W board. We utilize Agilent DSO-X 3034A oscilloscope whose working rate is 50 MSa/s. The sampling rate is set to 200 MSa/s. We use this setup to analyze the unmasked and masked scenarios.

For the unmasked AES implementation, 200 power traces are measured and analyzed by CPA and ACPPA which measurement is separate in CPA and ACPPA performs both operations together. In addition, the total number of sample points in a trace is 50,000. The first S-box key retrieving results shown in Fig. 4 (a) and (b), the black line indicates the correlation coefficients of the correct key and the gray lines indicate wrong key candidates. For ACPPA, the highest correlation coefficient occurs for the correct key after 60 traces, with a magnitude of 0.6. Compared to the 117 traces needed with a magnitude of 0.4 for CPA, ACPPA performs more efficient.

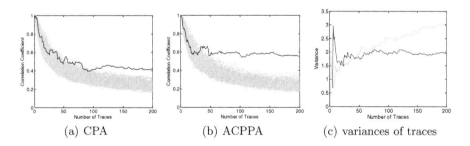

(a) CPA   (b) ACPPA   (c) variances of traces

Fig. 4. Correlation coefficient values and variances of power traces of unmasked AES

In addition, we give the variances of Hamming weight of the intermediate values to correct key. The results are indicated in Fig. 4 (c). The blue line indicates the variances in CPA while the red line indicates them in ACPPA. With traces increasing, the variance randomly measured tends to 2. However, the variance of traces measured by our method is about 3 and it becomes larger than 2 when 55 traces. By increasing the SNR, ACPPA can quickly distinguish the correct key candidates among others.

In the masked scenario, we carry out the implementation of Coron's masking scheme [25]. A random number is generated in this implementation. We focus on the two shares output of RefreshMasks. For the masked implementation, 1,000 power traces are measured and analyzed by CPA and ACPPA. The total number of sample points in a trace is 50,000. Since the number of samples is too large to combine leakages, we choose a subset of these sample points using POI methods [22]. Then, we perform the second-order CPA and ACPPA with two combining functions. Figure 5 (a) and (b) show the results of CPA and ACPPA using product combining, respectively. The black line indicates the correlation coefficients of the correct key and the gray lines indicate those of wrong key candidates. As shown in the figures, we successfully improved the correlation coefficients with ACPPA.

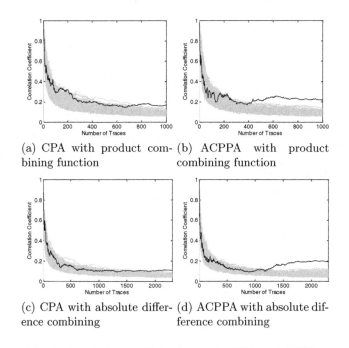

(a) CPA with product combining function

(b) ACPPA with product combining function

(c) CPA with absolute difference combining

(d) ACPPA with absolute difference combining

Fig. 5. Correlation coefficient values in CPA and ACPPA

To illustrate the efficiency under different combining functions, we perform the two attacks on the masked implementation using absolute difference combining function. As shown in Fig. 5 (c) and (d), the number of traces needed to recover the correct key for ACPPA is 1230, which is less than 1656 for CPA. In addition, the correlation coefficients of the correct key have been improved in ACPPA with the above two combining functions. The efficiency of this method has been verified by the smartcard, which has relative high SNR. The performance on other hardware platforms will be one of our future work.

5 Conclusions

The data complexity and time complexity are the main issues of the side-channel analysis. Chosen plaintext analysis can be regarded as the more threaten and efficient attack against cipher algorithm. In this paper, we proposed an adaptive chosen plaintext side-channel attack (ACPPA) to improve the efficiency of the existing SCA. ACPPA exploits the results of distinguishers to bias the distribution of power traces corresponding to the chosen plaintexts. It reduces the number of traces in both the measurement and analysis. Our chosen plaintext strategy improves the efficiencies of attacks on the unprotected designs and masked designs, which is adaptive to the different combining functions of the higher-order analysis. The SNR of power traces in ACPPA becomes higher so that the correct key can be distinguishable earlier than the traditional SCAs and has been verified by the experiments on the smartcard.

Acknowledgements. This work was supported by the National Natural Science Foundation of China under Grant (NO.62072247, NO.61972295).

References

1. Ge, C., Susilo, W., Liu, Z., Xia, J., Szalachowski, P., Liming, F.: Secure keyword search and data sharing mechanism for cloud computing. IEEE Trans. Dependable Secure Comput. https://doi.org/10.1109/TDSC.2020.2963978
2. Ge, C., Susilo, W., Baek, J., Liu, Z., Xia, J., Fang, L.: Revocable attribute-based encryption with data integrity in clouds. IEEE Trans. Dependable Secure Comput. https://doi.org/10.1109/TDSC.2021.3065999
3. Ge, C., Liu, Z., Fang, L., Ling, H., Zhang, A., Yin, C.: A hybrid fuzzy convolutional neural network based mechanism for photovoltaic cell defect detection with electroluminescence images. IEEE Trans. Parallel Distrib. Syst. **32**(7), 1653–1664 (2021). https://doi.org/10.1109/TPDS.2020.3046018
4. Kim, Y., Sugawara, T., Homma, N., Aoki, T., Satoh, A.: Biasing power traces to improve correlation power analysis attacks. In: First International Workshop on Constructive Side Channel Analysis and Secure Design (COSADE 2010), pp. 77–80 (2010)
5. Kim, Y., Ko, H.: Using principal component analysis for practical biasing of power traces to improve power analysis attacks. In: Lee, H.-S., Han, D.-G. (eds.) ICISC 2013. LNCS, vol. 8565, pp. 109–120. Springer, Cham (2014). https://doi.org/10.1007/978-3-319-12160-4_7
6. Zhou, X., et al.: An adaptive singular value decomposition-based method to enhance correlation electromagnetic analysis. In: IEEE International Symposium on Electromagnetic Compatibility (EMC). IEEE 2016, pp. 170–175 (2016)
7. Mangard, S.: Hardware countermeasures against DPA – a statistical analysis of their effectiveness. In: Okamoto, T. (ed.) CT-RSA 2004. LNCS, vol. 2964, pp. 222–235. Springer, Heidelberg (2004). https://doi.org/10.1007/978-3-540-24660-2_18

184   Y. Li et al.

8. Bleichenbacher, D.: Chosen ciphertext attacks against protocols based on the RSA encryption standard PKCS #1. In: Krawczyk, H. (ed.) CRYPTO 1998. LNCS, vol. 1462, pp. 1–12. Springer, Heidelberg (1998). https://doi.org/10.1007/BFb0055716
9. Joux, A., Martinet, G., Valette, F.: Blockwise-adaptive attackers revisiting the (in)security of some provably secure encryption modes: CBC, GEM, IACBC. In: Yung, M. (ed.) CRYPTO 2002. LNCS, vol. 2442, pp. 17–30. Springer, Heidelberg (2002). https://doi.org/10.1007/3-540-45708-9_2
10. Kiltz, E., O'Neill, A., Smith, A.: Instantiability of RSA-OAEP under chosen-plaintext attack. In: Rabin, T. (ed.) CRYPTO 2010. LNCS, vol. 6223, pp. 295–313. Springer, Heidelberg (2010). https://doi.org/10.1007/978-3-642-14623-7_16
11. Peng, X., Wei, H., Zhang, P.: Chosen-plaintext attack on lensless double-random phase encoding in the fresnel domain. Opt. Lett. **31**(22), 3261–3263 (2006)
12. Bergen, H.A., Hogan, J.M.: A chosen plaintext attack on an adaptive arithmetic coding compression algorithm. Comput. Secur. **12**(2), 157–167 (1993)
13. Schindler, W.: A timing attack against RSA with the Chinese remainder theorem. In: Koç, Ç.K., Paar, C. (eds.) CHES 2000. LNCS, vol. 1965, pp. 109–124. Springer, Heidelberg (2000). https://doi.org/10.1007/3-540-44499-8_8
14. Veyrat-Charvillon, N., Standaert, F.-X.: Adaptive chosen-message side-channel attacks. In: Zhou, J., Yung, M. (eds.) ACNS 2010. LNCS, vol. 6123, pp. 186–199. Springer, Heidelberg (2010). https://doi.org/10.1007/978-3-642-13708-2_12
15. Ou, C., Wang, Z., Sun, D., Zhou, X., Ai, J., Pang, N.: Enhanced correlation power analysis by biasing power traces. In: Bishop, M., Nascimento, A.C.A. (eds.) ISC 2016. LNCS, vol. 9866, pp. 59–72. Springer, Cham (2016). https://doi.org/10.1007/978-3-319-45871-7_5
16. Prouff, E., Rivain, M., Bevan, R.: Statistical analysis of second order differential power analysis. IEEE Trans. Comput. **58**(6), 799–811 (2009)
17. Chari, S., Jutla, C.S., Rao, J.R., Rohatgi, P.: Towards sound approaches to counteract power-analysis attacks. In: Wiener, M. (ed.) CRYPTO 1999. LNCS, vol. 1666, pp. 398–412. Springer, Heidelberg (1999). https://doi.org/10.1007/3-540-48405-1_26
18. Mangard, S., Oswald, E., Popp, T.: Power Analysis Attacks: Revealing the Secrets of Smart Cards, vol. 31. Springer, Boston (2008). https://doi.org/10.1007/978-0-387-38162-6
19. Kocher, P., Jaffe, J., Jun, B.: Differential power analysis. In: Wiener, M. (ed.) CRYPTO 1999. LNCS, vol. 1666, pp. 388–397. Springer, Heidelberg (1999). https://doi.org/10.1007/3-540-48405-1_25
20. Brier, E., Clavier, C., Olivier, F.: Correlation power analysis with a leakage model. In: Joye, M., Quisquater, J.-J. (eds.) CHES 2004. LNCS, vol. 3156, pp. 16–29. Springer, Heidelberg (2004). https://doi.org/10.1007/978-3-540-28632-5_2
21. Messerges, T.S.: Using second-order power analysis to attack DPA resistant software. In: Koç, Ç.K., Paar, C. (eds.) CHES 2000. LNCS, vol. 1965, pp. 238–251. Springer, Heidelberg (2000). https://doi.org/10.1007/3-540-44499-8_19
22. Oswald, E., Mangard, S., Herbst, C., Tillich, S.: Practical second-order DPA attacks for masked smart card implementations of block ciphers. In: Pointcheval, D. (ed.) CT-RSA 2006. LNCS, vol. 3860, pp. 192–207. Springer, Heidelberg (2006). https://doi.org/10.1007/11605805_13
23. Clavier, C., et al.: Practical improvements of side channel attacks on AES: feedback from the 2nd DPA contest. J. Cryptogr. Eng. **4**(4), 259–274 (2014)

24. Standaert, F.-X., Malkin, T.G., Yung, M.: A unified framework for the analysis of side-channel key recovery attacks. In: Joux, A. (ed.) EUROCRYPT 2009. LNCS, vol. 5479, pp. 443–461. Springer, Heidelberg (2009). https://doi.org/10.1007/978-3-642-01001-9_26
25. Coron, J.-S.: Higher order masking of look-up tables. In: Nguyen, P.Q., Oswald, E. (eds.) EUROCRYPT 2014. LNCS, vol. 8441, pp. 441–458. Springer, Heidelberg (2014). https://doi.org/10.1007/978-3-642-55220-5_25

Mind the Amplification: Cracking Content Delivery Networks via DDoS Attacks

Zihao Li and Weizhi Meng$^{(\boxtimes)}$

Department of Applied Mathematics and Computer Science,
Technical University of Denmark, Lyngby, Denmark
weme@dtu.dk

Abstract. A content delivery network (CDN) refers to a geographically distributed network of web servers, aiming to enhance the website performance and reliability, i.e., providing fast delivery of the Internet content. CDN is often part of a mature enterprise level network, but due to the distributed nature, CDN may be vulnerable to a distributed denial-of-service attack (DDoS), in which the cyber-attackers try to flood the victim with overloaded traffic or requests. In the literature, the impact of DDoS on CDN has not been widely studied. Motivated by this challenge, in this work, we emulate a CDN environment and investigate the effect of a particular DDoS attack on the environment. It is found that free CDN clusters could be destroyed by only several Gigabyte traffic. In the end, we also discuss some potential solutions to help defend against DDoS attacks.

Keywords: Content delivery network · Distributed Denial-of-Service Attack · Website server · Network security · Emulation and evaluation

1 Introduction

With the popularity of smartphones and social networking applications like Netflix and Facebook [3], users are likely to be streaming a longer video using the device. Also, the COVID-19 pandemic has created significant disruption on different organizations including enterprises and government. More and more people have the need to work from home and attend online meetings everyday [2]. This can increase the network traffic and cause delivery delay.

To minimize the delay, content delivery network (CDN) is used for the quick transfer of traffic needed for loading the Internet content, such as images, videos and webpages. That is, CDN represents a geographically distributed network of servers with the purpose of distributing web content to users with acceptable delay. It aims to reduce the physical distance between the server and the user, i.e., providing the high-quality content and fast loading speed [18]. With the rising need for live and uninterrupted content delivery over a high-speed data network, the global CDN market size was expected to grow from USD 14.4 billion in 2020 to USD 27.9 billion in 2025 [2].

© Springer Nature Switzerland AG 2021
Z. Liu et al. (Eds.): WASA 2021, LNCS 12938, pp. 186–197, 2021.
https://doi.org/10.1007/978-3-030-86130-8_15

In addition, a properly configured CDN is believed to help safeguard websites against some typical attacks such as Distributed Denial of Service (DDoS) attacks [4]. DDoS attacks aim at consuming finite network and system resources with a huge amount of trash data and preventing legitimate users from being able to access websites. For example in 2018, Github was hit with a 1.3 Tbps DDoS attack, which was caused by WebStresser, an online service that permits any people to launch attacks who do not have to learn knowledge about Botnet or writing scripts [5].

Motivation and Contributions. In the literature, many research studies are focusing on how to improve the performance and privacy of CDN [7,10,18], but few studies explore the potential impact of DDoS on CDN. With the development of cloud computing, most large-sized companies like Amazon, Alibaba and Huawei had deployed their own CDN network and even provided those cloud services to individuals. Some other small or medium sized companies were still facing the challenge of DDoS attack even they had deployed CDN nodes.

Motivated by this issue, in this work, we aim to explore and analyze the impact of DDoS on CDN. Our contributions can be summarized as follows.

– We emulate a CDN using Elastic cloud services provided by AliCloud. The selection of AliCloud is based on that its CDN has over 2800 nodes all over the world covering more than 70 countries.
– We investigate the impact of a particular DDoS attack (called UDP NTP amplification reflection DDoS attack) on the performance of CDN. For a real test, the DDoS attack was launched by using the tools from dark web.
– We introduce some potential solutions to mitigate DDoS on CDN, i.e., by using a cloud security architecture.

The reminder of this article is structured as follows. We introduce the background of CDN and our network environmental setup in Sect. 2. Section 3 introduces the UDP NTP amplification reflection DDoS attack and showcases the result. In Sect. 4, we introduce and discuss some potential solutions against DDoS, including a cloud security architecture. Section 5 reviews relevant studies on CDN and Sect. 6 concludes our work.

2   CDN and Network Environmental Setup

2.1   CDN Background

Content delivery network is a key element of many successful websites. As a geographically distributed network of proxy servers and their data centers, many nodes are usually deployed in multiple locations to reduce bandwidth costs and provide server acceleration to solve the overload problem caused by large amount of user requests. Those nodes are often called "edge servers" as they should be the closest edge of CDN to the end servers. Essentially, CDN can deploy cache server clusters for load balancing.

This virtual distributed network can intelligently cache the content of the source website (including all kinds of dynamic and static resources) to the edge servers in the world and can share the pressure of the source website. Taking AliCloud as an example, its CDN consists of more than 2800 nodes around the world across over 70 countries. All AliCloud nodes use a 10G network card, and a single node has storage capacity of 40TB-1.5PB, bandwidth load of 40–200 Gbps and bandwidth reservation of 130 Tbps. Below are the main application scenarios of CDN:

1. Small image files: the main business of websites is to download images and small files including all types of images, HTML, CSS, JS files, etc.
2. Large file downloading: another main business of websites is to download large files, i.e., the size of each single file over 20 Mb, such as games, various client downloads and application downloads.
3. Video and Audio data flow: CDN supports MP4, FLV and other mainstream video formats.
4. Website scalability: hide the source IP address to protect websites from DoS attack and implement load balancing. CDN can be expanded to a specifically professional extent or just reach a basic level with high scalability.

2.2   Target Web Servers Setup

To explore the impact of DDoS on CDN, there is a need to setup a proper environment. Due to implementation costs, it is hard to deploy a network with complete hardware or software resources at enterprise-level. However, cloud devices and services are mostly elastic, which provides enough flexibility on configuration selection. To make the emulated environment closer to real scenarios, we adopt AliCloud and rent cloud services online. Below are the deployment details of our target web servers.

Entities: We rent Elastic Compute Service (ECS) with Windows Server 2008 R2 Enterprise 64-bit. Its concrete configuration information was shown in Fig. 1. All servers were configured with the same settings.

Network: Two ECSs without assigning public IP addresses have been placed in the same virtual private cloud (VPC) network with two private IP addresses 172.31.17.130 and 172.31.17.129. Due to the cost limitation, their available bandwidth is 1Mbps. There is only one routing table, one switch and two security groups in the VPC.

Two entries have been added in routing table, the first one is created manually with destination network segment 172.31.16.0/20. The second entry is created by our system with destination network segment 100.64.0.0/10, referring to another private network inside the whole system. AliCloud has already deployed default NAT on public network gateways. Another NAT in the VPC is used for NAT proxy (SNAT and DNAT) to enforce management and security of ECS. To reduce the high costs of creating and renting additional NAT services, we adopted the default NAT provided by public network gateways. The only switch associated with routing table directly connects with all ECS entities.

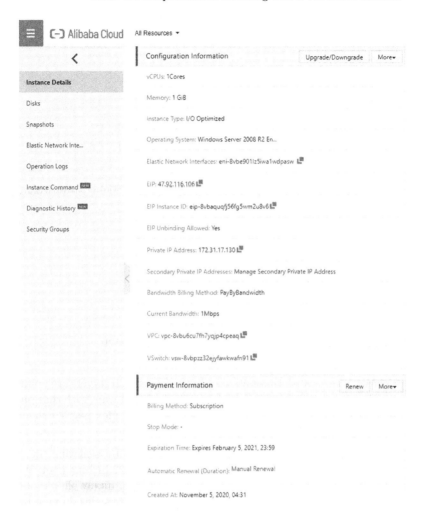

Fig. 1. Configuration information of Elastic cloud servers

Security Group Strategies: To ensure security and publish rented ECS as web servers to the external network, inbound rules can define ports using TCP protocol, only 80, 3389 and 22 were open for external access, in addition to ICMP. As for outbound rules, only port 80 was allowed to respond. Due to that the scale of established network is small, and there is only one switch to use, it is unnecessary to set network ACL (access control list) again. Security group strategies can achieve the same result.

Website Publishing: To simplify the process of establishing website, PHP-Study [1] was used, which is a program debugging integration package in PHP environment. It is able to integrate apache with others such as php, mysql, phpmyadmin and zendoptimizer. Once installed, users can directly call graphical user interface to reduce time consumption. Thus, users can copy their own website under

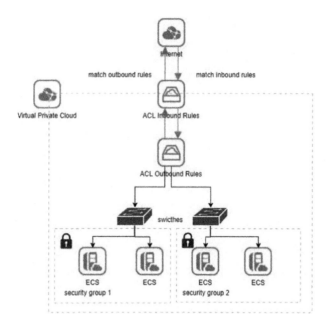

Fig. 2. The overall network environment setup

WWW directory, and publish the contents of website easily. If servers are bounded with public IP address, websites can be accessed over the Internet with that public IP address. It is also suggested to modify default path of index pages, otherwise hackers can easily temper files using the default file path.

Domain Name Service: To make websites accessible by searching domain names, we rent two domains: dns21.hichina.com and dns22.hichina.com. While it is noted that due to the regulation issues, all rent domain names should obtain ICP filing and pass real name authentication, in order to transfer domain name to be associated with Public IP address of web servers.

Figure 2 shows the overall network environmental setup, where websites can be accessed by domain names or public IP address.

3   Evaluation: DDoS on CDN Environment

In the experiment, we simulate a real attack scenario and conduct a special type of DDoS attack (called UDP NTP Amplification Reflection DDoS attack) by using a hacker-class attack tool. The first step was to scan NTP server lists and the second step was to send malicious requests.

3.1   UDP NTP Amplification Reflection DDoS Attack

NTP amplification is a DDoS attack based on UDP, attacker can use the publicly accessible NTP (Network Time Protocol) server to attack the target server with a large number of UDP traffic, making it impossible for regular traffic to access the target and surrounding infrastructure.

Network Time protocol is one of the earliest network protocols to synchronize the clocks of internet-connected devices. The common used port is UDP 123. In addition to clock synchronization, older versions of NTP also support monitoring services that allow administrators to monitor traffic on a given NTP server. This command, called *monlist*, can send a list of the last 600 hosts connected to the query server and the requester. For most basic types of NTP amplification attacks, attackers can repeatedly send a "get *monlist*" request to the NTP server, using the victim's server IP address as the IP address of the requesting server. Then the NTP server responds by sending the list to the spoofed IP address. As the response is far more than the number of requests, it can amplify the traffic to the target server and ultimately render the legitimate request service unavailable.

By taking advantage of the *"monlist"* command on some NTP servers, an attacker can multiply its initial request traffic to produce a larger response. By default, enabling this command on old devices allows to respond with the last 600 source IP addresses that have sent requests to the NTP server. A *monlist* request from a server with 600 IP addresses in its memory would be 200 times larger than the origin request. This means that an attacker with 1GB of Internet traffic can cause a significant increase of attacking traffic, i.e., more than 200 GB of traffic. NTP amplification attack can be divided into 4 steps:

- Attacker uses zombie hosts in Botnet to send UDP packets with deceptive IP addresses to the NTP server with *"monlist"* command. The spoofed IP address on each packet can point to the victim's real IP address.
- Each UDP packet makes a request to the NTP server using its *monlist* command, resulting in a large number of responses.
- The server then responds to the victim's IP address with large traffic.
- The target's IP address receives the response, and the surrounding network infrastructure becomes overwhelmed with traffic.

As the attacking traffic is the same as the legitimate traffic from valid server, it is difficult to mitigate such traffic without blocking legitimate activity from a real NTP server. In addition, UDP packets do not require a handshake; thus, the NTP server sends a large number of responses to the target server without verifying that the request is trustworthy. This makes the NTP server an excellent source of reflection for DDoS amplification attacks.

3.2   The First Step

Our DDoS attack can be divided into two steps. In the first step, we used the tool *masscan*, an Internet-scale port scanner to scan the entire Internet and find out servers that open UDP port 123 with command:

sudo ./masscan -pU:123 -oX NTP.xml –rate 10000 47.92.0.0-47.92.255.255

```
li@li-dev:~/masscan/bin$ sudo ./masscan -pU:123 -oX result.xml --rate 100000 101
.0.0.0-110.0.0.0

Starting masscan 1.0.6 (http://bit.ly/14GZzcT) at 2020-12-31 18:41:28 GMT
-- forced options: -sS -Pn -n --randomize-hosts -v --send-eth
Initiating SYN Stealth Scan
Scanning 150994945 hosts [1 port/host]
rate: 67.24-kpps,  6.28% done,   0:42:53 remaining, found=0
```

Fig. 3. Port scanning rate of Masscan

Active Servers

	Africa.	54
	Asia.	282
	Europe.	2880
	North america.	946
	Oceania	135
	South america.	60
	Global.	4069
	All library servers	4346

As of 2020-12-31

Fig. 4. Distribution of global NTP servers

We found that personal host with limited bandwidth, even with a much higher scanning rate, would not affect the final result. This is because if the speed was too fast, a large number of hosts might be missed. With *masscan*, scanning the entire network with one port should cost around 10 h at the max speed. Figure 3 shows that the practical max-speed of scanning was limited by the user bandwidth and nothing was found. To get over 2 million packets per second, users have to get an Intel 10-gbps Ethernet adapter and a specific driver known as "PF_RING ZC".

Figure 4 shows the number of active NTP servers across the world. We can scan all the hosts with open UDP port 123, but it is unclear whether the target hosts were running NTP services. Thus, raw data of *monlist* request should be constructed to check if servers will return data. A lot of NTP servers may have filtering mechanism, for example, UDP packets with a payload of 50 bytes will be dropped (as shown below).

$\backslash$x17$\backslash$x00$\backslash$x03$\backslash$x2a" . " $\backslash$x00" x4

Therefore, we can construct raw data with more than 80 bytes, according to the concrete conditions. One example is given as below.

rawData $=$ " $\backslash$x17$\backslash$x00$\backslash$x03$\backslash$x2a" $+$ " $\backslash$x00" $*$ 80

As all returned data should be monitored, we can define a function called "detect" (as shown in Fig. 5), which can monitor UDP data on a specific port. The selected port should be the source port sending *monlist* request as well. Any responded NTP server will be mapped to the selected port. Usually, selected port with a large number may not be used commonly. The destination network address should be the attacker's IP.

```
def detect():
    DetectedResult = sniff(filter"=udp port 50001 and dst net "47.92.137.85,
        store=0, prn=filerer)
```

Fig. 5. The function of "detect"

As long as a NTP server responded to the *monlist* requests, the replied data will be caught by *detect()*, which can put all received data into *filterer function* to handle. The function of "filterer" will check if the size of captured data packets is bigger than 200 bytes. This is because when NTP servers responded *monlist* requests, the returned packages would be larger. In our settings, we used 200 as a threshold to filter unrecognized packages.

3.3 The Second Step

This step aims to conduct NTP DDoS attack by using the collected IP addresses of NTP servers. Figure 6 shows the process of conducting DDoS attacks by the script. It is worth noting that many NTP servers may have been upgraded to NTP version 4 and close port 123 by default. Based on the statistical data, the ratio of old NTP servers is around 30%.

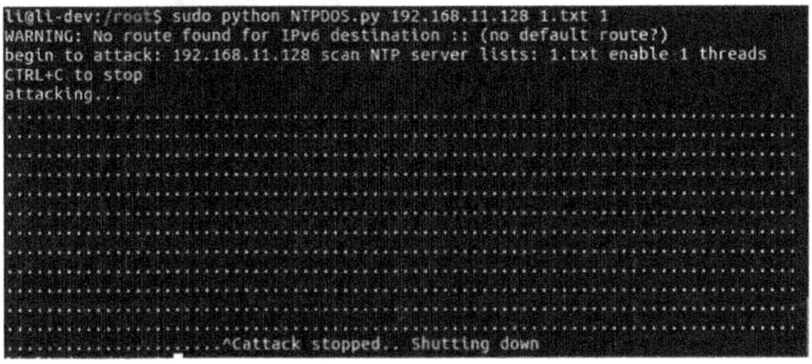

Fig. 6. Attacking process of NTP DDoS script

Our hacker-class DDoS tool can generate DDoS traffic of 300G or even 1 T.[1] It has the capability to launch the attack by combining both TCP and UDP DDoS attack techniques. Figure 7 shows the CPU usage of target server under the DDoS attack, and Fig. 8 presents the black hole state when the server was crashed down. Our results demonstrate that a CDN could be destroyed by only several Gigabyte traffic under the UDP NTP amplification reflection DDoS attack, and

---

[1] More details about the hacking tool test can check our demo at https://www. youtube.com/watch?v=cRXGIWcHX0g&feature=youtu.be.

Fig. 7. CPU usage of target server under the DDoS attack

Fig. 8. Crashed server with black hole state

there is a need to enhance the security of CDNs. According to the protection mechanism provided by AliCloud, all crashed servers under the DDoS would close all open ports and set in black hole state for a specific time period.

4   Potential Countermeasures Against DDoS

DDoS defence is not easy, and below are some common rules to mitigate DDoS attacks from different aspects.

- *Reduce exposure, isolate resources and unrelated businesses to reduce risk of attack.* We need to avoid exposing non-business necessary service ports to the public network and avoid non-business related requests and access. We can also achieve logic isolation within the network through the VPC, aiming to prevent attacks from zombie machine of internal network.

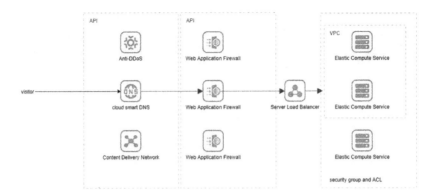

Fig. 9. Cloud security architecture against DDoS attack

- *Optimize the business architecture and design the system of disaster recovery switching.* We need to avoid a single point of failure in a business architecture through load balancing or a geographically multi-centric architecture. We can apply load balancing to implement multi-point concurrent business access of multiple servers, evenly distribute the user access traffic to each server and reduce the pressure of a single server. Another way is to purchase high enough bandwidth aiming to handle requests as much as possible.
- *Server security reinforcement.* Security reinforcement should be carried out for the operating system and software services on the server, aiming to reduce vulnerable sites and increase the cost of attackers. For example, we need to ensure that the server's system files are latest and updated in time.
- *Traffic cleaning.* DDoS defence methods should combine IP reputation, network traffic cleaning, fingerprint detection, user behavior detection and content features inspection to filter malicious traffic, i.e., constructing a suitable packet filter [11–14].

Figure 9 shows a mitigation solution based on cloud security architecture. The first layer applies Anti-DDoS IP, domain name cloud resolution and CDN network technologies. The second layer utilizes WAF (web application firewall) security devices to filter bad requests. To make the overall processing more efficient, load balancing should be established based on the existing servers. Load balancing is a promising solution to solve the high payload and concurrency of large websites. It does mitigate DDoS attack in essence and improve the performance of whole network. ECSs as the backend servers in VPC network of SLB (server load balancing) can be finally under protection of network security group strategies and network layer ACL.

5   Related Work

CDN can provide a geographically distributed network of web servers to deliver their content to end users, which is especially useful for businesses that have to handle a large amount of web traffic, such as Netflix, Facebook and Amazon.

Due to the pressure of minimizing delivery content and increasing download rates, many existing research studies focus on the CDN improvement. Thomdapu et al. [17] formulated the content placement problem from an optimization perspective and introduced an online algorithm to handle time-varying content popularity, with a very low computational cost. Nishimuta et al. [16] presented an adaptive server and path switching scheme that is based on the estimated acquisition throughput of each path. They assumed the use of a single-domain network in which CDNs are composed of OpenFlow-based SDNs. It can compute the estimated acquisition throughput of the path between the client and the server to against the flow quality degradation. Bannour et al. [6] introduced a deployment solution for CDN with the SDN technology. The main goal is to find at run-time appropriate partial Quorum configurations, which could achieve a balance between the SDN application's continuous performance and consistency requirements. Hassine et al. [9] focused on how to predict the videos' popularity at CDN, and introduced a two-level prediction approach. The goal is to find the best trade-off between complexity and prediction accuracy. More related work can refer to the survey [18].

Recently, the security and privacy issues of CDN have received much attention. Cui et al. [7] found that CDN providers could infer user preferences and the popularity of objects, and introduced a privacy-preserving encrypted CDN system to hide both the content of objects and user requests. The system is designed with a scalable key management approach for multi-user access. Hao et al. [8] explored the security implications of dynamic mapping that remain understudied in the CDN community. They figured out that attackers can hijack CDN's request redirection and nullify the benefits offered by CDNs. Nishiyama et al. [15] studied the issue of trusted video delivery and introduced a content-leakage detection scheme to handle the variation of the video length. In the literature, the impact of DDoS attacks has not been widely studied, which motivates our work with the aim to investigate the security of CDN.

6   Conclusion

To meet the demand for high-speed digital content, the CDN market is expected to grow at a rapid growth rate. It mainly provides a geographically distributed network of servers, which can bring web content closer to the geographic location of customs. In addition, CDN is believed to help protect websites against some common attacks, e.g., DDoS attacks. However, the impact of DDoS attacks on CDN has not been widely studied. In this work, we aim to emulate a CDN environment and explore the effect of UDP NTP amplification reflection DDoS attack on the environment. It is found that under such particular attack, free CDN clusters could be destroyed by using only several Gigabyte traffic. Then we discuss some potential solutions to safeguard CDN against DDoS attacks, including the protection of real IP addresses, optimization of the business architecture and the use of cloud security architecture. Our work attempts to attract more attention on enhancing the security of CDN.

References

1. PHPStudy. https://www.xp.cn/
2. Content Delivery Network Market. https://www.marketsandmarkets.com/Market-Reports/content-delivery-networks-cdn-market-657.html. Accessed Feb 2021
3. How does CDN work? https://www.cdnetworks.com/web-performance-blog/how-content-delivery-networks-work/. Accessed Feb 2021
4. What is a CDN? — How do CDNs work? https://www.cloudflare.com/learning/cdn/what-is-a-cdn/. Accessed Mar 2021
5. Police are now targeting former WebStresser DDoS-for-hire users. https://www.zdnet.com/article/police-are-now-targeting-former-webstresser ddos for hire-users/. Asscessed Mar 2021
6. Bannour, F., Souihi, S., Mellouk, A.: Adaptive distributed SDN controllers: application to content-centric delivery networks. Future Gener. Comput. Syst. **113**, 78–93 (2020)
7. Cui, S., Asghar, M.R., Russello, G.: Multi-CDN: towards privacy in content delivery networks. IEEE Trans. Dependable Secur. Comput. **17**(5), 984–999 (2020)
8. Hao, S., Zhang, Y., Wang, H., Stavrou, A.: End-users get maneuvered: empirical analysis of redirection hijacking in content delivery networks. In: USENIX Security Symposium, pp. 1129–1145 (2018)
9. Hassine, N.B., Minet, P., Marinca, D., Barth, D.: Popularity prediction-based caching in content delivery networks. Ann. des Telecommun. **74**(5–6), 351–364 (2019)
10. Hu, X., et al.: STYX: a hierarchical key management system for elastic content delivery networks on public clouds. IEEE Trans. Dependable Secur. Comput. **18**(2), 843–857 (2021)
11. Meng, Y., Kwok, L.F: Enhancing list-based packet filter using IP verification mechanism against IP spoofing attack in network intrusion detection. In: Proceedings of the 6th International Conference on Network and System Security (NSS), pp. 1–14 (2012)
12. Meng, Y., Kwok, L.F.: Adaptive non-critical alarm reduction using hash-based contextual signatures in intrusion detection. Comput. Commun. **38**, 50–59 (2014)
13. Meng, W., Li, W., Kwok, L.F.: Towards effective trust-based packet filtering in collaborative network environments. IEEE Trans. Netw. Serv. Manage. **14**(1), 233–245 (2017)
14. Meng, W.: Intrusion detection in the era of IoT: building trust via traffic filtering and sampling. IEEE Comput. **51**(7), 36–43 (2018)
15. Nishiyama, H., Fomo, D., Fadlullah, Z.M., Kato, N.: Traffic pattern-based content leakage detection for trusted content delivery networks. IEEE Trans. Parallel Distrib. Syst. **25**(2), 301–309 (2014)
16. Nishimuta, H., Nobayashi, D., Ikenaga, T.: Adaptive server and path switching for content delivery networks. IEICE Trans. Inf. Syst. **103-D**(11), 2389–2393 (2020)
17. Thomdapu, S.T., Katiyar, P., Rajawat, K.: Dynamic cache management in content delivery networks. Comput. Networks **187**, 107822 (2021)
18. B. Zolfaghari, et al.: Rai: content delivery networks: state of the art, trends, and future roadmap. ACM Comput. Surv. **53**(2), 34:1–34:34 (2020)

A Verifiable Federated Learning Scheme Based on Secure Multi-party Computation

Wenhao Mou, Chunlei Fu$^{(\boxtimes)}$, Yan Lei, and Chunqiang Hu$^{(\boxtimes)}$

School of Big Data and Software Engineering, Chongqing University,
Chongqing, China
{mwh,clfu,yanlei,chu}@cqu.edu.cn

Abstract. Federated learning ensures that the quality of the model is uncompromised while the resulting global model is consistent with the model trained by directly collecting user data. However, the risk of inferring data considered in federated learning. Furthermore, the inference to the learning outcome considered in a federated learning environment must satisfy that data cannot be inferred from any outcome except the owner of the data. In this paper, we propose a new federated learning scheme based on secure multi-party computation (SMC) and differential privacy. The scheme prevents inference during the learning process as well as inference of the output. Meanwhile, the scheme protects the user's local data during the learning process to ensure the correctness of the results after users' midway exits through the process.

Keywords: Federated learning · Secure multi-party computation · Differential privacy · Verification

1 Introduction

In a traditional machine learning process, training data is saved by the organization that performs the learning algorithm. While in a distributed learning system, the central node that saves the data sends the data to learning node, or the learning node directly accesses the shared data, given the learning nodes all are trusted [1, 2].

The current existing research on privacy protection in federated learning has yielded some results. The works are based on a partial or full homomorphic threshold encryption [1, 3], secret sharing [4–6], and differential privacy [7]. The current federated learning process that incorporates privacy protections is shown in Fig. 1. In this paper, we specifically consider the case that a data holder exits early in the training process, making the system robust to users who exit at any time.

Compared with pooling all user data for training, the traditional federated learning process significantly enhances privacy protection. However, federated learning still

Supported by the National Key Research and Development Project under Grant 2020YFB 1711900, National Natural Science Foundation of China under Grant 62072065, the Key Project of Technology Innovation and Application Development of Chongqing under Grant cstc2019jscx-mbdxX0044, and the Overseas Returnees Innovation and Entrepreneurship Support Program of Chongqing under Grant cx2020004 and cx2018015.

Z. Liu et al. (Eds.): WASA 2021, LNCS 12938, pp. 198–209, 2021.
https://doi.org/10.1007/978-3-030-86130-8_16

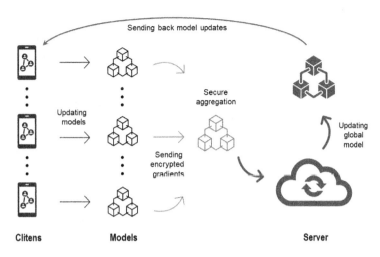

Fig. 1. A federated learning process that incorporates privacy protections.

has many security issues. Since the central server in federated learning is responsible for aggregating and distributing data, the central server may be exploited by attackers; there are many clients involved in learning in federated learning, and attackers can infer the training data of other users through the global model or parameters passed by users [8,9]. In addition, an attacker may launch Membership inference attacks or reconstruction through inference, Membership inference attacks are a method to infer training data details by checking the training data the presence or absence of specific data on the training data set to obtain information [10]. Reconstruction through inference, on the other hand, is a method that reconstructs the training data of other clients through the global model [11].

Therefore, we propose a new federated learning system that combines traditional federated learning with secure multi-party computation (SMC) and differential privacy to prevent inference during the learning process as well as inference on the output, which can provide sufficient privacy guarantees. In this system, third parties securely obtain model parameters from each data holder and the global model is updated in a secure aggregated manner. In this process, no data from any party is compromised and private data cannot be inferred from the global model.

2 Related Works

In this section, we will compare the existing work based on the features in our system. Federated learning is a decentralized and collaborative machine learning aimed primarily at protecting the privacy of users' data. Shokri and Shmatikov proposed a method for training neural networks on horizontally segmented data by exchanging update parameters [7,12]. The method could protect the privacy of the participants' training data, without sacrificing the accuracy of the resulting model case. Phong et al. [13] have proposed a new deep learning system that uses additive methods for protecting gradients from curious servers compromising user privacy, given the assumption of not degrading the accuracy of deep learning Homomorphic encryption. Truex et al. [1] propose a method to generate a joint learning method model that combines differential privacy and SMC to prevent inference threats and can guarantee high accuracy of the model. Hu et al. [14] find a method that can effectively perform distributed user data learning method for protecting user privacy to ensure that user data satisfies differential privacy.

Compared to existing approaches, our system mainly extends the security of the learning process, combines secure multi-party computing techniques such as homomorphic encryption with differential privacy, protects against inference threats, and effectively protects the privacy of users' private data while allowing users to quit midway through the learning process.

3   Preliminaries

In this section, we will first introduce the main concepts of federated learning and then outline the cryptographic source languages and modules that have been used in this system.

3.1   Federated Learning

In a traditional machine learning environment, there is often only one participant $\mathcal{U}$, which applies the machine learning algorithm F_m on the data set D to obtain the model M, i.e., $F_m(D) = M$. In this process, P has access to all the data sets D. While in a federate learning environment, there are multiple participants $\mathcal{U}_1, \mathcal{U}_2, ..., \mathcal{U}_n$. Each participant has its own data sets $D_1, D_2, ..., D_n$, who runs learning algorithms on their respective datasets to obtain the model, and transfer the parameters of the model to server S. Eventually the server will aggregate all the parameters and update the model M. All participants (including the server) have no access to the data of other users during this process.

3.2   Differential Privacy

The most recent model for quantifying and limiting the disclosure of personal information is Differential Privacy (DP), a rigorous mathematical framework that aims to introduce a degree of uncertainty into the published model in order to adequately obscure the contribution of any individual user [15]. DP theoretically limits the influence of a single individual, thus limiting the ability of an attacker to infer the identity of the members. Differential privacy is quantified by the privacy loss parameter (ϵ, δ), where smaller (ϵ, δ) corresponds to enhanced privacy. More formally, for all $S \subseteq Range(A)$, and for all adjacent datasets D and D', the randomization algorithm A is said to be (ϵ, δ)-differential privacy if the following equation is satisfied [15]:

$$P(A(D) \in S) \leq e^{\epsilon} P(A(D') \in S) + \delta$$

3.3 Secret Sharing

The secret sharing used in this system is based on Shamir's t-out-of-n secret sharing [16], which allows the user to split the secret s he wants to share into n pieces and hand them over to n other people to save. When such arbitrary t individuals take out their own fragment s_i, the individual can reconstruct s, but when there are fewer than t fragments, the person cannot get any information about s.

The secret sharing scheme is parameterized on an initial F whose size is at least $l \geq 2k$, where k is a security parameter. Secret sharing consists of two algorithms, **SS.share** and **SS.recon**. The sharing algorithm **SS.share**$(s, t, \mathcal{U}) \rightarrow (u, s_u)_{u \in U}$ takes the shared secret s, the shared user $\mathcal{U}$, and the threshold $t \leq |\mathcal{U}|$ as inputs, and generates a set of the secret fragments s_u, which is associated with the shared user u. The recombination algorithm **SS.recon**$((u, s_u)_{u \in V}, t) \rightarrow s$, takes the threshold t and the secret fragment s_u collected from V users as input, and outputs the secret s.

3.4 Key Agreement

The key agreement method in this system uses Diffie-Hellman key agreement [17], which is composed of **KA.param, KA.gen, KA.agree**. **KA.param** $\rightarrow pp$ takes security parameter k as input and generates some public parameters for subsequent algorithms. **KA.gen**$(pp) \rightarrow (s_u^{SK}, s_u^{PK})$ generates a set of key pairs for user u. **KA.agree**$(s_u^{SK}, s_v^{PK}) \rightarrow (s_{u,v})$ takes the private key of user u and the public key of user v as input, and generates the negotiation key of user u and v. These agreement keys will be used to transfer information between users during the learning process.

3.5 Threshold Homomorphic Encryption

An additive homomorphic encryption scheme guarantees the following: for some predefined function, **Enc**$(m1) \circ$ **Enc**$(m2) =$ **Enc**$(m1 + m2)$. This function indicates that the value obtained after encrypting $(m1+m2)$ using the algorithm **Enc**$(.)$ is the same as the sum of the values obtained after encrypting $m1$ and $m2$ separately using this algorithm. Such scheme is popular in privacy-preserving data analysis because untrusted parties can perform operations on encrypted values. An example of the additive homomorphic scheme is the Paillier cryptosystem [18], which is a probabilistic encryption scheme based on calculations in the group $\mathbb{Z}_{n2}^*$, where n is the RSA modulus. In [19], the authors extend this encryption scheme and propose a threshold variant. In the threshold variant, a set of participants is able to share the key such that no subset of parties smaller than a predetermined threshold can decrypt the value.

3.6 Homomorphic Hash Functions

The message M is encrypted in this system using a collision-resistant homomorphic hash function [20, 21]:

$$HF(M_i) = (A_i, B_i) = (g^{HF_{\delta, \rho}(M_i)}, h^{HF_{\delta, \rho}(M_i)})$$

where both δ and ρ are the secret key randomly selected in $\mathbb{Z}_q$. This homomorphic hash function has the following properties:

1. $HF(M_1 + M_2) \leftarrow (g^{HF_{\delta,\rho}(M_1)+HF_{\delta,\rho}(M_2)}, h^{HF_{\delta,\rho}(M_1)+HF_{\delta,\rho}(M_2)})$.
2. $HF(\alpha M_1) \leftarrow (g^{\alpha HF_{\delta,\rho}(M_1)}, h^{\alpha HF_{\delta,\rho}(M_1)})$.

Other properties of this homomorphic hash function can be found in [20–22].

3.7 Threat Model

Our system is designed to defend against three adversaries, 1) aggregators, 2) data providers, and 3) outsiders.

An aggregator is a central server that aggregates n data providers together using parameters passed by the Federated Learning System. In our system, TAs are trusted and do not collude with other entities.

Aggregators and all other participants are considered to be honest but curious. They will follow the protocol description correctly, but may also attempt to infer the private data of other users [23,24]. Thus, the aggregator will not deviate from the intended ML algorithm but will attempt to infer private information using all data received throughout the protocol execution.

In particular, we allow cloud servers to conspire with multiple users for maximum attack capability. Furthermore, we allow cloud servers to forge **Proof** (no conspiracy to forge **Proof**) and modify calculations to deceive users.

4 Our Scheme

In this section, we will present some of the details of the implementation of our federated learning system. The system mainly solves four privacy issues in the federated learning environment. The first issue is to protect the user's local data during the learning process. The second is to prevent the leakage of the intermediate results or the final model. Thirdly, to ensure the results after the user exits halfway. And the fourth is to support users to verify the results returned by the server.

We summarize our scheme in Fig. 2. The system consists of six rounds of interaction to complete the above tasks. First, the system starts to initialize and generates all public and private keys required by users and servers. Then, each user P_i encrypts its local gradient x_u and submits it to the cloud server. After receiving enough messages from all online users, the cloud server will summarize the gradients of all online users and return the results to each user along with **Proof**. Finally, each user decides to accept or reject the calculation result by verifying **Proof**, and then returns to **Round 0** to start a new iteration.

4.1 Share Decryption and Share Combining

To protect the user's local data during the learning process, we encrypted the model parameters of each user u using a threshold homomorphic encryption method. And to

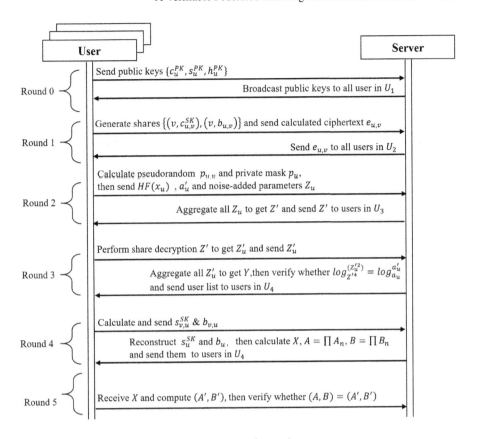

Fig. 2. Flow chart of our scheme.

prevent leakage of the intermediate results of learning and the final model, we add Gaussian noise to the model parameters y_u that need to be encrypted. Also by constructing a Fiat-Shamir zero-knowledge proof [25], the server can authenticate the user identity.

In **Round2**, each user encrypts the already-noised data y_u using their own public key h_u^{PK} for:

$$Z_u = \mathbf{Enc}_{pk}(y_u + noise(\epsilon, t'))$$

where ϵ is privacy guarantee, t' is non-colluding parties.

According to the Paillier cryptosystem, the user needs to calculate:

$$Z_u = g^{(y_u + noise(\epsilon, t'))} r^n$$

where n is the product of two prime numbers, i.e., $n = p \cdot q$ and $r \in Z_{n^2}^*$ is a random number.

In **Round3**, the server chooses $\bar{t} = n - t' + 1$ users to share decryption on Z' of the service aggregate.

Each user first calculates:

$$a'_u = a^{\Delta f(u)} \bmod n^2, \qquad f(x) = \sum_u^{k-1} x^u$$

and sends it to the server. After receiving them, the server returns the aggregated encrypted value $Z' = \mathbf{Enc}_{pk}(y_1 + y_2 + ... + y_n) \leftarrow Z_1 \circ Z_2 \circ ... \circ Z_n$. That is, $Z' = g^Y r^n$, where $Y = \sum_{u \in \mathcal{U}_3} y_u$.

After that, the user calculates $Z'_u = Z'^{2\Delta f(u)}$ on the returned Z' and sends it to the server. Finally, the server receive these data then proof the correctness:

$$\begin{aligned} \log_{Z'^4} (Z'^2_u) &= \log_{Z'^4} (Z'^{4\Delta f(u)}) \\ &= \log_{a_u} (a^{\Delta f(u)}) \\ &= \log_{a_u} (a'_u) \end{aligned}$$

If server have the required number of shares with a correct **Proof**, server can combine them into the result by taking a subset S of $\bar{t}$ shares and combine them to:

$$M = \prod_{u \in S} Z'^{2\lambda^S_{0,u}}_u \bmod n^2$$

where $\lambda^S_{0,u} = \Delta \prod_{u' \in S_1} \frac{-u}{u - u'} \in \mathbb{Z}$.

The value of M will have the form $M = Z'^{4\Delta^2} \bmod n^2$. Noting that $4\Delta^2 = 0 \bmod \lambda$, server can conclude that $M = (1 + n)^{4\Delta^2 Y} \bmod n^2$. Since $(1 + n)^{(x)} \equiv 1 + nx \bmod n^2$, so $1 + 4n\Delta^2 Y$, the server can calculate $Y = \frac{M-1}{4n\Delta^2}$.

4.2   Reducing Noise with SMC

In our system, the SMC framework can effectively reduce the noise added by DP. We assume that σ_s and S_s are the noise parameters in the federated learning algorithm and the sensitivity of the allocated budget, respectively. When using only differential privacy, each user adds noise $N(0, S_s^2, \sigma_s^2$ to the data y_u that needs to be sent to the server using the Gaussian mechanism of DP. The noise will be reduced by a factor of $t - 1$. Instead of sending $y_u + N(0, S_s^2, \sigma_s^2$, each user send $Enc(y_u + N(0, S_s^2, \frac{\sigma_s^2}{t-1}))$.

When the server aggregates these data sent by the user, it ends up with $\sum_{i-1}^n y_{u_i} + y_i$, where y_i is obtained from a Gaussian distribution with standard deviation $S_s \frac{\sigma_s}{\sqrt{t-1}}$. This is equivalent to $N(0, S_s^2, \frac{n\sigma_s^2}{t-1}) \sum_{i-1}^n y_{u_i}$. Since $t - 1 < n$, the noise in the value obtained by server aggregation strictly satisfies the DP requirement. In addition, since the number of colluders in the SMC framework is max $\bar{t}$, it is not possible to decrypt the private data of other users. In summary, the noise added by differential privacy can be effectively reduced by the SMC framework, and the security of the federated learning system can be ensured.

5   Security Analysis

5.1   Correctness Verification

In **Round 5** of this system, each remaining user receives the final σ, A, B, L, Q sent by the server and verifies $\phi = e(A, h)\dot{e}(L, h)^d$ by the l-BDHI assumption [21]. if ϕ verifies correctly then the user can infer A and L and verify $e(A, h) = e(g, B)$, $e(L, h) = e(g, Q)$ based on the DDH assumption [26]. From this, the user can conclude that the server computes the correct B and Q, which means that the aggregation result X returned by the server is correct.

By using the l-BDHI [21] and DDH [26] assumptions we can easily perform the proof, so the detailed proof process is omitted here.

5.2   Threshold Homomorphic Encryption

In **Round 2** and 3 of this system, each user sends a'_u, Z'_u to the server, and the server computes Z'. Then the server performs a zero-knowledge proof to verify that $\log_{Z'^4}\left(Z_u'^2\right) = \log_{a_u}(a'_u)$. Since each user shares the unique public value a_u with the server during the preparation phase, this leads the server to believe that the identity of the user is not forged by the adversary.

The non-interactive zero-knowledge proof mentioned above has used the Fiat-Shamir heuristic [25].

6   Performance Evaluation

In this section, we evaluate the performance of our system in terms of computation at different gradients and number of users during execution, and summarize the computational overhead of the system at each stage. Our system supports user validation of the aggregated results and ensures the security of the user's private data during and after the execution. Also, the system allows the user to exit at any point of the system execution and guarantees the correctness of the final results.

Since the accuracy of the model output in federated learning is related to the number of users involved in the training and the size of the local gradient that each user has, we recorded the number of users and the size of the gradient in each experiment to analyze the relationship between these factors with model accuracy and system overhead.

Figure 3 shows the classification accuracy and the running time required for the system to perform at different gradients in our experiments. In Fig. 3, we set up three sets of data with different number of gradients for our experiments, and it can be seen from Fig. 3(a) that the higher the number of local gradients owned by the user, the higher the accuracy of the model output. Accordingly, it can be seen from Fig. 3(b) that the more the number of local gradients the user has, the higher the computational overhead of each round. And when the number of iterations reaches a certain level, the accuracy of the model will stabilize.

Figure 4 shows the computational overhead of the users during the system execution, which we measure in terms of running time and data volume, respectively.

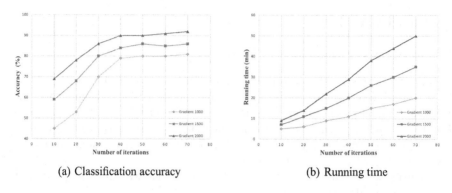

(a) Classification accuracy   (b) Running time

Fig. 3. No dropout, $|\mathcal{U}| = 100$, classification accuracy and running time with the different number of gradients per user.

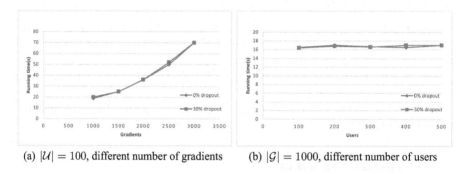

(a) $|\mathcal{U}| = 100$, different number of gradients   (b) $|\mathcal{G}| = 1000$, different number of users

Fig. 4. Total running time of each user (Verification part) with the different number of gradients per user and different number of users respectively.

In Fig. 4, we set up two different sets of data with different dropout rates and used the control variable method to vary the number of users or the number of gradients for the experiment. As can be seen from Fig. 4, the computational overhead required is higher when the number of local gradients owned by users increases, but remains essentially constant when only the number of users increases, and the low dropout rate does not affect the computational overhead. These overheads are mainly related to the number of user ladders, so when the number of user ladders increases, the total overhead increases as well.

Figure 6 shows the computational overhead of the server during the execution of the system. From Fig. 6, we can see that, unlike the changing pattern of the computational overhead of the users, the computational overhead of the server is linearly related to both the number of local gradients and the number of users. As the number of gradients or users increases, the computational overhead required by the server also increases, and a low dropout rate decreases the total running time. In addition, Fig. 5 shows that the number of users that quit greatly affects the server's computation overhead. In general, the main computation and communication overhead of the server throughout the

	Num.Clients	Dropout	Advertise Keys	Share Keys	Masking	User Authentication	Secure aggregation	Correctness verification	Total
Client	100	0%	100(ms)	1502(ms)	4250(ms)	980(ms)	532(ms)	6712(ms)	14076(ms)
Server	100	0%	1(ms)	203(ms)	560(ms)	248(ms)	1432(ms)	0(ms)	2444(ms)
Server	100	30%	1(ms)	198(ms)	524(ms)	244(ms)	9648(ms)	0(ms)	10615(ms)
Client	300	0%	100(ms)	3638(ms)	7425(ms)	1452(ms)	841(ms)	8521(ms)	21977(ms)
Server	300	0%	5(ms)	347(ms)	821(ms)	274(ms)	2680(ms)	0(ms)	4127(ms)
Server	300	30%	5(ms)	325(ms)	789(ms)	252(ms)	23167(ms)	0(ms)	24538(ms)

Fig. 5. The computation overhead per round for the client and server in different scenarios.

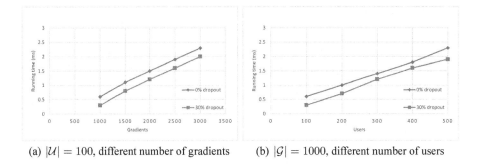

(a) $|\mathcal{U}| = 100$, different number of gradients   (b) $|\mathcal{G}| = 1000$, different number of users

Fig. 6. Total running time of the server (Verification part) with the different number of gradients per user and different number of users respectively.

execution of the system comes from aggregating the gradients transmitted by the users and removing the masks.

7   Conclusion

In this paper, we propose a federated learning system based on secure multi-party computation and differential privacy to enhance the privacy of the learning process and learning results. In addition, our system supports for users who exit midway using variants of secret sharing techniques and key protocols, and it also supports user verification of server aggregation results via homomorphic hash functions and pseudo-random functions. The security analysis demonstrates that our system is highly secure in guaranteeing the various supports for users. Based on our evaluation using real data, our system maintained good performance during the learning process. In the future, we will focus on reducing the computation and communication overhead of the system while maintaining security.

References

1. Truex, S., et al.: A hybrid approach to privacy-preserving federated learning. In: Proceedings of the 12th ACM Workshop on Artificial Intelligence and Security, pp. 1–11 (2019)
2. Xiong, Z., Cai, Z., Takabi, D., Li, W.: Privacy threat and defense for federated learning with non-iid data in AIoT. IEEE Trans. Industr. Inform. (2021)

3. Yuwen, P., Chunqiang, H., Deng, S., Alrawais, A.: R^2peds: a recoverable and revocable privacy-preserving edge data sharing scheme. IEEE Internet Things J. **7**(9), 8077–8089 (2020)

4. Chunqiang, H., Liao, X., Cheng, X.: Verifiable multi-secret sharing based on LFSR sequences. Theoret. Comput. Sci. **445**, 52–62 (2012)

5. Bonawitz, K., et al.: Practical secure aggregation for privacy-preserving machine learning. In: Proceedings of the 2017 ACM SIGSAC Conference on Computer and Communications Security, pp. 1175–1191 (2017)

6. Hu, C., Cheng, X., Tian, Z., Yu, J., Lv, W.: Achieving privacy preservation and billing via delayed information release. IEEE/ACM Trans. Netw. (2021)

7. Shokri, R., Shmatikov, V.: Privacy-preserving deep learning. In: Proceedings of the 22nd ACM SIGSAC Conference on Computer and Communications Security, pp. 1310–1321 (2015)

8. Kairouz, P., et al.: Advances and open problems in federated learning. arXiv preprint arXiv:1912.04977 (2019)

9. Pang, J., Huang, Y., Xie, Z., Han, Q., Cai, Z.: Realizing the heterogeneity: a self-organized federated learning framework for IoT. IEEE Internet Things J. **8**(5), 3088–3098 (2020)

10. Zheng, X., Cai, Z.: Privacy-preserved data sharing towards multiple parties in industrial IoTs. IEEE J. Sel. Areas Commun. **38**(5), 968–979 (2020)

11. Cai, Z., Xiong, Z., Xu, H., Wang, P., Li, W., Pan, Y.: Generative adversarial networks: a survey towards private and secure applications. ACM Comput. Surv. (CSUR) (2021)

12. Cai, Z., He, Z., Guan, X., Li, Y.: Collective data-sanitization for preventing sensitive information inference attacks in social networks. IEEE Trans. Dependable Secure Comput. **15**(4), 577–590 (2016)

13. Aono, Y., Hayashi, T., Wang, L., Moriai, S.: Privacy-preserving deep learning via additively homomorphic encryption. IEEE Trans. Inf. Forensics Secur. **13**(5), 1333–1345 (2018)

14. Hu, R., Guo, Y., Li, H., Pei, Q., Gong, Y.: Personalized federated learning with differential privacy. IEEE Internet Things J. **7**(10), 9530–9539 (2020)

15. Dwork, C.: Differential privacy: a survey of results. In: Agrawal, M., Du, D., Duan, Z., Li, A. (eds.) TAMC 2008. LNCS, vol. 4978, pp. 1–19. Springer, Heidelberg (2008). https://doi.org/10.1007/978-3-540-79228-4_1

16. Shamir, A.: How to share a secret. Commun. ACM **22**(11), 612–613 (1979)

17. Diffie, W., Hellman, M.: New directions in cryptography. IEEE Trans. Inf. Theory **22**(6), 644–654 (1976)

18. Paillier, P.: Public-key cryptosystems based on composite degree residuosity classes. In: Stern, J. (ed.) EUROCRYPT 1999. LNCS, vol. 1592, pp. 223–238. Springer, Heidelberg (1999). https://doi.org/10.1007/3-540-48910-X_16

19. Damgård, I., Jurik, M.: A generalisation, a simplification and some applications of Paillier's probabilistic public-key system. In: Kim, K. (ed.) PKC 2001. LNCS, vol. 1992, pp. 119–136. Springer, Heidelberg (2001). https://doi.org/10.1007/3-540-44586-2_9

20. Yun, A., Cheon, J.H., Kim, Y.: On homomorphic signatures for network coding. IEEE Trans. Comput. **59**(9), 1295–1296 (2010)

21. Fiore, D., Gennaro, R., Pastro, V.: Efficiently verifiable computation on encrypted data. In: Proceedings of the 2014 ACM SIGSAC Conference on Computer and Communications Security, pp. 844–855 (2014)

22. Xing, K., Chunqiang, H., Jiguo, Y., Cheng, X., Zhang, F.: Mutual privacy preserving k-means clustering in social participatory sensing. IEEE Trans. Industr. Inf. **13**(4), 2066–2076 (2017)

23. Agrawal, R., Srikant, R.: Privacy-preserving data mining. In: Proceedings of the 2000 ACM SIGMOD International Conference on Management of Data, pp. 439–450 (2000)

24. Chunqiang, H., Li, W., Cheng, X., Jiguo, Yu., Wang, S., Bie, R.: A secure and verifiable access control scheme for big data storage in clouds. IEEE Trans. Big Data **4**(3), 341–355 (2017)
25. Shoup, V.: Practical threshold signatures. In: Preneel, B. (ed.) EUROCRYPT 2000. LNCS, vol. 1807, pp. 207–220. Springer, Heidelberg (2000). https://doi.org/10.1007/3-540-45539-6_15
26. Boneh, D., Franklin, M.: Identity-based encryption from the weil pairing. In: Kilian, J. (ed.) CRYPTO 2001. LNCS, vol. 2139, pp. 213–229. Springer, Heidelberg (2001). https://doi.org/10.1007/3-540-44647-8_13

TX-RSA: A High Performance RSA Implementation Scheme on NVIDIA Tegra X2

Jiankuo Dong[1,2], Guang Fan[3,5], Fangyu Zheng[3,5(✉)], Jingqiang Lin[4], and Fu Xiao[1]

[1] School of Computer Science, Nanjing University of Posts and Telecommunications, Nanjing, China
[2] Guangxi Key Laboratory of Cryptography and Information Security, Guilin, China
[3] Institute of Information Engineering, Chinese Academy of Sciences, Beijing, China
zhengfangyu@iie.ac.cn
[4] School of Cyber Security, University of Science and Technology of China, Hefei, China
[5] Data Assurance and Communication Security Research Center, Chinese Academy of Sciences, Beijing, China

Abstract. Driven by computer vision and autopilot industries, embedded graphics processing units (GPUs) are now rapidly achieving extraordinary computing power, such NVIDIA Tegra K1/X1/X2, which are widely used in embedded environments such as mobile phones, game console and vehicle-mounted systems. Such performance advantages give embedded GPUs the possibility of accelerating cryptography that also requires high-density computing. In this paper, we implement TX-RSA in embedded GPU platforms, i.e., NVIDIA TX2, to accelerate the most prevailing public-key cryptosystem, RSA. Various optimization methods are employed to promote the efficiency, including multi-threaded Montgomery multiplication and CRT implementation on the resource-constricted embedded GPUs. Within 20 W of power consumption, TX-RSA can deliver 6,423 ops/s of RSA encryption and 131,324 ops/s of RSA decryption, which outperforms implementations in the desktop GPUs and embedded CPUs in the perspective of performance-to-power ratio.

Keywords: RSA · CUDA · Embedded GPU

1 Introduction

With the rapid development of all kinds of network services, a huge number of transactions are generated in electronic commerce, digital publishing, software

This work was partially supported by National Natural Science Foundation of China under Award No. 61902392 and Guangxi Key Laboratory of Cryptography and Information Security (No. CIS202120).

© Springer Nature Switzerland AG 2021
Z. Liu et al. (Eds.): WASA 2021, LNCS 12938, pp. 210–222, 2021.
https://doi.org/10.1007/978-3-030-86130-8_17

distribution, etc. For instance, the peak order processing speed of Tmall, a main-stream online shopping application in China, reached 583,000 orders per second during an online shopping festival on November 11, 2020 [1].

Behind those online services, securing the interchange of information through computing networks, cryptography system is playing a more important role than ever before. Actually, the increase in the number of transactions also means an increase in computing load. Some of the cryptographic algorithms involved have high computing requirements, especially those related to public-key cryptography. RSA is currently the most widely used public-key cryptographic algorithm. Compared with symmetric cryptographic algorithms and hashing algorithms, the calculations of modular exponentiation based on RSA signatures take up the main computational time in various cryptographic services (SSL/TLS [15], HTTPS).

It is necessary to use a hardware accelerator to unload those workloads for CPU. The prevailing platforms to implement cryptographic algorithms are mainly FPGA, GPU, CPU, ASIC, etc. Recently, embedded GPU offers another possibility. Driven by the rapid development of deep learning and edge computing, the capabilities of those devices are swiftly increasing. To meet the requirement of real-time tasks on mobile devices, like self-driving, the embedded GPU systems not only have high computing power, but also achieve low energy consumption. For example, declared as "the ideal platform for compute-intensive embedded projects", NVIDIA proposed a series of mobile processors named Tegra, which provide the most advanced GPU architecture for embedded GPUs and have been widely used in the field of computer vision and deep neural networks. One of their product, Jetson TX2, only takes about 15 W to provide 0.75 TFLOPS (10^{12} floating-point operations per second, which is implemented in a card-sized module.

However, high-performance public-key cryptography implementations on embedded GPU are still in their infancy. Although there are some hardware limitations, the embedded GPU has great potential in flexibility and low energy consumption.

1.1   Related Work

For RSA implementation, many previous works on different processors are reported. OpenSSL [7] is one of the most famous representatives. The CPU implementation of RSA is well optimized, and the FPGA solutions realize high speed and low power consumption. Nevertheless, limited by the comparatively low parallelism of the hardware, those schemes cannot adapt to large-scale computing scenarios.

Besides, previous studies [6,12,16] evaluate RSA performance on discrete GPUs. Their works show high throughput. Our previous works [4,5] utilized the double-precision floating-point computing power of discrete GPU to achieve higher performance. It is worth noting that these implementations need not only GPUs but also a complete set of facilities such as CPU, motherboard, memory, and fans, which consume a lot of power.

In terms of embedded GPUs, there are fewer researches on cryptography implementation, which are faced with many technical challenges. Firstly most embedded GPUs lack sufficient registers, making the general implementation, which launches a single thread for each RSA instance, suffer a severe performance penalty. Parallel processing algorithms for multi-thread RSA implementation are required. Moreover, the floating-point computing is not supported on embedded GPUs for cost considerations. Thus the floating-point implementations are inapplicable to embedded GPUs.

1.2 Contributions and Paper Organization

The contributions of this paper are threefold:

- First, we propose a suitable GPU-accelerated Montgomery multiplication algorithm by fully mining the exceptional speed and power-efficiency Embedded GPU TX2, with the approach called the Jetson-TX2-based RSA (TX-RSA) method. Compared with traditional desktop GPUs, NVIDIA company has made hardware tailoring for embedded GPUs. We design a state-of-the-art 4-thread parallel computing method for 1024-bit Montgomery multiplication to reduce the negative impact of insufficient registers. At the same time, we use the lower-level PTX ISA instruction set for the core calculations.
- Second, we provide an integral implementation of RSA algorithm, including public and private key operations. For RSA private key operation, we also provide an elaborate design for modular exponentiation, which is space to exchange for time. A modular subtraction and a multiply-add function are additionally implemented using efficient CUDA PTX ISA instructions. For 2048-bit RSA public key operation, we offer a well-designed 2048-bit Montgomery multiplication which is executed 19 times. Our RSA implementation is systematic, efficient and ready-to-use.
- Third, after a lot of experiments, we find the optimal performance parameters. And we also use the multi-stream method to overlap the memory copy latency. This scheme can improve the performance of public key cryptosystem with uncomplicated computation. Finally, on an embedded device with less than 20W power consumption, our RSA encryption and decryption operations reach 6423/131324 ops/s respectively. Compared with related works, our results have significant advantages in power consumption ratio. We believe our results have shown all the components to build a practical embedded GPU RSA accelerator.

The rest of our paper is organized as follows. Section 2 presents background material. Section 3 describes our proposed algorithms (Montgomery multiplication, modular exponentiation, and RSA) in detail. Section 4 analyses the performance of the proposed algorithm and compares it against previous works. Section 5 concludes the paper.

2   Preliminaries

In this section, we provide necessary backgrounds on embedded GPUs and CUDA, RSA acceleration methods, and data Sharing Functions.

2.1   Embedded GPUs and CUDA

NVIDIA Jetson TX2. The embedded platform used in the paper is NVIDIA Jetson TX2 (short for TX2), which is armed with a System on Chip (SoC) called Tegra X2 that integrates an NVIDIA GPU and ARM CPU clusters. The chip is implemented in a highly energy-efficient way and emphasizes performance for gaming and deep learning applications. It also supports other general-purpose computing scenarios like cryptographic processing. NVIDIA provides an SDK for Tegra SoCs, called JetPack, containing a customized Linux operating system, L4T (Linux for Tegra), and CUDA Toolkit.

Figure 1 shows the main components of the TX2. The most important part is the integrated GPU, which is revised from a version of the discrete Pascal GPU with micro-architecture GP10B (Compute Capability 6.2). It owns 2 streaming multiprocessors (SMs) for data processing. Each SM contains 128 single-precision CUDA cores. TX2 also integrates a dual-core Denver CPU and a quad-core A57 CPU. These 2 SMs can offer over 0.75 TFLOPS of single-precision floating-point arithmetic within about 15 W. With all those powerful computing units, the size of TX2 module is only 69.6 mm × 45 mm.

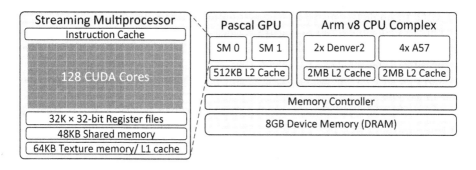

Fig. 1. Main components of NVIDIA Jetson TX2

CUDA. NVIDIA Compute Unified Device Architecture (CUDA) is a toolkit making it possible to perform general-purpose computation on GPUs. Jetson platform can use the CUDA integrated in JetPack SDK, so it can emphasize performance for gaming, deep learning, as well as cryptographic processing applications. Through the CUDA development toolkit, a CUDA-based program can use a set of C, C++, or CUDA assembly codes to finely utilize the GPU's storage and computing resources and complete specified operations.

In CUDA programming model, 32-thread is the minimum scheduling unit, which is also called a *warp*. Instructions are dispatched concurrently to all threads in the warp. Warps are further grouped into *blocks* and *grids*. Blocks are assigned to individual SMs and grids are spread across all the SMs on a GPU device. See [13] for a complete description of the GPU architecture and programming model.

2.2 RSA Acceleration Methods

There are two different methods to accelerate the RSA signature generation and verification respectively.

On the one hand, the Chinese Remainder Theorem (CRT) [14] is widely used to promote the efficiency for signature generation. Instead of calculating a $2n$-bit modular exponentiation directly, two n-bit modular exponentiations (Equation (a) & (b)) and the Mixed-Radix Conversion (MRC) algorithm [10] (Equation (c)) can be subsequently performed to conduct the RSA signature generation:

$$P_1 = C^{d \mod (p-1)} \mod p; \qquad (a)$$
$$P_2 = C^{d \mod (q-1)} \mod q; \qquad (b)$$
$$P = P_2 + [(P_1 - P_2) \cdot (q^{-1} \mod p) \mod p] \cdot q, \qquad (c)$$

where p and q are n-bit prime numbers chosen in private key generation ($M = p \times q$). Compared with calculating $2n$-bit modular exponentiations directly, the CRT technology can reduce the computational cost by 75% [14].

On the other hand, for signature verification, the acceleration solution is to choose an exponent (i.e., public key) with as few '1's in its binary representation as possible. The smallest exponent that is considered secure now is $2^{16} + 1$ (65,537) [3, §3.1]. Thus the exponentiation calculation requires only 17 modular multiplications.

Even with the CRT and the small public exponent trick, there is a bottleneck restricting the overall performance – modular multiplication, which is the core operation of RSA. In 1985 Peter L. Montgomery proposed an algorithm [11] to remove the costly division operation from the modular reduction, well known as Montgomery multiplication. Let $\bar{A} = AR(mod\ M), \bar{B} = BR(mod\ M)$ be the Montgomery form of A, B modulo M, where R and M are co-prime and $M \leq R$. Montgomery multiplication defines the multiplication of two numbers that are in Montgomery form, $MonMul(\bar{A}, \bar{B}) = \bar{A}\bar{B}R^{-1}(mod\ M)$. Even though the algorithm works for any R which is relatively prime to M, it is more useful when R is taken to be a power of 2, which leads to a fast division by R.

2.3 Data Sharing Functions in Target GPU

To improve the synchronize efficiency, We use a kind of data sharing function, *shuffle* instruction in our implementation, which *shuffle* uses a full cross-bar

Algorithm 1. Montgomery Multiplication (Coarsely Integrated Operand Scanning, CIOS)

Input:

$M > 2$ with gcd(M,2)=1, positive integers l, w such that $2^{wl} > M$;

$M' = -M^{-1} \mod 2^w$, $R^{-1} = (2^{wl})^{-1} \mod M$;

Integer multiplicand A, where $0 \le A < M$;

Integer multiplier B, where $B = \sum_{i=0}^{l-1} b_i 2^{wi}$, $0 \le b_i < 2^w$ and $0 \le B < M$;

Output:

An integer S such that $S = ABR^{-1} \mod M$ and $0 \le S < M$;

1: $S = 0$

2: **for** $i = 0$ *to* $l - 1$ **do**

3:    $S = S + A \times b_i$

4:    $Q = ((S \mod 2^w) \times M')(\mod 2^w)$

5:    $S = S + M \times Q$

6:    $S = S/2^w$

7: **end for**

8: **if** $S \ge M$ **then**

9:    $S = S - M$

10: **end if**

11: **return** S

switch and allows each thread to exchange a 32-bit value with any other thread within the warp. NVIDIA GPUs of compute capability 3.0 and above support those functions.

3   Methodology

In this section, we mainly introduce the integrated RSA implementation process. From the perspective of developers, this section is divided into three parts: Montgomery multiplication, modular exponentiation, and complete RSA signature algorithm. The involved symbols are explained in Table 1

Table 1. Symbol explanation

Symbol	Explanation
k	Thread ID where $0 \le k \le t - 1$
n	The bit length of the modulus, which is $w = 2048$
w	The window size of fixed window exponentiation algorithm
l	Number of integer limbs of the modulus, where $l = \frac{1024}{32} = 32$
t	Number of threads per Montgomery multiplication, where $t = 4$
h	Number of DPF limbs per thread, where $h = \lceil \frac{l}{t} \rceil$

3.1   Montgomery Multiplication

Montgomery multiplication is a modular multiplication method proposed by
Peter L. Montgomery [11] in 1985. From the perspective of security and performance improvement, Montgomery multiplication, avoiding complicated time-
consuming reduction calculation, got public since its foundation. This algorithm
is very efficient for both software and hardware implementation.

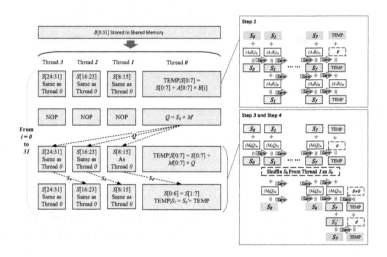

Fig. 2. Montgomery multiplication

Based on the TX2 platform, we use $t = 4$ threads to handle Algorithm 1.
Because the Chinese Remainder Theorem is used in our implementation, we only
need to compute 1024-bit ($n = 1024$) modular multiplication operation instead
of 2048-bit. From Algorithm 1, we find the core calculation is the loop operation
of Step (2–6), and the number of loops is $l = 32$. In our embedded device Jetson
TX2, the shared memory has higher access efficiency than device memory [13],
so we store the larger integer B of Montgomery multiplication in shared memory
to improve the overall implementation. For the convenience of description, we
divide the 1024-bit Montgomery multiplication cycle operation process into four
steps, which are shown as follows:

Step 1: In this Step, we should complete the operation $S = S + A(1024 - bit) \times$
$b_i(32 - bit)$. There are 8 limbs in each thread which is shown in Table 1. And we
use the underlying PTX ISA instruction $madc$ [13]. As shown in Fig. 2, we need
to execute 8 $madc.lo.cc.u32$ instructions and 8 $madc.lo.cc.u32$ instructions in our
integrated implementation for this step. After Step 1, we will get $(1024 + 32)$-bit
result S.

Step 2: The second step is a very concise step. Only Thread 0 is required to execute $Q = S_0 \times M^{-1}$. Because in the next step, we only use the lower 32 bits of the product result. We only need to use instructions $mul.lo.u32$ to get the first 32 bits of the multiplication result $Q = S_0 \times M^{-1}$. And then, we send Q to each thread using the shuffle instruction $\_\_shfl$ to prepare for subsequent calculations.

Step 3 and Step 4: It is easy to see that the process of Step 3 is similar to Step 1. We need to use the mad instruction to obtain the multiplication product which is 1056 bits length. As for Step 4, due to the principle of the algorithm, the lower 32 bits are zero and can be reduced. The large integer product S needs to be shifted right 32 bits.

As shown in Fig. 2, to simplify the calculation process as much as possible and combine the characteristics of CUDA PTX ISA instruction set, we propose an optimized implementation scheme that combines Step 3 and 4. Firstly, each thread executes 8 $madc.lo.cc.u32$ which is $S[i] = madc.lo.cc.u32(S[i], M[i], Q)$. And we use the shuffle instruction to pass $S[0]$ from Thread k to Thread $(k-1)$, and save the 32-bit integer into the temporary variable $TEMP$. Finally, we execute the 8 $madc.hi.cc.u32$ instructions which is $S[i] = madc.hi.cc.u32(S[i+1], M[i], Q)$ to complete this part of the process. Through the above optimization, we avoid the shift operation in Step 4 and improve the performance of the algorithm.

It can be seen from the Algorithm 1, after the above process is executed, there is an if branch judgment operation $if(S \geq M)$. In order to avoid the warp fork [5] from computing performance degradation, we perform the subtraction operation for all requests. When result is $(S \geq M)$, the $S = S - 0$ is carried out.

3.2   Montgomery Exponentiation

The most common algorithm of Montgomery Exponentiation operation is binary square-multiply. If using this method, we need $1024 + 1024/2 = 1536$ Montgomery multiplications. In order to reduce this number, we use the $m - ary$ method in [8]. Based on this scheme, when $m = 6$, the number of Montgomery multiplication is the least, which is $1024 + 26 + \lceil \frac{1024}{6} \rceil = 1259$. The main idea of this scheme is to use space for time, which is especially suitable for GPU devices with larger device memory.

The $m - ary$ method is also implemented in [5] and [4], which can reduce the number of Montgomery multiplication by 18%. The sliding window technology Constant Length Nonzero Windows (CLNW) [9] is another widely used method. However, the sliding window method is not suitable for GPU devices with parallel programming ideas because the possible warp bifurcation will reduce the overall implementation performance.

3.3 RSA Implementation

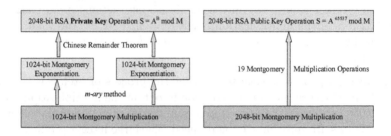

Fig. 3. RSA multiplication

As shown in Fig. 3, due to the different composition of RSA public key and private key, we adopt different optimization schemes to the implementation. For RSA algorithm, the private key operation is more complex than public key. Using the Chinese Remainder Theorem, we can get a 2048-bit modular exponentiation result through two 1024-bit ones. Our implementation is similar to the previous work [5]. The difference is that all our implementation is based on PTX ISA integer instruction rather than double-precision floating-point. Therefore, we also implemented 1024-bit modular subtraction and multiplication-add operations for CRT. For RSA public key operation ($S = A^{65537} mod M$), we use 19 Montgomery multiplication operations. And one is to turn A to Montgomery form $\bar{A} = Mont(A, R2M)$, and 16 operations is for exponentiation, the last one is to turn $\bar{A}$ back to normal form A which is $A = Mont(\bar{A}, 1)$.

Oriented to the parallelism policies, we use 4 threads to realize the 1024-bit Montgomery multiplication for 2048-bit RSA private key operations, and 8 threads for public key. This is because the public key operation implementation is much easier than private one. Compared with complex large integer exponentiation and CRT of RSA private key operation, the public key only relies on 19 multiplication. Based on these parallelism policies, 2048-bit private/public operations are executed by 8 threads in parallel. We ensure that the number of limbs processed by each thread is consistent ($l = 8$), and make sure the data will not be overflowed into the device memory.

The work [2] provides a solution named multi-stream, which is suitable for GPU program execution. It takes full advantage of the stream feature of CUDA. With this method, we can overlap the data transfer time between CPU and GPU. It has important performance improvement significance for the task whose kernel calculation latency is equivalent to memory copy, for example, the RSA public key operation or symmetric cryptographic algorithm.

4 Performance Evaluation and Related Work Comparison

In this section, we discuss the implementation performance and summarize the results for the proposed algorithm. There are two performance evaluation items, throughput and latency. The throughput means the numbers of RSA signature generation/verification completed in one period (e.g., 60 s) divided by the period. The latency is that the waiting interval from copying the data into GPU memory to getting the computed results from GPU. There are also some parameters that can affect the performance, and they are shown here.

- *Batch Size*: the number of RSA operations for GPU kernel.
- *Threads/RSA*: the number of CUDA threads assigned for each RSA signature generation/verification.
- *Threads/Stream*: the number of CUDA threads contained in a CUDA stream.
- *RSAs/Stream*: the number of RSA requests contained in a CUDA stream.

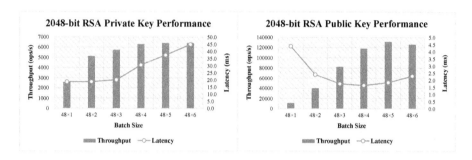

Fig. 4. RSA throughput and latency

4.1   Performance Evaluation

In our experiment, the batch size represents the total number of RSA calculation requests. It is also *the number of Stream(Stream No.)* × (*RSAs/Stream*). Figure 4 presents the performance of our TX-RSA implementation. For 2048-bit RSA public key operation, the trend of calculation latency is decreasing at the beginning and increasing at the end. When the number of streams is not enough, the delay consumption of memory copy can not be covered up, which has a great impact on the simple kernel computing of public key cryptography, but has little impact on the complex private key computing.

Table 2. The peak performance of 2048-bit TX-RSA

RSAs/Stream	Stream No.	Pri. Key Op. Throughput (ops/s)/Latency (ms)	Pub. Key Op. Throughput (ops/s)/latency(ms)
48	5	**6423/37.36**	**131324/1.83**

As shown in Table 2, our best performance of 2048-bit RSA public key operation is 131324 ops/s, and the latency is 1.83 ms. For private key operation, our TX-RSA can export 6423 ops/s with the latency 37.36 ms.

Table 3. Performance comparison

	Platform	Power (W)	Pri. Key Op. Throughput (ops/s)	Pub. Key Op. Throughput (ops/s)
OpenSSL [7]	(4+2)core ARM CPU in Tegra TX2	11	1762	67700
Dong et al. [4]	GTX Titan Black	245	52747	1237694
Emmart et al. [6]	GTX Titan Black	245	66250	–
Ours	2 Pa SMs in Tegra TX2	19	6423	131324

4.2   Related Work Comparison

vs. OpenSSL. The OpenSSL [7] algorithm library is one of the most widely used cryptographic libraries, and supports RSA cryptographic algorithms with multiple bit lengths. As shown in the Table 3, we use the command "*openssl speed rsa2048 -multi 6*" to test the 2048-bit RSA encryption/decryption performance on $(4+2)$ ARM CPU cores of TX2. We compare our results against OpenSSL. Our public/private key operation (encryption/decryption) performance is about 1.92/3.64 times that of this library. On embedded platforms, power consumption is also an important factor to consider. On the same platform, the OpenSSL library calls the ARM CPU cores, but TX-RSA calls the GPU Pascal cores, so there are also differences in power consumption. Even considering power consumption, our unit power consumption (1 W) performance is 1.5/2.1 (public/private) times that of OpenSSL.

vs. Desktop GPU. Within the scope of our knowledge, there is no query related implementation technology of RSA cryptography based on embedded GPUs. Therefore, we will compare our results with the existing desktop GPU results [4,6]. This work [6] is the fastest RSA cryptographic algorithm implementation to the best of our knowledge. Based on GTX Titan Black, its 1024-bit modular exponentiation performance reached 132500 ops/s. It is unfair to compare our results with desktop GPU platform directly. In the same method as Sect. 4.2, we also take power consumption into consideration. Our proposed RSA encryption (private key) implementation is 338 ops/s per watt. The work [6] only provides the performance of 1024-bit modular exponentiation with CRT for complete RSA algorithm. Even if our implementation includes the CRT algorithm, our private key operation throughput-to-power is still 1.25 times that of [6].

5 Conclusion

In this paper, we implement a novel, systematic and efficient implementation of RSA scheme (named TX-RSA) based on the exceptional speed and power-efficiency embedded computing device NVIDIA Jetson TX2. Our primary motivation is mining the computing power of embedded GPU platform TX2 and providing a high-throughput public key cryptography accelerator. As we all know, the desktop GPU is an excellent platform to improve the performance of public key cryptographic algorithms. Our work proves that although the embedded GPU TX2 has done hardware tailoring to a certain extent, it has significant advantages in terms of performance and power consumption ratio. Furthermore, not all scenarios require millions of public key cryptography computation requests. Our TX-RSA scheme can provide a brand new and efficient solution for the Internet of Things and edge computing.

Our future work will focus on providing high-performance network solutions for TX-RSA, and making TX2 an edge computing node to offer security supports for IoT devices.

References

1. China Briefing: (2021). https://www.china-briefing.com/news/chinas-double-11-shopping-festival-tests-consumption-strength-after-covid-19/
2. Cheng, W., Zheng, F., Pan, W., Lin, J., Li, H., Li, B.: Building your private cloud storage on public cloud service using embedded GPUs. In: Beyah, R., Chang, B., Li, Y., Zhu, S. (eds.) SecureComm 2018. LNICST, vol. 254, pp. 512–528. Springer, Cham (2018). https://doi.org/10.1007/978-3-030-01701-9_28
3. U.S. Department of Commerce/National Institute of Standards and Technology: Digital Signature Standard (DSS) (2013). http://nvlpubs.nist.gov/nistpubs/FIPS/NIST.FIPS.186-4.pdf
4. Dong, J., Zheng, F., Emmart, N., Lin, J., Weems, C.: sDPF-RSA: utilizing floating-point computing power of GPUs for massive digital signature computations. In: 2018 IEEE International Parallel and Distributed Processing Symposium (IPDPS), pp. 599–609. IEEE (2018)
5. Dong, J., Zheng, F., Pan, W., Lin, J., Jing, J., Zhao, Y.: Utilizing the double-precision floating-point computing power of GPUs for RSA acceleration. Secur. Commun. Netw. **2017** (2017)
6. Emmart, N., Zheng, F., Weems, C.: Faster modular exponentiation using double precision floating point arithmetic on the GPU. In: 2018 IEEE 25th Symposium on Computer Arithmetic (ARITH), pp. 130–137. IEEE (2018)
7. OpenSSL Software Foundation: OpenSSL Cryptography and SSL/TLS Toolkit (2016). http://www.openssl.org/
8. Knuth, D.E.: The Art of Computer Programming: Seminumerical Algorithms, vol. 2, p. 116. Addison-Wesley, Boston (1981)
9. Koç, C.K.: Analysis of sliding window techniques for exponentiation. Comput. Math. Appl. **30**(10), 17–24 (1995)
10. Koç, C.K.: High-speed RSA implementation. Technical report, RSA Laboratories (1994)

11. Montgomery, P.L.: Modular multiplication without trial division. Math. Comput. **44**(170), 519–521 (1985)
12. Neves, S., Araujo, F.: On the performance of GPU public-key cryptography. In: 2011 IEEE International Conference on Application-Specific Systems, Architectures and Processors (ASAP), pp. 133–140. IEEE (2011)
13. NVIDIA: CUDA C programming guide 9.0 (2017). https://docs.nvidia.com/cuda/cuda-c-programming-guide/
14. Quisquater, J.J., Couvreur, C.: Fast decipherment algorithm for RSA public-key cryptosystem. Electron. Lett. **18**(21), 905–907 (1982)
15. Rescorla, E.: The transport layer security (TLS) protocol version 1.3. RFC 8446, pp. 1–160 (2018). https://doi.org/10.17487/RFC8446
16. Yang, Y., Guan, Z., Sun, H., Chen, Z.: Accelerating RSA with fine-grained parallelism using GPU. In: Lopez, J., Wu, Y. (eds.) ISPEC 2015. LNCS, vol. 9065, pp. 454–468. Springer, Cham (2015). https://doi.org/10.1007/978-3-319-17533-1_31

Data Center Networks and Cloud Computing

Short Term Voltage Stability Assessment with Incomplete Data Based on Deep Reinforcement Learning in the Internet of Energy

Anqi Liu[1], Xin Guan[1(✉)], Di Sun[2], Haiyang Jiang[2], Chen Cui[1], and Dawei Fang[1]

[1] School of Data Science and Technology, Heilongjiang University, Harbin 150080, China
{20172901,2181782}@s.hlju.edu.cn, 2018012@hlju.edu.cn
[2] State Grid Heilongjiang Electric Power Company Limited, Harbin 150080, China

Abstract. Short-term voltage stability (STVS) assessment is one of the important challenges in the power system. With the wide application of phasor measurement units (PMUs), STVS assessment based on data-driven has attracted more and more attentions. In fact, some of the PMU data may be lost when used for STVS assessment, and it may affect the accuracy of STVS assessment. In this paper, we focus on assessing the STVS with incomplete PMU data based on data-driven method. Firstly, long short term memory (LSTM) network is adopted to fill the missing PMU data. Secondly, double deep Q-Learning (DDQN) is used for STVS assessment. The effectiveness of the proposed intelligent evaluation model is verified on the New England 39-bus system. As the experimental results shows, the deviation degree between the predicted PMU data and the true PMU data is small with a 20% data missing rate. Moreover, proposed STVS assessment model can achieve good performance when using the predicted PMU data.

Keywords: Short-term voltage stability · PMU data missing · Deep learning · Deep reinforcement learning

1 Introduction

In the internet of energy, many related problems have been raised. For example, data aggregation of renewable energy [6] and privacy protection [2,22] have been well solved. The stability of power grid is also a problem worthy of attention. In order to ensure stable operation of the power system, it is necessary to monitor the power system to prevent catastrophic problems. Short-term voltage stability is one of the main problems that threaten the power system security. Short-term voltage stability refers to the fact that the power system can still remain

Supported by organization x.

Z. Liu et al. (Eds.): WASA 2021, LNCS 12938, pp. 225–236, 2021.
https://doi.org/10.1007/978-3-030-86130-8_18

within the acceptable voltage range when the power system is subject to large disturbances [11]. One of the reasons for short-term voltage instability is the imbalance between the generated power of the system and the power required by the load [7]. However, the load continues to increase. Equipment such as generators cannot be added together due to economic reasons. These reasons aggravate the uncertainty of power generation on the power generation side. This makes STVS assessment particularly important.

At present, the mainstream dynamic methods for analyzing STVS are divided into three categories: energy function based method [5], time domain simulation based method [23], and data-driven based method [16]. Among them, the energy function based method cannot have high accuracy. For different power systems, it is difficult to establish the energy function. Therefore, the energy function based method cannot become the mainstream industrial method. The time domain simulation based method has a wide range of applications in actual power system analysis. However, the time domain simulation based method has the disadvantage of low computational efficiency. This makes it is not suitable for the scenario of STVS assessment. In the wide area measurement system (WAMS), the PMUs enable the system to obtain the voltage data after the fault in time and assess the STVS. Therefore, the data-driven based STVS assessment has gradually become a research hotspot.

With the development of artificial intelligence, It has related research in many fields. [12] use Deep Learning (DL) to identify the user's tap position information. In [18], Federated learning (FL) is used for privacy protection analysis. In [14], the optimal coalition of clients is carried out based on FL and Reinforcement Learning (RL). [3] not only can improve efficiency but also protect user's privacy. Simultaneously, artificial intelligence can also solve the STVS problem. In [19], an integrated machine learning method is proposed to solve the problem of STVS assessment, but its application background is the event-based STVS assessment. Taking into account the Fault-Induced delayed voltage recovery phenomenon in the STVS assessment, a Random Vector Functional Link (RVFL) model is applied to predict the stability of the power system [20].

However, the above-mentioned methods can only achieve good performance when PMU data is available and complete. In fact, some of the PMU data may be lost after the power system fails [17]. Once the data is incomplete, the above methods will not achieve good performance. In [10], they use existing data to fill the missing data. However, the computing efficiency of this kind of method is too low to solve the problem of short-term voltage stability assessment. In [21], a method is proposed to assess the short-term voltage stability using the incomplete data.

At present, only a few methods are proposed to solve the problem of PMU data missing when assess the short-term voltage stability. In this paper, we first focus on how to fill the missing PMU data when assess the short-term voltage stability. Taking into account the sequentiality of PMU data, Long Short-Term Memory (LSTM) model is applied to predict the missing PMU data based on the available PMU data. After the system obtains the complete data, the

STVS assessment is performed. Deep Reinforcement Learning (DRL) can make corresponding decisions and select suitable actions based on current state conditions, achieving a certain expected goal through the maximum reward value obtained [9]. DRL is a combination of DL and RL. RL extracts the observed state information, and DL uses the information extracted by RL to select the next action to achieve the final goal. Value-based Double Deep Q-Networks (DDQN) is a DRL algorithm with high-dimensional state input and low-dimensional state output. Therefore, the classification tasks can be performed well. Due to the problems of existing methods, this paper proposes a method based on DL and DRL which can fill the missing PMU data and solve the problem of STVS assessment.

The contributions of this paper are listed as follows. Firstly, the LSTM model is used to fill the missing PMU data based on the available PMU data in real time without taking into account the problems caused by changes of the grid topology, which can makes the performance of STVS assessment more stable. Secondly, a DDQN based evaluation model is proposed to solve the problem of STVS assessment. Compared with the traditional machine learning based evaluation model, proposed evaluation model can achieve better performance.

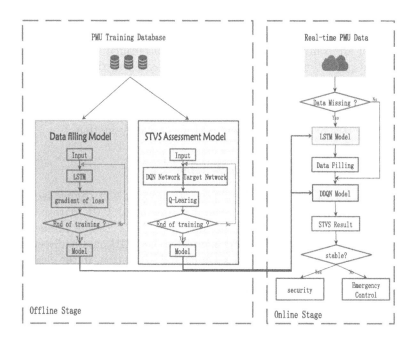

Fig. 1. Framework of the proposed intelligent scheme.

2   Proposed Intelligent Scheme

This paper needs to solve two problems. One is the problem of filling the missing data, and the other is STVS assessment. An intelligent scheme for STVS assessment with incomplete PMU data is designed. The overall framework is shown in Fig. 1.

2.1   Short-Term Voltage Stability

This paper focuses on the assessment of STVS, distinguish the unstable state from the stable state. Therefore, the research scope considered is a few seconds after the fault is cleared (the research time in this article is 5 s). The steady state means that all bus voltages after the fault are re-balanced to an acceptable state (the bus voltage after the fault is not less than 75% of the bus voltage before the fault in the industry). The unstable state refers to the voltage collapse during the transient period, which means the voltage is no longer able to maintain balance.

2.2   Offline Stage of Intelligent Scheme

In the offline stage, two models are trained at the same time. Firstly, the prediction model based on LSTM is trained for filling the missing data. The parameters of this model are continuously updated to get an optimal state, which enables the model to predict missing data more accurate. Then, the STVS evaluation model is trained. DDQN calculates the Q value through neural networks. With the Temporal-Difference (TD) algorithm to update the parameters, the trained model can get more rewards. This makes the obtained STVS assessment model can achieve better performance when used for online evaluation.

2.3   Online Stage of Intelligent Scheme

In the online stage, the model trained in the offline stage is first imported into the online stage. Firstly, the integrity of the real-time input PMU data is checked. If the some of the PMU data is lost, the LSTM model is used for prediction and filling the missing data. If the data is complete, the PMU data is directly input into the STVS assessment model for training and evaluation. In the case of complete data, the STVS evaluation model determines whether the current system is stable or not. If the unstable situation occurs, the system can immediately activates the emergency control device to ensure the safety of power system.

3   Data Filling Based on LSTM

In this paper, the proposed data filling method has good adaptability to solve the problem of data missing with different missing ratios. Here is an introduction to the basis of LSTM and processing for missing data.

3.1   Time Series Data

The PMU data used for STVS assessment is a time series data. The missing data is not only related to the data of the previous time but also related to the data before the failure. Since LSTM is good at dealing with the problems that need long term memory [8], LSTM model is used to fill the missing PMU data in this paper.

3.2   Long Short Term Memory Network

In order to solve the problem of filling the missing PMU data, LSTM model is applied for data prediction and filling. The flow of the sequential logic is shown in Fig. 2. For time t, there are k sequential PMU data input in the order of time and connected to their input layers respectively, then the input layer is connected to the LSTM layer. By a series of learning, the LSTM layer is connected with the output layer, and the predicted missing values are output through the output layer. Finally, these values are used for filling the missing PMU data.

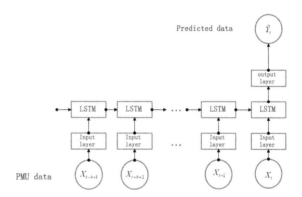

Fig. 2. The sequential structure of LSTM.

The LSTM unit is composed of cell state C_t, forget gate F_t, input gate I_t, output gate O_t, candidate memory cell $\widetilde{C}_t$, hidden state H_t, and input X_t. The information carried by the past time series data and the current time data can be transferred to the next time. This avoids the problem of vanishing gradients, and the dependence of the longer time step distance in the time series data can be better learned. However, the three gates F_t, I_t and O_t only allow information to pass through them selectively, ignoring useless information and accepting useful information. H_t can be the output of this LSTM unit and the input of the next LSTM unit. $\widetilde{C}_t$ is regarded as the new information input. X_t is the actual input data. The input X_t in this article is the status data of the PMU.

The first step is to determine the information that needs to be discarded from the cell state. The information is forgotten through the forget gate F_t. F_t

controls the influence of the last moment $C_t - 1$ on this moment C_t. The second step determines how much information needs to be stored in the cell state at the current time. This step includes the formation of input gate I_t and candidate memory cell $\widetilde{C}_t$. The third step uses the results from the previous two steps to update the cell state. In the final step, the output H_t is determined, and the information in the cell state is passed to H_t by controlling O_t. The corresponding calculation formula is as follows:

$$F_t = \sigma \left(X_t W_{xf} + H_{t-1} W_{hf} + b_f \right) \tag{1}$$

$$I_t = \sigma \left(X_t W_{xi} + H_{t-1} W_{hi} + b_i \right) \tag{2}$$

$$\widetilde{C}_t = \tanh \left(X_t W_{xc} + H_{t-1} W_{hc} + b_c \right) \tag{3}$$

$$C_t = F_t \odot C_{t-1} + I_t \odot \tilde{C}_t \tag{4}$$

$$O_t = \sigma \left(X_t W_{xo} + H_{t-1} W_{ho} + b_o \right) \tag{5}$$

$$H_t = O_t \odot \tanh \left(C_t \right) \tag{6}$$

Where W_{xf}, W_{hf}, W_{xi}, W_{hi}, W_{xc}, W_{hc}, W_{xo} and W_{ho} are weight parameters, respectively. b_f, b_i, b_c and b_o are deviation parameters. σ and $\tanh$ are activation functions.

Model Parameter Update. The parameters in LSTM need to be updated through repeated training to obtain the optimal model. θ is defined as the required update parameter. The back propagation through time (BPTT) algorithm is used to update the model. In order to update the model, the loss function is first defined. The mean square error (MSE) is used to calculate the loss. The loss function calculation formula is as follows:

$$loss_\theta = \frac{\sum_{i=1}^{N} \left(Y_i - \tilde{Y}_i \right)^2}{N} \tag{7}$$

Where N is the total number of training samples. Y_i is the real PMU data. $\tilde{Y}_i$ is the predicted PMU data.

4   STVS Assessment Based on DDQN

In different fault situations, the DDQN-based method proposed in this paper can maintain high performance for STVS evaluation. The following describes the basis of DDQN and the STVS evaluation model.

4.1   Deep Reinforcement Learning

The core of DRL is the Markov Decision Process (MDP). In this paper, we assume that the continuously generated PMU data is the environment, each PMU sample data is the state given by the environment. Action refers to the result of assessment (stable or unstable). The goal of the agent is to learn to assess STVS with PMU data. The correct decision is rewarded with 1, and the wrong decision is rewarded with −1.

$$R_t = \begin{cases} 1 & \text{Correct classification} \\ -1 & \text{Wrong classification} \end{cases} \tag{8}$$

4.2   Double Deep Q-Learning

The PMU data used for STVS assessment is a high-dimensional state input, and the assessment result is a discrete action output (stable or unstable). The DRL-based algorithm proposed in this paper uses deep learning to extract state features to fit the value function, making the assessment more accurate. The DDQN algorithm [15] is an improved algorithm based on the DQN algorithm [13].

In order to evaluate the quality of the actions of the agent, the assessment is performed through the Discounted Return. The calculation formula is as follows:

$$U_t = R_t + \gamma R_{t+2} + \gamma^2 R_{t+3} + \cdots = \sum_{k=0}^{\infty} \gamma^k R_{t+k} \tag{9}$$

Where U_t is the sum of rewards at time t and the time after t. $\gamma \in [0, 1]$ is the discount factor.

In order to maximize U_t, Action-Value Function $Q_\pi (s_t, a_t; w)$ is used to evaluate the quality of the action. As shown in Fig. 3, this paper uses PMU data as the input of RL, and the output of the fully connected layer is the Q value corresponding to each action.

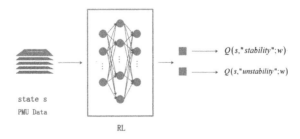

Fig. 3. The structure of DDQN.

4.3   Model Update

The update of DDQN relies on the TD algorithm. The TD algorithm uses the subsequent state Q^* to estimate the current Q^*. The parameters are updated by continuously reducing the TD error δ_t.

$$y_t = r_t + \gamma \cdot \max_a Q\left(s_{t+1}, a; w\right) \tag{10}$$

$$\delta_t = Q\left(s_t, a_t; w\right) - y_t \tag{11}$$

Where y_t is the TD target. The y_t is based on the real observation, which is more accurate than the value of $Q^*\left(s_t, a_t\right)$ based on guess. Therefore, y_t is the target, and $Q^*\left(s_t, a_t\right)$ is infinitely close to y_t.

However, the TD algorithm may causes DQN to overestimate the real action value. DDQN is a good way to reduce the problems caused by overestimation. Traditional DQN uses the same network for action selection and TD target calculation. Double-DQN uses the DQN network for action selection and use the target network to calculate the TD target. Therefore, the formula (10) is divided into two parts as shown below:

$$a^* = \arg\max_a Q\left(s_{t+1}, a; w\right) \tag{12}$$

$$y_t = r_t + \gamma \cdot Q\left(s_{t+1}, a^*; w'\right) \tag{13}$$

Where w is the parameter of the DQN network. w' is the parameter of the target network.

In order to reduce δ_t, the parameter w needs to be updated continuously. The gradient descent is used to update the parameter w and the loss function L_t is calculated to make the model more accurate as shown below:

$$L_t = \frac{1}{2}[Q\left(s_t, a_t; w\right) - y_t]^2 \tag{14}$$

$$w_{t+1} \leftarrow w_t - \alpha \cdot \frac{\partial L_t}{\partial w}\Big|_{w=w_t} \tag{15}$$

Where w_t is the parameter of the neural network at time t, and w_{t+1} is the parameter of the neural network at time $t + 1$. α is the learning rate of DDQN.

When the time of updating w' is reached, the value of parameter w in DQN network is assigned to w', and the updating of target network is completed. Since each PMU data sample is independent and identically distributed, the empirical playback is not needed in this paper.

5   Numerical Tests

The New England 39-bus system [1] is used to demonstrate the validation of the proposed intelligent scheme. The simulation is executed on a PC with Intel Core i7-8550U CPU (1.80 GHz) and 2.00 GB RAM. The software Power Factory is used for time-domain simulation to generate data. In this paper, the experiments is based on one kind of PMU placement strategy [4], and the sates of PMU placement strategy are shown in Table 1.

5.1   Data Generation

As shown in Table 2, 4 types of fault events are selected in this paper, there are short-circuit event, load event, switching event, and synchronous generator event. The fault clearing time is 0.21 s after the fault occurs. The simulation time step is 0.01 s. The simulation duration is 5 s. For generating the LSTM database, the voltage in the PMU data are selected for experiments. The total number of samples in this database is 540, and proportion of training set and test set is 7:3. For generating the DDQN database, 3580 samples are generated. The proportion of the training set and the test set are randomly divided into 7:3.

Table 1. PMU placement strategy.

Strategy	PMU installation bus	Quantity
1	3 8 10 16 20 23 25 29	8

Table 2. Fault set

Fault event	Short circuit	Switch	Load	Synchronous generator
Stability	539	418	413	421
Instability	718	358	354	359

Table 3. LSTM performance.

Missing rate	bus3	bus8	bus10	bus16	bus20	bus23	bus25	bus29
20%	1.5454%	0.4327%	0.7927%	1.6478%	1.7937%	0.9361%	0.8071%	0.575%

5.2   Parameter Selection

For LSTM Model. Since the number of PMUs placed in this paper is 8 in total, 8 models are trained separately for different buses. The learning rate of LSTM model is set to 0.0001. The sequence length is set to 20. The number of hidden layer units are set to 64. The batch size is set to 64.

For DDQN Model. The Learning rate of DDQN model is set to 0.01. Number of iterations is set to 40. In DDQN, action Set $A = \{0, 1\}$. 0 means that the agent judges that the current state is unstable. 1 means that the agent judges that the current state is stable. Discount factor is set to 0. The update frequency of the target network parameter is set to 5.

5.3   Experimental Results

Missing Data Filling. In this paper, the data missing rate is set to 20%. The Mean Absolute Percentage Error (MAPE) is used to evaluate the deviation degree between the predicted value and the true value. The small MAPE value proves that the LSTM model has better prediction performance for missing data. For lack of space, this paper only shows the results on bus2, as shown in Fig. 4. Table 3 shows the MAPE value under the PMU placement condition mentioned above. It is clear that missing data filling based on LSTM still maintains a good performance with a 20% data missing rate.

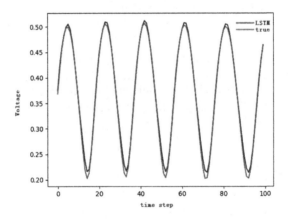

Fig. 4. PMU predicted result.

STVS Assessment. The assessment method proposed in this paper is compared with SVM based method. In order to verify the performance of the STVS assessment results of these two methods, 5 evaluation indicators for verification are adopted: Accuracy, Recall, Precision, F1-score and ROC curve. Table 4, Table 5, Table 6, Fig. 5 and Fig. 6 show the performance comparison between the SVM based model and the proposed model, respectively. It is clear that the evaluation performance of the proposed model is better than that of SVM based model.

Table 4. Accuracy of different methods

	SVM	DDQN
Accuracy	97.75%	100%

Table 5. Evaluation index of SVM

Category	Precision	Recall	F1-score
0	0.97	0.99	0.98
1	0.99	0.97	0.98

Table 6. Evaluation index of DDQN

Category	Precision	Recall	F1-score
0	1	1	1
1	1	1	1

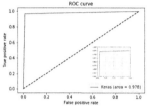

Fig. 5. ROC curve of SVM model.

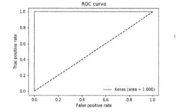

Fig. 6. ROC curve of DDQN model.

6   Conclusion

This paper presents a data-driven based STVS assessment model. In the actual process of power system evaluation, it is not necessary to consider the observability of PMU data and the topology of power grid. LSTM model is used to fill the missing PMU data without considering the physical information of the missing data. Then, DDQN is used to assess the STVS with complete PMU data. Experimental results show that the proposed method can not only fill the missing data with low error, but also evaluate STVS with high accuracy.

References

1. Athay, T., Podmore, R., Virmani, S.: A practical method for the direct analysis of transient stability. IEEE Trans. Power Appar. Syst. **2**, 573–584 (1979)
2. Cai, Z., He, Z.: Trading private range counting over big IoT data. In: 2019 IEEE 39th International Conference on Distributed Computing Systems (ICDCS), pp. 144–153. IEEE (2019)
3. Cai, Z., Zheng, X.: A private and efficient mechanism for data uploading in smart cyber-physical systems. IEEE Trans. Netw. Sci. Eng. **7**(2), 766–775 (2018)
4. Chakrabarti, S., Kyriakides, E.: Optimal placement of phasor measurement units for power system observability. IEEE Trans. Power Syst. **23**(3), 1433–1440 (2008)
5. Chang, H.D., Chu, C.C., Cauley, G.: Direct stability analysis of electric power systems using energy functions: theory, applications, and perspective. Proc. IEEE **83**(11), 1497–1529 (1995)

6. Chen, Q., Gao, H., Cai, Z., Cheng, L., Li, J.: Energy-collision aware data aggregation scheduling for energy harvesting sensor networks. In: IEEE INFOCOM 2018-IEEE Conference on Computer Communications, pp. 117–125. IEEE (2018)
7. Glavic, M., et al.: See it fast to keep calm: real-time voltage control under stressed conditions. IEEE Power Energ. Mag. **10**(4), 43–55 (2012)
8. Hochreiter, S., Schmidhuber, J.: Long short-term memory. Neural Comput. **9**(8), 1735–1780 (1997)
9. Ivanov, S., D'yakonov, A.: Modern deep reinforcement learning algorithms. arXiv preprint arXiv:1906.10025 (2019)
10. James, J., Lam, A.Y., Hill, D.J., Hou, Y., Li, V.O.: Delay aware power system synchrophasor recovery and prediction framework. IEEE Trans. Smart Grid **10**(4), 3732–3742 (2018)
11. Kundur, P., et al.: Definition and classification of power system stability IEEE/CIGRE joint task force on stability terms and definitions. IEEE Trans. Power Syst. **19**(3), 1387–1401 (2004)
12. Liang, Y., Cai, Z., Yu, J., Han, Q., Li, Y.: Deep learning based inference of private information using embedded sensors in smart devices. IEEE Network **32**(4), 8–14 (2018)
13. Mnih, V., et al.: Playing atari with deep reinforcement learning. arXiv preprint arXiv:1312.5602 (2013)
14. Pang, J., Huang, Y., Xie, Z., Han, Q., Cai, Z.: Realizing the heterogeneity: a self-organized federated learning framework for IoT. IEEE Internet Things J. **8**(5), 3088–3098 (2020)
15. Van Hasselt, H., Guez, A., Silver, D.: Deep reinforcement learning with double q-learning. In: Proceedings of the AAAI Conference on Artificial Intelligence, vol. 30 (2016)
16. Wang, B., Fang, B., Wang, Y., Liu, H., Liu, Y.: Power system transient stability assessment based on big data and the core vector machine. IEEE Trans. Smart Grid **7**(5), 2561–2570 (2016)
17. Wang, Y., Li, W., Lu, J.: Reliability analysis of wide-area measurement system. IEEE Trans. Power Deliv. **25**(3), 1483–1491 (2010)
18. Xiong, Z., Cai, Z., Takabi, D., Li, W.: Privacy threat and defense for federated learning with non-iid data in AIoT. IEEE Trans. Industr. Inform. (2021)
19. Xu, Y., et al.: Assessing short-term voltage stability of electric power systems by a hierarchical intelligent system. IEEE Trans. Neural Netw. Learn. Syst. **27**(8), 1686–1696 (2015)
20. Zhang, Y., Xu, Y., Dong, Z.Y., Zhang, P.: Real-time assessment of fault-induced delayed voltage recovery: a probabilistic self-adaptive data-driven method. IEEE Trans. Smart Grid **10**(3), 2485–2494 (2018)
21. Zhang, Y., Xu, Y., Zhang, R., Dong, Z.Y.: A missing-data tolerant method for data-driven short-term voltage stability assessment of power systems. IEEE Trans. Smart Grid **10**(5), 5663–5674 (2018)
22. Zheng, X., Cai, Z.: Privacy-preserved data sharing towards multiple parties in industrial IoTs. IEEE J. Sel. Areas Commun. **38**(5), 968–979 (2020)
23. Zhizhong, G., Wendong, Z., Zhuo, L., Xueyun, C., Daozhi, X., Kui, Z.: Fast judgment of power system transient stability by time domain simulation. Trans. China Electrotech. Soc. **3**, 47–49 (1994)

RDMA Based Performance Optimization on Distributed Database Systems: A Case Study with GoldenX

Yaofeng Tu[1,2], Yinjun Han[2(✉)], Hao Jin[2], Zhenghua Chen[2], and Yanchao Zhao[1]

[1] Nanjing University of Aeronautics and Astronautics, Nanjing, China
[2] ZTE Corporation, Shenzhen, China
han.yinjun@zte.com.cn

Abstract. The performance of distributed database system heavily relies on network to assist collaboration among nodes, while the traditional TCP/IP network has become the major bottleneck of the distributed database. Meanwhile, the emerging technology RDMA, featured with CPU offloading, bypassing the operating system kernel and zero copy, is envisioned to achieve low latency and high throughput data transmission between nodes. For this purpose, in this paper, we design and implement a high performance data transmission scheme based on RDMA and apply it to the distributed database system. Firstly, the paper analyzes the application scenarios and internal communication requirements of distributed database systems, combined with RDMA hardware characteristics. Secondly, based on the analysis results, we perform targeted design optimizations in three aspects, RDMA data transmission and memory region management, data placement, and congestion control. We propose efficient variable length data transmission mechanism based on the sliding window, application friendly data placement mechanism, and priority based adaptive congestion control mechanism to optimize the three aspects respectively. We further implement our idea with the typical distributed database GoldenX, and perform comprehensive experiments. Results shows that, compared with using RDMA network directly, the performance of GoldenX integrated with the optimizations is increased to 2.95 times, and the throughput is up to 2.61 times.

Keywords: RDMA · Database · Distributed system · Latency

1 Introduction

In the era of big data, the amount of global data is growing rapidly [2,7]. Traditional database systems are facing the challenges of massive data, high concurrency, fast processing and so on. The goal of DBMS software is to optimize the algorithm and data structure to adapt to the characteristics of hardware, so as to

© Springer Nature Switzerland AG 2021
Z. Liu et al. (Eds.): WASA 2021, LNCS 12938, pp. 237–248, 2021.
https://doi.org/10.1007/978-3-030-86130-8_19

squeeze out the raw hardware performance [8]. Both multi-core processors and non-volatile memory have greatly improved the performance of a stand-alone database, but the scale-up method still cannot meet the industry's demand for database performance. The database system is undergoing the transition from single machine to cluster, distributed database and cloud native database.

In the distributed database environment, the traditional TCP/IP network has become one of the main performance bottlenecks. The limited transmission capacity and the huge consumption of CPU load greatly affect the performance of the distributed database. With the development of high-performance network technologies, RDMA (Remote Direct Memory Access) have greatly improved the interconnection network environment that server clusters rely on. Beyond ultra-low latency and high throughput, RDMA also supports zero copy and kernel bypass, and hence can reduce the overhead associated with traditional network protocol stacks including context switch, interrupt and data copy.

The usage of RDMA is different from the traditional TCP network. There are many complicated processes such as memory registration, information synchronization, memory allocation, and data handling. Simply replacing the TCP network with the RDMA network cannot fully utilize the potential of RDMA to improve the performance of the distributed database system. According to the characteristics of the application scenario, the optimized use of RDMA technology is a key method to efficiently use RDMA to accelerate the existing system [4]. We designed an optimized RDMA data transmission mechanism based on the requirements among the access layer, compute layer, and DB cluster of the distributed database system.

The paper makes the following contributions:

- A variable-length data transmission mechanism based on sliding window is proposed. Both sides allocate and recycle memory through memory pools, and effectively reduce memory registration and synchronization overhead.
- Realize an application-friendly data placement mechanism. Based on a storage and network friendly data structure, it realizes the friendly data alignment of control plane, data plane and storage device plane, avoiding invalid memory copy.
- A priority-based adaptive congestion control method is proposed, which dynamically adjusts the recv instructions of the receiver according to the queue backlog of the sender, and avoid the recv resource exhaustion and latency increase during transmission.

2   Related Work

In recent years, academia and industry have proposed a series of distributed systems based on RDMA, and explored how to give full play to the hardware performance of RDMA through the redesign of existing systems. Binnig et al. [1] showed that the database system needs to make full use of the high bandwidth of the RDMA network. It is not enough to use faster network hardware, and the software must also be changed to solve the new bottleneck. X-RDMA

[6] integrated necessary functions that are not available in the current RDMA ecosystem, freeing developers from complex and imperfect details, while simplifying the programming model and extending the RDMA protocol to achieve application awareness. FaSST [4] recommended using UD (Unreliable Datagram) to implement RPC when using send/recv to improve scalability. Fan Lu et al. [5] proposed a MongoDB design scheme that supports RDMA. Compared with the existing socket version, the program has lower latency and higher throughput. Erfan Zamanian et al. [9] proposed a new high-availability scheme called active memory replication, which effectively uses RDMA to completely eliminate processing redundancy in replication. Through active memory, all replicas use their processing power to execute new transactions instead of performing redundant calculations, which effectively improves overall performance. Philipp Fent et al. [3] reconsidered the data flow inside and outside the database system, and accelerated the ODBC-like interface through a unified, message-based communication framework.

Different from the above research, this article carefully analyzes the communication characteristics of different scenarios in the distributed database, and combines the multiple access methods of RDMA to optimize remote memory management, data placement, and congestion control. While achieving performance improvement, it has high compatibility and strong versatility for distributed database systems.

3   Experimental Observations

GoldenX is a financial-level strong consistent relational database, which provides high performance and high availability for industries such as finance and telecom.

Fig. 1. Distributed database performance on RDMA and TCP

In the real database system, we observed that the performance improvement is not significant when the TCP network is directly replaced by the RDMA network under the same bandwidth. As shown in Fig. 1, we compared and analyzed the performance of the distributed database under the three network modes of TCP, ipoib and VMA. The performance of TCP is basically the same as that of ipoib, and the performance of VMA is significantly improved under low load, but when the load increases, the performance drops sharply, even lower than that of TCP and ipoib. It can be seen that using RDMA directly in the distributed database system can not give full play to the advantages of RDMA network. This is because the TCP stack used in these three modes brings extra consumption, while the zero copy and CPU offload features of RDMA network are not fully utilized. RDMA one-sided operation is the key to improve the performance of the network. In order to give full play to the advantages of RDMA network, we must customize and optimize the RDMA network according to the characteristics of the communication between nodes of the distributed database system.

4   System Design

GoldenX is a transaction-intensive application, which consumes a lot of CPU and is very sensitive to latency. Through the use of RDMA network, combined with GoldenX communication scenarios, we have carried out targeted design and optimization, which greatly improving the performance of GoldenX.

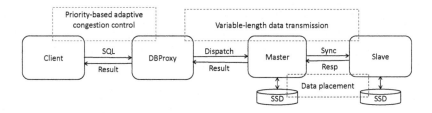

Fig. 2. The framework of RDMA based distributed database

As shown in Fig. 2, The GoldenX network communication consists of three levels. For the communication between computing layer DBProxy and database layer, there are massive, multiple length, and many rounds of data transmission, resulting in high resource consumption and latency. Therefore, we need to reduce message interaction and improve remote memory management to reduce resource consumption and latency. For the communication within the database cluster, there are multiple point-to-point data replication streams and a large number of data copies, that cause high CPU and memory overhead. Then, it is necessary to achieve zero-copy network transmission and data persistence at the transport layer and application layer to reduce system consumption. At the application layer, a large number of connections are needed to improve concurrency so that the capability of the database server can be fully utilized. Faced with numerous client connections and burst data requests, the DBProxy has the problems of large memory consumption and low resource utilization. Here we need to dynamically adjust server resources based on changes in client requests.

4.1   Efficient Variable-Length Data Transmission Mechanism

RDMA Write/Read primitives are the key to improve RDMA performance, it can access remote memory without peer side CPU involvement and reduce latency significantly. However, the RDMA specification does not define a remote memory management method, and applications need to handle remote memory allocation and recycling operations by themselves. Using RDMA one-sided operation requires at least 3 network interactions, including memory address notification, remote data reading or writing, and completion notification. At the same time, each data transmission needs to allocate a new memory of different sizes according to the size of the transmitted data, which has a large performance overhead.

We propose a variable-length data transmission method based on sliding window, which supports concurrent transmission of multiple lengths of data. It requires only two RDMA interactions for one transmission and avoids frequent memory allocation and release. Thus, it improves transmission efficiency greatly. As shown in Fig. 3(a), this method consists of two stages: initialization and data transmission.

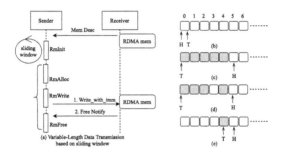

Fig. 3. Transmission based on the sliding window

The initialization stage mainly completes the creation of the sliding window. The receiver allocates a memory pool that is registered to the RDMA network card. The memory pool is composed of n consecutive memory units, and the unit size is fixed at m bytes. In the process of establishing RDMA connection, the receiver sends the memory pool information (address, length, KEY) to the sender who will invoke the memory pool initialization interface RmInit according to the received memory pool information to create the sliding window. As shown in Fig. 3(b), the sliding window is implemented by a circular queue composed of n members, with the base address equaling the address of the memory pool. Each member of the sliding window corresponds to a memory unit of the memory pool and uses 0/1 to indicate whether the corresponding unit is occupied. The sender uses the head pointer and tail pointer of the sliding window to identify the usage of the memory pool. At the beginning, both pointers point to position 0. The data transmission stage mainly includes two RDMA network interactions. Before sending the data, the sender invokes the memory allocation interface RmAlloc to allocate a segment of remote memory from the sliding window. The method supports allocation of continuous space with variable length. To transmit L bytes data, x contiguous members should be allocated from the sliding window and the value of x is round_up(L/m). The start position p is the index of head pointer, as shown in Fig. 3(b). During data transmission, the sender invokes the remote memory write interface RmWrite to write data to the target address of the receiver, and the offset of the target address $DataAddr$ relative to the base address $BaseAddr$ is $p * m$. RmWrite uses the immediate data of the write_with_imm verb to transfer data information to the receiver. The RDMA immediate data is a 32-bit integer, whose high 16 bits are used to store the starting position p, the low 16 bits are used to store the data length x, and the immediate data is calculated as $(p \ll 16) + x$. The receiver calculates the data address as $BaseAddr + (Imm \gg 16) * m$ and length $(Imm \& 0xFF)$ according to the received immediate data.

After the data is processed, the receiver sends the FREE notification to confirm that the memory can be freed. The sender invokes the remote memory release interface RmFree to update the sliding window status according to the memory location and length carried in the FREE message, As shown in Fig. 3(c). Figure 3(d) shows the sliding window state after executing RmFree to release unit 3, the head pointer and tail pointer remain unchanged, and the value of position 3 is set to 0. Figure 3(e) release units 0, 1 and 2, the tail pointer moves four positions to the right to merge adjacent free spaces.

The GoldenX supports high-concurrency distributed queries, which require a large number of data shuffling and aggregation operations. There are a large number of messages and frequent data exchanges between nodes, and the length of the message varies widely. This method effectively meets the needs of data transmission between computing nodes and data nodes of distributed database.

4.2   Application-Friendly Data Placement Mechanism

RDMA reduces the network latency to the μs level, the data processing overhead of the host software stack has become the main bottleneck of the system. We propose an application-friendly data placement mechanism which can ensure that the sender writes data to the receiver according to the data placement rules that the receiver's application can directly access. The memory data sharing between RDMA transport stack and application software is realized. Figure 4 shows the process of the application-friendly data placement method.

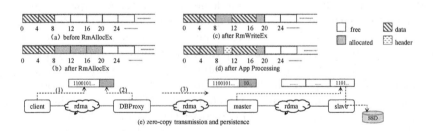

Fig. 4. Application-friendly data placement

The initial state is shown in Fig. 4(a), the memory allocation unit is 4 KB, and the used memory space is the first 8 KB. Assuming that the sender wants to send 6 KB of application data to the receiver, the sender specifies 4 KB alignment when calling the enhanced memory allocation interface RmAllocEx and reserves extra 1 KB of header space. The actual allocation is shown in Fig. 4(b), the whole allocated space is a 12 KB continuous space starting from the 8 KB offset of the memory pool, and the actual data space is the 6 KB continuous space starting from the 12 KB offset. The sender calls the enhanced interface RmWriteEx to write 6 KB data into the 12KB offset address, as shown in Fig. 4(c). After receiving the data, the receiver writes the 1 KB application's message header to the 11 KB offset of the memory pool according to the service flow, and combines the header with the subsequent 6 KB data into a continuous service message, as shown in Fig. 4(d). The head or tail reserved space and data alignment method are specified by parameters, and the application may construct a message that conforms to service rules in the RDMA memory without copying any data, which realizing application-friendly data placement.

DBProxy needs to dispatch the received SQL request to multiple target master nodes. Then the master processes and sends it to the slave, they persist the data locally if necessary. During this period, there are multiple message copy operations. This problem can be resolved by the application-friendly data placement mechanism shown in Fig. 4(e). (1) The client invokes RmAllocEx to allocate RDMA memory, reserves a specified length of head space, and calls RmWriteEx to write the content of the request into the remote memory of the DBProxy. (2) The DBProxy node receives the request and locates the target master node, fills the necessary information such as session ID into the reserved header space, then the new session message is constructed. (3) The DBProxy node sends the constructed session message to the target master nodes. Similarly, as shown in Fig. 4(e), the slave node receives the synchronized data and calls the DirectIO interface to directly write the 4KB aligned data in the memory to the storage device. Therefore, the application-friendly data placement mechanism realizes zero copy of RDMA network data transmission and persistence, which greatly improves system performance.

4.3   Priority-Based Adaptive Congestion Control

RDMA two-sided operations include send and recv instructions. The receiver needs to submit the recv instructions before the sender can submit the send instructions. Otherwise, the RNR (Receiver Not Ready) error will be triggered, resulting in abnormal QP (Queue Pair) status. We apply the idea of network layer congestion control based on PFC to the application layer, and propose a priority-based adaptive congestion control algorithm to solve the recv instructions exhaustion and latency increase in the process of data sending and receiving in the application layer. After detecting the message backlog at the sender, the sender sends a FCM (Flow Control Message) to notify the current backlog. The receiver dynamically adjusts the number of recv instructions based on the backlog in the flow control message and the queue priority.

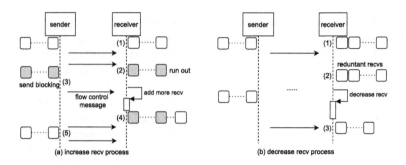

Fig. 5. Example of data transmission in GoldenX

As shown in Fig. 5(a), the process of expanding recv instruction resources is, (1) Normally, the receiver submits the recv instruction of the lowest water level, and submits a new recv instruction immediately after processing one recv message to ensure that the total number of recvs remains unchanged; (2) As the system traffic increases, the receiver consumes all recv operations, and no idle recv operation is available; (3) There is a backlog in the send queue at the sender, if the number of blocked operations exceeds the flow control threshold, the flow control mechanism is triggered. The sender sends a FCM to receiver to notify that there are N messages backlogged; (4) On receiving FCM, the receiver immediately increases the quantity of recv instructions to K. Considering that the number of subsequent backlog messages may be larger, we submit more recv than the actual demand number N each time. The number of over-allocations is proportional to the number of additions $\Delta K_{(i-1)j}$ last time, and is inversely proportional to the total number of recv operations $K_{(i-1)j}$ last time, and the formula for K is as follows:

$$K_{ij} = min(K_{(i-1)j} + (1 + \frac{\Delta K_{(i-1)j}}{K_{(i-1)j}}) * N_{ij}P_j, Max) \qquad (1)$$

Among them, i is the sequence number of recv quantity adjustment; j is the RDMA connection index number; N_{ij} is the recv backlog quantity when the connection j is backlogged for the i-th time; K_{ij} is the recv quantity of connection j after the i-th adjustment, and the initial value is the low water level value 8; ΔK_{ij} is the incremented quantity of recv during the i-th adjustment of connection j, and the initial value is 0; P_j is the weight of connection j, which ranges from 0 to 1. Max is the upper limit of the number of connection recvs. (5) The congestion of the sending queue is gradually relieved until it disappears completely. More data can be sent from the sender.

As shown in Fig. 5(b), the receiver reduces the recv operations: (1) In the running process, the traffic decreases, and the send instructions submitted by the sender decrease; (2) More and more recv operations become idle. When the number of idle operations exceeds the threshold, the flow control mechanism is triggered to stop issuing the new recv instruction. (3) As messages are sent and received, the recv operations gradually decrease until the total number of recv instructions drops to a lower level.

As a high-concurrency database, GoldenX has a large number of burst connection requests and large service fluctuations. After adopting priority-based adaptive congestion control method, the database can increase the recv operations during service peaks to improve receiving and sending capabilities, and decrease the recv operations when the service is low to reduce resource occupation. It helps the database to improve resource utilization under the premise of satisfying various burst requests, and provides more system resources for other tasks such as database space reclamation and data replication.

5   Implementation with GoldenX and Evaluation

In this section, we test the performance of three innovative mechanisms and the GoldenX integrated with the above-mentioned RDMA network optimization. The experimental cluster consists of 4 nodes with dual Intel Xeon(R) Gold 6230N and 384G DRAM. The nodes are connected to each other through Mellanox ConnectX-3 Pro 40G NIC. Each node runs CentOS Linux version 7.9, and Intel P4610 NVMe SSD is used to persist the data generated in the test.

5.1   Efficient Variable-Length Data Transmission Mechanism Evaluation

The efficient variable-length data transmission mechanism based on sliding window is named Wr_2step, and the traditional RDMA read mechanism is named Rd_3step. This test evaluates the latency and bandwidth of the two transmission modes. Figure 6(a) shows that the Wr_2step has a better latency than the Rd_3step. The transmission latency of the 1 KB packet is only 71% of the Rd_3step. Obviously, this is because Wr_2step reduces one network interaction. With the increase of packet size, as the data transmission overhead ratio increases, the latency advantage of Wr_2step gradually decreases.

For the bandwidth test, as shown in Fig. 6(b–f), for a 1KB packet, both methods reach the maximum bandwidth at 16 concurrent, Wr_2step leads by about 100%. The 4KB data packet test shows a similar trend to the 1KB data packet, and the peak bandwidth of Wr_2step leads by about 71%.

5.2   Application-Friendly Data Placement Mechanism Evaluation

In this test, the network transmission uses the Wr_2step method. After the data arrives at the receiver, one type of application uses the traditional memory copy method to obtain the data from RDMA buffer, and the other type of application uses the application-friendly data placement mechanism to access the data in a zero copy method. During the test, the request concurrency is fixed to 1, data packets of 1–1024 KB are tested one by one, and the average latency and bandwidth of the two applications are recorded and analyzed.

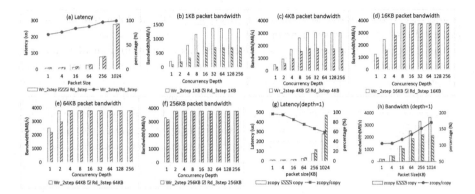

Fig. 6. Bandwidth and latency of different packets

As shown in Fig. 6(g–h), the latency of both modes increases with the increase of packet size. Compared with zcopy, the latency under copy mode is about 5% higher for 4 KB packets and 41% higher for 1024 KB packets. Similarly, the overhead of memory copy also affects bandwidth of data transmission. Compared with the copy mode, the zcopy mode increases the bandwidth by 5%–70%.

5.3 Evaluation of Priority-Based Adaptive Congestion Control Method

The packet size is 64 bytes in this test. To simulate the fluctuation of service load, the number of concurrent requests is gradually increased from 1 to 2048, and then decreased from 2048 to 1. The bandwidth of the following three solutions are tested respectively: (1) 8_recv: The receiver always uses 8 recv instructions to receive data; (2) auto_recv: The receiver uses the priority-based adaptive congestion control algorithm to dynamically adjust the number of recv instructions; (3) 32_recv: The receiver always uses 32 recv instructions to receive data.

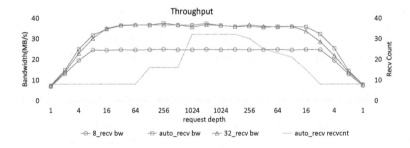

Fig. 7. priority-based adaptive congestion control

As shown in Fig. 7, in all test scenarios, as the concurrent depth of requests increases, the bandwidth increases gradually. The second half of the test shows a reverse trend. In the 8_recv scenario, the performance is the worst. Its peak bandwidth is only about 67% of the 32_recv scenario. The auto_recv scenario has the same performance as the 32_recv. The auto_recv recvcnt curve shows the actual change trend of the number of recv instructions. At the end of the test, the number of recv instructions is reduced to the low water level, and the memory resource is recycled. At the beginning and end of the test, the actual number of recv instructions is obviously lower than 32, which can save the memory. That is to say, the priority-based adaptive congestion control can achieve the performance similar to that of pre-allocated memory with less memory.

5.4 GoldenX Database Performance Evaluation

GoldenX is deployed on 4 nodes, one node deploys the client, one node deploys DBProxy, and 2 nodes deploy the DB cluster. We tested the performance of ipoib, vma and the optimized RDMA communication modes on RDMA network.

First, we use YCSB (Yahoo Cloud Serving Benchmark) to test the performance of different types of operations in the database. The database contains one table, and each record contains a primary key and 10 data columns of 64-byte string. Before the test, insert 1 million records first, and then test the database with different number of threads.

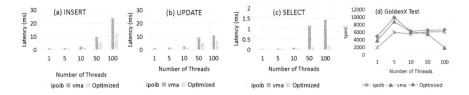

Fig. 8. GoldenX performance test

As shown in Fig. 8(a–c), the performance of the GoldenX based on the optimized RDMA communication mode is far better than that based on the native ipoib. The single thread scenario has the best performance up to 2.95 times in the INSERT scenarios. This is because the latency of RDMA network primitives is low, thus avoiding the overhead of TCP protocol stack. Compared with vma, the RDMA-specific optimization for database communication has further reduced the communication latency.

Then we use the TPC-C test set. As shown in Fig. 8(d), as the number of threads increases, the overall latency of database transactions increases. When there are 5 threads, the throughput reaches the maximum value. In the case of single thread and 5 threads, the performance advantage of the optimized RDMA is particularly obvious, which is 2.61 times of the original RDMA network.

6   Conclusion

This paper studies how to integrate RDMA high-performance network in the distributed database system, so that the hardware characteristics of RDMA and the internal communication requirements of the distributed database can be well adapted. We propose three algorithms, which utilize reliable transmission services, one-sided and two-sided RDMA primitives to implement variable-length data transmission based on the sliding window, application-friendly data placement, and priority-based adaptive congestion control. Experiments show that the concurrent access performance of GoldenX in the optimized RDMA network is up to 2.95 times higher than that in the direct RDMA network; In the TPC-C test set, its throughput is up to 2.61 times.

Acknowledgement. This work was supported in part by the National Key Research and Development Program of China under Grant 2019YFB2102000; in part by the Natural Science Foundation of Jiangsu Province under Grant BK20200067.

References

1. Binnig, C., Crotty, A., Galakatos, A., Kraska, T., Zamanian, E.: The end of slow networks: it's time for a redesign. arXiv preprint arXiv:1504.01048 (2015)
2. Chen, J., et al.: A parallel random forest algorithm for big data in a spark cloud computing environment. IEEE Trans. Parallel Distrib. Syst. **28**(4), 919–933 (2016)
3. Fent, P., van Renen, A., Kipf, A., Leis, V., Neumann, T., Kemper, A.: Low-latency communication for fast DBMS using RDMA and shared memory. In: 2020 IEEE 36th International Conference on Data Engineering (ICDE), pp. 1477–1488. IEEE (2020)
4. Kalia, A., Kaminsky, M., Andersen, D.G.: Fasst: fast, scalable and simple distributed transactions with two-sided (RDMA) datagram RPCS. In: 12th USENIX Symposium on Operating Systems Design and Implementation ({OSDI} 2016), pp. 185–201 (2016)
5. Lu, F., et al.: Improving the performance of MongoDB with RDMA. In: 2019 IEEE 21st International Conference on High Performance Computing and Communications (HPCC/SmartCity/DSS), pp. 1004–1010. IEEE (2019)
6. Ma, T., et al.: X-RDMA: effective RDMA middleware in large-scale production environments. In: 2019 IEEE International Conference on Cluster Computing (CLUSTER), pp. 1–12. IEEE (2019)
7. Peng, S., et al.: An immunization framework for social networks through big data based influence modeling. IEEE Trans. Dependable Secure Comput. **16**(6), 984–995 (2017)
8. Yu, S., Liu, M., Dou, W., Liu, X., Zhou, S.: Networking for big data: a survey. IEEE Commun. Surv. Tutor. **19**(1), 531–549 (2016)
9. Zamanian, E., Yu, X., Stonebraker, M., Kraska, T.: Rethinking database high availability with RDMA networks. Proc. VLDB Endow. **12**(11), 1637–1650 (2019)

A LambdaMart-Based High-Accuracy Approach for Software Automatic Fault Localization

Yunhao Xiao[1], Xi Xiao[2,4], Fang Tian[1], and Guangwu Hu[3]([✉])

[1] College of Informatics, Huazhong Agricultural University, Wuhan, China
[2] Tsinghua Shenzhen International Graduate School, Tsinghua University, Shenzhen, China
[3] School of Computer Science, Shenzhen Institute of Information Technology, Shenzhen, China
hugw@sziit.edu.cn
[4] Peng Cheng Laboratory, Shenzhen, China

Abstract. Software debugging or fault localization is a very significant task in software development and maintenance, which directly determines the quality of software. Traditional methods of fault localization rely on manual investigation, which takes too much time in large-scale software development. To mitigate this problem, many automatic fault localization techniques have been proposed which can effectively lighten the burden of programmers. However, the quality of these techniques is not enough to meet the practical requirements. In order to improve the accuracy of fault localization, we propose LBFL, a LambdaMart-based high-accuracy approach for software automatic fault localization, which can integrate software's diversified features and achieve very high accuracy. To realize that, LBFL first extracts the static and dynamic features and normalizes them. Then these features are gathered on LambdaMart algorithm for training. Finally, LBFL sorts the code statements according to the model and generates a list which can help developers to locate faults. Exhaustive experiments indicate that LBFL can locate 76 faults in Top-1, which has at least 217% improvements over nine single techniques and has 55% improvements over ABFL approach on the Defects4J dataset.

Keywords: Fault localization · Software engineering · Learning to rank · LambdaMart

1 Introduction

Software debugging or fault localization is a very significant task in software development and maintenance, which directly determines the quality of software. The traditional methods of fault localization rely on manual investigation, which costs too much time in large-scale software development. Therefore, many researchers have proposed software automatic fault localization methods, which have greatly facilitated developers. In recent years, some of them have also assisted in determining the location of fault by assigning suspicious program elements with suspicious scores and sorting them into list according to the scores.

© Springer Nature Switzerland AG 2021
Z. Liu et al. (Eds.): WASA 2021, LNCS 12938, pp. 249–261, 2021.
https://doi.org/10.1007/978-3-030-86130-8_20

Current fault localization techniques can be classified into three types: static techniques, dynamic techniques and fault localization with combined static and dynamic features. Static techniques extract features from the source code without information about execution. Dynamic techniques use information related to software execution. Spectrum-based fault localization (SBFL) [1–3] approaches collect spectrum information and compute suspicious scores for program elements. Mutation-based fault localization (MBFL) [4, 5] approaches use mutation operators to implant several bugs in the program under test to form mutant. Fault localization with combined features approaches makes full use of both of the dynamic and static features. The effectiveness of single technique in fault localization is limited, and an increasing number of people are looking for ways to combine different techniques. It is feasible to fit the formula manually if we consider few features. However, if we combine more features, manual fitting is obviously not feasible, while machine learning is suitable for using many features to fit the formula. Existing methods do not consider enough features [6, 7] and we attempt to extract more features. We use Learning To Rank (LTR) algorithm to get a ranking model. There are three types of LTR algorithms: Pointwise approach, Pairwise approach and Listwise approach. Pairwise approaches have better performance than other approaches because the goal of the ranking is closer to predict relative orders. Therefore, we use LambdaMart, a Pairwise method that has performed well in information retrieval in recent years, to train the model. It is also the first to apply this popular algorithm to the field of software automatic fault localization.

In order to take full advantage of different techniques, we propose a LambdaMart-based high-accuracy approach for software automatic fault localization (LBFL), which can integrate software's diversified features and achieve very high accuracy of debugging. We use Defects4J benchmark, which contains 357 real faults of 5 different Java projects, to evaluate LBFL. The experimental result shows that in the first position, LBFL can significantly provide improvement over the existing state-of-the-art techniques and approach.

In summary, the main contributions of this paper are as follows:

(1) We propose LBFL, a LambdaMart-based approach for software fault localization. Lambdamart model has performed well in the competition in recent years and supports incremental learning, which is of great significance in practical application of fault localization. It is the first attempt to apply LambdaMart model that originates information retrieval into the field of fault location approach.
(2) LBFL considers 11 static features and 20 dynamic features and gets them properly integrated by the proposed LTR algorithm. It assigns LBFL greatest advantage of fault localization accuracy improvement than the previous approaches, since among which the classic approach ABFL only considers 1 static feature and 14 dynamic features.
(3) The experiment shows that LBFL outperforms 9 state-of-the-art techniques (e.g., Ochiai, DStar, Metallaxis and MUSE) at least 217% in terms of Top-1, and surpasses the classic approach ABFL 55% in Top-1.

The rest of this article is arranged as follows: We discuss related work in Sect. 2 and elaborate the 3 steps of LBFL in Sect. 3. The experiences and findings are presented in

Sect. 4. Finally, we summarize the whole paper and put forward the prospect of future research in Sect. 5.

2 Related Work

2.1 Static Techniques

Static techniques don't take advantage of the information when the software is running. TR-based approaches leverage the full textual content of fault reports, and the source code or past bug reports. Chaparro et al. [8] consider that specific content from bug reports can improve TR-based approaches. IR-based fault localization is a popular static strategy in the recent years. Rahman et al. [9] proposed a novel technique named BLIZZARD, which uses appropriate query reformulation and effective information retrieval to localize bugs from project source and improves IR-based approach. Zhang et al. [10] use deep learning and knowledge graph to obtain interrelations of code for fault localization, which outperforms the state-of-the-art IR-based approaches and approaches based on deep learning.

2.2 Dynamic Techniques

(a) SBFL techniques locate faults according to the coverage information generated during executing. Christi et al. [11] used delta-debugging to reduce failing test cases and this method can meliorate the effect of spectrum-based localization. Aribi et al. [12] tackle the various metrics by combining them into a single metric which uses a weighted linear formula and remain the right expected weights of criteria through learning. This technique has higher precision than SBFL. Kim et al. [13] leveraged the coverage of variables instead of statements to improve SBFL techniques and came up with a variable-based fault localization technique named VFL. It is lightweight and is a technique which can improve the ability to localize bugs.

(b) MBFL conducts variation testing and analysis on software to determine whether the execution of a code statement will affect the execution result of a test case. The application of mutation and fault localization techniques has an excellent performance in automatic program repair. However, there is a problem of high execution cost in large industrial programs, because the number of mutants increases exponentially. Sun et al. [14] proposed a search-based program automatic repair method using mutation and fault location technique, which take advantage of fault localization, that is, mutant individuals can build an initial population based on statements with high suspicious value, and can quickly find patch. Wang et al. [15] proposed IETCR method for MBFL, which can reduce cost effectively while keeping the same accuracy.

(c) In addition to the above two methods, there are other run-time information based techniques. Neighbor-based fault localization (NFL) proposed by Vancsics et al. [16] is a graph-based algorithm which converts the coverage matrix to a graph and sorts methods according to their relationship to the passed and failed tests. Li et al. [17] proposed a novel technique based on information retrieval (IRBFL) and the technique firstly employs TF-IDF toward the software spectrum information to find fault. This method extracts information from execution frequencies of program entities and performs better than others in single fault localization. Nguyen et al. [18] proposed COFL, which identifies and analyzes suspicious feature interactions that cause the fault in configurable systems and ranks statements according to existing techniques such as SBFL to localize configuration-dependent bugs.

2.3 Fault Localization with Combined Static and Dynamic Features

In practical applications, fault localization with static and dynamic combined features has excellent results. Horváth et al. [19] put forward iFL. This method uses SFL to sort, and modifies the suspicious scores of the contextual knowledge of the statements with the feedback of the developer and it significantly improves the accuracy of fault localization. Li et al. [20] proposed DeepFL, a deep learning method to gather static and dynamic features to locate bug, which has great effectiveness. Li et al. [21] put forward a strategy of fault localization combining ATL transformation as static analysis and spectrum based information as dynamic analysis and assigning rule weight. Weighted spectrum information is used to update rule rank list. This strategy improves the effect of fault localization techniques.

3 Methodology

3.1 Overview

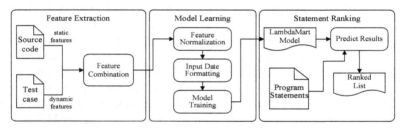

Fig. 1. Overview of LBFL

In order to get effective information about the various code statements, we need to extract the features of level, nLines, nComments, nTokens, nChars, nKeyword, isStatement, isAssignment, is Annotation, nSeparator and nOperator as static features and obtain spectrum information, SBFL formulas, MBFL techniques, stack trace analysis and dynamic slicing as dynamic features. Our goal is locating faults at the level of statement granularity and getting a ranked list according to suspicious scores, so we gather features to get a model and predict results depending on this model. Inspired by the ABFL approach, we change the rank SVM algorithm to the current popular LambdaMart algorithm and add more features. Our method consists of three parts: feature extraction, model learning and statement ranking. In the feature extraction step, we extract the static and dynamic features from the source code. In the second step, the features obtained in previous work are normalized. In addition, we format input data before training and use LambdaMart model for learning. Finally, according to the model, a ranked list with suspicious scores of code statements, which stands for the possibility of new error causing this failure, is generated. Our approach's diagram is depicted in Fig. 1.

3.2 Feature Extraction

(1) **Static Features**

Static features are extracted from the source code and are significant for improving results. Static analysis is an important factor in software fault localization, which has also been confirmed by Neelofar et al. [22] and others. But the previous work did not fully consider the static features, so it is necessary to introduce more static features and we add level, the number of lines, comments, tokens, chars, keyword, annotation, separator and operator as static features, which contribute to the results in our experiment. In our method, the static features in Table 1 are adopted.

Table 1. Static features in our approach

Static features	Descriptions
Level	The level of indentation of the statement
nLines	The number of lines in which the code statement resides
nComments	The number of comments in the file in which the statement resides
nTokens	The number of tokens in the statement
nChars	The number of characters in the statement
nKeyword	The number of keywords in the statement
isStatement	Whether the element is statement
isAssignment	Whether the code statement is assignment
nAnnotation	The number of annotations in the statement
nSeparator	The number of separators in the statement
nOperator	The number of operators in the statement

(2) **Dynamic Features**

Dynamic features are derived from information that software executes. Zou et al. [23] demonstrated the effectiveness of several features in dynamic techniques, so we use spectrum information, SBFL formulas, MBFL techniques, stack trace analysis and dynamic slicing mentioned in Zou's paper as dynamic features in our approach.

a) Spectrum information is collected when program is running, which is the number of passed or failed test cases executing this element or not. (e_p, e_f, n_p, n_f) is a tuple of four values as raw spectrum information. e_p and e_f are the numbers of the passed test cases and the failed test cases that execute the statement. n_p and n_f are the numbers of the passed test cases and the failed test cases that do not execute the statement. These four values are used as features in our approach.

b) Spectrum-based fault localization (SBFL) is particularly lightweight, which applies ranking formulas to compute suspicious scores based on the spectrum information. Eleven of these formulas are used in our method as dynamic features, which are Tarantula [24], Jaccard [25], Ochiai [2], Barinel [26], DStar [27], ER [28] and GP [29] and their specific definitions are shown in Table 2.

Table 2. Elven SBFL formulas

Techniques	Definitions
Tarantula	$S_{Tarantula} = \dfrac{\frac{e_f}{e_f+n_f}}{\frac{e_f}{e_f+n_f} + \frac{e_p}{e_p+n_p}}$
Jaccard	$S_{Jaccard} = \dfrac{e_f}{e_p+e_f+n_f}$
Ochiai	$S_{Ochiai} = \dfrac{e_f}{\sqrt{(e_p+e_f)(e_f+n_f)}}$
Barinel	$S_{Barinel} = 1 - \dfrac{e_p}{e_p+e_f}$
DStar$_2$	$S_{DStar2} = \dfrac{e_f^2}{e_p+n_f}$
ER1$_a$	$S_{ER1_a} = \begin{cases} -1 & n_f > 0 \\ n_p & otherwise \end{cases}$
ER1$_b$	$S_{ER1_b} = e_f - \dfrac{e_p}{e_p+n_p+1}$
GP$_2$	$S_{GP_2} = 2(e_f + \sqrt{n_p}) + \sqrt{e_p}$
GP$_3$	$S_{GP_3} = \sqrt{\left|e_f^2 - \sqrt{e_p}\right|}$
GP$_{13}$	$S_{GP13} = e_f + \dfrac{e_f}{2e_p+e_f}$
GP$_{19}$	$S_{GP19} = e_f\sqrt{\left|e_p - e_f + n_f - n_p\right|}$

c) Mutation-based fault localization (MBFL) is a new technique in recent years. MBFL uses statements covered by failed test cases to get and execute mutants and the features are obtained by MBFL techniques. Our approach selects Predicate Switching [23], Metallaxis [30] and Muse techniques to obtain dynamic features.

Predicate Switching technique traces the execution of the failed test case and executed predicates recorded. The technique switches the executing branch until covering all branches. It is a critical predicate if the failed test case can pass when we do predicate switching.

Metallaxis formula is computed as follows:

$$S_{Metallaxis}(m_i) = \frac{failed(m_i)}{totalfailed \times (failed(m_i) + passed(m_i))} \tag{1}$$

where $passed(m_i)$ is the number of test cases that passed on the original statements but failed on the mutant m_i, and similarly for $failed(m_i)$. The total number of test cases that fail on the original program is defined as $totalfailed$.

MUSE calculates the suspicious score of each mutant as follows:

$$S_{MUSE} = failed(m_i) - \frac{f2p}{p2f} \times passed(m_i) \tag{2}$$

where $p2f$ is the number of test cases that change from pass to fail, and $f2p$ is similar. Each statement has multiple mutants and suspiciousness values, and we take their average as features.

d) In a program where an error has occurred, we can check the stack information. The topper a program element is, the more likely it causes fault directly. We give the element a score of $1/d$ when it is at depth d. If an element is given multiple score, we select maximum value as the dynamic feature.

If there is a single failed test throwing an exception, the execution of the statement throwing the exception is used as the slicing criterion. If there is more than one test case that failed, three strategies are applied in our approach to handle multiple slices: union, intersection, and frequency. If a statement is frequently included in the slice of test that can't pass, it is the suspicious statement which causes fault.

e) Thanks to Zou et al. [23] for providing open source data about dynamic features mentioned above, which provides convenience for our work.

3.3 Model Learning

3.3.1 Feature Normalization

Our approach does min-max normalization on the features before using features. This step can speed up our training procedure, which rescales the feature values to a range of [0, 1].The formula below can help us to normalize features:

$$v_i = \frac{u_i - \min(u)}{\max(u) - \min(u)} \tag{3}$$

where v_i is raw value of the ith feature and u_i is the normalized values of the ith feature. $min(u)$ means minimum and $max(u)$ is maximum of original feature.

3.3.2 Input Data Formatting

Before model learning, we format features and labels of statements. Table 3 shows the input format. Program ID is the index of the buggy project from which the statement is derived and its values range from 1 to 357. The label value indicates whether the project's bug was caused by this statement. The value of 1 indicates it is a buggy statement, while the value of 0 means contrary.

Table 3. The input format

Label	Program ID	Features of Statement		
		1	2	......
1	1	$x_{(1,1)}$	$x_{(1,2)}$	......
0	1	$x_{(2,1)}$	$x_{(2,2)}$	......
......	......	......	......	......

3.3.3 Model Training: LambdaMart

LambdaMart [31], a pairwise LTR approach, which combines MART and LambdaRank, is the boosted tree version of LambdaRank based on RankNet. It has proved to solve ranking problems with good performance in real world. Lambdamart has many advantages over the traditional LTR model. It has the ability of feature selection, which is also the advantage of Mart. In addition, LambdaMart is an incremental learning approach, which means it can constantly learn from new samples, and can preserve much of what has been learned before and this is in line with the real-world application of fault localization. We select LambdaMart and take the format data as input to train model which is used to find faults in new buggy projects.

3.4 Statement Ranking

In this step, we predict new bugs on the basis of the trained model. Then, we get a list of statements in descending order of suspicious scores and the statement has topper rank, the more likely it is to cause fault. Programmers can locate faults according to this list, which can greatly reduce cost.

4 Experiments

4.1 Experimental Settings

We evaluate LBFL on a dataset of Defects4J (V1.0.1) benchmark, containing 357 real faulty programs of 5 Java projects. The projects include plenty of test cases, and each bug corresponds to at least one failed test case. Table 4 describes the bugs and projects in this dataset. In addition, we use RankLib, which is a Java library of learning to rank algorithms, to train LambdaMart model.

Table 4. Defects4J dataset

Project	The num of faults	The average num of statements
JFreeChart	26	4073.8
Closure compiler	133	17469.5
Apache commons-Lang	65	812.7
Apache commons-Math	106	2323.5
Joda-Time	27	5307.3
Total	357	8044.2

4.2 Metrics

(a) 'Top-N' is a metric representing the number of bugs that have been localized within the top N positions of the ranked lists of statements.
(b) 'The EXAM score' presents the percentage of statements that must be inspected until finding a buggy statement.
(c) 'Average Precision' (AP) is used to evaluate the accuracy of ranked list, and its formula is shown as follows:

$$AP = \sum_{i=1}^{M} \frac{P(i) \times faulty(i)}{The\ number\ of\ faulty\ statements} \tag{4}$$

$P(i)$ is the value of the number of faulty statements in the ith position divided by i. M stands for the number of code statements in the ranked list, $faulty(i)$ indicates whether the ith code statement is faulty. For all faults, we calculate Mean Average Precision (MAP).

4.3 Research Questions and Findings

RQ1: How Effective is LBFL?
We used the metrics mentioned above to evaluate the effectiveness of LBFL, which means Top-N, EXAM, and MAP score for faults in 357 projects are calculated.

   To evaluate the effectiveness of LBFL, we use different features and parameters. Different parameters will affect the effectiveness of the training model. In our experiments, we adjust the parameters and finally set the number of trees as 110, the number of leaves as 50, and the learning rate as 0.1.

   The results show that, 76, 124, 149 faults in position 1, 3 and 5 can be located by LBFL. In addition, EXAM is 0.019, and the MAP score is 0.269.

RQ2: Do Different LambdaMart Model Parameters Have Impacts on the Effectiveness of LBFL?
In this question, we discuss the effects of different LambdaMart model parameters including the number of trees, the number of leaves and the learning rate. We set the number

of tree as 110, the number of leave as 50 and learning rate as 0.1 and they are changed in follow-up experiments to explore their impact.

Figure 2 presents the results of different number of trees. By comparison, it can be found that the ability to localize faults is the best when the number of trees is 110, and 76, 124 and 149 faults can be located at Top-1,Top-3 and Top-5.

We can summarize the effects of the number of leaves on the performance of LBFL from the Fig. 2. It can be concluded from the results that the number of leaves is best to set to 50.

Finally, different learning rates have been used to evaluate effect of model parameters. We select 0.001, 0.01, 0.1, 0.3 and 0.5 as the learning rate to discuss its impacts. Figure 2 shows that LBFL has the best performance on Top-1 when the learning rate is 0.1.

It can be concluded from the experimental results that different parameters have a certain influence on the fault localization effectiveness of LBFL, and the appropriate parameters can give full play to its effect.

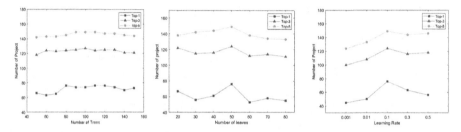

Fig. 2. The results of different parameters

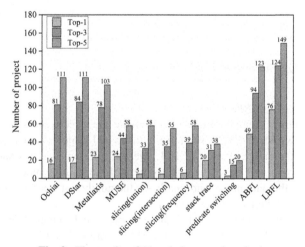

Fig. 3. The results of 11 techniques and methods

RQ3: How does LBFL Stack up against other Techniques or Methods?
To further demonstrate the effectiveness of LBFL, we compare LBFL with single state-of-the-art techniques and ABFL [6] approach using the LTR algorithm. We use Top-N metric to compare the results of LBFL with those of other techniques or methods on Defects4J, where Ochia and DStar are two SBFL techniques, Metallaxis and MUSE are two MBFL techniques. Some of the data comes from Zou [23]'s experiments. Figure 3 reports the results of LBFL and the results show that LBFL is better than any single technique in fault localization and SBFL techniques are the most effective single fault localization techniques. In addition, LBFL is 55%, 31% and 21% better than ABFL in Top-1, Top-3 and Top-5 respectively.

5 Conclusions

In this paper, we propose LambdaMart-based high-accuracy approach for software fault localization (LBFL), which leverages LambdaMart algorithm to integrate software's multiple static features and dynamic features. The most exciting characteristic in our proposal is that LBFL achieves the highest accuracy among single techniques in Top-1, which also has 55% improvement over the classical approach ABFL. Next, we will take more software features into account and combine them to improve the accuracy and effectiveness at the same time.

Acknowledgment. This work is supported in part by the National Natural Science Foundation of China (62004077, 61972219), the RD Program of Shenzhen (JCYJ20190813174403598, SGDX20190918101201696), the National Key Research and Development Program of China (2018YFB1800601), the Overseas Research Cooperation Fund of Tsinghua Shenzhen International Graduate School (HW2021013).

References

1. Jones, J.A., Harrold, M.J.: Empirical evaluation of the tarantula automatic fault-localization technique. In: IEEE/ACM International Conference Automated Software Engineering, pp. 273–282 (2005)
2. Abreu, R., Zoeteweij, P., Van Gemund, A.J.: On the accuracy of spectrum-based fault localization. In: TAICPART-MUTATION, pp. 89–98 (2007)
3. Jones, J.A., Harrold, M.J., Stasko, J.: Visualization of test information to assist fault localization. In: Proceedings International Conference Software Engineering, pp. 467–477 (2002)
4. Papadakis, M., Le Traon, Y.: Using mutants to locate unknown faults. In: Proceedings of IEEE International Conference Software Testing Verification Validation, pp. 691–700 (2012)
5. Papadakis, M., Le Traon, Y.: Effective fault localization via mutation analysis: a selective mutation approach. In: Proceedings of ACM Symposium Applied Computing, pp. 1293–1300 (2014)
6. Peng, Z., Xiao, X., Hu, G., Sangaiah, A.K., Atiquzzaman, M., Xia, S.: ABFL: an autoencoder based practical approach for software fault localization. Inf. Sci. **510**, 108–121 (2020)
7. Kim, Y., Mun, S., Yoo, S., Kim, M.: Precise learn-to-rank fault localization using dynamic and static features of target programs. ACM Trans. Softw. Eng. Methodol. **28**(4), 1–34 (2019)

8. Chaparro, O.: Improving bug reporting, duplicate detection, and localization. In: IEEE/ACM 39th International Conference on Software Engineering Companion (ICSE-C), pp. 421–424 (2017)
9. Rahman, M.M., Roy, C.K.: Improving IR-based bug localization with context-aware query reformulation. In: Proceedings of the 2018 26th ACM Joint Meeting on European Software Engineering Conference and Symposium on the Foundations of Software Engineering, pp. 621–632 (2018)
10. Zhang, J., Xie, R., Ye, W., Zhang, Y., Zhang, S.: Exploiting code knowledge graph for bug localization via bi-directional attention. In: Proceedings of the 28th International Conference on Program Comprehension, pp. 219–229 (2020)
11. Christi, A., Olson, M.L., Alipour, M.A., Groce, A.: Reduce before you localize: delta-debugging and spectrum-based fault localization. In: IEEE International Symposium on Software Reliability Engineering Workshops, pp. 184–191 (2018)
12. Aribi, N., Lazaar, N., Lebbah, Y., Loudni, S., Maamar, M.: A multiple fault localization approach based on multicriteria analytical hierarchy process. In: IEEE International Conference on Artificial Intelligence Testing, pp. 1–8 (2019)
13. Kim, J., Kim, J., Lee, E.: Poster: a novel variable-centric fault localization technique. In: Proceedings of International Conference Software Engineering, pp. 252–253 (2018)
14. Sun, S., Guo, J., Zhao, R., Li, Z.: Search-based efficient automated program repair using mutation and fault localization. In: Proceedings of International Computing Software Applied Conference, vol. 1, pp. 174-183 (2018)
15. Wang, H., Du, B., He, J., Liu, Y., Chen, X.: IETCR: an information entropy based test case reduction strategy for mutation-based fault localization. IEEE Access **8**, 124297–124310 (2020)
16. Vancsics, B.: NFL: neighbor-based fault localization technique. In: IEEE 1st International Workshop on Intelligent Bug Fixing (IBF), pp. 17–22 (2019)
17. Li, Z., Bai, X., Wang, H., Liu, Y.: IRBFL: an information retrieval based fault localization approach. In: COMPSAC, pp. 991–996 (2020)
18. Nguyen, S.: Configuration-dependent fault localization. In: ICSE-Companion, pp. 156–158 (2019)
19. Horváth, F., Lacerda, V.S., Beszédes, Á., Vidács, L., Gyimóthy, T.: A new interactive fault localization method with context aware user feedback. In: IEEE 1st International Workshop on Intelligent Bug Fixing (IBF), pp. 23–28 (2019)
20. Li, X., Li, W., Zhang, Y., Zhang, L.: DeepFL: integrating multiple fault diagnosis dimensions for deep fault localization. In: Proceedings of ACM SIGSOFT International Symposium Software Testing Analysis, pp. 169–180 (2019)
21. Li, P., Jiang, M., Ding, Z.: Fault localization with weighted test model in model transformations. IEEE Access **8**, 14054–14064 (2020)
22. Neelofar, N., Naish, L., Lee, J., Ramamohanarao, K.: Improving spectral-based fault localization using static analysis. Softw. Pract. Exper. **47**(11), 1633–1655 (2017)
23. Zou, D., Liang, J., Xiong, Y., Ernst, M.D., Zhang, L.: An empirical study of fault localization families and their combinations. IEEE Trans. Softw. Eng. (2019)
24. Jones, J.A., Harrold, M.J.: Empirical evaluation of the Tarantula automatic fault-localization technique. In: IEEE/ACM International Conference Automation Software Engineering, pp. 273–282 (2005)
25. Chen, M.Y., Kiciman, E., Fratkin, E., Fox, A., Brewer, E.: Pinpoint: problem determination in large, dynamic internet services. In: Proceedings of International Conference on Dependable Systems and Networks, pp. 595–604 (2002)
26. Abreu, R., Zoeteweij, P., Van Gemund, A.J.: Spectrum-based multiple fault localization. In: Proceedings of IEEE/ACM Interanational Conference Automation Software Engineering, pp. 88–99 (2009)

27. Naish, L., Lee, H.J., Ramamohanarao, K.: A model for spectra-based software diagnosis. ACM Trans. Softw. Eng. Methodol. (TOSEM) **20**(3), 1–32 (2011)
28. Xie, X., Chen, T.Y., Kuo, F.C., Xu, B.: A theoretical analysis of the risk evaluation formulas for spectrum-based fault localization. ACM Trans. Softw. Eng. Methodol. **22**(4), 1–40 (2013)
29. Yoo, S.: Evolving human competitive spectra-based fault localisation techniques. In: International Symposium on Search Based Software Engineering, pp. 244–258 (2012)
30. Papadakis, M., Le Traon, Y.: Metallaxis-FL: mutation-based fault localization. Softw. Test. Verification Reliab. **25**(5–7), 605–628 (2015)
31. Burges, C.J.: From ranknet to LambdaRank to LambdaMart: an overview. Learning **1123–581**, 81 (2010)

ParkLSTM: Periodic Parking Behavior Prediction Based on LSTM with Multi-source Data for Contract Parking Spaces

Taiwei Ling[1], Xin Zhu[1], Xiaolei Zhou[1,2(✉)], and Shuai Wang[1]

[1] School of Computer Science and Engineering, Southeast University, Nanjing, China
{213170098,zhuxin,shuaiwang}@seu.edu.cn
[2] The Sixty-Third Research Institute, National University of Defense Technology,
Changsha, China
zhouxiaolei@nudt.edu.cn@seu.edu.cn

Abstract. With the rapid development of urbanization and the swift rising of the number of vehicles in cities, the process of finding a suitable parking space not only wastes a lot of time but also indirectly aggravates the problem of traffic congestion. To assist the decision-making and alleviate the pain of parking, researchers propose a variety of methods to improve the parking efficiency of existing parking lots. Different from existing studies, we address the parking issue from an incremental rather than a stock perspective. In this paper, we propose a LSTM-based prediction model to make full use of contract parking spaces, which are characterized by the periodic departure time and complementary to the idle space during the peak period of the city. In addition, we utilize multi-source data as the input to improve the prediction performance. We evaluate our model on real-world parking data involved with nearly 14 million parking records in Wuhan. The experimental results show that the average accuracy of the ParkLSTM prediction reaches 91.091%, which is 11.19%–19.70% higher than other parking behavior prediction models.

Keywords: Intelligent transportation · Contract parking spaces · Multi-source data · Periodic · LSTM

1 Introduction

With the rapid development of modern industry, the problem of parking difficulties has increasingly become a major problem in the process of global urbanization. In China, according to the Ministry of Public Security, the total number of private vehicles in the country reaches 260 million while in the United States it is 281 million. According to a recent survey, due to the growth of a large number of vehicles and insufficient parking space infrastructures, nearly 30% of traffic

© Springer Nature Switzerland AG 2021
Z. Liu et al. (Eds.): WASA 2021, LNCS 12938, pp. 262–274, 2021.
https://doi.org/10.1007/978-3-030-86130-8_21

congestion during the peak period of urban traffic is caused by vehicles unable to find parking spaces in time [1]. The traffic congestion results in wasting a lot of time and fuel, which indirectly aggravates the risk of environmental pollution and traffic accidents.

To alleviate this problem, a few studies have proposed some solutions such as predicting the number of parking in the parking lot or releasing the pressure of parking scheduling to improve it. Parking guidance systems are proposed to achieve efficient scheduling of existing parking lots, thereby reducing the time for drivers to find parking spaces [3,9]. Researchers propose neural network prediction methods to judge the future status of the idle parking space in the parking lot, thereby assisting the decision-making of parking scheduling and improving the efficiency of the decision-making results [6,12,13].

Inspired by existing studies on parking behavior modeling [2,7,10,13,14], we propose a new parking behavior prediction model called ParkLSTM which is based on the LSTM model with multi-source data: (i) It predicts the travel time of the owner of a parking space from the perspective and data characteristics of a single contract (i.e., private) parking space; (ii) It is based on the LSTM model which is considered suitable for predicting periodic models as its basic framework; (iii) It fully considers the impact of multi-source data such as weather factors and holiday factors on the parking behavior of a single parking space in the model design and solves the problems of multiple periodicity and large volatility in a single parking space caused by these factors. The main contributions of this work are summarized as follows.

- To the best of our knowledge, this is the first work that attempts to combine the LSTM periodic prediction model and multi-source data as input to predict the departure time of a contracted parking space.
- We analyze nearly 19 million parking records in Wuhan, especially explaining the influence of holidays and weather factors on the distribution of user travel time. We propose and implement an improved LSTM model with multi-source data, and analyze the architecture and design ideas of the model.
- To verify the performance of the new model effectively, we utilize 14 million contract parking space records in Wuhan to evaluate the prediction effect. The experimental results show that the average accuracy of the multi-source data ParkLSTM reaches 91.091%, which is 11.19%–19.70% higher than other parking behavior prediction models like single-source data LSTM and Prophet Model. In addition, the 24-h average root mean square error of ParkLSTM is 2.585, which is 54.10%–61.68% lower than existing prediction models. To benefit the research community and make our work reproducible, we will release one-week data utilized in this paper.

The rest of the paper is organized as follows. Section 2 introduces our formulation and motivation. Section 3 describes the design of ParkLSTM and Sect. 4 analyzes the performance of ParkLSTM through experiments and comparison. Section 5 discusses limitations and potential problems. In Sect. 6, we review the related work, followed by the conclusion in Sect. 7.

2 Formulation and Motivation

In this section, we define the parking behavior of contract parking spaces and analyze the periodic characteristics of it. Then we clarify the reason for utilizing multi-source data.

2.1 Definition of Parking Behavior

The main task of this work is to accurately predict the future travel time of the owner of the contract parking space. Contract parking spaces refer to parking spaces that are privately owned by private individuals through signing contracts, such as residential parking spaces purchased by the head of a community. To dig out the potentially available parking behavior. Our available data is the time at which each car passes through the gate of the community, as well as information such as weather and statutory holidays. So we define the multi-data source of parking behavior as follows:

- **Departure Time Factor:** We define the sequence of the departure time in the lb past days of the t-th day is $X_t = \{x_t^1, x_t^2, \cdots, x_t^{lb}\}$, where lb is the number of the day we look back to predict the future departure time.
- **Weather Factor:** According to the degree of the influence of the weather on the parking behavior on the t-th day, we define the weather factor as $q_t = 0$ if it is pleasant weather while $q_t = 1$ if it is heavy weather on that day.
- **Holiday Factor:** Similar to the weather factor, the p_t which means the holiday factor on the t-th day is defined as follows: $p_t = 1$ if it is public holidays or weekends while $p_t = 0$ if it is workday.

2.2 Parking Behavior Analysis

To describe the parking behavior, taking [5] as a reference, we adopt the entropy and the JS divergence to analyze the periodic law of parking and the impact of multi-source data on the parking behavior.

- **Entropy:** Entropy is a common parameter utilized to measure the distribution of information. When the distribution is more regular, the value of entropy is smaller. IN this paper, if the distribution of departure time is more regular, the corresponding entropy value is smaller.

$$E(P) = -\sum P(x) log P(x) \tag{1}$$

- **JS divergence:** JS divergence is a variant of Kullback–Leibler divergence (KL Divergence). KL divergence, also known as relative entropy, is utilized to measure the similarity of two probability distributions. Like the KL divergence, the JS divergence decreases as the degree of similarity increases.

$$KL(P||Q) = \sum P(x) log \frac{P(x)}{Q(x)} \tag{2}$$

$$JS(P||Q) = \frac{1}{2}KL(P(x)||\frac{P(x)+Q(x)}{2}) + \frac{1}{2}KL(Q(x)||\frac{P(x)+Q(x)}{2}) \quad (3)$$

The departure time distribution regular pattern is a major feature of contract parking spaces. We judge the regulation of a parking space by calculating the entropy of the departure time distribution. Figure 1(a) and Fig. 1(b) show two parking spaces with different departure time distribution rules, where the x-axis is the date and the y-axis is the departure time. The seven small sub-pictures above respectively depict images connected by dates with the same week number, so that it is more clearly seen that the period of the series is seven days. From these two figures, we find that the departure time of the contracted parking space has a significant periodicity with the entropy of each picture low.

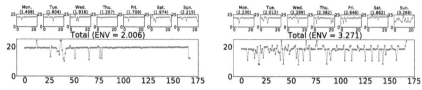

(a) Weekends and weekdays have the same periodic distribution

(b) Weekends and weekdays have different periodic distributions

Fig. 1. Entropy analysis of departure time distribution

2.3 Potential of Using Multi-source Data

Multi-source data mainly includes historical data of the departure time of vehicles, weather data, and holiday data. We utilize the JS divergence method to demonstrate the impact of multi-source data on parking distribution.

- **Departure Time Factor:**
  Departure time is the most basic data in parking behavior prediction. The model with single-source data to predict the future departure time is based on the historical departure time series.
- **Weather Factor:**
  When analyzing the impact of weather factors on the travel time of the owner of vehicles, to minimize the number of features input later, we divide the weather factor into two main parts. One part is called pleasant weather, which does not affect the transportation choices of people, such as sunny, cloudy, etc. The other part is some relatively severe weather conditions that always lead to changes in personnel travel, such as rain, snow, and fog. From Fig. 2(a), we find that firstly, the travel of contract parking space users has a high regularity, especially during workday; Secondly, due to the influence of weather factors, the JS divergence has reached 0.254, which shows that weather factors have affected vehicle travel to a certain extent.

- **Holiday Factor:**
  Compared with weather factors, the influence of holiday factors on people's travel schedule is more obvious and significant. Due to the characteristics of the holiday, the holiday factors have a great impact on the prediction results of vehicle travel. From Fig. 2(b) we find that the time distribution of holiday in orange and of the workday in blue are obviously different, which means that legal holidays have a quite large impact on users' parking behavior, resulting in the JS divergence of travel distribution during workday time and holidays reaching 0.441. Therefore, the holiday factor has become a factor that cannot be ignored in the prediction of departure time.

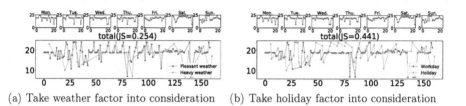

(a) Take weather factor into consideration   (b) Take holiday factor into consideration

Fig. 2. Influence of multi-source data

Through the above analysis, we get the following two conclusions: (i) The parking behavior of a contract parking space has a relatively high regularity; (ii) Multi-source data affects the parking behavior. Therefore, how to predict the parking behavior by combining periodicity and multi-source data has become a point worthy of research.

3   Proposed Model

As mentioned in Sect. 2, our requirements for the prediction model are mainly reflected in two aspects. One is the ability to effectively fit the periodic characteristics of parking data and to grasp the parking law on a weekly basis; The other is to effectively grasp the multi-source data such as the weather of the parking data and the holiday features to achieve accurate forecasts. Therefore, we put forward the idea of combining multi-source data with the LSTM model to achieve accurate prediction.

3.1   Model Overview

The LSTM (Long Short-Term Memory) model is a variant of RNN. It is characterized by adding valve nodes of each layer in addition to the RNN structure to achieve long-term and short-term memory functions, so it performs multi-step predictions of multivariable time series. It has a good effect on the problem of cyclical time series forecasting. And the awareness gate enhances the awareness of specific parameters on the basis of the original LSTM model.

Based on the above considerations, we design an LSTM model with holiday and weather awareness modules. This model is based on the traditional LSTM model with two special modules added. One module is to find the cyclical law, and the other module is to grasp the characteristics of the holiday and weather. The specific design of the model is introduced below.

3.2   ParkLSTM Model Design

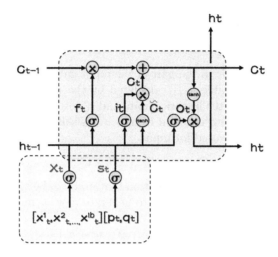

Fig. 3. ParkLSTM model

As shown in Fig. 3, the core module of ParkLSTM mainly consists of two parts. The part in the blue area is the basic LSTM model framework, and the part in the orange area is two perception modules added for the above two problems.

$$X_t = \sigma(W_x \cdot [x_t^1, x_t^2, \cdots, x_t^{lb}] + b_x) \qquad (4)$$

Equation 4 corresponds to the part of the orange area X_t, where $[x_t^1, x_t^2, \cdots, x_t^{lb}]$ is utilized to grasp the periodicity of vehicle travel historical data. lb is the number of historical data that needs to be taken into consideration, and finally, a characteristic value of historical data X_t is obtained through a sigmoid function.

$$s_t = \sigma(W_s \cdot [p_t, q_t] + b_s) \qquad (5)$$

Equation 5 corresponds to the part of the orange area s_t, where p_t and q_t respectively represent the weather feature data and holiday feature data of the corresponding date. We utilize a sigmoid function to get a holiday and weather eigenvalue s_t.

$$f_t = \sigma(W_f \cdot [h_{t-1}, X_t] + b_f) \qquad (6)$$

Equation 6 corresponds to the part of the forget gate in the blue area. It is based on the output value h_{t-1} calculated by the previous module and the X_t

which is just calculated (i.e. the first lb parking data). Then make it through the sigmoid function to get f_t which is utilized to determine whether to memorize the data C_{t-1} coming from the previous module.

$$i_t = \sigma(W_i \cdot [h_{t-1}, X_t, s_t] + b_i) \qquad (7)$$

Equation 7 corresponds to the part of the input gate in the blue area, which is based on the output value h_{t-1} calculated by the previous module and the characteristic value X_t of the historical data and the holiday-and-weather characteristics s_t. Through the sigmoid function, we get i_t. i_t is used to determine what data needs to be entered in the next C_t.

$$\tilde{C}_t = tanh(W_c \cdot [h_{t-1}, X_t] + b_c) \qquad (8)$$

Equation 8 corresponds to the part of the input gate in the blue area, which is based on the output value h_{t-1} calculated by the previous module and the characteristic value X_t of the historical data and s_t getting from the weather and holidays characteristics. But different from i_t, $\tilde{C}_t$ is solved by the tanh function, which is the data content used for input.

$$C_t = f_t * C_{t-1} + i_t * \tilde{C}_t \qquad (9)$$

Equation 9 realizes that the information that needs to be memorized and new input information are pieced together to generate new memorized information C_t.

$$o_t = \sigma(W_o \cdot [h_{t-1}, X_t, s_t] + b_o) \qquad (10)$$

Equation 10 corresponds to the part of the output gate in the blue area, which is similar to i_t. Based on the output value h_{t-1} calculated by the previous module and the characteristic value of the historical data X_t and holiday-weather characteristics s_t. It is calculated by the sigmoid function to get o_t which is used to determine which data needs to be output below.

$$h_t = o_t * tanh(C_t) \qquad (11)$$

Equation 11 corresponds to the output part in the blue area, which is solved according to the obtained memory information C_t and judgment information o_t.

4   Evaluation

4.1   Dataset

The datasets of our experiment include nearly 19,000,000 parking records of contract parking spaces in Wuhan from 2016-01 to 2017-12. The recording locations are mainly concentrated in areas such as communities, apartments, and office buildings. After data processing, we finally utilize about 14,000,000 parking records from 239 blocks. In addition, we crawl Wuhan's weather data and holiday information within the corresponding time range from the official website of the Wuhan Meteorological Bureau. An example of parking datasets is shown in Table 1. We conduct experimental evaluations on the performance of the three models based on the above data.

Table 1. Example of parking datasets

Record Id	Parking space Id	Parking lot Id	Departure time	Back time
3027226	420105000004	120008	2015-12-18 10:14:47	2016-01-15 15:56:24

4.2 Baselines

○ **Prophet Model with Single-source Data:** The Prophet model [13] is a commonly used time series forecasting model. The core formula is shown in Eq. 12. Among them, $g(t)$ is the trend function, which is used to describe the aperiodic changes in the time series. $s(t)$ is used to fit the model through the fourier series, which represents the periodic changes contained in the sequence with weekly or monthly cycles. $h(t)$ represents the influence caused by holidays or other accidental factors. ϵ is the error term, which represents the influence of the error that this model does not consider. Because the prophet model has the characteristics of strong interpretability, high flexibility, and fast fitting speed, it is often utilized in commercial forecasting models.

$$y(t) = g(t) + s(t) + h(t) + \epsilon \tag{12}$$

○ **LSTM Model with Single-source Data:** LSTM model, the long and short term memory neural network model, is a modification of the recurrent neural network, which learns the long-term laws better, so it has significant advantages in text recognition, image processing, and sequence prediction. However, in the absence of a perceptual door, the LSTM model makes predictions based on historical travel data, which often leads to unsatisfactory prediction results.

4.3 Performance Metrics

Our model is evaluated with two metrics. The accuracy rate is utilized to reflect the correctness of the model prediction result. The root mean square error is utilized to measure the degree of fluctuation between the predicted result and the actual result.

○ **Accuracy:**
We calculate the accuracy of the model by subtracting the Mean Absolute Error (MAE) from 1. The accuracy measures the similarity well between the predicted data and the actual data. In Eq. 13, P_i is the predicted data, and R_i is the actual observed data.

$$Accuracy = 1 - \frac{1}{N} \sum |P_i - R_i| \tag{13}$$

○ **RMSE:**
The root mean square error, which represents the sample standard deviation of the difference (called residual) between the predicted value and the

observed value to measure the degree of fluctuation of the predicted data around the actual data.

$$RMSE = \sqrt{\frac{1}{N}\sum(P_i - R_i)^2} \tag{14}$$

4.4 Experiment Results

∘ **Forecast Results:** As follows, we have drawn the prediction results of three methods for the same parking space. The blue line is the actual observation data, the red line is the predicted result, the x-axis is the serial number of the date, and the y-axis is the owner's departure time every day. At the time of the parking space, if you do not leave the house that day, it will be regarded as leaving at 24 o'clock. From the comparison of the experimental results in Fig. 4(a), Fig. 4(b) and Fig. 4(c), we clearly find that the prediction image of ParkLSTM with multi-source data is more consistent with the observation than the prediction results of the Prophet model and the LSTM model with single-source data. As a result, especially at some points with large fluctuations, the latter two models failed to fit well, while ParkLSTM, which takes more multi-source data such as weather and holiday into consideration, captures these characteristics well, thus achieving a good performance in fitting and prediction.

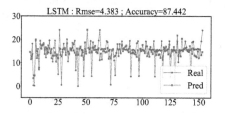

(a) LSTM with Single-source Data

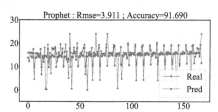

(b) Prophet with Single-source Data

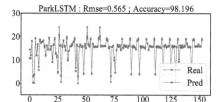

(c) ParkLSTM with Multi-source Data

Fig. 4. Comparison of the experimental results of the three methods

In summary, in this paper, we first try to design and implement an LSTM model with multi-source data including weather and holiday factors.

○ **More Experiment Cases:** In addition to the experimental image results, we enumerate the case of 10 contract parking spaces as shown in Table 2, 3 and 4. From Table 2, we find that the accuracy of ParkLSTM is basically above 90%, and the distribution is quite even. Besides, there are few cases of extreme deviation, while the accuracy rate of the Prophet model and the LSTM model is mostly around 70% to 80% and fluctuating greatly, which means that their prediction results are more unstable. Similarly, from Table 3 we find that the root mean square error of the ParkLSTM model is always about 2 of the lower level in the three models. The 24-h root mean square error of the Prophet model is around 4–7, and the LSTM is even greater. We count the average performance data of all contract parking spaces as shown in Table 4. We find that the performance of ParkLSTM is significantly better than the other two models.

Table 2. Comparison of the **Accuracy** of the three methods

Methods	Cases								
	Case01	Case02	Case03	Case04	Case05	Case06	Case07	Case08	Case09
LSTM	74.677	71.536	82.519	78.376	67.963	69.102	**94.078**	49.964	83.780
Prophet	91.690	84.057	83.766	84.139	83.518	77.850	92.953	61.596	83.936
ParkLSTM	**98.436**	**95.272**	**96.278**	**85.552**	**84.882**	**95.484**	93.622	**94.279**	**86.806**

Table 3. Comparison of the **RMSE** of the three methods

Methods	Cases								
	Case01	Case02	Case03	Case04	Case05	Case06	Case07	Case08	Case09
LSTM	7.305	8.777	5.330	7.198	10.22	10.70	2.346	16.35	4.818
Prophet	3.911	6.000	5.057	5.491	5.066	6.881	2.325	11.26	**4.512**
ParkLSTM	**0.527**	**1.716**	**1.296**	**5.296**	**4.514**	**1.445**	**2.049**	**2.075**	4.755

Table 4. Comparison of the average performance of the three methods (Total Cases)

Methods	Average	
	Accuracy	RMSE
LSTM	76.094	7.459
Prophet	81.927	5.633
ParkLSTM	**91.091**	**2.858**

○ **CDF of Accuracy and RMSE:**

Finally, we predict all the contract parking spaces and plot the predicted results into a cumulative distribution function (CDF) image. From Fig. 5(a), we find that most of the prediction accuracy of the ParkLSTM model is higher than 90%, which is significantly better than the 80% of the Prophet model and the 70% of the LSTM model. From Fig. 5(b), we find that the 24-h root mean square error of most of the predictions of the ParkLSTM model is less than 4, which is significantly less than the prediction results of the Prophet model and the LSTM model.

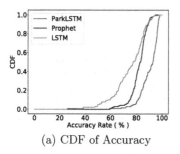
(a) CDF of Accuracy

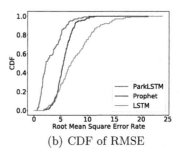
(b) CDF of RMSE

Fig. 5. CDF of results of three models

5 Discussions

Although ParkLSTM with multi-source data has achieved good experimental performance, there are still some limitations and potential problems that deserve further consideration and improvement:

- **Limitations:** The limitations of the ParkLSTM are mainly reflected in the requirements for computing power. Because more features are considered, the calculation time utilized by ParkLSTM is generally higher than that of the LSTM and the Prophet model with single-source data, which is improved by optimizing the model code and improving the efficiency of parallel computing.
- **Potential problems:** Since the ParkLSTM is aimed at private contract parking spaces, if it is put into a real application, the protection of privacy in the process of data processing should be paid attention to. This problem can be improved through encryption or anonymity services. In addition, data aggregation is utilized to avoid collecting the data of the specific user.

6 Related Work

The prediction of parking behavior has always been the focus of parking research, and because the parking behavior has the characteristics of (i) obvious periodicity (ii) being easily affected by Multiple factors. In Table 5, we divide it according to whether periodicity is emphasized. For example, in [4], although the author utilized the LSTM method to predict the phenomenon, the focus was on clustering enhancement and other aspects, which is a different perspective. In Table 6, we classify according to whether utilize multi-source data or not. For example, in [4,13], due to the usage of the prophet model, weather factors in multi-source data are not taken into consideration. [13] proposed to improve the efficiency of neural networks by adding weather awareness.

Table 5. Different prediction models with periodicity taken into consideration

Categories	Consider periodicity	Regardless of periodicity
LSTM-based models	[13] [this Work]	[4]
Other-based models	[11,14]	[6,8]

Table 6. Different prediction models with multi-source data taken into consideration

Categories	Single-source data	Multi-source data
LSTM-based models	[4,13]	[this Work]
Other-based models	[11]	[14]

In summary, in this paper, we first try to design and implement an LSTM model with multi-source data including weather and holiday factors in the prediction of the departure time of contracted parking spaces.

7   Conclusion

In this paper, we propose an improved LSTM called ParkLSTM which is suitable for predicting the departure time of contract parking spaces. The model improves performance by using multi-source data. We verify the model with 14 million parking record data in Wuhan and set accuracy and root mean square error as measurement indicators. Then we make an objective comparison with the single-source data LSTM model and Prophet model. The experimental results show that ParkLSTM with multi-source data significantly improves the forecast accuracy rate of departure time series and reduces the root mean square error, which is consistent with the expected results of our proposed model.

Acknowledgments. This work was supported in part by National Natural Science Foundation of China under Grant No. 61902066, Natural Science Foundation of Jiangsu Province under Grant No. BK20190336, China National Key R&D Program 2018YFB2100302 and Fundamental Research Funds for the Central Universities under Grant No. 2242021R41068.

References

1. Arnott, R., Rave, T., Schb, R.: Alleviating Urban Traffic Congestion. MIT Press, Cambridge (2005)
2. Cfa, B.: Predicting excess stock returns out of sample: can anything beat the historical average? (digest summary). Weather **18**(2), 42–54 (2008)

3. Geng, Y., Cassandras, C.G.: A new "smart parking" system based on optimal resource allocation and reservations. In: 2011 14th International IEEE Conference on Intelligent Transportation Systems - (ITSC 2011) (2011)
4. Ghosal, S.S., Bani, A., Amrouss, A., Hallaoui, I.E.: A deep learning approach to predict parking occupancy using cluster augmented learning method. In: 2019 International Conference on Data Mining Workshops (ICDMW) (2019)
5. Haykin, S.S., Gwynn, R.: Neural networks and learning machines. In: Neural Networks and Learning Machines (2009)
6. Qiu, R.Q., Zhou, H.P., Hui, W.U., Yi-Quan, R., Shi, M.: Short term forecasting of parking demand based on LSTM recurrent neural network. Tech. Autom. Appl. (2019)
7. Sathyanarayana, A., Joty, S., Fernandez-Luque, L., Ofli, F., Taheri, S.: Sleep quality prediction from wearable data using deep learning. JMIR mHealth uHealth 4(4), e125 (2016)
8. Shen, X., Batkovic, I., Govindarajan, V., Falcone, P., Darrell, T., Borrelli, F.: Parkpredict: motion and intent prediction of vehicles in parking lots. In: 2020 IEEE Intelligent Vehicles Symposium (IV), pp. 1170–1175 (2020). https://doi.org/10.1109/IV47402.2020.9304795
9. Shin, J.H., Jun, H.B.: A study on smart parking guidance algorithm. Transp. Res. Part C Emerg. Technol. 44, 299–317 (2014)
10. Tax, N., Verenich, I., La Rosa, M., Dumas, M.: Predictive business process monitoring with LSTM neural networks. In: Dubois, E., Pohl, K. (eds.) CAiSE 2017. LNCS, vol. 10253, pp. 477–492. Springer, Cham (2017). https://doi.org/10.1007/978-3-319-59536-8_30
11. Taylor, S.J., Letham, B.: Forecasting at scale. Am. Stat. 72(1), 37–45 (2018)
12. Ye, J., Sun, L., Du, B., Fu, Y., Tong, X., Xiong, H.: Co-prediction of multiple transportation demands based on deep spatio-temporal neural network. In: The 25th ACM SIGKDD International Conference (2019)
13. Zhang, F., Feng, N., Liu, Y., Yang, C., Du, X.: PewLSTM: periodic LSTM with weather-aware gating mechanism for parking behavior prediction. In: Twenty-Ninth International Joint Conference on Artificial Intelligence and Seventeenth Pacific Rim International Conference on Artificial Intelligence IJCAI-PRICAI-20 (2020)
14. Zhu, X., Wang, S., Guo, B., Ling, T., He, T.: Sparking: a win-win data-driven contract parking sharing system. In: UbiComp/ISWC 2020: 2020 ACM International Joint Conference on Pervasive and Ubiquitous Computing and 2020 ACM International Symposium on Wearable Computers (2020)

Privacy-Aware Computing

Cost-Sharing Mechanism Design for Social Cost Minimization in Ridesharing Systems

Yangsu Liu, Chaoli Zhang, Zhenzhe Zheng[✉], and Guihai Chen

Department of Computer Science and Engineering, Shanghai Jiao Tong University, Shanghai, China
{liu_yangsu,chaoli_zhang,zhengzhenzhe}@sjtu.edu.cn, gchen@cs.sjtu.edu.cn

Abstract. Ridesharing, as an emerging efficient solution for transportation congestion, has achieved great business success in recent years. A critical issue in the ridesharing system is to determine a group of passengers to share a ride and the corresponding payments to charge them to cover the cost of drivers. We present the desired properties of a cost-sharing mechanism in ridesharing systems, namely *economic efficiency*, *incentive compatibility*, *individual rationality* and *budget balance*. However, the existing classic mechanisms do not achieve these properties even in a simple case. In this work, we formulate a cost-sharing model for ridesharing systems, and design two VCG-based mechanisms for the simple case and the general case, respectively. The simple case can capture the ridesharing problem with a symmetric cost function, while the general case describes a more general ridesharing problem with a submodular cost function. We theoretically demonstrate that these two mechanisms are approximately economic efficient with other desirable properties guaranteed. Finally, we evaluate the proposed mechanisms on a real-world dataset. The evaluation results show that our mechanism could increase the user experience of passengers as well as the efficiency of the ridesharing system.

Keywords: Ridesharing · Smart transportation · Cost-sharing mechanism

1 Introduction

With the explosion of population and rapid development of urbanization in recent years, transportation services play a more and more significant role in urban management. In the past decade, ridesharing services, which group passengers with similar routes, were considered as an effective and efficient transportation solution to alleviate the problems of natural resource depletion, transportation congestion and air pollution [4]. The emerging ride-hailing platforms, such as Didi, Uber and Lyft, also provide various types of ridesharing services.

There are two compelling research problems in the context of ridesharing. One is how to efficiently match a group of passengers to a vehicle with variable objectives, such as maximizing the revenue of the platforms or minimizing the travel cost of the drivers. The other problem is determining the payments to passengers to cover

© Springer Nature Switzerland AG 2021
Z. Liu et al. (Eds.): WASA 2021, LNCS 12938, pp. 277–289, 2021.
https://doi.org/10.1007/978-3-030-86130-8_22

the travel cost. Even though these two problems are highly correlated, most works are only dedicated to the first optimization problem from the perspectives of demand prediction [12,24], dispatching [9,18,26] and online route selection [25,28], paying less attention to the second pricing problem. On the other hand, existing pricing mechanisms, which provide the same fare rate for all passengers [21,23], ignore different travel costs and willingness-to-pay of passengers. In this work, we jointly consider the passengers assignment and cost allocation, and design a cost-sharing mechanism to minimize the social cost in ridesharing systems.

Designing an efficient and effective cost-sharing mechanism needs to consider the following three challenges. The first challenge comes from the heterogeneity of passengers in terms of willingness-to-pay. For example, some impatient passengers would like to pay more to prioritize their routes. In this case, it is necessary to take the utilities of passengers into consideration during the process of passengers assignment. We resort to the auction mechanism, in which passengers submit a bid to reveal their maximum willingness-to-pay. Considering the strategic behaviors of passengers, passengers would manipulate the bids to take advantages of the passengers assignment. It is non-trivial to design a mechanism to guarantee incentive compatibility and individual rationality[1].

The second challenge is due to the complexity of travel cost in ridesharing systems. A desirable cost-sharing mechanism should satisfy the property of budget balance, *i.e.*, the total payments of passengers should at least cover the travel cost of the driver. However, the incurred travel cost could be influenced by diverse factors like detour, congestion or travel time. As we will show in Sect. 3, classic incentive compatible mechanisms cannot guarantee budget balance even in a simple case with a symmetric cost function.

The third challenge is to maximize the social welfare of the ridesharing system, which is defined as the difference between the passengers' valuations and the incurred cost of the system. Unfortunately, it has been proved that there exists no such a mechanism [13]. Furthermore, there is no efficient mechanism with guaranteed approximation ratio [22]. Thus, we need to find another metric to measure the efficiency loss of the ridesharing system.

In this paper, we conduct a study on the problem of cost-sharing mechanism design for social cost minimization in ridesharing systems. First, we explore the desirable properties that a desirable cost-sharing mechanism is supposed to satisfy, including economic efficiency, incentive compatibility, individual rationality and budget balance. Second, we demonstrate disadvantages of the classical mechanisms, and give an impossibility result of designing a mechanism satisfying the above four desirable properties simultaneously, even for a simple case. Then, we relax the constraint of economic efficiency and turn to a new metric, social cost, to measure the approximate efficiency of the ridesharing system. Based on this metric, we design a VCG-based cost-sharing mechanism for the simple case, and extend it to the general case with the general submodular cost function. We theoretically prove that these two mechanisms are $O(n)$ and $\mathcal{H}_n$ approximately economic efficient with other the desirable properties guaranteed,

---

[1] Please refer to Sect. 2 for the detailed definitions.

respectively. The n is the number of candidate passengers and $\mathcal{H}_n = \sum_{l=1}^{n} \frac{1}{l}$ denotes the sum of the first nth Harmonic number.

In summary, our main contributions are shown as follows:

- We formulate a cost-sharing model for ridesharing systems and show that existing mechanisms are not qualified for desirable properties in ridesharing systems.
- We introduce the social cost metric to measure efficiency of ridesharing systems and propose two incentive compatible, budget balanced, individually rational and guaranteed approximately efficient mechanisms for the simple and general scenarios, respectively.
- We evaluate the performance of the proposed mechanisms on a real-world dataset, and evaluation results shows that our mechanism could increase user experience and efficiency of ridesharing system.

This paper is structured as follows: In Sect. 2, we present a cost sharing model of ridesharing and introduce basic notions of the cost-sharing mechanism. We discuss some existing truthful mechanisms in the context of cost-sharing problem in Sect. 3. In Sect. 4, we design two VCG-based mechanisms for the simple case and general case, respectively. We show our evaluation results in Sect. 5, and briefly review the related works in Sect. 6. Finally, we conclude this paper in Sect. 7.

2 Preliminaries

In this section we briefly introduce the notions used in this paper and give an overview of the cost-sharing problem.

We focus on an under-supply scenario during rush hour, where drivers are much more than drivers. In this case, maximizing the efficiency of the system is approach to maximizing the efficiency of each driver. Thus, we reduce the problem with multiple drivers to the mechanism design problem with single driver. Assuming that a set $U = \{1, 2, \ldots, n\}$ of passengers are requiring to be lifted. The travel cost of the driver is associated with the selected passenger set $W \subseteq U$ with a set function $C : 2^U \rightarrow R$. The cost function is defined as a general set function which may depend on travel time, travel distance or other factors of passengers. We assume that $C(\emptyset) = 0$ and that C is monotonically non-decreasing, implying that $\forall T \subseteq S, C(T) \leq C(S)$. Furthermore, we note that the cost of a group $S \cup T$ would be less than the sum of the separate cost of them, i.e., $C(S \cup T) \leq C(S) + C(T)$. Otherwise, passengers in S and T would not be willing to share the ride as it takes less to ride separately.

Each passenger $i \in U$ has a fixed private valuation v_i for getting the travel service, i.e., she is willing to pay at most v_i to get lifted. Since passengers only care about whether arriving at their destinations or not, the fixed valuation v_i of the passenger i would not be affected by other passengers. Without loss of generality, we assume that passengers are sorted in descending order of their valuations, i.e., $v_i \geq v_j$ for any $i < j$.

Now we demonstrate the cost-sharing problem in the ridesharing system. As illustrated in the Fig. 1, the ridesharing platform first collects a non-negative valuation v_i from each passenger $i \in U$ for one ride. Then, the platform selects a set $W \subseteq U$ of passengers to share the ride, and finally charges every selected passenger $i \in W$ with a

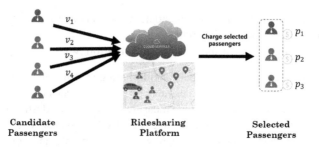

Fig. 1. An example of ridesharing system

non-negative payment p_i. The goal of every passenger i is to maximize her quasi-linear utility $u_i = (v_i - p_i)x_i$, where $x_i = 1$ if the passenger i gets served and $x_i = 0$ otherwise. For the sustainable development and economic efficiency of the system, the goal of the platform is to select the passenger set which maximizes the social welfare of the system and distribute incurred cost among passengers. Formally, the *Social Welfare* of the ridesharing system is defined as $SW(W) = \sum_{i \in W} v_i - C(W)$, where W is the set of passengers being served. With private valuations of passengers, truthfulness of the mechanism is necessary for the economic efficiency, because only when passengers report true valuation we can get real social welfare. Both budget balance and individual rationality are basic properties in ridesharing systems as the platform aims at gaining profit and the passenger would not accept a negative utility. Totally, we have identified four desirable properties that a cost-sharing mechanism for ridesharing systems should have: *incentive compatibility, budget balance, individual rationality* and *economic efficiency*, which are defined as follows:

Definition 1 (Truthfulness or Incentive Compatibility). *A mechanism satisfies incentive compatibility if truthfully bidding is the dominant strategy for every passenger. Formally, for any passenger* $i \in U$*, with others' valuation unchangeable,* $v_i - p_i \geq v_i - p_i'$ *where* p_i *and* p_i' *are the payments of* i *when truthfully bidding* v_i *and misreporting* v_i'*, respectively.*

Definition 2 (Individual Rationality). *A mechanism satisfies individual rationality if passengers never pay more than their willingness-to-pay, i.e.,* $(v_i - p_i)x_i \geq 0, \forall i \in U$*.*

Definition 3 (Budget Balance). *A mechanism satisfies budget balance if the whole platform having no deficit. That means that the sum of payments from passengers should cover the travel cost, i.e.,* $\sum_{i \in W} p_i \geq C(W)$ *where* W *is the set of passengers served.*

Definition 4 (Economic Efficiency). *A mechanism satisfies economic efficiency if the mechanism selects the subset of passengers that maximizes the social welfare.*

As we will show in the Sect. 3, designing a cost-sharing mechanism satisfying these four properties simultaneously is not trivial even in a very simple case and we will relax the economic efficiency property in Sect. 4.

Algorithm 1. Maximal Social Welfare Algorithm for The Simplified Case

---

Input: Sorted passengers' valuations: $\{v_1, v_2, \cdots, v_n\}$, where $v_i \geq v_j$ if $i < j$.
Output: Maximal social welfare SW and corresponding passengers Set W

1: Initialize $SW \leftarrow 0$, $W \leftarrow \emptyset$, $S \leftarrow \emptyset$, $i \leftarrow 1$.
2: **while** $i \leq n$ **do**
3:    $S \leftarrow S \cup \{i\}$
4:    **if** $SW \leq \sum_{j \in S} v_i - C(i)$ **then**
5:        $SW \leftarrow \sum_{j \in S} v_i - C(i)$
6:        $W \leftarrow S$
7:    **end if**
8:    $i \leftarrow i + 1$
9: **end while**
10: **return** SW, W

---

3   Discussion of Existing Mechanisms

It is non-trivial to maximize social welfare with all the critical properties guaranteed. In this section, we will discuss some widely used truthful mechanisms. We will show that all of them are not feasible for the ridesharing system even in a simplified case.

3.1   Simplified Case

We first consider a simple case where the cost function is symmetric and monotone, i.e., $C(S) = C(T)$ whenever $|S| = |T|$ and $C(S) < C(T)$ where $|S| < |T|$. By abuse of notation, we write $C(|S|) = C(S)$ in the simple case. This scenario could be described as a special case in a prioritized ridesharing problem [27]. With such an assumption, as long as the number of passengers in the group does not change, neither will the incurred cost. When considering social welfare maximization, it is simplified in the sense that we can mainly focus on valuations of passengers, assuming that we have got the real valuations from passengers. To choose the passenger group with maximal social welfare, we greedily pick the passengers with maximal social welfare as winners (as shown in Algorithm 1). It makes the problem much easier and clearer. Even in such a setting, we will show that existing widely used mechanisms fail to satisfy budget balance and incentive compatibility simultaneously.

3.2   Critical Payment Method

First, we show that the critical payment method, which plays a significant role in truthful mechanisms, fails to guarantee budget balance. By critical payment method, the platform charges every winner with the highest valuation of passengers who do not win. We give a simple example to illustrate the mechanism.

Example 1. There are four passengers $\{1, 2, 3, 4\}$ with true valuations $v_1 = 10, v_2 = 6, v_3 = 3, v_4 = 1$ and $C(0) = 0, C(1) = 1, C(2) = 2, C(3) = 3, C(4) = 5$.

Assuming that all passengers report truthfully, we will select $W = \{1, 2, 3\}$ as the winner set. By the critical payment technique, the payments are $p_1 = v_4 = 1, p_2 = v_4 = 1, p_3 = v_4 = 1$, while the social welfare is still maximized. The utilities are $u_1 = v_1 - p_1 = 9, u_2 = v_2 - p_2 = 5, u_3 = v_3 - p_3 = 2$.

However, the critical payment based mechanism cannot guarantee budget balance. For example, we keep the same setting in Example 1 except that $v_4 = 0.9$. In this case, $\{1, 2, 3\}$ are picked as winners with $p_1 = p_2 = p_3 = 0.9$. Thus, $p_1 + p_2 + p_3 - C(3) < 0$, indicating the mechanism does not satisfy budget balance.

3.3 VCG Mechanism

We consider another general incentive compatible mechanism, the VCG mechanism, which also guarantees the optimal social welfare. The payment of the passenger $i \in W$ is given as

$$p_i = \sum_{j \in W_i'} v_j - h(W_i') - (\sum_{j \in W \setminus \{i\}} v_j - h(W)), \tag{1}$$

where $h : 2^U \to R$ is any set function that is independent of v_i and W_i' denotes the winner set generated by the Algorithm 1 by setting $v_i = 0$ and other valuations identical. When the function h is the cost function C, the passenger i pays the "damage" she causes, $i.e.$, the difference between the optimal social welfare when i does not participate and social welfare of other passengers in the outcome decision. In such case, the mechanism satisfies both economic efficiency and incentive compatibility [20]. Unfortunately, we will show that budget balance is not guaranteed by the following example:

Example 2. Keep the main setting of Example 1 except that $v_4 = 0.9$ and $C(0) = 0, C(1) = 2, C(2) = 3, C(3) = 4, C(4) = 6$.

By the VCG mechanism, $\{1, 2, 3\}$ will be picked as winners and $p_1 = (v_2 + v_3 - C(2)) - (v_1 + v_2 + v_3 - C(3) - v_1) = 1, p_2 = 1, p_3 = 1, p_4 = 0$. Thus, $p_1 + p_2 + p_3 - C(3) = -1 < 0$. Thus, the budget balance is not guaranteed.

4   Modified VCG Mechanism

In this section, we first try to modify the VCG mechanism to satisfy budget balance. Unfortunately, we show an impossibility result for maximizing social welfare while keeping budget balance, even in the simple case. Thus we resort to another metric, social cost, to measure the loss of efficiency in the ridesharing system and design two modified VCG mechanisms satisfying budget balance, incentive compatibility, individual rationality and approximate economic efficiency for the simple case and the general case, respectively.

4.1 Beneficial Attempt on Budget Balance

First, we modify the VCG mechanism to satisfy budget balance. Note that W_i' is the winner set without participation of the passenger i. We can get that $\sum_{j \in W_i'} v_j - h(W_i') \geq \sum_{j \in W \setminus \{i\}} v_j - h(W \setminus \{i\})$. Combining it with the Eq. (1), we have $p_i \geq h(W) - h(W \setminus \{i\})$. Therefore, if the function h satisfies that

$$\sum_{i \in W} h(W) - h(W \setminus \{i\}) \geq C(S), \tag{2}$$

the mechanism could guarantee budget balance. Therefore, we can define a simple function $h(W) = \mathcal{H}(W) = \sum_{l=1}^{|W|} \frac{C(l)}{l}$. Thus, the payment p_i is

$$p_i = \sum_{j \in W_i'} v_j - \mathcal{H}(W_i') - \left(\sum_{j \in W \setminus \{i\}} v_j - \mathcal{H}(W) \right). \tag{3}$$

We demonstrate the mechanism by an example shown below (Example 3).

Example 3. There are five passengers $\{1, 2, 3, 4, 5\}$ with valuations $v_1 = 20, v_2 = 18, v_3 = 15, v_4 = 10, v_5 = 5$. The cost is only decided by the number of passengers where $C(0) = 0, C(1) = 10, C(2) = 19, C(3) = 27, C(4) = 34, C(5) = 40$.

With the definition of $\mathcal{H}$, we get $\mathcal{H}(0) = 0$, $\mathcal{H}(1) = 10$, $\mathcal{H}(2) = 19.5$, $\mathcal{H}(3) = 28.5$, $\mathcal{H}(4) = 37$, $\mathcal{H}(5) = 45$. To maximize social welfare, we still pick passengers $\{1, 2, 3, 4\}$ as the winner set with $p_1 = (v_2 + v_3 + v_4 - \mathcal{H}(3)) - (v_2 + v_3 + v_4 - \mathcal{H}(4)) = 8.5$, $p_2 = 8.5$, $p_3 = 8.5$ and $p_4 = 8.5$. Here, $p_1 + p_2 + p_3 + p_4 - C(4) = 0$.

In the above example, we achieve optimal social welfare and budget balance at the same time if passengers report truthfully. Unfortunately, the mechanism cannot guarantee the individual rationality and incentive compatibility although the payment is independent of the passenger's reporting valuation. For example, if we set $v_5 = 7$ in Example 3, we have $p_5 = (\sum_{i=1}^{4} v_i - H(4)) - (\sum_{i=1}^{5} v_i - H(5) - v_5) = 8$. Thus, the utility of the passenger 5 is negative, so that the truth-telling is not the dominant strategy of the passenger 5. This is due to that the allocation algorithm cannot guarantee maximization of social welfare and $\sum_{i \in W} v_i - \mathcal{H}(W)$ simultaneously.

Actually, as pointed out by Green [13], there is no cost-sharing mechanism satisfying the truthfulness, budget balance, individual rationality and economic efficiency simultaneously. This impossibility result indicates that we should relax at least one of our desirable properties. As a consequence, we turn to looking for a mechanism approximately maximizing social welfare. Unfortunately, another impossibility result given by Feigenbaum [11] implies that there is no such approximation guarantee of social welfare. The hardness of approximating efficiency is mainly due to mixed-sign property of social welfare. Hence, we need measure the efficiency loss of the mechanism in another way. For this purpose, we refer to the social cost metric proposed by Roughgarden [22]. Formally, the social cost $SC(W)$ of selected passenger set W is defined as

$$SC(W) = C(W) + \sum_{i \in U \setminus W} v_i \tag{4}$$

Algorithm 2. VCG-Based Mechanism for Simplified Case

Input: Sorted passengers' valuation profiles:$\{v_1, v_2, \cdots, v_n\}$, where $v_i \geq v_j$ if $i < j$.
Output: Passenger set W and corresponding Payment vector $\mathcal{X} = \{p_i | i \in W\}$

1: Compute $\mathcal{H}(|I|) \leftarrow \sum_{l=1}^{|I|} \frac{C(l)}{l}$ as: $\{\mathcal{H}(0), \mathcal{H}(1), \mathcal{H}(2), ..., \mathcal{H}(n)\}$.
2: Initialize $i \leftarrow 1$, $SW \leftarrow 0$, $W \leftarrow \emptyset$, $S \leftarrow \emptyset$, $\mathcal{X} \leftarrow \emptyset$.
3: **while** $i \leq n$ **do**
4:     $S \leftarrow S \cup \{i\}$
5:     **if** $SW \leq \sum_{i \in S} v_i - \mathcal{H}(i)$ **then**
6:         $SW \leftarrow \sum_{i \in S} v_i - \mathcal{H}(i)$
7:         $W \leftarrow S$
8:     **end if**
9:     $i \leftarrow i + 1$
10: **end while**
11: **for** $i \in W$ **do**
12:     Recompute W_i' by setting $v_i = 0$ for each passenger $i \in W$
13:     $p_i \leftarrow \sum_{j \in W_i'} v_j - \mathcal{H}(|W_i'|) - (\sum_{j \in W \setminus \{i\}} v_j - \mathcal{H}(|W|))$
14:     $\mathcal{X} \leftarrow \mathcal{X} \cup \{p_i\}$
15: **end for**
16: **return** $W, \mathcal{X}$

Social cost is the sum of incurred cost and valuations fail to receive the service (*i.e.*, opportunity cost). As the sum of social welfare and social cost is a constant, minimizing social cost is equivalent to maximizing social welfare. Definitely, the two objectives are not equivalent from an approximation perspective. Thus, we give another definition of approximate economic efficiency with the social cost, which is commonly adopted by other cost-sharing mechanisms [10].

Definition 5 (α-**approximate economic efficiency**). *The α-approximately efficient allocation satisfies that, $SC(W) \leq (\alpha + 1)SC(W^*)$, where W^* is the set minimizing the social cost and W denotes the set generated by the allocation algorithm.*

4.2 Mechanism Design for Simplified Case

For the simple case where the cost function is symmetric, we design a VCG-based mechanism similar to the method in Sect. 4.1. As shown in Algorithm 2, we first select the passenger set W with

$$W = \arg \max_{W \subseteq U} \sum_{j \in W} v_j - \mathcal{H}(W), \tag{5}$$

and charge the passenger $i \in W$ with the Eq. (3), where W_i' is the outcome of allocation by setting $v_i = 0$. Then, we briefly demonstrate the desirable properties guaranteed by Algorithm 2.

Theorem 1. *The VCG-based mechanism described in Algorithm 2 is truthful, individually rational, budget balanced and provides an approximation ratio of $O(n)$ in social cost where the cost function is symmetric.*

The proof is included in our technical report [17] but is omitted in this work due to space limitations.

4.3   Mechanism Design for General Case

Now we extend the mechanism to the general case where cost function is extremely complex due to the complexity of travel routing. Unfortunately, not every cost function can lead to a well-performed mechanism. It has been shown that if the cost function C is supermodular, no mechanism can achieve a guaranteed social cost approximation ratio [10]. Except for supermodular cost function, another class of general cost function satisfies submodularity, *i.e.*, for any $S \subseteq T \subseteq U$ and $i \in U \backslash T$, $C(S \cup \{i\}) - C(S) \geq C(T \cup \{i\}) - C(T)$. It is consist with the practice that the marginal cost is always monotonically decreasing in the ridesharing system.

For a general submodular cost function, we use Hart and Mas-Colell's potential function [14] to define the function $h(W)$ in the Eq. (3), which is defined as:

$$h(W) = \sum_{S \subseteq W} \frac{(|S| - 1)!(|W| - |S|)!}{|W|!} C(S),$$

where W is the allocation outcome. Similar to the mechanism for the simple case, the allocation outcome is

$$W = \arg \max_W \sum_{i \in W} v_i - h(W). \tag{6}$$

Due to the generality of cost function, here we skip the discussion on the complexity of calculating the optimal result and focus on designing the cost-sharing mechanism.

Theorem 2. *The VCG-based mechanism for general case satisfies the truthfulness, budget balance, individual rationality and provides an approximation ratio of $\mathcal{H}_n$ in the social cost.*

Due to the limitation of space, we leave the detailed proof in our technical report [17].

5   Evaluations

In this section, we conduct evaluations to demonstrate the performance of the VCG-based mechanisms for the general case in different levels of supply and demand. We first describe our simulation setup and then present simulation results.

5.1   Evaluation Setup

We evaluate the cost-sharing mechanism on a real taxi dataset of New York, which contains information of individual taxi rides in New York city [1]. Each entry in the dataset records information including start location, destination location, passenger number, travel time, travel distance. For studying the situation during rush hour, we sample the records in (10:00:00–10:02:00) on Jan 1st 2019 and Jan 2nd 2019 as our experiment data. We regard each entry as an individual request of a passenger. The individual valuation v_i of passenger i is sampled from a Gaussian distribution whose mean value is μ_i and variance $\delta_i = 10$. We let μ_i be linear with the travel distance of her request.

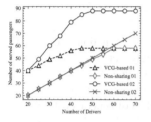 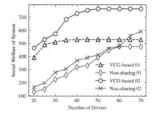 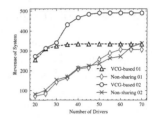

Fig. 2. The effect of supply on user experience

Fig. 3. The effect of supply on social welfare

Fig. 4. The effect of supply on revenue

To investigate the influence of the vehicle supply on the performance of our mechanism, we set different numbers of drivers for the rush hour setting in random location which is in range [20] with step 5. We define the cost function for each driver as $C(S) = \sum_{i \in S} dis(s_i, d_i)$, where S is the group of passengers share the same ride and the $dis(s_i, d_i)$ denotes the distance between the start point of the first passenger and the destination of the last passenger in a ride. We adopt the bipartite graph matching algorithm for vehicle sharing to allocate candidate passengers to each driver in advance.

5.2 Evaluation Results

We compare the performance of the VCG-based mechanism with the non-sharing mechanism which adopts a fixed rate of charge for the single passenger. The Fig. 2 shows the number of served passengers with different riding resource supplies, where the *VCG-based 01* and *Non-sharing 01* represent results conducted by the VCG-based mechanism and non-sharing mechanism using dataset on Jan 1st 2019, respectively. Similarly, the *VCG-based 02* and *Non-sharing 02* represent results using dataset on Jan 2nd 2019. Although the demand levels are different on these two days, it leads to the similar overall trend. The number of served passengers climbs and stay stable with the number of drivers rises except that the number of served passenger keep rising with the increasing number of drivers in Non-sharing 02. This is due to that 70 drivers cannot serve all passengers over the Non-sharing mechanism on the second day while all passengers get served with 50 drivers over VCG-based mechanism. Moreover, more passengers get serviced in VCG-based mechanism in comparison to the non-sharing mechanism, indicating that the experience of passengers are better by adopting VCG-based mechanism.

In our second simulation, we investigate the influence of riding resource on the social welfare and revenue of the system. As the Fig. 3 and Fig. 4 illustrate, both social welfare and revenue of the system first increases and then stay stable with drivers increasing. And the system could get extremely more social welfare and revenue by adopting VCG-based mechanism comparing to Non-sharing mechanism.

6   Related Works

We briefly review related works in this section. The most related topic is pricing and dispatching in ridesharing systems [3,5,6], which focused on optimizing efficiency of ridesharing systems. However, they all provide fixed fare rate and dismiss the heterogeneity of passengers' willingness-to-pay. There are a line of works based on the auction to recognize the heterogeneity of passengers. Kleiner *et al.* [15] proposed an incentive compatible mechanism based on parallel auctions considering the individual preference of passengers. Based on the Vickery auction, Asghari *et al.* [2] designed a truthful and individually rational mechanism for online ridesharing. Chen and Wang [7] proposed a pricing scheme aiming at optimizing social welfare of ridesharing system. But neither of them considers the travel cost of drivers.

Cheng *et al.* [8] proposed a fare splitting mechanism for last-mile ride-sharing which satisfies budget balance, individual rationality and incentive compatibility. Zhao *et al.* [29] showed that the VCG mechanism in ridesharing system results in a high deficit and proposed a mechanism with deficit control. However, these works ignore the efficiency of the ridesharing system.

There are several works designing the cost-sharing mechanism from a perspective of fairness [16,19]. They turned to cooperative game theory solution concepts, the Shapley value and the nucleolus, to allocate incurred cost fairly. However, the Shapley value and nucleolus cannot guarantee neither individual rationality nor incentive compatibility.

7   Conclusion

In this work, we have proposed a cost-sharing framework based on VCG mechanism to recognize the heterogeneity of passengers' willingness-to-pay and approximately minimize social cost of systems. First, we explored desirable properties for ridesharing and demonstrated why existing mechanisms fail. We have proposed two VCG-based mechanisms for the simple case and general case to guarantee the incentive compatibility, budget balance, individual rationality and provide a guaranteed approximation ratio for the economic efficiency. Finally, we evaluated the performance of our mechanism over a real-world data set. The evaluation results showed that the cost-sharing mechanism could increase the efficiency of the system as well as the user experience of passengers.

Acknowledgements. This work was supported in part by National Key R&D Program of China No. 2019YFB2102200, in part by China NSF grant No. 62025204, 62072303, 61972252, and 61972254, in part by Alibaba Group through Alibaba Innovation Research Program, and in part by Tencent Rhino Bird Key Research Project. The opinions, findings, conclusions, and recommendations expressed in this paper are those of the authors and do not necessarily reflect the views of the funding agencies or the government.

References

1. Taxi and limousine commission: Tlc trip record data. https://www1.nyc.gov/site/tlc/about/tlc-trip-record-data.page

2. Asghari, M., Shahabi, C.: An on-line truthful and individually rational pricing mechanism for ride-sharing. In: Proceedings of SIGSPATIAL, pp. 1–10 (2017)
3. Banerjee, S., Johari, R., Riquelme, C.: Pricing in ride-sharing platforms: a queueing-theoretic approach. In: Economics and Computation, p. 639 (2015)
4. Caulfield, B.: Estimating the environmental benefits of ride-sharing: a case study of Dublin. Transp. Res. Part D: Transp. Environ. **14**(7), 527–531 (2009)
5. Chen, L., Zhong, Q., Xiao, X., Gao, Y., Jin, P., Jensen, C.S.: Price-and-time-aware dynamic ridesharing. In: Proceedings of ICDE, pp. 1061–1072 (2018)
6. Chen, M., Shen, W., Tang, P., Zuo, S.: Dispatching through pricing: modeling ride-sharing and designing dynamic prices. In: Proceedings of IJCAI, pp. 165–171 (2019)
7. Chen, Y., Wang, H.: Pricing for a last-mile transportation system. Transp. Res. Part B: Methodol. **107**, 57–69 (2018)
8. Cheng, S., Nguyen, D.T., Lau, H.C.: Mechanisms for arranging ride sharing and fare splitting for last-mile travel demands. In: Proceedings of AAMAS, pp. 1505–1506 (2014)
9. Dickerson, J.P., Sankararaman, K.A., Srinivasan, A., Xu, P.: Allocation problems in ride-sharing platforms: online matching with offline reusable resources. In: Proceedings of AAAI (2018)
10. Dobzinski, S., Ovadia, S.: Combinatorial cost sharing. In: Proceedings of EC, pp. 387–404 (2017)
11. Feigenbaum, J., Papadimitriou, C.H., Shenker, S.: Sharing the cost of multicast transmissions. J. Comput. Syst. Sci. **63**(1), 21–41 (2001)
12. Geng, X., et al.: Spatiotemporal multi-graph convolution network for ride-hailing demand forecasting. In: Proceedings of AAAI (2019)
13. Green, J., Kohlberg, E., Laffont, J.J.: Partial equilibrium approach to the free-rider problem. J. Public Econ. **6**(4), 375–394 (1976)
14. Hart, S., Mas-Colell, A.: Potential, value, and consistency. Econometrica: J. Econom. Soc. **57**, 589–614 (1989)
15. Kleiner, A., Nebel, B., Ziparo, V.A.: A mechanism for dynamic ride sharing based on parallel auctions. In: Proceedings of IJCAI, Spain, July 16–22, 2011, pp. 266–272 (2011)
16. Levinger, C., Hazon, N., Azaria, A.: Fair sharing: the Shapley value for ride-sharing and routing games. arXiv preprint arXiv:1909.04713 (2019)
17. Liu, Y., Zhang, C., Zheng, Z., Chen, G.: Cost-sharing mechanism design for ridesharing systems. In: Technical report (2021). https://www.dropbox.com/s/rjb5x3fzb48q6pe/WASA_2021_full
18. Liu, Y., Skinner, W., Xiang, C.: Globally-optimized realtime supply-demand matching in on-demand ridesharing. In: Proceedings of WWW, pp. 3034–3040 (2019)
19. Lu, W., Quadrifoglio, L.: Fair cost allocation for ridesharing services - modeling, mathematical programming and an algorithm to find the nucleolus. Transp. Res. Part B-Methodol. **121**, 41–55 (2019)
20. Suzuki, M., Vetta, A.: How many freemasons are there? The consensus voting mechanism in metric spaces. In: Harks, T., Klimm, M. (eds.) SAGT 2020. LNCS, vol. 12283, pp. 322–336. Springer, Cham (2020). https://doi.org/10.1007/978-3-030-57980-7_21
21. Pandit, V.N., Mandar, D., Hanawal, M.K., Moharir, S.: Pricing in ride sharing platforms: static vs dynamic strategies. In: Proceedings of COMSNETS, pp. 208–215 (2019)
22. Roughgarden, T., Sundararajan, M.: Quantifying inefficiency in cost-sharing mechanisms. J. ACM (JACM) **56**(4), 1–33 (2009)
23. Sun, L., Teunter, R.H., Babai, M.Z., Hua, G.: Optimal pricing for ride-sourcing platforms. Eur. J. Oper. Res. **278**(3), 783–795 (2019)
24. Tong, Y., et al.: The simpler the better: a unified approach to predicting original taxi demands based on large-scale online platforms. In: Proceedings of SIGKDD, pp. 1653–1662. ACM (2017)

25. Xu, Y., Tong, Y., Shi, Y., Tao, Q., Xu, K., Li, W.: An efficient insertion operator in dynamic ridesharing services. In: Proceedings of ICDE, pp. 1022–1033 (2019)
26. Xu, Z., et al.: Large-scale order dispatch in on-demand ride-hailing platforms: a learning and planning approach. In: Proceedings of SIGKDD, pp. 905–913 (2018)
27. Yengin, D.: Characterizing the Shapley value in fixed-route traveling salesman problems with appointments. Int. J. Game Theory 41(2), 271–299 (2012)
28. Yuen, C.F., Singh, A.P., Goyal, S., Ranu, S., Bagchi, A.: Beyond shortest paths: route recommendations for ride-sharing. In: Proceedings of WWW, pp. 2258–2269 (2019)
29. Zhao, D., Zhang, D., Gerding, E.H., Sakurai, Y., Yokoo, M.: Incentives in ridesharing with deficit control. In: Proceedings of AAMAS, pp. 1021–1028 (2014)

Privacy Protection Framework for Credit Data in AI

Congdong Lv, Xiaodong Zhang$^{(\boxtimes)}$, and Zhoubao Sun

Nanjing Audit University, Nanjing 211815, China
270050@nau.edu.cn

Abstract. Rich and fine personal and enterprise data are being collected and recorded, so as to provide big data support for personal and enterprise credit evaluation and credit integration. In this process, the problem of data privacy is becoming more and more prominent. For example, the user's location data may be used to infer address, behavior and activity, and the user's service use records may reveal information such as gender, age and disease. How to protect data privacy while meeting the needs of credit evaluation and credit integration is one of the great challenges in the era of big data. In this paper, we propose a security privacy protection framework in artificial intelligence algorithm, analyze the possibility of privacy leakage from data privacy security, model privacy security and environment privacy security, and give the corresponding defense strategy. In addition, this paper also gives an example algorithm of data security level, which can ensure the security of data privacy.

Keywords: Privacy protection framework · Credit data ·
Privacy-preserved · Differential private · AI security

1 Introduction

With the widespread application of information technology, various information systems have stored and accumulated a wealth of personal data, such as patient diagnosis and treatment records kept by medical institutions, and customer online transaction data collected by e-commerce companies. These data contain great value. The underlying laws and knowledge based on data extraction is not only an important means to assist scientific research, such as exploring the causes of diseases through the mining and analysis of patient medical records and genetic data; it is also widely used in production and life to promote social development, for example, more Personalized recommendation systems, smart meters, face recognition, etc. in the field. Data has become a basic resource in many fields such as academics, industry, and social services. Although with the popularization of personal mobile devices and the development of mobile group sensing technology, data acquisition has become easier, but the process

Supported by National Key R&D Program (Grant Nos. 2019YFB1404602).

Z. Liu et al. (Eds.): WASA 2021, LNCS 12938, pp. 290–302, 2021.
https://doi.org/10.1007/978-3-030-86130-8_23

of data collection, cleaning, and storage will give many data application institutions, such as government departments and information consulting organizations, Bring many unnecessary burdens. Data publishing technology for the purpose of data application provides a solution to this problem. The technology uses statistical analysis methods to extract the underlying laws of the data according to the data application requirements, and publish the analysis results. It can avoid the waste of resources caused by repeated data collection, while making the value of data more widely used. The released information itself also provides a reliable channel for understanding group characteristics and needs. For example, statistical analysis of aggregated individual user data has become an important means for service providers to design personalized services and improve service quality.

The security and privacy risks of artificial intelligence systems are mainly reflected in the three levels of data, models, and systems. a) Data is the input of various artificial intelligence algorithms to mine valuable features. Almost every large company wants to collect as much data as possible to improve the competitiveness of their AI technology. More and more personal data, including location information, online search behaviors, user calls, user preferences, etc., are being silently collected by sensors built into the products of these large companies, which brings a huge risk of privacy leakage to data owners. In addition, the use of these data is not under the control of its owners, because there is currently no reliable way to record how the data is used and who uses it, so there is almost no way to track or punish violators who misuse the data. At the same time, the lack of immutable records in data usage increases the risk of data misuse. Increase the risk of data misuse. b) At present, many AI models themselves are hosted in a secure cloud service or deployed on end-user devices, and can allow customers to inquire about the usage model through the API interface after paying. In these scenarios, the AI model is the core, which embodies the business value, and its confidentiality is essential. At present, there are increasing attacks on AI-based systems. One of these attacks is to forge adversarial examples. These examples are specially made samples to deceive the target AI model. The attacker uses samples to iteratively query the target model. These samples are specially designed to extract information about the model's interior to the maximum extent through the prediction of the model's return value. The attacker uses this information to gradually train an alternative model. The alternative model itself can be used to construct future queries, and the response of the query will be used to further refine the alternative model. The adversary uses the alternative model to bypass the original model, thereby depriving its original owner of the business advantage, constructing a transferable hostile sample, which can deceive the original model to make correct predictions. c) Data on the Internet is scattered in various places and controlled by different stakeholder who do not trust each other. It is difficult to authorize or verify the use of data in complex cyberspace. Therefore, for real big data and real powerful artificial intelligence, it is very difficult to realize data sharing in cyberspace. During the training and application of the AI system, there are a series of operations such as the distribution, aggregation, and deployment of data, parameters, and models, and each step has the risk of privacy leakage. The whole process will not only be attacked by attackers at the software level, but also at the hardware level, such as side-channel attacks, which poses the risk of privacy leakage.

2 Related Works

2.1 Defense Strategies for Adversarial Attacks

At present, artificial intelligence technologies represented by deep learning generally have problems such as robustness and interpretability limitations. People have insufficient understanding of the inherent vulnerabilities of most artificial intelligence algorithms, and lack effective security verification, testing and enhancement methods. This will seriously hinder the widespread application of artificial intelligence technology.

Its targeted defense plan also aroused great attention and key research of researchers. The existing methods of defending against attacks mainly include: training anti-disturbance neural networks, detecting input, correcting input or denoising, gradient masking, hybrid methods, etc.

Training anti-disturbance neural network defense attempts to design special network architectures or elaborate training procedures to make the network robust to attacks. Adversarial training [1–4] is one of the most widely studied defense methods against adversarial attacks. Its goal is to train a robust model from scratch on a training set containing adversarial disturbance data [2,4]. Adversarial training [2,5–7] trains the network by using the generated adversarial images during the training process, provides regularization for the network, and achieves the purpose of defending against adversarial disturbances, especially against white box attacks. Robustness against confrontation. Adversarial training improves the classification accuracy of the target model in adversarial examples [1,4]. On some smaller image data sets, it can even improve the accuracy of clean images [2,3], although in ImageNet [8] data There is no such effect on the set.

Many scholars have proposed various adversarial training algorithms to improve the robustness of the model, based on the method of adversarial logit pairing (ALP). It is an effective adversarial training strategy. ALP uses logit predictions of adversarial images for "denoising", using logit of clean images as a "noise-free" reference, and encouraging similar adversarial predictions for clean and adversarial samples of the network. Goodfellow et al. [2] and Huang et al. [7] studied and evaluated their adversarial training on the MNIST dataset, and Kurakin et al. [3] proposed a comprehensive analysis of adversarial training on the ImageNet dataset. Madry et al. [5] believe that training with adversarial samples generated by "Projected Gradient Descent" (Projected Gradient Descent, PGD) is one of the most effective methods for adversarial training, which can effectively improve the robustness of the model. Tramr et al. [4] proposed "integrated adversarial training", which uses disturbance inputs transferred from some fixed pre-training models to enhance training data. On the

ImageNet dataset, integrated adversarial training greatly improves the robustness against black box attacks. However, because online generation of adversarial examples requires additional calculations and more epochs are required to fit adversarial examples, adversarial training is more time-consuming than pure image training [4]. These limitations hinder adversarial training. Use stronger attacks. Network distillation is also an effective adversarial training strategy, which can be used to defend against adversarial sample attacks. Hinton et al. [9] originally designed a distillation technique to transfer knowledge from a complex network to a simpler network, with the purpose of reducing the model size. For distillation, high temperature will increase the ambiguity of the softmax output. Applying this feature, Papernot et al. [10] further proved that high temperature softmax reduces the sensitivity of the model to small disturbances. Since the attack mainly depends on the sensitivity of the model, the result is unfavorable to the adversary. Therefore, they proposed defensive distillation to improve the robustness of the model to adversarial samples. In subsequent work, Papernot et al. [11] solved the numerical instability problem encountered in [10], thereby extending the defensive distillation method.

The defense method based on detecting adversarial samples is also an adversarial training strategy. This method achieves the purpose of defense by detecting and filtering out adversarial samples to prevent the network from further reasoning. Metzen et al. [12] proposed to use a small sub-network to enhance a target network. The sub-network is trained, and the output and input examples are the probability of adversarial samples, which are used to distinguish between real data and data containing anti-disturbance. Research has shown that attaching such a network to the internal layers of a deep network can help detect disturbances caused by FGSM, BIM, and DeepFool attacks. Grosse et al. [13] enabled their model to classify all adversarial examples into a special category by adding additional categories of the target network. Feinman et al. [14] believed that the uncertainty of adversarial data was higher than that of legal data from the Bayesian point of view, and used Bayesian neural network to estimate the uncertainty of the input data to detect the uncertainty of the adversarial data. Sexual input data. Xu et al. [15] introduced feature compression, which includes two heuristics for processing input images: reducing the color depth at the pixel level by encoding colors with fewer values, and filtering the image with a smoothing filter. Then, the adversarial examples are detected by comparing the predictions of the target network on the original input and the compressed input. Fan et al. [16] proposed a comprehensive detection framework consisting of a statistical detector and a Gaussian noise injection detector to filter out adversarial samples with different disturbance characteristics.

The defense method based on input conversion is also an adversarial training strategy. This method restores the original image through adversarial samples. This defense system attempts to change the input and then sends these inputs to the target model, aiming to reduce the adversarial interference before the target model. Osadchy et al. [17] applied a set of filters to remove anti-noise, such as median filter, mean filter and Gaussian low-pass filter. Graese et al. [18] evaluated the defensive performance of a set of MNIST digits [19] preprocessing transformation, including disturbances introduced by the image acquisition process, crop fusion, and binarization. Das et al. [20] performed JPEG compression preprocessing on the image to reduce the impact of adversarial noise. Meng et al. [21] proposed a two-step defense model called MagNet, which detects adversary input and then reconstructs it based on the difference between clean and adversary input. Gu et al. [22] proposed a variant of autoencoder network. In reasoning, the network is used to encode adversarial samples to eliminate adversarial disturbances. Wang et al. [23] used a separate data conversion module to convert the input image to eliminate anti-interference. Guo et al. [24] proposed several non-differentiable image preprocessing to defend against adversarial samples, including image cropping and rescaling, bit depth reduction, and JPEG compression. The indistinguishability and inherent randomness of this method make it difficult for adversaries to bypass Over defense. Xie et al. [25] proposed to add a randomization layer to defend against adversarial attacks. This layer randomly scales the image, and then randomly zero-fills the image. This method can effectively defend against single-step and iterative attacks. Jia et al. [26] proposed an image compression framework to defend against adversarial samples, called ComDefend. This method is a preprocessing module that consists of a compressed convolutional neural network and a reconstructed convolutional neural network, which can be combined with specific Combine with the defense model of the model to improve the robustness of classification. Xie et al. [27] proposed a feature denoising method to defend against PGD white box attacks. Yuan et al. [28] proposed a generative cleaning network based on quantized nonlinear transformation. The network has a trainable quantized nonlinear transformation block, which can destroy the complex noise pattern against attacks and restore the original image content. Fan et al. [29] proposed a hybrid defense framework that integrates detection and removal of anti-disturbance. The detection part consists of a statistical detector and a Gaussian noise injection detector. They are adapted to the disturbance feature to detect the countermeasure samples, and the cleaning part is used for Eliminate or mitigate the deep residual generation network against disturbances. Doan et al. [30] proposed Februus to deal with backdoor attacks against deep neural networks, purifying the input of classification tasks by removing potential trigger artifacts, thereby effectively mitigating backdoor attacks. Sun et al. [31] first used statistics and small change detectors to detect and filter out the obvious and insignificant interference adversarial samples, and then integrated the detector, the deep residual generation network (ResGN) and the target network for adversarial training Together, build a complete defense framework. Su et al. [32] studied a defensive method in face verification scenarios, trained a deep residual generation network (ResGN) to clear the opponent's interference, and proposed a new training framework.

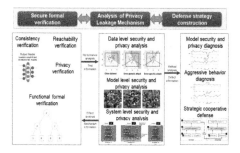

Fig. 1. Privacy protection framework

3   Privacy-Preserved Algorithm with Differential Privacy

The existing defense strategies for adversarial attacks are highly targeted, and usually design defense schemes for a specific type of attack. This paper studies the vulnerability analysis method based on static and dynamic theoretical analysis, and uses the model enhancement method to adjust the model parameters to repair its vulnerability. In order to further enhance the robustness of the model, this paper studies the defense model enhancement technology based on generative countermeasure network, the defense model enhancement technology based on robust model integration, and the adaptive defense model enhancement technology based on reinforcement learning. These three enhancement technologies can enhance the robustness of the model from different angles, and the three technologies work together to comprehensively enhance the self-confidence of the artificial intelligence system Adaptive defense capability. In the online defense phase, in order to ensure that the input samples do not contain anti noise, we study the corresponding anti noise detection and anti noise erasure scheme, and detect and erase the anti noise from multiple perspectives. The online collaborative defense strategy combines the above defense schemes to protect the input samples of the prediction tasks at multiple levels to ensure the accuracy of the prediction results. Combined with the enhancement model of offline defense and real-time prevention and control of online defense, the defense strategy can guarantee the security of intelligent recognition system in the whole life cycle, as shown in Fig. 1.

3.1   Secure Formal Verification of the Model

It condenses the application and security requirements of AI model security performance verification, flexible response to security threats, and coordinated deployment of defense strategies. It focuses on solving technical difficulties such as the analysis and detection of complex and diverse adversarial attacks, and the combination of advantages of different defense strategies. According to the research ideas and the main research content of the subject, the model is based on key technologies such as breaking through the model structure and simplifying the coding, complete test case dynamic generation, input sample high-dimensional feature analysis, model decision-making process understanding, defense mechanism optimization and combination and other key technologies. Formal verification of security.

3.2 Analysis of the Generation Mechanism of Adversarial Attacks

Poisoning/backdoor attacks distort the overall distribution of training data by constructing malicious samples and injecting them into training data, thereby causing abnormal decision-making behaviors of the model. Therefore, analyze its attack mechanism from the perspective of the high-dimensional features of the input samples and the decision boundary of the model. However, due to the huge sample input space of the AI model, it is difficult to carry out theoretical analysis. Based on the manifold hypothesis, most training data used for machine learning has a low-dimensional subspace structure inside. Therefore, finding a low-dimensional spatial mapping of an input sample is a prerequisite for the study of geometric spatial distribution. The project team intends to use natural sample data to study feature compression algorithms based on manifold learning, such as local linear embedding, isometric mapping, Hessian feature mapping, and Laplacian feature mapping, to form a manifold space mapping method based on natural samples.

3.3 Security Defense Strategy Construction

The project team intends to use static and dynamic theoretical analysis methods to analyze the vulnerability of the trained model, and use model enhancement methods to adjust model parameters to repair its vulnerability. In order to further enhance the robustness of the model, the research group proposed defense model enhancement technology based on generative confrontation network, defense model enhancement technology based on robust model integration, and adaptive defense model enhancement technology based on reinforcement learning. These three enhancement technologies The robustness of the model can be enhanced from different angles, and the three technologies work together to comprehensively enhance the adaptive defense capabilities of the artificial intelligence system. In the online defense stage, in order to ensure that the input samples do not contain anti-noise, the research team plans to design an adaptive anti-input detection and anti-noise erasing scheme to detect and erase anti-noise from multiple angles. The online collaborative defense strategy combines the above-mentioned defense schemes to protect the input samples for the execution of the prediction task at multiple levels to ensure the accuracy of the prediction results. Combining the enhanced model of offline defense and the real-time prevention and control of online defense, this collaborative defense framework can fully guarantee the security of the intelligent identification system throughout the entire life cycle.

3.4 Our Data Level Privacy Protection Algorithm

Algorithm 1 is an integrated algorithm for data privacy protection, providing users with a calling interface, including:

Algorithm 2: Single column privacy protection algorithm. For all the data in this column, use uniform privacy protection parameters to perform calculations to obtain new data and then send it to the data user. Algorithm

Algorithm 3: Multi-column privacy protection algorithm. For all the data in each column, use uniform privacy protection parameters, perform calculations, and obtain new data before sending it to the data user.

Algorithm 4: Privacy protection algorithm for multiple columns with different parameters. For all the data in each column, use uniform privacy protection parameters for calculations, use different privacy protection parameters for different columns, and finally transmit the data to the data user.

Algorithm 5: Single row and multiple column privacy protection algorithm. Different privacy protection parameters are used to calculate the data in different columns of the row to obtain new data and then send it to the data user.

Refer to Algorithm 2, a single column of privacy protection algorithms.

(1) The user specifies the column number. If the user does not specify the column number, a random function is used to randomly generate the column number;

(2) The user specifies privacy protection parameters. If the user does not specify privacy protection parameters, a random function is used to randomly generate privacy protection parameters;

(3) Read the value of each cell in the column, and then use the Laplace function and the privacy protection parameters in step (2) to calculate;

(4) Write the new data back to the table.

Refer to Algorithm 3, a multi-column privacy protection algorithm.

(1) The user specifies multiple column numbers. If the user does not specify a column number, a random function is used to randomly generate multiple column numbers;

(2) The user specifies the privacy protection parameter. If the user does not specify the privacy protection parameter, a random function is used to randomly generate a privacy protection parameter;

(3) For each column, read the value in each cell in the column, and then use the Laplace function and the privacy protection parameters in step (2) to calculate;

(4) Write the new data back to the table.

Referring to Algorithm 4, multiple columns of privacy protection algorithms with non-identical parameters

(1) The user specifies multiple column numbers. If the user does not specify a column number, a random function is used to randomly generate multiple column numbers;

(2) The user specifies multiple privacy protection parameters. If the user does not specify the privacy protection parameters, a random function is used to randomly generate multiple privacy protection parameters;

(3) For each column, read the value in each cell in the column, and then use the Laplace function and the privacy protection parameters in step (2) to calculate;

(4) Write the new data back to the table.

Refer to Algorithm 5, a single row and multiple column privacy protection algorithm.

(1) The user specifies the row number and multiple column number. If the user does not specify the row number and column number, a random function is used to randomly generate the row number and multiple column number;

(2) The user specifies multiple privacy protection parameters. If the user does not specify the privacy protection parameters, a random function is used to randomly generate multiple privacy protection parameters;

(3) Read the value of each cell in the column, and then use the Laplace function and the privacy protection parameters in step (2) to calculate;

(4) Write the new data back to the table.

Algorithm 1. Differential Private Cluster.

Require:
    The set of credit data, C;
    The private request, Req;
    The number of the column , r;
    The number of the column , i or the number vector of the column, Vec_i;
    The private protection parameter, ϵ or the vector of private protection parameters, Vec_ϵ;

Ensure: C'
1: **if** $Req = 1$ **then**
2:    $C'' = SigCP(C, \epsilon)$;
3: **end if**
4: **if** $Req = 2$ **then**
5:    $C'' = MulCP(C, \epsilon, i)$;
6: **end if**
7: **if** $Req = 3$ **then**
8:    $C'' = MulCDP(C, Vec_\epsilon, Vec_i)$;
9: **end if**
10: **if** $Req = 4$ **then**
11:    $C'' = SigRP(C, r, Vec_\epsilon, Vec_i)$;
12: **end if**
13: $C' = KMeans(C'')$;
14: **return** C';

Algorithm 2. Single Column Differential Privacy Protection $SigCP$.

Require:

    The set of credit data, C;

    The number of the column , i or the number vector of the column, Vec_i;

    The private protection parameter, ϵ or the vector of private protection parameters, Vec_ϵ;

Ensure: C'

  1: $C_i = C_{1i}, C_{2i}, ..., C_{ni} \in C$

  2: **for** each item $c \in C_i$ **do**

  3:   $c = c + Laplase(s/\epsilon)$;

  4: **end for**

  5: **return** C';

Algorithm 3. Multi column differential privacy protection $MulCP$.

Require:

    The set of credit data, C;

    The number of the column , i or the number vector of the column, Vec_i;

    The private protection parameter, ϵ or the vector of private protection parameters, Vec_ϵ;

Ensure: C'

  1: **for** each $i \in Vec_i$ **do**

  2:   **for** each item $c \in C_i$ **do**

  3:      $c = c + Laplase(s/\epsilon)$;

  4:   **end for**

  5: **end for**

  6: **return** C';

Algorithm 4. Multi column differential privacy protection with different ϵ $MulCDP$.

Require:

    The set of credit data, C;

    The number of the column , i or the number vector of the column, Vec_i;

    The private protection parameter, ϵ or the vector of private protection parameters, Vec_ϵ;

Ensure: C'

  1: **for** each $i \in Vec_i$ **do**

  2:   **for** each item $c \in C_i$ **do**

  3:      $c = c + Laplase(s/Vec_\epsilon[i])$;

  4:   **end for**

  5: **end for**

  6: **return** C';

Algorithm 5. Single row differential privacy protection with different ϵ *SigCDP*.

Require:
    The set of credit data, C;
    The number of the column , r;
    The number of the column , i or the number vector of the column, Vec_i;
    The private protection parameter, ϵ or the vector of private protection parameters, Vec_ϵ;
Ensure: C'
1: $C_r = C_{r1}, C_{r2}, ..., C_{rn} \in C$
2: **for** each $i \in Vec_i$ **do**
3:    $c[r][i] = c[r][i] + Laplase(s/Vec_\epsilon[i])$;
4: **end for**
5: **return** C';

4 Conclusion

In this paper, we propose a privacy protection framework in artificial intelligence algorithm to provide guidance for the privacy protection of credit data. Under the guidance of the framework, we give the privacy protection algorithm at the data level.

In the future, data privacy and model privacy need to be further discussed at the model level.

References

1. Szegedy, C., Zaremba, W., Sutskever, I., et al.: Intriguing properties of neural networks. arXiv preprint arXiv:1312.6199 (2013)
2. Goodfellow, I.J., Shlens, J., Szegedy, C.: Explaining and harnessing adversarial examples. arXiv preprint arXiv:1412.6572 (2014)
3. Kurakin, A., Goodfellow, I., Bengio, S.: Adversarial machine learning at scale. arXiv preprint arXiv:1611.01236 (2016)
4. Tramr, F., Kurakin, A., Papernot, N., et al.: Ensemble adversarial training: attacks and defenses. arXiv preprint arXiv:1705.07204 (2017)
5. Madry, A., Makelov, A., Schmidt, L., et al.: Towards deep learning models resistant to adversarial attacks. arXiv preprint arXiv:1706.06083 (2017)
6. Kannan, H., Kurakin, A., Goodfellow, I.: Adversarial logit pairing. arXiv preprint arXiv:1803.06373 (2018)
7. Huang, R., Xu, B., Schuurmans, D., et al.: Learning with a strong adversary. arXiv preprint arXiv:1511.03034 (2015)
8. Deng, J., Dong, W., Socher, R., et al.: ImageNet: a large-scale hierarchical image database. In: 2009 IEEE Conference on Computer Vision and Pattern Recognition, pp. 248–255. IEEE (2009)
9. Hinton, G., Vinyals, O., Dean, J.: Distilling the knowledge in a neural network. arXiv preprint arXiv:1503.02531 (2015)
10. Papernot, N., McDaniel, P., Wu, X., et al.: Distillation as a defense to adversarial perturbations against deep neural networks. In: 2016 IEEE Symposium on Security and Privacy (SP), pp. 582–597. IEEE (2016)

11. Papernot, N., McDaniel, P.: Extending defensive distillation. arXiv preprint arXiv:1705.05264 (2017)
12. Metzen, J.H., Genewein, T., Fischer, V., et al.: On detecting adversarial perturbations. arXiv preprint arXiv:1702.04267 (2017)
13. Grosse, K., Manoharan, P., Papernot, N., et al.: On the (statistical) detection of adversarial examples. arXiv preprint arXiv:1702.06280 (2017)
14. Feinman, R., Curtin, R.R., Shintre, S., et al.: Detecting adversarial samples from artifacts. arXiv preprint arXiv:1703.00410 (2017)
15. Xu, W., Evans, D., Qi, Y.: Feature squeezing: detecting adversarial examples in deep neural networks. arXiv preprint arXiv:1704.01155 (2017)
16. Fan, W., Sun, G., Su, Y., et al.: Integration of statistical detector and Gaussian noise injection detector for adversarial example detection in deep neural networks. Multimed. Tools Appl. **78**(14), 20409–20429 (2019)
17. Osadchy, M., Hernandez-Castro, J., Gibson, S., et al.: No bot expects the Deep-CAPTCHA! Introducing immutable adversarial examples, with applications to CAPTCHA generation. IEEE Trans. Inf. Forensics Secur. **12**(11), 2640–2653 (2017)
18. Graese, A., Rozsa, A., Boult, T.E.: Assessing threat of adversarial examples on deep neural networks. In: 2016 15th IEEE International Conference on Machine Learning and Applications (ICMLA), pp. 69–74. IEEE (2016)
19. LeCun, Y., Bottou, L., Bengio, Y., et al.: Gradient-based learning applied to document recognition. Proc. IEEE **86**(11), 2278–2324 (1998)
20. Das, N., Shanbhogue, M., Chen, S.T., et al.: Keeping the bad guys out: protecting and vaccinating deep learning with jpeg compression. arXiv preprint arXiv:1705.02900 (2017)
21. Meng, D., Chen, H.: MagNet: a two-pronged defense against adversarial examples. In: Proceedings of the 2017 ACM SIGSAC Conference on Computer and Communications Security, pp. 135–147 (2017)
22. Gu, S., Rigazio, L.: Towards deep neural network architectures robust to adversarial examples. arXiv preprint arXiv:1412.5068 (2014)
23. Wang, Q., Guo, W., Zhang, K., et al.: Learning adversary-resistant deep neural networks. arXiv preprint arXiv:1612.01401 (2016)
24. Guo, C., Rana, M., Cisse, M., et al.: Countering adversarial images using input transformations. arXiv preprint arXiv:1711.00117 (2017)
25. Xie, C., Wang, J., Zhang, Z., et al.: Mitigating adversarial effects through randomization. arXiv preprint arXiv:1711.01991 (2017)
26. Jia, X., Wei, X., Cao, X., et al.: ComDefend: an efficient image compression model to defend adversarial examples. In: Proceedings of the IEEE/CVF Conference on Computer Vision and Pattern Recognition, pp. 6084–6092 (2019)
27. Xie, C., Wu, Y., Maaten, L., et al.: Feature denoising for improving adversarial robustness. In: Proceedings of the IEEE/CVF Conference on Computer Vision and Pattern Recognition, pp. 501–509 (2019)
28. Yuan, J., He, Z.: Generative cleaning networks with quantized nonlinear transform for deep neural network defense (2019)
29. Fan, W., Sun, G., Su, Y., et al.: Hybrid defense for deep neural networks: an integration of detecting and cleaning adversarial perturbations. In: 2019 IEEE International Conference on Multimedia & Expo Workshops (ICMEW), pp. 210–215. IEEE (2019)
30. Doan, B.G., Abbasnejad, E., Ranasinghe, D.C.: Februus: Input purification defense against trojan attacks on deep neural network systems. In: Annual Computer Security Applications Conference, pp. 897–912 (2020)

31. Sun, G., Su, Y., Qin, C., et al.: Complete defense framework to protect deep neural networks against adversarial examples. Math. Probl. Eng. **2020**, 17 (2020)
32. Su, Y., Sun, G., Fan, W., et al.: Cleaning adversarial perturbations via residual generative network for face verification. In: 2019 IEEE International Conference on Acoustics, Speech and Signal Processing (ICASSP), ICASSP 2019, pp. 2597–2601. IEEE (2019)

A Secret-Sharing-based Security Data Aggregation Scheme in Wireless Sensor Networks

Xiaowu Liu[1](✉), Wenshuo Ma[1], Jiguo Yu[2,3,4], Kan Yu[1](✉), and Jiaqi Xiang[1]

[1] School of Computer Science, Qufu Normal University,
Rizhao 276825, People's Republic of China
{liuxw,kanyu}@qfnu.edu.cn
[2] School of Computer Science and Technology, Qilu University of Technology
(Shandong Academy of Sciences), Jinan 250353, People's Republic of China
[3] Shandong Computer Science Center (National Supercomputer in Jinan),
Jinan 250014, People's Republic of China
[4] Shandong Provinical Key Laboratory of Computer Networks,
Jinan 250014, People's Republic of China
jiguoyu@sina.com

Abstract. The reliable and secure data transmission is the essential attribute in Wireless Sensor Networks (WSNs). However, the attackers try to analyze the sensing data in a WSN, which may compromise the security of network. Meanwhile, the message sent by sensor node may be deserted and it can cause a negative effect on data accuracy. Based on the secret sharing and the privacy protection mechanism, we design a novel framework called the Secret-Sharing-based Security Data Aggregation scheme (S^3DA) in this paper. In S^3DA, a secret sharing algorithm and a data aggregation scheme are discussed. The former can promote the security and accuracy of sensing data and the latter may reduce the energy consumption in data transmission. The simulation experiments prove the effectiveness and the validity of our proposed framework.

Keywords: Wireless sensor networks · Data aggregation · Secret sharing

1 Introduction

Wireless Sensor Networks (WSNs) play an significant role in solving key issues such as the early event detection [1], the climate change [2] and the natural disasters relief [3]. They are also considered to be an effective way to improve the performance of many other applications, such as the health care [4], the process monitoring [5] and the smart grid [6]. However, the security and the data accuracy are critical challenges in a WSN when the sensing technique is applied into the a specific field.

This work was supported in part by the National Natural Science Foundation of China under Grants 61672321, 61832012, 61771289, 61373027 and the Shandong Graduate Education Quality Improvement Plan SDYY17138.

Data encryption techniques can improve the security of WSNs and thereby ensure that the sensing data will not be obtained by attackers [7–12]. There are two ways to protect sensing data from being revealed through data encryption [13], the hop-by-hop encryption [14] and the end-to-end encryption [15]. As the term suggests, the hop-by-hop mechanism means that the sensing data will be encrypted and decrypted in each hop, which may increase the energy consumption of sensor nodes and reduce the lifetime of network. Different from the hop-by-hop encryption, the end-to-end scheme can ensure that no additional operations(encryption and decryption) are performed during the transmission of encrypted data. Therefore, the less energy will be consumed and the lifetime of network will be prolonged. However, in the end-to-end scheme, it is necessary to carefully design an effective Data Aggregation (DA) method to fuse the encrypted data in relay nodes in order to avoid the additional transmission overhead [16,17]. The homomorphic encryption can meet the demand of end-to-end transmission and we will discuss a novel homomorphic-based Security Data Aggregation (SDA) scheme in this paper.

In addition to the security of DA, the data accuracy is also one of the important goals of DA. In a traditional WSN transmission scheme, sensor nodes attach the authentication code or the data error correction code to the sensing data with the aim of verifying or correcting the errors in receiving data at the Base Station (BS). However, the additional codes will extend the data length and place a non-ignorable burden on the limited energy of sensor node. What is worse, the data error correction code itself may yield wrong result. Therefore, how to improve the data accuracy is a meaningful and valuable topic in SDA.

Taking the security and accuracy into consideration, we propose a Secret-Sharing-based Security Data Aggregation scheme (S^3DA) in WSNs. The main idea of S^3DA is to search for a tradeoff between security and accuracy in a WSN without losing the effectiveness of network. The main contributions of S^3DA are as follows.

- An improved Shamir secret sharing scheme is proposed. This scheme can decrease the computation complexity in WSNs and effectively defend against the known plaintext attack.
- S^3DA can perform DA operations (such as linear function and non-linear function) depending on the encrypted data. Therefore, the energy consumption and the end-to-end security will be improved.
- A (t, n)−piecing mechanism is discussed in which the sensing data are divided into n pieces and the BS can accurately recover the original sensing data even if a part of correct pieces (more than a predefined threshold t) arrives at the BS.

The rest of the paper is arranged as follows: Sect. 2 summarizes the related works. Section 3 describes the network topology and preliminaries. Section 4 discusses the S^3DA framework. Section 5 present the performance evaluation. We conclude this paper in Sect. 6.

2   Related Work

The privacy protection and the traffic reduction, as effective measures to improve the performance of WSNs, have attracted great attention in recent years. Many techniques, such as data encryption and data aggregation, have been widely discussed in both academic and commercial worlds [18,19].

Data aggregation can significantly improve the energy consumption of sensor node through reducing the communication without sacrificing the security in a WSN. Generally speaking, many sensor nodes may acquire duplicated or redundant data in a monitored area, i.e. several sensors are deployed around a fire-prone spot and they may detect almost the same temperature in a certain time slot, and separately transmitting all sensing data to the BS by each node may consume overwhelming energy. Therefore, fusing all sensing data to an approximate result maybe a good choice. P. Zhang et al. [20] designed several multi-functional DA schemes (MODA, RODA and CODA) which provided a reasonable tradeoff among effectiveness, accuracy and security. Compared with traditional DA mechanisms, these schemes made two important contributions: (i)The proposed mechanisms can support more DA functions such as SUM, MEAN, MAX and MIN; (ii) The aggregation function can be performed on cipertext and the decryption is not indispensable in relay nodes so that the end-to-end confidentiality is assured. H. Zhong et al. proposed a secure data aggregation scheme that the sensing data can be recovered at the BS which provided a good reference for this paper [21]. The proposed scheme may eliminate the in-network false data and provide higher effectiveness and accuracy. Similar to [20], it can also ensure the end-to-end data confidentiality and the integrity security services under the support of homomorphic encryption. Hua et al. proposed an energy-efficient Adaptive Slice-based Secure Data Aggregation scheme (ASSDA) which can improve network performance on condition that the node resources are limited [22]. To be specific, ASSDA may reduce the energy consumption of nodes by improving the slicing technique and prolong the lifetime of network while maintaining an acceptable level of privacy protection.

3   Network Topology and Preliminaries

3.1   Network Topology

In this paper, we design a tree topology to organize the nodes in a WSN. S^3DA must ensure that the slices of a node reaches the BS through different paths. However cluster topology will collect information of all nodes in the cluster. So S^3DA is only suitable for tree topology. Sensor nodes are divided into three categories, the Leaf Nodes (LN), the Intermediate Node (IN) and the Base Station (BS). LNs are responsible for collecting environmental information of monitored area, such as temperature, humidity, smog and fire. After simply cutting the sensing data into several slices and sending them to different neighboring nodes, LNs mix all the received data slices and transmit them to the upstream nodes, INs. INs are in charge of aggregating the data slices received from downstream

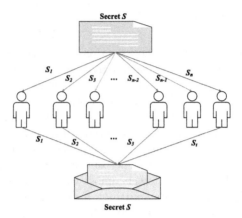

Fig. 1. Shamir secret sharing scheme

nodes, LNs. After the slices are aggregated, IN sends the fused data to its parent nodes until the BS arrives.

3.2 Shamir Secret Sharing Algorithm

In the classic Shamir secret sharing scheme [23], a message (private data), S, is divided into n pieces which are distributed among participants in a communication system. The secret message, S, can be recovered at the receiver if the number of participants is greater than or equal to t. Namely, the secret message, S, can be recovered if we randomly choose k participants from n participants (C_n^k). If the number of participants is less than t, the secret message, s, cannot be correctly recovered. We illustrate the process of Shamir secret sharing in Fig. 1.

The (t, n) secret sharing scheme proposed by Shamir is constructed based on the Lagrange interpolation formula and its specific steps are as follows.

(i) Initialization stage. The secret distributor, D, randomly selects n different non-zero elements, $x_1, x_2, \ldots, x_n$, from a finite field $GF(p)$. These elements respectively identify each shadow secret holder, $U_r = U_1, U_2, \cdots U_n (r = 1, 2, \cdots, n)$. Each shadow secret holder U_r discloses the corresponding identification x_r.

(ii) Secret distribution stage. D sends the secret $S \in Z_q$ (q is a large prime number) to the secret holder and randomly selects $t - 1$ elements $a_i (r = 1, 2, \cdots, t-1)$ in $GF(p)$ to construct a $(t-1) - order$ polynomial as shown in Eq. (1).

$$f(x) = a_0 + \sum_{i=1}^{t-1} a_i x^i \ (mod \ p) \tag{1}$$

where p is a large prime number, $p > S$ and the secret $S = f(0) = a_0$. The value of t is calculated according to Eq. (2).

$$t = \lfloor n/2 \rfloor + 1 \tag{2}$$

The distributor D generates the shadow secret S_r for all shadow secret holders according to Eq. (3).

$$S_r = f(x_r) = a_0 + \sum_{i=1}^{t-1} a_i x_r^i \ (mod\ p) \tag{3}$$

(iii) Secret recovery stage. Any t shadow secret holders $\{U_1, U_2, \cdots, U_t\}$ can recover the secret S using the Lagrange interpolation formula in Eq. (4).

$$S = f(0) = \sum_{i=1}^{t} f(x_i) \prod_{v=1, v \neq l}^{t} \frac{-x_v}{x_l - x_v} \ (mod\ p) \tag{4}$$

If there are less than t shadow secrets, no information about S can be obtained.

4 Secret-Sharing-based Security Data Aggregation

In this section, we will discuss our proposed S³DA scheme in detail. There are four steps in demonstrating the core mechanisms of S³DA, i.e., the aggregation tree construction, the data encryption in LN, the aggregation and encryption in IN and the data encryption in BS. For easy reading and understanding, we also demonstrate an illustrative example at the end of this section.

4.1 Aggregation Tree Construction

Firstly, the BS sends query information to select an aggregation node in a WSN. When a node receives the query, it elects itself as an IN with a certain probability (a predefined value). The IN continues to send the query received from the BS to its neighboring nodes (LNs). If an LN receives multiple queries, it randomly selects one of INs as its IN. This process continues until all nodes are joined in an aggregation tree.

4.2 Data Encryption in LN

We improve the Shamir secret sharing scheme and reduce the complexity in order to promote the effectiveness of S³DA.

(i) Key generation. The BS generates a group of keys and these keys are broadcasted to the sensor nodes in a WSN. Assumed that the key group generated by the BS is $\{\tau_1, \tau_2, \cdots, \tau_n\}$. The sensing data are divided into n pieces and the data can be recovered if more than t pieces are transmitted to the BS.

(ii) Encryption. After it receives the key, an AN divides the sensing data S into pieces. The sensing data S are cut into j pieces, $\{S_1, S_2, \cdots, S_j\}$ (j represents the number of pieces and $j = \lfloor n/2 \rfloor$). The LN generates a random number, r. r is inserted into a specific polynomial as a constant term and $S_1, S_2, \cdots, S_j$ are regarded as the coefficients of non-constant term of the polynomial. In addition, we need to choose a modulo p according to the size of sensing data S. Then, all data pieces of LN are encrypted using Eq. (5).

$$\begin{cases} g(\tau_1) = r + S_1\tau_1 + S_2\tau_1^2 + \cdots + S_j\tau_1^j \ (mod\ p) \\ g(\tau_2) = r + S_1\tau_2 + S_2\tau_2^2 + \cdots + S_j\tau_2^j \ (mod\ p) \\ \quad\quad\quad\vdots \\ g(\tau_n) = r + S_1\tau_n + S_2\tau_n^2 + \cdots + S_j\tau_n^j \ (mod\ p) \end{cases} \tag{5}$$

where $g(\tau_i)$ represents the ciphertext of S_i. The computational complexity will increase dramatically when the exponential calculation is performed in Eq. (5). Therefore, we should appropriately control the number of polynomial terms with the aim of reducing the computation complexity. In addition, each LN needs to add a flag K_i (key sequence number) in the front of $g(\tau_i)$ in order to identify different pieces at the BS. Then, an encrypted piece is expressed as $h_i = (K_i|g(\tau_i))$. An LN retains an encrypted piece, h_0, in itself and transmits others to its neighboring nodes.

4.3   Data Aggregation and Encryption in IN

After an IN receives the data of LNs, the data with the same key sequence number will be aggregated. The homomorphic addition aggregation can be expressed using Eq. (6).

$$\begin{cases} g_{IN}(\tau_1) = h_1^1 + \cdots + h_1^i = r^{agg} + \cdots + S_j^{agg}\tau_1^j \ (mod\ p), K_n = 1 \\ g_{IN}(\tau_2) = h_2^1 + \cdots + h_2^i = r^{agg} + \cdots + S_j^{agg}\tau_2^j \ (mod\ p), K_n = 2 \\ \quad\quad\quad\vdots \\ g_{IN}(\tau_n) = h_n^1 + \cdots + h_n^i = r^{agg} + \cdots + S^{agg}\tau_n^j \ (mod\ p), K_n = n \end{cases} \tag{6}$$

where $g_{IN}(\tau)$ is the ciphertext in an IN. S_j^{agg} is the sum of polynomial coefficients (i.e., $S_j^{agg} = S_j^1 + S_j^2 + \cdots + S_j^i$, where S_j^m represents the jth data sent by the ith node.). After the encryption aggregation is completed, the IN sends the encrypted data piece to the upstream IN or the BS.

4.4   Data Decryption in BS

After receiving the encrypted pieces, the BS decrypts them according to the nonlinear regression equation. The BS checks whether it has collected enough shared secrets (i.e. at least t shared encrypted pieces). Then, the BS decrypts the ciphertext and recovers the original data according to Eq. (7).

$$S^{agg} = \sum_{i=1}^{j+1} g(\tau_i)\prod_{v=1,v\neq l}^{j+1} \frac{x - x_v}{x_l - x_v} \ (mod\ p) \tag{7}$$

The BS randomly selects $(j+1)$ data pieces and substitutes them into Eq. (7). And the recovered data S^{agg} is obtained. Noticed that we may generate multiple S^{agg} for we have C_n^{j+1} different combinations when we select $j+1$ data pieces from n pieces. We will choose a specific "S^{agg}" as the final result which appears more frequent in the C_n^{j+1} final results.

5 Performance Evaluation

In this section, we evaluate the performance of S^3DA in terms of computation overhead, communication cost and accuracy and compare S^3DA with other classic DA schemes, such as CPDA [24], EEHA [25] and SMART [25]. In CPDA, the algebraic properties of polynomials are used among nodes to fuse sensing data collected from sensor nodes and it can guarantee that a node cannot know the sensing data of its neighboring nodes. In SMART, each node protects the privacy of sensing data through dividing them into slices and sending the encrypted slices to different aggregators. Different from CPDA and SMART, EEHA only slices the sensing data of LNs.

We deployed the OMNet++ simulator to verify our model and schemes. In the following simulation experiments, we considered a network with 120, 150 and 180 sensor nodes. These nodes are randomly scattered in an area of 100×100 m^2. The transmission range of the sensor node is 50 m, and the data rate is 1 Mbps.

5.1 Computation Overhead

In our simulation experiments, each node can exchange data with four neighboring nodes. Therefore, a node can divide its sensing data into five pieces (one piece is left by the node itself and the other four pieces are sent to the neighboring nodes) and this means n is 5 in a (t, n) piecing mechanism. For an easy comparison, the same data length is adopted in all schemes (CPDA, EEHA, SMART and S^3DA). We evaluate the computational cost through calculation operations (i.e., Addition, Multiplication, Exponentiation, Module, etc.) according to the method used by [26]. Figure 2 shows the comparison of computation overhead. EEHA, CPDA and SMART need additional encryption operations to ensure the privacy of sensing data, which need complex computation for encryption and decryption. However, S^3DA ensure the privacy of sensing data depending on the random number, the piecing technique and the polynomial, which is a prominent advantage over other DA schemes.

We also compared the computation overhead of S^3DA when a different n is chosen. As shown in Fig. 3, the computation complexity increases when the sensing data are cut into more pieces.

5.2 Communication Cost

We verified the four aforementioned schemes in the same aggregation tree. The ciphertext size of S^3DA partly depends on the value of p. However, the ciphertext sizes of CPDA, SMART and EEHA are closely related to the encryption algorithm. Therefore, we set the value of p in S^3DA as long as the ciphertext of CPDA, SMART and EEHA. We run the simulation 50 times and the average of communication cost was shown in Fig. 4 when $n = 5$. The simulation results can be explained by analyzing the number of messages exchanged in each scenario. In CPDA, a cluster head sends six messages and a cluster member

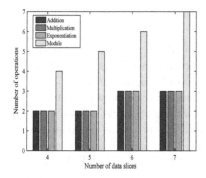
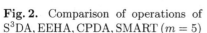

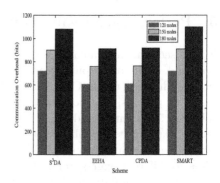

Fig. 2. Comparison of operations of S³DA, EEHA, CPDA, SMART ($m = 5$)

Fig. 3. The communication cost of S³DA, EEHA, CPDA and SMART ($m = 5$)

sends five messages for private data aggregation. In SMART, each node needs to send four pieces and one message for data aggregation. In EEHA, only the leaf nodes divide their sensing data into slices and send at most $(n - 1)$ pieces to their selected neighbors. Therefore, the communication overhead of EEHA is lower than that of SMART and it is the best one in the four schemes. The communication overhead of EEHA is related to the number of leaf nodes in the aggregation tree.

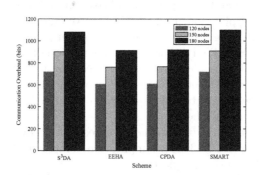

Fig. 4. The communication cost of S³DA, EEHA, CPDA and SMART ($m = 5$)

The piecing and transmission mechanisms of S³DA are similar to those of SMART. Therefore, the communication cost of S³DA is roughly equal to SMART. However, CPDA, EEHA and SMART cannot support the unique properties of S³DA. S³DA has the best robustness if some data pieces are lost in the process of data transmission. The BS can recover the original data as long as it receives part of data slices. And S³DA is also capable of protecting the sensing data in case of key leakage. The attacker needs to obtain a certain number of data pieces to recover the original data. In addition, the decryption operation is not indispensable in a relay node (IN) and the end-to-end privacy preserving can be ensured. Therefore, it is a good tradeoff between the security and the communication cost.

5.3   Accuracy

We adopt the definition of accuracy as the ratio of the sum collected by the data aggregation scheme to the actual sum of all individual sensor nodes [24]. Taking the real link into consideration, we set the bit error rate at 5%. An accuracy value of 1.0 represents an ideal situation. We considered a network with 120 sensor nodes.

Figure 5 shows the accuracy of four schemes, CPDA, SMART, EEHA and S^3DA when $n = 5$. We can observe that as the time elapses, the accuracy improves for the four schemes. In [25], H. Li et al. analyzed this phenomenon that conflicts between data packets will decrease as time passes. In addition, as the simulation runs, more data pieces will arrive at the BS before the deadline and S^3DA demonstrates better accuracy. Noticed that S^3DA does not show the high accuracy at the initial stage. This is because the BS cannot receive enough pieces (no less than t, $t = 3$ in this simulation) to verify the final aggregation result. However, the BS can provide sufficient combinations (C_5^3) for aggregation verification and the accuracy of aggregation remarkably improves after the initial stage.

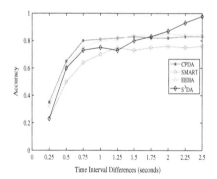

Fig. 5. Accuracy comparison of CPDA, SMART, EEHA, ISSA ($n = 5$)

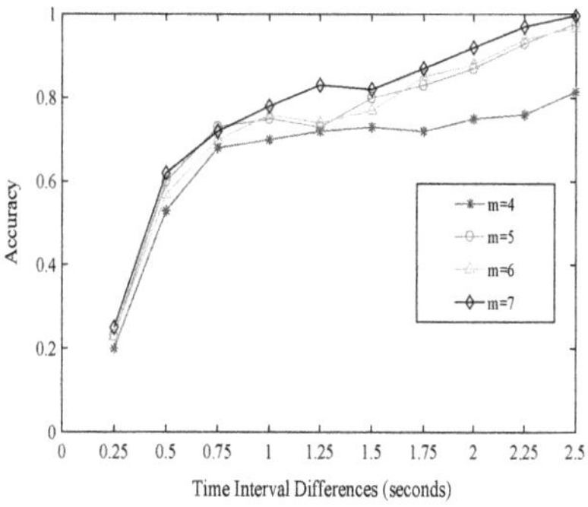

Fig. 6. Accuracy of S^3DA wit different data piece

We also tested whether the number of pieces can affect the aggregation accuracy of S^3DA as shown in Fig. 6. As n increases, the aggregation accuracy also improves. This demonstrates that more pieces have a positive impact on the aggregation accuracy.

6   Conclusion

In this paper, we propose a novel security mechanism for data aggregation in WSNs. Based one the Shamir secret sharing scheme, a homomorphic encryption scheme called S^3DA is explored which can guarantee the end-to-end privacy of sensing data and higher aggregation accuracy at the price of relatively low computation overhead and communication cost. In S^3DA, the BS can recover the original sensing data even if some pieces are deserted in a WSN. This property is particularly suitable for WSNs deployed in harsh environments which provides a new measure for the packet-loss-sensitive applications. Although our scheme may provide a solution for security aggregation in WSNs, there are still many meaningful topics to be studied in the future. We should verify the impact of different packet-loss-rates on the aggregation accuracy and design a more robust homomorphic encryption scheme. The decrease in communication cost is also a huge challenge in subsequent studies.

References

1. He, Z., Cai, Z., Cheng, S., Wang, X.: Approximate aggregation for tracking quantiles and range countings in wireless sensor networks. Theoret. Comput. Sci. **607**, 381–390 (2015)
2. Yu, K., Wang, Y., Yu, J., Yu, D., Cheng, X., Shan, Z.: Localized and distributed link scheduling algorithms in IoT under Rayleigh fading. Comput. Netw. **151**, 232–244 (2019)
3. Sharma, N., Gupta, V.: Meta-heuristic based optimization of WSNs localisation problem-a survey. Procedia Comput. Sci. **173**, 36–45 (2020)
4. Muralitharan, K., Sangwoon, Y., Yoon, M.J.: Enhanced clustering and ACO-based multiple mobile sinks for efficiency improvement of wireless sensor networks. In: Computer Networks, vol. 160, pp. 33–40. Elsevier (2019)
5. Zheng, X., Cai, Z.: Privacy-preserved data sharing towards multiple parties in industrial IoTs. IEEE J. Sel. Areas Commun. **38**(5), 968–979 (2020)
6. Yu, K., Yan, B., Yu, J., Chen, H., Dong, A.: Methods of improving secrecy transmission capacity in wireless random networks. Ad Hoc Netw. **117**, 102492 (2021)
7. Cai, Z., He, Z.: Trading private range counting over big IoT data. In: 2019 IEEE 39th International Conference on Distributed Computing Systems (ICDCS), pp. 144–153. IEEE (2019)
8. Yu, J., et al.: Efficient link scheduling in wireless networks under Rayleigh-fading and multiuser interference. IEEE Trans. Wirel. Commun. **19**(8), 5621–5634 (2020)
9. Cheng, S., Cai, Z., Li, J., Gao, H.: Extracting kernel dataset from big sensory data in wireless sensor networks. IEEE Trans. Knowl. Data Eng. **29**(4), 813–827 (2016)
10. Li, J., Cheng, S., Cai, Z., Yu, J., Wang, C., Li, Y.: Approximate holistic aggregation in wireless sensor networks. ACM Trans. Sens. Netw. (TOSN) **13**(2), 1–24 (2017)
11. Cheng, S., Cai, Z., Li, J.: Curve query processing in wireless sensor networks. IEEE Trans. Veh. Technol. **64**(11), 5198–5209 (2014)
12. Ilgi, G.S., Ever, Y.K.: Critical analysis of security and privacy challenges for the Internet of drones: a survey. In: Drones in Smart-Cities, pp. 207–214. Elsevier (2020)

13. Wang, X., Zhou, Q., Cheng, C.T.: A UAV-assisted topology-aware data aggregation protocol in WSN. Phys. Commun. **34**, 48–57 (2019)
14. Tirani, S.P., Avokh, A.: On the performance of sink placement in WSNs considering energy-balanced compressive sensing-based data aggregation. J. Netw. Comput. Appl. **107**, 38–55 (2018)
15. Zhang, J., Hu, P., Xie, F., Long, J., He, A.: An energy efficient and reliable in-network data aggregation scheme for WSN. IEEE Access **6**, 71857–71870 (2018)
16. Padmaja, P., Marutheswar, G.: Energy efficient data aggregation in wireless sensor networks. Mater. Today: Proc. **5**(1), 388–396 (2018)
17. Sharma, N., Bhatt, R.: Privacy preservation in WSN for healthcare application. Procedia Comput. Sci. **132**, 1243–1252 (2018)
18. Zhang, Q., Liu, X., Yu, J., Qi, X.: A trust-based dynamic slicing mechanism for wireless sensor networks. Procedia Comput. Sci. **174**, 572–577 (2020)
19. Kaur, M., Munjal, A.: Data aggregation algorithms for wireless sensor network: a review. Ad Hoc Netw. **100**, 102083 (2020)
20. Zhang, P., Wang, J., Guo, K., Wu, F., Min, G.: Multi-functional secure data aggregation schemes for WSNs. Ad Hoc Netw. **69**, 86–99 (2018)
21. Zhong, H., Shao, L., Cui, J., Xu, Y.: An efficient and secure recoverable data aggregation scheme for heterogeneous wireless sensor networks. J. Parallel Distrib. Comput. **111**, 1–12 (2018)
22. Hua, P., Liu, X., Yu, J., Dang, N., Zhang, X.: Energy-efficient adaptive slice-based secure data aggregation scheme in WSN. Procedia Comput. Sci. **129**, 188–193 (2018)
23. Haseeb, K., Islam, N., Almogren, A., Din, I.U., Almajed, H.N., Guizani, N.: Secret sharing-based energy-aware and multi-hop routing protocol for IoT based WSNs. IEEE Access **7**, 79980–79988 (2019)
24. He, W., Liu, X., Nguyen, H., Nahrstedt, K., Abdelzaher, T.: PDA: privacy-preserving data aggregation in wireless sensor networks. In: IEEE INFOCOM 2007–26th IEEE International Conference on Computer Communications, pp. 2045–2053. IEEE (2007)
25. Li, H., Lin, K., Li, K.: Energy-efficient and high-accuracy secure data aggregation in wireless sensor networks. Comput. Commun. **34**(4), 591–597 (2011)
26. Girao, J., Westhoff, D., Schneider, M.: CDA: concealed data aggregation for reverse multicast traffic in wireless sensor networks. In: 2005 IEEE International Conference on Communications, ICC 2005, vol. 5, pp. 3044–3049. IEEE (2005)

Fast Application Activity Recognition with Encrypted Traffic

Xue Liu[1], Shigeng Zhang[1,2(✉)], Huihui Li[1], and Weiping Wang[1]

[1] School of Computer Science, Central South University, Changsha 410000, China
{liuxue,sgzhang,huihuili,wpwang}@csu.edu.cn
[2] Institute of Information Engineering, Chinese Academy of Sciences,
Beijing 100093, China

Abstract. With the popularity and development of mobile devices, the types and number of mobile applications are increasing, and people will perform different activities in the same application (e.g., refreshing the page, sending messages, browsing). Obtaining network traffic in real-time is an important foundation for network content supervision. Identifying application activity based on network traffic helps network managers understand user behaviors better and improve the quality of service. The widespread use of encrypted traffic in Mobile Applications presents a challenge to accurately identify application activities. Due to the low recognition speed of the existing application action recognition work for encrypted traffic, it is difficult to meet the real-time requirements. Therefore, we propose a fast application activity recognition method based on encrypted traffic. We extract the trend characteristics of the traffic generated by the application activity and use machine learning to identify the activity. The experimental results show that our method can identify user activities effectively. In addition, we have improved the existing method in real-time, and experiments show that our method is two orders of magnitude faster than the existing method when the recognition rate is similar to that of the existing methods.

Keywords: Mobile application · Activity recognition · Encrypted traffic

1 Introduction

The applications in mobile devices provide a wide range of functions, covering all aspects of people's lives, such as entertainment, finance, medical care, and so on. People perform different activities in different applications, such as editing messages, receiving messages in social applications, refreshing pages in search applications. Most of these different activities will interact with the network and generate traffic. Mobile application activity recognition is the process of automatically classifying network traffic into different application activities based on some parameters or characteristics of traffic generated by application activities.

Supported by organization x.

© Springer Nature Switzerland AG 2021
Z. Liu et al. (Eds.): WASA 2021, LNCS 12938, pp. 314–325, 2021.
https://doi.org/10.1007/978-3-030-86130-8_25

A good application activity identification method can help network managers to understand users' behavior habits clearly, which is helpful to network operation, network development planning and network traffic scheduling, to improve the quality of service. Moreover, it can be used to scan and filter illegal and unhealthy network behaviors, which is a supplement to other network security protection technologies.

Traditional mobile application classification methods, such as port-based classification methods and Deep Packet Inspection (DPI)-based classification methods, are only applicable to unencrypted traffic and cannot analyze encrypted traffic. Nowadays, with the popularity of privacy protection awareness of users, more and more mobile applications use the Secure Sockets Layer (SSL)/Transmission Control Protocol (TLS) protocol for network communication, and the encryption traffic generated by mobile applications increases. After the SSL/TLS protocol encrypts the transmitted data, network management software and network administrators are unable to analyze the packet contents, so the research on the recognition and classification method based on encrypted traffic is increasingly important.

Many scholars have studied the identification methods for encrypted traffic, mostly by extracting the characteristics of the traffic, and then using machine learning for training and classification recognition. These methods solve the problems in traditional classification methods effectively, but there are still some deficiencies, which cannot have high recognition rate and high real-time performance at the same time.

In this paper, we propose a fast application activity recognition method based on encrypted traffic. By analyzing the flow change trend of different activities, we find that the flow change trend of the same activity is very similar, while the flow change trend of different activities is obviously different. Therefore, we use the trend characteristics of traffic and machine learning methods to identify activities. Our method can identify application activities in real-time and achieve high recognition accuracy.

The rest of this article is organized as follows: In Sect. 2, we introduced related work on application classification and application activity recognition based on encrypted traffic. In Sect. 3, we introduced in detail our proposed method for implementing application activity recognition based on encrypted traffic. In Sect. 4, we present our experimental results and comparative analysis. Finally, we conclude this article.

2 Related Work

Many researchers focus on the classification of mobile applications based on traffic. Some work [5,9,15–18] use unencrypted traffic for application classification, mainly by using deep packet inspection to analyze the content of Hypertext Transfer Protocol (HTTP) traffic to construct application fingerprints. The method based on encrypted traffic for application classification [1,6,11–14] mainly uses the statistical characteristics of traffic or the characteristics of the handshake phase of Transport Layer Security (TLS) encrypted sessions.

Some researchers have done more fine-grained research on the classification of mobile application activities [2–4,7,8,10]. Conti et al. [3,4] found that different application activities generate different network traffic patterns. Firstly, they use clustering to gather the flow of similar network patterns, construct feature vectors based on clustering results, and then use the machine learning model to classify application activities. Their approach requires accurate access to multiple flows generated by the same activity, which is not always possible in the real environment. And they used Dynamic Time Warping (DTW) as the distance measurement method in the clustering stage, which is very time-consuming. Saltaformaggio et al. [10] proposed the NetScope method. They analyze IP packet headers, extract some statistical characteristics from them, then cluster activities based on these characteristics to generate behavior models, and then classify activities based on behavior models. Ata et al. [2] proposed an application activity recognition method based on multiple flows, which first extracted 48 statistical features from each flow, then calculated behavioral features from multiple flows in a given time period, and then used supervised learning methods for activity recognition.

3   Method

In general, we extract the fine-grained behavior characteristics of the packet length sequence of the session by wavelet decomposition, then train and classify them using machine learning algorithms. The recognition process is shown in Fig. 1.

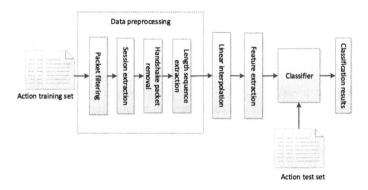

Fig. 1. Application activity recognition process.

3.1   Related Definitions

Flow: A set of unidirectional packets generated by a pair of communication nodes in one interaction, recorded as flow {srcIP, dstIP, srcPort, dstPort, Protocol}, where srcIP is the source Internet Protocol(IP) address, dstIP is the destination IP address, srcPort is the source port number, dstPort Is the destination port number, and Protocol is the transport layer protocol. All packets in a flow have the same quintuple.

Session: A set of two-way network packets generated by the interaction of a pair of communication nodes, that is, a two-way stream, which is a source and destination interchangeable flow that srcIP, srcPort and dstIP, dstPort are interchangeable. A session is a complete process from establishing a connection to completing the data transfer between the client and the server.

Sequence of Packet Lengths: A sequence of packet lengths in a TCP session considering the direction of the packet. Each value in the sequence represents the size and transmission direction of the packet. The arrangement order is the same as the data packet transmission order in a TCP session. Since the session consists of two unidirectional flows, in order to reflect the direction of the packets in the vector better, we record the packet size sent by the client as a positive value and the packet received by the client as a negative value. The sequence of packet lengths is represented by $S = \{P_1, P_2, \ldots, P_n\}$. If the i-th data packet is a data packet sent by the client, $P_i\{i \in [1, n]\}$ is the packet length of the i-th packet in the TCP session, otherwise $P_i\{i \in [1, n]\}$ is the opposite of the packet length of the i-th packet in the TCP session.

3.2   Data Preprocessing

After getting the traffic generated by each application, it needs to be preprocessed. The specific operation consists of four steps that we describe below.

1) Packet Filtering. Due to network congestion, application failures, and other unpredictable network behavior, data packets transmitted by applications may be lost, duplicated, and out of order. In this case, to ensure the reliability of its transmission, the TCP protocol will request retransmission of the lost data and reorder the out-of-order data. The collection of duplicate data will bring redundant information, increase the complexity of the analysis, and affect the processing performance of the algorithm. Therefore, to ensure the accuracy of the analysis, we remove this part of the redundant data, and also filter the bad packets during transmission.
2) Session Extraction. A session is a complete interaction process. To gain a clearer understanding of each active transport mode, we extract all sessions from the traffic.
3) TCP Handshake Packet Removal. TCP is a connection-oriented communication protocol. At the beginning of communication, a connection is established through a three-way handshake. After the communication ends, the

connection needs to be disconnected. We observe that the traffic generated by different activities of the same application may have the same three-way handshake process. In order to avoid interference, we remove the TCP handshake packet. Since our method is based on a sequence of packet lengths, packets with a zero payload are not useful to us, so we also remove packets with a zero payload during transmission.

4) Sequence of Packet Lengths Extraction. After we get the TCP session, we extract the sequence of packet lengths for each session. If the original packet length sequence is {200, 50, 150, 20}, where the second and fourth data packets are data packets received by the client, and the other two are opposite, the processed sequence of packet lengths is {200, −50, 150, −20}. Then, we use the sequence of packet lengths for feature extraction.

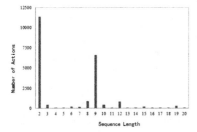

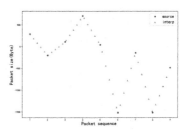

Fig. 2. Distribution of number of packets in sequences of packet lengths.

Fig. 3. Interpolation result.

3.3   Feature Extraction

Linear Interpolation. As shown in Fig. 2, after the above pre-processing process, there is a case that the sequence of packet lengths is too short. To facilitate feature extraction, we use the characteristics of time series data to interpolate the sequence of packet lengths to obtain the sequence information approximately and enrich its information.

The sequence of packet length is one-dimensional data, so we use the common linear interpolation method to estimate the value according to the two adjacent data points. Suppose that the two points adjacent to the left and right are (x_0, y_0) and (x_1, y_1), the interpolation point is (x, y), and the interpolation formula is:

$$y = \frac{x - x_1}{x_0 - x_1} y_0 + \frac{x - x_0}{x_1 - x_0} y_1 \tag{1}$$

As shown in Fig. 3, the interpolated sequence can approximately replace the original sequence.

Construct Feature Vector. The object of our analysis is the traffic generated by various activities in the application. After pre-processing the traffic, the corresponding Sequences of packet lengths are extracted. We analyze the traffic generated by different activities of the same application. As shown in Fig. 4, we use a line chart to draw the sequences of packet lengths of three different activities. The abscissa represents the order of the packet in the sequences of packet lengths, and the ordinate represents the size and the direction of the packet. By comparing the Sequences of packet lengths of different activities, we can find that the changing trend of the packet length of different activities in the same application is different, that is, the session transmission mode generated by different activities is different. We also analyzed the traffic generated by the same activity in the same application, and we plotted the sequences of packet lengths of three different sessions generated by the same activity. As shown in Fig. 5, we find that the trend of sessions generated by the same activity in the same application is similar. Although the packet lengths may be somewhat different, the trend and fluctuation of the sequences are basically the same. It can be seen that the transmission pattern of the same activity is similar. Since the trend of sequences of packet lengths of different activities is different, and the trend of sequences of packet lengths of the same activity is similar, we consider to extract the trend characteristics of sequences of packet lengths.

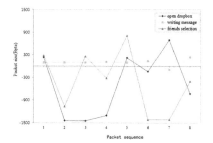 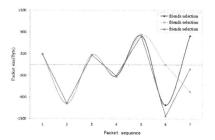

Fig. 4. Sequences of packet lengths for different activities in the same application. **Fig. 5.** Sequences of packet lengths for the same activity of the same application.

We use wavelet decomposition to extract the trend feature of the sequence of packet length. Wavelet decomposition reflects the process of people's step-by-step identification of shapes, and it reflects a principle of low-to-high resolution. Multi-scale transformation can decompose a sequence of packet lengths onto different channels of each frequency for easy analysis.

Figure 6 depicts the original sequence of packet lengths of an activity and the result of the first level decomposition using the db1 wavelet. There are three subgraphs, among which s represents the original sequence of packet lengths, a1 represents the level 1 approximation of reconstruction, i.e. the low-frequency part, and d1 represents the level 1 detail of reconstruction, i.e. the high-frequency part. As can be seen from Fig. 6, the low-frequency part of wavelet decomposition well represents the trend of the activity, so we use the low-frequency part sequence after wavelet decomposition as the feature vector to identify the application activities. We choose Coif5 as the wavelet basis function for recognition. The wavelet decomposition formula we use is:

$$\psi_{a,b}(x) = \frac{1}{\sqrt{a}}\psi(\frac{x-b}{a}) \quad (a \neq 0, b \in R) \tag{2}$$

Where $a = a_0^j, a_0 > 1, j \in Z$, is the scaling parameter for scaling, reflecting the scale of the specific basis function, b is the translation parameter for translation, $b = ka_0^j b_0, b_0 > 0, k \in Z$.

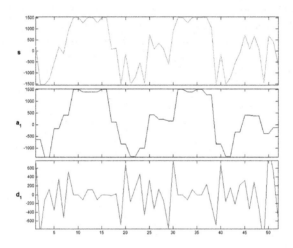

Fig. 6. First-level decomposition of a sequence of packet lengths.

3.4   Classification

Finally, we build a feature vector based on the sequence of packet lengths generated by each activity and use the machine learning algorithm to train a classifier, and then use this classifier to identify the feature vector constructed from the session of unknown activity.

4   Experiment

4.1   Dataset

The dataset we used is the dataset published by Conti et al. in 2016 [4], which contains activity data of seven applications [16]: Gmail, Facebook, Twitter, Tumblr, Drop-box, Google+ and Evernote. The seven applications have high popularity. To collect a wealth of real-world traffic, the author ran seven applications on a

Galaxy Nexus (GT-I9250) mobile phone and used scripts to call Android Debug Bridge(ADB) commands to perform specific activities on the mobile phone. At the same time, they used a server equipped with Wireshark to monitor the WiFi access point to capture mobile phone traffic and marked the traffic data according to the time recorded by the script. The detailed information of the data set is shown in Table 1, where the number of activities refers to the number of different activities performed in each application, and the number of sessions refers to the number of sessions generated by each application.

4.2   Experimental Setup

Our experiments were performed on an Intel Xeon E5-2620 v2 professional server, the operating system was Windows Server 2019 Datacenter, and the physical memory was 112G.

There are four cases for the classification results of the sample. True positives (TP) and true negatives (TN) are cases where the samples are correctly classified. False positives (FP) and false negatives (FN) are misclassified situations. We also used related evaluation indicators: Precision.

4.3   Experimental Evaluation

Table 1. Activity dataset.

Application	Number of activities	Number of sessions
Gmail	38	9924
Twitter	33	36259
Facebook	40	50320
Tumblr	47	56702
Dropbox	33	48462
Google+	38	33470
Evernote	32	17014

Selection of Machine Learning Algorithm. After extracting the trend features of traffic generated by activities, we select the appropriate classification algorithm through experiments. We select all the sessions of Dropbox in the dataset to experiment. Some activities have too few sessions, so we refer to the configuration in [16], focusing on the 7 sensitive and special activities in Dropbox, and the other activities are uniformly marked as other dropbox. The experimental data is shown in Table 2.

Machine learning algorithms are widely used in various classification tasks, among which are commonly used include linear regression, decision trees, support vector machines, random forests, Bayesian networks and neural networks.

Table 2. Dropbox's activity data.

Activity	Number of sessions
Open dropbox	3877
Folder creation	3193
File text input	2329
File favorited	1513
Favorites page	776
Open file	1091
Delete file	1151
Other dropbox	34532

In order to select the appropriate machine learning algorithm for training the classification and recognition model, we use different machine learning algorithms on the application activity data set to perform a ten-fold cross-validation experiment, record the precision, TPR, and FPR of the ten tests, and then calculate them separately average value. We select C4.5, logistic regression, SVM and random forest for the experiment, and select the optimal classification algorithm according to the experimental results.

Table 3. Experimental results of different machine learning algorithms.

Machine learning algorithms	TPR	FPR	Precision
C4.5	0.800	0.481	0.733
Logistic regression	0.765	0.547	0.673
SVM	0.732	0.644	0.649
Random forest	0.996	0.009	0.996

The experimental results are shown in Table 3. It can be seen that the classification effect of random forest is the best, so we choose random forest as the classification algorithm for activity recognition.

Classification Experimental Results. Since some activities of application have few sessions, we refer to the configuration in [16] and focus only on the more sensitive and special activities in each application, while the remaining activities are classified as other. So we pay attention to 4 activities of Gmail, 6 activities of Twitter, 6 activities of Facebook, 9 activities of Tumblr, 7 activities of Dropbox, 10 activities of Google+, 6 activities of Evernote.

The classification results are shown in Table 4. Among the seven applications, Dropbox and Gmail have the best multi-class classification results, the precision and TPR of which exceed 0.99. Tumblr has the worst multi-class classification performance, with a precision of 0.698 and a TPR of 0.708.

Table 4. Multi-classification results.

Application	TPR	FPR	Precision
Gmail	0.991	0.016	0.991
Twitter	0.717	0.331	0.763
Facebook	0.878	0.418	0.886
Tumblr	0.708	0.374	0.698
Dropbox	0.996	0.009	0.996
Google+	0.704	0.142	0.737
Evernote	0.797	0.096	0.824

Comparison with Other Methods. We compare our recognition method with the method proposed by Conti et al. [4] in 2016, which we call Conti's method. By analyzing the transmission mode of each activity, they use the DTW algorithm to calculate the distance between the time series generated by different activities, perform hierarchical clustering, construct feature vectors based on the clustering results, and then use the random forest algorithm to train the classifier.

Conti's method has a good recognition effect, but the method of calculating the similarity between time series using the DTW algorithm makes the calculation amount large and the running speed slow. In the clustering stage, the DTW distance needs to be calculated for every two-time series, and In the recognition phase, the DTW distance needs to be calculated for each time series generated by the activity to be recognized and each cluster center. As the number of time series increases, the recognition speed of this method cannot meet the real-time requirements. Our method uses wavelet decomposition to extract features, which is very fast.

Conti's method identifies the activity based on all sessions generated by an activity, while our method identifies the activity that generated the session based on only one session generated by the activity. This also makes our method recognition faster than Conti's method.

The comparison of the recognition speed of the two methods is shown in Fig. 7. It can be seen that the recognition speed of our method is faster than Conti's method when the difference is the largest, our method is 339 times faster than Conti's method. In addition, we also made statistics and comparisons of the recognition precision of the two which is shown in Fig. 8.

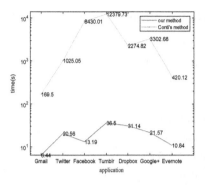 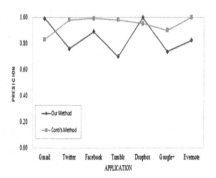

Fig. 7. Comparison of recognition speed between Conti's method and our method.

Fig. 8. Comparison of recognition rate between Conti's method and our method.

5 Conclusion

In this paper, to understand user behavior, we propose a new fast and accurate application activity recognition algorithm based on encrypted traffic. In this algorithm, we use wavelet decomposition to extract the trend features of each session to construct feature vectors. Then we use the random forest as a classification algorithm to train a classifier and identify the session to be detected. Compared with other methods, our method has better real-time performance and is more suitable for actual activity recognition.

Acknowledgments. This work was supported by in part by the National Natural Science Foundation of China (Grant Nos. 61772559, 61602167).

References

1. Alan, H.F., Kaur, J.: Can android applications be identified using only TCP/IP headers of their launch time traffic? In: Proceedings of the 9th ACM Conference on Security & Privacy in Wireless and Mobile Networks, pp. 61–66 (2016)
2. Ata, S., Iemura, Y., Nakamura, N., Oka, I.: Identification of user behavior from flow statistics. In: 2017 19th Asia-Pacific Network Operations and Management Symposium (APNOMS), pp. 42–47. IEEE (2017)
3. Conti, M., Mancini, L.V., Spolaor, R., Verde, N.V.: Can't you hear me knocking: identification of user actions on android apps via traffic analysis. In: Proceedings of the 5th ACM Conference on Data and Application Security and Privacy, pp. 297–304 (2015)
4. Conti, M., Mancini, L.V., Spolaor, R., Verde, N.V.: Analyzing android encrypted network traffic to identify user actions. IEEE Trans. Inf. Forensics Secur. **11**(1), 114–125 (2015)
5. Dai, S., Tongaonkar, A., Wang, X., Nucci, A., Song, D.: NetworkProfiler: towards automatic fingerprinting of android apps. In: 2013 Proceedings IEEE INFOCOM, pp. 809–817. IEEE (2013)

6. Korczyński, M., Duda, A.: Markov chain fingerprinting to classify encrypted traffic. In: IEEE INFOCOM 2014-IEEE Conference on Computer Communications, pp. 781–789. IEEE (2014)

7. Kulkarni, R.A.: Scrutinizing action performed by user on mobile app through network using machine learning techniques: a survey. In: 2018 2nd International Conference on Inventive Systems and Control (ICISC), pp. 860–863. IEEE (2018)

8. Park, K., Kim, H.: Encryption is not enough: inferring user activities on KakaoTalk with traffic analysis. In: Kim, H., Choi, D. (eds.) WISA 2015. LNCS, vol. 9503, pp. 254–265. Springer, Cham (2016). https://doi.org/10.1007/978-3-319-31875-2_21

9. Ranjan, G., Tongaonkar, A., Torres, R.: Approximate matching of persistent lexicon using search-engines for classifying mobile app traffic. In: IEEE INFOCOM 2016-The 35th Annual IEEE International Conference on Computer Communications, pp. 1–9. IEEE (2016)

10. Saltaformaggio, B., et al.: Eavesdropping on fine-grained user activities within smartphone apps over encrypted network traffic. In: 10th {USENIX} Workshop on Offensive Technologies ({WOOT} 16) (2016)

11. Shen, M., Wei, M., Zhu, L., Wang, M.: Classification of encrypted traffic with second-order Markov chains and application attribute bigrams. IEEE Trans. Inf. Forensics Secur. **12**(8), 1830–1843 (2017)

12. Shen, M., Wei, M., Zhu, L., Wang, M., Li, F.: Certificate-aware encrypted traffic classification using second-order Markov chain. In: 2016 IEEE/ACM 24th International Symposium on Quality of Service (IWQoS), pp. 1–10. IEEE (2016)

13. Taylor, V.F., Spolaor, R., Conti, M., Martinovic, I.: AppScanner: automatic fingerprinting of smartphone apps from encrypted network traffic. In: 2016 IEEE European Symposium on Security and Privacy (EuroS&P), pp. 439–454. IEEE (2016)

14. Taylor, V.F., Spolaor, R., Conti, M., Martinovic, I.: Robust smartphone app identification via encrypted network traffic analysis. IEEE Trans. Inf. Forensics Secur. **13**(1), 63–78 (2017)

15. Wang, S., Yan, Q., Chen, Z., Yang, B., Zhao, C., Conti, M.: TextDroid: semantics-based detection of mobile malware using network flows. In: 2017 IEEE Conference on Computer Communications Workshops (INFOCOM WKSHPS), pp. 18–23. IEEE (2017)

16. Xu, Q., Erman, J., Gerber, A., Mao, Z., Pang, J., Venkataraman, S.: Identifying diverse usage behaviors of smartphone apps. In: Proceedings of the 2011 ACM SIGCOMM Conference on Internet Measurement Conference, pp. 329–344 (2011)

17. Xu, Q., et al.: Automatic generation of mobile app signatures from traffic observations. In: 2015 IEEE Conference on Computer Communications (INFOCOM), pp. 1481–1489. IEEE (2015)

18. Yao, H., Ranjan, G., Tongaonkar, A., Liao, Y., Mao, Z.M.: Samples: self adaptive mining of persistent lexical snippets for classifying mobile application traffic. In: Proceedings of the 21st Annual International Conference on Mobile Computing and Networking, pp. 439–451 (2015)

A Privacy-Preserving Peer-to-Peer Accommodation System Based on a Credit Network

Songwei Li[1], Zhen Wang[1], Chi Zhang[1]([✉]), Lingbo Wei[1], Jianqing Liu[2], Ying Ma[3], and Yuguang Fang[3]

[1] School of Cyberspace Science and Technology, University of Science and Technology of China, Hefei, Anhui 230027, People's Republic of China
{bgplsw,wang1992}@mail.ustc.edu.cn, {chizhang,lingbowei}@ustc.edu.cn
[2] Department of Electrical and Computer Engineering, University of Alabama in Huntsville, Huntsville, AL 35899, USA
jiangqing.liu@uah.edu
[3] Department of Electrical and Computer Engineering, University of Florida, Gainesville, FL 32611, USA
mayinggator@ufl.edu, fang@ece.ufl.edu

Abstract. While Peer-to-peer (P2P) accommodations like Airbnb bring huge convenience and unique experiences to our daily life, a guest taking a P2P accommodation may face great risks, because he/she cannot check the quality of the accommodation before it starts, resulting in a bad experience. Although current P2P accommodation platforms use rating systems and arbitrations to solve the problems, they may not be practical in reality, since interpersonal expectations and interactions between a guest and a host play an important role in rating a P2P accommodation. In this paper, we introduce a new technique based on a credit network to solve these problems. A credit network is a network that uses currency to model transitive trust (or credit) between different users in a distributed fashion. It is modified from the current Bitcoin-based credit network by using a trusted hardware and a protocol for a guest to book a P2P accommodation without revealing unnecessary private information of either the guest or the host with high efficiency. Security and performance analysis shows that our scheme can help a guest find a trustworthy host in a privacy-preserving way, while still achieving high efficiency.

Keywords: P2P accommodation · Credit network · Blockchain · Bitcoin · Privacy-preserving

1 Introduction

P2P accommodations are growing at a steadily increasing rate as of today. Users can register in a P2P accommodation platform, like Airbnb, as guests or hosts

This work was supported by the Natural Science Foundation of China (NSFC) under grants 62072426, U19B2023, and 61871362.

Z. Liu et al. (Eds.): WASA 2021, LNCS 12938, pp. 326–337, 2021.
https://doi.org/10.1007/978-3-030-86130-8_26

to find or provide accommodations [1]. Unfortunately, guests and hosts may also face great risks during a P2P accommodation. A guest may land a low quality accommodation which does not match his/her expectation [2], since he/she cannot verify its quality in person before checking in. To make matters worse, a guest even faces the risk of personal safety if the host is malicious, since the guest has to live with the host during the accommodation. Thus, a guest needs methods to check whether a host is trustworthy or not, to prevent the risks of poor services and personal safety.

Guests in current P2P accommodation systems use rating systems to find trustworthy hosts, and ask for compensation from the platform for a bad experience. On the one hand, a rating system only gives all guests the same view of a host [3]. Yet, when rating an accommodation, the interpersonal expectations and interactions between a guest and a host play an important role, which suggests that different guests have different views on the same host. For example, a host will be more trusted by his relatives than other people, but a rating system cannot show this difference. On the other hand, a guest may not be satisfied with the compensation from the platform, since the cost for appealing to the platform may far exceed the compensation.

Credit networks have been considered as an attractive solution to overcoming the shortcomings of current P2P accommodation systems. A credit network is a weighted, directed graph, where users use currency (fund) to model transitive trust between them in a distributed fashion. In a credit network, a user can declare his/her trust in another user by sharing the control of his/her fund to that user, which represents the trust. A guest can determine if a host is trustworthy by finding paths from the guest to the host in the credit network. Unlike rating systems, different users can have different views on the same host, since they would find different paths to the host that contains different level of trust. When a guest books an accommodation, the funds on the paths to the host becomes the guarantees of the accommodation. The guest can simply withdraw his funds on the paths as compensation for a bad experience. Since the original credit network [4] suffers from security issues, where a malicious user can fake or disclose contradictory trust amounts to different users, Litos et al. [5] propose a new model of a credit network, and build its first prototype on Bitcoin. The trust relationships are recorded in the Bitcoin blockchain which is public to everyone, thus such malicious behaviors can be prevented.

Unfortunately, the efficiency of booking an accommodation, as well as the privacy of guests and hosts will be challenged if we directly apply such Bitcoin-based credit network to P2P accommodations. In terms of efficiency, such credit network is restricted by low throughput and high transaction fees in Bitcoin, which could cause high latency and extra transaction fees to P2P accommodations. In terms of privacy, the trust relationship of a guest or host is recorded in the Bitcoin blockchain, and thus anyone can analyze the blockchain to collect the trust relationships of them [6]. Moreover, a malicious host can even collect private information, like personally identifiable information, of guests by publishing fake house resources, waiting for guests' requests, and then canceling the requests after getting the private information of guests at almost no cost. To overcome these issues, we build a new credit network which can mask the trust relationships of its users, as well as decreasing latency and transaction fees when using the credit network. Moreover, we use this credit network to build a P2P accommodation system where guests can find trustworthy hosts with high efficiency, and prevent the malicious behaviors of hosts.

Our main contributions are highlighted as follows:

- We re-design the Bitcoin-based credit network by using Intel Software Guard Extensions (SGXs) [7], a kind of trusted hardware that provide integrity and confidentiality of code and data. Our credit network ensures that the trust relationships of its users cannot be known by irrelevant people unless a dispute on the accommodation happens. Moreover, our credit network achieves high efficiency and decreases the transaction fees when maintaining trust or finding paths for guarantees of accommodations.
- We design a privacy-preserving P2P accommodation system based on our credit network. In our system, a guest can determine whether a host is trustworthy or not by finding paths from the guest to the host in the credit network. The funds on the paths are used as guarantees of the accommodation, and thus the guest can simply withdraw his funds on the paths as compensation for a bad experience. Our system can also prevent malicious hosts from collecting private information of guests, so that the private information of a guest would not be known by others until the accommodation begins.

The rest of this paper is organized as follows. Section 2 overviews the required basic ideas of credit networks and SGXs. Section 3 presents the system model, threat model, and the design goals. Section 4 describes the construction of our re-designed credit network. Section 5 details the privacy-preserving P2P accommodation system based on our credit network. Section 6 and 7 discuss the security analysis and performance evaluation of our system, and Sect. 8 concludes this paper.

2   Background

Credit networks are used to model trust among users in a distributed fashion to build transitive trust models which are robust against intrusions. We begin our discussion by describing the concept of credit networks, and how a credit network is built on Bitcoin. We then introduce the SGXs that we use in our credit network.

2.1   Credit Networks

A credit network is a weighted, directed graph $G = (V, E)$, where V is the set of vertices representing users in the credit network, and E is the set of edges representing the trust between users, which is modeled by currency. User n_i directly trusts user n_j, if and only if $(n_i, n_j) \in E$. The level of the direct trust is equal to $w(n_i, n_j)$, which is the weight of edge (n_i, n_j). Moreover, user n_i indirectly trusts user n_k if and only if $(n_i, n_k) \notin E$ and there exists several users $n_1, n_2, \ldots, n_m$ satisfying $(u_i, n_1), (n_1, n_2), \ldots, (n_m, n_k) \in E$. The total level of the trust (direct and indirect) is the maximum flow from n_i to n_k.

The work in [5] builds a prototype of a credit network on Bitcoin based on the multisignature that Bitcoin provides. In the credit network, the trust of user n_i in n_j is defined as the amount of bitcoins that n_i can lose when n_j betrays n_i and steals the bitcoins. Assume that n_i thinks his/her trust in n_j values 10 bitcoins (10 BTC). To achieve this trust, first n_i and n_j need to generate a 1-of-2 multisignature address $1/\{n_i, n_j\}$, which is a special Bitcoin address that is controlled by two private keys that belong to n_i and n_j, respectively. The signature of either n_i or n_j is sufficient to transfer bitcoins from $1/\{n_i, n_j\}$ to any other address. After generating $1/\{n_i, n_j\}$, n_i transfers 10 BTC from his/her own address to it. In such a case, either n_i or n_j can transfer these 10 BTC to his/her own address, thus n_i would lose up to 10 BTC if n_j betrays n_i and steals these 10 BTC, equivalent to say, the level of the trust.

2.2 Intel Software Guard Extension

An SGX is a modern CPU that provides integrity and confidentiality of code and data. An SGX can create a secure container called enclave in its secure memory, where the owner of the SGX can load codes in it. These codes can only be called by given interfaces defined by the owner. Once initialized, both the codes and the interfaces cannot be tampered. Moreover, the communication between two enclaves is encrypted with a secret key shared between them, thus the integrity and confidentiality of the communication can be ensured.

3 Problem Statement

3.1 System Model

As shown in Fig. 1, our scheme involves two parts: a credit network and an accommodation information system involving hosts, guests, and a platform. The guest Alice and the host Bob are users in the Bitcoin-based credit network. In order to participate in the credit network, each user should have an enclave, which is used to maintain his/her direct trust in others. All users can execute remote attestation to validate the integrity and confidentiality of the codes in enclaves and construct secure connections with others.

As a host, Bob puts a description of his house resource on the platform to attract guests for accommodations, while Alice pulls all descriptions from the platform and searches the house resources she wants from these descriptions. The platform is only used for publishing the descriptions from hosts and it provides no guarantees on service qualities and personal security. When Alice finds an accommodation from Bob that she wants to book, she checks whether the level of her trust in Bob is more than the rent of the accommodation by using a distributed algorithm in the credit network. If Alice has enough trust in Bob, she sends messages through the paths from her to Bob to make sure that the funds that represent the trust on the paths can be used as guarantees for the accommodation. Alice then can pay Bob the rent directly, and wait for the start of the accommodation. After the accommodation, Alice can withdraw her trust as compensation if she thinks the quality of the accommodation is poor. Any other user on the paths decides whether to supplement the loss of trust, resulting in the redistribution of trust on the paths.

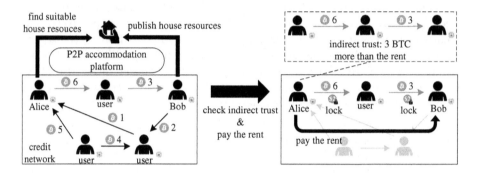

Fig. 1. The system model of P2P accommodation services.

3.2   Threat Model

We consider an attacker with the ability to access the full Bitcoin blockchain. The attacker can analyze the transactions in the blockchain, trying to infer the trust relationships of a guest or a host. Moreover, the attacker can be a user in the credit network, who can steal the funds from others who trust the attacker. Since a guest uses a distributed algorithm to find paths to a host, the attacker will try to figure out the accommodation between them by using the messages delivered in the credit network which go through the attacker. To take a further step, the attacker can also act as a host in our system, who can publish fake house resources, wait for accommodations of guests, and collect the private information of the guests.

In addition, we make the assumption that the enclaves in our scheme are trustworthy, i.e., the integrity and confidentiality of code and data in them can be ensured.

3.3   Design Goals

In light of the above threat model, we present the design goals of our P2P accommodation system as follows.

- **Security.** The credit network used in our P2P accommodation should achieve fund security. Namely, the maximum amount of funds of a guest or a host that get lost in the credit network equals to the level of the direct trust he/she has in others, which is the risk to trust others. Moreover, a guest can get compensation after a poor accommodation in an efficient way according to his/her expectation.
- **Privacy.** Trust relationships of guests or hosts, as well as the level of the trust, cannot be known by irrelevant people unless a dispute on an accommodation happens. In addition, even if a malicious host publishes fake house resources for collecting private information of guests, the guest being cheated can withdraw his/her rent and punish the host.
- **Efficiency.** On the one hand, when a guest wants to calculate his/her trust in a host, he/she can do it with high efficiency. On the other hand, no transaction needs to be recorded on the blockchain when using funds as guarantees for an accommodation unless a dispute happens, which overcomes the challenges of low throughput and high transaction fees of Bitcoin.

4 The Re-design of the Bitcoin-Based Credit Network

The Bitcoin-based credit network [5] also brings concerns on both efficiency and privacy if we directly apply it to P2P accommodation services. Before booking an accommodation, a lot of transactions need to be recorded in the blockchain to make sure that the funds used as guarantees cannot be stolen by any others before the accommodation ends (or to say, lock the funds). These transactions not only bring huge latency when booking accommodations, but also expose the trust relationships of users. Thus, we re-design the Bitcoin-based credit network so that it is suitable in P2P accommodations. By using enclaves, users in our credit network can maintain their trust without involving the blockchain. In addition, funds that represent trust can be locked off-chain, which improves efficiency and privacy at the same time.

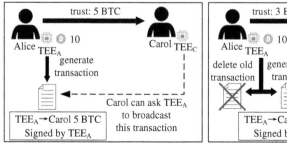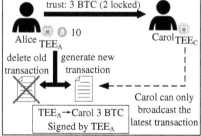

(a) Alice trusts Carol that values 5 BTC.   (b) Alice locks 2 BTC funds.

Fig. 2. The construction of our credit network.

Figure 2(a) shows an example where Alice directly trusts Carol, and the level of the trust is 5 BTC. Alice uses her enclave TEE_A to generate a Bitcoin account to maintain her trust. Then Alice transfers enough funds, e.g., 10 BTC, to TEE_A. After that, Alice uses TEE_A to generate a transaction, which transfers 5 BTC from TEE_A to Carol, and signs it by TEE_A. This transaction is stored in TEE_A, and TEE_A sends the level of trust, 5 BTC, to Carol's enclave TEE_C. Carol can use TEE_C to communicate with TEE_A to let TEE_A broadcast the transaction, so that Carol can borrow these 5 BTC which equals to Alice's trust values. Carol can later transfer funds to TEE_A to return the borrowed funds, or he can choose not to do so, which means that Carol betrays Alice's trust and steals her funds.

In our credit network, locking funds is achieved by generating new transactions. Figure 2(b) shows an example where Alice locks her trust in Carol which values 2 BTC. Alice uses TEE_A to generate a new transaction, which transfers 3 BTC (5 minus 2) from TEE_A to Carol, and deletes the previous one. Then TEE_A sends the level of trust to TEE_C. If Carol wants to steal these funds, he can use TEE_C to communicate with TEE_A and steal 3 BTC from Alice, but the remaining 2 BTC are still controlled by TEE_A. This method can also be used for releasing funds, which means removing the lock of the funds. If Alice uses TEE_A to generate a new transaction which transfers 5 BTC from TEE_A to Carol and sends the new level of trust to TEE_C, it means that Alice releases the locked 2 BTC funds.

5   The Peer-to-Peer Accommodation Protocol

In this section, we propose our P2P accommodation system based on the re-designed credit network above. The working process of our P2P accommodation system includes four steps: initialization, finding an accommodation, locking funds for the accommodation, and the accommodation aftermath. We will describe how the guest Alice, the host Bob, and other users in the credit network interact with each other during each step.

5.1   Initialization

The first step of our P2P accommodation system is the initialization, where all users in the credit network should generate necessary information so that finding paths in the credit network can be achieved without revealing privacy of any users.

We use SpeedyMurmurs [6], an efficient distributed routing algorithm in path-based transaction networks, to build our algorithm, where each user in the credit network needs to have several coordinates. We need to randomly choose L users in advance, called landmarks. A landmark sends an INIT message to all neighbors, inviting them to become child nodes of the landmark, to generate a spanning tree of the network. This INIT message is flooded over the network till all users have joined the spanning tree. Finally, every user generates a coordinate. The coordinate of the landmark is (), an empty vector. The coordinate of any other user is the coordinate of his/her parent concatenating a random b-bit number. After the initialization, each user will have L coordinates, since there are L different landmarks chosen, and thus each user joins L different spanning trees. Algorithm 1 describes how a user works during the initialization. Notice that the credit network is a dynamic network, any user that newly joins the credit network also needs to perform Algorithm 1. Also, a user needs to change the coordinate if his/her parent is absent.

Algorithm 1. Initialization at user n_i

Require: randomly choose L landmarks in advance
1: Init:
2:    $isroot_i[L] = \{0\}$
3:    **if** n_i is the l-th landmark **then** $isroot_i[l] = 1$
4:    $id_i[L] =$ **null**
5: Upon receiving nothing:
6:    **if** $isroot_i[l] = 1$ **then**
7:        $id_i[l] = ()$
8:        **for all** $n_j \in N(n_i)$ **do**
9:            send $\langle INIT, l, id_i[l] \rangle$ to n_j
10:      **end for**
11:   **end if**
12: Upon receving $\langle INIT, l, id_j[l] \rangle$ from a neighbor n_j:
13:   **if** $id_i[l] =$ **null then**
14:      generate a b-bit random number r
15:      $id_i[l] = concatenate(id_j[l], r)$
16:      **for all** $n_k \in N(n_i)$ except n_j **do**
17:         $//N(n_i)$ is the set of all neighbors of n_i
18:         send $\langle INIT, l, id_i[l] \rangle$ to n_k
19:      **end for**
20:   **end if**

Moreover, as a host, Bob puts a description of his house resource on the platform to attract guests for his accommodations.

5.2 Finding an Accommodation

When Alice wants to book an accommodation, she pulls all descriptions and return addresses from the platform, and searches for suitable house resources from them. Alice will choose one of these house resources according to the descriptions and whether she has enough trust in the hosts.

Specifically, for each host, Alice needs to check whether her trust in the host is more than the rent of the accommodation. For each host, Alice communicates with the host and get all his return addresses. A return address is a special coordinate calculated by VOUTE [8], which allows Alice to find paths to the host correctly without revealing the real coordinate of the host. Alice then randomly splits the rent into shares $s[1], s[2], \ldots, s[L]$. Then for each return address $addr[l]$, Alice sends a message, including $s[l]$ and $addr[l]$, to one of her neighbor, trying to find a path to the host in the l-th spanning tree. Each user that receives the message selects the neighbor which has the minimum distance to the host with sufficient trust as the next hop. The distance of two users is represented by the number of hops between them in the spanning tree, which can be easily calculated by their coordinates and return addresses. When the host receives this message. The host sends an acknowledgement message backward through the path to notify the success of the path establishment. Thus, Alice can determine that she has enough trust if she receives L messages from all L paths. If Alice does not receive all these messages, she can re-split the rent and try another time, or she indeed does not have enough trust.

With such a method, Alice can filter those hosts with insufficient trust. Finally, for the remaining hosts, the guest checks their descriptions and chooses the accommodation she wants.

5.3   Locking Funds for the Accommodation

Assume that Alice chooses the accommodation provided by Bob. After choosing an accommodation, Alice communicates with Bob by his phone number for more details of the accommodation. If Alice decides to take the accommodation, Bob sends a payment method to Alice to let her pay the rent.

Before paying the rent, Alice should lock enough funds in the credit network as guarantees so that she can get compensation if necessary. Alice splits the rent into L shares $s[1], s[2], \ldots, s[L]$ as in the last subsection. Then for each share $s[l]$, Alice uses the same method as in the last subsection to find L paths to Bob. When Bob sends messages that go through these paths acknowledging the success, a user that receives such a message therefore can lock his/her funds on the path, i.e., generating a new Bitcoin transaction and sending the level of the trust to the neighbor. Alice can assert that all users on the paths have finished locking when receiving L messages from all L paths. She can then pay the rent to Bob with the given payment method, and notify Bob that the payment is finished. After the payment, Alice can give her personally identifiable information to Bob, e.g., phone number or real name, and waits for the start of the accommodation.

5.4   The Accommodation Aftermath

Finally, Alice meets with Bob offline, and the accommodation begins. When the accommodation ends, if Alice thinks the quality of the accommodation matches her expectation, she can sends messages through the credit network to release the locked funds so that the credit network resets to whatever before the accommodation happens. If Alice thinks the quality of the accommodation is under her expectation, she can withdraw part of her locked funds as compensation from the credit network, and only release the remaining part of it. Any other user that on the paths decides whether to use the locked funds to supplement the loss of trust from the last hop or not, resulting in the redistribution of trust on the paths. After the redistribution, Alice's trust in Bob decreases, since there are less funds on the paths.

6 Security Analysis

6.1 Security

Based on the above design, our P2P accommodation system achieves security goal mentioned in Sect. 3.3. Initially, the underlying credit network used in our system can achieve fund security. A malicious user can steal the funds of his/her neighbor by broadcasting the transaction in the enclave of the neighbor, which is allowed in the credit network. However, the enclave prevents a malicious user from stealing the locked funds of his/her neighbor since only the latest transaction can be broadcasted by the enclave, which achieves fund security. Moreover, a guest that took a poor accommodation can simply get compensation from his/her locked funds. Since it is decided by the guest that how much funds should be withdrawn, the guest can always get enough compensation based on his/her expectation.

6.2 Privacy

In our system, the funds that represent trust relationships of guests or hosts are maintained by Bitcoin addresses controlled by enclaves. Compared with multisignature addresses, such Bitcoin addresses do not have any features which indicate if such addresses maintain funds representing trust relationships. Thus, an attacker cannot infer the trust relationships of guests or hosts by analyzing the transactions in the blockchain. Even if the attacker is a user in the credit network and he/she transfers messages, which indicates he/she is on a path from a guest to a host, the attacker cannot figure out the accommodation between them unless a dispute happens. The messages that go through the attacker do not contain the coordinates or any other personally identifiable information of the guest. Although the messages contain the return addresses of the host, the attacker cannot use them to infer the real coordinates or other information of the host. Therefore, our system hides the accommodation between a guest and a host even if an attacker is on the path between them.

Although a malicious host can collect personally identifiable information of guests by publishing fake house resource in our system, the guest can withdraw his/her rent and punish the host. The guest withdraws all his locked funds, which equals to the rent, as his/her compensation, and other users redistribute their trust on the paths. In such situation, the users on the paths that directly trust the host will use the locked funds to supplement the loss of trust from the last hop, meaning that the host loses the trust of others because of his malicious behavior.

7   Performance Analysis

In this section, we discuss the performance analysis of our P2P accommodation system. Compared with current P2P accommodation system, the extra overhead of our system mainly comes from the usage of our credit network. Thus, we evaluate the efficiency when finding paths and locking funds in our credit network, as well as the blockchain cost (the transaction fees) during an accommodation.

7.1   Performance of the Credit Network

We evaluate the efficiency when finding path and locking funds in our credit network. Since our algorithms are mainly built on SpeedyMurmurs, we explore how SpeedyMurmurs can show its advantages in our scheme. We implement a framework for graph analysis called GTNA, as well as obtaining the datasets from crawling Ripple (https://ripple.com). We simulate the performance of our scheme and compare it with the SilentWhispers [9] and Ford-Fulkerson algorithm [10], which is known as the baseline.

We use the parameter $L = 3$ as SpeedyMurmurs advises, i.e., there are three spanning trees in the credit network, and the evaluation result is shown in Table 1. While Ford-Fulkerson achieves the best success ratio for finding paths from a guest to a host with sufficient trust, it has huge time and communication overheads. Compared with Ford-Fulkerson, our scheme has much lower overhead while its success ratio is very close to Ford-Fulkerson. Moreover, our scheme shows better performance than SilentWhispers in all the three aspects. Thus our scheme can help a guest determine whether a host is trustworthy or not, by finding paths in the credit network with high success ratio and high efficiency.

Table 1. Performance for different schemes

Scheme	Success ratio	Delay (ms)	Communication overhead (the number of messages)
Our scheme $(L = 3)$	0.90	52.37	22.3
SilentWhispers [9]	0.66	82.48	28.7
Ford-Fulkerson [10]	1.00	249690	28700

7.2   Blockchain Cost

We evaluate the number of transactions that need to be recorded in the blockchain for an accommodation. Table 2 shows the numbers of transactions in our scheme and in the credit network proposed in [5]. Obviously, our scheme has fewer transactions when maintaining the trust and performing payment through a credit network. Thus, our scheme can achieve lower transaction fee for using a credit network.

Table 2. Blockchain cost of different credit networks

Credit network	The number of transactions (adjusting trust values)	The number of transactions (performing a payment)
Our scheme	1 for initialization, 0 for each adjustment	0
Trust is risk [5]	1 for initialization, 1 for each adjustment	18

8   Conclusion

A guest often takes great risks when he/she wants to book a P2P accommodation like from Airbnb, and the private information of a host can be collected easily today. In this paper, we apply a credit network to solve these problems. By using enclaves, we optimize the current credit network, and demonstrate how to book a P2P accommodation while revealing no private information. The performance analysis shows that our scheme only introduces little latency and communication overhead for a P2P accommodation while maintaining very low transaction fee.

References

1. Hamari, J., Sjöklint, M., Ukkonen, A.: The sharing economy: why people participate in collaborative consumption. J. Assoc. Inf. Sci. Technol. **67**(9), 2047–2059 (2016)
2. Ert, E., Fleischer, A., Magen, N.: Trust and reputation in the sharing economy: the role of personal photos in Airbnb. Tour. Manage. **55**, 62–73 (2016)
3. DeFigueiredo, D., Barr, E., Wu, S.F.: Trust is in the eye of the beholder. In: International Conference on Computational Science and Engineering, Vancouver, BC, Canada, August 2009
4. Fugger, R.: Money as IOUs in social trust networks & a proposal for a decentralized currency network protocol (2004). http://ripple.ryanfugger.com/decentralizedcurrency.pdf
5. Thyfronitis Litos, O.S., Zindros, D.: Trust is risk: a decentralized financial trust platform. In: Kiayias, A. (ed.) FC 2017. LNCS, vol. 10322, pp. 340–356. Springer, Cham (2017). https://doi.org/10.1007/978-3-319-70972-7_19
6. Roos, S., Moreno-Sanchez, P., Kate, A., Goldberg, I.: Settling payments fast and private: efficient decentralized routing for path-based transactions (2017). arXiv preprint arXiv:1709.05748
7. I. R: Software guard extensions programming reference. Intel Corporation (2014)
8. Roos, S., Beck, M., Strufe, T.: Anonymous addresses for efficient and resilient routing in F2F overlays. In: IEEE INFOCOM 2016 - The 35th Annual IEEE International Conference on Computer Communications, San Francisco, CA, USA, April 2016
9. Malavolta, G., Moreno-Sanchez, P., Kate, A., Maffei, M.: SilentWhispers: enforcing security and privacy in decentralized credit networks. Cryptology ePrint Archive, Report 2016/1054 (2016). http://eprint.iacr.org/2016/1054
10. Ford, L.R., Fulkerson, D.R.: Maximal flow through a network. Can. J. Math. **8**, 339–404 (1956)

Private Frequent Itemset Mining in the Local Setting

Hang Fu, Wei Yang$^{(\boxtimes)}$, and Liusheng Huang

School of Computer Science and Technology, University of Science
and Technology of China, Hefei, China
`qubit@ustc.edu.cn`

Abstract. Set-valued data, which is useful for representing user-generated data, becomes ubiquitous in numerous online services. Service provider profits by learning patterns and associations from users' set-valued data. However, it comes with privacy concerns if these data are collected from users directly. This work studies frequent itemset mining from user-generated set-valued data meanwhile locally preserving personal data privacy. Under local d-privacy constraints, which capture intrinsic dissimilarity between set-valued data in the framework of differential privacy, we propose a novel privacy-preserving frequent itemset mining mechanism, called PrivFIM. It provides rigorous data privacy protection on the user-side and allows effective statistical analyses on the server-side. Specifically, each user perturbs his set-valued data locally to guarantee that the server cannot infer the user's original itemset with high confidence. The server can reconstruct an unbiased estimation of itemset frequency from these randomized data and then combines it with the Apriori-based pruning technique to identify frequent itemsets efficiently and accurately. Extensive experiments conducted on real-world and synthetic datasets demonstrate that PrivFIM surpasses existing methods, and maintains high utility while providing strong privacy guarantees.

Keywords: Local differential privacy · Frequent itemset mining · Crowdsensing · Randomized response

1 Introduction

Nowadays, with the prevalence of big data analytics, it becomes ubiquitous to improve the quality of services through collecting and analyzing user data. Frequent itemset mining (FIM) is a well-recognized data mining problem, which aims to discover groups of items that occur frequently in user data. The discovery of frequent itemsets is of significance to valuable economic and research purposes, such as mining association rules [3], predicting user behavior [2], and finding correlations [6]. However, directly collecting set-valued data (e.g., web browsing history and medical records) from users comes with privacy concerns, since these set-valued data may reveal sensitive information about individuals.

Differential privacy is the de facto standard privacy notion that provides provable privacy protection without any assumptions on the adversary's background knowledge. Several works have been studied on mining frequent itemsets in the context of centralized differential privacy, such as injecting noises to

© Springer Nature Switzerland AG 2021
Z. Liu et al. (Eds.): WASA 2021, LNCS 12938, pp. 338–350, 2021.
https://doi.org/10.1007/978-3-030-86130-8_27

itemset frequencies [13], filtering unpromising candidates [14], and constructing a basis set [11]. In the centralized differential privacy model, a trustable data curator is assumed and users' raw data are collected and processed by the trusted data curator. However, the assumption of trustable data curators or third parties is unpractical, since data curators may trade user's privacy unlawfully and third parties might be cracked or corrupted.

As an answer to privacy protection in local settings, local differential privacy (LDP) [8] has been proposed for the scenario that users take full control of their raw data without the trust of any party. Users sanitize their data by a randomized algorithm independently and locally before sending them to the untrusted collector. Then all the perturbed data are aggregated by the untrusted collector to estimate statistical analysis results about the original data. Due to the practical setting and protective strength of LDP, it has been widely deployed in popular systems, such as Google Chrome browser [9] and Windows systems [7].

Unfortunately, existing LDP mechanisms for set-valued data [15,16] fail to achieve high utility for complex statistical analysis tasks, such as frequent itemset mining, as they ignores the intrinsic structure of set-valued data. Specifically, LDP guarantees the same distinguishability for any two set-valued data x, x'. This implies that the group structure of set-valued data cannot be preserved under LDP-based perturbation. Recently, local d-privacy [4,5] is proposed as an extension of LDP with distance metrics, which is more applicable for structured data. Local d-privacy ensures low distinguishability between similar set-valued data for strong privacy preservation and high distinguishability between dissimilar set-valued data for high data utility.

Motivated by the facts above, we propose PrivFIM, a novel privacy-preserving algorithm for mining frequent itemsets. Specifically, the set-valued data is sanitized as a random subset of items. The subset is randomly output with a high probability to preserve the information of the input itemset while satisfying the constrain of local d-privacy. Furthermore, the unbiased estimation of itemset frequencies can be inferred from all randomized subsets. Finally, we adopt the search space pruning technique of Apriori algorithm to mining the frequent itemsets on these randomized subsets efficiently and accurately. Experimental results in both synthetic datasets and real-world datasets show that PrivFIM outperforms the existing solutions.

2   System Model

2.1   Set-Valued Data

Set-valued data is a set of items or elements. Let $\mathcal{I} = \{a_1, a_2, ..., a_g\}$ denote the item domain, the set-valued data x is a subset of the domain $\mathcal{I}$ (i.e., $x \subseteq \mathcal{I}$). For simplicity, we assume that the size of each set-valued data (i.e., m) is the same across all users. Though the cardinality of users' set-valued data could be different in practice, all set-value data can be pre-processed to a fixed size through padding or truncating [15].

In order to quantitatively measure the dissimilarity between set-value data, we need to introduce a distance metric d onto the domain of set-value data. Intuitively, the fewer two itemsets intersect, the less similar they are. When two m-sized set-value data x and x' are encoded in bit-vector forms, the hamming distance of two encoded bit-vectors is denoted as $d_{ham}(x, x')$, which equals to $2 \cdot (m - |x \cap x'|)$. Since it captures intrinsic dissimilarity between set-valued data, the distance metric is defined as $d = \frac{d_{ham}}{2}$ in this paper.

2.2 Privacy Definition

The data collector is assumed to be untrusted because the privacy leakage can be caused by unauthorized data trading or unpredictable hacking activities. Each user's data privacy is supposed to be preserved independently in the local setting (e.g., on mobile devices). Local differential privacy (ϵ-LDP) emerges as the de facto data privacy notion which ensures up to e^ϵ distinguishability of outputs for any pair of two inputs x and x'. When applying to set-value data, LDP ignores the dissimilarity between set-valued data, thus fails to achieve high utility for complicated statistical analysis tasks, such as frequent itemset mining. Local d-privacy further relaxes the distinguishability of outputs to $\epsilon \cdot d(x, x')$, for the purpose of providing strong privacy protection for similar inputs meanwhile allowing high data utility for dissimilar inputs. Formally, the definition of local d-privacy for set-valued data is described as follows:

Definition 1 (Local d-Privacy). *A randomization mechanism $\mathcal{M}$ satisfies local d-privacy if and only if for any pairs of set-valued data x, x' (here $|x| = m, |x'| = m$ as assumed) in the domain $\mathcal{X}$, and for any possible output $z \in \mathcal{Z}$, it holds:*

$$Pr[\mathcal{M}(x) = z] \leq e^{\epsilon \cdot d(x,x')} \cdot Pr[\mathcal{M}(x') = z]$$

The parameter ϵ is called the *privacy budget* that quantifies the strength of privacy protection. When ϵ is small, the adversary cannot distinguish between the input tuple x and x' with high confidence. Thus, it provides plausible deniability for individuals involved in the sensitive set-valued data.

2.3 Aggregation Model

The data aggregation model (shown in Fig. 1) involves one data aggregator $\mathcal{A}$ and a set of users $\mathcal{U}$ with size $|\mathcal{U}| = n$. Assuming that each user u^i possesses a m-sized set-valued data x^i, To preserve privacy locally, each user u^i independently randomizes his set-valued data x^i to a privatized view z^i through a local d-privacy mechanism and then sends it to the aggregator. After collecting the privatized data $Z = \{z^1, z^2, \cdots, z^n\}$ from all users, the server needs to estimate the frequency of itemsets and mine frequent itemsets from these privatized data. To be formal, the true frequency of an itemset s on the raw set-valued dataset $X = \{x^1, x^2, \cdots, x^n\}$ is:

$$f(s) = \frac{\#\{u^i | s \subseteq x^i, 1 \leq i \leq n\}}{n} \tag{1}$$

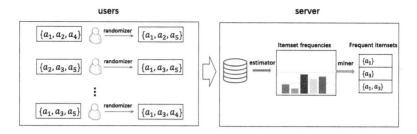

Fig. 1. System model.

Accordingly, the exact result of top-k frequent itemset mining consists of the k itemsets with the highest frequencies. Our goal is to estimate the frequency of itemsets and find frequent itemsets with high accuracy under the required privacy constraint (i.e., satisfying local d-privacy).

3   PrivFIM

In this section, we describe the details of the proposed mechanism, including the itemset randomizer for the protection of users' privacy, the itemset frequency estimator for the estimation of itemset frequency, and the frequent itemset miner for the selection of frequent itemsets.

3.1   Itemset Randomizer

To sanitize user's set-valued data locally, the itemset randomizer randomly responses with a fixed-size subset z of the item domain $\mathcal{I}$. According to the Exponential Mechanism [12], when the input set-valued data is $x \subseteq \mathcal{I}$, the output probability of the subset $z \subseteq \mathcal{I}$ is defined as follows:

$$Pr[R(x) = z] \propto \exp(\epsilon \cdot \frac{u(x, z)}{2\Delta u})$$

where Δu is the global sensitivity of utility function $u(x, z)$ and its value equals $max_{x, x' \subseteq \mathcal{I}, z \subseteq \mathcal{I}} \frac{|u(x,z) - u(x,z')|}{d(x,x')}$. If all users' set-valued data have the same cardinality, then one can remove the factor of $1/2$ in the exponent of $\exp(\epsilon \cdot \frac{u(x,z)}{2\Delta u})$ and return z with proportional to $\exp(\epsilon \cdot \frac{u(x,z)}{\Delta u})$. This improves the statistical utility of outputs.

The utility function $u(x, z)$ maps input/output pairs to utility scores which determine the probability that maps x to z. In PrivSet [15], the utility function is defined as an indicator function of whether x and z have common items. It is designed for the problem of item frequency estimation, which measures the existence of an item after perturbing the input itemset. Intuitively, after randomization, the larger the randomized output intersects with the input itemset, the more information the output will preserve. For estimation of itemset frequency, we should allocate a larger probability to the subset that intersects more with input. Formally, we define the utility function as the size of the intersection between the m-sized input x and the k-sized output z, that is $u(x, z) = |x \cap z|$. Herein, the sensitivity of the utility function is $\Delta u = max_{x,x' \subseteq \mathcal{I}, z \subseteq \mathcal{I}} \frac{|u(x,z) - u(x,z')|}{d(x,x')} = 1$. Hence the probability normalizer can be calculated as $\Omega = \sum_{i=0}^{k} \binom{g-m}{k-i} \cdot \binom{m}{i} \cdot e^{i \cdot \epsilon}$. Consequently, the itemset randomizer will random output a k-size subset z of $\mathcal{X}$ with probability:

$$Pr[R(x) = z] = \frac{\exp(\epsilon \cdot u(x, z))}{\Omega}, \ z \subseteq I \ and \ |z| = k \qquad (2)$$

Theorem 1. *The itemset randomizer satisfies local d-privacy.*

Proof. Given the output z, for any two possible m-sized itemset x, x', we have

$$\frac{Pr[R(x) = z|x]}{Pr[R(x') = z|x']} = \frac{\exp(\epsilon \cdot u(x, z))/\Omega}{\exp(\epsilon \cdot u(x', z))/\Omega}$$
$$= \exp\left(\epsilon \cdot (u(x, z) - u(x', z))\right)$$
$$\leq \exp(\epsilon \cdot d(x, x') \cdot \Delta u)$$
$$= \exp(\epsilon \cdot d(x, x')) \qquad (3)$$

According to the definition of local d-privacy, Theorem 1 holds.

Consider the implementation of the itemset randomizer, its output domain size is $\binom{g}{k}$, thus naively random sampling an element from the domain is computationally expensive when g and k are relatively large. The efficient implementation of the itemset randomizer is presented in Algorithm 1. Note that the output probability of z is determined by the number of intersected items between x and z. We first decide the number of intersected items (i.e., l) between x and z at lines 3−9. Then, l items are sampled from the set-valued data x, and the remaining $k - l$ items are sampled from the rest of the item domain $\mathcal{I} - x$, to finally constitute the private view z at lines 10−11. It reduces the computational complexity of randomization from $O(\binom{g}{k})$ to $O(g)$, which is linear to the size of item domain. Therefore, the itemset randomizer component is extremely efficient on the user-side.

3.2 Itemset Frequency Estimator

After the aggregator collects all perturbed data, we focus on how to estimate the frequency from these perturbed data. Our estimation procedure starts by estimating 1-sized itemsets and iteratively combines them to estimate the larger ones.

Consider an l-sized itemset s_l and a user's set-valued data x. Given the output probabilities in Eq. (2), if $u(s_l, x) = t$ (i.e., $|s_l \cap x| = t$), then we consider the

---

Algorithm 1. Itemset Randomizer

Input: User's set-valued data $x \subseteq \mathcal{I}$, privacy budget ϵ;
Output: A privatized view $z \subseteq \{c | c \subseteq \mathcal{I}, |c| = k\}$;
  1: $z = \emptyset$
  2: $\Omega = \sum_{i=0}^{k} \binom{g-m}{k-i} \cdot \binom{m}{i} \cdot e^{i \cdot \epsilon}$
  3: $r = uniform\ random(0.0, 1.0)$
  4: $l = 0$
  5: $p = \binom{g}{k}/\Omega$
  6: **while** $p < r$ **do**
  7:     $l = l + 1$
  8:     $p = p + \binom{g-m}{k-i} \cdot \binom{m}{i} \cdot e^{i \cdot \epsilon}$
  9: **end while**
10: $z = z \cup sample(x, l)$
11: $z = z \cup sample(\mathcal{I} - x, k - l)$
12: **return** z

---

probability that s_l shows up in the output z (i.e., $s_l \subseteq z$). Since $|s_l \cap x| = t$ and $s_l \subseteq z$, there must be t intersected items between x and z. Except for the t intersected items, the possible number of intersected items between x and z ranges from 0 to $k - l$. Combining all these possible situations, the probability can be derived as:

$$Pr[s_l \subseteq R(x) | u(s_l, x) = t] = \frac{\sum_{i=0}^{k-l} \binom{g+t-m-l}{k-l-i} \cdot \binom{m-t}{i} \cdot e^{(i+t) \cdot \epsilon}}{\Omega} \quad (4)$$

Herein, we denote it as $P_{l,t}$ for short. Let $C(s_l)$ denote the times of s_l that occurs in the perturbed data, then the expectation of $C(s_l)$ is:

$$\mathbb{E}(C(s_l)) = n \cdot \sum_{t=0}^{l} Pr[s_l \subseteq R(x) | u(s_l, x) = t] \cdot Pr[u(s_l, x) = t] \quad (5)$$

Now we start with two examples of the frequency estimation for 1-sized itemset and 2-sized itemset, respectively, and then generalize it to the l-sized case.

Frequency Estimation for 1-Sized Itemset. Consider a 1-sized itemset $s_1 \subseteq \mathcal{I}$ and a user's original set-valued data x, the situation when $u(s_1, x) = 1$ implies $s_1 \subseteq x$ (i.e., $Pr(u(s_1, x) = 1) = f(s_1)$). Similarly, we also have $Pr(u(s_1, x) = 0) = 1 - f(s_1)$. Combining with Eqs. (4) and (5), the unbiased estimation of $f(s_1)$ can be derived as:

$$\tilde{f}(s_1) = \frac{C(s_1)/n - P_{1,0}}{P_{1,1} - P_{1,0}} \quad (6)$$

Frequency Estimation for 2-Sized Itemset. Consider a 2-sized itemset $s_2 \subseteq \mathcal{I}$ and a user's original set-valued data x, the situation that $u(s_2, x) = 2$

implies $s_2 \subseteq x$ (i.e., $Pr(u(s_2,x) = 2) = f(s_2)$). According to inclusion-exclusion principle, we have $Pr(u(s_2,x) = 1) = \sum_{s \subseteq s_2,|s|=1} f(s) - 2f(s_2)$ and $Pr(u(s_2,x) = 0) = 1 - \sum_{s \subseteq s_2,|s|=1} f(s) + f(s_2)$. Since we have obtained the unbiased estimation of frequency for all 1-sized itemset, the unbiased estimation of $\sum_{s \subseteq s_2,|s|=1} f(s)$ is $\sum_{s \subseteq s_2,|s|=1} \tilde{f}(s)$. Combining with Eqs. (4) and (5), the unbiased estimation of $f(s_1)$ can be derived as:

$$\tilde{f}(s_2) = \frac{C(s_2)/n - P_{2,0} + (P_{2,0} - P_{2,1}) \cdot \sum_{s \subseteq s_2,|s|=1} \tilde{f}(s)}{P_{2,2} - 2P_{2,1} + P_{2,0}} \tag{7}$$

Now we present the frequency estimation for l-sized itemset in the general case.

Frequency Estimation for l-Sized Itemset. Note that before we begin to estimate the frequency of l-sized itemsets, we have obtained the unbiased estimation for itemsets whose size is smaller than l. Consider a l-sized itemset $s_l \subseteq \mathcal{I}$, we denote the sum of the estimated frequency of all k-sized subset of s_l as $\tilde{N}_{s_l}(k) = \sum_{s \subseteq s_l,|s|=k} f(s)$, then the estimation of $f(s_l)$ is:

$$\tilde{f}(s_l) = \frac{C(s_l)/n - \sum_{m=0}^{l} P_{l,m} \cdot \sum_{i=0}^{l-m-1} (-1)^i \binom{m+i}{m} \tilde{N}_{s_l}(m+i)}{\sum_{m=0}^{l} P_{l,m} \cdot (-1)^{l-m} \binom{l}{m}} \tag{8}$$

Theorem 2. $\tilde{f}(s_l)$ is an unbiased estimation of $f(s_l)$.

Proof. According to inclusion-exclusion principle, we have

$$Pr[u(s_l,x) = m] = \sum_{i=0}^{l-m} (-1)^i \binom{m+i}{m} \sum_{s \subseteq s_l,|s|=m+i} f(s), 0 \le m \le l \tag{9}$$

Plugging to Eq. (5), we have

$$\mathbb{E}(C(s_l)) = n \cdot \sum_{m=0}^{l} P_{l,m} \cdot \sum_{i=0}^{l-m} (-1)^i \binom{m+i}{m} N_{s_l}(m+i)$$

$$= n \cdot \sum_{m=0}^{l} P_{l,m} \cdot [f(s_l) + \sum_{i=0}^{l-m-1} (-1)^i \binom{m+i}{m} N_{s_l}(m+i)] \tag{10}$$

Recall that $\tilde{N}_{s_l}(k)$ is the unbiased estimation of $N_{s_l}(k)$. Combining together, $f(s)$ is unbiasedly estimated as

$$\tilde{f}(s_l) = \frac{C(s_l)/n - \sum_{m=0}^{l} P_{l,m} \cdot \sum_{i=0}^{l-m-1} (-1)^i \binom{m+i}{m} \tilde{N}_{s_l}(m+i)}{\sum_{m=0}^{l} P_{l,m} \cdot (-1)^{l-m} \binom{l}{m}} \tag{11}$$

To summarize up, we present the implementation of itemset frequency estimator in Algorithm 2, which records the itemset frequency in private itemsets at lines 2−6, then derives the unbiased estimation of itemset frequency at line 7.

Algorithm 2. Itemset Frequency Estimator

Input:

    Private itemsets $Z = \{z^1, z^2, \cdots, z^n\}$ from n users, The l-sized itemset s_l;

Output:

    Unbiased estimation $\tilde{f}(s_l)$ of s_l

1: set $\tilde{f}(s_l) = 0.0$ and $C(s_l) = 0$

2: **for** $i = 1$ to n **do**

3:     **if** $s_l \subseteq z^i$ **then**

4:         $C(s_l) = C(s_l) + 1$

5:     **end if**

6: **end for**

7: $\tilde{f}(s_l) = \dfrac{C(s_l)/n \quad \sum_{m=0}^{l} \Gamma_{l,m} \cdot \sum_{i=0}^{l-m-1} (-1)^i \binom{m+i}{m} \tilde{N}_{s_l}(m+i)}{\sum_{m=0}^{l} P_{l,m} \cdot (-1)^{l-m} \binom{l}{m}}$

8: **return** $\tilde{f}(s_l)$

3.3 Frequent Itemset Miner

We now show how to discover frequent itemsets from all privatized views. The classic Apriori algorithm exploits the monotonicity of frequency. Specifically, given an itemset s and one of its subsets $s' \subseteq s$, their frequencies $f(s)$ and $f(s')$ satisfy $f(s) \leq f(s')$. There are several benefits by leveraging the monotonicity: (1) Starting from frequent singleton itemsets and iteratively combine them to form larger ones, many itemsets can potentially be avoided when exploring the search space. (2) The estimation error increases with the size of itemset. By eliminating the larger itemset through more accurate estimation of the smaller itemset, the mining result achieves higher utility. Algorithm 3 shows the details of mining frequent itemsets on all collected privatized views.

Algorithm 3. Frequent Itemset Miner

Input:

    Privatized views $Z = \{z^1, z^2, \cdots, z^n\}$ from n users; top-k

Output:

    The set of top-k frequent itemsets F;

1: $l = 1$

2: $F_0 \leftarrow$ all 1-sized itemsets

3: **while** $F_{l-1} \neq \emptyset$ **do**

4:     $\mathcal{C}_l \leftarrow$ generate candidate l-sized itemsets from F_{l-1}

5:     **for** itemset $s_l \in \mathcal{C}_l$ **do**

6:         $\tilde{f}(s_l) \leftarrow$ apply itemset frequency estimator

7:     **end for**

8:     $F = F \cup \mathcal{C}_l$

9:     $F \leftarrow$ select the k most frequent itemsets in F

10:     $F_l = \{s | s \in F, |s| = l\}$

11:     $l = l + 1$

12: **end while**

13: **return** F

---

4   Experiments

4.1   Experimental Setup

Datasets. For evaluation of the itemset frequency estimation performance, several datasets are generated by IBM synthetic Data Generation Code for Associations and Sequential Patterns with different item domain size g and different fixed cardinality m. For evaluation of frequent itemset mining performance, we run experiments on two real-world datasets: Online dataset and Retail dataset [1]. A summary of these two datasets is reported in Table 1.

Table 1. Datasets.

Dataset	Users	Items	Average length
Online	541909	2603	4.36
Retail	88162	16470	10.31

Competitors. We compare PrivFIM with the following two state-of-the-art mechanisms. (a) *PrivSet* [15]: It is a local differentially private set-valued data aggregation mechanism, which is designed for item distribution estimation. (b) *PSFO* [16]: It proposed a padding-and-sampling frequency oracle for frequent item mining and further adapted it to find frequent itemsets through mapping itemsets to items. In PrivFIM, the size of the output subset is set to be 3, which is enough to identify the most frequent itemsets meanwhile avoids introducing too much noise. We run each algorithm several times and report its average results.

Metrics. For evaluation of itemset frequency estimator, the itemsets considered in these experiments include all 1-sized itemsets and 2-sized itemsets. We use the Mean Squared Error (MSE) to evaluate the performance of itemset frequency estimation. Specifically, f is the true frequency and $\tilde{f}$ is the estimated frequency. Let S denote the set of all considered itemsets, then MSE is defined by:

$$MSE(\tilde{f}) = \frac{1}{|S|} \sum_{x \in S} (f(x) - \tilde{f}(x))^2 \tag{12}$$

We use the Normalized Cumulative Gain [10] (NCG) to evaluate the performance of frequent itemset mining. Define s_i as the i-th most frequent itemset. Let the ground truth for top k itemsets as $S_t = \{s_1, s_2, ..., s_k\}$. Denote the k itemsets identified by our algorithm using S_r. According to the rank of itemset, each itemset s_i in the S_t is assigned with a quality score $q(s_i) = k + 1 - i$. The highest ranked itemset has a score of k, the next one has a score $k - 1$, and so on; and all other itemsets have a score of 0. To normalize this into a value between 0 and 1, we divide the sum of scores by the maximum possible score (i.e., $\frac{k(k+1)}{2}$). Formally, NCG is defined as:

$$NCG = \frac{\sum_{x \in S_r} q(x)}{\sum_{x \in S_t} q(x)} \tag{13}$$

4.2 Evaluation of Itemset Frequency Estimator

In this subsection, we evaluate the accuracy of the itemset frequency estimation on various synthetic datasets.

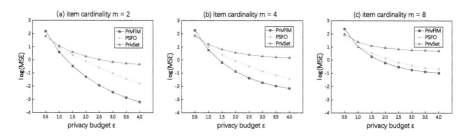

Fig. 2. Mean squared error with $n = 10000$ users, domain size $g = 32$ and set cardinality m ranges from 2 to 8.

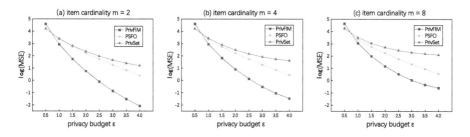

Fig. 3. Mean squared error with $n = 10000$ users, domain size $g = 128$ and set cardinality m ranges from 2 to 8.

Varing Item Domain Size. Simulated with 10000 users, Figs. 2, 3 show the logarithm of MSE for itemset frequency estimation with different item domain sizes. PrivFIM has a much lower estimation error than the other two solutions when the privacy budget is relatively large (e.g. $\epsilon > 1$). When the itemset cardinality m is fixed, the error reductions grow with the privacy budget ϵ and the domain size d. The main reason is that the item domain size and the itemset cardinality of the transformed frequent item mining problem is exponential times of the original item domain size. Our method is able to reconstruct the itemset frequency directly without such a transformation.

Varing Itemset Cardinality. Simulated with 10000 users, Figs. 2, 3 show the logarithm of MSE for itemsets frequency estimation with different itemset cardinality. Similarly, in all these settings, our proposed mechanism has a much lower estimation error than the other two solutions when the privacy budget is relatively large (e.g. $\epsilon > 1$). When the domain size d is fixed, the error reduction is more evident when the itemset cardinality m is small. The main reason is that the randomized output preserves more information when the itemset cardinality m is small.

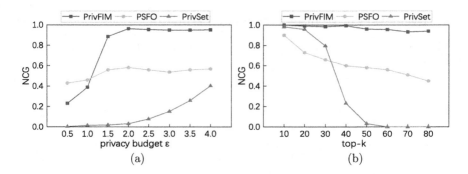

Fig. 4. Results on online.

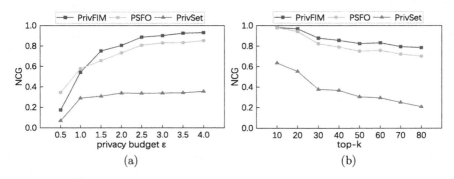

Fig. 5. Results on retail.

4.3   Evaluation of PrivFIM

Figure 4(a) and Fig. 5(a) show the accuracy of top-50 frequent itemsets mining with respect to different privacy budget ϵ. It can be observed that PrivFIM substantially outperforms the other two compared methods. In common sense, the larger the privacy budget, the more accurate the results should be. However, the performance of PSFO and PrivSet do not get improved as the privacy budget increases. PrivFIM gets significantly improved as the privacy budget increases. When ϵ is fixed at 2, Fig. 4(b) and Fig. 5(b) show the accuracy of frequent itemsets mining with different top-k. Our proposed mechanism still works persistently better. On the Online dataset, PrivFIM is able to achieve high utility while the utility of the other two mechanisms drops dramatically, especially when k is greater than 50.

5   Conclusions

In this paper, we present PrivFIM, which is an effective and accurate privacy-preserving mechanism for frequent itemset mining in the local setting. It provides rigorous data privacy protection on the user-side and allows effective statistical analyses on the server-side. Experimental results in both synthetic datasets and real datasets show that PrivFIM outperforms the state-of-the-art solutions. Future research directions include improving the communication cost of our mechanism and extending the proposed mechanism to privacy-preserving frequent sequence mining.

References

1. Frequent itemset mining dataset repository. http://fimi.ua.ac.be/data/
2. Adar, E., Weld, D.S., Bershad, B.N., Gribble, S.D.: Why we search: visualizing and predicting user behavior. In: Proceedings of the 16th International Conference on World Wide Web, pp. 161 170 (2007)
3. Agrawal, R., Srikant, R.: Fast algorithms for mining association rules in large databases. In: Proceedings of 20th International Conference on Very Large Data Bases, pp. 487–499 (1994)
4. Alvim, M.S., Chatzikokolakis, K., Palamidessi, C., Pazii, A.: Metric-based local differential privacy for statistical applications. CoRR (2018). http://arxiv.org/abs/1805.01456
5. Andrés, M.E., Bordenabe, N.E., Chatzikokolakis, K., Palamidessi, C.: Geo-indistinguishability: differential privacy for location-based systems. In: 2013 ACM SIGSAC Conference on Computer and Communications Security, CCS 2013, Berlin, Germany, 4–8 November 2013, pp. 901–914 (2013)
6. Brin, S., Motwani, R., Silverstein, C.: Beyond market baskets: generalizing association rules to correlations. In: SIGMOD 1997, Proceedings ACM SIGMOD International Conference on Management of Data, pp. 265–276 (1997)
7. Ding, B., Kulkarni, J., Yekhanin, S.: Collecting telemetry data privately. In: Advances in Neural Information Processing Systems, pp. 3571–3580 (2017)
8. Duchi, J.C., Jordan, M.I., Wainwright, M.J.: Minimax optimal procedures for locally private estimation. J. Am. Stat. Assoc. **113**(521), 182–201 (2018)
9. Erlingsson, Ú., Pihur, V., Korolova, A.: RAPPOR: randomized aggregatable privacy-preserving ordinal response. In: Proceedings of the 2014 ACM SIGSAC Conference on Computer and Communications Security, pp. 1054–1067. ACM (2014)
10. Järvelin, K., Kekäläinen, J.: Cumulated gain-based evaluation of IR techniques. ACM Trans. Inf. Syst. **20**(4), 422–446 (2002)
11. Li, N., Qardaji, W.H., Su, D., Cao, J.: PrivBasis: frequent itemset mining with differential privacy. In: Proceedings of the VLDB Endowment, vol. 5, no. 11, pp. 1340–1351 (2012)
12. McSherry, F., Talwar, K.: Mechanism design via differential privacy. In: 48th Annual IEEE Symposium on Foundations of Computer Science (FOCS 2007), pp. 94–103 (2007)
13. Su, S., Xu, S., Cheng, X., Li, Z., Yang, F.: Differentially private frequent itemset mining via transaction splitting. In: 32nd IEEE International Conference on Data Engineering, ICDE 2016, pp. 1564–1565 (2016)
14. Wang, N., Xiao, X., Yang, Y., Zhang, Z., Gu, Y., Yu, G.: PrivSuper: a superset-first approach to frequent itemset mining under differential privacy. In: 33rd IEEE International Conference on Data Engineering, ICDE 2017, San Diego, CA, USA, 19–22 April 2017, pp. 809–820 (2017)

15. Wang, S., Huang, L., Nie, Y., Wang, P., Xu, H., Yang, W.: PrivSet: set-valued data analyses with locale differential privacy. In: 2018 IEEE Conference on Computer Communications, INFOCOM 2018, pp. 1088–1096 (2018)
16. Wang, T., Li, N., Jha, S.: Locally differentially private frequent itemset mining. In: 2018 IEEE Symposium on Security and Privacy, SP 2018, Proceedings, San Francisco, California, USA, 21–23 May 2018, pp. 127–143 (2018)

Internet of Vehicles

DAFV: A Unified and Real-Time Framework of Joint Detection and Attributes Recognition for Fast Vehicles

Yifan Chang⬤, Chao Li⬤, Zhiqiang Li⬤, Zhiguo Wang⬤,
and Guangqiang Yin$^{(\boxtimes)}$⬤

University of Electronic Science and Technology of China, Chengdu, China
yfchang@std.uestc.edu.cn, {zgwang,yingq}@uestc.edu.cn

Abstract. In the past decade, with the development of computing equipment and CNN, target detection has made great progress, which has promoted the development of specific target detection. The purpose of vehicle detection is not only to extract the vehicle from a large number of traffic surveillance cameras, but also for some follow-up research, such as the structured storage of vehicle information, which needs to quickly identify the attributes of the vehicle. Based on those demands, we propose a method of joint Detection and Attributes recognition for Fast Vehicles (DAFV). Firstly, we present Feature Rapidly Extract Module (FREM), which is to quickly shrink the feature map size and enhance the runtime efficiency. Secondly, we present Feature Refinement Module (FRM) to increase feature utilization rate and improve the performance. Lastly, we present the Cross-Stage and Multi-Scale (CS-MS) Module to optimize scale-invariant design. Related experiments based on UA-DETRAC dataset proves that DAFV is a feasible and effective method. The DAFV is fast and the speed does not change with the number of vehicles. For 416 × 416 pictures, DAFV can reach 53 FPS with only 775 Mib GPU memory, which can meet the needs of real-time applications.

Keywords: Vehicle detection · Attributes recognition · Real-time

1 Introduction

With the increasing number of vehicles and the proliferation of video surveillance data, intelligent transportation system is becoming more and more important in our life. By collecting real-time road traffic images, video surveillance can provide real and reliable information for road traffic management, assist in research and judgment, effectively improve the efficiency of road management and reduce the work pressure of management. However, the rapid growth of video surveillance data makes it difficult to extract and use effective information. The traditional video surveillance strategy can not meet the daily needs of road managers. Therefore, advanced tools are needed to extract effective information from massive videos and filter redundant and low value information. Therefore, it is very

© Springer Nature Switzerland AG 2021
Z. Liu et al. (Eds.): WASA 2021, LNCS 12938, pp. 353–365, 2021.
https://doi.org/10.1007/978-3-030-86130-8_28

important to detect the vehicles in real-time and identify the vehicle attributes. They can effectively extract useful information from video surveillance.

In the past decade, the methods based on convolutional neural network have been widely used in the field of vehicle detection [7], and the mainstream algorithms can be divided into two types: two-stage detection and one-stage detection. For two-stage detection algorithms, such as R-CNN [1], SPP-Net [2], Fast R-CNN [3] and Faster R-CNN [4], the main idea is to generate a series of sparse candidate boxes by Selective Search [5] or Region Proposal Network (RPN) [6], and then detect them. However, two-stage detection has a large amount of computation and can not meet the requirements of real-time detection, for example, the detection speed of Faster R-CNN is not faster than 12FPS at Titan X. In order to solve this problem, in recent years, people have adopted one-stage algorithm to balance the speed and accuracy, such as YOLOv2 [8], YOLOv3 [9] and SSD [10], whose main idea is to carry out dense sampling in different positions of the picture, using different scales and aspect ratio, then using convolution neural network to extract features, and finally directly performing classification and regression. YOLOv3 [9] uses residual network for feature extraction and is robust to vehicle detection, especially for small vehicle targets. Although YOLOv3 [9] has a good performance in speed and accuracy, it ignores the information exchange between darknet-53 fragments, and it is even difficult to train.

In urban traffic monitoring, extracting different semantic information from the detected vehicles is an interesting and valuable task [31–33], that is, vehicle attribute recognition. Every vehicle on the road has its own special properties: driving direction, its own color, vehicle type, etc. If we can accurately identify the vehicle attributes, it will be helpful for us to find a fixed target vehicle. The previous method is often to design a network for each attribute of the vehicle to identify the single attribute, which makes the utilization of visual information low. There are often strong correlations between vehicle attributes. And vehicle attribute recognition is helpful to vehicle detection, so we think that multi-task learning can be used to jointly train vehicle detection and attribute recognition, and a unified detection and recognition framework model can significantly improve efficiency [15,16].

In this paper, we propose a new convolutional neural network Detection and Attributes for Fast Vehicles (DAFV) for real-time vehicle detection and attribute recognition in traffic system, illustrated in Fig. 1. DAFV consists of three parts: Feature Rapidly Extract Module (FREM), Feature Refinement Module (FRM), Cross-Stage and Multi-Scale (CS-MS). With FREM, DAFV is able to run quickly and efficiently, extracting all the features of the vehicle with less calculation. Then the vehicle features are introduced into FRM, and through the design of the two-stream crossover unit, the utilization rate of the features is improved. It is worth noting that the lower feature map can obtain higher positioning accuracy, and the upper feature map can obtain better recognition accuracy. Therefore, the CS-MS module combines the lower features with the upper features to improve the accuracy of vehicle detection and attribute recognition.

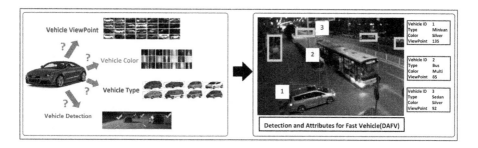

Fig. 1. Illustration of DAFV.

To sum up, the main contributions of our work are as follows:

1. A fast feature extraction module (FREM) is proposed. It reduces the size of the feature graph quickly by using three down-sampling, and uses more convolution kernels of 1×1 size to reduce the computational overhead, thus significantly improving the speed of feature extraction.
2. The Feature Refinement Module (FRM) is proposed. It increases the width of the network by using two double-flow crossing units (TS-DC units) to improve the feature utilization and performance, so as to achieve accurate classification of fine-grained vehicles.
3. A Cross-Stage and Multi-Scale (CS-MS) is proposed. Through the short connection, it introduces the deep features of the detection objects into the shallow features, increases the effective feature number of small targets in the network, and improves the feature quality, so as to obtain more meaningful semantic information and achieve accurate detection of fast vehicles.

Experiments are carried in UA-DETRAC dataset, and the accuracy and speed are compared with the existing methods. For 416×416 images, DAFV can reach 55FPS with 775 Mib memory consumption.

2   Method

The architecture of our proposed DAFV method is illustrated in Fig. 2. The bottom number in the figure represents the size of the current feature map, which helps us analyze the entire architecture of DAFV more directly. The pink area in the figure represents four tasks.

2.1   Feature Rapidly Extract Module

As shown in Fig. 2, FREM consists of a CBM, RE_1 and RE_2. CBM represents a group of basic operations, including convolution, Batch Normalization, and Mish activation functions [11]. Mish activation functions allow better information to penetrate deep into the neural network, resulting in better accuracy and generalization. The main difference between RE_1 and RE_2 is that RE_1 uses maximum pooling, and RE_2 uses a convolution kernel with a step size of 2 and a size of 3×3.

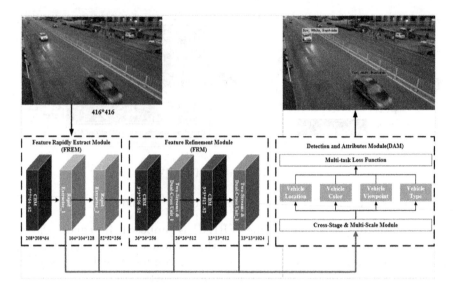

Fig. 2. The architecture of DAFV.

In the RE, there are two ResEXBlocks and three CBMs, which are an important part of DAFV. We add a shortcut connection CBM, after down-sampling, the shallow and deep features were fused through channel fusion, and the number of features were doubled.

Inspired by Inception [12–14] and ResNeXt [34], we redesign the ResNet [17] module (As shown in Fig. 3). There are two obvious differences between ResNeXt [34] and our ResEXBlock:

1. The number of channels. Unlike ResNeXt [34], the previous layer and the last layer have different channel numbers, and our ResEXBlock keeps the number of channels in each layer the same;
2. Activation function. In ResNeXt [34], the activation function is executed after the shortcut. In ResEXBlock, we add an activation function in the last layer before the shortcut. In addition, the activation functions used are different. We use Mish on the last layer.

FREM is designed to make DAFV run quickly and efficiently. We adopt the following two measures to reduce the number of parameters and the calculation cost to achieve the speed of real-time detection.

1. Reduce the size of feature map. In FREM, we use three down-sampling to reduce the size of the feature map to eight times the original size.
2. Use more 1×1 convolution kernels. Large convolution kernels will lead to more computational overhead, so we use more 1×1 convolution kernels to reduce the amount of computation while ensuring accuracy. The convolution of 1×1 adds nonlinear excitation to the learning representation of the previous layer to improve the expressive ability of the network. We have counted the number and proportion of different convolution kernels in the network, As shown in Table 1.

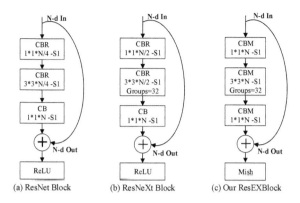

Fig. 3. Comparison of ResNet Block, ResNeXt Block and Our ResEXBlock. CBR represents a group of basic operations, including convolution, Batch Normalization, and ReLu activation functions [18].

Table 1. The numbers of different convolution kernel in FREM.

Kernel size	1×1	3×3	5×5	7×7	Sum
Number	14	5	0	1	20
Rate	72.727%	22.727%	0	4.545%	100%

2.2 Feature Refinement Module

As shown in Fig. 2, FRM contains two CBMs and two Two-Streams & Dual-Cross Units (TS-DC Units). Two of the CBMs have a convolution kernel step size of 2, which are used for down-sampling. Two TS-DC Units are used to extract more detailed features. At the head of FRM, we first add a pooling layer to reduce the size and computational cost of the feature map. At this time, the size of the feature map has been reduced by 16 times.

TS-DC is the core component of FRM and is used to increase the utilization rate of features. We divide the feature (2N dimension) after 1×1 CBL into two parts (A stream and B stream), as shown in the Fig. 5. CBL represents a group of basic operations, including convolution, Batch Normalization, and

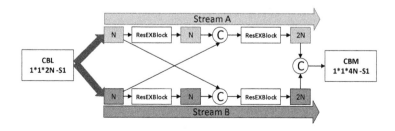

Fig. 4. The architecture of Two Streams & Dual-Cross Unit. Note: The highlighted boxes represent the features dimension.

Linear activation functions. After the first ResEXBlock, we add shortcuts to both streams to make full use of 2N-dimensional features. However, in order to control the feature dimension, we delete the shortcut between the second ResEXBlock groups. After being processed by TS-DC unit, the feature dimension only doubled. Finally, we add a 1×1 convolution to fuse features that have previously experienced channel fusion.

2.3   Detection and Attributes Module

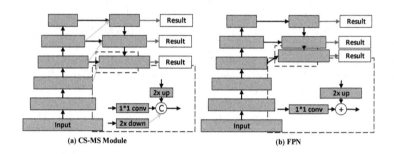

Fig. 5. The architecture of CS-MS Module and FPN.

In order to deal with the variable scale problem of vehicles under the surveillance camera, we have made some improvements on the basis of FPN [6], as shown in the Fig. 5.

1. Add three additional paths from shallow to deep features.
   Shallow features are low-level semantics and contain more location information. This information can be used for the precise positioning of vehicles, because the number of down-sampling is small. In addition, these shallow features also contain some simple information, such as color, texture and shape, which can help DAFV identify the attributes of the vehicle.
2. Change the way of feature fusion from element fusion to channel fusion.
   We sample the top-down features by doubling the spatial resolution (Linear interpolation), and sample the top-down features by convolution kernel with step size of 2 and a size of 3×3. Then we fuse these two types of features with corresponding horizontal (Same spatial resolution) features (Applicable to 1×1 convolution to reduce channel size by half).

2.4   Loss Function

Unlike most common object detection, Because of three attribute recognition tasks and one vehicle detection task, DAFV has own multi-task loss function which can be defined as follows.

$$L_{DAFV} = L_{cls} + L_{det} + L_{conf} \qquad (1)$$

L_{cls} is the attributes recognition loss. We use standard binary cross entropy loss with sigmoid function instead of softmax as L_{cls} for multi-label classification, where I_i^{obj} means if object appears in cell i, I_{ij}^{obj} means that the j_{th} bounding box predictor in cell i is "responsible" for that object, $\hat{p}$ means the prediction, and p means the ground truth. $S \times S$ represents the number of Cells, generally 13×13, 26×26, 52×52, B represents the number of anchors on each CELL, generally 3, and Classes represents the total number of attributes.

$$L_{cls} = \sum_{i=0}^{S \times S} \sum_{j=0}^{B} I_{ij}^{obj} \sum_{c \in class} [\hat{p}_i(c) \log(p_i(c)) + (1 - \hat{p}_i(c)) \log(1 - p_i(c))] \quad (2)$$

L_{det} is the bounding box regression loss, and we use CIOU loss [19] as L_{det} for accurate localization, where pre and gt represent prediction and ground truth, d_{L2} is the Euclidean distance, b^{pre} and b^{gt} denote the central points of predicted box and ground truth box, c is the diagonal length of the smallest enclosing box covering the two boxes, a is a positive trade-off parameter, and v measures the consistency of aspect ratio.

$$L_{det} = \sum_{i=0}^{S \times S} \sum_{j=0}^{B} I_{ij}^{obj}[1 - IoU_{gt}^{pre} + \frac{d_{L2}(b^{pre}, b^{gt})}{c^2} + \alpha v] \quad (3)$$

$$\alpha = \frac{v}{(1 - IoU_{gt}^{pre}) + v} \quad (4)$$

$$v = \frac{4}{\pi^2} \left(\arctan \frac{w^{gt}}{h^{gt}} - \arctan \frac{w^{pre}}{h^{pre}} \right)^2 \quad (5)$$

λ_{noobj} indicates penalty term, it is a penalty factor, usually a small number, with a typical value of 0.1, which is used to reduce the loss of an anchor without objects. All the anchors without objects are negative samples, so the number of negative samples is absolutely dominant. We must reduce their proportion to prevent the positive samples containing objects from being submerged in the negative samples. I_{ij}^{noobj} has opposite meaning form I_{ij}^{obj}, which indicates that the j_{th} bounding box predictor in cell i is "irresponsible" for object, if the box at i, j has no target, its value is 1, otherwise it is 0.

$$L_{conf} = - \sum_{i=0}^{S \times S} \sum_{j=0}^{B} I_{ij}^{obj} \left[\hat{C}_i \log(C_i) + \left(1 - \hat{C}_i\right) \log(1 - C_i) \right]$$
$$- \lambda_{noobj} \sum_{i=0}^{S \times S} \sum_{j=0}^{B} I_{ij}^{noobj} \left[\hat{C}_i \log(C_i) + \left(1 - \hat{C}_i\right) \log(1 - C_i) \right] \quad (6)$$

3 Experiments

In this section, we experiment with our proposed DAFV framework on UA-DETRAC dataset [20]. All the experiments were carried on the Darknet framework, running on Intel Xeon CPU E5-2630 and 8 NVIDIA GTX 1080Ti GPU.

3.1 Experimental Setup

We train DAFV by parameters random initialization, because DAFV is a new CNN, and we cannot fine-tune from other models trained in Imagenet or similar benchmark dataset. During training, we adopt some strategies to accelerate the loss convergence and improve the performance of DAFV. Note that while training, those settings (Mini-Batch size, learning rate) should multiplicate the number of GPUs. Mini-Batch size = 64, 80k iterations. Weights are initialized by Xavier. Biases are initialized to zero; Adam [21] with momentum = 0.949, and weight decay = 0.0005; Learning rate warm up and Multi-Steps decay schedule with an initial learning rate of 0. 005. First 4k iterations ($1k \times 4$GPUs), we use warming up to make the learning rate of DAFV gradually increase from 0 or a very small constant (0.00001) to the initial value, then after 20k iterations, the learning rate is reduced by half to 0.0025. After 55k iterations, it is reduced to 0.00025. After 70k iterations, it is reduced to 0.000025; Label smoothing [22]. A small constant = 0.01; Multi-Scale Training. By every 10 batches, our DAFV randomly chooses a new image spatial resolution. DAFV uses 416×416 as default input resolution; Data augmentation, including Color distortion (Saturation, Exposure, Hue, Mosaic) and Geometric transformation (Random cropping, Random rotating, Horizontal flipping, Resize); We use k++ means to generate anchor box priors on the train dataset. The 9 clusters are (14, 20), (23, 31), (36, 41), (58, 48), (42, 73), (74, 78), (55, 141), (117, 106), (135, 213), and the average IoU between 9 clusters and the ground truth is 0.7546.

3.2 Performance

Ablation Study. To better understand DAFV, we ablate each component or strategy to examine how it affects the final performance. All ablation experiment results are listed in Table 2.

IoU threshold, NMS threshold and Conf threshold are respectively set to 0.5, 0.45 and 0.5 as default. We use COCO-101 point mAP@0.5 (AP50) as default metric, and COCO-101 points mAP@0.75 (AP75) as strict metric [23].

Table 2. Ablation study (AP50).

Model	AP50	GPU memory	FPS
DAFV (Baseline)	60.67	775 MiB	53
Large input size (608 × 608)	61.02	1143 MiB	36
Focal loss	49.78	734 MiB	54
Color related data augment	60.30	775 MiB	53
Extra pathways in CS-MS module	60.42	721 MiB	56
Leaky ReLU	60.24	663 MiB	59

(1) Input size. Larger input size, richer feature map which can affect detection and recognition precision, especially for small vehicles. We use a maximum input size (608 × 608) to evaluate DAFV, and the AP just increase about 0.3%–0.4%.

(2) Focal Loss. As discussed in Section C, we apply Focal Loss to reduce the effect of class imbalance. And we trained DAFV with Focal Loss several times, even we changed some hyperparameters and strategies, but it still does not work as expected and drops the mAP seriously.

(3) Color related data augment. As our works involve vehicle color recognition, so we train DAFV without those methods (Saturation, Exposure, Hue, Mosaic) to check how they affect mAP.

(4) Feature fusion. We add some extra pathways which are marked red in the CS-MS Module as shown in Fig. 5. We trained DAFV without those extra pathways to show the effect of this design.

(5) Different activation function. In DAFV, we mainly use Mish instead of ReLU or Leaky ReLU, so we replace Mish with Leaky ReLU and retrained DAFV, while another factors keep the same.

Evaluation of DAFV. We evaluate DAFV on the test dataset. As can be seen in Table 3 and 4, from AP50 to AP75, the mAP of DAFV drops by 8.98%, the mAP of Sunny and Cloudy drop by 5.21% and 8.32%, the mAP of Rainy and Night drop by 7.62% and 9.38%. We run our model five times on test dataset and calculate the average FPS.

Table 3. The performance of DAFV (AP50).

Condition	mAP	P	R	Average IOU	F1-score	FPS
Test dataset	60.67	72	68	62.68	70	53
Sunny	53.36	77	70	66.26	73	
Cloudy	61.09	73	70	62.03	72	
Rainy	71.83	70	77	58.50	73	
Night	41.57	68	53	56.12	60	

Table 4. The performance of DAFV (AP75).

Condition	mAP	P	R	Average IOU	F1-score
Test dataset	51.69 (−8.98)	67	63	59.14	65
Sunny	48.24 (−5.21)	69	64	60.64	66
Cloudy	52.77 (−8.32)	71	65	59.77	68
Rainy	64.21 (−7.62)	68	71	54.21	69
Night	32.19 (−9.38)	58	48	49.67	53

Since no relevant works are found, comparisons with other methods could not be carried out. So we use three tables (Table 5, 6 and 7) to show the specific performance of DAFV.

Table 5. The performance of vehicle type recognition.

	Sedan	SUV	Van	Taxi	Bus	Truck
AP 50	73.83	52.09	73.45	83.09	85.41	57.37
AP 75	64.89	45.93	55.94	70.58	67.71	44.82

Table 6. The performance of vehicle viewpoint recognition.

	Front	Rear	Side	Front-side	Rear-side
AP 50	50.59	33.24	68.74	71.74	70.85
AP 75	42.17	27.72	60.83	64.15	66.74

Table 7. The performance of vehicle color recognition.

	White	Silver	Black	Gray	Blue	Red	Brown	Green	Yellow	Multi	Beige
AP 50	74.40	73.51	76.85	48.97	41.86	81.66	21.94	15.35	73.42	80.41	26.02
AP 75	65.40	66.50	68.28	39.19	32.28	74.43	17.85	9.74	64.87	66.15	21.01

Those tables above demonstrate that our methods for joint detection and attributes for fast vehicles are feasible and can be performed in real-time speed. But they also illustrate a problem that being sensitive to illumination, occlusion and truncation with a few instances, makes those classes (Such as Brown, Green, Beige, Rear) hard to distinguish, so their performance is a little bit low.

In order to visually show what our works can do in practical use, we choose some qualitative images to show the results of our DAFV. Figure 6 shows some qualitative results on the test dataset that we divided.

Evaluation of Vehicle Detection. In order to evaluate the performance of vehicle detection, we delete the task of attribute identification and only train the vehicle detection task. We continue to train on the UA-DETRAC Dataset. And compare with existing vehicle detection, as shown in Fig. 7. The accuracy of DAFV was 5.42% lower than the current best accuracy (SpotNet) and 2.1% lower than the second best (SSD_VDIG). But our FPS is 53, 33 higher than YOLOv2's. Therefore, our DAFV has good application value and can be applied to real-time vehicle detection on the road.

As shown in Table 8, compared with other models, our DAFV model can achieve overall 81.38% mAP and 53 FPS, and its comprehensive performance is far better than that of other models, and can still perform well in complex road conditions or bad weather.

Fig. 6. Qualitative results of vehicle detection and attribute recognition.

Table 8. Comparison of DAFV results with other models.

Model	Overall	FPS	Easy	Medium	Hard	Cloudy	Night	Rainy	Sunny
YOLOv2 [8]	57.72	20	83.28	62.25	42.44	57.97	64.53	47.84	69.75
Faster R-CNN [4]	58.45	11.11	82.75	63.05	44.25	66.29	69.85	45.16	62.34
EB [24]	67.96	10	89.65	73.12	53.64	72.42	73.93	53.40	83.73
R-FCN [25]	69.87	6	93.32	75.67	54.31	74.38	75.09	56.21	84.08
HAT [26]	78.64	3.6	93.44	83.09	68.04	86.27	78.00	67.97	88.78
DCN [27]	79.05	8	93.85	85.07	69.00	85.55	82.38	68.95	89.08
FG-BR-Net [28]	79.96	10	93.49	83.60	70.78	87.36	78.42	70.50	89.89
ME-Net [29]	80.76	14	94.56	85.90	69.72	87.19	80.68	71.06	89.74
SSD_VDIG [30]	82.68	2	94.60	89.71	70.65	89.81	83.02	73.35	88.11
SpotNet [31]	86.80	14	97.58	92.57	76.58	89.38	89.53	80.93	91.42
Ours (DAFV)	**81.38**	**53**	**92.90**	**88.12**	**75.99**	**88.62**	**88.77**	**75.46**	**80.54**

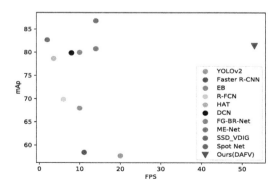

Fig. 7. The effects of DAFV and other models are compared in the UA-DETRAC dataset.

4 Conclusion

Those three attributes of vehicle: color, type and viewpoint are not strictly independent. The rich correlation information contained in these attributes cannot be ignored, and they together play an important role in detection task. So we propose to integrate attribute recognition tasks into the detection task, which is called DAFV.

The DAFV, a feasible method that can detect vehicles and recognize attributes directly from images/videos in a single stage (or in one evaluation), is a single CNN, and it can be trained end-to-end, unlike two-stage methods. Meanwhile it is fast, achieving 53 FPS with 775 MiB GPU memory cost for 416×416 images, which is important for ADAS, real-time surveillance and some practical use.

References

1. Girshick, R., Donahue, J., Darrell, T., et al.: Rich feature hierarchies for accurate object detection and semantic segmentation. In: IEEE Conference on Computer Vision and Pattern Recognition (CVPR), pp. 580–587 (2014)
2. He, K., Zhang, X., Ren, S.: Spatial pyramid pooling in deep convolutional networks for visual recognition. IEEE Trans. Pattern Anal. Mach. Intell. **37**(9), 1904–1916 (2015)
3. Girshick, R.: Fast R-CNN. In: IEEE International Conference on Computer Vision (ICCV), pp. 1440–1448 (2015)
4. Ren, S., He, K., Girshick, R., et al.: Faster R-CNN: towards real-time object detection with region proposal networks. IEEE Trans. Pattern Anal. Mach. Intell. **39**(6), 1137–1149 (2016)
5. Uijlings, J.R.R., Sande, K.E.A.V.D., Gevers, T., et al.: Selective search for object recognition. Int. J. Comput. Vis. **104**, 154–171 (2013). https://doi.org/10.1007/s11263-013-0620-5
6. Lin, T.Y., Dollár, P., Girshick, R., et al.: Feature pyramid networks for object detection. In: IEEE Conference on Computer Vision and Pattern Recognition (CVPR), pp. 936–944 (2017)
7. Xiong, Z., Xu, H., Li, W., et al.: Multi-source adversarial sample attack on autonomous vehicles. IEEE Trans. Veh. Technol. **70**(3), 2822–2835 (2021)
8. Redmon, J., Farhadi, A.: YOLO9000: better, faster, stronger. In: IEEE Conference on Computer Vision and Pattern Recognition (CVPR), pp. 6517–6525 (2017)
9. Redmon, J., Farhadi, A.: YOLOv3: an incremental improvement. In: IEEE Conference on Computer Vision and Pattern Recognition (CVPR) (2018)
10. Liu, W., et al.: SSD: single shot multibox detector. In: Leibe, Bastian, Matas, Jiri, Sebe, Nicu, Welling, Max (eds.) ECCV 2016. LNCS, vol. 9905, pp. 21–37. Springer, Cham (2016). https://doi.org/10.1007/978-3-319-46448-0_2
11. Misra, D.: Mish: a self regularized non-monotonic neural activation function (2019)
12. Szegedy, C., Liu, W., Jia, Y., et al.: Going deeper with convolutions. In: IEEE Conference on Computer Vision and Pattern Recognition (CVPR), pp. 1–9 (2015)
13. Loffe, S., Szegedy, C.: Batch normalization: accelerating deep network training by reducing internal covariate shift (2015)
14. Szegedy, C., Loffe, S., Vanhoucke, V., et al.: Inception-v4, inception-ResNet and the impact of residual connections on learning. In: AAAI Conference on Artificial Intelligence (2016)

15. Wang, J., Cai, Z., Yu, J.: Achieving personalized k-anonymity-based content privacy for autonomous vehicles in CPS. IEEE Trans. Ind. Inform. **16**(6), 4242–4251 (2020)
16. Xiong, Z., Cai, Z., Han, Q., et al.: ADGAN: protect your location privacy in camera data of auto-driving vehicles. IEEE Trans. Ind. Inform. **17**(9), 6200–6210 (2020)
17. He, K., Zhang, X., Ren, S., et al.: Deep residual learning for image recognition. In: IEEE Conference on Computer Vision and Pattern Recognition (CVPR), pp. 770–778 (2016)
18. Krizhevsky, A., Sutskever, I., Hinton, G.: ImageNet classification with deep convolutional neural networks. In: Neural Information Processing System Foundation (NIPS), pp. 1097–1105 (2012)
19. Zheng, Z., Wang, P., Liu, W., et al.: Distance-IoU loss: faster and better learning for bounding box regression. In: AAAI Conference on Artificial Intelligence, pp. 12993–13000 (2020)
20. Wen, L., Du, D., Cai, Z., et al.: UA-DETRAC: a new benchmark and protocol for multi-object detection and tracking. Comput. Vis. Image Underst. **93**, 102907 (2015)
21. Kingma, D., Ba, J.: Adam: a method for stochastic optimization. In: International Conference on Learning Representations (2014)
22. Szegedy, C., Vanhoucke, V., Loffe, S.: Rethinking the inception architecture for computer vision (2016)
23. Lin, Tsung-Yi., et al.: Microsoft COCO: common objects in context. In: Fleet, David, Pajdla, Tomas, Schiele, Bernt, Tuytelaars, Tinne (eds.) ECCV 2014. LNCS, vol. 8693, pp. 740–755. Springer, Cham (2014). https://doi.org/10.1007/978-3-319-10602-1_48
24. Wang, L., Lu, Y., Wang, H., et al.: Evolving boxes for fast vehicle detection, pp. 1135–1140 (2020)
25. Dai, J., Li, Y., He, K., et al.: R-FCN: object detection via region-based fully convolutional networks(2016)
26. Wu, Shuzhe, Kan, Meina, Shan, Shiguang, Chen, Xilin: Hierarchical attention for part-aware face detection. Int. J. Comput. Vis. **127**(6), 560–578 (2019). https://doi.org/10.1007/s11263-019-01157-5
27. Cao, W.M., Chen, X.J.: Deformable convolutional networks tracker. DEStech Trans. Comput. Sci. Eng. (2019)
28. Fu, Z., Chen, Y., Yong, H., et al.: Foreground gating and background refining network for surveillance object detection. IEEE Trans. Image Process. **28**(12), 6077–6090 (2019)
29. Yang, Y., Zhang, G., Katabi, D., et al.: ME-Net: towards effective adversarial robustness with matrix estimation (2019)
30. Kim, K., Kim, P., Chung, Y., et al.: Multi-scale detector for accurate vehicle detection in traffic surveillance data. IEEE Access **7**, 78311–78319 (2019)
31. Perreault, H., Bilodeau, G. A., Saunier, N., et al.: SpotNet: self-attention multi-task network for object detection, pp. 230–237 (2020)
32. Cai, Z., Zheng, X.: A private and efficient mechanism for data uploading in smart cyber-physical systems. IEEE Trans. Netw. Sci. Eng. **7**(2), 766–775 (2018)
33. Cai, Z., Zheng, X., Yu, J.: A differential-private framework for urban traffic flows estimation via taxi companies. IEEE Trans. Ind. Inform. **15**(12), 6492–6499 (2019)
34. Xie, S., Girshick, R., Dollár, P., et al.: Aggregated residual transformations for deep neural networks. In: IEEE Conference on Computer Vision and Pattern Recognition (CVPR), pp. 5987–5995(2017)

Vehicular Path Planning for Balancing Traffic Congestion Cost and Fog Computing Reward: A Routing Game Approach

Man Xiong, Changyan Yi, and Kun Zhu[✉]

Nanjing University of Aeronautics and Astronautics, Nanjing 211100, China
{xiongman,changyan.yi,zhukun}@nuaa.edu.cn

Abstract. With the rapid development of Internet-of-Vehicle (IoV) technologies (such as autonomousdriving and electrical vehicles), more and more smart vehicles are emerging on the road, resulting in not only traffic congestion, but also a waste of resource. In this paper, we study a novel vehicular path planning scheme, which aims to well balance each vehicle's traffic congestion cost (incurred by the travelling delay between its origin and destination) and fog computing reward (obtained from providing its redundant computing resource to road-side units). Different from the existing work, we consider that vehicles with different driving speeds contribute differently to the traffic congestion (e.g., slower vehicles may lead to more severe traffic congestion), and at the same time they can act as mobile fog nodes while driving in exchange for certain rewards. To characterize the competition among multiple vehicles due to their strategic path planning and investigate the inherent tradeoff between the congestion cost and computing reward for each individual, an atomic pure strategy routing game is formulated. Then, we analyze the equilibrium performance and propose an efficient algorithm to derive the corresponding solution. Theoretical and simulation results examine the feasibility of our proposed scheme, and demonstrate its superiority over the counterparts.

Keywords: Vehicular path planning · Vehicular fog computing · Traffic congestion · Routing game · Nash equilibrium

1 Introduction

The recent development of the Internet of Things (IoT) and smart vehicle technologies have led to the emergence of a new concept called Internet of Vehicle (IoV) [2], which is envisioned to make smart transportation services more convenient. Meanwhile, smart vehicles equipped with on-board computers or on-board equipment units in IoV have abundant computing resource, and such resource may be wasted or underutilized when vehicles are running light-duty applications. Therefore, given a certain reward, a smart vehicle may be willing to provide its redundant computing resource to road-side units (RSUs) by acting as a

© Springer Nature Switzerland AG 2021
Z. Liu et al. (Eds.): WASA 2021, LNCS 12938, pp. 366–377, 2021.
https://doi.org/10.1007/978-3-030-86130-8_29

mobile fog computing [13–15] node. To build an efficient transportation system with a joint consideration of the traffic congestion and fog computing capability, one may notice that path planning is a natural and fundamental issue.

Due to its importance, path planning has gained substantial research attentions. Recent studies in this area include path planning with the consideration of driver characteristics [16,17] and path planning after natural disasters [10]. However, most of existing work focused on optimal path selection for a single vehicle only, while ignoring the traffic congestion cost caused by the mutual impacts of different vehicles' path selections. Although some recent papers [3,4] have started to investigate this problem in path planning, they commonly ignored a fact that vehicles with different speeds may contribute differently to the traffic congestion, and they did not consider that vehicles may serve as mobile fog nodes to provide computing resource during their trips.

In fact, a careful study of multi-vehicle path planning with a joint consideration of traffic congestion cost and fog computing reward is imperative and crucial because of the following reasons. 1) There will be a huge number of smart vehicles in the future, and the exploitation of their underutilized vehicular computing resource can largely expand the network computing capacity. However, when acting as a mobile fog node, each vehicle may prefer a longer travel time for obtaining more reward, while this may also lead to a higher traffic congestion cost. Thus, an optimal path planning scheme should be designed by jointly taking these two into account. 2) Owing to the high device intelligence, smart vehicles may behave strategically and selfishly in their path selections, causing severe traffic congestion if they are not well coordinated. This motivates an equilibrium study of the path planning involving multiple vehicles.

Nevertheless, addressing all aforementioned features in multi-vehicle path planning raises additional challenges. 1) It is very difficult to find an equilibrium optimal path planning for all vehicles because the path selections among vehicles are mutually influencing with heterogenous impacts. 2) We are required to design a new routing algorithm for balancing the tradeoff between the congestion cost of each vehicle's selected path and the reward obtained from providing fog computing resource, which cannot be easily solved by the conventional shortest-path searching algorithm.

To tackle these challenges and fill the gap in the literature, a routing game approach is proposed in this paper to produce the optimal path planning among multi-vehicles, considering the traffic congestion cost (incurred by the travelling delay between its origin and destination) and fog computing reward (obtained from providing its redundant computing resource to RSUs). In our considered model, vehicles that are about to make their path selection decisions form a group. They communicate with each other's route choices through the information center, and choose their own optimal path based on other vehicles' path selections. Even if the vehicle knows the path selections of other vehicles, it does not know which vehicle a certain path selection belongs to, so that the privacy issue may not be a primary concern. For each individual vehicle, it will select the path that maximizes its utility consisting of the traffic congestion cost and fog computing reward. Since road resource (i.e., the capacity of the road) is limited and shared, there is a competitive relationship among vehicles. Therefore, we propose a routing game to obtain the equilibrium optimal path for each vehicle. Then we prove the existence of the equilibrium solution of the game, design an efficient algorithm, and analyze the corresponding performance.

The main contributions of this paper are summarized in the following.

1. Considering the objective of maximizing the utility of each individual vehicle, consisting of the traffic congestion cost and fog computing reward, a pure-strategy atomic game is proposed.
2. We prove the existence of the game equilibrium, and propose an algorithm for vehicular path planning. Then, we theoretically show that the algorithm can converge to the equilibrium solution in a finite number of iterations.
3. Numerical simulations are conducted to examine all theoretical analyses and demonstrate the superiorities of the proposed algorithms over the counter-parts.

The rest of the paper is organized as follows. Section 2 presents the system model and problem formulation for multi-vehicle path planning considering both the traffic congestion cost and fog computing reward. In Sect. 3, we define the Nash equilibrium of the game and then propose a distributed algorithm to find the equilibrium solution of the game. Simulation results and analysis are given in Sect. 4, followed by conclusions in Sect. 5.

2   System Model and Problem Formulation

In this section, the network model of multi-vehicle path planning for fog computing enabled connected vehicle system is first described. Then, with the objective of jointly optimizing the traffic congestion cost and fog computing reward of each individual vehicle in path planning, a pure strategy atomic game is formulated.

2.1   System Model

We consider an IoV system consisting of a number of smart vehicles and RSUs, as illustrated in Fig. 1. The transportation network is divided into disjoint road segments. Each disjoint segment is regarded as a link l. Each smart vehicle has its own origin and destination, and they can choose any one of the several potential paths to reach the destination, while each path can be seen as a combination of links (disjoint segments). Notice that since the travel time of a certain vehicle is affected by the total number of vehicles on the link of its selected path, as more vehicles will cause more serious traffic congestion, the traffic congestion cost (incurred by the travelling delay between its origin and destination) of each vehicle depends on not only its own path selection, but also the path selections of other vehicles.

Meanwhile, we consider that each smart vehicle can act as a mobile fog node to provide its redundant computing resource to the RSUs during its trip, in exchange for some rewards. Therefore, besides taking into account the traffic congestion cost, vehicles may determine their path selections based on fog computing rewards they can obtain.

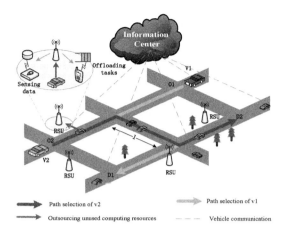

Fig. 1. An illustration of fog computing enabled connected vehicle systems.

2.2   Problem Formulation

The transportation network can be modelled as a directed graph $G(N, A)$, where N represents the set of nodes (intersections) and A stands for the set of arcs (links). Denote the number of arcs by $L = |A|$ and the total number of nodes by $n = |N|$. Suppose that there are m smart vehicles, labeled by $v = 1, \cdots, m$, in a coordinated group. As discussed above, these vehicles are on the way and about to make route decisions (i.e., path selections) within a short time period. Each vehicle v has a specific origin-destination (OD) pair given by $(o_v, d_v) \in N \times N$ with a set of k_v potential paths connecting them, denoted by $P_v = \{p_v^1, \cdots, p_v^{k_v}\}$, where p_v^i is the ith potential path of vehicle v. We consider that two pieces of real time traffic information are available to all vehicles: (i) the real-time traffic congestion caused by vehicles of each link; (ii) real-time summary information on the tentative path selections of other vehicles. Each vehicles is able to determine its self-preferred path by predicting the suffered congestion cost and the obtained fog computing reward on each link l with information (i) and (ii).

Let f_l be the congestion condition of link $l \in A$ caused by all vehicles' route choices/path selections. Particularly, denote each vehicle v's path selection by $p_v \in P_v, \forall v = 1, 2, \cdots, m$. Different from the existing work which commonly assumed that $f_l, l \in A$, is a function of the number of vehicles choosing link l in their path selections (meaning that vehicles contribute equally to the traffic congestion) [4], we define that the contribution of each vehicle v to the traffic congestion is denoted by σ_v. This describes the fact in reality that vehicles with different driving speeds may result in different impacts to the traffic congestion (e.g., slower vehicles may led to more severe traffic congestion). Then the congestion condition of link $l \in A$ can be defined as

$$f_l(p_1, p_2, \cdots, p_m) = \sum_{v=1}^{m} \sigma_v^l, \tag{1}$$

where

$$\sigma_v^l = \begin{cases} \sigma_v, & \text{if } l \in p_v; \\ 0, & \text{otherwise.} \end{cases} \tag{2}$$

Since the congestion that each vehicle v experiences on each link $l \in p_v$ depends on not only its own path selection but also the other vehicles', we denote the congestion (measured by the travel time) of vehicle v on link l by $C_{v,l}(f_l(p_v, p_{-v}))$, where p_{-v} represents the path selection of vehicles other than vehicle v. We assume that $C_{v,l}(\cdot)$ follows the well-known Bureau of Public Roads (BPR) [1] function for estimating the travel time of US federal highways, i.e.,

$$C_{v,l}(f_l(p_v, p_{-v})) = t_l(1 + \alpha(f_l/c_l)^\beta), \tag{3}$$

where t_l is link l's free flow time (i.e., road travel time when there is no congestion on link l), and c_l stands for the capacity of link l. Obviously, $C_{v,l}$ increases as f_l increases, but decreases with increasing c_l. In addition, α and β are the given positive scalars, especially, β is normally greater than 3 to cater the essence of traffic congestion. Generally speaking, the value of α and β are suggested to be 0.15 and 4 respectively [3].

Thus, the travel time of vehicle v on path p_v, given the path selections of all other vehicles, is formulated as

$$T_v(p_v, p_{-v}) = \sum_{l \in p_v} C_{v,l}(f_l(p_v, p_{-v})). \tag{4}$$

Accordingly, the congestion cost of vehicle v selecting the path p_v is defined as

$$F_v = T_v \cdot E, \tag{5}$$

where E is the energy consumption cost of vehicles per unit of time.

Besides the induced congestion cost, we consider that vehicles can also obtain rewards from providing their redundant computing resources to RSUs along their trips. Define that the available computing resources provided by different vehicles are heterogenous, denoted by r_v. Then the reward of choosing link l by vehicle v can be calculated as

$$R_{v,l} = r_v \cdot q \cdot C_{v,l}(f_l(p_v, p_{-v})), \tag{6}$$

where q is the unit computing resource price, and $C_{v,l}(f_l)$ is the travel time of vehicle v on link l as shown in (3). It can be observed the reward R_v, l increases with both the offered computing resource r_v and the travel time of link l.

Based on (6), the reward that can be obtained by vehicle v during its entire journey is

$$R_v = \sum_{l \in p_v} R_{v,l}. \tag{7}$$

By jointly taking into account the congestion cost and fog computing reward, the utility function of each vehicle v can be written as

$$U_v = R_v - F_v. \tag{8}$$

Clearly, there is a tradeoff in maximizing U_v for each vehicle v. Specifically, the longer the vehicle v is congested, the lager traffic cost F_v it suffers. However, a larger travel time also brings a higher reward R_v to vehicle v. Therefore, each vehicle will try its best to balance such tradeoff so as to reduce its congestion cost while increasing the reward it obtained.

Substitute (5) and (7) into (8) and then we get

$$\begin{aligned}
U_v &= R_v - F_v \\
&= \sum_{l \in p_v} r_v q C_{v,l}(f_l(p_v, p_{-v})) - E \sum_{l \in p_v} C_{v,l}(f_l(p_v, p_{-v})).
\end{aligned} \tag{9}$$

Recall that $f_l(p_v, p_{-v}) = \sum_{v=1}^{m} \sigma_v$ according to (1). Thus, by some simple mathematical manipulations, we have

$$U_v = E \sum_{l \in p_v} (\frac{r_v q}{E} - 1) C_{v,l}(\sum_{v \in \{1, \cdots, m\} : l \in p_v} \sigma_v). \tag{10}$$

It is worth nothing that vehicles which can offer more computing resources have the potential to earn more fog computing rewards. As a result, to exploit such benefits, these vehicles (i.e., vehicle with larger values of r_v) may tend to drive slower, leading to a greater traffic congestion. This implies that the contribution of each vehicle v to the traffic congestion increases with r_v. To match this fact, we define the contribution of each vehicle v to the traffic congestion in a form by

$$\sigma_v = (\frac{r_v q - E}{E}), \tag{11}$$

which essentially characterizes the unit gain of fog computing reward over the congestion cost. Then, U_v in (10) can be rewritten as

$$U_v = E \sum_{l \in p_v} \sigma_v C_{v,l}(\sum_{v \in \{1, \cdots, m\} : l \in p_v} \sigma_v). \tag{12}$$

Consider that vehicles that will make their path selection decisions in a short time period form a communication group, in which they negotiate future path selections by proposing and re-proposing their tentative path selections according to the aggregated path selection information from other vehicles. As a smart and rational individual, each vehicle $v = 1, 2, \cdots, m$ will try to maximize its utility function U_v by selecting an optimal path given all other vehicles' path selections. Obviously, the change in path selection of vehicle v may affect the congestion condition of link l. Since the link capacity are limited (i.e., each road can only support a limited number of vehicles) and shared, this may further trigger frequent changes in path planning of all vehicles for maximizing their utilities. Such path selection process in which vehicles compete for road resources can by formulated by a routing game. To be more specific, the game is a pure-strategy atomic routing game, which can be formally defined as

$$\mathcal{G} = \{\mathcal{V}, \mathcal{P}, \{U_v(p_v)\}_{v \in \mathcal{V}}\}, \tag{13}$$

where smart vehicles in set $\mathcal{V} = 1, 2, \cdots, m$ act as players in the game; $\mathcal{P}$ signifies the strategy set of vehicles, i.e., $\{P_v\}_{v=1}^m$; and $U_v(p_v)$ is the utility of vehicle v choosing any path $p_v \in P_v$.

Note that different from the traditional congestion game, solving the formulated game problem $\mathcal{G}$ is very challenging because (i) each vehicle can provide fog computing resource to obtain a reward, resulting in one more decision variable in our problem than a traditional congestion game, which make it hard to find an equilibrium solution; (ii) compared to general congestion games, we consider that different vehicles have different contributions to the traffic congestion, which will cause the congestion degree of each vehicle on a same link to be different. In the following section, to tackle these difficulties, we will propose a distributed algorithm to derive the corresponding solution (i.e., the optimal path selection of each individual vehicle).

3   Equilibrium Solution of the Routing Game

In this section, we first define the equilibrium of the formulated routing game $\mathcal{G}$, and then prove its existence. After that, an efficient algorithm is proposed to find the equilibrium solution followed by corresponding theoretical analysis.

3.1   Nash Equilibrium and Its Existence

The solution of the routing game $\mathcal{G}$ is an equilibrium path selection, i.e., a combination of all vehicles' path selections $p^* \triangleq \{p_v^*\}_{v=1}^m$, in which for all vehicles $v \in \mathcal{V}$, we have

$$U_v(p_v^*, p_{-v}^*) \geq U_v(p_v, p_{-v}^*), \forall p_v \in P_v. \tag{14}$$

When this equilibrium is reached, all vehicles do not have the motivation to deviate from their current path selections unilaterally.

Theorem 1. *There are always an equilibrium path selection p^* existing for the routing game $\mathcal{G}$.*

Proof. Define the function $H : \mathcal{P} \to \mathbb{R}$ as

$$H(\mathbf{p}) = E \sum_{l \in A} \sum_{v \in \mathcal{V}: l \in p_w} \sigma_v C_{v,l} (\sum_{w \in \{1, \cdots, v\}: l \in p_w} \sigma_w), \tag{15}$$

where $\mathbf{p} \in \mathcal{P}$ is a strategy profile of the path selection by all vehicles. The function H corresponds to an approximation of the integral over the utility function.

Notice that $f_l \leq c_l$ in function $C_{v,l}(\cdot)$ as the congestion of the link never exceeds its maximum capacity and β in function $C_{v,l}(\cdot)$ is small so that f_l approaches c_l in heavy traffics, meaning that $(f_l/c_l)^{\beta}$ can be approximated to be f_l/c_l in function $C_{v,l}(\cdot)$. Then, we expand $C_{v,l}(\cdot)$ in function H and get

$$
\begin{aligned}
H(\mathbf{p}) &= E\sum_{l \in A}(t_l f_l(\mathbf{p}) + \sum_{v,w \in \mathcal{V}:l \in p_v \cap p_w, v \leq w} \frac{\alpha t_l}{c_l}\sigma_v\sigma_w) \\
&= E\sum_{l \in A}(t_l f_l(\mathbf{p}) + \frac{1}{2}\sum_{v,w \in \mathcal{V}:l \in p_v \cap p_w} \frac{\alpha t_l}{c_l}\sigma_v\sigma_w + \frac{1}{2}\sum_{v \in \mathcal{V}:l \in p_v} \frac{\alpha t_l}{c_l}\sigma_v^2) \\
&= \frac{E}{2}\sum_{l \in A}(C_{v,l}(f_l(\mathbf{p})) + C_{v,l}(0))f_l(\mathbf{p}) + \frac{E}{2}\sum_{v \in V}\sum_{l \in p_v}(C_{v,l}(\sigma_v) - C_{v,l}(0))\sigma_v.
\end{aligned}
$$
(16)

Let us define $\mathbf{p}_{-v}$ be the path selection of all vehicles except vehicle v. Then, by replacing the path selection of vehicle $v \in \mathcal{V}$ from p_v to p_v' in function H, we have

$$
\begin{aligned}
H(p_v', \mathbf{p}_{-v}) &= H(\mathbf{p}) + E\sigma_v\sum_{l \in p_v' \backslash p_v}C_{v,l}(f_l(p_v', \mathbf{p}_{-v})) - E\sigma_v\sum_{l \in p_v \backslash p_v'}C_{v,l}(f_l(\mathbf{p})) \\
&= H(\mathbf{p}) + U_v(p_v', \mathbf{p}_{-v}) - U_v(\mathbf{p}).
\end{aligned}
$$
(17)

This indicates that function H is a potential function, and thus the formulated routing game $\mathcal{G}$ is a potential game [9]. Knowing that the potential game has a pure Nash Equilibrium [11], the equilibrium path selection p^* in game $\mathcal{G}$ can be expressed as $p^* \triangleq \{p_v^*\}_{v=1}^m$.

3.2   Optimal Path Selection Algorithm

In order to find the equilibrium optimal path selection, an optimal path selection algorithm (OPLSA) is proposed, in which vehicles select the optimal path locally based on the given other vehicles' path selections. This process continues until an equilibrium path decision is reached among all vehicles, i.e., all vehicles do not have the motivation to further change their selected paths.

Compared with algorithms generally used to solve congestion games, the proposed OPLSA is not to find the shortest path, but to find the path with the largest utility value. As the path planning we studied considers both the traffic congestion cost and fog computing reward, the calculation of U_v needs to consider the combination of both. Therefore, we modify the general shortest path algorithm from selecting the shortest path according to the traffic congestion cost to choosing the path which maximizes the utility. In the process to find a new path, only one vehicle is enable to select its optimal path at each iteration, given that all other vehicles' path selections are known and fixed. After a new path selection is made, this information will be instantaneously shared with other vehicles. Detailed steps of the proposed OPLSA is summarized in Algorithm 1.

In the procedure of OPLSA, all vehicles can receive other vehicles' path decisions from the RSUs or the nearby vehicles and then they can make their decisions based on such information. The algorithm is executed until there is no vehicle changing its path selection. In each iteration, each vehicle chooses its locally optimal path. The codes from line 6 to 12 in Algorithm 1 are used to find the optimal path for each vehicle and to determine whether the path selection changes. Then the codes from 14 to 17 determine whether the algorithm has reached the termination condition. If all vehicles do not change their path selections in m consecutive iterations, the algorithm finally terminates.

Algorithm 1. Optimal Path Selection Algorithm (OPLSA)

1: Input: Transportation network with traffic conditions and computing resource owned by vehicles.
2: Output: Equilibrium path selection for each vehicle.
3: Initialize: Each vehicle chooses a random path and then calculate σ_v.
4: **while** $balance < 1$ **do**
5:     Set a flag $flag$ to judge whether equilibrium of the game is reached;
6:     **for all** $i = 1 : v$ **do**
7:         Find the shortest path for each vehicle $sp\{i\}$ with the largest utility value.
8:         **if** $sp\{i\}$ hasn't been changed **then**
9:             $flag(i) = 0$;
10:        **else**
11:            $flag(i) = 1$;
12:        **end if**
13:    **end for**
14:    **if** $sum(flag) == 0$ **then**
15:        $balance = balance + 1$;
16:    **else**
17:        $balance = 0$.
18:    **end if**
19: **end while**

The advantages of the proposed OPLSA are three-folds. First, as will be shown in the next subsection, the algorithm has a good convergence performance, which is very important in practical implementations. Second, it dose not require any additional computational cost, because the algorithm is not executed at the information center, but it is distributed to each vehicle. Third, since computational complexity of the algorithm does not increase exponentially as the number of vehicles increases, OPLSA also has a good scalability.

3.3   Convergence of the OPLSA

To show that the proposed OPLSA algorithm has a good convergence performance, here we first give its termination condition.

Lemma 1. *If all vehicles do not change their path selections in m consecutive iterations, then the proposed OPLSA terminates and all vehicles end up by taking their equilibrium path selection.*

Proof. This proof is omitted due to the page limit.

The vehicles' strategies which are best-reply response strategies in our algorithm lead to the NE, and this has already been proved in [12]. The main idea of proving the convergence is to show that the value of the potential function increases as the algorithm proceeds.

Theorem 2. *The proposed algorithm converges to an equilibrium path selection in a finite number of iterations with the termination condition in Lemma 1.*

Proof. This proof is omitted due to the page limit.

4   Simulation Results and Analysis

In this section, numerical simulations are conducted to evaluate the performance of the proposed OPLSA algorithm. All experimental results are obtained by taking averages over 100 runs with various system parameters.

4.1   Simulation Settings

Consider a MATLAB-based simulation environment for the transportation network of Sioux Falls city [3], which includes 24 nodes and 76 links. We use the BPR function in (3) to calculate the link travel time. t_l in the BPR function is the free flow link travel time and it is randomly distributed between 2 ro 5. Meanwhile, c_l stands for the link capacity, the size of which can be adjusted [3]. According to [6], the computing resource r_v of each vehicle randomly chosen from 40 to 60 MHz. In addition, following the conventions in [5,7], we set the price of computing resource per unit time $q = 0.2$ and the energy consumption cost per unit of time $E = 47.6$. Note that some parameters may be varied for different evaluation purposes.

4.2   Performance Evaluations

Figure 2 examines the convergence of the proposed OPLSA for solving the formulated routing game $\mathcal{G}$ with the number of vehicles $m = 400$. From this figure, we can observe that the proposed algorithm converges very quickly. Consistent to the theoretical analyses in Sect. 3, the average utility value. Moreover, notice that when the fog computing reward dominates the traffic congestion cost, each vehicle is willing to select the path that maximizes the utility value.

In Fig. 3, the superiority of applying the proposed OPLSA compared to the existing independent routing mechanism (IRM) [8] is demonstrated. In IRM, each vehicle only considers to maximize the individual utility in its own path

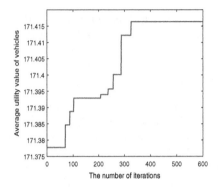

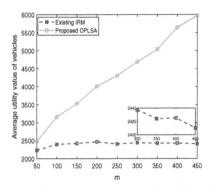

Fig. 2. Convergence of OPLSA.   **Fig. 3.** Performance of OPLSA.

planning regardless of other vehicles' path selections. This figure shows that, since a larger number of vehicles implies more congested traffic and leads to more fog computing reward, the utility value of each vehicle increases as m increases for the proposed OPLSA. However, since a larger m resulting in much more severe traffic congestion for the existing IRM due to the lack of multi-vehicle coordination, the average utility value of vehicles increases slightly or even decreases. This indicates that the OPLSA can effectively alleviate traffic congestion compared to the existing IRM, and thus reduce the traffic congestion cost. One can also see that such superiority becomes much more obvious when the number of vehicles is relatively large, and this implies that the proposed OPLSA is more suitable to be applied in scenarios with bad traffic conditions.

5   Conclusion

In this paper, by jointly considering the traffic congestion cost and fog computing reward, a novel path planning scheme is studied. The novelties of this work mainly rely on two aspects: i) a practical transportation system with vehicles in different speeds contributing differently to the traffic congestion is modeled; ii) vehicles are enabled with fog computing capabilities and can offer computing resources in exchange for certain rewards. An atomic pure-strategy routing game is formulated to describe the competitive relationship among vehicles in strategic path planning, and an efficient algorithm is designed to find the corresponding equilibrium. Theoretical analyses and simulation results show the convergence of the proposed algorithm, and show that it can alleviate the traffic congestion and improve the average utility of all vehicles compared to the counterparts.

Acknowledgement. This work was supported by the National Natural Science Foundation of China (No. 62071230, No. 62002164).

References

1. BPR. Traffic Assignment Manual: Bureau of Public Roads, U.S. Department of Commerce (1964)
2. Ang, L., Seng, K.P., Ijemaru, G.K., Zungeru, A.M.: Deployment of IoV for smart cities: applications, architecture, and challenges. IEEE Access **7**, 6473–6492 (2019)
3. Du, L., Chen, S., Han, L.: Coordinated online in-vehicle navigation guidance based on routing game theory. Transp. Res. Rec. J. Transp. Res. Board **2497**, 106–116 (2015)
4. Du, L., Chen, S., Han, L.: Coordinated online in-vehicle routing balancing user optimality and system optimality through information perturbation. Transp. Res. Part B Methodol. **79**, 121–133 (2015)
5. Guo, D., et al.: A vehicle path planning method based on a dynamic traffic network that considers fuel consumption and emissions. Sci. Total Environ. **663**, 935–943 (2019)
6. Madan, N., Malik, A.W., Rahman, A.U., Ravana, S.D.: On-demand resource provisioning for vehicular networks using flying fog. Veh. Commun. **25**, 100252 (2020)
7. Mahmud, R., Srirama, S., Ramamohanarao, K., Buyya, R.: Profit-aware application placement for integrated fog-cloud computing environments. J. Parallel Distrib. Comput. **135**, 177–190 (2020)
8. Minciardi, R., Gaetani, F.: A decentralized optimal control scheme for route guidance in urban road networks. In: ITSC 2001. 2001 IEEE Intelligent Transportation Systems. Proceedings (Cat. No. 01TH8585), pp. 1195–1199 (2001)
9. Monderer, D., Shapley, L.: Potential games. Games Econ. Behav. **14**, 124–143 (1996)
10. Muhuri, S., Das, D., Chakraborty, S.: An automated game theoretic approach for cooperative road traffic management in disaster. In: 2017 IEEE International Symposium on Nanoelectronic and Information Systems (iNIS), pp. 145–150 (2017)
11. Rosenthal, R.W.: A class of games possessing pure-strategy nash equilibria. Int. J. Game Theory **2**(1), 65–67 (1973)
12. Scutari, G., Barbarossa, S., Palomar, D.P.: Potential games: a framework for vector power control problems with coupled constraints. In: 2006 IEEE International Conference on Acoustics Speech and Signal Processing Proceedings, vol. 4, pp. IV–IV (2006)
13. Yi, C.: A queueing game based management framework for fog computing with strategic computing speed control. IEEE Trans. Mob. Comput. (2020)
14. Yi, C., Cai, J., Su, Z.: A multi-user mobile computation offloading and transmission scheduling mechanism for delay-sensitive applications. IEEE Trans. Mob. Comput. **19**(1), 29–43 (2019)
15. Yi, C., Huang, S., Cai, J.: Joint resource allocation for device-to-device communication assisted fog computing. IEEE Trans. Mob. Comput. (2019)
16. Zhang, K., Wang, J., Chen, N., Cao, M., Yin, G.: Design of a cooperative v2v trajectory-planning algorithm for vehicles driven on a winding road with consideration of human drivers' characteristics. IEEE Access **7**, 131135–131147 (2019)
17. Zhang, K., Wang, J., Chen, N., Yin, G.: A non-cooperative trajectory-planning method for vehicles with consideration of drivers' characteristics. In: 2017 Chinese Automation Congress (CAC), pp. 5956–5961 (2017)

Distributed Collaborative Anomaly Detection for Trusted Digital Twin Vehicular Edge Networks

Jiawen Liu[1], Shuaipeng Zhang[1], Hong Liu[1(✉)], and Yan Zhang[2(✉)]

[1] School of Software Engineering, East China Normal University, Shanghai, China
hliu@sei.ecnu.edu.cn
[2] The Department of Informatics, University of Oslo, Oslo, Norway
yanzhang@ieee.org

Abstract. The vehicular networks are vulnerable to cyber security attacks due to the vehicles' large attack surface. Anomaly detection is an effective means to deal with this kind of attack. Due to the vehicle's limited computation resources, the vehicular edge network (VEN) has been proposed provide additional computing power while meeting the demand of low latency. However, the time-space limitation of edge computing prevents the vehicle data from being fully utilized. To solve this problem, a digital twin vehicular edge networks (DITVEN) is proposed. The distributed trust evaluation is established based on the trust chain transitivity and aggregation for edge computing units and digital twins to ensure the credibility of digital twins. The local reachability density and outlier factor are introduced for the time awareness anomaly detection. The curl and divergence based elements are utilized to achieve the space awareness anomaly detection. The mutual trust evaluation and anomaly detection is implemented for performance analysis, which indicates that the proposed scheme is suitable for digital twin vehicular applications.

Keywords: Anomaly detection · Digital twin · Trust evaluation

1 Introduction

Vehicles are becoming more and more connected and intelligent with the advances in 5G and big data technologies. However, due to the vehicles' large attack surface, cybersecurity attacks can cause life-threatening situations, which highlights the need for efficient security monitoring and intrusion detection systems. Given the vehicles' limited computing resources, dedicated server is needed to complete the computation work. High real-time performance, as a key guarantee for vehicular security, makes the traditional cloud computing, which can cause high latency and instability, unsuitable for IoV's stable services [1,2]. Trying to solve this problem, some studies have proposed Vehicular Edge Network (VEN) by combining vehicular network with edge computing. By deploying edge computing units at the edge of the network, the vehicles' data can be processed

© Springer Nature Switzerland AG 2021
Z. Liu et al. (Eds.): WASA 2021, LNCS 12938, pp. 378–389, 2021.
https://doi.org/10.1007/978-3-030-86130-8_30

and analyzed at the edge of the network, which brings it the strengths of low latency and bandwidth cost saving.

Digital twin, as a technology that creates a real-time connected virtual object for a physical entity through machine learning and physical modeling, was initially designed for industrial manufacturing to realize intelligent manufacturing, and is gaining more and more attention to its application in smart cities [3–5]. Bring digital twin to VEN can break through the limitations of current vehicular networks by constructing a virtual intelligent network space, which can make the network architecture become time-space unconstrained. Each node (vehicle) in the network will be created a corresponding digital twin, and the information interaction between vehicles can be transferred from the physical world to the digital world through the digital twin in the digital world. In this way, the limitation of time and space of traditional vehicle-mounted edge network can be eliminated, and the potential value of data can be played to a greater extent.

The current anomaly detection mechanisms focus on the vehicle data in a short time and the specific vehicle instead of majority of vehicles [6,7]. The attacker would act as the normal vehicle temporarily which could be found out based on the history data stored in the digital twin. If the behavior of specific vehicle is observed alone, its negative effect on other vehicles might be ignored. In this work, the authors propose a time-space awareness anomaly detection method, which is based on the time and space awareness. Thereinto, time awareness is to detect the anomalies according to the vehicle history data; space awareness is to detect the anomalies according to the transmission and driving conditions.

Ensuring the credibility of the anomaly detection model is also critical to driving safety, which makes the trust assessment necessary. Data collected from vehicles for digital twin creation is transmitted to the edge computing unit through the open wireless communication network, which makes the data vulnerable to wireless attacks [8]. For example, the adversary may deliberately steal and modify the vehicles' data that the vehicle sends to the edge computing units for creating or updating the its digital twin. Once these data are maliciously modified, the digital twin cannot reflect the real state of the physical entity, which will affect the accuracy of anomaly detection results. At the same time, the attacker may modify the feedback, causing the vehicle to make wrong decisions, which pose a huge threat to road safety. It is important to conduct trust assessment to ensure the credibility of anomaly detection model.

The main contributions of this paper are as follows.

- An architecture of trusted digital twin vehicular edge networks (DITVEN) is proposed, by integrating digital twin with VEN to establish an efficient mapping between vehicles and cyber systems. To the best of our knowledge, the novel architecture in this article is the first in the literature to combine digital twin with TVEN to solve the limitations of time and space.
- The trust evaluation is established for edge computing units and digital twins to ensure the credibility of the anomaly detection model. The digital twins are separated into different groups with dynamic trust values. The edge

computing units evaluate digital twins from the sight of group and digital twin respectively. The digital twins also evaluate each other, in which trust chain transitivity and aggregation are designed.

– The anomaly detection is achieved with both time awareness and space awareness. The time awareness refers to the observation towards the history data of vehicles. The space awareness refers to the observation towards the whole picture of the vehicles on specific roads.

The remainder of this paper is organized as follows. Section 2 outlines the related work. Section 3 presents the system model including various components used in the solution. Section 4 describes the proposed solution. The implementation and performance analysis are discussed in Sect. 5. Finally, Sect. 6 summarizes the conclusion.

2   Related Work

V. Reddy *et al.* [9] proposed a similarity model to mitigate badmouthing and collusion attacks. The impact of malicious recommendations was removed upon trust computation. H. Choi *et al.* [10] proposed the hierarchical trust chain framework for secured and reliable internet of things (IoT) service provisioning, which includes local trust chains and global distributed trust chain for scalable and trusted services. There into, time slot based delayed verification algorithm and the blockchain configuration method are proposed for trust analysis. However, the approaches above rely on the centralized certificate authority directly. If the authorities is manipulated by the attackers, the trust management system is faced with risk and the vehicles might be in danger.

A new architecture of digital twin enabled industrial IoT is also considered, where digital twins captured the characteristics of industrial devices to assist federated learning [11]. However, the digital twin network mentioned above do not consider the security of networks. The digital twins contain full information, so the safety of digital network is important.

In the approach we proposed, we applied the digital twins towards the vehicular network. The following methods are taken to ensure the safety of digital twin vehicular network. We design the distributed trust evaluation towards digital twins, which does not rely on centralized authorities only. The mutual evaluation is introduced. Meanwhile, we also take the time and space awareness anomaly detection to classify the malicious digital twins.

3   System Model

Figure 1 illustrates the architecture of DITVEN, which is divided into two layers: the physical edge layer and the digital twin layer.

The physical layer consists of two main types of entities: physical vehicles (PVs) and edge computing units. PVs are the main data source of the system.

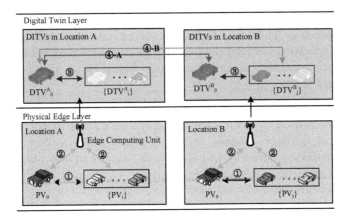

Fig. 1. The system model.

The following manipulation is based on the sensor data from the on-board device. The vehicles contain ultrasonic sensors, long-range radar, laser scanner, corner radar, Front camera, roof antenna, rear radar, and central driver assistance controller. The digital twins are updated with the latest vehicle sensor data such as location, velocity, and acceleration. Edge computing units act as the container of the digital twins within the road, which distributes the computation and storage resource among the digital twins. During the trust evaluation, the edge computing units play the role as the authorities to evaluate the vehicles on basis of the contact between vehicles and edge computing units. The edge computing units would generate the score towards to digital twins group and digital twins only, and give the trust assessment as to some digital twins. The computing units filters out the trustworthy entities for the following process. The edge computing unit take the responsibility of constructing time series to detect anomalies from the time dimension and constructing the real-time road model to detect anomalies from the space dimension.

Digital twins are the dynamic copies of the real entities. The introduction of digital twins reduces the transmission cost between the vehicles and edge computing units. Previously, the vehicle needs to upload the sensor data to the edge computing units through intermediates, and the edge computing units need to distribute the commands among the vehicles through intermediates, which leads to transmission latency. In the proposed scheme, the interconnection between digital twins and edge computing units is within the edge computing units, which make improvements on the efficiency. The digital twins are synchronized with the real entities through intermediates. Digital twin is used for the following purposes. First, the inner structure of the digital twin includes the power module, transmission module, and user experience module. The inner structure constructs the copies of these modules, and the related parameters are monitored to detect the inner faults. Second, the digital twin is taken as an integrated entity and focus on the properties from a holistic point of view such as location, velocity, and acceleration. Third, the digital twin keeps connections with others such as the synchronization between the real entities and the digital twins through an edge computing unit, the transmission among digital twins, and the connection between digital twins and edge server.

Figure 1 shows the four main cooperative contexts.

- *Cooperative context* ① : Although physical autonomous driving vehicles are equipped with sensors, radars, and other equipment to collect surrounding data, these devices have physical limitations, which can only obtain the environmental conditions within a certain range but cannot obtain the traffic conditions of the road beyond a certain distance. On the highway, if the self-driving car makes a wrong decision, it will cause other vehicles to make a wrong decision, which poses a great threat to traffic safety. This requires vehicles to interact with each other to ensure road safety and improve traffic efficiency.

- *Cooperative context* ② : refers to the cooperation between PVs the edge computing unit. In our architecture, the creation and maintenance of the digital twin of PVs is completed by the edge computing units. When a PV is driving on the road, its own state information needs to be uploaded to the nearby edge computing unit. After evaluating the reliability of the vehicle and verifying the data, the edge computing unit updates the status of its digital twin. At the same time, the feedback information of the digital twin is also fed back to the vehicle by the edge computing unit.

- *Cooperative context* ③ : Depending on the digital twin type of interaction, the cooperation between physical vehicles and digital twin vehicles can be divided into two types: cooperation between the physical vehicle and the unique digital twin and cooperation between the physical vehicle and the temporary digital twin. The unique digital twin updates its autonomous driving decision model based on data collected by the physical vehicle as it runs, and pushes the model to the physical vehicle when it is idle.

- *Cooperative context* ④ : Cooperation between digital twins is also divided into two types, namely cooperation between temporary (④-A) and cooperation between unique digital twins (④-B). When a vehicle enters a certain edge network region for the first time, the edge computing node of the region will request its unique digital twin, and the collected data of the vehicle will update its digital twin. The updated digital twin acts as a temporary digital twin for the vehicle in this edge area.

Trust of digital twins is evaluated from two dimensions. The edge server will evaluate the digital twins as the authorities from the reached transmission rate. The digital twins could be grouped as to the different brands. Within the group, the digital twins obtain mutual evaluations. The digital twins within the group could construct mutual evaluation with the part of the trust values. The trust value towards digital twins decides whether the digital twins could be involved in the following process.

- *Time awareness anomaly detection:* The time awareness anomaly detection ensures safety from the time dimension. During the time cycle, each point is equipped with a series of historical digital twin data, which constructs the time series. The digital twins which deviate with the prediction from the time series would be labeled as suspicious objects.
- *Space awareness anomaly detection:* The digital twins within the road could construct a whole picture. Two metrics are taken into the picture. From the view of the physical point, the location and velocity describe the physical vector field. From the view of the transmission point, the location and the transmission path describe the transmission vector field. Divergence and curl could be introduced to make judgments toward the whole picture of the road condition. For example, the curl describes the driving conditions of vehicles within the road to judge whether the vehicles are entering into a correct way and the divergence describes the transmission conditions of vehicles within the road to judge whether there are black holes which could be labeled as attackers.

4 Trust Evaluation and Anomaly Detection

4.1 Trust Evaluation Towards Digital Twins

The edge computing unit monitors the digital twin network in real-time. The edge computing units take snapshots of the network, and computes two types of trust values as shown in Fig. 2. The edge server calculates the authority trust value. The authority trust value is based on the interaction between the edge server and the digital twins. The edge server calculates the mutual trust value. Digital twins evaluate each other, and the trust chain is established within the digital twin group for the trust paths aggregation. The main notations are listed in Table 1.

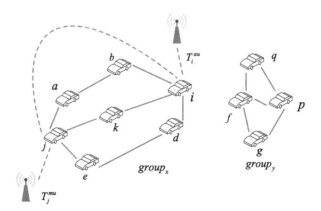

Fig. 2. The trust evaluation towards digital twin vehicles.

Table 1. Notations

Notation	Description
DT_*	The digital twin of V_*
$group_*$	The digital twin group *
$score_g, score_p$	The group score, the personal score
F_*	The normal behavior rate
T_*^{au}	The authority trust towards DT_*
f_c	The calculation method defined to connect the edges
f_a	The calculation method defined to aggregate the paths
T_*^{mu}	The trust evaluation based on the mutual evaluation
η_{data_*}	The weight of $data_*$
$k - ditance(o)$	The distance from the point o to the point the kth far from the point o
$d(p, o)$	The distance from the point o to the point p
lrd	The local reachability density
LOF	The local outlier factor

The digital twins are separated according to these criteria: official, public service, and civilian. The civilian digital twins could be separated according to different brands. $Group = [group_1, group_2, \ldots, group_n]$, $group_i$ represent the particular digital twin group. The trust evaluation from the authorities towards digital twins lies in group score and personal score.

$$score_* = mean(F_* + \omega \cdot score_*^h) \tag{1}$$

Here, $*$ refers to $group$ and $person$. $score_g^h$ and $score_p^h$ refer to the last group score and personal score. $score_g^h$ and $score_p^h$ are initialized manually. $\omega = exp(\frac{\alpha}{t_c - t_0})$ refers to the time decay factor, that the historical score is decreasing over time, and α refers to the rate adjustment factor. The group score and personal score are influenced by the digital twins' behaviors and decreases as time goes.

F_g and F_p refer to the normal behavior rate, that the digital twin interacts with the authorities. The authorities would judge the normal and abnormal interactions, high normal behavior rate leads to high score as a reward, low normal behavior rate leads to low score as a punishment. The trust evaluation based on authorities T_j^{au} is composed of group scores and personal scores.

Within the digital twin group, $DT_i, DT_j \in group_x$, the digital twins have their own trust evaluation method. The trust evaluation $opinion_{ij}$ from DT_i to DT_j is assigned with (t_{ij}, c_{ij}), t_{ij} refers to the trust value and c_{ij} refers to confidence. The digital twins within the same group construct a graph. From

DT_i to DT_j, there are many paths such as $(v_0 = DT_i, v_1, ..., v_n = DT_j)$, and (v_i, v_{i+1}) is labeled with t, c.

There are two calculation methods are defined as f_c and f_a.

- f_c is applied to connect the trust chain. The trust evaluation from DT_i to DT_j is labeled with trust value t_{ij} and confidence c_{ij}. The trust evaluation from DT_j to DT_k is labeled with trust value t_{jk} and confidence c_{jk}. f_c connects these two trust evaluations. The trust evaluation from DT_i to DT_k is labeled with trust value $t_{ik} = t_{ij}t_{jk}$ and confidence $c_{ik} = c_{ij}c_{jk}$.
- f_a is applied to aggregate the trust chains. The trust chain from DT_i to DT_j has two paths $chain_x, chain_y$ labeled with trust value and confidence. The aggregation result is $chain_z$. The trust chain with high confidence decides the trust value of $chain_z$. If the confidences of $chain_x, chain_y$ are the same, the $chain_z$ is labeled with the higher trust of the $chain_x, chain_y$. Thus, mutual evaluations are obtained within the digital twin group. These evaluations are aggregated according to the T^{au} of the digital twins. The highly trusted DT is assigned with high weight.

$$T_j^{mu} = \sum_{k \in group_x} \frac{T_k^{au}}{\sum_{d \in group_x} T_d^{au}} eval_{kj} \tag{2}$$

$$H(T_j^*) = -T_j^* ln(T_j^*) - (1 - T_j^*) ln(1 - T_j^*) \tag{3}$$

Here, $*$ refers to au(authorities) and mu(mutual). Information entropy could reflect the degree of disorder of information. Therefore, the weights can be modified according to the difference between T_j^{au} and T_j^{mu} to realize adaptive weight distribution, so as to make full use of effective information to solve the limitation of empirical weight.

$$\omega_* = \frac{e^{-H(T_j^*)}}{e^{-H(T_j^{au})} + e^{-H(T_j^{mu})}} \tag{4}$$

$$T_j^c = \omega_{au} T_j^{au} + \omega_{mu} T_j^{mu} \tag{5}$$

Here, $*$ refers to $group$ and $person$. The authorities judge the digital twins according to the T_j^c. The threshold η is manually set. The digital twins labeled abnormal entities would be coped with further.

4.2   Time-Space Awareness Anomaly Detection

The vehicles upload data such as velocity, location and acceleration to the digital twin, denoted as $\{x_i\}$, thereinto x_0 refers to velocity, x_1 refers to acceleration, and so on. Actually, the data varies with the time, which constructs the time series. As to the time series, the Local Outlier Factor is taken to determine whether there are anomalies within the time series.

$$reach - distance_k(p, o) = max\{k - distance(o), d(p, o)\} \tag{6}$$

Algorithm 1: The trust evaluation towards digital twins

1: // The authority trust evaluation;
2: **for** each DT_i within the road **do**
3:     calculate T_i^{au};
4: **end for**
5: // The mutual trust evaluation;
6: **for** each DT_j within the road **do**
7:     $DT_j \in group_x$;
8:     **for** each $DT_i \in group_x$ within the road **do**
9:         **while** *path* between DT_i and DT_j **do**
10:             $f_c((v_0, v_1), (v_1, v_2), \ldots, (v_{n-1}, v_n))$;
11:         **end while**
12:         $f_a(path_0, path_1, \ldots, path_n)$;
13:         get $eval_{ij}$;
14:     **end for**
15:     calculate T_j^{mu};
16: **end for**
17: // The comprehensive trust evaluation;
18: **for** each DT_i within the road **do**
19:     calculate ω_{au}, ω_{mu};
20:     calculate T_i^c;
21: **end for**

$k - distance(o)$ refers to the distance from one point to another point with the kth far from the point o. $d(p, o)$ refers to the distance from the point o to the point p. As for the k nearest points from the point o, the $reach - distance_k(p, o)$ refers to $k - distance(o)$. As for the other points, the $reach - distance_k(p, o)$ refers to $d(p, o)$.

$$lrd_k(p) = \frac{|N_k(p)|}{\sum_{o \in N_k(p)} reach - distance_k(p, o)} \quad (7)$$

lrd refers to the local reachability density. $N_k(p)$ refers to the k nearest from the point p. The $|N_k(p)|$ is actually equal to k. $\sum_{o \in N_k(p)} reach - distance_k(p, o)$ implies that if the point o is the neighbor to the point p, but the point p is not the neighbor to the point o, the $lrd_k(p)$ gets smaller, which means the point p is anomaly point.

$$LOF_k(p) = \frac{\sum_{o \in N_k(p)} \frac{lrd(o)}{lrd(p)}}{|N_k(p)|} \quad (8)$$

LOF refers to the local outlier factor, and $LOF_k(p)$ gets larger, which means that the neighbor of point p is a dense point, and the point p might be an anomaly point. The particular road is taken as the object of analysis from two dimensions in order to detect anomalies within the road.

- First, the vector field is constructed in the way of transmission. That is, the vector come from the source of transmission to the destination of the transmission, noted as v_t. Several areas are taken within the road randomly, and calculate the divergence $div = \frac{\oint v_t\, dl}{\triangle S}$ of these areas. If there are any area which div is under zero to a large extent, the area might contain an attacker that implement the black hole attack.

- Second, the vector field is constructed in the way of physics. That is, the vector starts from the location of the vehicle, and the direction and value is consistent with the velocity, noted as v_p. Several areas are taken within the road to calculate the curl $curl = \frac{\oint v_p\, dl}{\triangle C}$. Under normal circumstances, the absolute value of value is large. If there are any vehicles deliver the wrong motion data, the $curl$ would be close to an anomalous value.

The local outlier factor is applied for the time series of the multiple-dimensional variable. Two parameters curl and divergence which describe the driving and transmission condition hold the vehicles within the road as a whole picture and generate the anomaly alarms.

5   Implementation and Performance Analysis

The trust evaluation is separated into two parts: the trust evaluation from authorities and the trust evaluation based on the mutual evaluation. The trust evaluation from authority is influenced by F and ω, the normal behavior rate and time decay factor.

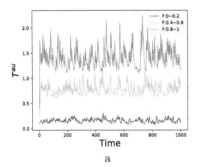
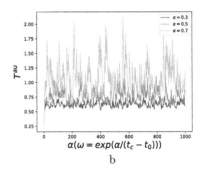

a   b

Fig. 3. The influence of F (a) and ω (b) towards trust value.

The influence of F towards trust value would be explored. The time range is set as 0–1000. The record time is randomly set. The F is set as 0–0.2, 0.4–0.6, and 0.8–1. From Fig. 3-a, the DT with a high normal behavior rate is labeled with a high trust value.

The influence of ω towards trust value should be considered. The time range is set as 0–1000. The record time is randomly set. The F is set as 0.4–0.6. From Fig. 3-b, the DT with a high time decay factor is labeled with a high trust value.

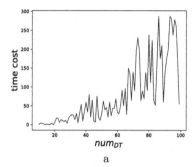 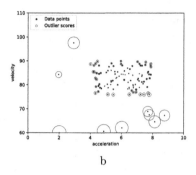

a   b

Fig. 4. a) The time cost varying with the number of digital twins; b) The LOF anomaly detection.

From Fig. 4-a, the trust evaluation based on mutual evaluation is time-consuming. The time cost varying with the number of digital twins would be explored. In detail, the trust evaluation between DT_i and DT_j is based on the chain connection and chain aggregation. The former is involved with multiple f_c calculations. The latter is involved with f_a calculation.

The multi-dimension variable is taken as the object, such as acceleration and velocity. LOF is taken to detect the anomalies. As the Fig. 4-b describes, the radius of the point is proportional to the local outlier factor. Around the corner of the figure, there are several outliers which might be anomalies.

Experiments are performed for trust evaluation and anomaly detection. For the trust evaluation, the performance analysis shows that the behavior rate and time decay rate have a positive effect on the trust value, and the relation curve of time cost and the digital twin number is obtained. For the anomaly detection, the proposed anomaly detection successfully identifies the potential anomalies.

6   Conclusions

This work proposed a distributed collaborative anomaly detection scheme for digital twin vehicular networks. Digital twins are used for real-time scheduling within the vehicular network. The trust evaluation is based on trust from authorities and mutual evaluation, which filter out the trustworthy digital twins. The edge computing unit generates the score towards the vehicle group and the vehicle only, based on the contact history between the edge server and vehicles. The mutual evaluation is conducted based on the existing assessment within the vehicle group. The comprehensive trust assessment filters out trustworthy vehicles and providing the sensor data for anomaly detection. The edge computing unit detect anomalies from time and space dimensions. The performance analysis shows that the behavior rate and time decay rate have a positive effect on the trust value, and the relation curve of time cost and the digital twin number is obtained.

Acknowledgment. This work is funded by the National Key R&D Program of China (2020AAA0107800), National Natural Science Foundation of China (62072184). This work is partially supported by the Project of Science and Technology Commitment of Shanghai (19511103602, 20511106002).

References

1. Zhang, K., Zhu, Y., Maharjan, S., Zhang, Y.: Edge intelligence and blockchain empowered 5G beyond for the industrial internet of things. IEEE Network **33**(5), 12–19 (2019)
2. Kang, J., Lin, D., Bertino, E., Tonguz, O.: From autonomous vehicles to vehicular clouds: challenges of management, security and dependability. In: 2019 IEEE 39th International Conference on Distributed Computing Systems (ICDCS), pp. 1730–1741. IEEE (2019)
3. Ríos, J., Mas, F., Oliva, M., Hernandez-Matias, J.: Framework to support the aircraft digital counterpart concept with an industrial design view. Int. J. Agile Syst. Manag. **9**, 212–231 (2016)
4. Rassõlkin, A., Vaimann, T., Kallaste, A., Kuts, V.: Digital twin for propulsion drive of autonomous electric vehicle. In: 2019 IEEE 60th International Scientific Conference on Power and Electrical Engineering of Riga Technical University (RTUCON), pp. 1–4 (2019)
5. Marti, S., Giuli, T.J., Lai, K., Baker, M.: Mitigating routing misbehavior in mobile ad hoc networks, pp. 255–265 (2000)
6. Wang, Y., Ming Chia, D.W., Ha, Y.: Vulnerability of deep learning model based anomaly detection in vehicle network. In: 2020 IEEE 63rd International Midwest Symposium on Circuits and Systems (MWSCAS), pp. 293–296. IEEE (2020)
7. Bose, B., Dutta, J., Ghosh, S., Pramanick, P., Roy, S.: D&RSense: detection of driving patterns and road anomalies. In: 2018 3rd International Conference On Internet of Things: Smart Innovation and Usages (IoT-SIU), pp. 1–7. IEEE (2018)
8. Sassi, M.S.H., Fourati, L.C.: Investigation on deep learning methods for privacy and security challenges of cognitive IoV. In: 2020 International Wireless Communications and Mobile Computing (IWCMC), pp. 714–720. IEEE (2020)
9. Reddy, V.B., Negi, A., Venkataraman, S., Venkataraman, V.R.: A similarity based trust model to mitigate badmouthing attacks in internet of things (IoT). In: 2019 IEEE 5th World Forum on Internet of Things (WF-IoT), pp. 278–282 (2019)
10. Choi, H., Lee, G.M., Rhee, W.: Hierarchical trust chain framework for IoT services. In: 2019 Eleventh International Conference on Ubiquitous and Future Networks (ICUFN), pp. 710–712 (2019)
11. Sun, W., Lei, S., Wang, L., Liu, Z., Zhang, Y.: Adaptive federated learning and digital twin for industrial internet of things. IEEE Trans. Industr. Inform. **17**(8), 5605–5614 (2020)

Optimal Resource Allocation
in Time-Varying Vehicular Networks
with Delay Constraints

Xiying Fan[1]([✉])[ID] and Bin Fu[2][ID]

[1] University of Science and Technology Beijing, Beijing, China
xiyingfan@ustb.edu.cn
[2] University of Texas Rio Grande Valley, Edinburg, USA

Abstract. To provide data transmission with high quality of service, we aim to adaptively allocate network resources in vehicular networks. Considering the temporal property of the dynamic networks, we propose the concept of delay-constrained temporal varying graphs based on the concept of time-varying graphs. By adding the delay factor to the original graph model, it is more general and can be applied to a wide range of delay-tolerant applications. On this basis, we formulate the resource allocation problem, then apply the technique of Lagrange duality to decompose the problem and obtain the optimal transmission rate and transmit power. Accordingly, an efficient resource allocation scheme is proposed, which can obtain the exact solutions. We evaluate the proposed algorithm using realistic vehicular mobility traces. Simulation results show the effectiveness of the proposed scheme in terms of data delivery ratio and network throughput.

Keywords: VANETs · Resource allocation · Time-varying graph · Delay-constrained

1 Introduction

As an important infrastructure of Intelligent Transportation System (ITS), vehicular networks (VANETs) mainly provide services such as safety management, traffic control and entertainments, which requires real-time data transmission with reliability [1]. However, the rapid movement of vehicles will lead to highly time-varying network topology, which will cause increased communication delay and reduced transmission ratio. This brings a variety of challenges to the data transmission in VANETs [2,3]. Meanwhile, computing-intensive and time-sensitive vehicular applications focus on either energy consumption or service delay of application requests, thus improve the Quality-of-Service (QoS) of the network. However, the network resources, such as computing and communication resources, are limited. Due to the limited network resources, in delay-tolerant applications, we might need to make a tradeoff between factors such as the transmission rate and end-to-end delay, to fully exploit the available network resources. Therefore, how to adaptively jointly allocate network resources in the network is the key to providing data transmission with better QoS [4]. As it is

© Springer Nature Switzerland AG 2021
Z. Liu et al. (Eds.): WASA 2021, LNCS 12938, pp. 390–401, 2021.
https://doi.org/10.1007/978-3-030-86130-8_31

mentioned, VANETs are highly dynamic, which will cause that the communication links between vehicles change rapidly, such that the resource allocation is a challenging issue [5].

To portray the characteristics of VANETs, existing studies mainly model the network topology as different types of graphs utilizing graph theory [6]. In this way, graph theory can be applied to solve various problems in dynamic networks. Currently, there are mainly three approaches to model the topology of vehicular networks, including instantaneous, aggregated, and time-varying. The instantaneous approaches consider the network topology at a time constant, however, the temporal characteristic is not included. The aggregated approaches study the topology graph in a time interval, which can be treated as a static network. As it is known, the links of VANETs change rapidly, which results that the links might only exist in only a small duration other than the considered aggregated period. Therefore, we characterize the VANETs as time-varying graphs, depends on which the network behavior will be evaluated.

In this context, we study the efficient resource allocation in time-varying vehicular networks. We formulate the resource allocation problem, and apply the technique of Lagrange duality to solve the problem.

The main contributions of our work are described as follows.

- We propose the concept of delay-constrained temporal varying graphs based on the concept of time-varying graph, which is more general and can be applied to a wide range of delay-tolerant applications.
- We formulate the resource allocation problem, and apply the technique of Lagrange duality to decompose the problem. Then, we propose an efficient resource allocation algorithm for the time-varying VANETs.
- We evaluate the proposed scheme through simulations and show the effectiveness of the proposed method in terms of data delivery ratio and network throughput.

The remainder of the paper is organized as follows. Section 2 overviews the related work. Section 3 describes the system model and problem formulation. Section 4 proposes a resource allocation scheme and describes the detailed process of the proposed scheme. Section 5 presents the performance evaluation. Finally, Sect. 6 concludes the paper.

2 Related Work

Extensive research has been done to study efficient and reliable resource allocation algorithms for VANETs. Ashraf et al. [7] presented a proximity-aware resource allocation scheme for V2V communications, which could satisfy the safety services requirements and reduce the signaling overhead and interference from other pairs by enabling zone formation. Lin et al. [8] proposed an SMDP model for VCC resource allocation considering heterogeneous vehicles and RSUs, and presented an approach for finding the optimal resource allocation strategy. Jiang et al. [9] considered the frequency point allocation problem in VANETs, and proposed a graph coloring-based frequency allocation scheme, which considered connectivity degree as allocation priority. Liu et al. [10] proposed an architecture of NOMA-based autonomous driving vehicular networks to satisfy the communication requirements such as cross-layer interference, and investigated the subchannel and power allocation in the NOMA system. Ao et al. [11] studied the effect of channel state information (CSI) on overheads of resource allocation in VANETs, and proposed a permutation model, in which the nodes with good CSI had higher priority to occupy resources and the nodes with bad CSI were not able to participate in resource allocation, leading to a decrease in the overheads of resource allocation. Costa et al. [12] designed a task allocation scheme, which utilized the technique of combinatorial optimization to exploit network computational resources in vehicular cloud environment. Abbas et al. [13] investigated an effective cluster-based resource management mechanism and analyzed the performance for Vehicle-to-Everything (V2X) networks, which could cope with the fast channel deviations caused by high mobility. With the increasing shared traffic data in VANETs, similar data download requests vehicles might affect the efficiency of resource allocation. To alleviate the issue, Cui et al. [14] proposed an efficient edge-computing based data downloading scheme, in which the infrastructure could cache the popular data in qualified edge computing vehicles. Wang et al. [15] aimed to optimize the social welfare of resource allocation in mobile crowdsourcing on the basis of Walrasian equilibrium. Yu et al. [16] presented a stochastic load balancing method to alleviate the resource overloading with virtual machine migration and minimize the total migration overhead. LiWang et al. [17] presented a novel framework for graph jobs to service providers via opportunistic V2V communication. Considering the vehicles' contact duration and resources, the authors formulated the job allocation problem as a nonlinear integer programming, which mainly included low-traffic and high volume scenarios. To minimize task completion delay, Dai et al. [18] studied computation offloading in mobile edge computing (MEC) - assisted network, which considered task coordination, and heterogeneous abilities of servers. On this basis, the authors formulated a cooperative computation offloading problem and proposed an efficient scheduling algorithm.

Considering the communication energy, Kui et al. [19] introduced Energy-aware Temporal Reachability Graphs (ETRG) to characterize the connectivity of mobile opportunistic networks. Then the authors proposed an effective algorithm to calculate ETRG based on TVGs. Jia et al. [20] presented the time-sharing graph and proposed a collaboration scheme that allowed satellites to use inter-satellite links (ISLs) for data offloading. Jiang et al. [21] considered the routing problem in earth-observation satellite network, and proposed a joint spatio-temporal routing framework, in which the time-varying topology was modeled as a spatio-temporal graph. The authors proposed a multi-path routing algorithm with cost constraint to find available routing in tolerant delay. Zhu et al. [22] studied cooperative transmission and resource allocation in cloud-based terrestrial-satellite networks, and proposed a resource allocation problem based on a two-tier game.

Most existing resource allocation research assumes that the network topology is abstracted as static or instantaneous graphs. To better reflect the dynamic characteristics of VANETs, this study takes the temporal property of the dynamic networks into account to study efficient resource allocation in VANETs.

3   System Model and Problem Formulation

3.1   Time-Varying Graph Model

Although most studies utilize static graphs to model the networks at one instant moment, time-varying graphs are obviously more suitable to represent the characteristics of vehicular networks. Moreover, time-varying graphs are also useful to abstract the network topology, and investigate network connectivity and reachability. We refer to literature [19] and present our time-varying model. The basic notions and definitions are described as below.

Definition 1. *Time-varying graphs (TVG): Let V be a set of vertices, where $|V| = N$ denotes the number of vertices in the graph, and $E \subseteq V \times V$ be the set of edges in the network. Here, V, E denote the nodes and the links between the nodes in the network, respectively. Assume the dynamic events happen during a time span $T \subseteq \mathbb{T}$ which is called the lifetime of the network. A general TVG can be modeled as $G = (V, E, T, \rho(.), d(.))$, where*

- *$\rho(.) : E \times T \to \{0, 1\}$ is a presence function, indicating whether a given edge $e \in E$ exists at a given time $t \in T$.*
- *$d(.) : E \times T \to \mathbb{T}$ is a delay function, denoting the time needed for data transmission on a given edge.*

Then, we define the notion of delay-constrained time-varying graphs (DTVG) by extending the mentioned two functions with transmission rate and transmission delay as parameters. Based on Definition 1, the concept of DTVG is shown as Definition 2.

Definition 2. *Delay-constrained Time-varying graphs: Let V be a set of vertices and $E \subseteq V \times V$ be the set of edges. The lifetime of network will be divided into n time intervals with the same length presented as $t_1, t_2, \cdots, t_n$. DTVG can be modeled by $G = (V, E, T, f(r_l), \zeta)$, where $f(r_l)$ indicates the utility function of transmission rate over link l, and ζ indicates the transmission latency if a path exists.*

3.2   Link Capacity

In this section, we define the relevant parameters to formalize the problem more intuitively. The set of data flow in the network is denoted by S, $s \in S$ represents the sth flow in S. L represents the set of links in the network while V is the set of nodes. The delay of data flow s from node i to node j is expressed as d_{ij}^s, and the transmit power used for transmission on link l is p_l. In order to effectively improve the transmission reliability, each sender needs to evaluate the quality of transmission link to reduce transmission failures.

We calculate the cumulative interference value of each node, for node i, the value is calculated as (1).

$$I_i(t_0) = \sum_{j=1}^{|V|} |h_{ji}|^2 \cdot g\left(d_{ij}(t)\right) \tag{1}$$

where $|h_{ji}|^2$ represents the multipath attenuation gain that is independent of the distance between i and j at time t denoted as $d_{ij}(t)$. We have $E\left[|h_{ji}|^2\right] = 1$. $g(.)$ represents the path loss function, and $d_{ji}(t)$ is the distance from node i to node j at time t. According to the calculation of cumulative interference, the instantaneous signal to interference plus noise ratio (SINR) of node j at time t is shown as (2).

$$SINR_j^i(t) = \frac{|h_{ji}|^2 \cdot g\left(d_{ij}(t)\right)}{N_0 + I_j(t)} \tag{2}$$

In a fading environment, the maximum capacity on link l at time t is defined as (3), where W denotes the bandwidth.

$$c_l(t) = W \log\left(1 + SINR_j^i(t)\right) \tag{3}$$

3.3   Problem Formulation

Before formulating the problem, we define the functions $U(r_l^s)$ and $V(p_l)$ to represent the bounded, smooth and convex cost functions with transmission rate and power as parameters, respectively. We assume that both functions have first-order derivatives. Therefore, the resource allocation problem can be expressed as (4).

$$
\begin{aligned}
min \sum_{l\in L} V(p_l) - \sum_{s\in S}\sum_{l\in L(s)} U(r_l^s) \\
s.t. \sum_{s\in S} r_l^s \le c_l, \forall l \in L, \forall s \in S \\
\sum_{l\in L} d_l^s \le \zeta, \forall l \in L, \forall s \in S \\
p_{min} \le p_l \le p_{max}, \forall l \in L
\end{aligned} \tag{4}
$$

where r_l^s represents the transmission rate of the sth data flow passing through link l, and d_l^s represents the delay of the data flow passing through link l. The optimization goal of the formulated problem is to minimize the cost of transmit power on each link while ensuring the maximum network utility. The first constraint denotes that the total amount of data passing through the link cannot exceed the maximum link capacity. The second constraint means that the data delivery delay should be no greater than the threshold ζ. The third constraint shows that the transmit power shall be within a range of $[p_{min}, p_{max}]$ to reduce the interference.

4   Algorithm Design

As there exists the coupling of transmission rate and transmit power, the dual method is applied to decompose the coupling constraints [23].

First, we introduce two Lagrange multiplier vectors $\boldsymbol{\lambda} = \{\lambda_1, \lambda_2, \cdots, \lambda_L\}$ and $\boldsymbol{\mu} = \{\mu_1, \mu_2, \cdots, \mu_S\}$. Then, the formulated problem can be transformed into the following form (5).

$$L(r_l^s, p_l) = \min \sum_{l \in L} V(p_l) - \sum_{s \in S} \sum_{l \in L} U(r_l^s) + \sum_{l \in L} \left(\sum_{s \in S} \lambda_l r_l^s - \lambda_l c_l \right) + \sum_{s \in S} \mu_l \left(\sum_{l \in L} d_l^s - \zeta \right)$$
(5)

We reorganize expression (5) and have a new form as (6).

$$L(r_l^s, p_l) = \min \left\{ \sum_{l \in L} (V(p_l) - \lambda_l c_l) - \sum_{s \in S} \sum_{l \in L} (U(r_l^s) - \lambda_l r_l^s - \mu_l d_l^s) \right\}$$
(6)

According to (6), we decompose the formulated optimization problem into two subproblems, shown as (7) and (8).

$$L^1(r_l^s, \boldsymbol{\lambda}, \boldsymbol{\mu}) = \min \left\{ - \sum_{s \in S} \sum_{l \in L} (U(r_l^s) - \lambda_l r_l^s - \mu_l d_l^s) \right\}$$
(7)

$$L^2(p_l, \boldsymbol{\lambda}) = \min \sum_{l \in L} (V(p_l) - \lambda_l c_l)$$
(8)

By observing (7) and (8), it can be seen that both subproblems are convex optimization problems.

The subproblem $L^1(r_l^s, \boldsymbol{\lambda}, \boldsymbol{\mu})$ can be regarded as a real-time data transmission problem. By decomposing the problem, we can obtain a local optimal solution at each node. Then each node exchanges the value of the dual variables to reach the global optimal solution. In this way, the optimization problem at link l is expressed as (9).

$$L^1(r_l^s, \boldsymbol{\lambda}, \boldsymbol{\mu}) = \min \left\{ - (U(r_l^s) - \lambda_l r_l^s - \mu_l d_l^s) \right\}$$
(9)

According to the values of dual parameters, the optimal solution should satisfy (10) and (11).

$$r_l^{s*} = \arg \min \left\{ - (U(r_l^s) - \lambda_l r_l^s - \mu_l d_l^s) \right\}$$
(10)

$$p_l{}^* = \arg\min \sum_{l \in L} (V(p_l) - \lambda_l c_l) \tag{11}$$

Based on the traditional dual-based optimization method, the update operation of $\boldsymbol{\lambda}$ and $\boldsymbol{\mu}$ at each iteration can be obtained as equations (12) and (13).

$$\lambda_l(t + 1) = [\lambda_l(t) + \epsilon(r_l^s - \sum_{l \in L} c_l)]^+ \tag{12}$$

$$\mu_l(t + 1) = [\mu_l(t) + \gamma(d_l^s)]^+ \tag{13}$$

where ϵ and γ represent the step size of the update operations. As the dynamic network topology will cause dynamic changes in link connectivity, selecting a constant step size can ensure the convergence of the optimization problem.

The optimization problem (9) is a completely distributed problem, which can be solved independently at each link without the information of other links. Therefore, the decomposed problem is more suitable for the dynamic topology of VANETs. In order to speed up the convergence, the sub-gradient descent method is used to update the two dual vectors. Then, we combine equations (12) and (13) to obtain the optimal transmit power and transmission rate.

The proposed resource allocation algorithm is shown as Algorithm 1.

Algorithm 1. Resource allocation scheme in time-varying VANETs

---

Require: Delay-constrained Time-varying graphs $G = (V, E, T, f(r_l), \varsigma)$
Ensure: transmission rate r_l^s and transmit power p_l
1: Initialization
2:     Assign initial values to $\boldsymbol{\lambda}$ and $\boldsymbol{\mu}$;
3: Obtain the neighbor set of node i as $N_i{}^t$
4:     Neighbor nodes exchange information with each other and store the information of neighbor nodes in list $N_i{}^t$;
5: **for** $j \in N_i{}^t$ **do**
6:     Calculate the SINR and the maximum capacity of link l;
7: **end for**
8: **repeat**
9:     Update the Lagrange multipliers λ_l and μ_l ;
10:     Update the transmission rate r_l^s and transmit power p_l;
11: **until** (r_l^s and p_l are fixed or the values of λ_l and μ_l are equal to zero)
12: Obtain the optimal transmission rate r_l^s and transmit power p_l;

The specific process of the proposed scheme is described as follows.

- In network initialization phase, each node i broadcasts a HELLO packet to its neighbors. When the neighbor node j receives the HELLO packet from i, it returns a packet containing its own ID and other related information. According to the information, node i could obtain its neighbor list, and calculate the corresponding SINR and link capacity.

- Initialize the dual vectors $\boldsymbol{\lambda}$ and $\boldsymbol{\mu}$, and calculate the transmission rate r_l^s and transmit power p_l according to (10) and (11). On this basis, the dual vectors will be updated. The update process will be terminated until the transmission rate and transmit power are fixed or λ_l and μ_l are equal to zero.
- When node i transmits a data packet, it will first judge whether the packet is valid. If the total transmission delay of the packet exceeds the given threshold, the received packet will be discarded. Otherwise, it will adopt the calculated transmission rate r_l^s and transmit power p_l for packet transmission, and repeat the above process until the data packet is transmitted successfully.

5   Performance Evaluation

In this study, we use OMNeT++ 5.0 to simulate the realistic network scenario and then evaluate the performance of the proposed scheme. The selected area is $2\,\text{km} \times 2\,\text{km}$ shown as Fig. 1. The map file is derived from OpenStreetMap [24] and then we use Simulation of Urban Mobility (SUMO) to convert the extracted area to the road network [25] shown as Fig. 2. The realistic mobility traces of vehicles are generated by SUMO. In the simulations, the number of vehicles varies from 100 to 600 and vehicular speed varies from $8\,\text{m/s}$ to $18\,\text{m/s}$. The communication range of the nodes is set to $200\,\text{m}$. The transmission frame duration is set to $1\,\text{ms}$. The average encounter duration is related to the vehicles' velocity and density. The MAC layer protocol follows 802.11p, with the distributed coordination function enabled.

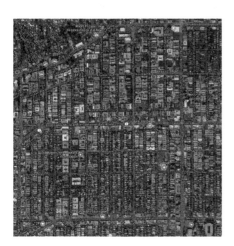
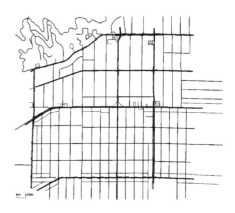

Fig. 1. Google map   **Fig. 2.** Road network

As [26], when there is a data packet transmission, the node transmits the packet according to the optimized transmission rate and power, and the selection range of transmit power is $[0.5\,\text{w}, 1\,\text{w}]$. In addition, the step sizes in the update operations are both set to 0.01. In order to ensure the accuracy of the simulation results, 20 experiments are carried out with different parameter settings, and the average value of the simulation results is obtained as the final results.

The proposed resource allocation scheme is compared with the dynamic proximity-aware resource allocation algorithm proposed by Ashraf et al. [7] and the graph-based resource allocation by Jiang et al. [9]. The performance of the schemes is evaluated by comparing the effects of number of network nodes and the vehicular speed on data delivery ratio and network throughput.

Figure 3 describes data delivery ratio of the compared algorithms when the number of nodes increases from 100 to 600. It can be observed that as the node density increases, the data delivery ratio of all the compared schemes increases. This is because the increasing number of nodes results that the neighbor nodes within the transmitter's communication range increases such that more nodes are involved in data transmission. Particularly, when the scenario is sparse, the increasing number of nodes can greatly improve the successful rate of data transmission, and the growth will slow down when the density becomes larger. The delivery ratio of the proposed resource allocation scheme is superior to the compared schemes.

Figure 4 illustrates how the number of vehicles impacts the network throughput of the compared algorithms. It is shown in the figure that when the node density increases, the network throughput of the compared schemes will be improved. As the increasing node density can significantly increase the data delivery ratio shown in Fig. 3, the network throughput increases accordingly. Besides, it can be observed that the throughput of the proposed scheme shows more improvement compared with other schemes for the reason that it considers the time-varying characteristic of VANETs.

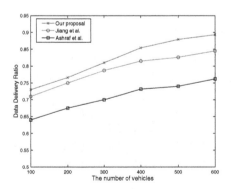
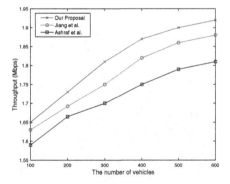
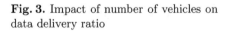

Fig. 3. Impact of number of vehicles on data delivery ratio

Fig. 4. Impact of number of vehicles on throughput

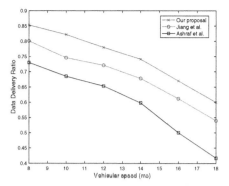 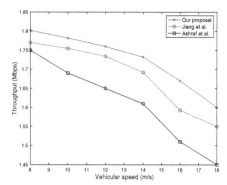

Fig. 5. Impact of vehicular speed on data delivery ratio

Fig. 6. Impact of vehicular speed on throughput

Figure 5 evaluates the impact of vehicular speed on data delivery ratio of the compared schemes. It can be seen from the figure that when the vehicles accelerate, the data delivery ratio of the schemes decreases. It is because that the increasing vehicular speed will result in shorter connection time between vehicles. As this study applies time-varying graphs to abstract the network topology and investigate network connectivity, it can be observed that our proposal achieves higher delivery ratio compared with the other two schemes.

Figure 6 presents the relationship between the changing vehicular speed and network throughput of the compared algorithms. Due to the higher vehicular speed, more communication handovers will occur and the delivery ratio of the schemes will be effected. Therefore, the network throughput of the schemes decreases when the vehicular speed increases. Besides, the network throughput of the proposed resource allocation scheme outperforms the compared schemes.

6 Conclusion and Future Prospect

In this work, we focus on efficient resource allocation in time-varying VANETs. To describe the temporal feature of VANETs, we present delay-constrained time varying graphs based on time-varying graphs. In this context, we study how to adaptively allocate network resources and improve the quality of data transmission. We apply the technique of Lagrange duality to decompose the problem and obtain the optimal transmission rate and transmit power. The proposed scheme is evaluated using realistic vehicular mobility traces and simulation results show the effectiveness of the proposed resource allocation scheme in terms of data delivery ratio and network throughput. In future work, we will consider more complex network conditions and extend our proposal such that it can be applied to more vehicular applications.

Acknowledgement. This work is supported by the Fundamental Research Funds for the Central Universities (No. FRF-TP-20-065A1Z).

References

1. Zhang, Y., Zhang, H., Long, K., Zheng, Q., Xie, X.: Software-defined and fog computing based next generation vehicular networks. IEEE Commun. Mag. **56**(9), 34–41 (2018)
2. Ahmed, E., Gharavi, H.: Cooperative vehicular networking: a survey. IEEE Trans. Intell. Transp. Syst. **19**(3), 996–1014 (2018)
3. Xing, M., He, J., Cai, L.: Utility maximization for multimedia data dissemination in large-scale VANETs. IEEE Trans. Mob. Comput. **16**(4), 1188–1198 (2017)
4. Abbas, F., Fan, P., Khan, Z.: A novel low-latency V2V resource allocation scheme based on cellular V2X communications. IEEE Trans. Intell. Transp. Syst. **20**(6), 2185–2197 (2019)
5. Singh, P.K., Nandi, S.K., Nandi, S.: A tutorial survey on vehicular communication state of the art, and future research directions. Veh. Commun. **18**, 1–39 (2019)
6. Zhu, J., Huang, C., Fan, X., Fu, B., Guo, S.: EDDA: an efficient distributed data replication algorithm in VANETs. Sensors **18**, 547 (2018)
7. Ashraf, M.I., Bennis, M., Perfecto, C., Saad, W.: Dynamic proximity-aware resource allocation in vehicle-to-vehicle (V2V) communications. In: 2016 IEEE Globecom Workshops (GC Wkshps), Washington, DC, USA, pp. 1–6 (2016)
8. Lin, C., Deng, D., Yao, C.: Resource allocation in vehicular cloud computing systems with heterogeneous vehicles and roadside units. IEEE Internet Things J. **5**(5), 3692–3700 (2018)
9. Jiang, Y., Hao, S., Han, Q.: Graph-based resource allocation for V2X communications in typical road scenarios. In: 2020 IEEE/CIC International Conference on Communications in China (ICCC), Chongqing, China, pp. 657–662 (2020)
10. Liu, Y., Zhang, H., Long, K., Nallanathan, A., Leung, V.C.M.: Energy-efficient subchannel matching and power allocation in NOMA autonomous driving vehicular networks. IEEE Wirel. Commun. **26**(4), 88–93 (2019)
11. Ao, M., Zhang, X.: Analysis of resource allocation overheads in vehicle ad hoc network considering CSI. In: 2020 IEEE International Conference on Smart Internet of Things (SmartIoT), Beijing, China, pp. 323–327 (2020)
12. da Costa, J.B.D., Meneguette, R.I., Rosario, D., Villas, L.A.: Combinatorial optimization-based task allocation mechanism for vehicular clouds. In: 2020 IEEE 91st Vehicular Technology Conference (VTC2020-Spring), Antwerp, Belgium, pp. 1–5 (2020)
13. Abbas, F., Liu, G., Fan, P., Khan, Z.: An efficient cluster based resource management scheme and its performance analysis for V2X networks. IEEE Access **8**, 87071–87082 (2020)
14. Cui, J., Wei, L., Zhong, H., Zhang, J., Xu, Y., Liu, L.: Edge computing in VANETs-an efficient and privacy-preserving cooperative downloading scheme. IEEE J. Sel. Areas Commun. **38**(6), 1191–1204 (2020)
15. Wang, Y., Cai, Z., Zhan, Z., Zhao, B., Tong, X., Qi, L.: Walrasian equilibrium-based multi-objective optimization for task allocation in mobile crowdsourcing. IEEE Trans. Comput. Soc. Syst. (TCSS) **7**(4), 1033–1046 (2020)
16. Yu, L., Chen, L., Cai, Z., Shen, H., Liang, Y., Pan, Y.: Stochastic load balancing for virtual resource management in datacenters. IEEE Trans. Cloud Comput. (TCC) **8**(2), 459–472 (2020)
17. LiWang, M., Hosseinalipour, S., Gao, Z., Tang, Y., Huang, L., Dai, H.: Allocation of computation-intensive graph jobs over vehicular clouds in IoV. IEEE Internet Things J. **7**(1), 311–324 (2020)

18. Dai, P., Hu, K., Wu, X., Xing, H., Teng, F., Yu, Z.: A probabilistic approach for cooperative computation offloading in MEC-assisted vehicular networks. IEEE Trans. Intell. Transp. Syst. (2020). https://doi.org/10.1109/TITS.2020.3017172
19. Kui, X., Samanta, A., Zhu, X., Zhang, S., Li, Y., Hui, P.: Energy-aware temporal reachability graphs for time-varying mobile opportunistic networks. IEEE Trans. Veh. Technol. **67**(10), 9831–9844 (2018)
20. Jia, X., Lv, T., He, F., Huang, H.: Collaborative data downloading by using inter-satellite links in LEO satellite networks. IEEE Trans. Wireless Commun. **16**(3), 1523–1532 (2017)
21. Jiang, F., Zhang, Q., Yang, Z., Yuan, P.: A space-time graph based multipath routing in disruption-tolerant earth-observing satellite networks. IEEE Trans. Aerosp. Electron. Syst. **55**(5), 2592–2603 (2019)
22. Zhu, X., Jiang, C., Kuang, L., Zhao, Z., Guo, S.: Two-layer game based resource allocation in cloud based integrated terrestrial-satellite networks. IEEE Trans. Cogn. Commun. Netw. **6**(2), 509–522 (2020)
23. Qiu, F., Bai, J., Xue, Y.: Optimal rate allocation in wireless networks with delay constraints. Ad Hoc Netw. **13**, 282–295 (2014)
24. Haklay, M., Weber, P.: OpenStreetMap: user-generated street maps. IEEE Pervasive Comput. **7**(4), 12–18 (2008)
25. SUMO-Simulation of Urban Mobility. http://sumo.sourceforge.net. Accessed 1 Jan 2001
26. Wen, S., Deng, L., Liu, Y.: Distributed optimization via primal and dual decompositions for delay-constrained FANETs. Ad Hoc Netw. **109**, Article ID 102288 (2020)

Deep Reinforcement Learning for Resource Allocation in Multi-platoon Vehicular Networks

Hu Xu, Jiequ Ji, Kun Zhu$^{(\boxtimes)}$, and Ran Wang

College of Computer Science and Technology, Nanjing University of Aeronautics and Astronautics, Nanjing, China
{xuhu1998,jiequ,zhukun,wangran}@nuaa.edu.cn

Abstract. Grouping vehicles into different platoons is a promising cooperative driving application to enhance the traffic safety and traffic capacity of future vehicular networks. However, fast-changing channel conditions in high mobility multi-platoon vehicular networks cause tremendous uncertainty for resource allocation. Moreover, the increasing popularity of various emerging vehicle-to-infrastructure (V2I) applications may results in some service demands with conflicting quality of experience. In this paper, we formulate a multi-objective resource allocation problem, which maximizes the transmission success rate of intra-platoon communications and the capacity of V2I communications. To efficiently solve this problem, we formulate the long-term resource allocation problem as a partially observable stochastic game, where each platoon acts as an agent and each resource allocation solution corresponds to an action taken by the platoon. Then a Contribution-based Parallel Proximal Policy Optimization (CP-PPO) method is employed so that each agent learns subchannel selection and power allocation strategies in a distributed manner. In addition, we propose a deep reinforcement learning (DRL) based framework to achieve a good tradeoff in the multi-objective problem. Under appropriate reward design and training mechanism, extensive simulation results demonstrate the significant performance superiority of our proposed method over other methods.

1 Introduction

The rapid proliferation of vehicles has lead to increasingly congested traffic on highways and in big cities, raising concerns about traffic safety and environmental pollution [1]. Fortunately, grouping vehicles into different platoons has been recognized as a prospective solution for traffic management in future vehicle networks. In particular, vehicles in one platoon can accelerate and brake at the same time in a train-like manner. With the assistance of cellular-based vehicle-to-vehicle (C-V2X) communication technology, a fleet of vehicles share their driving information to predict traffic conditions and optimize their own decisions, which can improve traffic capacity and traffic safety [2].

© Springer Nature Switzerland AG 2021
Z. Liu et al. (Eds.): WASA 2021, LNCS 12938, pp. 402–416, 2021.
https://doi.org/10.1007/978-3-030-86130-8_32

Despite the numerous advantages of platooning, several technical challenges should be carefully addressed before it becomes a commonplace. Generally, vehicle-to-vehicle (V2V) connections share spectrum with vehicle-to-infrastructure (V2I) links in a vehicle network [3]. Since vehicles in different platoons interfere with each other within their communication range over the same subchannel, the resource allocation of one platoon will affect that of other platoons. In order to ensure the quality of intra-platoon communication in each platoon, the resource allocation of other platoons needs to be considered to alleviate the interference between different platoons. Therefore, it is crucial to strengthen the cooperation between platoons and between vehicles within each platoon. Moreover, time-varying changing channel conditions in high-mobility vehicular networks bring considerable uncertainty for resource allocation. In particular, the inaccuracy of collected instantaneous channel state information will make it impossible to conduct resource allocation properly. Inspired the aforementioned facts, how to develop an effective resource allocation strategy in a multi-platoon vehicular network remains to be addressed.

The work in [4] proposed a proximity and quality-of-service-aware resource allocation strategy for V2V communication systems to minimize the total transmission power of all V2V links under the constrains of reliability and queuing latency, where a Lyapunov-based stochastic optimization method was used to solve this problem. In [5], a graph-based resource allocation algorithm was proposed to maximize the sum V2I capacity. In recent years, reinforcement learning (RL) has been employed in many works to resolve resource allocation in vehicular networks [6–8]. The work in [6] proposed a deep reinforcement learning (DRL) based resource allocation algorithm to improve spectrum efficiency. An optimal resource scheduling mechanism was proposed in [7] to minimize transmission delay in software-defined vehicular networks. The work in [9] proposed a RL-based algorithm to minimize the overhead of resource provisioning for vehicular clouds.

Unfortunately, the above-mentioned works did not consider the impact of platoon formation and cooperation among multiple platoons on the reliability and efficiency of vehicle networks. In this paper, we consider cooperation not only between vehicles within each platoon but also between different platoons. Under this setup, a multi-objective optimization problem is proposed that maximizes the transmission success rate of intra-platoon communications and the capacity of V2I communications by jointly optimizing subchannel allocation and power control. However, considering the uncertainty in the environment (e.g., high mobility of vehicles and dynamicity of platoons), it is extremely difficult to solve using traditional optimization techniques. Therefore, we develop a Contribution-based Parallel Proximal Policy Optimization (CP-PPO) algorithm for resource allocation in multi-platoon enabled vehicular networks. Specifically, we formulate the resource allocation problem as a partially observable stochastic game and measure the contribution of each platoon agent to the global reward. On this basic, a DRL-based framework is proposed to solve the resulting multi-objective optimization problem. This framework is beneficial for achieving a good tradeoff between intra-platoon communications and V2I communications while ensuring the transmission delay and reliability requirements. Simulation results demonstrate that the reward performance of our proposed CP-PPO algorithm is better than that of PPO algorithm without considering credit assignment and distributed mode.

2   System Description

Consider a cellular-based multi-platoon vehicular communication network as shown in Fig. 1, where vehicles sharing the same route are adaptively planned into a platoon and drive cooperatively. For ease of exposition, a predecessor-leader following control strategy is adopted where each platoon member (PM) communicates with the preceding platoon leader (PL) and PM. Thus, there are two communication modes in each intra-platoon, namely, PM-to-PM communications (M2M) in unicast manner and PL-to-PMs (L2M) communications in multicast manner. During time slot t, cooperative awareness messages are disseminated circularly in each platoon. According to 3GPP cellular V2X architecture in [10], V2I links provide simultaneous support for mobile high date rate entertainment and V2V connections guarantee reliable periodic safety message sharing for safety driving.

Assume that there are M channels and each of them is occupied by M V2I links. We define the set of platoons as $\mathcal{N} = \{1, \ldots, N\}$ and the set of V2I links as $\mathcal{M} = \{1, \ldots, M\}$, respectively. We consider a platoon as a device-to-device (D2D) group and use $\mathcal{D} = \{1, \ldots, D\}$ to denote the set of L2M receivers. Then the set of L2M receivers in the n-th platoon is denoted as $\mathcal{D}_n$. Denote a set of M2M links in the n-th platoon as $\mathcal{K}_n$ and a set of all M2M links in multiple platoons as $\mathcal{K}$. This system adopts an orthogonal frequency domain multiplexing (OFDM) protocol. We consider a case where M orthogonal spectrum subchannels have been allocated in advance to M V2I links with fixed transmission power. Specifically, the m-th V2I link occupies the m-th subchannel. Moreover, L2M and M2M links reuse the frequency resources allocated to V2I links.

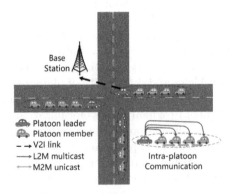

Fig. 1. System description of multi-platoon vehicular networks.

2.1   Communication Model and Channel Model

Let P_m^{V2I} denote the uplink transmission power of V2I transmitter m. In addition, the transmission powers of L2M leader n and M2M transmitter k over the m-th subchannel are respectively denoted as $P_{n,m}^{\text{L2M}}$ and $P_{k,m}^{\text{M2M}}$, which are subject to the following constraints

$$0 \le P_{n,m}^{\text{L2M}} \le P_{\max}^{\text{L2M}}, \quad 0 \le P_{k,m}^{\text{M2M}} \le P_{\max}^{\text{M2M}}. \tag{1}$$

We model the spectrum allocation as $\{a_n[m], b_k[m]\}$, with $a_n[m] = 1$ (or $b_k[m] = 1$) indicates that the n-th L2M leader (or the k-th M2M link) reuses the m-th subchannel, otherwise $a_n[m] = 0$ (or $b_k[m] = 0$). The transmission rate of the m-th V2I link can be expressed as

$$R_m^{\text{V2I}}[m] = \log_2(1 + \frac{P_m^{\text{V2I}} G_m^{\text{BS}}[m]}{P_{\text{noise}} + I_m[m]}), \tag{2}$$

$$I_m[m] = \sum_{n \in \mathcal{N}} a_n[m] P_{n,m}^{\text{L2M}} G_n^{\text{L2B}}[m] + \sum_{k \in \mathcal{K}} b_k[m] P_{k,m}^{\text{M2M}} G_k^{\text{M2B}}[m], \tag{3}$$

where P_{noise} denotes the noise power; $G_m^{\text{BS}}[m]$ is the channel gain from the m-th V2I transmitter to the BS over the m-th subchannel; $G_d^{\text{L2B}}[m]$ and $G_k^{\text{M2B}}[m]$ denote the channel gains from the d-th L2M transmitter to the BS and from the k-th M2M transmitter to the BS over the m-th subchannel, respectively.

The channel quality of vehicle receiver d in the n-th L2M multicast link over the m-th sub- channel is given by

$$\beta_{n,d}^{\text{L2M}}[m] = \frac{G_{n,d}^{\text{L2M}}[m]}{P_{\text{noise}} + I_{n,d}[m]}, \tag{4}$$

$$I_{n,d}[m] = P_m^{\text{V2I}} G_{m,d}^{\text{V2I}}[m] + \sum_{k \in \mathcal{K}} b_k[m] P_{k,m}^{\text{M2M}} G_{k,d}^{\text{M2M}}[m] + \sum_{n' \neq n} a_{n'}[m] P_{n',m}^{\text{L2M}} G_{n',d}^{\text{L2M}}[m], \tag{5}$$

where $G_{n,d}^{\text{L2M}}[m]$ denotes the channel gain of L2M receiver d from the L2M transmitter n over the m-th subchannel; $G_{m,d}^{\text{V2I}}[m]$ and $G_{k,d}^{\text{M2M}}[m]$ denote the channel gains from V2I transmitter m and M2M transmitter k to L2M receiver d over the m-th subchannel, respectively; $G_{n',d}^{\text{L2M}}[m]$ denotes the channel gain from L2M transmitter n' in the n'-th platoon to receiver d over the m-th subchannel.

For the n-th L2M multicast, its transmission condition in the m-th subchannel is determined by the receiver with the worst condition [11]:

$$\beta_n^{\text{L2M}}[m] = \min_{d \in D_n} \beta_{n,d}^{\text{L2M}}[m]. \tag{6}$$

The normalized transmission rate of the n-th L2M is given by

$$r_n^{\text{L2M}}[m] = \log_2(1 + P_{n,m}^{\text{L2M}} \beta_n^{\text{L2M}}[m]). \tag{7}$$

Thus the aggregate transmission rate of the n-th L2M multicast is given by

$$R_n^{\text{L2M}}[m] = |D_n| r_n^{\text{L2M}}[m]. \tag{8}$$

The transmission rate of the k-th M2M link over the m-th subchannel can be expressed as

$$R_k^{\text{M2M}}[m] = \log_2(1 + \frac{P_{k,m}^{\text{M2M}} G_{k,k}^{\text{M2M}}[m]}{P_{\text{noise}} + I_k[m]}), \tag{9}$$

$$I_k[m] = P_m^{\text{V2I}} G_{k,m}^{\text{V2I}}[m] + \sum_{n \in \mathcal{N}} a_n[m] P_{n,m}^{\text{L2M}} G_{k,d}^{\text{L2M}}[m] + \sum_{k' \neq k} b_{k'}[m] P_{k',m}^{\text{M2M}} G_{k,k'}^{\text{M2M}}[m], \tag{10}$$

where $G_{k,k}^{\text{M2M}}[m]$ denotes the channel gain of M2M receiver from M2M transmitter over the m-th subchannel; $G_{k,m}^{\text{V2I}}[m]$ and $G_{k,d}^{\text{L2M}}[m]$ denote the channel gains from the m-th V2I link and the d-th L2M transmitter to M2M receiver k over the m-th subchannel, respectively; $G_{k,k'}^{\text{M2M}}[m]$ denote the channel gain from the k'-th M2M transmitter to M2M receiver k over the m-th subchannel.

2.2   Problem Formulation

A constant duration T is divided into discrete time slots with equal length. Accordingly, the subchannel selection and power allocation of intra-platoon communications in the n-th platoon are expressed as $\mathbf{A_n} = \{(a_n[m]^{(1)}, P_{n,m}^{\text{L2M}(1)}), \ldots, (a_n[m]^{(t)}, P_{n,m}^{\text{L2M}(t)}), \ldots, (a_n[m]^{(T)}, P_{n,m}^{\text{L2M}(T)})\}$ and $\mathbf{B_n} = \{(b_k[m]^{(1)}, P_{k,m}^{\text{M2M}(1)}), \ldots, (b_k[m]^{(t)}, P_{k,m}^{\text{M2M}(t)}), \ldots, (b_k[m]^{(T)}, P_{k,m}^{\text{M2M}(T)}), k \in \mathcal{K}_n\}$.

The index t is added in $a_n[m]^{(t)}$ or $P_{n,m}^{\text{L2M}(t)}$ to indicate the subchannel selection and power control at different time slots, and $T = |\mathcal{T}|$ is the scheduling horizon indicating the number of time slot ahead for resource allocation decision making. $\mathbf{A_n}$ and $\mathbf{B_n}$ represent the subchannel and power control of the L2M link and M2M links in n-th platoon respectively.

In this system model, V2V communication links are mainly responsible for delivering cooperative awareness messages (CAM) periodically among neighboring vehicles for advanced driving services. Therefore, we define a function $\mathcal{S}$ to judge whether the transmission can be completed within a time slot t:

$$\mathcal{S}(R_n^{\text{L2M}}[m]^{(t)}) = \begin{cases} 1, & \text{if } R_n^{\text{L2M}}[m]^{(t)} * t \geq B, \\ 0, & \text{otherwise.} \end{cases} \tag{11}$$

On this basic, we present a new problem that maximizes the transmission success rate of intro-platoon communications in each platoon, which is mathematically described as

$$\max_{\mathbf{A}, \mathbf{B}} f_1 = \sum_{t \in \mathcal{T}} \frac{\sum_{n \in \mathcal{N}} \mathcal{S}(R_n^{\text{L2M}}[m]^{(t)}) + \sum_{k \in \mathcal{K}} \mathcal{S}(R_k^{\text{M2M}}[m]^{(t)})}{|\mathcal{N}| + |\mathcal{K}|}, \tag{12}$$

where $\mathbf{A} = [\mathbf{A_1}, \mathbf{A_2}, \ldots, \mathbf{A_n}, \ldots]$ and $\mathbf{B} = [\mathbf{B_1}, \mathbf{B_2}, \ldots, \mathbf{B_n}, \ldots]$ are matrixes of decision vectors $\mathbf{A_n}$ and $\mathbf{B_n}$ for $n \in \mathcal{N}$ respectively.

Moreover, V2I communication links are designed to provide entertainment services with high mobile transmission rate. As such, a sum-capacity maximization problem is formulated as follows

$$\max_{\mathbf{A},\mathbf{B}} f_2 = \sum_{t \in \mathcal{T}} \sum_{m \in \mathcal{M}} R_m^{\mathrm{V2I}}[m]^{(t)}. \tag{13}$$

Toward that end, the resource allocation problem investigated in this work aims to simultaneously maximize the transmission success rate of intra platoon communications and the capacity of V2I communications by jointly designing subchannel selection and power allocation. Mathematically, this problem can be written as

$$\max_{\mathbf{A},\,\mathbf{B}} \quad f = [f_1, f_2] \tag{14a}$$

$$\text{s. t} \quad a_d[m] = \{0,1\}, \forall m \in \mathcal{M} \tag{14b}$$

$$b_k[m] = \{0,1\}, \forall k \in \mathcal{K} \tag{14c}$$

$$\sum_{m \in \mathcal{M}} a_d[m] \leq 1, \forall d \in \mathcal{D}, \tag{14d}$$

$$\sum_{m \in \mathcal{M}} b_k[m] \leq 1, \forall k \in \mathcal{K}, \tag{14e}$$

$$0 \leq P_{n,m}^{\mathrm{L2M}} \leq P_{\max}^{\mathrm{L2M}}, \tag{14f}$$

$$0 \leq P_{k,m}^{\mathrm{M2M}} \leq P_{\max}^{\mathrm{M2M}}. \tag{14g}$$

where (14b)–(14e) impose the spectrum allocation constraints that each L2M or M2M link only reuses at most one subchannel. (14f) and (14g) represent the transmission power constraints of L2M and M2M links. However, due to the uncertainty in our considered vehicular environment (e.g., high mobility of vehicles and dynamicity of platoons), it is challenging and impractical to solve using traditional optimization techniques.

The work in [12] modeled the resource allocation in high mobility vehicular environments as a multi-agent reinforcement learning (MARL) problem, which was then solved using fingerprint-based deep Q-network method. However, such a method is only appropriate for the situation where the number of V2V and V2I communication links is small and fixed. In particular, when the number of vehicles increases or decreases (i.e., the number of agents changes), the neural network trained previously is not suitable for the new scenario. In our model, we also consider the dynamics of platoons. When the number of vehicles in a platoon changes, the input and output dimensions of this agent also change, leading to the retraining of the neural network. Therefore, we proposed a Contribution-based Parallel Proximal Policy Optimization (CP-PPO) algorithm to solve our formulated optimization problem. Specifically, we restrict the input and output of the neural network to remain constant by fixing the maximum size of a platoon.

Thus, the proposed algorithm can be applied to the situation with a large number of vehicles and the number of platoons and the number of vehicles in a platoon changes dynamically.

3 Proposed Resource Allocation Method

In this section, we describe how to use the CP-PPO based algorithm to address the spectrum section and power allocation problem in our considered multi-platoon vehicular network. On this basic, we propose a DRL-based framework for solving the multi-objective optimization problem.

3.1 Preliminaries

In the multi-platoon vehicular networks, we consider each platoon as an agent learning to access limited spectrum and control transmission power for all L2M and M2M links in the platoon. Resource allocation in multi-platoon can be modelled as a Partially Observable stochastic game (POSG) solved with reinforcement learning. Formally, the POSG can be defined as a tuple $(\mathcal{N}, \mathcal{S}, \{\mathcal{A}^n\}_{n=1}^N, \{\mathcal{O}^n\}_{n=1}^N, \mathcal{P}, \{\mathcal{R}^n\}_{n=1}^N)$, where $\mathcal{N}$ represents the set of agents; $\mathcal{S}$ denotes the state space set; $\mathcal{A} = \mathcal{A}^1 \times \mathcal{A}^2 \times ... \times \mathcal{A}^N$ is the action space set; $\mathcal{O} = \mathcal{O}^1 \times \mathcal{O}^2 \times ... \times \mathcal{O}^N$ is the observation space set; $\mathcal{P}(s'|s, a)$ represents the transition probability; $\mathcal{R}^n : S \times \mathcal{A} \times \mathcal{S} \to \mathcal{R}$ denotes the reward function of the nth agent, and $\mathcal{R}$ is the reward for joint action. When all agents share the same global reward function, i.e., $\mathcal{R}^1 = \mathcal{R}^2 = ... = \mathcal{R}^N$, the MARL problem is fully cooperative. Multiple platoons need to perform cooperatively to reduce interference, i.e., all agents need to work together for a global goal according to (14a).

Independent Q-learning [13] is one of the most popular MARL algorithms, but it cannot handle the non-stationary environment. Besides, if we simply set a common global reward for all agents, some platoon agents are hard to realize how much they have contributed to the global reward and the contribution itself is difficult to quantify, leading to the so-called credit assignment problem. Some agents may become lazy and will not explore because other agents have learned good strategies and have a greater contribution to the global reward. In other words, since other agents have done so well, the exploration of the agent may reduce the performance, thus the exploration of this lazy agent becomes daunting. Therefore, we quantify the contribution of each platoon to the global reward through the transmission success rate of intra-platoon communications.

3.2 Algorithm Design

The details of the POSG model and our CP-PPO are presented as follows:

Agent: $n \in \mathcal{N}$, where n is a platoon existing in the multi-platoon vehicular network.

State and Observation Space: The environment state S_t includes global channel conditions, which is unknown to each platoon agent. Each agent can only observe local channel information about the intra-communication in each platoon, the observation space of nth platoon is summarized as

$$\mathcal{O}^n = \{n, G_n, B_n, t\}, \tag{15}$$

$G_n = \{G_{n,d}^{L2M}, G_{m,d}^{V2I}, G_k^{M2M}, G_{k,n}^{L2M}, G_{k,d}^{M2M}, G_{n,m}^{L2B}, G_{k,m}^{M2B}\}$, $B_n = \{B_{L2M_n}, B_{M2M_1}, \ldots, B_{M2M_k}\}$, $\forall k \in \mathcal{K}_n, \forall m \in \mathcal{M}, \forall d \in \mathcal{D}_n$. The intra-platoon communications is composed of one L2M link and several M2M links. The observation space of an individual n^{th} platoon agent contains signal channels, interference channel from other L2M or M2M transmitters, all V2I transmitters and from own transmitter to the BS. Note that, $G_{n,m}^{L2B}$ and $G_{k,m}^{M2B}$ are estimated at the BS and transmitted to PL, which incurs small signalling overhead. In essence, the remaining channel information is correctly estimated by all PMs as the receiver of L2M or M2M links at the beginning of each time slot t and then can be transmitted to the PL through delay-free feedback [14]. These observations are normalized by subtracting the mean and

---

Algorithm 1. CP-PPO Based Resource Allocation In Multi-Platoon Networks.

1: **Input:**
2:     Environment **E**;
3:     Observation Space $\mathcal{O}$;
4:     Action Space $\mathcal{A}$;
5: **Process:**
6: Initialize state-value function ϕ and policy function π randomly;
7: **for** each iteration **do**
8:     **while** Platoons are within the range of BS **do**
9:         Update vehicles in platoon position and channel large-scale fading
10:        Reset B_n, for all $n \in N$
11:        **for** timeslot t=1,..., T **do**
12:            # *Collect experiences in parallel*
13:            **for** each platoon agent n **do**
14:                Observe $\mathcal{O}_t^{(n)}$ and choose action $\mathcal{A}_t^{(n)}$
15:            **end for**
16:            Update channel small-scale fading
17:            All agents perform a joint action $\mathcal{A}_t$ and interact with environment to receive a global reward $\mathcal{R}_{t+1}$
18:            **for** each platoon agent n **do**
19:                Calculate $\mathcal{R}_{t+1}^{(n)}$ according to (19), compute advantages $\hat{A}_i^t$ using GAE
20:            **end for**
21:        **end for**
22:    **end while**
23:    **for** each platoon agent n **do**
24:        # *Update policy and value function*
25:        Update θ by Adam w.r.t $L_{policy}^{PPO}(\pi)$
26:        Update ϕ by Adam w.r.t $L_{value}^{PPO}(\phi)$
27:    **end for**
28: **end for**

---

dividing by the standard deviation using the statistics aggregated over the course of entire training. We use one-hot encode to record the nth platoon. B_n are the remaining CAM data size per cent value of L2M and all M2M links in intra-platoon communication and t is the percentage of the time remaining over the transmission latency.

Action Space: $\mathcal{A}^n = \{A_{L2M_n}, A_{M2M_1}, \ldots, A_{M2M_k}\}, \forall k \in \mathcal{K}_n$. A_{L2M} or A_{M2M_k} is a two-tuple:$\{S, P\}$, S represents the subchannel that the L2M or M2M link selects, which is an integer value in the range of $[1, M]$. P is the L2M or M2M transmission power which is continuous and satisfy the constraint (14f) and (14g). When the power is selected as zero, we set the transmission power to -100 dBM. Note that, S is a continuous action value in the training, we divide various intervals and then map the value to an integer value for subchannel selection.

Reward Design: Reward design is essential for solving problems with hard-to-optimize objectives and the system performance is closely related to the reward designed. Our bi-objective optimization problem includes maximizing transmission success rate of all intra-platoon communications in platoons and the sum capacity of V2I links. In achieve the first objective, we set the reward equal to the L2M and M2M transmission rate until the CAM is delivered, after which the reward of L2M and M2M is set to a constant number of α and β respectively, that is larger than the largest possible L2M and M2M transmission rate. We encourage each L2M and M2M transmission being finished as soon as possible, so the reward design is not only simply about transmission rate but also attempts to achieve more rewards of α and β. In response to the second objective, we simply include the instantaneous sum capacity of all V2I links. As such, the global reward $\mathcal{R}_{t+1}$ at each time slot is set as:

$$\mathcal{R}_{L2M_n}^{(t)} = \begin{cases} R_n^{L2M}[m]^{(t)}, & \text{if } B_{L2M_n} > 0, \\ \alpha, & \text{otherwise.} \end{cases} \tag{16}$$

$$\mathcal{R}_{M2M_k}^{(t)} = \begin{cases} R_k^{M2M}[m]^{(t)}, & \text{if } B_{M2M_k} > 0, \\ \beta, & \text{otherwise.} \end{cases} \tag{17}$$

$$\mathcal{R}_{t+1} = \lambda_1 (\sum_{n \in \mathcal{N}} \mathcal{R}_{L2M_n}^{(t)} + \sum_{k \in \mathcal{K}} \mathcal{R}_{M2M_k}^{(t)}) + \lambda_2 \sum_{m \in \mathcal{M}} R_m^{V2I}[m]^{(t)}, \tag{18}$$

where λ_1 and λ_2 are positive weights to balance two objectives.

To avoid lazy agent as mentioned before, we consider each agent's contribution to the global reward and utilize the transmission success rate of communications in each platoon to quantify the contribution. The reward of nth platoon agent is defined as:

$$\mathcal{R}_{t+1}^{(n)} = \frac{\mathcal{R}_{L2M_n}^{(t)} + \sum_{k \in \mathcal{K}_n} \mathcal{R}_{M2M_k}^{(t)}}{\alpha + |\mathcal{K}_n|\beta} \mathcal{R}_{t+1}. \tag{19}$$

Reinforcement learning aims to find an optimal policy π_* maximizing the cumulative discounted rewards with a discount factor γ. The number of episodes or time slots T is the radio of transmission latency to a subframe. The cumulative discounted reward is hence defined as:

$$G_t = \sum_{k=0}^{T} \gamma^k \mathcal{R}_{t+k+1}, 0 \le \gamma \le 1. \tag{20}$$

Learning Algorithm: Our proposed CP-PPO is summarized in Algorithm 1. We adopt a robust policy gradient algorithm, Proximal Policy Optimization (PPO), to resource allocation in multi-platoon vehicular networks. Our approach adapts the centralized learning, decentralized execution paradigm. Each platoon receives its own observation $\mathcal{O}_t^{(n)}$ at each time slot and chooses the action generated from the shared policy π_θ, and the policy is trained with experiences collected by all platoons simultaneously. The training process alternates between collecting experiences by running the policy in parallel. Each platoon agent exploits the shared policy to access limited spectrum and control the transmission power of intra-platoon communications. All agents generate a joint action $\mathcal{A}_t$ to interact with the environment and receive a global reward $\mathcal{R}_{t+1}$. Each platoon agent gets $\mathcal{R}_{t+1}^{(n)}$ depending on the transmission success rate of intra-platoon communications. Then the sampled experiences are used to construct the loss and it is consist of two parts: $L_{value}^{PPO}(\theta)$ and $L_{policy}^{PPO}(\pi)$. The network structure of state-value function $V_\phi(s_i^t)$ is same with the network of policy function π_θ, except that it has only one unit in its last layer with a linear activation. The state-value function is used to estimate the advantage $\hat{A}_i^t$ using generalized advantage estimation (GAE) [15]. We construct the squared-error loss $L_{value}^{PPO}(\theta)$ and optimize it with the Adam Optimizer. The probability ratio between old and new policies is expressed as

$$r(\theta) = \frac{\pi_\theta(a|s)}{\pi_{\theta_{old}}(a|s)}, \tag{21}$$

PPO imposes the constraint by forcing $r(\theta)$ to stay within a small interval around 1, precisely $[1 - \epsilon, 1 + \epsilon]$, where ϵ is a hyperparameter.

$$L_{policy}^{PPO}(\pi) = E[\min(r(\theta)\hat{A}_{\theta_{old}}(s,a), \; \mathrm{clip}(r(\theta), 1 - \epsilon, 1 + \epsilon)\hat{A}_{\theta_{old}}(s,a))], \tag{22}$$

where the function $\mathrm{clip}(r(\theta), 1 - \epsilon, 1 + \epsilon)$ clips the ratio to be no more than $1 + \epsilon$ and no less than $1 - \epsilon$.

3.3   DRL for the Multi-objective Problem

In this subsection, we employ the decomposition strategy as the basic framework to decompose the multi-objective problem into a set of scalar problems. Specifically, the well-known Weighted Sum method is used, in which a set of uniform weight vectors $\lambda^1, ..., \lambda^N$ is adopted, e.g., $(1,0), (0.99, 0.01), \ldots, (0,1)$

for a bi-objective problem. Note that $\lambda^n = (\lambda_1^n, ..., \lambda_L^n)$, where L is the number of objectives. Thus the original multi-objective problem is divided into N scalar subproblems and each scalar subproblem is modelled and solved by CP-PPO algorithm with the assistance of other subproblems via the neighbourhood-based parameter transfer strategy. When all subproblems are solved, we will obtain the Pareto optimal solution and Pareto Front. Under such case, the objective of the nth subproblem is expressed as:

$$\max \quad \lambda^n \cdot f = \sum_{l=1}^{L} \lambda_l^n \cdot f_l. \tag{23}$$

According to (23), two neighbouring subproblems have adjacent weight vectors so that they may have very close solutions. Therefore, a subproblem can use its neighbouring subproblem' solutions to solve itself. For example, the $(n-1)^{th}$ subproblem has been optimized and its parameters are $[\omega_{\lambda^{n-1}}, b_{\lambda^{n-1}}]$, then the network parameters in the $(n-1)^{th}$ subproblem are loaded as the starting training point for n^{th} subproblem. In brief, the parameters are transferred from the previous subproblem to the next one sequentially, which save the amount of time compared with training all the N subproblems. Also, another advantage is that once the model has been trained well, we can obtain the Pareto Front directly and quickly through a simple forward propagation.

4   Simulation Results

In this section, we provide simulation results to demonstrate the system performance of multi-platoon vehicular networks. We consider a system with $M = 25$ vehicles that can randomly leave their original platoon and join another platoon. We consider not only the mobility of vehicles but also the dynamicity of platoons (i.e., vehicles leaving a platoon or new vehicles joining this platoon). Unless stated, basic simulation parameters are summarized in Table 1.

To illustrate the superiority of our proposed CP-PPO-based algorithm in terms of transmission success rate, we consider the following two benchmark algorithms: i) Proximal Policy Optimization (PPO) where agents share the same global reward and ii) Multi-Agent Reinforcement Learning (MARL) where a fingerprint-based deep Q-network is used for each agent learning in a distributed manner.

Figure 2 compares the performance of our proposed algorithm with the benchmark algorithms by plotting the reward curve versus the number of training iterations. For comparison, we exploit the same global reward mechanism in this simulation. It can be seen from Fig. 2 that our proposed algorithm achieves significantly higher reward as compared with the benchmark algorithms. In addition, we observe that our proposed algorithm converges in about 90 iterations while the PPO algorithm and MARL algorithm converge after 150 and 170 iterations, respectively. This means that our proposed algorithm is computationally efficient.

Table 1. Simulation parameters

Communication parameter	Value	Communication parameter	Value
Maximum of platoon size	8	Vehicle antenna height	1.5 m
Number of subchannels	25	Vehicle antenna gain	3 dBi
Carrier frequency	2 GHz	Vehicle receiver noise figure	9 dB
Total bandwidth	10 MHz	Lane width	3.5 m
V2I transmit power	23 dBm	Number of lanes	4 in each direction
L2M maximum transmit power	23 dBm	Number of direction	4
M2M maximum transmit power	23 dBm	Decorrelation distance	10 m
Noise power	−114 dBm	Path loss	LOS NLOS
BS antenna height	25 m	Shadowing distribution	Log-normal
BS antenna gain	8 dBi	Fast fading	Rayleigh fading
BS receiver noise figure	5 dB	Path loss and shadowing	Every 100 ms
Latency constraint	10 ms	Fast fading update	Every 1 ms

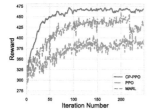 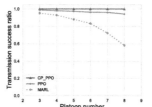 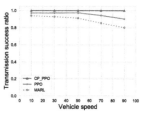

Fig. 2. Reward vs the number of training iterations for different algorithms.

Fig. 3. Transmission success rate vs platoon number for different algorithms.

Fig. 4. Transmission success rate vs vehicle speed for different algorithms.

Figure 3 illustrates the transmission success rate of intra-platoon communications versus platoon number. As the number of platoons increases, not only the training time increases, but also the convergence of the two benchmark algorithm becomes particularly poor, leading to a significant reduction of transmission success rate. This indicates that the MARL-based algorithm can not achieve better performance when the number of agents is large since each agent needs to carry on a new neural network training.

Figure 4 demonstrates the relationship between the transmission success rate intra-platoon communications and the moving speed of vehicles. For different values of vehicle speed, our proposed is observed to significantly outperform the two benchmark algorithms. In addition, the transmission success rate gap between our proposed algorithm and the MARL-based algorithm become obviously larger as vehicle speed grows, especially compared to that gap related to our proposed algorithm and the PPO-based algorithm. The reason is that the MARL-based algorithm has poor adaptability to highly dynamic vehicular environments.

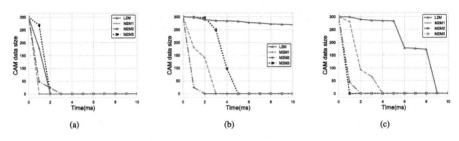

Fig. 5. The change of the remaining CAM data size of intra-platoon communications within the time constraint $T = 10$ ms for different vehicular environments and different algorithms.

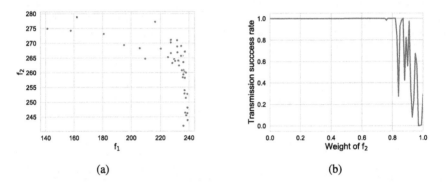

Fig. 6. Pareto Front achieved by using the proposed DRL-based framework in (a); Transmission success rate versus the weight of the optimization objective f_2.

To illustrate why our proposed algorithm can achieve better performance than the two benchmark algorithms, we consider an episode in which our proposed algorithm enables intra-platoon communications to successfully deliver the CAM data of 300 bytes while the benchmarks fail. Figure 5 plots the change of the remaining CAM data size of intra-platoon communications within the time constraint (i.e., $T = 10$ ms), for all L2M and M2M links. In Fig. 5(a), we illustrate the remaining CAM data size for our proposed algorithm in a general vehicular environment. It can be observed from Fig. 5(a) that both L2M and three M2M links finish CAM data delivery early in the episode. As mentioned in the reward design, we encourage intra-platoon communications to finish transmission as soon as possible by setting larger reward α and β after the CAM date L2M and M2M links is finished. However, traffic becomes heavy-crowded as multiple platoons get closer to each other, leading to serious interference. In this case, the PPO and MARL algorithms cannot satisfy the requirement of transmission delay. In Fig. 5(b) and Fig. 5(c), we demonstrate the remaining CAM data sizes for the PPO-based algorithm and our proposed CP-PPO algorithm in a crowded vehicular environment, respectively. From Fig. 5(b), we can see that all M2M links successively deliver all CAM data in the episode while the L2M link fails to transmit the required CAM data, which leads to the failed agent suffering from daunting exploration. Figure 5(c) shows that our proposed algorithm can guarantee the transmission delay in such an environment, which further confirms the tremendous benefits of our proposed algorithm.

With the DRL-based framework, the bi-objective resource allocation problem can be solved by the proposed neighbourhood-based parameter-transfer method. Figure 6(a) shows the Pareto Front achieved by using the proposed DRL-based framework. Moreover, the transmission success rate versus the weight of the optimization objective f_2 is depicted in Fig. 6(b). From these two figures, we can observe that when λ_2 is greater than 0.7, although the capacity of V2I links is high, this system cannot guarantee the transmission success rate of intra-platoon communications under the constraints of transmission delay. It is clear that a good tradeoff between the transmission success rate of intra-platoon communications and the capacity of V2I links can be achieved when the weighting factor is in the range of 0.4 to 0.6.

5   Conclusion

In this paper, we studied the real-time resource allocation in multi-platoon vehicular networks, where multiple V2V links reuse the spectrum preoccupied by V2I links. To model the uncertainty in high-mobility vehicular environments, we formulated the power allocation and subchannel selection for maximizing the success rate of intra-platoon transmissions and the capacity of V2I communications as a stochastic game. Then a CP-PPO-based resource allocation algorithm was proposed to search the optimal policy from the continuous state and action space. Moreover, we developed a DRL-based framework to solve the resulting multi-objective optimization problem. Simulation results shown that our proposed CP-PPO algorithm can effectively satisfy the transmission latency and reliability of communications in each platoon while strengthening the cooperation among platoons to mitigate interference. Simulation results shown that our proposed algorithm can achieve better performance than the PPO algorithm and MARL algorithm in terms of transmission success rate.

Acknowledgement. This work is supported by National Natural Science Foundation of China (No. 62071230).

References

1. Wang, F.: Parallel control and management for intelligent transportation systems: concepts, architectures, and applications. IEEE Trans. Intell. Transp. Syst. **11**(3), 630–638 (2010)
2. Nardini, G., Virdis, A., Campolo, C., Molinaro, A., Stea, G.: Cellular-V2X communications for platooning: design and evaluation. Sensors **18**(5), 1527 (2018)
3. Molina-Masegosa, R., Gozalvez, J.: LTE-V for sidelink 5G V2X vehicular communications: a new 5G technology for short-range vehicle-to-everything communications. IEEE Veh. Technol. Mag. **12**(4), 30–39 (2017)

4. Ashraf, M.I., Liu, C., Bennis, M., Saad, W., Hong, C.S.: Dynamic resource allocation for optimized latency and reliability in vehicular networks. IEEE Access **6**, 63:843-63:858 (2018)
5. Liang, L., Xie, S., Li, G.Y., Ding, Z., Yu, X.: Graph-based resource sharing in vehicular communication. IEEE Trans. Wirel. Commun. **17**(7), 4579–4592 (2018)
6. Liang, L., Ye, H., Li, G.Y.: Toward intelligent vehicular networks: a machine learning framework. IEEE Internet Things J. **6**(1), 124–135 (2019)
7. Zheng, Q., Zheng, K., Zhang, H., Leung, V.C.M.: Delay-optimal virtualized radio resource scheduling in software-defined vehicular networks via stochastic learning. IEEE Trans. Veh. Technol. **65**(10), 7857–7867 (2016)
8. Ye, H., Li, G.Y., Juang, B.F.: Deep reinforcement learning based resource allocation for V2V communications. IEEE Trans. Veh. Technol. **68**(4), 3163–3173 (2019)
9. Salahuddin, M.A., Al-Fuqaha, A., Guizani, M.: Reinforcement learning for resource provisioning in the vehicular cloud. IEEE Wirel. Commun. **23**(4), 128–135 (2016)
10. 3rd Generation Partnership, Technical Specification Group Radio Access Networks; Study enhancement 3GPP Support for 5G V2X Service; (Release 15). Document 3GPP TR 22.886 V15.1.0 (March 2017)
11. Meshgi, H., Zhao, D., Zheng, R.: Optimal resource allocation in multicast device-to-device communications underlaying LTE networks. IEEE Trans. Veh. Technol. **66**(9), 8357–8371 (2017)
12. Liang, L., Ye, H., Li, G.Y.: Spectrum sharing in vehicular networks based on multi-agent reinforcement learning. IEEE J. Sel. Areas Commun. **37**(10), 2282–2292 (2019)
13. Tan, M.: Multi-agent reinforcement learning: Independent vs. cooperative agents. In: Proceedings of the Tenth International Conference on Machine Learning, pp. 330–337 (1993)
14. Nasir, Y.S., Guo, D.: Multi-agent deep reinforcement learning for dynamic power allocation in wireless networks. IEEE J. Sel. Areas Commun. **37**(10), 2239–2250 (2019)
15. Schulman, J., Moritz, P., Levine, S., Jordan, M., Abbeel, P.: High-dimensional continuous control using generalized advantage estimation. arXiv preprint arXiv:1506.02438 (2015)

Revenue Maximization of Electric Vehicle Charging Services with Hierarchical Game

Biwei Wu, Xiaoxuan Zhu, Xiang Liu, Jiahui Jin$^{(\boxtimes)}$, Runqun Xiong, and Weiwei Wu

School of Computer Science and Engineering, Southeast University, Nanjing, China
{beilwu,xxuanzhu,xiangliu,jjin,rxiong,weiweiwu}@seu.edu.cn

Abstract. Electric Vehicle (EV) industry has ushered in rapid development recently, and many corporations such as Xingxing, State Grid, have built substantial charging stations (CSs) to supply charging services and gain charging revenues. In this paper, we focus on maximizing the sum of the revenues of all CSs managed by one corporation, assuming other corporations' pricing strategies are fixed. We model the EV charging and CS pricing problems as a hierarchical stackelberg game with the corporation at the upper layer as the leader and EV flows at the lower layer as followers. We first analyze the charging strategy equilibrium for EV flows, which however lacks closed-form expressions and thus the backward induction cannot be applied to solve the pricing optimization for the corporation. Therefore, we analyze the hierarchical game as a mathematical program with equilibrium constraints (MPEC). Additionally, a smooth algorithm is applied to solve the MPEC. Simulation results show that the smooth algorithm can achieve high revenues for the corporation.

Keywords: EV flows · Hierarchical game · Pricing optimization · Equilibrium

1 Introduction

In recent years, with the development of fast charging technology, the electric vehicle (EV) industry has ushered in rapid development [1]. As environmentally friendly transportation, EVs have drawn increasing attention from the public and markets [2,3]. Therefore, some corporations such as Xingxing, State Grid, have built substantial charging stations (CSs) to supply charging service in the EV charging market, where corporations compete with each other to gain charging revenues.

As the charging service supplier, corporations are looking for ways to make their business more profitable. There exists competition among different corporations in the charging market, and each corporation wishes to motivate more EVs to charge at CSs managed by it so as to boost revenues. Compared with changing the location of CSs [4], pricing is easier to implement without additional costs. The corporation thus usually adjusts the charging prices for CSs

© Springer Nature Switzerland AG 2021
Z. Liu et al. (Eds.): WASA 2021, LNCS 12938, pp. 417–429, 2021.
https://doi.org/10.1007/978-3-030-86130-8_33

overtime to attract more EVs, and a good pricing strategy can make the corporation more profitable. Additionally, as rational individuals, EVs prefer to choose the most suitable CS to minimize charging costs. They take into consideration the charging prices of CSs, distance to CSs, and queuing costs at different CSs while making their charging decisions. Furthermore, as the queuing cost depends on the number of EVs at the same CS, EVs can affect each other's decisions, and there exists a game among different EVs.

Some studies about EV charging and CS pricing have been conducted to maximize the revenues of the CSs [5–9]. However, these works only focus on the revenue of a single CS rather than the revenue of the corporation, and the amount of electric vehicles in these works is small, which is not consistent with the practical applications. In this paper, we consider the pricing optimization for all CSs managed by one corporation to maximize the total revenue of the corporation, assuming other corporations' pricing strategies are fixed. To optimize the pricing strategies for CSs, the corporation should consider the competitors' decisions and anticipate the EVs' charging behavior which may lack closed-form expressions due to the game among EVs. This makes it more challenging to analyze pricing strategies. Additionally, taking into account the great number of EVs in real urban environments further increases the challenge of solving the problem.

To tackle above challenges, we model the EV charging and CS pricing problems as a hierarchical stackelberg game [10]. Specifically, the corporation is the leader in the game, whose goal is to maximize its CSs' total revenues by setting the optimal price for each CS, and its pricing optimization is the upper layer problem. The EVs in the game aim at minimizing the total charging costs. As the pricing optimization is the main issue in the game, we analyze EVs' decisions with a coarser granularity to handle the large number of EVs to solve the hierarchical game effectively. Thus we divide the city into multiple regions, each of which contains a certain number of EVs. We treat the EV flows of regions as followers instead of individual EVs, the EV-flow is a certain number of EVs, whose charging costs optimization is the lower layer problem. As such, the game among EVs becomes the game among EV flows in different regions.

For this hierarchical game, the lower layer problem corresponds to a classical non-cooperative game [11] that is parameterized by the pricing strategies at the upper layer. As the lower equilibrium lacks closed-form expressions, and the upper problem is constrained by it, the upper problem cannot be solved through the classical backward induction method. We instead solve the hierarchical game as a mathematical program with equilibrium constraints (MPEC) [12], through which the hierarchical game can be transformed as a single-level optimization problem. Additionally, we analyze the existence of the equilibrium solution of the hierarchical game, and a smooth algorithm is applied to solve the MPEC. Finally, we compare the smooth algorithm with Block Coordinate Descent (BCD) method [6] and the fixed pricing method which includes the lowest pricing strategy and the highest pricing strategy. The simulation results show that the smooth algorithm can achieve higher revenues for the corporation.

The main contributions of this paper can be summarized as follows. 1) We model the EV charging and CS pricing problems as a hierarchical stackelberg game with the corporation as the leader and the EV flows as followers. 2) We jointly consider the charging costs optimization for EV flows and the pricing optimization for CSs managed by the considered corporation. 3) We analyze the existence of the equilibrium solution of the hierarchical game and formulate the hierarchical game as a MPEC. 4) We apply a smooth algorithm to solve the MPEC, and the simulation results verify the correctness of our theoretical analysis.

2   Related Work

Some previous works have been conducted to explore the EV charging and CS pricing problems. Most existing works mainly focus on two aspects. 1) Maximizing the revenues of the CSs [5–9]. 2) Minimizing the social costs [13–16].

Maximizing the Revenues of the CSs. Jan et al. [5] proposed a dynamic pricing method based on Markov Decision Process (MDP) to maximize the charging service provider's revenues. Cheng et al. [7] proposed a dynamic pricing incentive mechanism to encourage small merchants to install and share their charging equipment with others to adapt to the increasing charging market needs. Wei et al. [8] modeled the CS pricing problem as a multi-leader multi-follower stackelberg game to analyze the price competition among CSs, but the scenario in this paper is only one-dimensional. Woongsup et al. [9] also analyzed the pricing competition among heterogeneous CSs.

Minimizing the Social Costs. Yanhai et al. [13] proposed an algorithm to adjust the prices to incentivize EV flows in different areas to charge at different CSs to minimize the total social costs. Qiang et al. [14] also considered factors such as pricing and distance to model the overall charging problem as an optimization of social welfare. Gagangeet et al. [15] studied the issue of electric energy trading between EVs and CSs in the dynamic pricing charging market, and compared the two cases: modeling EVs as leaders and modeling CSs as leaders. Zeinab et al. [16] proposed a coordinated dynamic pricing model to reduce the overlap between the residential peak power consumption time and the charging station peak power consumption time during the evening peak power consumption period.

However, these works only consider the revenues of a single CS, without considering the corporation's revenues. As one corporation usually manages a certain number of CSs, and the pricing optimization for the multiple CSs is more challenging than for the single CS. Thus the optimization of the corporation's revenues is more intractable but more meaningful. Additionally, these works consider the strategies of individual EVs, but the number of EVs handled is very small, which is not consistent with the actual urban environment.

3 System Model and Game Formulation

3.1 System Model

In this subsection, we introduce the CS pricing and EV charging model. Formally, the city can be abstracted as n regions with N_i, $\forall i \in \{1, 2, ..., n\}$, EVs in region i to be charged, and there are m CSs managed by l corporations. The charging capacity of CS j is N_j^c, $\forall j \in \{1, 2, ..., m\}$, denoting the number of EVs that can be charged by CS j at the same time. Moreover, corporation s, $\forall s \in \{1, 2, ...l\}$, manages H_s CSs, whose charging prices are set by the corporation s, and the revenues of these CSs also belong to this corporation.

In our proposed model, we focus on maximizing the sum of revenues of all CSs managed by one corporation with the charging prices of other corporations' CSs fixed. The corporation can adjust the charging price for each CS dynamically to maximize its revenues by predicting the charging strategies of EV flows in different regions. Subsequently, the EV flows in region i ($\forall i \in \{1, 2, ..., n\}$) can determine the optimal number of EVs to CS j ($\forall j \in \{1, 2, ..., m\}$) based on the price p_j of CS j, the distance d_{ij} to CS j, and the queuing cost q_j at CS j. The goal of EV flows in each region is to ensure that all the charging demands are served and the charging costs are minimized. We then introduce the definition of EV flows' charging costs and the corporation's utility.

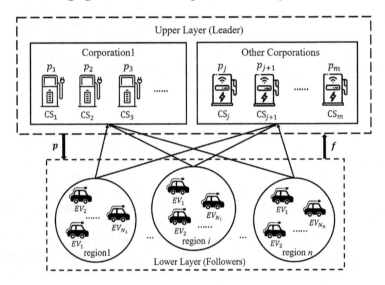

Fig. 1. System model.

EV Flows' Charging Costs. As the EV flows in each region wish to minimize the total charging costs, we first define the cost function of EV flows. Specifically, EV flows make decisions on the number of EVs to each CS according to the estimated charging costs, and the charging costs of EV-flow from region i to CS j is defined as follow

$$C_{ij} = (\omega_1 p_j + \omega_2 q_j + \omega_3 d_{ij}) f_{ij}, \tag{1}$$

where p_j denotes the charging price of CS j, q_j denotes the queuing cost of EV-flow at CS j, and d_{ij} denotes the distance from region i to CS j. Additionally, ω_1, ω_2, and ω_3 are weights assigned to the three types of costs respectively, and f_{ij} denotes the EV-flow from region i to CS j, $0 \leq f_{ij} \leq N_i$. Specifically, the queuing cost depends on the capacity of the CS and the number of EVs that come to the CS, we give a linear assumption about the queuing cost based on [13], which is defined as

$$q_j = \frac{f_j}{N_j^c} = \frac{\sum_{i=1}^n f_{ij}}{N_j^c}, \tag{2}$$

where f_j denotes the total EV flows coming to CS j from all the regions, which can be further denoted by $\sum_{i=1}^n f_{ij}$. Without loss of generalization, all the EV flows in each region choose different CSs rationally, and we define the cost function of EV flows in region i as

$$C_i = \sum_{j=1}^m C_{ij}. \tag{3}$$

Corporation's Utility. The goal of the corporation is to maximize its charging revenue, which comes from the CSs managed by it. For a single CS j, the utility is defined as

$$V_j = (p_j - \varepsilon_j) f_j, \tag{4}$$

where ε_j denotes the average operating cost at CS j. As CSs are managed by different corporations, we assume that the corporation s manages H_s charging stations, H_s should be less than m, and the corporation expects to maximize its revenues. Formally, the utility of corporation s is defined as follow

$$V_s = \sum_{j=1}^{H_s} V_j = \sum_{j=1}^{H_s} (p_j - \varepsilon_j) f_j. \tag{5}$$

3.2 Game Formulation

In this subsection, we investigate the interaction between the corporation and EV flows from a distributed perspective. Specifically, we adopt the stackelberg game which features the hierarchical game structure where the corporation is the leader at the upper layer and the EV flows are followers at the lower layer. We jointly consider the charging costs optimization for EV flows, and the pricing optimization for CSs managed by the corporation. Additionally, we also present the analysis regarding the structure of the game equilibrium.

In a distributed perspective, the EV flows and the corporation in the model determine their optimal strategies based on their interest. The corporation can determine pricing strategies for CSs managed by it, and the EV flows can determine their charging strategies by choosing different CSs. In the proposed game, the corporation is the leader and takes action first in the competition. The corporation can adjust CSs' charging prices first by anticipating the responses of

EV flows' charging behaviors. Upon receipt of all CSs' pricing strategy p, EV flows in each region can react to the leader's action and determine their charging strategies. Following the discussions above, we can specify the optimization problem for each participant in the game.

Corporation's Optimization Problem. At the upper layer, the corporation should anticipate the response strategies of the EV flows and consider the pricing strategies of the CSs managed by other corporations to set prices. According to the utility function (5), the optimization problem for corporation s, $\forall s \in \{1, 2, ..., l\}$, can be correspondingly given as

$$\max \quad V_s = \sum_{j=1}^{H_s} (p_j - \varepsilon_j) f_j \tag{6}$$

$$s.t. \quad \varepsilon_j < p_j \le p_j^{max},$$

where the charging price p_j of CS j, $\forall j \in \{1, 2, ..., H_s\}$, should be larger than the operating cost ε_j due to the individual rationality of the corporation. Additionally, each CS's charging price cannot increase indefinitely due to government management, which means that there is a price ceiling p_j^{max}.

EV Flows' Optimization Problem. At the lower layer, EV flows in region i, $\forall i \in \{1, 2, ..., n\}$, aim at minimizing their total charging costs. As the pricing mechanism provides a simple but effective way to control the EV flows' behavior, EV flows in region i, $\forall i \in \{1, 2, ..., n\}$, can decide on the optimal EV-flow f_{ij} to each CS j based on the CSs' pricing strategy p. According to the cost function (3), the optimization problem for EV flows in region i, can be given as

$$\min \quad C_i = \sum_{j=1}^{m} C_{ij} \tag{7}$$

$$s.t. \quad \begin{cases} \sum_{j=1}^{m} f_{ij} = N_i, \\ f_{ij} \ge 0, \forall j \in \{1, 2, ..., m\}, \end{cases}$$

where the constraint in (7) means that all the charging demand in each region should be served.

Lower Equilibrium Condition. As the goal of EV flows is to minimize total charging costs, their decisions are affected by each other due to the queuing cost in the CS. Therefore, the solution to the lower problem (7) can be characterized by the equilibrium. In an equilibrium state, no EV flows can decrease their charging costs by unilaterally changing their charging strategy. Specifically, this concept can be denoted as

$$C(f_i^*) \le C(f_i), \quad \forall i \in \{1, 2, ..., n\}, \tag{8}$$

where f_i^* denotes the optimal charging strategy of EV flows in region i, i.e., $f_i^* = [f_{i1}^*, f_{i2}^*, ..., f_{im}^*]^T$.

Reformulation of Corporation's Optimization. We have formulated the two-layer hierarchical game, which is constituted by the problem (6) at the leader and (7) at each follower. We have also specified the lower equilibrium condition. We then consider the upper problem, which handles one single optimization problem as we assume that there is only one corporation adjusting its CSs' pricing strategies while other corporations' strategies are fixed. Since the corporation needs to consider the response of the EV flows in different regions, the corporation's optimization can be reformulated as follow

$$\max \quad V_s = \sum_{j=1}^{H_s} (p_j - \varepsilon_j) f_j$$

$$s.t. \begin{cases} \varepsilon_j < p_j \leq p_j^{max}, \\ \boldsymbol{f}_i = \arg\min C_i(\boldsymbol{f}_i), \quad \forall i \in \{1, 2, ..., n\}, \\ \quad s.t. \begin{cases} \sum_{j=1}^{m} f_{ij} = N_i, \\ f_{ij} \geq 0, \forall j \in \{1, 2, ..., m\}, \end{cases} \end{cases} \quad (9)$$

where the lower layer equilibrium condition in (8) is a constraint of the upper optimization problem in (6).

4 Game Analysis and Solving as MPEC

4.1 Game Analysis

In this subsection, we first analyze the lower layer game for EV flows and the equilibrium of the hierarchical game. Then we analyze the optimality conditions at each follower and apply the Karush-Kuhn-Tucker (KKT) condition [17] to present them. Subsequently, we reformulate the hierarchical game as a MPEC. For the lower game, we have the following proposition.

Proposition 1 (Equilibrium of Lower Game). *There always exists a unique equilibrium in the lower game, and the optimization problem of each follower can converge to a unique solution in the equilibrium state, regardless of the pricing strategy $\boldsymbol{p}$ at the upper layer.*

Proof. The objective function of problem (7) is continuous, and the inequality and equality constraints are convex. Therefore, the feasible sets of (7) are closed, nonempty, and convex. The Hessian matrix of the utility function C_i is positive definite, which means that $\nabla^2 C_i \succ 0$. Therefore, the utility function C_i is strictly convex, therefore, the lower layer game always exists a unique equilibrium, and the optimization problem of each follower can converge to a unique solution in the equilibrium state, regardless of the pricing strategy $\boldsymbol{p}$ at the upper layer [11].   □

We have proved that the lower game always admits a unique equilibrium, which ensures that the optimization problem of each follower can converge to a unique solution in the equilibrium state when the leader's pricing strategy is given. For the equilibrium of the hierarchical game and the solution of the upper layer problem, we have the following proposition.

Proposition 2 (Equilibrium of Hierarchical Game). *There always exists an equilibrium in the hierarchical game, and the hierarchical game can always converge to a solution which can be denoted as $[\boldsymbol{p}^*, \boldsymbol{f}^*]$, where $\boldsymbol{p}^*$ is the solution of the upper problem, and $\boldsymbol{f}^*$ is the equilibrium solution of the lower game among EV flows.*

Proof. The feasible sets of the problem (9) are continuous, bounded, and convex. The objective function of the corporation is subject to $\boldsymbol{p}$ and the lower equilibrium $\boldsymbol{f}^*$, which is well-defined. For each CS, when the charging price is high, the EVs will become conservative in choosing that CS. Instead, when the charging price is low, the revenues may also be low due to the low charging price. Thus the optimal charging price $\boldsymbol{p}^*$ always exists. Additionally, since the lower game always admits a unique equilibrium, we can infer that there always exists an equilibrium in the hierarchical game, and the hierarchical game can always converge to a solution.   □

We have analyzed the characteristics of the hierarchical game. Due to the complicated game among the followers and the lack of closed-form equilibrium expressions in the lower game, the corporation's optimization problem cannot be solved through the classical backward induction method. Thus we solve the hierarchical game as a MPEC. As the best-response at each follower corresponds to a concave problem, we can apply the KKT condition [17] to equivalently present the optimality conditions $\boldsymbol{f}_i = \arg\min C_i(\boldsymbol{f}_i)$ at each follower. Therefore, the problem (9) can be reformulated as

$$\max \quad V_s = \sum_{j=1}^{H_s} (p_j - \varepsilon_j) f_j$$

$$\text{s.t.} \quad \begin{cases} \varepsilon_j < p_j \le p_j^{max}, \\ \nabla_{\boldsymbol{f}_i} L_i = 0, \quad \forall i \in \{1, 2, ..., n\}, \\ \sum_{j=1}^{m} f_{ij} = N_i, \quad \forall i \in \{1, 2, ..., n\}, \\ \nu_{ij} f_{ij} = 0, \quad \forall i \in \{1, 2, ..., n\}, \forall j \in \{1, 2, ..., m\}, \\ \nu_{ij} \ge 0, \quad \forall i \in \{1, 2, ..., n\}, \forall j \in \{1, 2, ..., m\}, \end{cases} \tag{10}$$

where L_i is the Lagrange function at the follower-i, given as

$$L_i(\boldsymbol{f}_i, \boldsymbol{\nu}_i, \lambda_i) = C_i - \boldsymbol{\nu}_i \boldsymbol{f}_i + \lambda_i (N_i - \sum_{j=1}^{m} f_{ij}), \tag{11}$$

where $\boldsymbol{\nu}_i = [\nu_{i1}, \nu_{i2}, ..., \nu_{im}]^T$ and λ_i are the corresponding Lagrange multipliers. As the constraints $\nu_{ij} f_{ij} = 0$ are complementary constraints which are very complicated and hard to handle, it is intractable to solve the MPEC directly. Additionally, if we enumerate each combination situation corresponding to the complementary constraints, although the problem in each situation is convex, there will be 2^{m*n} problems to be solved, which is extremely inefficient. Therefore, we perturb the original MPEC following [18] and obtain a sequence of smooth problems, the solutions of which converge to a solution of the original MPEC. The details of the smooth algorithm are presented in the next subsection.

4.2 Solution for MPEC

In this subsection, we perturb the original MPEC and consider a sequence of smooth and regular problems as stated above. Specifically, we consider the perturbed problem $\boldsymbol{P}(\mu)$ with parameter μ as follow:

$$\max \quad V_s = \sum_{j=1}^{H_s} (p_j - \varepsilon_j) f_j$$

$$s.t. \quad \begin{cases} \varepsilon_j < p_j \leq p_j^{max}, \\ \nabla_{f_i} l_{\cdot i} = 0, \quad \forall i \in \{1, 2, ..., n\}, \\ \sum_{j=1}^{m} f_{ij} = N_i \quad \forall i \in \{1, 2, ..., n\}, \\ \nu_{ij} \geq 0, \quad \forall i \in \{1, 2, ..., n\}, \forall j \in \{1, 2, ..., m\}, \\ f_{ij} - z_{ij} = 0, \quad \forall i \in \{1, 2, ..., n\}, \forall j \in \{1, 2, ..., m\}, \\ \sqrt{(z_{ij} - \nu_{ij})^2 + 4\mu^2} - (z_{ij} + \nu_{ij}) = 0, \end{cases} \quad (12)$$

where $\boldsymbol{z} \in \Re^{m*n}$ is an auxiliary variable. We can observe that the complementary constraints in (10) are replaced by the last two constraints in $\boldsymbol{P}(\mu)$. Specifically, when $\mu = 0$, the last constraint in $\boldsymbol{P}(\mu)$ may reduce to two cases: (1) $\nu_{ij} = 0$ and $\sqrt{z_{ij}^2} - z_{ij} = 0$, (2) $f_{ij} = 0$ and $\sqrt{(-\nu_{ij})^2} - \nu_{ij} = 0$. Since these two cases correspond to the complementary constraints in (10), $\boldsymbol{P}(\mu)$ is equal to the original MPEC. When $\mu > 0$, $\boldsymbol{P}(\mu)$ is a well-defined smooth problem, and it can be solved by standard optimization tools. When $\mu \to 0$, the solution of the MPEC will converge to a stationary point by [18]. The smooth algorithm is shown in Algorithm 1.

Algorithm 1. Smooth Algorithm for MPEC

1: Let $\{\mu^k\}$ be any sequence of nonzero numbers with $\lim_{k\to\infty} \mu^k = 0$;
2: choose $\omega^0 = (\boldsymbol{p}^0, \boldsymbol{f}^0, \boldsymbol{\nu}^0, \boldsymbol{z}^0, \boldsymbol{\lambda}^0) \in \Re^{H_s+3m*n+n}$, and set $k = 1$;
3: **while** $\|e\| > \epsilon$ **do**
4:    Find a stationary point ω^k of $\boldsymbol{P}(\mu^k)$;
5:    $e = \omega^k - \omega^{k-1}$;
6:    Set $k = k + 1$
7: **end while**;

As shown in Algorithm 1, we can solve a sequence of problems $\boldsymbol{P}(\mu)$ to obtain a solution of the original MPEC. As the pricing of CSs, the decisions of EV flows, the Lagrange multipliers, and the auxiliary variable are all variables in $\boldsymbol{P}(\mu)$, we choose an initial value of these variables $\omega^0 = (\boldsymbol{p}^0, \boldsymbol{f}^0, \boldsymbol{\nu}^0, \boldsymbol{z}^0, \boldsymbol{\lambda}^0)$ and solve $\boldsymbol{P}(\mu)$ by standard optimization tools. Then we calculate the Euclidean distance between two iterations which is denoted by $\|e\|$. When $\|e\|$ is lower than a threshold ϵ, the algorithm stops. Specifically, as μ is also a parameter of $\boldsymbol{P}(\mu)$, and for $\lim_{k\to\infty} \mu^k = 0$, the parameter μ should be initially set to a number which is close to 0 (e.g., 0.0001) and reduced at each iteration.

Table 1. The experimental parameters

Parameters	Description	Value	Parameters	Description	Value
ω_1, ω_2, ω_3	Different weights	0.6, 0.1, 0.3	μ	Algorithm parameter	0–10^{-4}
N_j^c	Charging capacity	4–32 piles	ϵ	Stopping parameter	10^{-4}
p_j	Charging price	0.8–1.8 RMB	n	Region number	11, 13
d_{ij}	Distance to CS	1–15 km	ε_j	Operating cost	0.2–0.4 RMB

5   Simulation Results

In this section, we design a simulation to validate the effectiveness of the model and the smooth algorithm. All computations are performed on a 64-bit machine with 16 GB RAM and a six-core Intel i7-8770 3.20 GHz processor. And the optimization problems are solved with python 3.8, scipy 1.5.2 and pyomo 5.7.3.

To better imitate the real environment, we collect the EVs and CSs data in Nanjing (NJ) and Wuhan (WH)[1]. We then generated some summary statistics based on real data in the two cities. We divide Nanjing into 11 regions and divide Wuhan into 13 regions according to the official administration information, and all CSs in one region are abstracted as one CS for simplicity. The number of EVs in Nanjing is about 130000, we suppose 5% of the 130000 EVs (6500 EVs) that charge in the charging game as [13] in Nanjing, and 4000 EVs (5% of the 80000 EVs) charge in the charging game in Wuhan. We assume that the EVs' distribution follows the residential population distribution, and the result of the two cities is shown in Fig. 2 and Fig. 3. The distance from each region to each CS is obtained according to the Google traffic map. Additionally, according to the data on Telaidian (www.teld.cn), the charging capacity at different CSs fluctuates from 4 to 32, and the pricing of each kilowatt-hour of electricity at different CSs fluctuates from 0.8 to 1.8 RMB. Thus the average charging fee of each EV when fully charged can be estimated within the range of 40 to 90 RMB, and we assume the operating cost is a quarter of the charging price. Additionally, the weights in (1) are set as $\omega_1 = 0.6$, $\omega_2 = 0.1$, $\omega_3 = 0.3$ as [13]. The parameter μ is initially set to 0.0001 and reduced by a factor of 100 at each iteration, and the stopping parameter ϵ is set to 10^{-4} as [18]. The experimental parameters are listed in Table 1.

We compare the smooth algorithm with Block Coordinate Descent (BCD) method [6] and the fixed pricing method which includes the lowest pricing strategy (PFix-min) and the highest pricing strategy (PFix-max). All the evaluations are performed based on the data generated from the real data in Nanjing and Wuhan as stated above. We first compare the running time of the smooth algorithm with the BCD algorithm based on the data in Nanjing and Wuhan. The results are shown in Fig. 4 and Fig. 5, from which we can observe that the smooth algorithm is faster than BCD algorithm obviously, and as the scale of the problem increases, the distinction becomes more obvious.

---

[1] http://www.cheyanjiu.com/info.php?CateId=19.

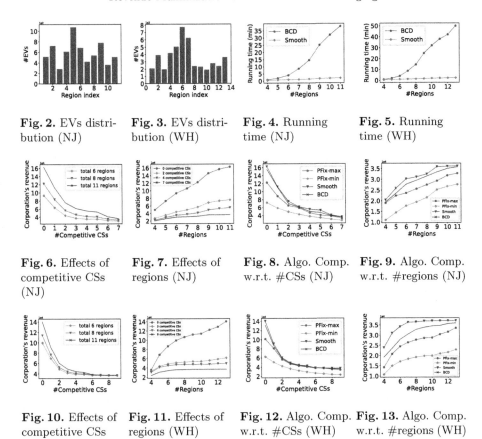

Fig. 2. EVs distribution (NJ)

Fig. 3. EVs distribution (WH)

Fig. 4. Running time (NJ)

Fig. 5. Running time (WH)

Fig. 6. Effects of competitive CSs (NJ)

Fig. 7. Effects of regions (NJ)

Fig. 8. Algo. Comp. w.r.t. #CSs (NJ)

Fig. 9. Algo. Comp. w.r.t. #regions (NJ)

Fig. 10. Effects of competitive CSs (WH)

Fig. 11. Effects of regions (WH)

Fig. 12. Algo. Comp. w.r.t. #CSs (WH)

Fig. 13. Algo. Comp. w.r.t. #regions (WH)

We then investigate the corporation's revenue based on the data in Nanjing. We first investigate the corporation's revenue calculated by the smooth algorithm under different number of total regions. As shown in Fig. 6, as the number of competitive CSs increases, the corporation's revenue becomes lower, because more CSs participate in the competition. We then investigate the corporation's revenue under the different numbers of competitive CSs. The result is given in Fig. 7, from which we can observe that when there are more regions considered, the CSs will be more heavily loaded, and the corporation has a higher chance to improve the total revenue. We then compare the smooth algorithm with the algorithms mentioned above. As shown in Fig. 8 and Fig. 9, the smooth algorithm can achieve higher revenue for the corporation in the cases where there are different number of competitive CSs and regions.

We then investigate the corporation's revenue based on the data in Wuhan. We also investigate the corporation's revenue under different cases. As shown in Fig. 10, as the number of competitive CSs increases, the corporation's revenue becomes lower. Figure 11 shows that when there are more regions considered, the corporation's revenue will be higher. The results are the same as the results in Nanjing. We then compare the smooth algorithm with other algorithms, Fig. 12 shows that the smooth algorithm can achieve higher revenue than other algorithms when the number of competitive CSs changes, and Fig. 13 shows that the smooth algorithm can achieve higher revenue for the corporation when the number of regions changes. All results above show the effectiveness of the smooth algorithm in our model.

6 Conclusion and Future Work

In this paper, we propose a hierarchical stackelberg game to investigate the EV charging market where CSs are managed by different corporations. Specifially, we study the pricing optimization problem for one corporation assuming other corporations' pricing strategies are fixed. In the proposed game, the corporation is the leader, whose goal is to maximize its total revenue by setting the most suitable price for each CS managed by it. To handle a large number of EVs in the urban environment, we treat the EV flows as followers instead of individual EVs. The EV flows can decide charging behavior to minimize their total charging costs. Due to the lack of closed-form expressions of the lower equilibrium, we analyze the hierarchical game as a MPEC and apply the smooth algorithm to find the solution for the MPEC. Simulation results have shown that the smooth algorithm can achieve high revenues for the corporation.

As the future work, we will investigate the equilibrium among different corporations, assuming all corporations can adjust the pricing strategies. This can be modeled as an equilibrium problem with equilibrium constraints (EPEC). Diagonalization methods have been widely used by researchers in engineering fields to solve EPECs [19], which inspires us to solve the equilibrium among different corporations.

Acknowledgments. This work is supported by the National Key R&D Program of China under grant 2018AAA0101200, National Natural Science Foundation of China under Grants No. 62072099, 61972086, Jiangsu Provincial Key Laboratory of Network and Information Security under Grants No.BM2003201, Key Laboratory of Computer Network and Information Integration of Ministry of Education of China under Grants No.93K-9, and partially supported by Collaborative Innovation Center of Novel Software Technology and Industrialization, Collaborative Innovation Center of Wireless Communications Technology and the Fundamental Research Funds for the Central Universities.

References

1. Bayram, S.I., Michailidis, G., Devetsikiotis, M., Granelli, F.: Electric power allocation in a network of fast charging stations. IEEE J. Selected Areas Commun. **31**(7), 1235–1246 (2013)
2. Chen, S., Chen, H., Jiang, S.: Optimal decision-making to charge electric vehicles in heterogeneous networks: Stackelberg game approach. Energies **12**(2), 325 (2019)

3. Xu, W., et al.: Internet of vehicles in big data era. IEEE CAA J. Autom. Sinica **5**(1), 19–35 (2018)
4. Xiong, Y., Gan, J., An, B., Miao, C., Bazzan, A.L.C.: Optimal electric vehicle charging station placement. In: Proceedings of the Twenty-Fourth International Joint Conference on Artificial Intelligence, IJCAI, Buenos Aires, Argentina, July 25–31, pp. 2662–2668 (2015)
5. Mrkos, J., Komenda, A., Jakob, M.: Revenue maximization for electric vehicle charging service providers using sequential dynamic pricing. In: Proceedings of the 17th International Conference on Autonomous Agents and MultiAgent Systems, AAMAS, Stockholm, Sweden, July 10–15, pp. 832–840 (2018)
6. Yu, Y., Su, C., Tang, X., Kim, B.G., Han, Z.: Hierarchical game for networked electric vehicle public charging under time-based billing model. IEEE Trans. Intell. Transp. Syst. **22**(1), 518–530 (2020)
7. Fang, C., Lu, H., Hong, Y., Liu, S., Chang, J.: Dynamic pricing for electric vehicle extreme fast charging. IEEE Trans. Intell. Transp. Syst. **22**(1), 531–541 (2020)
8. Yuan, W., Huang, J., Zhang, Y.J.: Competitive charging station pricing for plug-in electric vehicles. IEEE Trans. Smart Grid **8**(2), 627–639 (2017)
9. Woongsup, L., Robert, S., Wong, V.: An analysis of price competition in heterogeneous electric vehicle charging stations. IEEE Trans. Smart Grid **10**(4), 3990–4002 (2019)
10. Wu, W., et al.: Incentive mechanism design to meet task criteria in crowdsourcing: how to determine your budget. IEEE J. Selected Areas Commun. **35**(2), 502–516 (2017)
11. Rosen, J.B.: Existence and uniqueness of equilibrium points for concave n-person games. Econometrica **33**, 520–534 (1964)
12. Luo, Z.-Q., Pang, J.-S., Ralph, D.: Mathematical Programs with Equilibrium Constraints. Cambridge University Press, Cambridge (1996)
13. Xiong, Y., Gan, J., An, B., Miao, C., Soh, Y.C.: Optimal pricing for efficient electric vehicle charging station management. In: Proceedings of the 2016 International Conference on Autonomous Agents & Multiagent Systems, Singapore, May 9–13, pp. 749–757 (2016)
14. Tang, Q., Wang, K., Yang, K., Luo, Y.: Congestion-balanced and welfare-maximized charging strategies for electric vehicles. IEEE Trans. Parallel Distrib. Syst. **31**(12), 2882–2895 (2020)
15. Aujla, G.S., Kumar, N., Singh, M., Zomaya, A.Y.: Energy trading with dynamic pricing for electric vehicles in a smart city environment. J. Parallel Distrib. Comput. **127**, 169–183 (2018)
16. Moghaddam, Z., Ahmad, I., Habibi, D., Masoum, M.: A coordinated dynamic pricing model for electric vehicle charging stations. Transp. Electrification IEEE Trans. **5**(1), 226–238 (2019)
17. Boyd, S., Vandenberghe, L.: Convex Optimization. Cambridge University, Press (2004)
18. Facchinei, F., Jiang, H., Qi, L.: A smoothing method for mathematical programs with equilibrium constraints. Math. Program. **85**(1), 107–134 (1999)
19. Su, C.L.: Equilibrium problems with equilibrium constraints: stationarities, algorithms, and applications. Ph.D. thesis, Stanford University (2005)

Adaptive Uplink/Downlink Bandwidth Allocation for Dual Deadline Information Services in Vehicular Networks

Dong Li[1], Kai Liu[1(✉)], Feiyu Jin[1], Weiwei Wu[2], Xianlong Jiao[1], and Songtao Guo[1]

[1] College of Computer Science, Chongqing University, Chongqing, China
{cslidong,liukai0807,fyjin,xljiao,guosongtao}@cqu.edu.cn
[2] College of Computer Science and Engineering, Southeast University, Nanjing, China
weiweiwu@seu.edu.cn

Abstract. With recent advances in information and communication technologies, vehicular networks become a promising paradigm in enabling various intelligent transportation systems (ITS). Efficient data update and dissemination are one of the fundamental requirements for realizing emerging ITS applications. In this paper, we first propose a two-layer architecture for dual deadline information services in vehicular networks, in which bandwidth resources are expected to be allocated adaptively for soft deadline data update and hard deadline data dissemination. Subsequently, we present an Age of Information (AoI) model to capture the quality of soft deadline temporal information, and formulate a Data Update and Dissemination (DUD) problem, which aims to minimize the average AoI and maximize the system service ratio. Further, we propose an Adaptive Request Bandwidth Scheduling (ARBS) algorithm, which makes scheduling decisions with respect to uplink and downlink bandwidth allocation and the selection of corresponding data items to be updated and disseminated. Finally, we give an extensive performance evaluation, which conclusively demonstrates that the proposed algorithm is able to effectively improve the bandwidth efficiency and enhance the service quality.

Keywords: Temporal information · Bandwidth allocation · Dual deadline · Vehicular networks

1 Introduction

Recent advances in wireless communication technologies such as Dedicated Short Range Communication (DSRC) and Cellular-Vehicle-to-Everything (C-V2X) [1,2], have paved the way for the development of a new era of the vehicular ad-hoc networks (VANETs). Meanwhile, the rapid development on sensing, computation and control technologies has brought diverse intelligent transportation system (ITS) applications [3]. In particular, temporal data services are one of

This work was supported in part by the National Key Research and Development Program of China under grant No. 2019YFB2102200, and in part by the National Natural Science Foundation of China under Grant No.61872049 and No. 62072064.

Z. Liu et al. (Eds.): WASA 2021, LNCS 12938, pp. 430–441, 2021.
https://doi.org/10.1007/978-3-030-86130-8_34

the fundamental requirements on enabling many emerging ITS applications [4]. This work focuses on the dual deadline information services, where the freshness of data has a soft deadline, which means it is not a must to retrieve the latest version of the temporal data items to enable the applications, but the quality of the service will degrade with less fresh information. On the other hand, it is worth noting that the vehicular requests have hard deadlines, and the service would fail if the requested data items were not retrieved before the request deadline. The service data needs to be updated and disseminated for the limited wireless communication bandwidth. Clearly, it is imperative to strike a balance on service quality and service ratio by appropriately allocating the bandwidth resources and scheduling corresponding data items.

In previous research, great efforts have been made to improve the data quality in VANETs. W. Nie et al. [5] proposed a quality-oriented data collection scheme, which aims to effectively satisfy both the accuracy and real-time requirements stipulated by ITS applications. P. Dai et al. [4] proposed a system architecture, in which vehicles can sense and update information for the database via vehicle-to-infrastructure (V2I) communication. On the other hand, the Age of Information (AoI) [6–8] is an important metric to evaluate the data freshness. J. Liu et al. [9] studied the UAV-enabled data collection problem in wireless sensor networks, in which an iterative sensor node association and trajectory planning policy is proposed to find the age-optimal solution. C. Xu et al. [10] proposed a model-free reinforcement learning algorithm to minimize the long-term cumulative cost by jointly considering the user's AoI and the energy consumption of the sensors.

Furthermore, many studies have been put on data dissemination problems in VANETs. Liu et al. [11] investigated the cooperative data scheduling problem, in which an SDN-based scheduling framework is introduced in VANETs for the first time. Then, more following work [12–14] has been conducted to improve data dissemination efficiency in VANETs via SDN based scheduling. Further, Liu et al. [15] proposed a fog computing empowered architecture together with SDN based scheduling in heterogeneous VANETs. In addition, a few studies considered both the data update and dissemination in VANETs. S. Zhang et al. [16] designed a roadside unit centric (RSUC) scheme and a request adaptive (ReA) scheme to balance the AoI and latency. The RSUC scheme decouples cache update and content delivery through bandwidth splitting. The ReA scheme updates the cached content items upon user requests with certain probabilities.

Distinguishing from existing studies, this work considers synergistic effects of the following factors into scheduling, including uplink and downlink bandwidth allocation, AoI modelling, soft deadline temporal information and hard deadline service requests in VANETs. Moreover, a novel AoI model is defined to capture the freshness of the service data. The overall objective is to adaptively allocate the uplink and downlink bandwidth, as well as to schedule the corresponding data items to be updated and disseminated, so as to improve the service quality without jeopardizing the service of real-time requests.

The main contributions of this paper are summarized as follows:

- We present a two-layer service architecture to enable dual deadline information services in VANETs, where vehicles in the user layer can sense the up-to-date information, while the server in the cloud layer can update the database via the uplink channel, and serve vehicles' requests by disseminating corresponding data items via the downlink channel.

- We define the AoI model by taking into account the soft deadline of temporal information, and then by considering the hard deadline of vehicles' requests and the high mobility of vehicles, we formulate a Data Update and Dissemination (DUD) problem, which aims to minimize the average AoI and maximize the system service ratio.
- We propose an Adaptive Request Bandwidth Scheduling (ARBS) algorithm, by considering the significant factors including the broadcast productivity, the remaining available time, and the updatable data version set, which makes online scheduling decisions on uplink/downlink bandwidth allocation as well as the corresponding data items to be updated and disseminated.

The rest of this paper is organized as follows. Section 2 presents the service architecture. Section 3 defines the AoI model and formulates the DUD problem. Section 4 proposes the ARBS algorithm. Section 5 builds the simulation model and gives the performance evaluation. Section 6 concludes this work.

2   Service Architecture

As described in Fig. 1, the service architecture consists of two layers, including the cloud layer and user layer. In the cloud layer, the cloud node such as the cellular base station (BS) with a scheduler maintains the database and can update data (e.g., traffic information) via the uplink channel. Moreover, based on the vehicular request, the cloud node will disseminate the corresponding data via the downlink channel. In the user layer, the end-user (i.e., vehicle) can send a request to the cloud node, which corresponds to one data item in the database. In the dialog box of vehicles in Fig. 1, the question mark indicates the requested data item, and q_i means it is a request in the request queue. Specifically, vehicles can communicate with the cloud node via cellular interfaces such as Long-Term Evolution-Vehicle (LTE-V) and C-V2X. For simplicity, we call them vehicle-to cloud (V2C) communication. Furthermore, we assume that vehicles are equipped with different sensors and they are able to obtain the up-to-date information. Nevertheless, note that the data items maintained in the cloud may not be updated in time, which may result in stale data and compromise the service quality. Meanwhile, there are hard deadlines to serve the vehicles' requests, beyond which the service is failed. The Age of Information (AoI) of data measures the service quality of temporal information(detailed definition can be found in Sect. 3), and a smaller value of AoI gives the better service quality. Therefore, the objectives of the system are to minimize the mean AoI of the data requested by satisfied requests, and to maximize the service ratio of vehicular requests.

The service flow of the system is described in Fig. 1. Step 1: The cyber information (e.g., requested data) can be encapsulated into vehicles' control messages, and transmitted to the cloud node via the control channel. Step 2: At the beginning of each scheduling period, the cloud node makes scheduling decisions on uplink/downlink bandwidth allocation and corresponding data update/dissemination. Step 3: The scheduling decisions are encapsulated into the control message and disseminated to vehicles via the control channel. Step 4: During the scheduling period, the cloud node executes the data disseminating via the downlink channel, and the data update via the uplink channel.

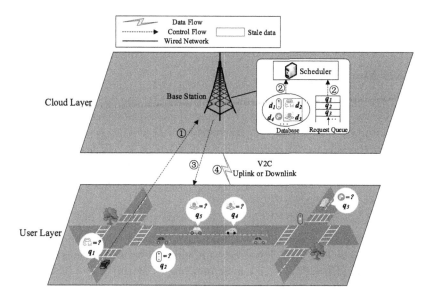

Fig. 1. The service architecture.

The system characteristics are discussed as follows. First, we consider a dual deadline for information services. On the one hand, the data item in database has a soft deadline, where its quality degrades over time since the latest update. On the other hand, a vehicular request has a hard deadline, before which the corresponding data has to be retrieved. Otherwise, the service would fail. Accordingly, in each time unit, given a total amount of available bandwidth, pending requests, as well as the AoI of data in the database, the cloud node should allocate appropriate portion of uplink and downlink bandwidth for data updating and dissemination, respectively, and determines the corresponding data to be updated and disseminated.

3   Problem Formulation

3.1   Notations

Denote the database as $D = \{d_1, d_2, d_3, \cdots, d_{|D|}\}$, and each data item d_i is characterized by a three-tuple $\langle V_{d_i}^{latest}(t), S_{d_i}, F_{d_i}\rangle$, where $V_{d_i}^{latest}(t)$ is the latest version of d_i at time t, S_{d_i} is the size of d_i, and F_{d_i} is the update frequency of d_i. The request queue at time t is denoted by $\Gamma(t) = \{q_1(t), q_2(t), \cdots, q_{|\Gamma|}(t)\}$, where each request q_k corresponds to a three-tuple $\langle R_{q_k}, t_{q_k}^{subm}, L_{q_k}\rangle$, where R_{q_k}

is the data required by q_k, and $t_{q_k}^{subm}$ and L_{q_k} represents the submission time and the hard deadline of q_k, respectively. The system time unit is τ and the bandwidth in this work refers to the number of bytes transmitted per unit time, namely, the unit is KB/τ. Let $B(t)$ denotes the total available bandwidth of the cloud node at time t, which is split into uplink and downlink channels working independently. $B^{up\text{-}avail}(t)$ and $B^{down\text{-}avail}(t)$ denote the uplink and downlink available bandwidth at time t.

3.2   AoI Model

In this part, we define the AoI model to quantify the freshness of the data required by the vehicles, which is the interval from the generation time of the sampled data version(i.e., $t_{R_{q_k}}^{gen}(t)$, the version in D at t) to the time the data is retrieved by the vehicle. Therefore, for q_k, the AoI of R_{q_k} is denoted by:

$$A_{R_{q_k}} = t_{R_{q_k}}^{dissem} + T_{R_{q_k}}^{down}\left(t_{R_{q_k}}^{dissem}\right) - t_{R_{q_k}}^{gen}\left(t_{R_{q_k}}^{dissem}\right) \tag{1}$$

where $t_{R_{q_k}}^{dissem} + T_{R_{q_k}}^{down}\left(t_{R_{q_k}}^{dissem}\right)$ is the completion time of q_k. $t_{d_i}^{dissem}$ is the time when the cloud node disseminates d_i, and $T_{d_i}^{down}(t)$ represents the transmission time of d_i with the allocated downlink bandwidth at time t. Given the allocated downlink bandwidth $B_{d_i}^{down}(t)$ for disseminating d_i at time t, we have

$$A_{R_{q_k}} = t_{R_{q_k}}^{dissem} + S_{R_{q_k}}/B_{R_{q_k}}^{down}\left(t_{R_{q_k}}^{dissem}\right) - t_{R_{q_k}}^{gen}\left(t_{R_{q_k}}^{dissem}\right) \tag{2}$$

Note that given the update frequency of d_i(i.e., F_{d_i}), although $A_{d_i} > F_{d_i}$, which means that the retrieved data is an outdated version, it is still acceptable for soft-deadline services.

3.3   Data Update and Dissemination (DUD) Problem

In this part, we formulate the Data Update and Dissemination (DUD) problem. First, given a requested data R_{q_k}, when R_{q_k} is scheduled to disseminate at time $t_{d_i}^{dissem}$, it must meet its hard deadline L_{q_k}:

$$t_{R_{q_k}}^{dissem} + T_{R_{q_k}}^{down}\left(t_{R_{q_k}}^{dissem}\right) \leq L_{q_k} \tag{3}$$

We assume that the set of requests that can be completed during $[t, t+1]$ is represented by $\Gamma^T(t) = \left\{q_k \middle| R_{q_k} \in D^{dissem}(t), \forall q_k \in \Gamma(t)\right\}$, where $D^{dissem}(t)$ is the scheduled dissemination list at time t. As a result, the set of completed requests during the service interval $[t_0, t_n]$ $(\forall n \in \mathbb{N})$ can be defined as follows:

$$CR = \left\{q_k \middle| q_k \in \Gamma^T(t), \forall t, t \in [t_0, t_n]\right\} \tag{4}$$

Accordingly, the number of completed request during interval $[t_0, t_n]$ is:

$$|CR| = \sum_{t=t_0}^{t_n}\left|\Gamma^T(t)\right| \tag{5}$$

The service ratio of system is the ratio of the number of completed requests to the total number of submitted requests, which is represented by:

$$SR = \frac{|CR|}{\sum_{t=t_0}^{t_n} N(t)} = \frac{\sum_{t=t_0}^{t_n} |\Gamma^T(t)|}{\sum_{t=t_0}^{t_n} N(t)} \tag{6}$$

where $N(t)$ is the number of requests submitted at time t. Then, the average AoI of each data during $[t_0, t_n]$ is computed by:

$$\overline{A} = \frac{1}{|CR|} \sum_{\forall q_k \in CR} A_{R_{q_k}} = \frac{1}{|CR|} \sum_{t=t_0}^{t_n} \sum_{\forall q_k \in \Gamma^T(t)} A_{R_{q_k}} \tag{7}$$

The objective of the DUD problem is to adaptively allocate uplink and downlink bandwidth and select corresponding data items to be updated and disseminated, so as to minimize the average AoI and maximize service ratio. The objective function is described as follows:

$$\underset{B^{up\_avail}(t), B^{down\_avail}(t), D^{update}(t), D^{dissem}(t)}{\arg\min} \overline{A}/SR \tag{8}$$

s.t.

$$B^{up\_avail}(t) + B^{down\_avail}(t) \le B(t) \tag{9}$$

$$\sum_{\forall d_i \in D^{update}(t)} B_{d_i}^{up}(t) \le B^{up\_avail}(t) \tag{10}$$

$$\sum_{\forall d_i \in D^{dissem}(t)} B_{d_i}^{down}(t) \le B^{down\_avail}(t) \tag{11}$$

where $B_{d_i}^{up}(t)$ is the allocated uplink bandwidth for update d_i at time t, $D^{update}(t)$ and $D^{dissem}(t)$ denote the update and dissemination list at time t. Constraint (9) ensures allocated uplink/downlink bandwidth will not exceed the capacity of the cloud node. Constraint (10) and (11) ensures the bandwidth allocated to data will not exceed the capacity of uplink and downlink.

4   Proposed Algorithm

In this section, we propose a heuristic algorithm called Adaptive Request Bandwidth Scheduling (ARBS). First, primary concepts are defined as follows.

Definition 1. *Broadcast productivity. At time t, the broadcast productivity of d_i, which is denoted by $\gamma_{d_i}(t)$, is defined as the set of requests that require d_i, which is represented by:*

$$\gamma_{d_i}(t) = \{q_k | R_{q_k} == d_i, \forall q_k \in \Gamma(t)\} \tag{12}$$

Note that $|\gamma_{d_i}(t)|$ is the number of requests that can be accomplished by the cloud node when the cloud node broadcasts d_i at time t. It is clear that the higher value of $|\gamma_{d_i}(t)|$ gives higher the priority of scheduling d_i.

Definition 2. *The remaining available time. At time t, for a request q_k, its remaining available time $t_{q_k}^{avail}$ is computed by:*

$$t_{q_k}^{avail} = L_{q_k} - t \qquad (13)$$

Clearly, we should give higher priority for q_k with lower values of $t_{q_k}^{avail}$, since it is more urgent to be served. With above analysis, we define the priority of q_k as $P_{q_k}(t) = |\gamma_{R_{q_k}}(t)| / t_{q_k}^{avail}$.

To improve the AoI, for a request q_k, we further define a set called *Updatable data version set* to determine whether the corresponding data should be updated at time t. First, we define the latest-data set, where the data is the latest version at time t, which is denoted by $D^{new}(t)$. The cloud node maintains $D^{new}(t)$ at each scheduling period.

Definition 3. *Updatable data version set. At time t, the updatable data version set for the request q_k, denoted by $\Psi_{q_k}(t)$, is the union of the version of R_{q_k} before L_{q_k}(e.g., $V_{R_{q_k}}^{latest}(t)$, $V_{R_{q_k}}^{latest}(t + F_{d_i})$), which is represented by:*

$$\Psi_{q_k}(t) = \left\{ V_{R_{q_k}}^{latest}(t') \,\middle|\, d_i \notin D^{new}(t'), (t') < L_{q_k}, t' = t + nF_{d_i}, \forall n \in \mathbb{N} \right\} \qquad (14)$$

With above definitions, details procedures of ARBS are presented as follows:

In Step 1, the cloud node traverses the database D and the request queue $\Gamma(t)$ to record the data version and remove expired requests.

In Step 2, we calculate the $P_{q_k}(t)$ of all requests in the request queue $\Gamma(t)$ and determine $D^{lower\_AoI}(t)$ and $\Gamma^{lower\_AoI}(t))$, which is the set of data (or requests) scheduled at time t can gain lower AoI. Specifically, a request q_k at t, if $V_{R_{q_k}}^{latest}(t)$ equals to t and R_{q_k} is not the latest version (i.e., $V_{R_{q_k}}^{latest}(t)$ in $\Psi_{q_k}(t)$), then add R_{q_k} to $D^{lower\_AoI}(t)$ and q_k to $\Gamma^{lower\_AoI}(t + \tau)$. We set the transmission time is τ, so we can disseminate R_{q_k} at time $(t + \tau)$ to obtain lower AoI (i.e., 2τ). Moreover, if R_{q_k} is already the latest version at time t and $t > V_{R_{q_k}}^{latest}(t) + \tau$, then disseminate with a version in $\Psi_{q_k}(t)$ can get a lower AoI (i.e., 2τ), otherwise the AoI obtained by disseminating R_{q_k} at time t is at least 3τ. And we choose the most recent version for update. If $\Psi_{q_k}(t)$ is null, we disseminate R_{q_k} according to $P_{q_k}(t)$.

In Step 3, we determine $B^{up\_avail}(t)$ and $B^{down\_avail}(t)$. We assume that the uplink bandwidth required by $D^{lower\_AoI}(t)$ at time t is $B^{uplink\_lower\_AoI}(t)$, and the downlink bandwidth required by $\Gamma^{lower\_AoI}(t)$ is $B^{down\_lower\_AoI}(t)$. The initial bandwidth of the uplink and downlink is $B^{uplink\_lower\_AoI}(t)$ and $B - B^{uplink\_lower\_AoI}(t)$, respectively. In the later period, we adaptively allocate bandwidth according to the uplink and downlink historical bandwidth utilization and current bandwidth demand. For the uplink, at time t, if the utilization of downlink in the last period is higher than that of uplink and $B^{uplink\_lower\_AoI}(t)$ is greater than 0, then we allocate bandwidth $B^{uplink\_lower\_AoI}(t)$ form $B^{down\_avail}(t)$ to $B^{up\_avail}(t)$. The same method is used for the downlink, but at least $B^{up\_avail}(t)$ reserves $B^{uplink\_lower\_AoI}(t)$

to ensure the freshness of the data. Moreover, if the $B^{up\_avail}(t)$ can meet $B^{uplink\_lower\_AoI}(t)$, we allocation bandwidth $B^{up\_avail}(t) - B^{uplink\_lower\_AoI}(t)$ to $B^{down\_avail}(t)$ to disseminate more requested data.

In Step 4, we determine the update data list $D^{update}(t)$ and dissemination data list $D^{dissem}(t)$. After determining the bandwidth allocation of uplink and downlink (i.e., $B^{up\_avail}(t)$ and $B^{down\_avail}(t)$), the $D^{update}(t)$ and $D^{dissem}(t)$ can be obtained. We set the transmission time is τ. Accordingly, the bandwidth allocation for R_{q_k} is $S_{R_{q_k}}/\tau$. The detail operation of calculating $D^{update}(t)$ is as follow: $\forall d_i \in D^{lower\_AoI}(t)$, check whether $B^{up\_avail}(t) - S_{d_i}/\tau$ is more than 0 and $d_i \notin D^{update}(t)$, if it is true, add d_i to $D^{update}(t)$ and $B^{up\_avail}(t)$ minus S_{d_i}/τ. Repeat this step until $B^{up\_avail}(t)$ cannot allocate bandwidth to d_i. Same as update, we insert $\Gamma^{lower\_AoI}(t)$ into the head of $\Gamma(t)$ and allocate "time unit" bandwidth to determine $D^{dissem}(t)$.

Last, the cloud node schedules data according to $D^{update}(t)$ and $D^{dissem}(t)$ with corresponding bandwidth, and then it updates data version and $\Gamma(t)$.

5   Performance Evaluation

5.1   Experimental Setup

Similar to typical settings in the relevant work [4], the time unit τ is set to 1s. The size of database is set to 400, and the size of each data is uniformly distributed in the range [200,300] KB, while the update frequency of each data is uniformly distributed in the range $[10,40]\tau$. The total available bandwidth for the cloud node is set to B = 60 Mbps. In addition, the map is extracted from a 1.5 km × 1.5km area in the center of Chengdu, and the coverage of the cloud node is 600 m. The vehicle arrival rate follows Poisson process with parameter λ and each vehicle may randomly submit [1, 20] requests at a time unit τ.

For performance comparison, we have implemented one of the most competitive solutions called PBS in [17], which schedules data according to priority, and data will be updated as long as it can get higher quality. In addition to the two primary metrics SR (Eq. 6) and average AoI (Eq. 7), we design another metric called Average Bandwidth Usage (ABU) to evaluate the algorithms performance on improving bandwidth efficiency, which is the mean value of bandwidth usage at each τ. The ABU is divided into uplink/downlink and is computed by:

$$ABU^{up/down}(t) = \frac{\sum_{t=t_0}^{t_n} \sum_{\forall d_i \in D^{update/dissem}(t)} B_{d_i}^{up/down}(t)/B}{|t_n - t_0|} \tag{15}$$

5.2   Experimental Results and Analysis

1) Effect of the vehicle arrival rate (λ): Fig. 2(a) shows the objective function of algorithms under different λ. Recall that the smaller objective function indicates the better performance. Clearly, compared with PBS, the proposed algorithm is more effective. The results shown in Fig. 2(b) and Fig. 2(c) explain the reason. In Fig. 2(b), the average AoI of both algorithms decrease with an increasing of λ. This is because as the traffic load becomes higher, more bandwidth is expected to allocate for data dissemination to keep decent service ratio, and inevitably, the service quality decreases. On the other hand, as expected, the SR of the two algorithms also decreases with an increasing of λ, which results the objective function value of both algorithms maintains relatively stable. To better understand the superiority of ARBS, we further investigate the ABU of algorithms. As shown in Fig. 2(d), there is not much difference between the uplink and downlink ABU of the two algorithms. However, ARBS considers $\Psi_{q_k}(t)$ of the scheduled request and will choose an appropriate time for data update and dissemination, while PBS only serves the requests of the current time unit while ignoring the request asking for the same data in the later time unit. On the other hand, PBS does not consider soft deadline feature of the temporal information, which may result the overestimate of the update operation, and accordingly, give unsatisfactory performance on balancing AoI and SR.

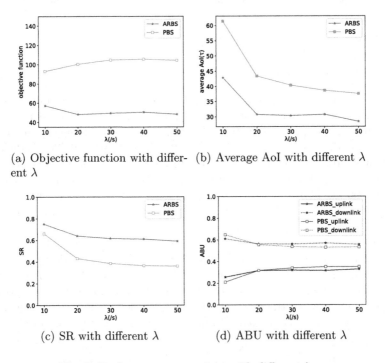

(a) Objective function with different λ

(b) Average AoI with different λ

(c) SR with different λ

(d) ABU with different λ

Fig. 2. Performance comparison with different λ.

2) Effect of the data size: Fig. 3(a) shows the effect of data sizes on system performance. As expected, the system performance on minimizing the objective function value decreases with an increasing of data sizes, as it gives higher overhead on both data update and dissemination. The average AoI and SR are shown in Figs. 3(b) and 3(c), where we note that ARBS outperforms PBS significantly on minimizing the average AoI and maximizing the SR. The ABU of uplink and downlink under different data sizes is shown in Fig. 3(d). As noted, the uplink ABU of PBS becomes higher with an increasing of data sizes. This is mainly because PBS may prefer to the schedule of data update, and thus excessively consume the uplink bandwidth. On the contrary, ARBS can adaptively adjust the uplink and downlink bandwidth in each time unit, which strikes better balance on data update and dissemination.

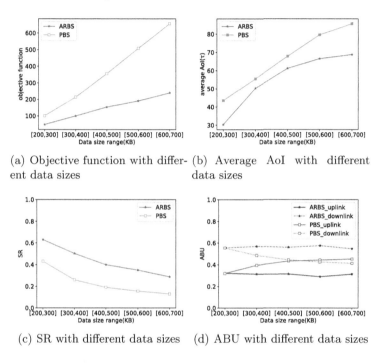

(a) Objective function with different data sizes

(b) Average AoI with different data sizes

(c) SR with different data sizes

(d) ABU with different data sizes

Fig. 3. Performance comparison with different data sizes.

3) Effect of the data update frequency: The last set of experiments evaluated the performance of algorithms under different update frequencies. As shown in Fig. 4(a), the objective function of the two algorithms decrease as the data update frequency increases. Obviously, ARBS has better system performance. Figure 4(b) and 4(c) shows the average AoI and SR of the two algorithms under different data update frequency. As the update frequency increases, the AoI of the two algorithms decreases, while the SR increases slowly. This is because a larger update frequency will not cause the system to fall into "busy update state", which provides the system with more bandwidth and opportunities to disseminate data with latest version, thereby improving the SR and AoI. Figure 4(d) is the uplink and downlink ABU of two algorithms under different update frequencies. As the update frequency increases, the bandwidth required by the uplink becomes lower in each time unit while the downlink disseminates data consume more bandwidth, as a result, the uplink ABU gradually becomes smaller, and the downlink ABU moderately becomes larger.

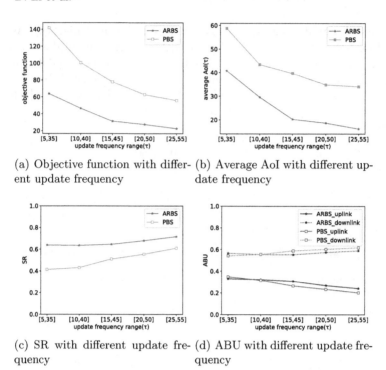

(a) Objective function with different update frequency

(b) Average AoI with different update frequency

(c) SR with different update frequency

(d) ABU with different update frequency

Fig. 4. Performance comparison with different update frequency.

6 Conclusion

In this paper, we first presented a two-layer service architecture for dual deadline information services where the cloud node maintains a database in the cloud layer and can update data via the uplink channel. Moreover, in the user layer, the vehicle can submit a request, and the cloud node will disseminate the data accordingly via the downlink channel. Then, we formulated a DUD problem which considering the soft deadline of temporal information and the hard deadline for vehicle requests. Further, by considering the broadcast productivity, the remaining available time, and the updatable data version set, we proposed an algorithm called ARBS, which makes scheduling decisions on uplink and downlink bandwidth allocation, as well as the corresponding data items to be updated and disseminated. Last, we gave a comprehensive performance evaluation under different circumstances. The results conclusively demonstrated the superiority of the proposed algorithm on enhancing both service quality and service ratio.

References

1. Qi, W., Landfeldt, B., Song, Q., Guo, L., Jamalipour, A.: Traffic differentiated clustering routing in dsrc and c-v2x hybrid vehicular networks. IEEE Trans. Veh. Technol. **69**(7), 7723–7734 (2020)

2. Chen, S., et al.: Vehicle-to-everything (v2x) services supported by lte-based systems and 5g. IEEE Commun. Standards Mag. **1**(2), 70–76 (2017)
3. Liu, C., Liu, K., Guo, S., Xie, R., Lee, V.C.S., Son, S.H.: Adaptive offloading for time-critical tasks in heterogeneous internet of vehicles. IEEE Internet of Things J. **7**(9), 7999–8011 (2020)
4. Dai, P., et al.: Temporal information services in large-scale vehicular networks through evolutionary multi-objective optimization. IEEE Trans. Intell. Transp. Syst. **20**(1), 218–231 (2019)
5. Nie, W., Lee, V.C.S., Niyato, D., Duan, Y., Liu, K., Nutanong, S.: A quality-oriented data collection scheme in vehicular sensor networks. IEEE Trans. Veh. Technol. **67**(7), 5570–5584 (2018)
6. Yates, R.D., Kaul, S.K.: The age of information: real-time status updating by multiple sources. IEEE Trans. Inform. Ther. **65**(3), 1807–1827 (2019)
7. Li, F., Sang, Y., Liu, Z., Li, B., Wu, H., Ji, B.: Waiting but not aging: optimizing information freshness under the pull model. IEEE/ACM Trans. Netw. **29**(1), 465–478 (2021)
8. Talak, R., Karaman, S., Modiano, E.: Optimizing information freshness in wireless networks under general interference constraints. IEEE/ACM Trans. Netw. **28**(1), 15–28 (2020)
9. Liu, J., Tong, P., Wang, X., Bai, B., Dai, H.: Uav-aided data collection for information freshness in wireless sensor networks. IEEE Trans. Wireless Commun. **20**(4), 2368–2382 (2021)
10. Xu, C., Wang, X., Yang, H.H., Sun, H., Quek, T.Q.S.: Aoi and energy consumption oriented dynamic status updating in caching enabled IOT networks. In: IEEE Conference on Computer Communications Workshops, pp. 710–715 (2020)
11. Liu, K., Ng, J.K.Y., Lee, V.C.S., Son, S.H., Stojmenovic, I.: Cooperative data scheduling in hybrid vehicular ad hoc networks: Vanet as a software defined network. IEEE/ACM Trans. Netw. **24**(3), 1759–1773 (2016)
12. Bhatia, J., Kakadia, P., Bhavsar, M., Tanwar, S.: SDN-enabled network coding-based secure data dissemination in VANET environment. IEEE Internet Things J. **7**(7), 6078–6087 (2020)
13. Liu, K., Xu, X., Chen, M., Liu, B., Wu, L., Lee, V.C.S.: A hierarchical architecture for the future internet of vehicles. IEEE Commun. Mag. **57**(7), 41–47 (2019)
14. Singh, A., Aujla, G.S., Bali, R.S.: Intent-based network for data dissemination in software-defined vehicular edge computing. IEEE Transactions on Intelligent Transportation Systems, pp. 1–9 (2020)
15. Liu, K., Xiao, K., Dai, P., Lee, V., Guo, S., Cao, J.: Fog computing empowered data dissemination in software defined heterogeneous VANETs. IEEE Transactions on Mobile Computing, pp. 1–1 (2020)
16. Zhang, S., Li, J., Luo, H., Gao, J., Zhao, L., Shen, X.S.: Low-latency and fresh content provision in information-centric vehicular networks. IEEE Transactions on Mobile Computing, pp. 1–1 (2020)
17. Dai, P., Liu, K., Sha, E., Zhuge, Q., Lee, V., Son, S.H.: Vehicle assisted data update for temporal information service in vehicular networks. In: 2015 IEEE 18th International Conference on Intelligent Transportation System, pp. 2545–2550 (2015)

A Local Collaborative Distributed Reinforcement Learning Approach for Resource Allocation in V2X Networks

Yue Zhang[1], Guoping Tan[1,2(✉)], and Siyuan Zhou[1,2]

[1] School of Computer and Information, Hohai University, Nanjing, China
[2] Jiangsu Intelligent Transportation and Intelligent Driving Research Institute, Nanjing, China
{yue.zhang,gptan,siyuan.zhou}@hhu.edu.cn

Abstract. In this paper, we propose a resource allocation approach for V2X networks based on distributed reinforcement learning with local collaboration. We construct a local collaborative mechanism for sharing information among vehicles. In this model each vehicle is able to obtain the instantaneously information of the environment shared by neighboring vehicles. By adopting proximal policy optimization algorithm, we addressed the issues of the joint allocation of spectrum and transmit power in a distributed manner. The simulation results show that agents can effectively learn an optimized strategy by cooperating with other vehicles in the adjacent area, so as to maximize the ergodic V2I capacity of the whole system while meeting the strict delay limits of the V2V link.

Keywords: V2X · Resource allocation · Local collaboration · Reinforcement learning

1 Introduction

As an instrumental enabler for Intelligent Transportation Systems (ITS), smart cities, and autonomous driving, vehicular networks have attracted significant research interests in recent years both from the academic and industrial communities [1]. Vehicular networks, commonly known as vehicle-to-everything (V2X) networks, connecting vehicles on the road as a dynamic communication network [2]. It supports efficient information exchange between vehicles or between vehicles and other road users and roadside infrastructures, which is expected to improve road safety, reduce traffic congestion and road infrastructure costs, and decrease air pollution etc. Due to high mobility of vehicles and complicated time-varying communication environments, it is very challenging to guarantee the diverse quality-of-service (QoS) requirements in vehicular networks, such as extremely large capacity, ultra reliability, and low latency [3]. To address such issues, efficient resource allocation for spectrum sharing becomes necessary in the V2X scenario.

This work was supported in part by the National Natural Science Foundation of China (No. 61701168, 61832005, 61571303), the China Postdoctoral Science Funded Project (No. 2019M651672).

© Springer Nature Switzerland AG 2021
Z. Liu et al. (Eds.): WASA 2021, LNCS 12938, pp. 442–454, 2021.
https://doi.org/10.1007/978-3-030-86130-8_35

The traditional resource allocation methods in V2X networks include Graph theory, Lyapunov optimization theory etc. A graph-based interference-aware resource allocation strategy is proposed in [4], which assigns the weights of edges based on the interference terms between the relevant vertices. In [5], Du et al. designed a heuristic resource allocation method based on two-sided cost minimization using Lyapunov optimization criterion to separate vehicle side and infrastructure side into independent per-frame optimization. The traditional methods mainly performing static optimization, which is difficult to adapt to the complex environment of vehicular networks with dynamic changes. In [6], Yang et al. developed a real-time adaptive resource allocation strategy based on deep reinforcement learning by considering both delay violation probability and decoding error probability in a MEC-enabled vehicular network operating with finite block-length coding to support low-latency communication. In the work of centralized resource allocation, the information of vehicles needs to be reported to a central controller in real time which leading to a high transmission overhead. Moreover, the high mobility of vehicles prevents the centralized controller from collecting the complete CSI. Recently, several distributed resource allocation mechanisms have been developed for V2X networks. Ye et al. proposed a distributed spectrum and power allocation algorithm based on deep reinforcement learning for cellular V2V communication in [7]. With the assumption that an orthogonal resource is allocated for V2I links beforehand, the study focuses on resource allocation for V2V links under the constraints of V2V link latency and minimized interference impact to V2I links. This work is extended in [8] to include a broadcast scenario. In [8], each vehicle is modelled as an agent and the number of times that the message has been received by the vehicle and the distance to the vehicles that have broadcast are additionally considered in defining the state. Then, each vehicle improves the messages broadcast and sub-channel selection policies through the learning mechanism. Liang et al. proposed a fingerprint-based Deep Q-network (DQN) method in [9] to solve the Radio Resource Management problems in vehicular networks. By giving all agents a common reward, it mitigates the instability of multi-agent environment. The work in [7–9] performed with distributed reinforcement learning which doesn't take into account the synergy among the vehicles and have an effective way to avoid conflicts in the process of resource competition.

However, the local state information of the environment obtained by a single vehicle is limited and the behavior of other vehicles is unknown and uncontrollable. Interference caused by the behavior of vehicles to compete for radio resource becomes more severe as the density of vehicles increasing. Thus, a mechanism based on information sharing among vehicles in an adjacent area is essential. Actually, a local joint cooperative learning method is proposed for distributed traffic control in [10], which can substantially improve the learning efficiency without high communication overhead by sharing information among vehicles in the adjacent area. The work in [10] aims to solve the control problem of vehicles in mixed-autonomy traffic scenarios and the communication process is not taken into account. Specifically, we proposed a distributed resource allocation approach based on LC-PPO in our work and committed to enhancing the collaboration among vehicles. Through information sharing in the adjacent area, more local state information about environment, such as real-time channel state and interference information can be obtained by a single vehicle in a time slot. In addition, vehicles can effectively avoid conflicts with vehicles nearby when making behavioral decisions based on more and richer observations.

The rest of the paper is organized as follows. In Sect. 2, the system model is introduced. A local collaborative distributed reinforcement learning based approach is highlighted in Sect. 3. In Sect. 4, the configuration of the experiments and the analysis of simulation results are presented. In Sect. 5, we make a summary.

2 System Model

It is assumed that there are several vehicles in the coverage region of a single base station type RSU (RSU positioned in the center). Some vehicles established connections with RSU for V2I communication, while others paired up with each other for V2V communication, which we called IUEs and VUEs, respectively. The IUEs demand V2I links to support high capacity communication with RSU while the VUEs need V2V links to share information for traffic safety management. A vehicle, as a transmitter, who communicates with a vehicle in the distance. Detecting other vehicles within a certain radius in an adjacent area, then collecting the local state information of the environment observed by the vehicles nearby, it's regarded that communication is not considered in the process.

2.1 Network Model

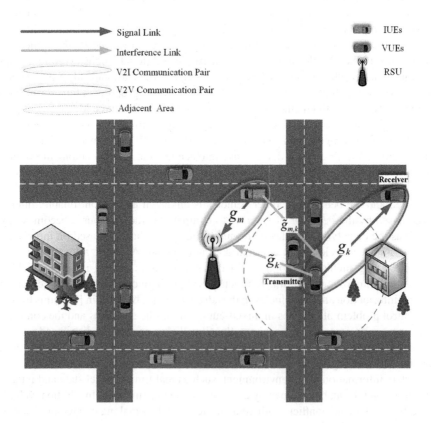

Fig. 1. Network model

In a Manhattan grid-type urban road scenario shown in Fig. 1. Considering a cellular V2X network that contains M IUEs denoted by $\mathcal{M} = \{1,...,M\}$ and K VUEs denoted by $\mathcal{K} = \{1,...,K\}$. Both of them use PC5 port for communication, and adopt Mode 4 under cellular V2X architecture, so that they can share spectrum resources in the same band. Supposing that M V2I links are assigned orthogonal spectrum sub-bands in advance with a fixed power, i.e., V2I number M occupies sub-band number m.

The SINR of the mth IUEs can be expressed as follows:

$$\gamma^I[m] = \frac{P_m^I g_m}{\delta^2 + \sum\limits_{k \in \mathcal{K}} \rho_k[m] P_k^v \tilde{g}_k} \tag{1}$$

where P_m^I and P_k^v are the transmit power of the mth IUEs and k^{th} VUEs, respectively. P_m^I is a fixed value while $P_k^v \in \mathscr{P}$, which is a set of power. g_m is the channel power gain of the mth V2I link and $\tilde{g}_k$ is the power gain of the interference channel for the mth V2I link from the kth V2V link. δ^2 is the noise power. The value of $\rho_k[m]$ can indicate whether the kth V2V link occupies the spectrum of the mth V2I link. If it is occupied then $\rho_k[m] = 1$, otherwise $\rho_k[m] = 0$.

Hence, according to *shannon formula*, the capacity of the mth V2I link is given by:

$$C^I[m] = W \cdot \log(1 + \gamma^I[m]) \tag{2}$$

where the W is the bandwidth of each spectrum sub-band.

Similarly, it can be deduced that the SINR of the kth VUEs can be expressed as follows:

$$\gamma^v[k] = \frac{P_k^v g_k}{\sigma^2 + G_I + G_d} \tag{3}$$

where, $G_I = \sum\limits_{m \in \mathcal{M}} \rho_k[m] P_m^I \tilde{g}_{m,k}$ denotes the interference power received by the kth V2V link from the V2I link sharing the same RB with it, $G_d = \sum\limits_{m \in \mathcal{M}} \sum\limits_{k \in \mathcal{K}, k \neq k'} \rho_k[m] \rho_{k'}[m] P_{k'}^v \tilde{g}_{k',k}^v$ represents the interference of all other V2V links that share the same sub-band with the kth V2V link, $\tilde{g}_{m,k}$ and $\tilde{g}_{k',k}^v$ are the power gain of the interference channel from the mth V2I link and the k'^{th} V2V link, respectively.

Then, the capacity of the kth V2V link is given by:

$$C^v[k] = W \cdot \log(1 + \gamma^v[k]) \tag{4}$$

2.2 Problem Formulation

Our goal is to design an effective spectrum and power selection approach based on local collaboration among vehicles for the V2V link, so as to meet the V2V link delay limit while improve the ergodic V2I capacity of the whole system. Due to the significant role of V2V communication in protecting the safety of vehicles, there are more stringent requirements of latency and reliability for V2V links. In contrast, regular cellular communication services performed in V2I links demand higher data rate to support the services of in-car entertainment. Hence, with the purpose of achieving the goal as envisioned, we formulate a joint spectrum and power allocation scheme as an optimization problem, which can be expressed as:

$$\max \left\{ \sum_{m \in \mathcal{M}} C^I[m] + \sum_{k \in \mathcal{K}} C^v[k] \right\}$$

$$s.t. \quad
\begin{aligned}
C1: & \quad \sum_{k \in \mathcal{K}} n_{k,t} \leq N_{RB} & n_{k,t} \in \{0,1\}, \, 0 \leq t \leq T_{\max} \\
C2: & \quad P_{k,t} \in \mathscr{P} & k \in \mathcal{K}, \quad 0 \leq t \leq T_{\max} \\
C3: & \quad T_{k,t} \leq T_0 & k \in \mathcal{K}, \quad 0 \leq t \leq T_{\max}
\end{aligned}
\tag{5}$$

where $n_{k,t}$, $P_{k,t}$ and $T_{k,t}$ denote the number of sub-bands occupied by k^{th} VUEs, the transmit power level selected by k^{th} VUEs and the time used for transmission, respectively at time slot t. N_{RB} is the number of resource blocks for allocation. $T_{\max}$ and T_0 denote the total number of time slots and the maximum tolerable latency, respectively. In (5), C1 and C2 are the constraints for the behavior of vehicles. C3 impose restrictions on the time used by the V2V link for load transmission to make sure that the transmission can be completed within the V2V delay limit T_0.

3   Local Collaborative PPO Based Resource Allocation Approach

In this section, the formulations of the key parts of reinforcement learning is shown and the proposed LC-PPO based resource allocation approach for V2X networks is described in detail.

The aforementioned optimization problem (5) is difficult to be solved by the conventional optimization-based methods which are unable to cope with the complicated channel condition of vehicular networks and fully exploit the information hidden in the massive data generated by on-board devices. Reinforcement Learning (RL), unlike learning methods that require pre-acquisition of data sets, generates data by interacting with a dynamic channel environment and learns strategies by utilizing the data to solve sequential decision problems, is a suitable candidate to deal with the radio resource management problems in V2X networks. With deep reinforcement learning, the constraints in (5) can be achieved by a reasonable setting of the reward function.

Considering the VUEs as RL agents in the network, the state space, action space and reward founction of RL approach are defined as follows:

(1) **State Space:** state is defined as s_t, which can be expressed as $\{G_t^v, G_t^I, I_{t-1}, P_{t-1}, U_t, L_t\}$, each item in it is as follows:

G_t^v: the real-time channel state information of the current V2V link at time t. For V2V link k, $G_t^v = \{g_k, \tilde{g}_{m,k}, g_{k',k}\}$.

G_t^I: the real-time channel state information of the sub-band shared by the current V2V link at time t. For the case where V2V link k occupies the frequency sub-band of V2I link m, $G_t^I = \{g_m, \tilde{g}_k\}$.

I_{t-1}: expressed as $I_{t-1} = (I_{t-1}[1], ..., I_{t-1}[M])$, each item of which represents the received interference power of the current V2V link for all V2I links at time $t - 1$.

P_{t-1}: expressed as $P_{t-1} = (P_{t-1}[1], ..., P_{t-1}[M])$, each item of which represents the number of times the sub-band is used by the partner at time $t - 1$

U_t: the remaining time to meet the maximum tolerable latency T_0.

L_t: the remaining load for transmission. If the V2V transmission is completed within the maximum tolerable latency T_0, then $L_t=0$, otherwise L_t is the amount of the load transferred during the timeout period.

Joint State: Due to the reasons that the limited ability of a single agent to obeserve environment and the information contained in obeservations has a great influence on the decision making, we introduced an idea of local cooperative learning, which aims to improve the information acquisition ability of the agent and help the agent making more informed decisions by enhancing the information sharing between the agent and the surrounding partners. The specific operations are as follows:

A joint policy in a smaller scale is defined with a local MDP$\langle D, S_J, A, \rho_0, P, r\rangle$, where D is the radius of the local network formed by the number of partners centered on the agent. Assuming that for the kth agent, the radius D of the local collaborative network centered on it is defined as n, that is, the number of its partners is n (the n cars closest to it).

At each time slot, agents observes the environment to obtain local state information. After receiving the obeservations from n partners in the local network centered on it, the agent will merge the data to form a joint state :

$$s_{J_k,t} = \left\{ s_{p_1,t}, s_{p_2,t}, ..., s_{p_n,t}, s_{k,t} \right\} \tag{6}$$

where $s_{k,t}$ presents the state observed by agent k at time t. $s_{p_1,t}, s_{p_2,t}, ..., s_{p_n,t}$ denotes the obervations of its n partners at time t, respectively.

(2) Action Space: At time slot t, the agent k observes the environmet to get an obeservation s_t ($s_t \in S$). Subsequently, it takes the joint state $s_{J_k,t}$ as input to performs an action a_t($a_t \in A$) which including the selection of a sub-band to share spectrum resources and the power level used for transmission according to the current strategy π. The transmit power is discretized into three levels, so the dimension of the action space is $3 \times N_{RB}$, where N_{RB} is the total number of resource blocks, which corresponds to the sub-band one to one.

(3) Reward Founction: The setting of the reward function is critical to the problem of reinforcement learning, since it will directly affect the convergence of the policy and the ability to achieve the desired training goal. The reward function shall include three components according to the restrictions shown in (5), e.t., the total traversal capacity of V2I and V2V and the remaining transmission time of V2V. The total traversal capacity of V2I and V2V links are used to measure the interference of the current V2V link to V2I and other V2V links, respectively, and the positive or negative remaining transmission time is corresponds to the success or otherwise of V2V transmission, respectively. Hence, the reward function can be expressed as:

$$r_t = \mu_I \sum_{m \in \mathcal{M}} C^I[m] + \mu_v \sum_{k \in \mathcal{K}} C^v[k] + \mu_t U_t \tag{7}$$

The coefficients μ_I, μ_v, and μ_t are the weights of the three components respectively. When V2V transmission exceeds the time delay limit, the value of U_t is negative, which means it is a penalty, and the more time exceeded, the greater the penalty the agent's behavior gets.In order to obtain good performance in the long term, both immediate and future rewards should be considered.

Therefore, the main goal of reinforcement learning is to find a strategy to maximize the desired cumulative discounted reward:

$$L(\pi_\theta) = E[\sum_{n=0}^{\infty} \beta^n r_{t+n}]$$ (8)

where π_θ is the parameterized strategy and θ is the parameter of the strategy. $\beta \in [0,1]$ is the discount factor.

(4) LC-PPO Based Approach: PPO (Proximal Policy Optimization) is a policy-based reinforcement learning algorithm with low computational complexity compared to other policy gradient methods so as we can achieve the convergence of the policy by adjusting fewer parameters. In addition, it facilitate the form of joint state in our work of local collaboration since the training data collected by PPO does not include the observations at the next moment.

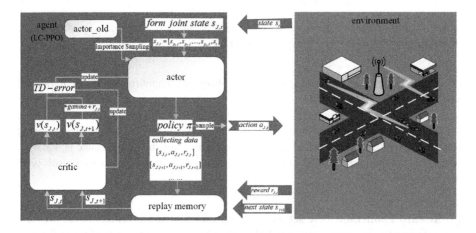

Fig. 2. Workflow of LC-PPO

Combining PPO with local collabration mechanism, the process of LC-PPO interacting with the environment is shown in Fig. 2. At time slot t, the agent (VUEs) observes the environment (everything outside the VUEs) to obtain the local state information s_t of the environment which including channel state information, interference conditions, etc. from within the state space S. Then the agent will form a joint state $s_{J,t}$ based on its own obeservations and the obeservations of n partners around it. Subsequently, the agent takes the joint state $s_{J,t}$ as the input of the actor network, and takes an action

$a_{J,t}$ i.e., selects a sub-band and transmit power from the action space A for transmission accordingly based on current policy π. After the agent feeds back its actions to the environment, then the environment jumps to the next state s_{t+1}, and agent will get a reward $r_{J,t}$.

Through the interaction process between the LC-PPO and the environment, the agent(k^{th} VUEs) collects n training data, all in the shape of: $[s_{J_k,t}, a_{J_k,t}, r_{J_k,t}]$. They are stored in a replay memory sequentially, and then retrieved in order from back to front during the training phase.

In the training phase, $s_{J_k,t}$ and $s_{J_k,t+1}$ are input to the critic network in turn, and the V-values of the two states are obtained separately. so that an advantage value($TD - error$) can be calculated, which is defined for each state-action pair to measure the superiority or inferiority of an action to the average performance of all actions in a given state. Regarding its specific calculation procedure as follows:

$$A(s_{J_k,t}, a_{J_k,t}) = Q(s_{J_k,t}, a_{J_k,t}) - V(s_{J_k,t}), Q(s_{J_k,t}, a_{J_k,t}) = r_{J_k,t} + \sum_{i=1}^{T-1} \gamma^i r_{J,t+i} + \gamma^{+T} V(s_{J_k,t+T})$$
(9)

where $Q(s_{J_k,t}, a_{J_k,t})$ represents the total expected discount reward that can be obtained by the vehicle in the state $s_{J_k,t}$ taking action $a_{J_k,t}$, $V(s_{J_k,t})$ is the estimated discount reward from state $s_{J_k,t}$ onwards. T is the time horizon, and γ is the discount factor.

Moreover, In order to update the current strategy π with the previous strategy π_{old} and to take advantage of the scarce training data, we adopt Improtance Sampling. Specifically. A policy ratio R_t is defined to evaluate the similarity between the updated policy and the previous policy at time step t as:

$$R_t(\theta) = \frac{\pi_\theta(a_{J_k,t}|s_{J_k,t})}{\pi_{\theta_{old}}(a_{J_k,t}|s_{J_k,t}) + 1e-8}$$
(10)

1e-8 is set for preventing the denominator from being 0.

In addition, We take some restrictions on the policy ratio R_t, which can limit the policy updates to a reasonable range, as follows:

$$clip(R_t(\theta)) \begin{cases} R_t(\theta), & 1 - \varepsilon \le R_t(\theta) \le 1 + \varepsilon \\ 1 - \varepsilon, & 1 - \varepsilon > R_t(\theta) \\ 1 + \varepsilon, & R_t(\theta) > 1 + \varepsilon \end{cases}$$
(11)

where ε is a tiny positive constant.

With the constrained policy update and clipping operation, the policy optimization objective function can be adapted from Eq. (8) as:

$$L^{clip}(\pi(\theta)) = E_\tau[\min(R_t A_t, (clip(R_t), 1 - \varepsilon, 1 + \varepsilon)A_t)]$$
(12)

where A_t abbreviates the advantage value $A_t(s, a)$ at time t, $clip(.)$ is the clipping function, and R_t is short for $R_t(\theta)$.

In particular, in the local network centered on the kth agent, each of its partners only plays the role of providing shared data. While they receive the local state information of the environment shared by their respective partners under their own local network as well, and store it in their own replay memory to support the training of them. The specific algorithm flow can be viewed in Table 1.

Table 1. Local cooperative based proximal policy optimization

Algorithm 1 LC-PPO
1:   Initialize policy network with random weighs θ_0 and clipping threshold $\in$.
2:   **for** episode = 1 ,..., N **do**
3:     Reset Environment, Replay Memory
4:     **for** step = 0 ,..., T **do**
5:       **for** k = 0 ,..., K **do**
6:         Detect partners within radius of D
7:         Form Joint states $s_{J_k,t} = \left\{ s_{p_1,t}, s_{p_2,t}, ..., s_{p_n,t}, s_{k,t} \right\}$
8:         Collect transition $[s_{J_k,t}, a_{J_k,t}, r_{J_k,t}]$ on policy $\pi(\theta)$
9:         Extend Replay Memory with transitions
10:    **end for**
11:    Estimate advantage A with Eq (9)
12:    Update the policy by $\theta \leftarrow \arg max_\theta \, L^{clip}(\theta)$ as Eq (12)
13: **end for**

4 Experiments and Results Analysis

In this section, we present simulation results to demonstrate the performance of the proposed method for resource allocation of V2X network, and given our own analysis of the results.

We consider a single cell system with the carrier frequency of 2 GHz. We follow the simulation setup for the Manhattan case detailed in 3GPP TR 36.885, where there are 9 blocks in all and with both line-of-sight (LOS) and non-line-of-sight (NLOS) channels. The vehicles are dropped on the roads randomly following the spatial Poisson process.

Our experiments are conducted on a PC with an Intel Core i7-8700H CPU whose frequency is 3.2 GHz. We use TensorFlow 2.1.0 with Python 3.6 on Ubuntu 20.04 LTS in the simulations to implement LC-PPO. The key parameters of simulations are shown in Table 2 and Table 3.

The proposed method is compared with other two benchmark algorithms. The first is a random resource allocation method. At each time, the agent randomly chooses a sub-band and a transmit power level for transmission. Based on the relevance of the research questions, the other method is developed in [7], where they designed a DQN-based resource allocation strategy.

As shown in Fig. 3, it can be seen that after the same number of iterations of training, our proposed resource allocation approach based on LC-PPO is able to make the agent get a higher average return value. The trend of convergence more obvious, which is about 1000 Step or so, the return value will stabilize at about 55.

Table 2. Simulation parameters

Parameter	Value
Number of lanes	8 in total
Number of vechicles	40
Number of partners	3
Vehicle speed	36 km/h
Number of RB	20
Carrier frequency	2 GHZ
Bandwidth per channel	1.5 MHZ
RSU antenna height	25 m
RSU antenna gain	8 dBi
RSU receiver noise figure	5 dB
Vehicle antenna height	1.5 m
Vehicle antenna gain	3 dBi
Vehicle receiver noise figure	9 dB
Latency constraints T_0 for V2V transmission	100 ms
Transmit power of IUEs, VUEs	23 dB, [5,10,23] dB
Noise power σ^2	-114 dBm
$[\mu_I, \mu_v, \mu_t]$	[0.1,0.9,1]

Table 3. Channel model parameters

Parameter	V2I Link	V2V Link
Path loss model	$128.1 + 37.6\log_{10}d$, d in km	LOS in WINNER+ B1 Manhattan
Shadowing distribution	Log-normal	Log-normal
Shadowing standard deviation ξ	8 dB	3 dB
Decorrelation distance	50 m	10 m
Path loss and shadowing update	Every 100 ms	Every 100 ms
Fast fading	Rayleigh fading	Rayleigh fading
Fast fading update	Every 1 ms	Every 1 ms

Figure 4 shows the performance comparison between our proposed approach and the two baseline algorithms in the test round in terms of average ergodic V2I capacity and average V2V failure rate. As we have seen, our proposed strategy has a huge improvement over the other two algorithms in these two aspects. The reasons may lie in the efforts made in our work for the collaboration among vehicle. By sharing information among vehicles in the adjacent area, the probability of conflict between agent and surrounding vehicles in sub-band selection is greatly reduced, and thus performance improvements in both aspects will occur.

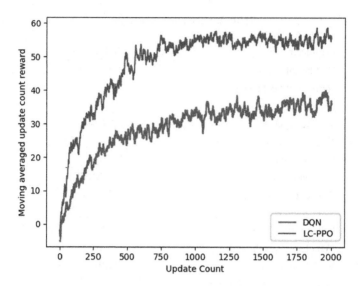

Fig. 3. Comparison of the changes in mean reward of DQN and LC-PPO

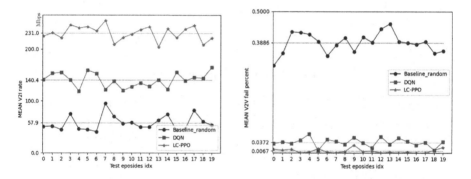

Fig. 4. Mean V2I rate and V2V fail percent during test phase

Figure 5 shows the relationship between the probability of three different power levels being selected and the remaining time. The probability of the lowest power level 5 dB being selected is always the lowest regardless of the remaining time. The reason may be that if the agent selects a power level 5 dB, it will most likely violate the delay limit of the V2V link, thus received a heavy punishment. In most of the time, the probability of the power level 23 dB being selected is higher than 10 dB due to reason that the higher the transmitting power is, the shorter the transmission time is. However, when the remaining time is depleted, the probability of 10 dB being selected will exceed 23 dB. We think it is a way for the agent to increase the reward. When the remaining time is not much left, even choosing the highest power level, the agent may still not be able to complete the V2V load transmission within the specified time. In contrast to this, it is better for the agent to reduce the interference by reducing the power to obtain a higher reward.

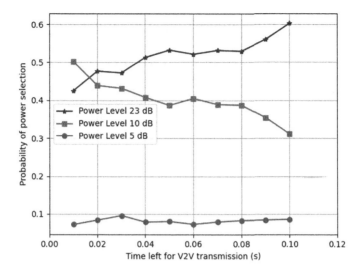

Fig. 5. Power selection probability versus remaining time

5   Conclusion

In this paper, we proposed a V2X network resource allocation strategy based on distributed reinforcement learning with local collaboration and apply it to a Manhattan grid-based urban road scenario. Due to the introduction of the idea of local cooperative learning, the agent in the distributed network resource allocation problem can obtain the local state information of the environment shared by the surrounding partners, and can make more informed behavioral decisions at each step based on richer information input. From the simulation results, each agent learns how to work together to improve the ergodic V2I capacity at the whole system level while minimizing the failure rate of V2V link transmission.

References

1. Noor-A-Rahim, M.: A survey on resource allocation in vehicular networks. IEEE Transactions on Intelligent Transportation Systems, pp. 1–21 (2020)
2. Wang, L.: Learn to compress CSI and allocate resources in vehicular networks. IEEE Trans. Commun. **68**(6), 3640–3653 (2020)
3. Guo, C.: Resource allocation for low-latency vehicular communications: an effective capacity perspective. IEEE J. Select. Areas Commun. **37**(4), 905–917 (2019)
4. Zhang, R.: Interference graph-based resource-sharing schemes for vehicular networks. IEEE Trans. Veh. Technol. **62**(8), 4028–4039 (2013)
5. Du, J.: Computation offloading and resource allocation in vehicular networks based on dual-side cost minimization. IEEE Tran. Veh. Technol. **68**(2), 1079–1092 (2019)
6. Yang, T., Hu, Y.: Deep reinforcement learning based resource allocation in low latency edge computing networks. In: 2018 15th International Symposium on Wireless Communication Systems (ISWCS), pp. 1–5. Lisbon, Portugal (2018). https://doi.org/10.1109/ISWCS.2018.8491089

7. He, Y., Li, Y.G.: Deep reinforcement learning for resource allocation in V2V communications. In: 2018 IEEE International Conference on Communications (ICC), pp. 1–6. Kansas City, MO, USA (2018). https://doi.org/10.1109/ICC.2018.8422586

8. He, Y.: Deep reinforcement learning based resource allocation for V2V communications. IEEE Trans. Veh. Technol. **68**(4), 3163–3173 (2019)

9. Liang, L.: Spectrum sharing in vehicular networks based on multi-agent reinforcement learning. IEEE J. Select Areas Commun. **37**(10), 2282–2292 (2019)

10. Wei, H., Liu, X.: Mixed-autonomy traffic control with proximal policy optimization. In: 2019 IEEE Vehicular Networking Conference (VNC), pp. 1–8. Los Angeles, CA, USA (2019). https://doi.org/10.1109/VNC48660.2019.9062809

Visual Computing for IoT

DDCAttNet: Road Segmentation Network for Remote Sensing Images

Genji Yuan[1], Jianbo Li[1,2(✉)], Zhiqiang Lv[2], Yinong Li[1], and Zhihao Xu[1]

[1] College of Computer Science and Technology, Qingdao University,
Qingdao 266071, China
{2020010029,lijianbo}@qdu.edu.cn
[2] Institute of Ubiquitous Networks and Urban Computing, Qingdao 266070, China

Abstract. Semantic segmentation of remote sensing images based on deep convolutional neural networks has proven its effectiveness. However, due to the complexity of remote sensing images, deep convolutional neural networks have difficulties in segmenting objects with weak appearance coherences even though they can represent local features of object effectively. The road networks segmentation of remote sensing images faces two major problems: high inter-individual similarity and ubiquitous occlusion. In order to address these issues, this paper develops a novel method to extract roads from complex remote sensing images. We designed a Dual Dense Connected Attention network (DDCAttNet) that establishes long-range dependencies between road features. The architecture of the network is designed to incorporate both spatial attention and channel attention information into semantic segmentation for accurate road segmentation. Experimental results on the benchmark dataset demonstrate the superiority of our proposed approach both in quantitative and qualitative evaluation.

Keywords: Remote sensing · Road segmentation · Attention mechanism

1 Introduction

Remote sensing image segmentation is a fundamental task of computer vision that assigns a specified category label to each pixel in an image [1–3]. Remote sensing image segmentation technology plays an important role in many fields

This research was supported in part by National Key Research and Development Plan Key Special Projects under Grant No. 2018YFB2100303, Shandong Province colleges and universities youth innovation technology plan innovation team project under Grant No. 2020KJN011, Shandong Provincial Natural Science Foundation under Grant No. ZR2020MF060, Program for Innovative Postdoctoral Talents in Shandong Province under Grant No. 40618030001, National Natural Science Foundation of China under Grant No. 61802216, and Postdoctoral Science Foundation of China under Grant No. 2018M642613.

© Springer Nature Switzerland AG 2021
Z. Liu et al. (Eds.): WASA 2021, LNCS 12938, pp. 457–468, 2021.
https://doi.org/10.1007/978-3-030-86130-8_36

such as urban planning, intelligent traffic, environmental protection, climate change and forest vegetation. Remote sensing images have many categories and complicated spatial information, which makes it a challenging task to segment remote sensing images effectively.

With the further improvement of remote sensing image resolution, the accuracy of traditional image segmentation methods can no longer meet the current requirements [4]. Therefore, the need to develop new methods of remote sensing image segmentation is greater than ever before. Fortunately, with the progress achieved with deep learning, investigations of remote sensing images segmentation have produced overwhelming analytical approaches to improve segmentation accuracy. Fully convolutional network (FCN) has greatly improved the state-of-art in image segmentation, and it also plays an important role in the remote sensing image segmentation. The development of a large number of semantic segmentation networks was born from FCN architecture. To aggregate multi-scale contexts, some methods generate feature maps by different expanded convolutions and pooling operations [5,6]. Some methods design novel encoder-decoder structure of networks to fuse mid-level and high-level semantic information [7–9]. Another works adopt more efficient basic classification models to capture richer global context features or [10,11]. These fusion methods for context facilitate the capture of different scale objects. However, the long-range dependencies between objects in a global view cannot be fully exploited due to the limitations of context information.

Recently, attention modules have been widely applied in the image vision field because of their flexible structure [12–14]. Attention mechanism has been proven to be an effective means to enhance the performance of a neural network [15]. The attention mechanisms explore long-range dependencies by generating weight feature maps and fusing feature maps. When designing the attention networks, one or more attention modules are integrated sequentially with each block in a basic backbone network, with each attention module focusing on channel or spatial information [17,18]. Most of the attention modules are learned by convolution layers with limited receptive fields, which makes it hard to exploit the original spatial information in a global scope [18]. Crucially, precise spatial information plays a fundamental role in the segmentation of remote sensing images. The complexity of network will increase significantly if deeper layers are stacked [19]. In addition, the effective receptive field of CNN only occupies a small portion of the full theoretical receptive field [20,21]. Consequently, the global information cannot be used effectively for remote sensing image segmentation [22–24].

In this paper, we present a Dual Dense Connected Attention network (DDCAttNet) to improve the segmentation accuracy of remote sensing images. In our work, both the spatial attention module and the channel attention module are used for remote sensing image segmentation to capture the features dependencies in the spatial and channel dimensions respectively. These two attention modules can effectively improve the accuracy of remote sensing image segmentation. Specifically, we applied two parallel attention modules between the convolution blocks, one of which is the spatial attention module and the other is the channel attention module. We introduce a series of skip connections among different attention modules to transfer the information gathered from the previous attention modules to the subsequent decoder modules, which thereby improving the learning ability of DDCAttNet. The outputs of attention modules between convolutional blocks are fused to further enhance the feature representations. Our method shows better performance when dealing with complex and diverse remote sensing images. Our network model can aggregate the features of the target from the global space to avoid the influence of occluded objects. Moreover, we explicitly consider the relationship between spatial attention and channel attention for understand the scene from the long-range dependence of the target. The contribution of this study primarily includes the following three points:

(1) We propose a Dual Dense Connected Attention network (DDCAttNet) that uses spatial and channel attention mechanisms to enhance the ability of features capture in the semantic segmentation of remote sensing images.
(2) We design a global attention module to extract pixel-level spatial information, and a lightweight channel attention module is utilized to model channel interdependencies. The performance of the semantic segmentation is significantly improved after modeling the long-range dependencies of target features.
(3) We combine skip connections between the decoder modules to enhance the learning capabilities of DDCAttNet.

2   Related Work

Semantic segmentation, as one of the challenging tasks based on pixel-level image classification, is a key approach to divide an image into a variety of coherent semantically-meaningful parts [25,26]. Methods of semantic segmentation can be roughly divided into two categories: traditional methods and ones based on deep learning. Traditional methods on image semantic segmentation have heavily relied on artificial design features, such as color, texture, shape and spatial position to extract features. However, with the improvement of image resolution, these algorithms show some bottlenecks. It is now well established from a variety of studies, that the method based on deep learning is a promising approach to solve image semantic segmentation problems. The FCN proposed by Shelhamer et al. [27] combines semantic information from a deep layer with appearance information from a shallow by the skip connections, uses convolutional layer to extract features, and fully convolutional layer to generate a segmentation image with accurate edges and detailed label. It is encouraging that compared with traditional methods, methods based on FCN can achieve sound semantic segmentation results on many representative image segmentation datasets. In recent years, there has been an increasing amount of literature on FCN extend models, such as SegNet [28], U-Net [29], DeepUNet [30], Y-Net [31] and DeepLab [32]. Among them, Badrinarayanan et al. [28] adopted a novel decoder structure of network, in which an up-sampling manner was proposed. The U-Net network has been proven to exhibit excellent performance in various semantic segmentation tasks. DeepLab acquired a larger receptive field by Atrous Spatial Pyramid Pooling (ASPP) composed of parallel convolution with different expansion rates. Semantic segmentation plays a significant role in the recognition of different types of targets in remote sensing images. In recent years, many state-of-the-art semantic segmentation methods have been proposed to segment remote sensing images effectively. Shuai et al. [33] used a directed acyclic graph recurrent neural network to capture long-range dependency information. However, although this method can capture rich contextual information, it is heavily dependent on models trained on large labeled datasets. In order to solve the problem of class imbalance in remote sensing images, Dong et al. [34] proposed a weighted focal loss. Chen et al. [35] effectively improved the performance of semantic segmentation based on the fusion of multi-modal data.

In addition, attention mechanisms have been designed to model long-range dependencies and have been successfully applied in many tasks. Vaswani et al. [36] first applied the attention mechanism to explore the global dependence of machine translation. Now, the attention mechanism has been widely used in image classification [37], image segmentation [38] and other fields [39]. Zhang et al. [40] introduced a self-attention mechanism to model attention-driven, long-range dependency for image generation tasks. Hu et al. [41] focused on the channel relationship and proposed the Squeeze-and-Excitation (SE) architectural unit, which can adaptively recalibrate the channel-wise feature response. Li et al. [42] constructed a Spatial Group-wise Rnhance (SGE) module that can adjust the weight of each sub-feature by generating an attention factor for each spatial location. Gao et al. [43] used Global Second-order Pooling (GSoP) to more effectively exploit holistic image information throughout a network. Cao et al. [43] developed a simplified network based on a query-independent formulation, resulting in a lightweight module to capture long-range dependencies. Chen et al. [45] proposed a a novel double attention block for image or video recognition, which can aggregate and propagate informative global features from the entire spatio-temporal space. Most non-local neural networks focused on creating sophisticated attention modules for better network performance [21].

3   Proposed Method

For a feature set $F = \{f_i \in \mathbb{R}^d, i = 1, ..., N\}$ of N correlated features with each of d dimensions, the attention models are used to learn the attention value ω_i of the ith feature. The local attention and the global attention are two common strategies utilized to construct the long-range dependencies of the ith feature. The attention mechanism mainly calculates the context information c_i of the encoder, and then connects c_i with the target hidden state h_i of the decoder [46]. Hence, overall, there is only a slight difference between the models in the calculation of context vector c_i. Global attention utilizes all hidden states together to jointly learn attention [47].

As illustrated in Fig. 1, we design two types of attention modules to capture global information by a residual network, thus obtaining better feature representations for pixel-level prediction. The framework proposed in this paper consists

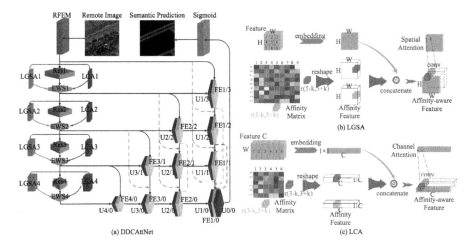

Fig. 1. The architecture of our DDCAttNet. LGSA (b) represents the lightweight global spatial attention module. LCA (c) represents the lightweight global channel attention module. U*/* represents upsampling layer, FE*/* represents feature extractor.

of the following components: residual blocks, spatial attention module, channel attention module, and densely-connected skip connections. We designed a raw feature extraction module (RFEM) to capture the feature information of the raw remote sensing images. Specifically, the RFEM module is convolution + batch normalization + ReLU + Max pooling. We aggregate the outputs of the two attention modules and the residual blocks to obtain better feature representations.

3.1 Spatial Attention Module

For a feature tensor $X = \mathbb{R}^{C \times H \times W}$ with width W, height H and channel C, we designed a lightweight global spatial attention module, namely LGSA, to learn a spatial attention map of size $H \times W$. Each C-dimensional feature vector is used as a feature node. We achieve local interaction through k neighbors without reducing the dimensionality. Such method is proven to guarantee both efficiency and effectiveness [15]. First, X is converted into two C-dimensional feature vectors $x_i, x_j \in \mathbb{R}^{HW \times C}$ by two convolutional layers. Then, the affinity matrix is constructed using these two C-dimensional feature vectors. In this paper, we have not applied the dimensionality reduction operation, but calculating the affinity matrix for all elements would be a much greater computational burden. Therefore, we consider cross-space interaction through each element and its $k(k \leq H, k \leq W)$ nearest neighbors. Specifically, $r_{i,j}$ denotes the affinity between the $i-th$ element and the $j-th$ element, which can be defined as the dot product affinity

$$r_{i,j} = \upsilon_s(x_i)^T \nu_s(x_j), \tag{1}$$

where υ_s, ν_s denote 1×1 $conv + BN + ReLU$. $\upsilon_s(x_i) = ReLU(W_\upsilon x_i)$, $\nu_s(x_i) = ReLU(W_\nu x_i)$, where $W_\upsilon \in \mathbb{R}^{C \times C}$, $W_\nu \in \mathbb{R}^{C \times C}$. For element x_i, the affinity vector is $r_i = [r_{i,i-k}, ..., r_{i,i+k}, r_{i-k,i}, ..., r_{i+k,i}]$. Note that $r_i = [r_{i,j}, r_{j,i}]$ here. $r_{j,i}$ denotes the affinity between the $j - th$ element and the $i - th$ element. k denotes the adaptive nearest neighbor element. We stack the elements pairwise relations with their k nearest neighbors according to a certain fixed order. The affinity vector r_i contains positional and relational information of the elements, providing a compact representation to capture spatial information.

In addition to the affinity vector r_i, we have considered the feature itself x_i. Because only spatial information needs to be extracted, the original feature map is converted into a $1 \times H \times W$ feature map after a layer of convolution. Then, the affinity matrix is connected to the feature map and the corresponding weight values are obtained by a global average pooling.

$$y = [g(\omega_s(x_i)), \psi_s(r_i)], \tag{2}$$

where ω_s, ψ_s denote 1×1 $conv + BN + ReLU$, i.e. 1×1 spatial convolution is first implemented, followed by batch normalization (BN) and ReLU activation. $\omega_s(x_i) = ReLU(W_\omega x_i)$, $\psi_s(x_i) = ReLU(W_\psi x_i)$. $g(\cdot)$ denotes global average pooling operation along the channel dimension to further reduce the dimension to 1.

Finally, the Sigmoid activation function is used to generate the corresponding weight maps.

$$att = \sigma(Wy), \tag{3}$$

where σ is a Sigmoid function, W is a parameter matrix. The band matrix W is used to learn attention weights by a strategy of shared parameters, i.e.,

$$att_i = \sigma\left(\sum_{j=1}^{2k+1} w^j y_i^j\right), \; y_i^j \in \Omega_i^{2k+1}, \tag{4}$$

where Ω_i^{2k+1} indicates the set of $2k$ affinity term of y_i.

The coverage of the nearest neighbor needs to be determined. It would take more effort to adjust the interaction range manually, so we set the interaction range by an adaptive method [48,49]. According to the shared similarity principle, it is reasonable that the nearest neighbor interaction range is proportional to the feature map size. We use nonlinear mapping to determine the interaction range of the nearest neighbors, i.e.,

$$S = 2^{(\eta * k - b)}. \tag{5}$$

Then, given feature map size S, Interaction range k can be adaptively determined by

$$k = \left| \frac{log_2(S)}{\eta} + \frac{b}{\eta} \right|_{odd}, \tag{6}$$

where $|\cdot|_{odd}$ denotes the nearest odd number. In this paper, if $S \geq 64$, $\eta = 2, b = 1$, else $\eta = 1, b = 0$. Clearly, better performance can be achieved with fewer parameters through nonlinear mapping.

3.2   Channel Attention Module

We designed a lightweight channel attention (LCA) module to learn the C-dimensional attention vector. Similar to spatial attention module, the affinity $r_{i,j}$ from element i to element j can be defined as a dot-product affinity:

$$r_{i,j} = v_c(x_i)^T \nu_c(x_j), \tag{7}$$

where v_c, ν_c denote 1×1 $conv + BN + ReLU$. First, input feature tensor $X = \mathbb{R}^{C \times H \times W}$ is flattened to $X' = \mathbb{R}^{HW \times C \times 1}$ and then using a BN followed by ReLU activation to perform a transformation on X'. We obtain the nearest neighbor k by equal (8).

$$k = \left| \frac{log_2(C)}{\eta} + \frac{b}{\eta} \right|_{odd}, \tag{8}$$

where C indicates the number of channels. When calculating the channel nearest neighbor, $\eta = 2, b = 1$. Then, the pairwise relationships between channels are represented by an affinity matrix. High-dimensional channels have a long interaction range, while the ground-low-dimensional channels achieve a shorter range of interaction through nonlinear mapping.

The subsequent operation is similar to the spatial attention module. For element, the affinity vector is $r_i = [r_{i,i-k}, ..., r_{i,i+k}, r_{i-k,i}, ..., r_{i+k,i}]$, to represent global structural information. When calculating the channel attention, we paid equal attention to the channel itself in addition to the affinity matrix. Similar to equal (2) and equal (3). Note that the weights are shared between channels.

For our lightweight attention module, the complexity of the model is increased as little as possible without dimensionality reduction. Our model adds few model parameters, while bringing clear improvement. Although the non-local approach uses global contextual information to determine attentional features, it ignores the structural information of the affinity relationships between different features. In this paper, we mine knowledge from global information through pairwise affinity relationships between features. In addition, since the training data has been desensitized, we extract the boundary information directly using the original images. Using only feature maps to determine the final prediction may be inaccurate. This is because information can be lost in the process of constant downsampling.

4   Experiment

We choose the remote sensing image dataset constructed by Liu et al. [6] as the benchmark, which is used to train and evaluate the DDCAttNet. The dataset contains several major urban areas in Ottawa, Cancda. The spatial resolution of the image is $0.21 - m$ per pixel. The images cover 21 areas about $8\,km^2$. The images contain multiple manual annotations, and we only used road surface annotations in this paper. The dataset has a lot of occulusions caused by cars and trees, so the dataset is more challenging. In our experiments, we used the

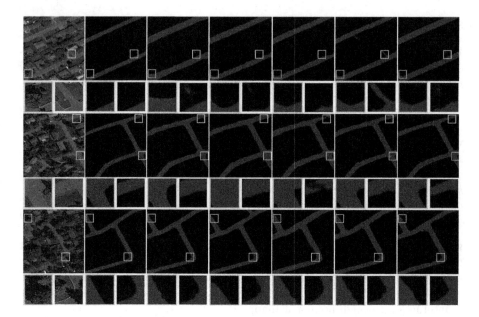

Fig. 2. The road segmentation results for several image patches of the benchmark test images. From left to right: Input image, ground truth, FCN++ [27], SegNet++ [50], UNet++ [29], RoadNet++ [6] and DDCAttNet++. The road and background are shown in blue and black, respectively. (Color figure online)

Adam optimizer with decay of 0.9 and $\epsilon = 1e - 3$. The learning rate is set to 0.001 and decays every 50 epoch.

To evaluate the performance of the method in this paper, we introduce metrics of common semantic segmentation evaluations [27,50]. Let n_{ij} denote the number of pixels predicted by class i to be class j, where there exist n_{cls} different classes. Let $t_i = \sum_j n_{ij}$ denote the total number of pixels of the i, including both true positives and false positives. Then, we can obtain the following evaluation metrics. (1) Global accuracy, which is used to evaluate the percentage of correctly predicted pixels, $\sum_i n_{ii} / \sum_i t_i$. (2) Class average accuracy, which indicates the prediction accuracy for all classes, $(1/n_{cls}) \sum_i n_{ii}/t_i$. (3) Mean intersection over union (I/U) over all classes, $(1/n_{cls}) \sum_i n_{ii}/(t_i + \sum_j n_{ji} - n_{ii})$.

Let TP, FP and FN denote the true positives, the false positives, and the false negatives, respectively. We can obtain three metrics that are common in the field of road detection. i.e., $Precision = TP/(TP + FP), Reacll = TP/(TP + FN), F - score = 2(precision \times recall)/(precision + recall)$.

Our method is compared with the other state-of-the-art methods, including FCN [27], SegNet [50], UNet [29], and RoadNet [6]. As shown in Table 1, DDCAttNet achieves the best segmentation results on all metrics. These evaluation results demonstrate the effectiveness of the method in this paper, which is significantly improved compared to most advanced methods. '+' denotes the spatial attention module. '++' not only contains the spatial attention module

Table 1. Road segmentation performance of different methods. The best performance indicators are highlighted in red color.

Method	Global accuracy	Class average accuracy	I/U	Precision	Recall	F-score	Parameter (M)
FCN	98.0	95.8	91.8	91.6	93.3	92.4	74.6
FCN++	98.5	95.9	90.8	94.5	90.3	92.4	226.8
FCN++(light)	98.2	96.1	92.3	92.5	92.3	92.4	96.2
SegNet	96.1	93.2	88.9	88.2	85.4	86.8	117.9
SegNet++	96.8	94.0	90.2	88.3	91.8	90.0	361.6
SegNet++ (light)	97.1	94.8	90.1	90.4	91.8	91.1	150.8
UNet	97.8	96.2	90.3	91.3	91.6	91.4	69.1
UNet++	98.1	95.8	93.2	92.6	93.4	93.0	286.2
UNet++ (light)	98.3	96.4	92.7	92.8	93.8	93.3	100.4
RoadNet	98.2	96.2	92.5	92.3	92.7	92.5	123.6
RoadNet++	97.9	96.8	93.1	93.6	92.8	93.2	462.4
RoadNet++ (light)	98.6	96.9	92.9	93.6	93.7	93.6	148.2
DDCAttNet+	98.3	96.6	93.0	93.6	93.4	93.5	68.9
DDCAttNet++	98.6	96.5	93.4	93.2	94.4	93.8	246.9
DDCAttNet++ (light)	98.6	96.8	93.5	93.8	94.2	94.0	82.3

but also the channel attention module. Specifically, DDCAttNet++ achieves the best road segmentation performance on all metrics and has different degrees of performance improvement for different segmentation methods, which demonstrates the effectiveness of the proposed spatial attention module and channel attention module. The road segmentation results for several image patches of the benchmark test images are shown in Fig. 2. As shown in Fig. 2, DDCAttNet++ shows a competitive performance in terms of visual effects, especially in the absence of road information.

5 Conclusion

In this paper, a novel end-to-end CNN network is applied to perform the remote sensing image road segmentation task. We propose two lightweight attention modules (spatial attention module and channel attention module). DDCAttNet automatically learns global features and establishes long-rang dependencies, and the network can better cope with road segmentation in complex scenes. Specifically, DDCAttNet presents more competitive results when the road is obscured by objects such as shadows, buildings and trees, or when the environment is similar to the road. Experiments have demonstrated that the network suggested in this paper is able to adapt to various scenarios and sizes of roads. Besides, the lightweight attention model we designed can be easily combined with advanced models and gain their performance. In the future, we plan to develop the remote sensing image road segmentation task from the aspect of loss function in order to segment the curved part of road better.

References

1. He, K., Zhang, X., Ren, S., Sun, J.: Identity mappings in deep residual networks. In: Leibe, B., Matas, J., Sebe, N., Welling, M. (eds.) ECCV 2016. LNCS, vol. 9908, pp. 630–645. Springer, Cham (2016). https://doi.org/10.1007/978-3-319-46493-0_38
2. Huang, G., Liu, Z., Van Der Maaten, L., Weinberger, K.Q.: Densely connected convolutional networks. In: Computer Vision and Pattern Recognition, pp. 4700–4708 (2017)
3. Sun, S., Pang, J., Shi, J., Yi, S., Ouyang, W.: FishNet: a versatile backbone for image, region, and pixel level prediction. Adv. Neural. Inf. Process. Syst. **31**, 754–764 (2018)
4. Zheng, P., Qi, Y., Zhou, Y., Chen, P., Zhan, J., Lyu, M.R.-T.: An automatic framework for detecting and characterizing performance degradation of software systems. IEEE Trans. Reliab. **63**(4), 927–943 (2014)
5. Chen, L.-C., Papandreou, G., Kokkinos, I., Murphy, K., Yuille, A.L.: DeepLAB: semantic image segmentation with deep convolutional nets, Atrous convolution, and fully connected CRFs. IEEE Trans. Pattern Anal. Mach. Intell. **40**(4), 834–848 (2017)
6. Liu, Y., Yao, J., Lu, X., Xia, M., Wang, X., Liu, Y.: RoadNet: learning to comprehensively analyze road networks in complex urban scenes from high-resolution remotely sensed images. IEEE Trans. Geosci. Remote Sens. **57**(4), 2043–2056 (2018)
7. Ding, H., Jiang, X., Shuai, B., Qun Liu, A., Wang, G.: Context contrasted feature and gated multi-scale aggregation for scene segmentation. In: Computer Vision and Pattern Recognition, pp. 2393–2402 (2018)
8. Zhang, H., et al.: Context encoding for semantic segmentation. In: Computer Vision and Pattern Recognition, pp. 7151–7160 (2018)
9. Lin, G., Milan, A., Shen, C., Reid, I.: RefineNet: multi-path refinement networks for high-resolution semantic segmentation. In: Computer Vision and Pattern Recognition, pp. 1925–1934 (2017)
10. Peng, C., Zhang, X., Yu, G., Luo, G., Sun, J.: Large kernel matters-improve semantic segmentation by global convolutional network. In: Computer Vision and Pattern Recognition, pp. 4353–4361 (2017)
11. Liu, Z., Li, X., Luo, P., Loy, C.-C., Tang, X.: Semantic image segmentation via deep parsing network. In: Computer Vision and Pattern Recognition, pp. 1377–1385 (2015)
12. Yu, F., Wang, D., Shelhamer, E., Darrell, T.: Deep layer aggregation. In: Computer Vision and Pattern Recognition, pp. 2403–2412 (2018)
13. Fu, J., Zheng, H., Mei, T.: Look closer to see better: recurrent attention convolutional neural network for fine-grained image recognition. In: Computer Vision and Pattern Recognition, pp. 4438–4446 (2017)
14. Cai, Y., et al.: Guided attention network for object detection and counting on drones. arXiv preprint arXiv:1909.11307 (2019)
15. Wang, Q., Wu, B., Zhu, P., Li, P., Zuo, W., Hu, Q.: ECA-Net: efficient channel attention for deep convolutional neural networks. In: Computer Vision and Pattern Recognition, pp. 11534–11542 (2020)

16. Li, J., Xiu, J., Yang, Z., Liu, C.: Dual path attention net for remote sensing semantic image segmentation. ISPRS Int. J. Geo Inf. **9**(10), 571 (2020)
17. Woo, S., Park, J., Lee, J.-Y., Kweon, I.S.: CBAM: convolutional block attention module. In: Ferrari, V., Hebert, M., Sminchisescu, C., Weiss, Y. (eds.) ECCV 2018. LNCS, vol. 11211, pp. 3–19. Springer, Cham (2018). https://doi.org/10.1007/978-3-030-01234-2_1
18. Zhang, Z., Lan, C., Zeng, W., Jin, X., Chen, Z.: Relation-aware global attention for person re-identification. In: Computer Vision and Pattern Recognition, pp. 3186–3195 (2020)
19. Wang, F., et al.: Residual attention network for image classification. In: Computer Vision and Pattern Recognition, pp. 3156–3164 (2017)
20. Luo, W., Li, Y., Urtasun, R., Zemel, R.: Understanding the effective receptive field in deep convolutional neural networks. Adv. Neural. Inf. Process. Syst. **29**, 4898–4906 (2016)
21. Wang, X., Girshick, R., Gupta, A., He, K.: Non-local neural networks. In: Computer Vision and Pattern Recognition, pp. 7794–7803 (2018)
22. Hu, J., Shen, L., Sun, G.: Squeeze-and-excitation networks. In: Computer Vision and Pattern Recognition, pp. 7132–7141 (2018)
23. Ma, X., et al.: DCANet: learning connected attentions for convolutional neural networks. arXiv preprint arXiv:2007.05099 (2020)
24. Ungerleider, S.K.L.G.: Mechanisms of visual attention in the human cortex. Annual Rev. Neurosci. **23**(1), 315–341 (2000)
25. Sharma, S., Ball, J.E., Tang, B., Carruth, D.W., Doude, M., Islam, M.A.: Semantic segmentation with transfer learning for off-road autonomous driving. Sensors **19**(11), 2577 (2019)
26. Chen, G., et al.: Fully convolutional neural network with augmented Atrous spatial pyramid pool and fully connected fusion path for high resolution remote sensing image segmentation. Appl. Sci. **9**(9), 1816 (2019)
27. Long, J., Shelhamer, E., Darrell, T.: Fully convolutional networks for semantic segmentation. In: Computer Vision and Pattern Recognition, pp. 3431–3440 (2015)
28. Badrinarayanan, V., Kendall, A., Cipolla, R.: SegNet: a deep convolutional encoder-decoder architecture for image segmentation. IEEE Trans. Pattern Anal. Mach. Intell. **39**(12), 2481–2495 (2017)
29. Ronneberger, O., Fischer, P., Brox, T.: U-Net: convolutional networks for biomedical image segmentation. In: Navab, N., Hornegger, J., Wells, W.M., Frangi, A.F. (eds.) MICCAI 2015. LNCS, vol. 9351, pp. 234–241. Springer, Cham (2015). https://doi.org/10.1007/978-3-319-24574-4_28
30. Li, R., et al.: DeepuNet: a deep fully convolutional network for pixel-level sea-land segmentation. IEEE J. Sel. Top. Appl. Earth Obser. Remote Sens. **11**(11), 3954–3962 (2018)
31. Li, Y., Xu, L., Rao, J., Guo, L., Yan, Z., Jin, S.: A Y-Net deep learning method for road segmentation using high-resolution visible remote sensing images. Remote Sens. Lett. **10**(4), 381–390 (2019)
32. Chen, L.-C., Papandreou, G., Schroff, F., Adam, H.: Rethinking atrous convolution for semantic image segmentation. arXiv preprint arXiv:1706.05587 (2017)
33. Shuai, B., Zuo, Z., Wang, B., Wang, G.: Scene segmentation with DAG-recurrent neural networks. IEEE Trans. Pattern Anal. Mach. Intell. **40**(6), 1480–1493 (2017)
34. Dong, R., Pan, X., Li, F.: DenseU-net-based semantic segmentation of small objects in urban remote sensing images. IEEE Access **7**, 65347–65356 (2019)

35. Chen, K., et al.: Effective fusion of multi-modal data with group convolutions for semantic segmentation of aerial imagery. In: IEEE International Geoscience and Remote Sensing Symposium, pp. 3911–3914 (2019)
36. Vaswani, A., et al.: Attention is all you need. Adv. Neural. Inf. Process. Syst. **30**, 5998–6008 (2017)
37. Anderson, P., et al.: Bottom-up and top-down attention for image captioning and visual question answering. In: Computer Vision and Pattern Recognition, pp. 6077–6086 (2018)
38. Fu, J., et al.: Dual attention network for scene segmentation. In: Computer Vision and Pattern Recognition, pp. 3146–3154 (2019)
39. Kuen, J., Wang, Z., Wang, G.: Recurrent attentional networks for saliency detection. In: Computer Vision and Pattern Recognition, pp. 3668–3677 (2016)
40. Zhang, H., Goodfellow, I., Metaxas, D., Odena, A.: Self-attention generative adversarial networks. In: International Conference on Machine Learning, pp. 7354–7363 (2019)
41. Hu, J., Shen, L., Albanie, S., Sun, G., Vedaldi, A.: Gather-excite: exploiting feature context in convolutional neural networks. Adv. Neural. Inf. Process. Syst. **31**, 9401–9411 (2018)
42. Li, X., Hu, X., Yang, J.: Spatial group-wise enhance: Improving semantic feature learning in convolutional networks. arXiv preprint arXiv:1905.09646 (2019)
43. Gao, Z., Xie, J., Wang, Q., Li, P.: Global second-order pooling convolutional networks. In: Computer Vision and Pattern Recognition, pp. 3024–3033 (2019)
44. Cao, Y., Xu, J., Lin, S., Wei, F., Hu, H.: GCNET: non-local networks meet squeeze-excitation networks and beyond. In: Computer Vision and Pattern Recognition (2019)
45. Chen, Y., Kalantidis, Y., Li, J., Yan, S., Feng, J.: A^2-nets: double attention networks. Adv. Neural. Inf. Process. Syst. **31**, 352–361 (2018)
46. Luong, M.-T., Pham, H., Manning, C.D.: Effective approaches to attention-based neural machine translation. arXiv preprint arXiv:1508.04025 (2015)
47. Bahdanau, D., Cho, K., Bengio, Y.: Neural machine translation by jointly learning to align and translate. arXiv preprint arXiv:1409.0473 (2014)
48. Ioannou, Y., Robertson, D., Cipolla, R., Criminisi, A.: Deep roots: improving CNN efficiency with hierarchical filter groups. In: Computer Vision and Pattern Recognition, pp. 1231–1240 (2017)
49. Xie, S., Girshick, R., Dollár, P., Tu, Z., He, K.: Aggregated residual transformations for deep neural networks. In: Computer Vision and Pattern Recognition, pp. 1492–1500 (2017)
50. Badrinarayanan, V., Handa, A., Cipolla, R.: SegNet: a deep convolutional encoder-decoder architecture for robust semantic pixel-wise labelling. arXiv preprint arXiv:1505.07293 (2015)

Fine-Grained Measurements of Repetitions on Performance of NB-IoT

Yusheng Qiu and Xiangmao Chang[✉]

Computer Science and Technology, Nanjing University of Aeronautics
and Astronautics, Nanjing, China
{qyusheng,xiangmaoch}@nuaa.edu.cn

Abstract. Narrowband-Internet of Things (NB-IoT) is an emerging cellular technology designed for Low-Power Wide-Area Network applications. To extend coverage, repetition scheme is introduced to boost the
signal during transmission. In this paper, we evaluate the effects of the
repetition number on the performance of NB-IoT networks under different signal conditions. Using an empirical approach, we perform extensive
field measurements of the critical characteristics such as power consumption and transmission reliability by setting up a software-defined base
station. We present detailed analysis of power consumption and packet
loss under different repetition settings and signal conditions from both
the overall and the phased perspectives. The results show that the repetition setting dramatically affects the power consumption of random
access and the data sending phases.

Keywords: Power consumption · Field measurement · NB-IoT

1 Introduction

Narrow-Band Internet of Things (NB-IoT) is a low-power wireless access technology based on cellular networks. It is developed by 3rd Generation Partnership
Project (3GPP) and released in 2016 [4]. NB-IoT has several advantages, such
as low power consumption, extended coverage, and reliable connections, which
make it a promising technology for a variety of IoT applications, such as smart
home, smart city, and smart industry [15].

To provide reliable connection with extended coverage, a repetition scheme
is applied during the transmission process. In other words, each transmission is
repeated for a dedicated number of times according to a repetition value configured by an evolved Node B (eNB). Obviously, increasing the repetition value can
increase transmission reliability and provide deeper coverage. However, unnecessary repetition can lead to power consumption wastage. Thus, a proper repetition
value is critical for both transmission reliability and power consumption.

This work was supported in part by the National Key Research and Development Program of China under Grant 2019YFB2102000; in part by the Natural Science Foundation of Jiangsu Province under Grant BK20200067.

© Springer Nature Switzerland AG 2021
Z. Liu et al. (Eds.): WASA 2021, LNCS 12938, pp. 469–480, 2021.
https://doi.org/10.1007/978-3-030-86130-8_37

Fig. 1. Example of UE's operational phases.

Several works have studied the relationships between the repetition value and network performance [9–11,13]. However, these works are all based on theoretical analysis which lacks field verification. In addition, none of them involves power consumption, which is a critical characteristic of NB-IoT. As a result, it is still unclear to what extent the repetition affects the power consumption and the transmission reliability in different signal conditions.

Field measurement is an efficient approach to understand network performance in different scenarios. However, there are several challenges for fine-grained measurement of repetitions on the performance of NB-IoT networks. First, NB-IoT is a closed cellular network deployed by operators on licensed spectrum, where the base station can not be accessed for public measurement. As a result, researchers can not control the repetition value for the measurement of different scenarios. Second, NB-IoT works on capacity-constrained embedded User Equipment (UE). It is hard to collect the low-level interaction information between the node and the base station. Third, the low-level transmission logs are not always consistent with the current series, which brings obstacles to power consumption analysis.

In this paper, we perform extensive field measurements of power consumption and transmission reliability under various repetition values and signal conditions based on a software-defined base station. Our analysis reveals the detailed power consumption and packet loss under different repetition settings and signal conditions. Furthermore, we analyzed the effect of the repetition on the power consumption of each transmission procedure. We find that the repetition setting mainly affects the power consumption of random access and the data sending procedures.

2   NB-IoT Primer

Assume an evolved Node B (eNB) with an NB-IoT network deployed as a cell, and one UE camping on it. The UE transfers Uplink (UL) data destined to an IoT server through the eNB periodically. To send these data, the UE will perform the CP procedure [6,7]. Where, the UE alternates between Connected and Idle states. When powered on or exiting from Idle state, the UE needs to first establish a control link with the network. In order to do that, it must scan and select a proper cell. Then, it needs to perform a Random Access (RA) procedure. Once the UE and eNB reestablish the connection, the UE switches to Connected state. During the Connected state, the UE maintains an Inactivity Timer, which will be restarted every time the UE ends its communication with the eNB. When the timer expires the

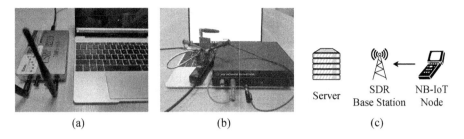

(a)   (b)   (c)

Fig. 2. Measurement platform: (a) SDR base station, (b) NB-IoT node and power monitor, (c) Network topology.

UE will perform a Release procedure to release the connection and enters the Idle state. While the Inactivity timer is counting down, the UE might keep listening, or perform Connected state Discontinuous Reception (C-DRX). In the Idle state, the UE may utilize two mechanisms: Extended Discontinuous Reception (eDRX) or Power Saving Mode (PSM). These mechanisms are designed to reduce the energy consumption of the UE in the absence of traffic while idle waiting for Downlink (DL) messages. A typical example of UE's operational phases is as shown in Fig. 1.

NB-IoT is designed to support IoT devices that operate in deep indoor or remote areas. To achieve this, two main mechanisms are introduced: 1) burst repetition and 2) the ability to allocate variable resources to UEs under different signal quality through the use of Extended Coverage Level (ECL), which provides efficient management of a massive number of IoT devices with various traffic and different coverage conditions.

3   Field Measurements

In this section, we first present the platform which we constructed for measurement, followed by the methodology and the results of the measurement.

3.1   Platform Construction

The value of Repetition is configured by the Base Station (BS). To study the relationship between the Repetition and the performance of NB-IoT, it is necessary to measure the performance of NB-IoT under various settings of Repetition. However, it is impossible to change the parameter settings frequently for a commercial BS. To address this issue, we construct a Software-Defined Radio (SDR) BS by combining Amerisoft SDR [1] and a Universal Software Radio Peripheral (USRP), as shown in Fig. 2(a). Amarisoft SDR fully supports the NB-IoT protocol (3GPP Release 13) and provides us with the ability to deploy an NB-IoT network with a specified configuration.

We use Quectel BC28 [2] for the measurement, which is an off-the-shelf NB-IoT module and compatible with 3GPP Release 13. This module is embedded on a development board that facilitates powering the module and interfacing

Table 1. Key parameters configurated in the SDR.

Parameter	Value range
Number of repetitions	[1, 4, 8, 16, 32, 64, 128]
Max power of transmitting	[23] dB
Modulation and coding scheme	[4]
Subcarrier spacing	[15] kHz
Number of subcarriers	[1]
Number of resource unit	[1]
SI periodicity	[640] ms
Max number of search space	[8]
Starting subframe	[2]
Inactivity timer	[10] s

with it via USB but also provides a jumper for a separate power supply to the module only. It supports controlling with AT command [5] and outputting the protocol interaction debug logs between UE and eNB.

We employ the Monsoon High Voltage Power Monitor [3] as the power measurement device to track the power consumption of the UE device. This tool can severe as both a power supply unit and a power measuring unit for the target device. The module is powered directly with this device using the jumper on the power path that isolates the module power supply from other components of the development board, so that we can measure the power consumption of the module only. The voltage of the UE device is set to 3.3 V and the current traces is sampled at a time interval of 1/5000 s throughout the measurements.

Both the UE and the power monitor are connected to a computer. The computer is used to control the UE through a set of AT commands while recording the debug logs and current traces, as shown in Fig. 2(b).

3.2 Methodology

To observe the impact of repetition on the performance of NB-IoT, we conduct measurement under different values of repetition. The value of repetition can be set as 2^i, where i is a nonnegative integer. It is set as $i = 0, 2, 3, 4, 5, 6, 7$ during the measurement. To simulate the various application conditions of NB-IoT, we also conduct the measurements under different signal qualities, which are created by using signal attenuators and placing the module at different distances away from the antenna of SDR. Other parameters of the BS are fixed and consistent with the settings of commercial BS, as shown in Table 1.

For each set of configuration, we first set it on the BS, and then power on the UE. At this time, it can only attach to the BS we deployed, as shown in Fig. 2(c), so that it is restricted to work under the configuration we specify. While the UE is continuously sending uplink data to the server, we change the signal quality between it and the BS by adjusting the signal attenuator. By repeating these procedures on each set of configuration, the current traces and debug logs of the UE working under different repetition values and signal qualities are collected.

3.3 Measurement Results

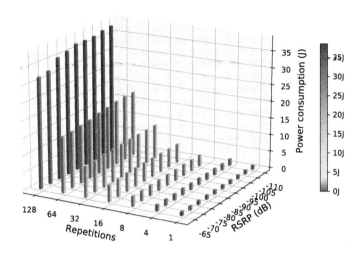

Fig. 3. Power consumption under different repetitions and signal qualities.

Figure 3 shows the overall power consumption of UE devices during each data transmission versus different Repetitions values and signal quality at the corresponding period. From the perspective of Repetitions, the power consumption of the UE devices increases sharply as the number of Repetitions increases. When the number of Repetitions is 128, the power consumption reached 35 times the number of 1. While from the perspective of signal quality, the power consumption of the UE devices increases as the signal quality deteriorates, but it is much gentler than when the number of Repetitions changes. The influence of the signal quality on the power consumption of the device is not obvious when the number of Repetitions is small, but as the number of Repetitions increases, its influence will become much more significant.

The packet loss rate is a key performance indicator that can reflect a network's availability. Unsuccessful transmission of a packet will cause the UE to retransmit, which will add additional power consumption, time delay, and resource occupation to UE and eNB.

Figure 4 shows the packet loss rate of each data transmission under different conditions. From both perspectives of parameter and signal quality, the packet loss rate of the UE devices increases as the signal quality deteriorates beyond a certain threshold, which becomes lower as the number of Repetitions decreases. When the signal quality is acceptable, there is almost no packet loss. When

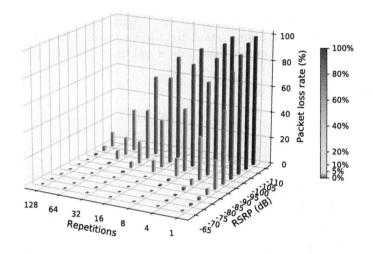

Fig. 4. Packet loss rate under different repetitions and signal qualities. (Color figure online)

RSRP is worse than −115 dB, all the data packets we send are lost, which determines the lower limit of the signal quality we can measure. The results in between shows that the increase in the number of Repetitions is of great help in reducing the packet loss.

Comparing Fig. 3 with Fig. 4, it can be observed that there is a trade-off between power consumption and packet loss rate. As shown the blue bars in Fig. 4, when the signal quality is better than −85 dB, even if the number of Repetitions is only 1, the packet loss rate can still be guaranteed to be less than 5%, which can be considered acceptable. Therefore, in this case, it will be unreasonable to use more repetition times, which would lead to extra waste of power of UE and resources of eNB without offering performance gains. However, when the signal quality does not meet this threshold, it is necessary to increase the number of Repetitions, otherwise, the packet loss rate of the UE devices will increase significantly and the service requirements cannot be met.

4   Fine-Grained Analysis

In a transmission cycle, there are several operational phases, which are synchronization, random access, data sending, inactivity, and release. Since the repetition has a great impact on the power consumption and packet loss during the transmission, we conduct fine-grained analysis on each procedure in this section.

A key challenge for this analysis is to match the debug log series and the current traces. First of all, the original data of both of them contain timestamps, but are both relative times of their first record. The first record of the current traces is generated at the moment when the UE is powered on, while the first record of the debug log is generated when the UE finishes the startup and initialization process. That is, the time start of the debug log is later than the

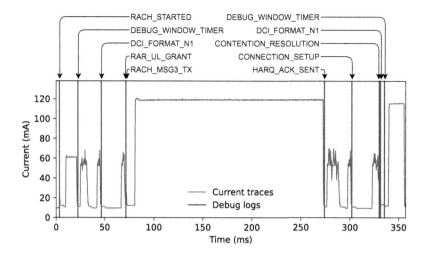

Fig. 5. UE's unified current traces and debug logs.

start time of the current traces. To make them match, an offset time needs to be added to the timestamps of the debug logs, i.e. the time from when the UE is powered on to when the first debug log is reported. Besides that, we also noticed that the timestamps of the debug logs reported by the UE may contain errors. The elapse speed of time of the debug logs is always a little different from the time of current traces, while the latter is consistent with reality. This leads to a gradual misalignment between them even if their start time is already aligned, requiring further correction manually.

After solving the above challenge, we put them together based on the unified timeline, as shown in Fig. 5, where the current traces that presents its power consumption can be mapped into the debug logs that records its instantaneous working environment (e.g. signal quality) and status (e.g. current operation, signaling messages). Putting them together gives us a new perspective to analyze the patterns in the current traces with ms-level accuracy, and the results of our analysis are presented in Sect. 4.1. However, although the debug logs can help us understand the relationship between the UE's behavior and the current traces, it can not be directly used to determine the range of each phase due to its diverse appearance times that may be at the beginning, middle, or end of a behavior. Based on the patterns of its current traces obtained from the mapping, we manually segmented and labeled the current traces as finely and accurately as possible into fine-grained phases whose states and conditions are identified, and then show the results in Sect. 4.2.

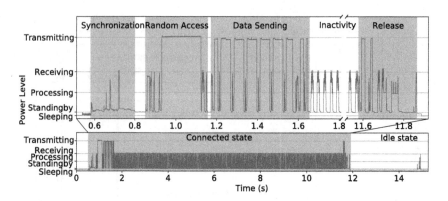

Fig. 6. Example of UE's current traces.

4.1 Current Patterns

This section describes the patterns of current traces by operational phases using a complete cycle as an example, as schematically illustrated in Fig. 6.

We find that the current magnitude of the UE is closely related to its behavior, and the current traces at different phases have different patterns. When the UE performs different behaviors, its current magnitude will be quite different. In order to facilitate the analysis, we summarize the current traces of the UE into the following power levels according to the magnitude of current to describe its behaviors:

1. Transmitting: The UE is actively transmitting a packet to the network, whose current traces often appears to be block-like.
2. Receiving: The UE is actively receiving information from the network, the current is usually lower than transmitting.
3. Processing: The UE is not transmitting or receiving, but processing some data. Typically peaks-like current traces preceding transmitting or closely following receiving.
4. Standingby: The UE is doing nothing except waiting for the timing to perform the next operation, which often appears to be a much lower but steady horizontal line, separating other parts.
5. Sleeping: The UE is inactive and sleeping, almost like powered off.

The UEs will enter standingby mode whenever possible (i.e. once the system is idle). Using it as a separator, we can divide the current traces into small pieces of behaviors and take an in-depth dissecting of them.

Synchronization. This phase occurs at the beginning of the entire cycle. During this phase, depending on the list of candidate cells, the current traces of the UE will be very diverse. Among them, several receiving behaviors of different levels will appear, but transmitting behaviors will not be observed.

Random Access. Between this phase and the previous Synchronization phase, there will be standingby behavior of varying duration. This can be used to help determine the end of the previous phase. This phase starts with a block-like transmitting behavior, followed by the corresponding receiving behaviors. Then there will be a relatively obvious transmitting behavior, and this phase ends when the subsequent receiving and processing behaviors are completed.

Data Sending. At the beginning of this phase there will be a receiving behavior, and then a set of shorter transmitting and receiving behaviors. After this, there will be a sequence of several transmitting behaviors of same duration and receiving interspersing among them, which is the most noticeable part of the entire cycle. The number of them depends on the amount of data needed to be sent. After the data is successfully sent, there will be another short transmitting behavior, which marks the end of this phase.

Inactivity. The current traces of this phase is very regular and will appear in a fixed pattern. As a transitional state between the Data Sending and Release, the UE in this phase remains in an inactive state, no transmitting will be observed. During this phase, the UE alternates between receiving, processing and standingby.

Release. This phase is entered as soon as the Inactivity phase is over. The UE will perform a set of Transmission and Reception to releases the connection. This phase is over when the power level enters the sleeping state.

4.2   Power Consumption Decomposition

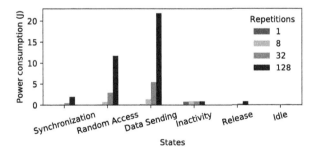

Fig. 7. The power consumption of operational phases under different repetitions.

As presented above, the number of Repetitions has a great impact on power consumption. In order to have a deeper understanding of it, we break down the power consumption of each data transmission cycle into small phases according to the states based on the patterns of the UE's current traces discussed

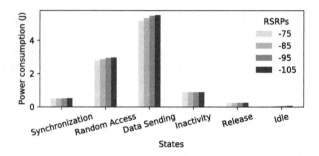

Fig. 8. The power consumption of operational phases under different signal qualities.

in Sect. 4.1 for further study. Figure 7 and Fig. 8 shows the power consumption breakdown by UE's operational phases, which are respectively slices of Repetitions is 32 and RSRP is −90 dB.

The power consumption in the Idle state only accounts for a small part of the overall consumption, which remains when condition changes and is almost negligible comparing. Therefore, the existing energy-saving mechanisms in the Idle state has been able to effectively reduce the power consumption during it. For further saving, the consumption generated during the Connected state should be paid more attention to.

When the number of Repetitions increases, it can be clearly seen that the power consumption of connection establishing and data sending grow with it and gradually become the dominant part. In the meanwhile, the consumption of other parts has not changed much, especially the Inactivity phase. Comparing their unified current traces, we found that this is mainly due to the extension of the duration of transmitting. On the other hand, as the signal quality deteriorates, these parts don't have much variation, comparing to when the number of Repetitions changes. When the signal quality approaches the lower limit, this change becomes even more gradual. This is due to the limit of transmit power of the UE to prevent it from increasing indefinitely. These can explain and support the previous findings of the overall power consumption.

4.3   Discussion

In summary, the increase in the number of Repetitions can effectively reduce the occurrence of packet loss and improve the stability of the network, but will also increase the duration of transmitting, resulting in a substantial increase in the overall power consumption. Under certain signal quality conditions, increasing the number of Repetitions will, instead of improving the performance of the network, only cause additional waste of power consumption. Therefore, blindly increasing the number of Repetitions is not a good choice, and it is necessary to explore the signal quality threshold of different Repetitions that can bring improvement to the performance of the network while not causing unnecessary power waste. Taking the signal quality of −90 dB as an example, a Repetitions of 8 can ensure the availability of the network, while producing the least power consumption, from the original maximum 37 J to a much lower 3.3 J, which will greatly extend the battery lifetime of the UE device. This threshold corresponds to the division threshold of the coverage level, with which different configurations can be assigned to different ranges of signal quality. It is apparent that a proper tuning of these is crucial to control the trade-off between performance and energy consumption, shedding light on these aspects is one of the goals of this work.

5   Related Work

In this section, we review related works about the energy efficiency of the NB-IoT network. A great deal of studies have investigated it through power measurement or modeling. Lauridsen et al. [8,12] conducted empirical power consumption measurements, and then proposed an analytical energy consumption model based on the Markov chain and validated it through these measurements. B Martinez et al. [14] empirically evaluated the performance bounds of NB-IoT by analyzing characteristics that end-user feels, such as energy consumption, reliability, and delays. Focusing on parameters that are within end-user's control, they conducted experiments to reveal the behavior of NB-IoT devices in actual operation, and found that UE's power consumption is greatly impacted by the active time of the transceiver. AK Sultania et al. [16] presented an energy consumption model for NB-IoT devices using PSM and eDRX with a Poisson arrival process for data transmission occasions, and analyzed impacts of different PSM timers, eDRX timers, and packet Inter-Arrival Times. Different from them, we examine the power consumption of the UE focusing on the Connected state which is its main source and configurations that are specified by eNB using an empirical approach in this paper.

6   Conclusion

In this work, we conduct a detailed analysis of energy consumption of UE devices in NB-IoT networks by mapping the measured power consumption and device's working status, and conduct the first experimental study to explore it under various Repetitions configurations and different signal quality through this mapping. To further analyze the collected data, we segment the current traces into small pieces whose states and conditions are identified. We find: 1) the energy consumption is mostly generated in the Connected state; 2) the energy consumption is strongly affected by Repetitions configured, especially the phases involving transmitting; 3) the energy consumption does not seem to be strongly affected by channel conditions, comparing to Repetitions; 4) under different configurations, the channel conditions have different effects on packet loss, depending on whether it is below a certain level. Based on such empirical observations, we provide indication for parameter configurations that prolong the device battery lifetime while satisfying the basic requirements of an NB-IoT application.

This paper uses an empirical approach to shed light on the performance of UE devices when deployed in real conditions, as a complement to related works. In future work, we will continue to study the impact of more parameter combinations on UE's power consumption and other performance indicators under different application cases at a finer level.

References

1. Amarisoft technology. https://www.amarisoft.com/products/network-deployment/
2. Bc-28. https://www.quectel.com/cn/product/bc28.htm
3. Monsoon high voltage power monitor. https://www.msoon.com/high-voltage-power-monitor
4. Standardization of NB-IOT completed. http://www.3gpp.org/newsevents/3gpp-news/1785-nb_iot_complete. Accessed 15 Feb 2020
5. 3GPP: AT command set for User Equipment (UE). Technical Specification (TS) 36.331, 3rd Generation Partnership Project (3GPP) (2018). Version 13.7.0
6. 3GPP: Evolved Universal Terrestrial Radio Access (E-UTRA); User Equipment (UE) procedures in idle mode. Technical Specification (TS) 36.304, 3rd Generation Partnership Project (3GPP) (2018). Version 13.8.0
7. 3GPP: Evolved Universal Terrestrial Radio Access (E-UTRA); Physical layer procedures. Technical Specification (TS) 36.213, 3rd Generation Partnership Project (3GPP) (2020). Version 13.16.0
8. Andres-Maldonado, P., Lauridsen, M., Ameigeiras, P., Lopez-Soler, J.M.: Analytical modeling and experimental validation of NB-IOT device energy consumption. IEEE Internet Things J. 6(3), 5691–5701 (2019)
9. Feltrin, L., et al.: Narrowband IoT: a survey on downlink and uplink perspectives. IEEE Wirel. Commun. 26(1), 78–86 (2019)
10. Harwahyu, R., Cheng, R.G., Tsai, W.J., Hwang, J.K., Bianchi, G.: Repetitions versus retransmissions: tradeoff in configuring NB-IOT random access channels. IEEE Internet Things J. 6(2), 3796–3805 (2019)
11. Harwahyu, R., Cheng, R.G., Wei, C.H., Sari, R.F.: Optimization of random access channel in NB-IOT. IEEE Internet Things J. 5(1), 391–402 (2017)
12. Lauridsen, M., Krigslund, R., Rohr, M., Madueno, G.: An empirical NB-IOT power consumption model for battery lifetime estimation. In: 2018 IEEE 87th Vehicular Technology Conference (VTC Spring), pp. 1–5. IEEE (2018)
13. Liu, Y., Deng, Y., Elkashlan, M., Nallanathan, A.: Random access performance for three coverage enhancement groups in NB-IOT networks. In: 2019 IEEE Global Communications Conference (GLOBECOM), pp. 1–6. IEEE (2019)
14. Martinez, B., Adelantado, F., Bartoli, A., Vilajosana, X.: Exploring the performance boundaries of NB-IOT. IEEE Internet Things J. 6(3), 5702–5712 (2019)
15. Mekki, K., Bajic, E., Chaxel, F., Meyer, F.: A comparative study of LPWAN technologies for large-scale IoT deployment. ICT Express 5(1), 1–7 (2019)
16. Sultania, A.K., Zand, P., Blondia, C., Famaey, J.: Energy modeling and evaluation of NB-IOT with PSM and EDRX. In: 2018 IEEE Globecom Workshops (GC Wkshps), pp. 1–7. IEEE (2018)

Deep Reinforcement Learning Based Intelligent Job Batching in Industrial Internet of Things

Chengling Jiang, Zihui Luo, Liang Liu[✉], and Xiaolong Zheng

Beijing Key Lab of Intelligent Telecommunication Software and Multimedia,
Beijing University of Posts and Telecommunications, Beijing, China
{jiangchengling,luozihui,liangliu,zhengxiaolong}@bupt.edu.cn

Abstract. The ever-developing Industrial Internet of Things (IIoT) is promoting the transformation of traditional manufacturers to intelligent manufacturing. Intelligent job batching, as one of the important parts of intelligent production in IIoT, is desired to group jobs with similar features into one batch under the constraint of batch capacity while considering the manufacturing target. This work formulates the job batching problem as a Markov Decision Process and proposes a deep reinforcement learning (DRL) based method to achieve intelligent job batching. The job batching model is based on the pointer network. The convergence of the model under different parameters is analyzed, and the performance of the method is evaluated by comparing it with the manual result, K-means algorithm, and multiple meta-heuristic algorithms via real production data. Experiments show that the proposed method can produce better solution in terms of the feature difference within a batch and the total batch number, especially in large-scale manufacturing scenarios.

Keywords: Job batching · Deep reinforcement learning · Industrial Internet of Things

1 Introduction

With the boom of Industrial Internet of Things (IIoT) [1,3], the traditional industry is upgrading towards intelligent manufacturing. The realization of multi-variety and small-batch flexible production is an essential part of intelligent manufacturing. To improve the utilization of equipments and production efficiency, jobs with similar features are grouped into a batch for processing.

The job batching process is usually conducted by manpower in practical production. Due to the large number of jobs, unknown batch number, multiple job features and constraints, it is difficult for technicians to generate a reasonable solution in an efficient manner. As shown in Fig. 1, in the envisioned smart factory of IIoT, through the comprehensive perception of production data by massive intelligent devices, the real-time transmission of production data by wireless communication and wireless sensor network, and the rapid calculation and decision-making

© Springer Nature Switzerland AG 2021
Z. Liu et al. (Eds.): WASA 2021, LNCS 12938, pp. 481–493, 2021.
https://doi.org/10.1007/978-3-030-86130-8_38

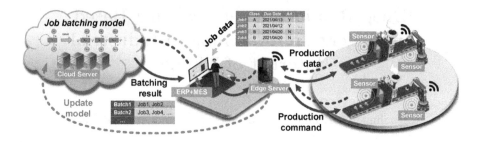

Fig. 1. The envisioned smart factory in Industrial Internet of Things

by job batching model in the cloud, the whole production process can be automatic, intelligent, and unmanned. Apparently, the results of the batching model in the cloud determines the performance of production plan, which directly affects the production efficiency. To achieve the vision of IIoT, an efficient job batching model is desired. Existing studies on job batching mainly focus on clustering algorithm [15,19] and meta-heuristic algorithm [5,6,10,15,20]. Both methods are not efficient in dealing with the batching problem with large number of jobs. Besides, the performance of both methods depends on human experience, which do not make use of the massive data to learn prior knowledge. Accordingly, designing an efficient and intelligent job batching method for IIoT scenario is of great urgency and practical significance.

The job batching problem can be regarded as a mapping from an input sequence of jobs to be batched to an output sequence of job batching result. Vinyals [18] proposed the pointer network base on the attention mechanism [8] to handle the sequence-to-sequence (Seq2Seq) scenario, which is consistent with the job batching process. However, the pointer network needs supervised training, whose performance heavily depends on the quality of labels. It is unrealistic to manually label massive data in IIoT scenario, making the supervised learning inapplicable. Reinforcement learning (RL) [17] is a data-driven method that can learns stable strategy by interacting with the environment without labels. However, each job has multi-dimensional features in job batching problem, which cannot be handled by RL. Recently, deep reinforcement learning (DRL) which combines the perceptual ability to process multi-dimensional features of deep learning (DL) [9] and the stable decision-making ability of RL, has successfully solved various practical problems [12–14,21]. Therefore, this work adopts a DRL based method to approach the job batching problem based on pointer network.

The main contributions of this paper are as follows.

1) We formulate the job batching problem as a Markov Decision Process and employ a DRL based method which can process multi-dimensional input data and does not need labels to approach the job batching problem in IIoT.
2) We consider the job batching process as a mapping from one sequence to another and propose a job batching model based on pointer network, with the objective of minimizing the batch number and the feature difference within a batch under the batch capacity constraint.

3) We compare the proposed method with manual result, K-means algorithm and multiple meta-heuristic algorithms using real production data. The experimental results show the superiority of our method.

2   Problem Description and Mathematical Model

2.1   Notation

M	Total number of jobs to be batched
N	Total number of batches (unknown in advance)
C	Maximum capacity of a batch
K	Number of job features
D	Total feature difference of all batches
x_i	The job i
w_i	Weight of job i
f_k	The $k\,th$ feature of job
c_k	Score of $k\,th$ feature of job
α, β	Score of two sub objectives
U_n	Set of jobs contained in batch n
$|U_n|$	Number of jobs contained in batch n
V_n	Remaining capacity of batch n
μ_{in}	Decision variable: is job i in batch n

2.2   Problem Formulation

In this paper, we mainly consider a typical job batching problem that must be faced under the multi-variety and small-batch flexible production in IIoT. Specifically, given a set of M jobs $X = \{x_i, i = 1, 2, \cdots, M\}$, each job x_i has K features $f_i = \{f_{ik}, k = 1, 2, \cdots, K\}$ such as the delivery date, length, width etc. which are defined by the actual application scenarios, and a weight w_i. So each job is defined as $x_i = \{f_i, w_i\}$. The maximum capacity of a batch is C. The total batch number is unknown in advance. The purpose of job batching problem is to group jobs with similar features into a batch under the constraint of batch capacity, so as to minimize the feature difference D of all batches and the total number of batches N. The mathematical model is as follows.

$$\min target = \alpha D + \beta N \tag{1}$$

$$\text{where } D = \sum_{n=1}^{N} \sum_{i=1}^{|U_n|} \sum_{j \neq i}^{|U_n|} \sqrt{c_1(f_{i1} - f_{j1})^2 + c_2(f_{i2} - f_{j2})^2 + \cdots + c_k(f_{ik} - f_{jk})^2}$$

$$0 \leq \alpha \leq 1, \ 0 \leq \beta \leq 1 \tag{2}$$

$$\sum_{k=1}^{K} c_k = 1 \tag{3}$$

$$0 < \sum_{i \in U_i} w_i \leq C \tag{4}$$

$$0 < \sum_{n=1}^{N} \mu_{in} \leq 1, \text{where } \mu_{in} = \begin{cases} 1, \text{job } i \text{ belongs to batch } n \\ 0, \text{otherwise} \end{cases} \tag{5}$$

Equation (1) is the objective function; Constraint (2) and (3) represent the importance of the two sub objectives in Eq. (1) and the importance of each feature respectively; Constraint (4) indicates that the total weight of jobs in a batch cannot exceed the maximum capacity; Constraint (5) indicates that one job can only be grouped into one batch.

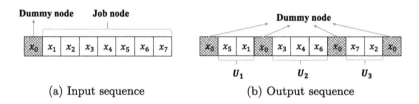

(a) Input sequence   (b) Output sequence

Fig. 2. A specific instance of input sequence and output sequence.

3   Job Batching Model

3.1   Markov Decision Process

This paper formulates the job batching problem as a Markov Decision Process (MDP). At each time step t, the agent observes current environment state S^t and take the action y_t. The agent can obtain the reward R from the environment according to its action. Then the environment state moves from S^t to S^{t+1}. The agent continuously interacts with the environment and batches jobs successively so as to obtain the maximum cumulative reward.

State. It is defined that when a job x_i is grouped into one batch, the weight of job x_i would change from w_i to 0 and the remaining capacity V_n of current batch n would change from C to $C - d_i$. So each job can be redefined as $x_i = \{f_i, w_i^t\}$, where f_i refers to the static features of job x_i, which remain unchanged at any time, w_i^t refers to the weight of job x_i, which changes with the action of agent. Accordingly, the current environment state at time t is $S^t = \{f, w^t, V_n^t\}$, where $f = \{f_i, i = 1, 2, \cdots, M\}$ refers to the static features of all jobs, $w^t = \{w_i^t, i = 1, 2, \cdots, M\}$ refers to the weights of all jobs at time t, and V_n^t refers to the remaining capacity of the current batch n at time t.

Action. The dummy node $x_0 = \{f_0, w_0\}$ is defined to separate each batch, the static features and weight of the dummy node are always 0. The dummy node x_0 and all jobs x_i ($i = 1, 2, \cdots, M$) serve as the input sequence. At each time step t, the action of agent is to select a node from the input sequence as the output node. The first output node is always dummy node, indicating the beginning of the batching. If the agent considers there are no available jobs to group into current batch, it would select the dummy node to end the current batch and start a new batch. When all jobs are batched, an output sequence can be obtained. A specific instance is shown in Fig. 2. The input sequence is x_i ($i = 0, 1, \cdots, 7$). Note that the dummy node is always at the first position in the input sequence. The output sequence is $\{x_0, x_5, x_1, x_0, x_3, x_4, x_6, x_0, x_7, x_2, x_0\}$, indicating that jobs are grouped into 3 batches: $U_1 = \{x_5, x_1\}$, $U_2 = \{x_3, x_4, x_6\}$, $U_3 = \{x_7, x_2\}$.

Reward. The reward reveals the quality of the action taken by the agent under the current environment state. The goal of the agent is to minimize the total number of batches (N) and the sum of feature difference of all batches (D). The smaller the target value, the better job batching decisions the agent makes and the greater the reward to the agent. Accordingly, the reward R is designed in Eq. (6):

$$R = -target = -(\alpha D + \beta N) \tag{6}$$

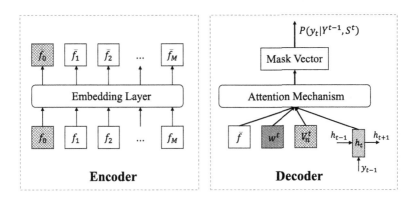

Fig. 3. Overall structure of job batching model

3.2 Overall Structure of the Model

The overall structure of the job batching model proposed is shown in Fig. 3. It is based on the pointer network, which includes an encoder and a decoder.

Encoder. In pointer network, the encoder is implemented based on Recurrent Neural Network (RNN) [16]. However, RNN is meaningful only when the permutation of the input sequence conveys certain information. In the input sequence, except that the first node is dummy node, the order of other job nodes has no meaning. Therefore, the job batching model omits the RNN in the encoder, and directly use a one-dimensional convolution layer as the embedding layer to map the static features $f = \{f_i, i = 0, 1, \cdots, M\}$ of nodes to a matrix $\bar{f} = \{\bar{f}_i, i = 0, 1, \cdots, M\}$, which reduces the computational complexity.

Decoder. The decoder includes a Long Short-Term Memory (LSTM) [4,23], an attention mechanism and a mask vector, the last two parts would be illustrated further in Sect. 3.3. At each time step t, the LSTM fetches hidden state h^{t-1} of LSTM and the output node y^{t-1}, and outputs the hidden state h^t. The output matrix $\bar{f}$ of the encoder, the dynamic weight feature w^t of all nodes in input sequence, the remaining capacity $V_n{}^t$ of the current batch n, and the hidden state h^t of LSTM are input to the attention mechanism. Then the probability distribution of each node can be obtained with the help of mask vector. Finally, the node with the highest probability is selected as the output node at time t. After the agent makes the decision at time t, the weights of jobs would be updated from w^t to w^{t+1}, the remaining capacity of the current batch would be updated from $V_n{}^t$ to $V_n{}^{t+1}$ and the mask vector would be updated according to the decision of agent. The updated vectors are input to the model at next time step $t + 1$.

Algorithm 1. DRL Based Job Batching Algorithm

1: initialize the parameters of actor network θ and critic network φ randomly
2: **for** *epoch* $= 1, 2, \cdots$ **do**
3:     reset gradients: $d\theta \leftarrow 0$, $d\varphi \leftarrow 0$
4:     sample J instances randomly from the training set
5:     **for** $j = 1, 2, \cdots, N$ **do**
6:         initialize time step $t \leftarrow 0$
7:         initialize the mask vector: $mask = [1, 0, \cdots 0]$
8:         construct the input sequence X_i $(i = 0, 1, 2, \cdots, M)$
9:         **repeat**
10:             observe state S_j^t, select output node y_t according to $P(y_t | Y^{t-1}, S^t)$
11:             update state $S_j^t \leftarrow S_j^{t+1}$, mask vector and time step $t \leftarrow t + 1$
12:         **until** all jobs are grouped into corresponding batches
13:         calculate actual reward R_j and the estimated reward $V(S_j^0; \varphi)$
14:     **end for**
15:     calculated $d\theta$ and $d\varphi$ and update actor network and critic network separately
16: **end for**

3.3   Attention Mechanism and Mask Vector

At each time step t, the attention mechanism calculates the probability distribution a^t of each node in the input sequence via Eq. (7), where v_a and ω_a are trainable variables. The probability distribution serves as the pointer to the node in input sequence.

$$a^t = \mathrm{Softmax}(v_a \tanh(\omega_a \left[\bar{f}; h^t; d^t; V_n{}^t\right])) \tag{7}$$

A mask vector which has the same length with the input sequence is introduced to constraint the agent decision. each element of the mask vector has one-to-one correspondence to the node in the input sequence. Each element value of the mask vector is either 0 or 1. The first element value of the mask vector which corresponds to the dummy node is always 1, enabling the agent to end the partition of the current batch at any time. At time step t, if one of the following situations are satisfied, the element values of the mask vector corresponding to the job node x_i $(i = 1, 2, \cdots, M)$ are set to zero: a) job node x_i is selected as the output node; b) the weight $w_i{}^t$ of job node x_i is larger than the remaining capacity $V_n{}^t$; c) at $t = 0$, the agent can only select the dummy node.

Combined with the mask vector, the final probability distribution of each node at time t is calculated in Eq. (8), where v_b are trainable variable and a^t is probability distribution calculated by Eq. (7). From Eq. (8), If the element value of the mask vector is 0, the probability of the node corresponding to the mask vector element as the output node is also 0. Finally, the node with the highest probability is taken as the output node.

$$P(y_t | Y^{t-1}, S^t) = \text{Softmax}(v_b a^t - \ln(mask)) \qquad (8)$$

3.4 DRL Based Algorithm

A DRL based job batching algorithm is employed to train the job batching model. It contains two network: an actor network and a critic network. The actor network is used to predict the output probability of each node in the input sequence at each time step t. Assuming the parameter of actor network is θ. The critic network is used to calculate the estimated reward of each input sequence. Assuming that the parameter of critic network is φ.

The specific steps of the DRL based job batching algorithm are shown in Algorithm 1. Firstly, the parameters of actor network and critical network are initialized randomly. At each epoch, J instances are sampled randomly from the training set (each instance is a set of M jobs). For each instance j, the time step t and mask vector is initialized, the input sequence is constructed. At each time step t, actor network observes current environment state S_j^t and selects the output node y_t according to Eq. (8), then the environment state, the mask vector and the time step are updated accordingly. When all jobs are grouped into corresponding batches in instance j, the actual reward R_j and the estimated reward $V(S_j^0; \varphi)$ are calculated respectively. After the batching task of J instances are terminated, the gradients of actor network and critic network are calculated and updated according to Eq. (9) and (10).

$$d\theta \leftarrow \frac{1}{J} \sum_{j=1}^{J} (R_j - V(S_j^0; \varphi)) \nabla_\theta \log P(Y_j | S_j^0) \qquad (9)$$

$$d\varphi \leftarrow \frac{1}{J} \sum_{j=1}^{J} \nabla_\varphi (R_j - V(S_j^0; \varphi))^2 \qquad (10)$$

In Eq. (9) and (10), S_j^0 refers to the environment state of jth instance at time step $t = 0$, Y_j refers to the output sequence with regard to S_j^0, R_j refers to the actual reward obtained in the jth instance, $P(Y_j|S_j^0)$ refers to the probability distribution of each node, $V(S_j^0; \varphi)$ refers to the estimated reward in the jth instance with regard to S_j^0.

4   Experimental Results

The experiments focus on two parts: analyzing convergence of the proposed method using different parameter settings; and comparing performance of the proposed method with manual result, K-means algorithm, and other meta-heuristic algorithms in terms of the total batch number, the feature difference of all batches, the target value, and the inference time.

4.1   Experimental Environment

The experiments are conducted on real production data provided by Nanjing Iron and Steel Co., Ltd. (NISCO). The production process of the steel plants in NISCO mainly includes four stages (Fig. 4): ironmaking, steelmaking, continuous casting and hot rolling. The production machines in the first three stages are batch processing machines (BPMs). According to the capacity constraint of BPMs (the maximum capacity of a batch), jobs with similar features are grouped into a batch to improve production efficiency. The job data of NISCO in the past six months are used for training the model, the results of manual batching of 50, 100, 200, 300 jobs are used for testing the model. We train the proposed model on NVIDIA Tesla P100-PCIE 16 GB GPU and evaluate the performance on Lenovo Intel(R) Core(TM) i7-6700 8 GB CPU @ 3.40 GHz.

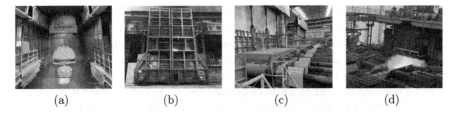

(a)   (b)   (c)   (d)

Fig. 4. Main production process and physical equipments of the steel plants in NISCO. (a) Iromaking; (b) Steelmaking; (c) Continuous casting; (d) Hot rolling.

The parameters used in this work are divided into two categories: i) Parameters that are set according to specific application scenario: the score of job's each feature; the score of two sub objectives. According to the NISCO's job batching requirements, each job has six features ($K = 6$), which are category, thickness, length, width, delivery date and processing technology. The score of job's features are: $c_1 = 0.2$, $c_2 = 0.2$, $c_3 = 0.08$, $c_4 = 0.16$, $c_5 = 0.16$, $c_6 = 0.2$; the score of two sub objectives are: α is 0.1–0.5, β is 0.1–0.5; the maximum capacity of a batch C is 180. ii) The parameters used in the DRL based algorithm for training: the number of neurons in the hidden layer is 10–256; the learning rate for updating the actor network and critic network is 0.00001–0.01; the batch size for one training is 1–128.

4.2 Convergence Analysis

This subsection analyzes the convergence of training the proposed model using different settings of four factors: number of neurons in the hidden layer, learning rate, batch size and different number of jobs.

Firstly, we analyze the convergence effect using different number of neurons in the hidden layer. Consider the problem instance with $M = 100$. Figure 5a shows the convergence effect when the number of neurons in the hidden layer is 8, 32, 64, 128, 256. Within limits, the more the number of neurons is, the more quickly the convergence is achieved. However, when the number of neurons is 256 which

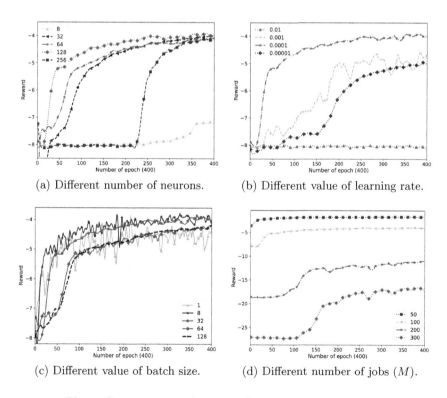

(a) Different number of neurons.   (b) Different value of learning rate.

(c) Different value of batch size.   (d) Different number of jobs (M).

Fig. 5. Convergence analysis on different parameter settings.

is too large, the model converges after 200 epoches. Accordingly, the number of neurons in the hidden layer is set to 128 which has the fastest convergence speed.

Secondly, we analyze the convergence effect using different learning rate. Consider the problem instance with $M = 100$. Figure 5b shows the convergence effect when the learning rate is 0.01, 0.001, 0.0001, 0.00001. When the learning rate is 0.00001, which is too small, it takes a very long time to converge (after 400 epoches). When the learning rate is 0.01 which is too large, the model cannot converge. So we set the learning rate to 0.0001 which converges fastest.

Thirdly, we conduct the convergence analysis on different value of batch size. Figure 5c shows the convergence analysis of the instance with $M = 100$ when the batch size is 1, 8, 32, 64, 128. The smaller the batch size is, the larger the gradient oscillation amplitude of the model is, which is not conducive to the convergence of the model; the larger the batch size is, the smaller the gradient oscillation amplitude of the model is, but the training is easy to fall into local optimum. When the batch size is 32, the oscillation amplitude of gradient is small and the model converges fast. Accordingly, the batch size is set to 32.

Lastly, we conduct the convergence analysis on different number of jobs. Figure 5d shows the convergence analysis of M is 50, 100, 200, 300. The more the number of jobs is, the more slowly the convergence is achieved. Although it takes hours to train the model, once the model is well trained, it can quickly solve the problems it has not encountered before in seconds or minutes.

Table 1. Comparision of the experimental results using the proposed method, manual result, the K-means method, and three meta-heuristic algorithms.

Size	Parameter (α,β)	Metrics	Method					
			Manual	K-means	GA	ACO	TS	Ours
50	(0.5, 0.2)	Batch number	4	4	4	4	4	4
		Difference value	5.79	5.70	**1.35**	4.02	1.37	**1.35**
		Target value	3.70	3.65	**1.48**	2.81	1.49	**1.48**
		Inference time (s)	–	**2.78**	10.08	6.45	86.94	13.00
100	(0.1, 0.3)	Batch number	10	10	10	10	10	10
		Difference value	6.34	5.58	8.37	7.44	6.42	**3.09**
		Target value	3.63	3.56	3.84	3.74	3.64	**3.31**
		Inference time (s)	-	**3.77**	34.61	46.25	406.58	35.00
200	(0.1, 0.5)	Batch number	22	**21**	22	22	22	**21**
		Difference value	16.00	16.61	66.88	14.30	14.05	**13.99**
		Target value	12.60	12.16	17.69	12.43	12.41	**11.90**
		Inference time (s)	–	**5.70**	135.19	380.31	2261.31	57.00
300	(0.1, 0.5)	Batch number	34	**32**	34	34	34	**32**
		Difference value	24.41	25.29	122.41	17.63	17.48	**17.36**
		Target value	19.44	18.53	29.24	18.76	18.75	**17.74**
		Inference time (s)	-	307.64	314.43	1386.12	6574.58	**93.00**

4.3   Performance Comparison

To evaluate the performance of proposed method, we compare our method with the manual result, K-means algorithm and several typical meta-heuristic algorithms which are Genetic Algorithm (GA), Ant Colony Optimization (ACO), and Tabu Search (TS). The experiments are conducted on different problem sizes with M is 50, 100, 200, 300. Table 1 shows the comparison results.

K-means algorithm needs the batch number in advance, which is unknown in practical production. For experimental comparison, this paper set the batch number of K-means algorithm to $n = \left\lceil \sum_{i=1}^{M} w_i / M \right\rceil$, which is the ideal minimum batch number. Since the results of meta-heuristic algorithm are unstable for its introduction of random factors, we run each meta-heuristic algorithm 10 times, and compare their optimal results with our proposed method. From Table 1, we know that our proposed method performs better than the manual result, K-means algorithm and other meta-heuristic algorithms in terms of the total batch number, the total feature difference of all batches and the target value. Especially, the inference time of our method does not increase significantly as the number of jobs increases. Therefore, our method can be used to deal with the job batching problem with large job number in actual production.

5   Related Work

Job batching problem exists widely in chemical, steelmaking, textile, semiconductor, and other fields. In recent years, scholars at home and abroad have made extensive researches on this problem.

In chemical field, [11] proposed the best priority and variable neighborhood search algorithm for furnace grouping in NdFeB enterprises; [22] proposed a novel Particle Swarm Optimization algorithm with Von Neumann Topology for the furnace-grouping in special aluminum alloy production. In steelmaking field, [20] proposed an improved compact genetic algorithm for the charge design in steelmaking and continuous casting; [15] proposed a fuzzy clustering algorithm based on an improved particle swarm optimization for the order batching in cold rolling. In textile field, [5] proposed a hybrid multi-subpopulation genetic algorithm for textile batch dyeing scheduling; [2] proposed a Multi-Agent Recurrent Proximal Policy Optimization (MA-RPPO) reinforcement learning based fully reactive scheduling method for the vats batching problem of textile dyeing workshop, which simplified the problem by only considering one job feature. In semiconductor field, [7] proposed an algorithm based on the hybrid ant colony optimization algorithm for the semiconductor furnace operation.

Most of the researches on job batching problem are based on meta-heuristic algorithms, whose performance depends heavily on human experience. Only few works attempt to use DRL to solve simplified job batching problem which deviates from actual production.

6   Conclusion

In this paper, we build a job batching model based on pointer network. We propose a DRL based method to achieve intelligent job batching, which can learn the stable strategy by making full use of the massive unlabeled data in IIoT and can handle multi-dimensional data. We analyze the convergence of the model and compare the performance with multiple methods. The experiments demonstrate that our method can produce stable and better solution. Especially, our method can produce faster solution even in the problem with large job number. In the future, we will focus on the study of using DRL method to achieve intelligent scheduling combined with the job batching problem in IIoT.

Acknowledgements. This work was supported in part by the National Key R&D Program of China 2017YFB1003000, NSFC 62061146002, 61632008, 61921003, and Fundamental Research Funds for the Central Universities (2019XD - A14).

References

1. Gilchrist, A.: Industry 4.0: The Industrial Internet of Things. Apress, Berkeley (2016). https://doi.org/10.1007/978-1-4842-2047-4
2. He, J.J., Zhang, J., et al.: Multi-agent reinforcement learning based textile dyeing workshop dynamic scheduling method. CIMS, pp. 1–31 (2021)
3. He, Y., Guo, J.C., Zheng, X.L.: From surveillance to digital twin: challenges and recent advances of signal processing for industrial IoT. IEEE Signal Process. Mag. **35**(5), 120–129 (2018). https://doi.org/10.1109/MSP.2018.2842228
4. Hochreiter, S., Schmidhuber, J.: Long short-term memory. Neural Comput. **9**(8), 1735–1780 (1997). https://doi.org/10.1162/neco.1997.9.8.1735
5. Huynh, N.T., Chien, C.F.: A hybrid multi-subpopulation genetic algorithm for textile batch dyeing scheduling and an empirical study. Comput. Ind. Eng. **125**, 615–627 (2018). https://doi.org/10.1016/j.cie.2018.01.005
6. Jia, S.J., Yi, J., Du, B.: A charge optimization algorithm based on column generation and linear programming. Metallur. Ind. Autom. **44**(262(03)), 35–40 (2020)
7. Jiang, X.K., Zhang, P., Lv, Y.L., et al.: Hybrid ant colony algorithm for batch scheduling in semiconductor furnace operation. J. Shanghai Jiaotong Univ. (8), 792–804 (2020). https://doi.org/10.16183/j.cnki.jsjtu.2018.232
8. Kool, W., Van, H., Welling, M.: Attention, learn to solve routing problems! In: ICLR (2018)
9. LeCun, Y., Bengio, Y., Hinton, G.: Deep learning. Nature **521**(7553), 436–444 (2015). https://doi.org/10.1038/nature14539
10. Liu, X.H., Zhang, T., et al.: Batch scheduling of parallel machines with different capacity for sterilization process in medical equipment enterprises. Ind. Eng. J. **24**(01), 82–89 (2021)
11. Liu, Y.F., Chai, T.Y.: The best priority and variable neighborhood search algorithm for production furnace grouping in NDFEB enterprises. CIESC J. (2018)
12. Luo, S.: Dynamic scheduling for flexible job shop with new job insertions by deep reinforcement learning. Appl. Soft Comput. **91**, 106208 (2020). https://doi.org/10.1016/j.asoc.2020.106208

13. Mnih, V., Kavukcuoglu, K., et al.: Playing Atari with deep reinforcement learning. Computer Science (2013)
14. Nazari, M., Oroojlooy, A., et al.: Reinforcement learning for solving the vehicle routing problem. In: NeurIPS (2018)
15. Pan, R.L., Wang, X.M., et al.: Optimization method of order batching for cold rolling based on fuzzy clusting. Control Decis. (1), 141–148 (2017). https://doi.org/10.13195/j.kzyjc.2015.1238
16. Schuster, M., Paliwal, K.: Bidirectional recurrent neural networks. IEEE Trans. Signal Process. **45**(11), 2673–2681 (1997). https://doi.org/10.1109/78.650093
17. Sutton, R., Barto, A.: Reinforcement Learning: An Introduction. MIT Press, Cambridge (2018)
18. Vinyals, O., Fortunato, M., Jaitly, N.: Pointer networks. In: NIPS (2015)
19. Wang, L., Gao, X.W., Wang, W., Wang, Q.: Order production scheduling method based on subspace clustering mixed model and time-section ant colony algorithm. IEEE/CAA JAS **40**(009), 1991–1997 (2014)
20. Yi, J., Du, B., et al.: An improved compact genetic algorithm for charge design problem. In: CCDC (2019)
21. Zhang, C., Song, W., et al.: Learning to dispatch for job shop scheduling via deep reinforcement learning. In: NIPS, vol. 33 (2020)
22. Zhang, H., Ku, T., Zhang, D.Y.: Furnace-grouping optimization with order-grouping for special aluminum ingots. Control Theory Appl. (2019)
23. Zhang, Y., Zheng, X.L., Liu, L., Ma, H.D.: Multivariate and multi-frequency LSTM based fine-grained productivity forecasting for industrial IoT. IEEE MSN (2020). https://doi.org/10.1109/MSN50589.2020.00058

ORMD: Online Learning Real-Time Malicious Node Detection for the IoT Network

Jingxiu Yang, Lu Zhou$^{(\boxtimes)}$, Liang Liu, and Zuchao Ma

Nanjing University of Aeronautics and Astronautics, Nanjing 210016, China
{jingxiuyang,liangliu,macher}@nuaa.edu.cn

Abstract. With the rapid development of the Internet of Things and its widespread deployment in daily life and production, malicious node detection is becoming more and more important. The attackers can invade the normal nodes to launch various attacks like dropping or tampering data packets. As the current approaches mainly rely on injecting and collecting data for a period of time and out-of-band communications between nodes and the sink node, it is lagging. In addition, these approaches rely on reliable source nodes and use offline data to calculate, which slows down the detection speed. In this paper, for the first time, we propose an Online learning Real-time Malicious node Detection scheme (ORMD) for IoT network. ORMD adopts an out-of-band-free data collection method, in which probe packets are injected from the sink node to randomly chosen source nodes. The source nodes return the probe packets back to the sink node. The sink node analyzes the returned probe packets to obtain the path's reliability which is used to derive the node's reliability. The derivation of the node's reliability is formalized as a multiple linear regression problem, which can be solved by online learning algorithm. Simulation results show that ORMD can detect malicious nodes in real time with a high accuracy, up to 96%.

Keywords: IoT network security · Malicious node detection · Online learning · Trust management

1 Introduction

The Internet of Things (IoT) is a kind of network that connects all the smart objects together [1]. The typical network in IoT is the wireless sensor network (WSN), which is mainly composed of sensor nodes with limited resources [2]. With the rapid development of internet technology, the IoT network have been used in

Supported by the National Key R&D Program of China (Grant No.2020AAA0107700), the National Natural Science Foundation of China (Grant 62076125, U20B2049, U20B2050), State Key Laboratory Foundation of smart grid protection and operation control, the Science and Technology Funds from National State Grid Ltd.

© Springer Nature Switzerland AG 2021
Z. Liu et al. (Eds.): WASA 2021, LNCS 12938, pp. 494–509, 2021.
https://doi.org/10.1007/978-3-030-86130-8_39

many fields like smart medical, military, urban transportation, etc. There are several types of topologies in IoT network, including the peer-to-peer topology, star topology and mesh topology. In the mesh network, the nodes communicate with each other, and forward data to the sink node through multiple routes. The sink nodes are used to connect the IoT network to the external network, and the processing and storage capacity of these sink nodes is relatively strong. Since the IoT network is open and can not deploy strong security mechanism, the attackers can easily introduce malicious nodes into the network or invade the normal nodes to launch various attacks, which disrupt network operation. These malicious nodes may be external or internal. Through investigation, the internal attacks are often more dangerous and difficult to detect [3]. The internal attacks include sink-hole attack, black-hole attack and selective-forwarding attack, etc. [4,5].

Currently, there are some researches on malicious nodes and attacks detection in [6,7], such as a detection method called Hard Detection (HD) [7]. These schemes all have their own limitations. Firstly they rely on the reliable source nodes. Additionally, the out-of-band communications between the source nodes and the sink must be secure, which is a strict restriction for IoT networks. Secondly, they use offline methods to collect data and calculate which can not guarantee real-time detection and slows down the detection speed. To solve these problems, we propose an Online learning Real-time Malicious node Detection scheme (ORMD). In ORMD, we propose a combination of trust model and online learning method to detect and locate malicious nodes. Through the analysis of experimental results, ORMD performs better than other approaches in terms of detection accuracy and error rate.

In summary, our work makes the following contributions:

1) We propose an Online learning Real-time Malicious node Detection scheme (ORMD), in which uses the nodes' trust value to represent the reliability of nodes. In ORMD, the sink nodes which have sufficient resources and memory are used to collect data and calculate.
2) We propose an out-of-band-free packets injection and collection method, in which injects probe packets from the sink node to the randomly selected source nodes. Then the source nodes return probe packets back to the sink node. This method does not require reliable source nodes and it is out-of-band-free, therefore it is feasible in the IoT networks.
3) We introduce an online learning model to derive node trust value. The sink nodes are used to receive probe packets and perform online learning algorithm to update detection model. There is a cluster analysis based on node's trust value to classify nodes.

The remaining of the paper is organized as follows: Sect. 2 deals with the related works of the malicious attack in the IoT network. We explains our threat model in Sect. 3. Section 4 describes our detection method (ORMD) in detail. Section 5 discusses our simulation setup and results, and finally Sect. 6 makes a conclusion.

2   Related Work

The malicious attacks and nodes detection in the IoT network has been extensively studied in recent years. The existing work can be divided into the following three categories: schemes based on reputation and trust model, schemes based on secure routing protocols and schemes based on machine learning. We give a comprehensive analysis of existing detection schemes and ORMD in Table 1.

Table 1. Comprehensive analysis of existing literature for malicious attack detection

References	Type of attack resolved	Schemes based on different technologies			
		Trust management	Secure routing protocol	Machine learning	The other
Xin liu [7]	Internal attack	✓	×	×	×
Yan S [8]	Malicious node attack	✓	×	×	×
Jaydip S [9]		✓	×	×	×
Tian [10]		✓	×	×	×
Nasser R [11]	Jamming and selfishness	✓	×	×	×
Wei Z [12]	Internal attack	✓	×	×	×
Mohammad [13]	On-off attacks	×	✓	×	×
Lwin M T [14]	Malicious attacks	✓	×	×	Blockchain
Fenye B [15]		✓	✓	×	×
S.Renubala [16]	Black hole and flooding attack	✓	✓	×	×
Semanti D [17]	Malicious internal node attack	×	✓	×	×
Hayajneh A [18]	Malicious or defective nodes	✓	✓	×	×
Hongjun D [19]	Selective forwarding attack and sinkhole attack	×	×	✓	×
Boqi G [20]	Internal node attack	×	×	✓	×
Elvin E [21]	Internal node attack	✓	×	✓	×
Ravi N [22]	DDoS attack	×	×	✓	×
ORMD	Internal attack	✓	×	✓	×

2.1   Schemes Based on Reputation and Trust Model

Many of the existing malicious node detection schemes are based on reputation and trust model. In [8], a trust model based on entropy was proposed to define the trust value of each node. This model enables nodes to respond quickly to heterogeneous attacks, but requires many hardware resources to calculate the trust values of neighbor nodes. In [9], a linear trust evaluation mechanism was proposed, which used linear functions and probabilities to calculate the reliability of nodes in the Ad-Hoc network. In [10], the authors provided a mechanism to predict their future trust using the node's past trust. The method in [11] assumed that all nodes collect basic communication statistical data related to their neighbors' communications, which were sent periodically to the base station. It evaluated nodes using trust measures to effectively detect concealed malicious nodes, which are based on current and past trust values.

In recent years, a trust management scheme in [12] based on Dempster-Shafer evidence theory for malicious node detection was proposed. By considering spatiotemporal correlation of the data collected by sensor nodes in adjacent area, the trust degree can be estimated. This may increase network consumption due to redundant information. In [13], the authors putted forward a comprehensive fuzzy-logic based trust management approach based on clustering of IoT nodes in detecting malicious nodes. The emergence of block-chain also gives a new way to trust management, as in [14], the block chain-based trust management system with a lightweight consensus algorithm in a mobile Ad-Hoc network (MANET) was introduced. The feasibility of this approach in a real network is unknown.

2.2   Schemes Based on Secure Routing Protocols

Malicious attack detection method in WSN can also be improved the detection performance from routing protocols. In [15], the authors presented a highly scalable hierarchical trust management protocol based on cluster analysis to deal with selfish or malicious nodes effectively. A fuzzy logic-based trust evaluation method in [16] was proposed to obtain secure routing. The method uses a Bio-Inspired Energy-Efficient Cluster (BEE-C) protocol and fuzzy logic to calculate node trust. In [17], Enhanced LEACH protocol and a modified cluster-head selection algorithm have been proposed, which bases on remaining battery life and distance to resist the malicious attacks. In [18], the authors developed a novel security protocol using a Message Authentication Code to verify authenticity of messages, and a reputation table to identify malicious or defective nodes. However, it is heavy for the limited resource IoT device.

2.3   Schemes Based on Machine Learning

There are also a lot of researches to improve malicious node detection performance by using machine learning. In [19], the proposed method learned the feature of known nodes, classified them by dynamic multivariate classification, and then established the sample space of all sensor nodes in the network to derive the malicious nodes. In [20], The authors putted forward environment-adaptive malicious node detection method based on ensemble learning. The authors took advantage of a machine/deep learning (ML/DL) trust model approach in [21]. It models trust as a classification process and the extraction of relevant features using a hybrid model like Bayesian Neural Network. And it combined deep learning with probabilistic model for intelligent decision and effective generalization in nodes' trust computation in the network. In [22], a novel mechanism named learning-driven detection mitigation that detects DDoS attack using a semi-supervised machine-learning algorithm and mitigation of attack was presented, which only mitigated the DDoS attack.

3   IoT Network and Threat Model

With the increase of connected IoT devices, the mesh networks have been widely studied. A mesh network is composed of different IoT devices (sensor nodes).

These nodes forward data through multiple routes to the destinations (sink node). As in the Fig. 1, packets can be transmitted to the sink node along multiple routes in a mesh IoT network.

In this paper, we assume that the attackers are those who pretend to be normal internal nodes or compromise normal internal nodes to launch internal attacks. Take the Fig. 1 as an example, N_6 is captured by the attacker, then it becomes a malicious node to launch attacks. In our threat model, malicious nodes can launch tampering attacks, black-hole attack and selective-forwarding attack. First of all, a tampering attack means that N_6 has a certain attack probability $ap(0 \leq ap \leq 1)$ to tamper with data packets. The initial set of packets $pk_1, pk_2, ..., pk_N$ might be $pk_1'', pk_2, ..., pk_i'', ..., pk_N$, in which pk_1'' is damaged. When the damaged packets arrives at the sink node, this attack can be detected by verifying the integrity of the data packet pk_i to discover damaged data packets. Black-hole attack is that a denial of service attack by dropping packets which drops packets selectively or in batches. The initial set of packets $pk_1, pk_2, ..., pk_N$ might be $pk_1, pk_5, ..., pk_N$ or be empty. Selective forwarding attack means malicious nodes N_6 can forward or discard specific packets with the certain attack probability $ap(0 \leq ap \leq 1)$, so that the data packets cannot reach the sink node, causing the network to fall into chaos. Black hole attacks and selective forwarding attacks can be detected by using the packet id at the sink node to compare the initial all packets set pk_{all} and the packets set received by the sink node pk_{rec}. Cooperative attacks are not within the scope of this paper, and the above attacks are independent of each other.

The current security requirements of IoT systems is that it can detect attacks and identify malicious nodes. In this paper, we propose ORMD based on trust management and online learning to detect malicious nodes, in which the nodes' trust value to represent the reliability of nodes

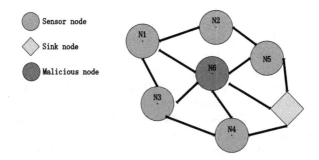

Fig. 1. An example of our mesh network and threat model.

4 Proposed Scheme ORMD

4.1 Workflow

As shown in Fig. 2, the workflow of ORMD are as follows:

Step1. The sink node chooses some source nodes $SS_1, SS_2, ...SS_k$ to inject probe packets, and the probe packets are forwarded to the source nodes through typical routing protocol, like RPL [23] and AODV [24].

Step2. After the source node $SS_i (1 \leq i \leq k)$ receives the probe packets, it continues to forward the packets back to the sink node. During transmission, ORMD uses the data provenance to record the routing path [25].

Step3. Once the sink node receives a probe packet, the sink extracts the recorded routing path P and calculates path's trust value, which is the ratio of probe packets successfully transmitted through the path P according to the packet's id and message digest verification.

Step4. We use path's trust value to derive node's trust value. The calculation of nodes' trust values is formalized as a multiple linear regression problem solved by online machine learning. That is to say, we use the trained online learning model to infer the node's trust value based on the path information and the path's trust value.

Step5. k-means clustering analysis based on node's trust value is used to classify malicious nodes which have lower trust values.

It can be seen from the workflow and the figure that ORMD contains three major parts: probe packets injection and collection, real-time nodes' trust value estimation and clustering of nodes based on trust value. This three parts are explained in detail in Sect. 4.2–4.4.

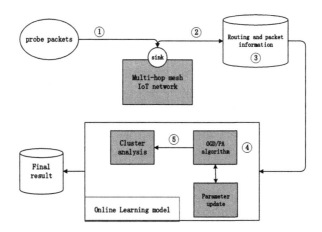

Fig. 2. The workflow of real-time malicious node detection scheme (ORMD)

4.2   Packets Injection and Collection

In this paper, we design an out-of-band-free packets injection and collection method. As shown in the Fig. 3, the method includes the following three phases:

1) **Packets injection:** Firstly, the sink node S randomly chooses some source nodes to inject probe packets. The probe packets are transmitted to the source nodes according to the typical routing protocol like RPL [23].
2) **Reverse packets transmission:** After receiving the probe packets, the source nodes return the packets back to the sink node. ORMD uses the data provenance technology [25] to record its routing path P in the transmission.
3) **Routing path extraction and integrity verification:** When the probe packets finally arrive at the sink node, the sink node analyzes the packets to extract the routing path P and checks packets' id and message digest to verify the packets' integrity.

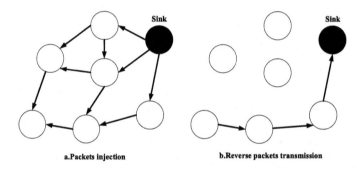

a.Packets injection   b.Reverse packets transmission

Fig. 3. The out-of-band-free packets collection method

Take Fig. 1 as an example, the sink node S has a private key k to signs probe packets, $N_1, N_2, ...$ are chosen as source nodes. First, the sink node generates probe packets and uses Hash algorithm to calculate its message digest: $MD = Hash(pk)$, and signs packets using its secret key: $E = enc(MD)_k$. The basic structure of the probe packet includes packets' id, source address(SS), destination address(D), path information(PI), message signature (E), data content(C) as shown Eq. (1). ORMD uses the data provenance technology to record the path information, which is represented by node sequence as (1).

$$pk = (id, SS, D, PI, E, C) \quad PI = <N_1, N_2, ...N_i> \tag{1}$$

When a probe packet $pk_1 = (id_1, S, N_1, PI, E, C)$ is injected from the sink node S, the probe packet pk_1 is forwarded by N_4, N_6 and arrives the source node N_1. Then the source node N_1 reverses the source and destination of pk_1 to generate reverse packet $pk_1' = (id_1, N_1, S, PI, E, C)$, the reverse packet pk_1' is returned to sink node S through the path N_2, N_5. During transmission, PI is recorded as $<N_4, N_6, N_1, N_2, N_5>$. After the sink node receives the packet pk'_1, it uses its private key k and HASH to calculate the message digest for verifying the integrity of the packet pk'_1. Then the sink node continues to select the source node and repeats the above packet injection process until all the probe packets are injected.

4.3   Real-Time Nodes' Trust Value Estimation

We use the trust value to represent the reliability of paths and nodes. We denote $P.TV$ as the trust value of the path P, and $N.TV$ as the trust value of the node N. We try to derive the node's trust value from the path's trust value, and find that the derivation of node's trust value is formalized as a multiple linear regression problem which is widely used machine learning to solve.

$$\{pk'_1.PI, pk'_2.PI, ..., pk'_i.PI\} = \{<N_4, N_6, , N_1, N_2, N_5>, <N_5, N_2, N_1, N_6>, ...\} \tag{2}$$

Once the sink node receives the reverse probe packet pk'_i, it extracts the path from the $pk'_i.PI$. The path information $pk'_1.PI =< N_4, N_6, N_1, N_2, N_5 >$can be represented as a vector $P_1 = [1, 1, 0, 1, 1, 1]$ to simplify the calculation, in which the number in P_1 indicates the number of times that a node appears in the path P_1.

After the sink node knows the routing path, it also gets the proportion of normal packets transmitted through the path by verifying the integrity of packets. This proportion is regarded as the trust value of the path. Therefore, we denote the trust value of the path P_1 as $P_1.TV$, which is equivalent to the number of normal packets received by the sink node (define as pk_{rec}) divided by the number of all packets (define as pk_{all}) transmitted through the path P_1. We can also use the trust value of all nodes on the path P_1 to represent the $P_1.TV$. For trust value $P_1.TV$ is expressed as:

$$P_1.TV = \frac{pk_{rec}}{pk_{all}} = N_1.TV * N_2.TV * N_4.TV * N_5.TV * N_6.TV$$

$$\ln P_1.TV = 1 * \ln N_1.TV + 1 * \ln N_2.TV + 0 * \ln N_3.TV + 1 * \ln N_4.TV +$$

$$1 * \ln N_5.TV + 1 * \ln N_6.TV = [1, 1, 0, 1, 1, 1] * \ln \begin{bmatrix} N_1.TV \\ N_2.TV \\ \vdots \\ N_6.TV \end{bmatrix} \tag{3}$$

For the entire network, We suppose there are n nodes and m paths. We can obtain all routing path represented as PM (Path Matrix). And the matrix of all routing path's trust value and the node's trust value are represented as PTM (Paths' trust value Matrix) and NTM (Nodes' trust value Matrix). In PM (Path Matrix), the a_{ij} indicates number of times that node N_j appears in path P_i:

$$PM = \begin{bmatrix} a_{11} & a_{12} & a_{13} \cdots & a_{1n} \\ a_{21} & a_{22} & a_{23} \cdots & a_{2n} \\ \vdots & \vdots & \ddots & \vdots \\ a_{m1} & a_{m2} & a_{m3} \cdots & a_{mn} \end{bmatrix} \quad NTM = \begin{bmatrix} N_1.TV \\ N_2.TV \\ \vdots \\ N_n.TV \end{bmatrix} \quad PTM = \begin{bmatrix} P_1.TV \\ P_2.TV \\ \vdots \\ P_m.TV \end{bmatrix}$$

(4)

According to the relationship between the routing path's trust value and the node's trust value, the relationship of different matrix can be expressed as:

$$PM * \ln NTM = \ln PTM \tag{5}$$

In the IoT network, as soon as a packet is arrived at the sink node, the routing path is extracted and the integrity verification is performed to update the PM and PTM. Using the above expression, the calculation of NTM is formalized as multiple linear regression problem, so we use online learning algorithm to estimate NTM (the node's trust value).

Because the sink nodes have enough memory and resources, online incremental machine learning can be implemented at the sink node for processing data in real time. The online learning model is updated every time when a new sample is received. Therefore, we use online machine learning model to estimate nodes' trust value in ORMD. In Algorithm 1, we first present a general algorithmic framework of online machine learning for node's trust value estimation. Then, we introduce several typical online learning algorithms which can be employed in ORMD, including Online Gradient Descent (OGD) and Passive-Aggressive Algorithm (PA). Then, we choose the one with better detection performance in experiments of Sect. 4.

Algorithm 1. Online Learning (x_t, y_t, w)

Input: feature matrix x_t at rounds t, target value matrix y_t
Output: Weight values w
1: math.ln(y_t)
2: predict value $y_t' = f(w, x_t)$
3: compute the loss $l(y_t', y_t)$
4: update the weight w

Nodes' Trust Value Learning Based on Online Gradient Descent (OGD): Gradient descent updating is an efficient approach for online learning. Assume $S \subset R^n$ is a closed convex set of diameter at most D. This means that for every $w, w' \in S, |w - w'| \leq D$. The loss function is basically similar to the stochastic gradient descent algorithm [26]:

$$l(x_t, w) = \log(1 + exp(-y_t(w_t \Delta x_t)))$$

$$W_{t+1} = W_t + \eta_t y_t x_t \Delta \frac{1}{1 + exp(y_t(w_t \Delta x_t))}, \qquad \eta_t = \frac{D}{L\sqrt{t}} \tag{6}$$

at $t = 1$, select any $w_1 \in S$, η_t is the learning rate at t times and assume that the norm of the gradients is bounded by L.

Nodes' Trust Value Learning Based on Passive-Aggressive Algorithm (PA):
Passive-Aggressive Learning Algorithm (PA) is one of classic online learning algorithm. It's based on a slightly different Hinge loss function (called ϵ-insensitive) [27]:

$$l(x_t, w) = max(0, |y_t - f(x_t, w)| - \epsilon)$$

$$w_{t+1} = w_t + \eta_t^{PA} y_t x_t \quad where \quad \eta_t^{PA} = \frac{l(x_t, w)}{||w_t||^2} \tag{7}$$

The parameter ϵ determines a tolerance for prediction errors. The update rule are the same which is adopted for classification problems.

As shown the Algorithm 1, the sink node extracts the packets' routing path and verify its integrity to update the PM and PTM in real time. Then we use these as the input of online learning model, the trust value of nodes matrix NTM can be estimated by online learning algorithm.

4.4 Clustering of Nodes Based on Trust Value

After all the nodes' trust values are estimated by online learning algorithm, we cluster and classify nodes based on trust value to detect malicious nodes. There are many clustering algorithms, and the choice of algorithms depends on the type of data, the purpose of clustering, and the specific application. Clustering algorithms are mainly divided into five categories: partition-based clustering method, hierarchical-based clustering method, density-based clustering method, grid-based clustering method and model-based clustering method. There are some widely used algorithms in each category, such as k-means algorithm, Agglomerative Hierarchical Clustering (AHC) algorithm, Density-Based Spatial Clustering of Applications with Noise (DBSCAN) algorithm, Clustering In QUEst (CLIQUE) algorithm and Gaussian Mixture Models (GMM) in model-based method. In this paper, we need to cluster the one-dimensional data of node's trust value, and the nodes need to be divided into two categories: malicious and benign. Through experiments in Sect. 4 and analysis, it can be known that the k-means algorithm is simple, efficient and easy to calculate.

In ORMD, We know that a node with low trust value indicates that it may be a malicious node. We choose the simple and efficient k-means algorithm to cluster the nodes into two categories based on the nodes' trust value, such as the set of benign and malicious nodes. In k-means algorithm, the k represents the final number of clustering which is determined in advance. In our algorithm, we set $k = 2$ to represent the set of benign and malicious nodes. First, the initial point is randomly selected as the cluster centroids. The similarity between trust value of each nodes with centroids' value is calculated, then the nodes are grouped into the most similar cluster. The centroid of each cluster is recalculated, and this process is repeated until the centroid is no longer changed. Finally, the cluster which each node belongs to is determined.

5   Simulation Results

In order to evaluate detection performance of ORMD, we simulate the IoT network and deploy our detection method (ORMD), and evaluate ORMD through different experiments, including the comparison of different online learning algorithms and clustering algorithms, the comparison with hard detection (HD) [7] and offline learning, and the influence of different factors on ORMD.

In the simulation, we assume that there are N nodes distributed with $10 \times 10\,\mathrm{m}^2$ rectangular network region. The sink node S is at the edge of the rectangle. The communication range of each node is $r = 2\,\mathrm{m}$. We generate random networks, and the simulation is repeated in 10 rounds. In each round, unless otherwise stated, we randomly select 30% of the nodes as malicious nodes. The attack probability ap_i of each malicious node is 30%. However, ap_i once is allocated, and it is fixed in the simulation. We use 1000 probe packets transmitted through routing path. In order to evaluate the performance of ORMD, we use the metrics shown in Table 2 and some metrics are explained as following:

FN: False Negative, identified as a benign node, but in fact it is a malicious node.

FP: False Positive, identified as a malicious node, but in fact it is a benign node.

TN: True Negative, identified as a benign node, and in fact it is also a benign node.

TP: True Positive, identified as a malicious node, and in fact it is also a malicious node.

Table 2. Simulation metrics

Precision	TP/(TP+FP)	Ratio of malicious nodes correctly identified in the detection results
Recall	TP/(TP+FN)	Ratio of malicious nodes correctly identified in the real malicious set
Accuracy	(TN+TP)/(TN+TP+FN+FP)	Ratio of benign nodes and malicious nodes correctly identified
Error rate	(FN+FP)/(TN+TP+ FN+FP)	Ratio of benign nodes and malicious nodes misidentified

5.1   Comparison of Different Online Learning Algorithms and Clustering Algorithms

Comparison of Different Online Learning Algorithms. In the Sect. 3, There are two classic online learning algorithms introduced: online gradient descent (OGD) and passive-aggressive learning algorithm (PA). Then we used these two algorithm to deploy in our ORMD. The simulation metrics above versus different proportions of malicious nodes in the network are plotted in Fig. 4(a). We evaluate the performance of the algorithm with detection accuracy and error rate. As shown in the Fig. 4(a), PA algorithm is significantly better than the OGD algorithm, and we can see the detection accuracy of PA is generally higher than that of OGD algorithm, up to more than 90%. Therefore, we use the PA algorithm for the following simulation experiments.

Comparison of Different Clustering Algorithms. In order to compare the effectiveness of various clustering algorithms, we have applied four clustering algorithms in ORMD, including k-means algorithm, Agglomerative Hierarchical Clustering algorithm (AHC), Density-Based Spatial Clustering of Applications with Noise (DBSCAN) algorithm, Clustering In QUEst (CLIQUE) algorithm. From Table 3, We can see that k-means can quickly and effectively identify malicious nodes in high accuracy, because the nodes' trust value is one-dimensional data, and the number of clusters can be determined.

Table 3. Comparison with different clustering algorithms

Clustering algorithm	k-means	AHC	DBSCAN	CLIQUE
Accuracy	0.915	0.893	0.867	0.933
Error rate	0.085	0.106	0.133	0.067
Time complexity	$O(n)$	$O(n^3)$	$O(n^2)$	$O(n^2)$

5.2   Comparison with Hard Detection (HD) and Offline Learning Algorithm

In this section, we study the detection performance of the hard-detected (HD), detection with offline machine learning algorithm (support vector machine) and our detection method (ORMD). The settings are unchanged, and HD and offline machine learning algorithm (SVM) are deployed in this experiment.

Comparison with Hard Detection (HD). In Hard detection (HD), they inject the probe packets from the reliable source node and assume that each node's trust values are the same on the same path, so one node's N_i trust value on different paths is solved directly with $\frac{1}{m}\sum_{j=1}^{m}\sqrt[n]{P_j.TV}$ (n is the number of all nodes on the path P_j and m is the number of path has the nodeN_i). Direct brute force solution leads to inaccurate calculation results. As shown in the Fig. 4(b), ORMD is significantly better than HD under different percentage of malicious nodes in the network. ORMD can reach up to 96% in detection accuracy and the error rate is as low as 0.1 or less.

Comparison with Offline Learning Algorithm. Offline learning algorithm (SVM) was used, which periodically collects large number of packets to learning the node's trust value. It repeatedly inject 1000 packets from the source node until all the collections at sink were successful, then learn the trust value of nodes using the SVM. The training time here includes injecting probe packets, collecting data and model training. In the offline learning model, after multiple rounds of network simulation results, we find the average detection time is 5.78 s and detection performance is not stable. From the Fig. 4(c), it can be seen that the detection accuracy of the online learning algorithm is relatively low at first but increases by the training time (ms) due to incremental update, finally close to stable detection. It can reach up to 92%. So ORMD which uses online learning algorithm is better than offline learning algorithm in detection speed, and ORMD can detect malicious nodes in real-time with high accuracy.

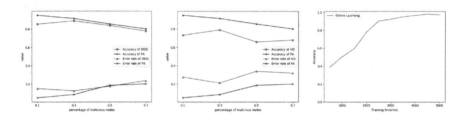

Fig. 4. Comparison with different online learning algorithm and other algorithm

5.3   The Influence of Different Factors on Detection Performance

In this section, we evaluate the effects of different factors on ORMD in detection performance. These factors include the number of nodes, percentage of malicious nodes, probability of malicious attack and nodes' communication radius.

Influence of the Number of Nodes. Here, we examine the impact of nodes' number on ORMD. The simulation metrics above versus the number of nodes N in the network are plotted in Fig. 8. We set the number of nodes to 5, 15, 25 and 35. The rest of the settings are unchanged. In the Fig. 5(a), it indicates that most malicious nodes are effectively identified which can account for most of the detection results and the detection accuracy of ORMD is relatively high, which can reach to 92% with error rate below 0.1 for different number of nodes. We find that when there are relatively few nodes and the limitation of communication radius, it cannot accurately identify malicious nodes.

Influence of the Ratio of Malicious Nodes. In the experiment, we show the impact of percentage of malicious nodes. We set the percentage of malicious nodes in all nodes to be 0.1, 0.3, 0.5 and 0.7. The rest of the settings are unchanged and number of nodes is 15. As shown in Fig. 5(b), when the number of malicious nodes in the network is too small or too large, the recall can be 90% that smaller than the medium number of malicious nodes. The increase of malicious nodes can lead to more malicious attacks and the increase of damaged data packets transmitted through routing paths, which lower the trust value of the normal nodes and reduce the detection accuracy. Also a small number of malicious nodes results in only a small number of malicious attacks, which can not accurately derive the trust value of the node.

Influence of the Probability of Malicious Attack. We set the malicious node attack probability to be 0.1, 0.3, 0.5 and 0.7. The rest of the settings are unchanged. In Fig. 5(c), we plot the simulation metrics above as functions of percentage of malicious nodes. This figure shows that our detection method can detect the malicious nodes efficiently in case of different probability of malicious attack, the accuracy all can reach up to 95%. Because the probability of attack increases, the number of damaged packets transmitted on routing path with the malicious node has increased, and the detection effect is more obvious, so we can find that the detection accuracy increases with the increase in attack probability.

Influence of Nodes' Communication Radius. The other settings are unchanged. In order to evaluate the influence of the node communication radius on the detection method in the network, we set the variables of the node communication radius, which are 1 m, 2 m, 3 m, and 4 m respectively. In Fig. 5(d), we plot the simulation metrics above as functions of node communication radius. The communication radius of nodes is closely related to the number of routing paths in the network. The larger node's communication radius, the more nodes can communicate with other nodes and the more paths to reach the sink. We can find that as the communication radius of nodes increases, the detection accuracy can reach up to 95% with lower error rate.

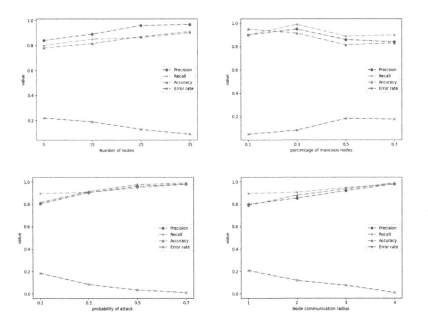

Fig. 5. The influence of different factors on detection performance

6 Conclusion

How to detect malicious nodes in the IoT network effectively and quickly is a key issue. To address this critical issue, we propose an Online learning Real-time Malicious Detection method (ORMD) based on trust model and online learning. In ORMD, the out-of-band-free packets injection and collection method is that the sink node injects and collects probe packets to randomly selected source nodes, then the source nodes return the probe packets back to the sink node to collect information about the routing paths, which are used to obtain path's trust value. Based on the path's trust value, the calculation of nodes' trust value is formalized as a multiple linear regression problem. Then we use online learning algorithm and cluster analysis algorithm to derive nodes' trust value and detect the malicious nodes. Simulation results show that ORMD successfully detects malicious nodes with a high accuracy in real-time. We explore a combination of reputation model and online learning method to detect and locate malicious nodes, and We regard this work as preliminary solution.

References

1. Gubbi, J., Buyya, R., Marusic, S., Palaniswami, M.: Internet of things (IoT): a vision, architectural elements, and future directions. Futur. Gener. Comput. Syst. **29**(7), 1645–1660 (2013)
2. Fantacci, R., Pecorella, T., Viti, R., Carlini, C.: A network architecture solution for efficient IoT WSN backhauling: challenges and opportunities. IEEE Wirel. Commun. **21**(4), 113–119 (2014)
3. Meddeb, R., Triki, B., Jemili, F., Korbaa, O.: A survey of attacks in mobile ad hoc networks. In: 2017 International Conference on Engineering & MIS (ICEMIS), pp. 1–7. IEEE (2017)
4. Ren, K., Lou, W., Zhang, Y.: LEDS: providing location-aware end-to-end data security in wireless sensor networks. IEEE Trans. Mob. Comput. **7**(5), 585–598 (2008)
5. Khan, M.A., Salah, K.: IoT security: review, blockchain solutions, and open challenges. Futur. Gener. Comput. Syst. **82**, 395–411 (2018)
6. Liu, L., Ma, Z., Meng, W.: Detection of multiple-mix-attack malicious nodes using perceptron-based trust in IoT networks. Futur. Gener. Comput. Syst. **101**, 865–879 (2019)
7. Liu, X., Abdelhakim, M., Krishnamurthy, P., Tipper, D.: Identifying malicious nodes in multihop IoT networks using diversity and unsupervised learning. In: 2018 IEEE International Conference on Communications (ICC), pp. 1–6. IEEE (2018)
8. Sun, Y.L., Yu, W., Han, Z., Liu, K.R.: Information theoretic framework of trust modeling and evaluation for ad hoc networks. IEEE J. Sel. Areas Commun. **24**(2), 305–317 (2006)
9. Sen, J., Chowdhury, P.R., Sengupta, I.: A distributed trust establishment scheme for mobile ad hoc networks. In: 2007 International Conference on Computing: Theory and Applications (ICCTA 2007), pp. 51–58. IEEE (2007)
10. Liqin, T., et al.: Computation and analysis of node intending trust in WSNs. In: 2010 IEEE International Conference on Wireless Communications, Networking and Information Security, pp. 496–499. IEEE (2010)

11. Rikli, N.-E., Alnasser, A.: Lightweight trust model for the detection of concealed malicious nodes in sparse wireless ad hoc networks. Int. J. Distrib. Sens. Netw. **12**(7), 1550147716657246 (2016)
12. Zhang, W., Zhu, S., Tang, J., Xiong, N.: A novel trust management scheme based on dempster-shafer evidence theory for malicious nodes detection in wireless sensor networks. J. Supercomput. **74**(4), 1779–1801 (2018)
13. Alshehri, M.D., Hussain, F.K.: A fuzzy security protocol for trust management in the internet of things (fuzzy-IoT). Computing **101**(7), 791–818 (2019)
14. Lwin, M.T., Yim, J., Ko, Y.-B.: Blockchain-based lightweight trust management in mobile ad-hoc networks. Sensors **20**(3), 698 (2020)
15. Bao, F., Chen, R., Chang, M.J., Cho, J.-H.: Hierarchical trust management for wireless sensor networks and its applications to trust based routing and intrusion detection. IEEE Trans. Netw. Serv. Manag. **9**(2), 169–183 (2012)
16. Renubala, S., Dhanalakshmi, K.S.: Trust based secure routing protocol using fuzzy logic in wireless sensor networks. In: 2014 IEEE International Conference on Computational Intelligence and Computing Research, pp. 1–5. IEEE (2014)
17. Das, S., Das, A.: An algorithm to detect malicious nodes in wireless sensor network using enhanced leach protocol. In: 2015 International Conference on Advances in Computer Engineering and Applications, pp. 875–881. IEEE (2015)
18. Al Hayajneh, A., Bhuiyan, M.Z.A., McAndrew, I.: A novel security protocol for wireless sensor networks with cooperative communication. Computers **9**(1), 4 (2020)
19. Dai, H., Liu, H., Jia, Z.: Dynamic malicious node detection with semi-supervised multivariate classification in cognitive wireless sensor networks. Concurr. Comput. Pract. Exp. **27**(12), 2910–2923 (2015)
20. Gao, B., Maekawa, T., Amagata, D., Hara, T.: Environment-adaptive malicious node detection in manets with ensemble learning. In: 2018 IEEE 38th International Conference on Distributed Computing Systems (ICDCS), pp. 556–566. IEEE (2018)
21. Eziama, E., Tepe, K., Balador, A., Nwizege, K.S., Jaimes, L.M.S.: Malicious node detection in vehicular ad-hoc network using machine learning and deep learning. In: 2018 IEEE Globecom Workshops (GC Wkshps), pp. 1–6. IEEE (2018)
22. Ravi, N., Shalinie, S.M.: Learning-driven detection and mitigation of DDoS attack in IoT via SDN-cloud architecture. IEEE Internet Things J. **7**(4), 3559–3570 (2020)
23. Kharrufa, H., Al-Kashoash, H., Al-Nidawi, Y., Mosquera, M.Q., Kemp, A.H.: Dynamic RPL for multi-hop routing in IoT applications. In: 2017 13th Annual Conference on Wireless On-demand Network Systems and Services (WONS), pp. 100–103. IEEE (2017)
24. Marina, M.K., Das, S.R.: Ad hoc on-demand multipath distance vector routing. Wirel. Commun. Mob. Comput. **6**(7), 969–988 (2006)
25. Wang, C., Hussain, S.R., Bertino, E.: Dictionary based secure provenance compression for wireless sensor networks. IEEE Trans. Parallel Distrib. Syst. **27**(2), 405–418 (2015)
26. Ying, Y., Pontil, M.: Online gradient descent learning algorithms. Found. Comput. Math. **8**(5), 561–596 (2008)
27. Lu, J., Zhao, P., Hoi, S.C.: Online passive-aggressive active learning. Mach. Learn. **103**(2), 141–183 (2016)

TFRA: Trajectory-Based Message Ferry Recognition Attack in UAV Network

Yuting Wu[1(✉)], Yulei Liu[1], Liang Liu[1(✉)], Feng Wang[1], Lihong Fan[1], and Qian Zhou[2]

[1] Nanjing University of Aeronautics and Astronautics, Nanjing, China
{yutingwu,liu_yulei,liangliu,lih}@nuaa.edu.cn
[2] Nanjing University of Posts and Telecommunications, Nanjing, China
zhouqian@njupt.edu.cn

Abstract. The introduction of ferry UAVs (message ferry) in the UAV network is an effective means to solve the cooperative communication of multiple UAVs. The ferry UAVs act as message collectors and throwers in the network to improve data transmission efficiency, the critical roles that ferry plays have made them the target of sophisticated attacks, ferry should be protected, otherwise, routing efficiency and data delivery of the network will be affected. Since the movement mode of ferry nodes is different from the ordinary nodes, this paper attempts to distinguish ordinary node and ferry node through trajectory analysis, then we propose a Trajectory-based message Ferry Recognition Attack (TFRA) which is easy for an attacker to implement, using the idea of trajectory clustering to distinguish the trajectory of the ferry node, and obtain the location for further attacks. At the same time, we conducted a systematic study on the existing path planning scheme of ferry node, and summarized several typical types of message ferry path planning schemes, then evaluated the performance of TFRA in these schemes. The results show TFRA can attack ferry nodes with high accuracy and recognition rate.

Keywords: UAV network · Message ferry recognition · Trajectory clustering

1 Introduction

In recent years, UAV (unmanned aerial vehicle) has become a promising new computing platform and has broad application prospects on search and rescue operations [18], forest fire automatic monitoring [20], ground target detection and tracking [29], and disaster monitoring [19], etc. The cooperative application of small multi-UAVs has the advantages of greater survivability, higher scalability, faster completion of tasks, smaller radar cross-sections, but it also faces some

Sponsored by the Natural Science Foundation of China (Grant No. 61902199); NUPTSF (Grant No. NY219142); State Key Laboratory for Novel Software Technology (Grant No. KFKT2019B13).

unique challenges. Among them, one of the most important design issues is collaborative communication between multiple UAVs.

It is an attractive scheme to establish connections by introducing message ferry. Message ferry is a mobile assistive technology whose existence promotes connections and solves the disconnection and sparsity of mobile ad hoc networks [11]. Message ferry is a delay-tolerant forwarding scheme that physically transfers data to the destination or the next relay node without an end-to-end routing path [21]. By using the ferry node as a relay, the node can communicate asynchronously with other disconnected nodes, or transmit the collected data to the ground station when other nodes perform normal data collection, which can increase routing path diversity and network delivery rate [7].

In a UAV network containing ferry node, the ferry node acts as data collector and data transmitter, its movement mode is well-designed to meet the needs of the network, and the critical roles that ferry nodes play have made them the target of sophisticated attacks, therefore its location anonymity is very important. If attacker attacks the ferry node, making it unable to work, then the routing efficiency of the network reduces. Or the ferry node is captured, attackers can carry out attacks such as the dissemination of false information, black hole, and gray hole attacks [4], making the network paralyzed or unable to work.

Using technology such as radar, an attacker can easily obtain UAV's position and depict their flight trajectory [10]. In the actual application of UAVs, the network may include different types of UAVs, such as ferry UAVs and ordinary UAVs. In this case, if the attacker can also distinguish the types of nodes in the network, they can easily attack important nodes such as ferry nodes to achieve the purpose of paralyzing the UAV network at a lower cost.

There have been many studies on the location anonymity of nodes in wireless sensor networks, and many kinds of attack methods and location anonymity protection methods have also been proposed. As far as we know, the research on ferry nodes' location anonymity in UAV network is still an open problem. In this paper, we aim to identify and attack ferry nodes in UAV network, our contributions can be summarized as follows:

- We systematically studied path planning methods of ferry nodes in UAVs and self-organizing networks, and have summarized several typical path planning methods of ferry nodes according to their main design ideas.
- The flight mode of the ferry node is different from the ordinary node. Based on this feature, we propose a Trajectory-based message Ferry Recognition Attack (TFRA). We design a global attacker who can observe near the UAV network and obtain the flight trajectory of UAVs through radar and other technologies, then the attacker identifies ferry nodes through trajectory clustering, and its location information is obtained to initiate further attacks.
- We conducted a performance evaluation on TFRA under three typical ferry node path planning schemes, the results show that TFRA can identify ferry nodes with high accuracy.

The rest of this paper is organized as follows. Section 2 outlines some related works on ferry path planning and location anonymity. Section 3 describes prerequisites including the network model, adversary model and ferry path planning schemes we used. Section 4 describes the details of TFRA. Section 5 analyzes and discusses our experimental results. Finally, Sect. 6 concludes this work.

2   Related Works

This paper is concerned with anonymity of nodes' location or indistinguishability of trajectory, which is similar to location privacy attacks on source nodes and sink nodes in wireless sensor networks, this type of attack requires finding the exact location of the source node or sink node. As far as we know, there are few studies on the attack of identifying ferry nodes in UAV network. Because the movement patterns of ferry and ordinary nodes are different, we aim to distinguish them from the perspective of trajectory, therefore we studied ferry path planning schemes as well.

2.1   Anonymity of Nodes' Location

To obtain the exact location of key nodes, the researchers suggested many types of attacks, such as passive attacks like wireless eavesdropping attacks, retrospective attacks, packet analysis attacks, and traffic analysis attacks; on the other hand, active attackers capture or cloning legal nodes to obtain the position information about a source or a base station [16].

In addition, according to the range of an adversary's monitoring area, the attack model can be classified into two categories: global attack and local attack. Local attackers in [13,24] can only monitor a few hops and track the angle and strength of the received signal with antennas and spectrum analyzers. Global attackers in [14,25] attack by monitoring the traffic of the entire network, analyze the content correlation, time correlation, and packet sending rate of the data packets.

2.2   Message Ferry Path Planning Schemes

The path planning schemes of ferry nodes can be divided into two categories: random path and planned path. In the case of the random path, the ferry node moves randomly and collects data from nodes within its communication range, for instance, MULEs in [23].

The planned path can be roughly divided into three categories: fixed path planning, global path planning, and distributed dynamic path planning.

Fixed Path Planning: the paths of all nodes are preset during network initialization to complete data collection and transmission, and the nodes move according to the preset paths during network operation [8,27].

Global Path Planning: the basic idea is to determine a series of points that the path of ferry node must contain through factors such as distance, energy, and node movement model. *Bin Tariq M M et al.* [11] propose an algorithm that ferry node passes a path which makes it touches each mobile node with a certain minimum probability. Similarly, in [26], the ferry nodes visit the exact rendezvous to collect data. In [5,17,22], the distance indicated by the hops, the number of packets forwarded to the nearest point by each node, energy, and total travel time of ferry node are suggested as factors to determine rendezvous.

Distributed Dynamic Path Planning: the above methods are all based on the prior knowledge (i.e. movement model) of other nodes, otherwise, they are not applicable. *Chin-Lin Hu et al.* in [15] designed a dynamic ferry node scheduling method that multiple ferry nodes tried to perceive the strength of information exchange in geographically adjacent places, found hot spots, and then independently planned travel paths through these hot spots. *JinYi Yoon et al.* [28] proposed a distributed path planning algorithm based on the weighted sum of travel time and the delivery deadline.

3   Network Model and Prerequisites

In this section, we will introduce the network model and prerequisites of message ferry path planning schemes.

3.1   Network Model

What we are considering is to apply UAV networks to search and rescue missions. As shown in Fig. 1(a), multiple ordinary searching nodes are sent to different locations in the mission area, the ferry nodes are introduced to establish connections between the ordinary searching nodes and the ground station. Data transmissions between nodes and the ground station use high-throughput links with limited range (Data Link). In addition, remote links (Control Link) are used for telemetry and control information.

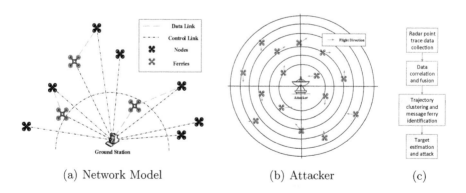

(a) Network Model   (b) Attacker   (c)

Fig. 1. Network and adversary model

Our network model can be abstracted into a weighted undirected graph G, which contains m mobile nodes, $G = <N, E>$, $N = \{n_i | 1 \le i \le m\}$, $E = \{e_{ij} | 1 \le$

$i, j \leq m$}. e_{ij} indicates that nodes n_i and n_j are within the communication range of each other. Each node has a geographic location (latitude, longitude, height), direction, and speed, making it possible to predict future movements. It is assumed that message unicast is used and the ferry node only carries or forwards messages and doesn't generate any messages. The message transmission time is ignored because it is much shorter than the time for the UAV to move between nodes.

3.2 Message Forwarding with Ferries Path Planning

In this paper, we mainly consider three types of the planned path scheme.

Fixed Path Planning: we use the network scenario in [8,27], the number of UAVs in the network ranges from 13 to 24, the number of ferry nodes is 4, the position and trajectory of the UAVs are both preset in advance, the ordinary searching node is placed outside the communication range of the ground station, but within the communication range of at least one ferry node, the symmetric ferry node in the network is always moving towards the opposite direction to generate more paths for forwarding decisions.

Global Path Planning [5,17,22,26]: we summarize the common points of global path planning in several references: it is assumed that the ground station continuously receives and buffers the data transmission requests from the UAVs. When the data transmission requests accumulate to a certain number or reach a transmission cycle, the ground station plans the flight path of the ferry node. When there are multiple ferry nodes, the ground station first allocates the tasks, clusters the tasks according to geographic location, and then finds the closest ferry node to the clustering center, then the tasks in this cluster are assigned to that ferry node. When there is a ferry node closest to multiple clustering centers, multiple clustering results are merged and then assigned to that ferry node. Ferry node then plans a optimal path to complete tasks.

Distributed Dynamic Path Planning: we adopt the scheme in [15], and during initialization, all UAVs are randomly distributed in a fixed area.

3.3 Adversary Model

The attacker's goal is to disrupt or affect the communication in the UAV networks then ultimately paralyze the network. We assume that the attacker equipped with radar, radiofrequency, and sensors observes near the UAV networks. The maximum detection distance of radar is 3 to 10 km [10] and the attacker also uses radiofrequency and sensors to compensate for radar blind spots.

Such that the attacker can collect UAV point trace data and then obtain the flight trajectory by correlating the data. Then the attacker analyzes these flight trajectory, distinguishes the trajectory of the ferry node through the trajectory clustering algorithm, and accurately estimates the location of the target (ferry node), then launches further attacks [2]. The attacker model is shown in Fig. 1(b), the attack method and process are shown in Fig. 1(c).

4   TFRA: Trajectory-Based Message Ferry Recognition Attack

In this section, we describe in detail the steps of our proposed trajectory-based message ferry recognition attack. After we obtain the flight trajectories of UAVs, we aim to distinguish the trajectory of the ferry node by analyzing the trajectory data, so as to identify the ferry node.

4.1   Trajectory Representation and Preprocessing

We represent the trajectory by its spatial position at each time interval in the form of $[t_i, x_i, y_i, z_i]$, $i = 1, 2, 3, ...$, where t_i represents the point-in-time and x_i, y_i, z_i represent coordinates of the position at time t_i.

To better represent the high-level meaningful movement patterns of the original trajectory, we convert the mission area to a pre-defined grid-based topology and transform the trajectory into a coarse-grained representation based on grid, that is, defined as a sequence of virtual grid IDs which are transformed from the corresponding coordinate points of the trajectory.

The paths of ferry nodes and ordinary nodes have different characteristics, including shapes of the trajectories curve and the flight area covered by the trajectories. Therefore, we normalize the trajectories by unifying the start point of each trajectory to remove the influence of the coordinates.

The clustering of the trajectories is more focused on the difference in movement patterns between trajectories. Therefore we pruned the trajectory to eliminate the impact of time. If nodes are in the same grid in continuous-time, only one grid is retained. The trajectory after pruning pays more attention to spatial distribution, and the removal of some points can also improve the clustering speed.

4.2   Trajectory Similarity Calculation

Trajectory similarity needs to be calculated to facilitate trajectory clustering, we adopted three typical similarity metrics including Euclidean distance [12], modified Hausdorff distance and Frechet distance [6], and the performance of these three metrics are evaluated through experiments in Sect. 5.

Hausdorff distance is generally used to measure the maximum mismatch between two trajectories, but it is defined on an unordered set of points, so even two completely different trajectory distances are likely to be very close. Therefore we adopt modified Hausdorff distance that considers the time series of the trajectories. As described in [9], for any point a_i in trajectory set A, first find the corresponding point b_i in trajectory set B. The search for corresponding point b_i is based on the length of the trajectory, according to the proportion of the distance from the starting point to the point a_i of the trajectory A to the total length of the trajectory A, find the corresponding point b_i in trajectory B that has the closest proportion. Then preset a range to find the neighbor node set N_{bi} of b_i, then the distance between point a_i and set B is $d_i = \min \{d(a_i, b_j) \mid b_j \in N_{bi}\}$. The distance between two points is calculated using the euclidean distance.

For two trajectories $t_1 = \{grid_i, grid_{i+1}, \ldots\}$ and $t_2 = \{gird_j, grid_{j+1}, \ldots\}$, we use the coordinates of the grid center to represent the grid, the distance between two grids is calculated according to the coordinate of the grid center.

4.3   Clustering and Identification

Our purpose is to distinguish ferry nodes and ordinary nodes, so first we need to distinguish the trajectories of ferry nodes and ordinary nodes. Trajectory clustering is used to cluster similar trajectories into one class. Some common clustering methods are adopted as follows: agglomerative clustering, GMM and Kmeans, and their performance will be evaluated through experiments.

After the trajectory clustering is completed, we need to distinguish the clusters to find which type is the trajectory set of the ferry node. In order to distinguish the trajectories of the two types of nodes, we use the ferry path planning scheme mentioned in Sect. 3.2 to generate a series of trajectory data for ordinary nodes and ferry nodes. We analyze these trajectories and extract the following trajectories features: (1) trajectory length, (2) the proportion of the minimum/maximum coordinates of the trajectory to the maximum/minimum coordinates of the flight region, (3) the proportion of the number of grids covered by the trajectory to the total number of grids, (4) the starting point of the trajectory, (5) the ending point of the trajectory, (6) the proportion of the maximum span of coordinates of the trajectory to the maximum span of the flight region, (7) the number of changes in the trajectory slope.

In the following we use machine learning methods to determine the importance of these features, the methods used are `SelectKBest` and `Recursive feature elimination(RFE)` [3], and the importance of each $feature_i$ is regarded as its corresponding weight w_i, the first k features selected based on weight are used as the features for subsequent judgment clustering. Then we extract the k features of each trajectory in the aforementioned cluster and take the average of the k features of all trajectories in the cluster as the feature of the cluster, we use KNN, SVM, Decision Tree (DT), Random Forest (RF), Logistic Regression (LR), etc. to train the above-mentioned trajectory feature set, and take the features of the cluster as input and judge whether each cluster is ferry nodes set or ordinary nodes set. The accuracy of these algorithms will be compared through experiment and it is found that the model trained by the random forest algorithm has high accuracy rate, so we use the random forest algorithm in the follow-up.

5   Performance Evaluation

In this section, we analyze and discuss the results of our proposed trajectory-based message ferry recognition attack scheme under three ferry node path planning methods, respectively.

Table 1. Parameters of three path planning scheme

	Fix_1	Fix_2	Fix_3	Global distributed dynamic
Simulation area (m^2)	800×800	1100×1100	1200×1200	800×800
Number of ordinary UAVs	9	11	20	20
Number of ferry UAVs	4	4	4	1 to 4
UAV speed (m/s)	5	5	5	5
Grid size (m)	20			
Communication range (m)	200			

5.1 Experiment Scenarios and Parameters

As shown in Sect. 3.2, we conducted simulation experiments on three types of ferry node path planning methods. The detailed experimental parameters of the three schemes are summarized as follows.

Fixed path planning: we carried out experiments in three scenarios with fixed path planning in [8,27], the specific parameters are shown in Table 1.

Global path planning and distributed dynamic path planning: the specific parameters are shown in Table 1. The ordinary nodes adopt random waypoint model or random range move model. In the random waypoint model, ordinary nodes can move randomly in the entire area. In the random range move model, ordinary nodes are only allowed to move randomly within a range. The ferry node moves according to the flight path control information sent by the ground station, otherwise, it adopts the random waypoint model or remains still. For different network settings, 20 networks are randomly generated, and the final result is averaged.

Experimental variables: we study the impact of four types of experimental variables, including type of trajectory, clustering algorithm, ordinary node movement mode, and similarity metric. The specific variables are shown in Table 2.

5.2 Performance Metrics

We use the following indicators to evaluate performance:

- Accuracy: accuracy is defined as the probability of correctly identifying the ferry node. This indicator can evaluate the feasibility of the trajectory-based message ferry identification attack method.
- Recognition Rate (RR): the recognition rate is defined as the proportion of the identified ferry nodes to all ferry nodes. The greater the number of ferry nodes that are attackable and the higher the chance of attackers making the network paralyzed.

Table 2. Experimental variables

Experimental variables	Parameters
Type of trajectory	1. Original trajectories 2. Coarse-grained and normalized trajectories 3. Fully processed trajectories (prunned trajectories)
Clustering algorithm	1. Kmeans 2. GMM 3. Agglomerative clustering
Ordinary node move mode	1. Random waypoint model 2. Random range move model
Similarity metric	1. Euclidean distance 2. Modified Hausdorff distance 3. Frechet distance

5.3   Accuracy Comparison of Different Models

In this part, we compare the accuracy of five classification models: KNN, SVM, Decision Tree (DT), Random Forest (RF), Logistic Regression (LR). We used the three ferry path planning algorithms mentioned above to generate 7200 trajectory data and trained them with the five classification algorithms mentioned above. The experimental results show that most of the algorithms can achieve high accuracy. Due to the length of the paper, we only give the experimental results of random forest in the subsequent experiments.

5.4   Simulation Experiment Results and Discussion

The Impact of Trajectory Clustering Algorithm and Trajectory Pre-processing: the trajectory data set used by the trajectory clustering algorithm is divided into three types, *Original* represents the original trajectory, *Normalization* represents the coarse-grained and normalized trajectory, and *Pruning* represents the fully processed trajectory. The similarity metric is euclidean distance. As shown in Fig. 2(a) that coarse-grained representation and normalization can significantly improve the accuracy of recognition. Pruning does not affect the accuracy of recognition, and this operation can reduce the time of clustering.

Different clustering algorithms have little effect on the accuracy of recognition, in order to simplify, in the subsequent comparison experiments, *Agglomerative Clustering* is adopted.

The Impact of Ferry Path Planning Scheme: we obtain the trajectories of UAVs under three different path planning algorithms: fixed path planning (*Fix*), global path planning (*Global*), and distributed dynamic path planning (*Distributed*). As can be seen from the results in Fig. 2(b), different ferry node path planning algorithms have no obvious effect on the results of cluster recognition, accuracy is high in all three scenarios.

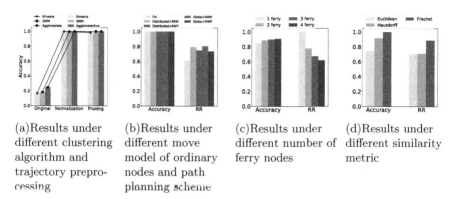

(a)Results under different clustering algorithm and trajectory preprocessing

(b)Results under different move model of ordinary nodes and path planning scheme

(c)Results under different number of ferry nodes

(d)Results under different similarity metric

Fig. 2. Experiment results

The Impact of Movement Mode of Ordinary Nodes: in this part, we study the impact of two typical movement modes of ordinary nodes: random waypoint model (RWP) and random range model (RRM). It can be seen from the results in Fig. 2(b) that the movement mode of ordinary nodes does not have much impact on recognition results, but when using RRM, the recognition rate is higher. This is because the moving range of ordinary nodes in RRM is small, and the trajectory similarity to the ferry node is lower.

In the above two experiments, three similarity metrics were adopted, the number of ferry nodes ranged from 1 to 4, and the trajectory data set was the trajectory after pretreatment.

The Impact of the Number of Ferrying Nodes: in the experiment, the number of ferry nodes is increased from 1 to 4. As can be seen from the results in Fig. 2(c) that as the number of ferry nodes increases, the accuracy of recognition continues to increase, while the recognition rate decreases. As the number of ferry nodes increases, the number of identifiable ferry nodes increases, and the similarity of elements in ferry clustering also increases, so the recognition accuracy increases, and at the same time, the difficulty of identifying all ferry nodes increases, so the recognition rate decreases.

The Impact of Similarity Metric: Euclidean distance, Frechet distance, and modified Hausdorff distance are respectively expressed by *Euclidean*, *Frechet* and *Hausdorff*. From the results in Fig. 2(d), it can be seen that the accuracy is much higher than the Euclidean distance when the modified Hausdorff distance and Frechet distance are used as the similarity metric, which can be basically close to 1. At the same time, using the modified Hausdorff distance and Frechet distance as the similarity metric, the recognition rate is also greatly improved, the highest average recognition rate can reach 0.88. Among the three methods adopted, the Euclidean distance only considers the actual distance between the coordinate points; the modified Hausdorff distance considers the maximum mismatch between the two trajectories considering the time factor; the Frechet distance gradually analyze from global to local which avoids judging the similarity of each sub-target only from the distance of point data, the closer the overall situation, the higher the similarity. Therefore, it can be seen from the experimental results that the Frechet distance has the best accuracy, followed by the Hausdorff distance, at the same time it has the reverse order in computing time. The descending order of recognition rate is $Frechet > Hausdorff > Euclidean$, but in terms of clustering time: $Frechet > Hausdorff > Euclidean$.

In the above two experiments, three similarity metrics were adopted, the number of ferry nodes ranged from 1 to 4, and the trajectory data set used by the trajectory clustering algorithm is divided into three types, including the same three types as in experiment one.

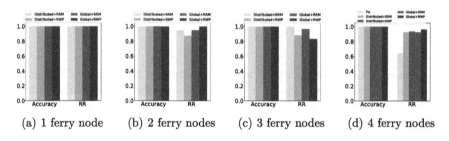

(a) 1 ferry node   (b) 2 ferry nodes   (c) 3 ferry nodes   (d) 4 ferry nodes

Fig. 3. Results on Agglomerative clustering with Frechet distance

Combining all the above experiments, we can know that the factors that have the greatest impact on recognition results are similarity metric and the number of ferry nodes, where the number of ferry nodes mainly affects recognition rate, and similarity metric has a great impact on both accuracy and recognition rate. Among all the experimental results, the results using *Agglomerate clustering* and *Frechet* distance are the best. The specific results of the experiment are shown in Fig. 3. The recognition rate of global path planning methods and distributed dynamic path planning method is above 90%, the average recognition rate reaches about 95%, and the accuracy is close to 1. For the fixed path planning, the accuracy is close to 1, and the recognition rate is above 60%.

6   Conclusion and Future Work

Ferry nodes play an important role and the exposure of their locations may cause serious consequences. Therefore in this paper, we propose a Trajectory-based message Ferry Recognition Attack (TFRA), using the difference between the flight mode of the ferry node and the ordinary node to identify ferry nodes in UAV network and get its location information to launch further attacks. At the same time, we have summarized ferry path planning schemes and performed performance evaluation of TFRA on three typical ferry path planning schemes, the results show the feasibility of our proposed method. In the future, we will investigate the online identification of ferry nodes, improving accuracy and recognition rate is also our goal.

References

1. Crazyflie 2.1. https://www.bitcraze.io/products/crazyflie-2-1/
2. Radar data processing. https://grasswiki.osgeo.org/wiki/Radar_data_processing
3. Sklearn:feature selection and recursive feature elimination. https://scikit-learn.org, https://www.scikit-yb.org
4. Agrawal, P., Ghosh, R.K., Das, S.K.: Cooperative black and gray hole attacks in mobile ad hoc networks. In: Proceedings of the 2nd International Conference on Ubiquitous Information Management and Communication, pp. 310–314 (2008)
5. Alnuaimi, M., Shuaib, K., Alnuaimi, K., Abdel-Hafez, M.: Data gathering in delay tolerant wireless sensor networks using a ferry. Sensors **15**(10), 25809–25830 (2015)
6. Alt, H., Godau, M.: Computing the fréchet distance between two polygonal curves. Int. J. Comput. Geomet. Appl. **5**(01n02), 75–91 (1995)
7. Ammar, M., Chakrabarty, D., Sarma, A.D., Kalyanasundaram, S., Lipton, R.J.: Algorithms for message ferrying on mobile ad hoc networks. In: IARCS Annual Conference on Foundations of Software Technology and Theoretical Computer Science. Schloss Dagstuhl-Leibniz-Zentrum für Informatik (2009)
8. Asadpour, M., Hummel, K.A., Giustiniano, D., Draskovic, S.: Route or carry: motion-driven packet forwarding in micro aerial vehicle networks. IEEE Trans. Mobile Comput. **16**(3), 843–856 (2016)
9. Atev, S., Miller, G., Papanikolopoulos, N.P.: Clustering of vehicle trajectories. IEEE Trans. Intell. Transp. Syst. **11**(3), 647–657 (2010)
10. Barton, D.K.: Modern radar system analysis. ah (1988)
11. Tariq, M.M.B., Ammar, M., Zegura, E.: Message ferry route design for sparse ad hoc networks with mobile nodes. In: Proceedings of the 7th ACM International Symposium on Mobile Ad Hoc Networking and Computing, pp. 37–48 (2006)
12. Deza, M.M., Deza, E.: Encyclopedia of distances. In: Encyclopedia of distances, pp. 1–583. Springer, Heidelberg (2009). https://doi.org/10.1007/978-3-642-00234-2
13. Guangjie Han, X., Miao, H.W., Guizani, M., Zhang, W.: CPSLP: a cloud-based scheme for protecting source location privacy in wireless sensor networks using multi-sinks. IEEE Trans. Veh. Technol. **68**(3), 2739–2750 (2019)
14. Han, G., Zhou, L., Wang, H., Zhang, W., Chan, S.: A source location protection protocol based on dynamic routing in WSNS for the social internet of things. Futur. Gener. Comput. Syst. **82**, 689–697 (2018)
15. Hu, C.-L., Lin, H.-Y., Hsu, Y.-F., Huang, S.-Z., Hui, L., Zhang, Z.: Message forwarding with ferries in delay-tolerant networks. In: 2019 28th Wireless and Optical Communications Conference (WOCC), pp. 1–5. IEEE (2019)
16. Jiang, J., Han, G., Wang, H., Guizani, M.: A survey on location privacy protection in wireless sensor networks. J. Netw. Comput. Appl. **125**, 93–114 (2019)
17. Konstantopoulos, C., Pantziou, G., Vathis, N., Nakos, V., Gavalas, D.: Efficient mobile sink-based data gathering in wireless sensor networks with guaranteed delay. In: Proceedings of the 12th ACM International Symposium on Mobility Management and Wireless Access, pp. 47–54 (2014)
18. Manathara, J.G., Sujit, P.B., Beard, R.W.: Multiple UAV coalitions for a search and prosecute mission. J. Intell. Robot. Syst. **62**(1), 125–158 (2011)
19. Maza, I., Caballero, F., Capitán, J., Dios, J.R.M., Ollero, A.: Experimental results in multi-UAV coordination for disaster management and civil security applications. J. Intell. Robot. Syst. **61**(1–4), 563–585 (2011)
20. Merino, L., Caballero, F., Ramiro Martínez-De-Dios, J., Maza, I., Ollero, A.: An unmanned aircraft system for automatic forest fire monitoring and measurement. J. Intell. Robot. Syst. **65**(1–4), 533–548 (2012)

21. Pu, C., Carpenter, L.: To route or to ferry: a hybrid packet forwarding algorithm in flying ad hoc networks. In: 2019 IEEE 18th International Symposium on Network Computing and Applications (NCA), pp. 1–8. IEEE (2019)
22. Salarian, H., Chin, K.-W., Naghdy, F.: An energy-efficient mobile-sink path selection strategy for wireless sensor networks. IEEE Trans. Veh. Technol. **63**(5), 2407–2419 (2013)
23. Shah, R.C., Roy, S., Jain, S., Brunette, W.: mules: modeling and analysis of a three-tier architecture for sparse sensor networks (2003)
24. Wang, H., Han, G., Zhang, W., Guizani, M., Chan, S.: A probabilistic source location privacy protection scheme in wireless sensor networks. IEEE Trans. Veh. Technol. **68**(6), 5917–5927 (2019)
25. Wang, H., Han, G., Zhou, L., Ansere, J.A., Zhang, W.: A source location privacy protection scheme based on ring-loop routing for the IoT. Comput. Netw. **148**, 142–150 (2019)
26. Xing, G., Wang, T., Xie, Z., Jia, W.: Rendezvous planning in wireless sensor networks with mobile elements. IEEE Trans. Mob. Comput. **7**(12), 1430–1443 (2008)
27. Peng, J., Gao, H., Liu, L., Wu, Y., Xu, X.: FNTAR: a future network topology-aware routing protocol in UAV networks. In: IEEE Wireless Communications and Networking Conference (WCNC) (2020)
28. Yoon, J., Lee, A.-H., Lee, H.: Rendezvous: opportunistic data delivery to mobile users by UAVs through target trajectory prediction. IEEE Trans. Veh. Technol. **69**, 2230–2245 (2019)
29. Zhu, S., Wang, D., Low, C.B.: Ground target tracking using UAV with input constraints. J. Intell. Robot. Syst. **69**(1–4), 417–429 (2013)

Mobile Ad-Hoc Networks

Scaling DCN Models for Indoor White Space Exploration

Yunlong Xiang, Zhenzhe Zheng, Yuben Qu$^{(\boxtimes)}$, and Guihai Chen

Department of Computer Science and Engineering, Shanghai Jiao Tong University, Shanghai, China
{xiangyunlong,zhengzhenzhe,quyuben}@sjtu.edu.cn, gchen@cs.sjtu.edu.cn

Abstract. With the fast growth of the wireless spectrum demand, people have been focusing on utilizing indoor white spaces. In the past few years, several indoor white space exploration methods have been proposed. These methods focus on the utilization of spatial and spectral correlations of white spaces. However, these correlations change over time. In this paper, we perform indoor white space synchronous measurement to demonstrate the volatility of white spaces. Then, we propose a DCN (Deep Convolutional Network)-based method to capture the statistical dependencies among the features and combinatorial features extracted from white spaces, which are not limited to spatial or spectral features, and construct the white space availability map. After demonstrating the instability of spectral and spatial correlations, we scale our DCN models to a time-agnostic model. We conduct real-world experiments to evaluate our system. The evaluation results show that our time-specific DCN model and time-agnostic model outperforms the state-of-the-art method.

Keywords: White space · DCN · Time-agnostic

1 Introduction

The advancement of wireless communications brings about the increasing demand for radio spectrum resources. Meanwhile, abundant licensed spectrums are not taken full advantage of [14]. These lead to spectrum shortage. In 2008, the Federal Communications Commission (FCC) proposed a resolution permitting unlicensed devices to access locally unoccupied TV spectrums, *i.e.* TV white spaces [2]. From then on, researchers have focused on the utilization of TV white spaces [1,4]. However, the unlicensed users are not supposed to interfere with the licensed transmissions. Thus, all users should achieve the white space availability information before using it.

Most existing works [7,9] focus on outdoor white space exploration. In fact, 70% of wireless spectrum demand comes from indoor environment [13], giving rise to a promising research filed of indoor white space exploration. However, there are only a few works on exploring indoor white spaces. WISER [13] is the first indoor white space exploration system. After that, FIWEX [6] was proposed

Z. Liu et al. (Eds.): WASA 2021, LNCS 12938, pp. 525–537, 2021.
https://doi.org/10.1007/978-3-030-86130-8_41

to improve the performance. These existing indoor white space exploration systems deploy a small number of RF-sensors at part of the candidate locations and reconstruct the map of the white space availability of all the candidate locations using the measurement results.

As the state-of-the-art method, FIWEX is based on the white space linear dependence of locations and channels. However, TV spectrums are highly complex due to unpredictable signal propagation and traffic dynamics. Thus, white spaces have more complex patterns (features) and corresponding correlations, such as temporal correlations [11]. If we can mine these correlations which are not utilized till now, the system performance will be improved. On the other hand, the white space linear dependence of locations and channels are not stable, which will be shown in this paper. In fact, the spectral and spatial dependence changes over time, making FIWEX a time-specific system. As a result, FIWEX cannot accurately construct the indoor white space availability map of the whole day. The map shows the white space distribution information at different locations.

Considering the two limitations above, we design a general, scalable system to construct the white space availability map indoors. We first build a special DCN model to automatically capture the features from white spaces and utilize the correlations among these features to construct the map. It is worth noting that these features extracted by DCN are not limited to the spectral and spatial ones which have been studied in prior works. Apart from extracting more complex features, DCN combines them and achieve the correlations among the combinatorial ones. Then, we scale our DCN model to a unified (*i.e.* time-agnostic) model by taking the temporal volatility of white space correlations into consideration. Our main contributions are as follows.

- We perform indoor white space synchronous measurement in a building. The measurement results demonstrate the drawbacks of asynchronous measurement, which make us only perform synchronous measurements for experiments and analysis.
- We propose a special DCN model for indoor white space exploration, *i.e.* constructing the white space availability map. This method can automatically extract features from white spaces apart from the spatial and spectral features, combine them and capture the statistical dependencies among these features, which gives rise to higher performance of our system.
- We prove the instability of the spatial and spectral linear correlations of white spaces, which motivates us to consider model scalability, *i.e.* how to train and deploy DCN models for different periods of a day. We address this challenge by focusing on the general, time-agnostic correlations and scaling our time-specific DCN models to a single, time-agnostic model.
- We evaluate our system in the real-world experiment. It is shown that our time-specific DCN model and time-agnostic model can identify 20.17% and 34.48% more indoor white spaces with 20.98% and 36.27% less false alarm rate, respectively, compared to the state-of-the-art method.

Area A

Fig. 1. Map of the lab room

2   Indoor White Space Synchronous Measurement

In this section, we perform our indoor white space **synchronous** measurement in a lab room of a building. The map is shown in Fig. 1. One purpose of the **synchronous** measurement is to explore the drawbacks of asynchronous measurement. Another purpose is to use these data to perform system evaluation in Sect. 5.

2.1   Measurement Setup

Our measurement equipment is composed of a USRP N210, an omni-directional log periodic PCB antenna, and a laptop. The daughter-board of our USRP N210 is SBX, the noise figure of which is 5–10 dBm. The TV channels we measured are 45 channels between 470 MHz–566 MHZ and 606 MHz–870 MHz. The channel bandwidth is 8 MHz.

We need to judge whether a channel is occupied. We compare the signal strength of a channel with a threshold. If it is lower than the threshold, the channel is vacant. Otherwise, the channel is occupied. Just the same as prior works [6,13], the threshold we adopted is -84.5dBm$/8$ MHz.

2.2   Synchronous Measurement

We choose 22 locations and deploy 22 sensors in the lab room. Then we perform synchronous measurement for a period of two weeks. Our observations are as follows:

There Exist Spatial and Spectral Correlations. We use our two-week measurement results to calculate the spectral and spatial correlations of TV spectrums. We choose Pearson product-moment correlation coefficients as the metric. We obtain a vector for each location based on the measurement results. The elements of the vector are the signal strength of all the TV channels in the two weeks. After that, for each pair of locations, we use the measurement results to calculate the Pearson correlation coefficients. As Fig. 2(a) shows, most

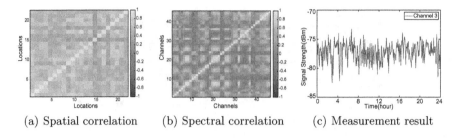

(a) Spatial correlation   (b) Spectral correlation   (c) Measurement result

Fig. 2. Observations of synchronous measurement

of the coefficients are large, which means most of the locations are tightly correlated. Similarly, we can get Fig. 2(b), which denotes the spectral correlations. In Fig. 2(b), we discover that a channel may have strong correlations with some channels. But the correlations between it and some other channels can be in a very low degree. Figure 2(a) and Fig. 2(b) verify the spatial and spectral correlations of TV spectrums. However, the correlations are unstable over time in a day, which will be shown in Sect. 4, leading to performance degradation of FIWEX and WISER if evaluated using data of the whole days.

Drawbacks of Asynchronous Measurement. In previous works [6,13], the training and testing process of systems are all performed based on asynchronous measurement results. They assume the signal strength of all the channels at all the locations are stable in some time (at least 1 h). Figure 2(c) illustrates the signal strength of Channel 3 at Location 1 within 24 h (a day). We observe that there exists too much significant signal fluctuation, leading to a significant change in signal strength even within several minutes. For example, in the third hour, a sudden fall of the signal strength happens. If we perform asynchronous measurement around the time at Location 1, a small time difference may produce significant variation in signal strength for Channel 3, which may result in performance degradation of our system. Thus, we abandon the asynchronous measurement and perform a fine-grained synchronous measurement for our system.

3   System Model

In this section, we describe our system model. First, we present our problem model in regard to reconstructing the white space availability map through the partial sensing results. Then, we introduce our DCN model to solve the problem.

3.1   Problem Model

Due to the cost consideration, we can't deploy sensors on every corner indoors to obtain the complete sensing results. Thus, our system aims to reconstruct the

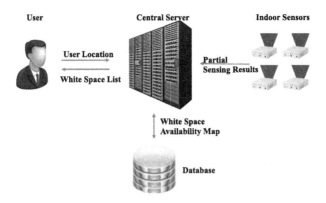

Fig. 3. System model

complete white space information indoors through the partial sensing results obtained by a few sensors. The system architecture is shown in Fig. 3. We select M indoor locations that cover the main indoor areas, which are referred to as candidate locations. In these candidate locations, we deploy $N(N<M)$ sensors to detect the TV spectrum signal strength. We denote the set of locations where we deploy sensors as

$$L = \{l_1, l_2, l_3, ..., l_N\} \tag{1}$$

where $1 \leq l_i \leq M, 1 \leq i \leq N$. We denote the number of channels as P. In our experiments, $P = 45$. The absolute signal strength of channels at location i is denoted by

$$\boldsymbol{m}_i = (m_{i,1}, m_{i,2}, m_{i,3}, ..., m_{i,P})^T \tag{2}$$

where $m_{i,j}$ is the absolute signal strength of Channel j at Location i. For the convenience of representation, we subtract the white space threshold (-84.5dBm) from the absolute signal strength to obtain the relative signal strength. The result is

$$\boldsymbol{x}_i = (x_{i,1}, x_{i,2}, x_{i,3}, ..., x_{i,P})^T \tag{3}$$

where $x_{i,j} = m_{i,j} - threshold, 1 \leq i \leq M, 1 \leq j \leq P$. Hence, the complete indoor TV spectrum relative signal strength at all the candidate locations is represented as:

$$\boldsymbol{x} = (\boldsymbol{x}_1^T, \boldsymbol{x}_2^T, \boldsymbol{x}_3^T, ..., \boldsymbol{x}_M^T)^T \tag{4}$$

However, considering the sensor cost, we do not have complete sensing results. What we get is incomplete white space information at N chosen candidate locations where sensors are deployed. The vector of incomplete white space information is denoted as

$$\boldsymbol{y} = (\boldsymbol{x}_{l_1}^T, \boldsymbol{x}_{l_2}^T, \boldsymbol{x}_{l_3}^T, ..., \boldsymbol{x}_{l_N}^T)^T. \tag{5}$$

The correlation between $\boldsymbol{x}$ and $\boldsymbol{y}$ is

$$\boldsymbol{y} = \boldsymbol{\Phi} \boldsymbol{x} \tag{6}$$

where $\boldsymbol{\Phi}$ is the measurement matrix ($\boldsymbol{\Phi} \in \mathbb{R}^{NP \times MP}$), denoted as

$$\boldsymbol{\Phi} = \begin{pmatrix} \boldsymbol{\Phi}_{l_1,1} & \boldsymbol{\Phi}_{l_1,2} & \cdots & \boldsymbol{\Phi}_{l_1,M} \\ \boldsymbol{\Phi}_{l_2,1} & \boldsymbol{\Phi}_{l_2,2} & \cdots & \boldsymbol{\Phi}_{l_2,M} \\ \vdots & \vdots & \ddots & \vdots \\ \boldsymbol{\Phi}_{l_N,1} & \boldsymbol{\Phi}_{l_N,2} & \cdots & \boldsymbol{\Phi}_{l_N,M} \end{pmatrix} \tag{7}$$

where $\boldsymbol{\Phi}_{i,j}$ is a $P \times P$ matrix

$$\boldsymbol{\Phi}_{i,j} = \begin{cases} I_P & i = j \\ \mathbf{0} & otherwise \end{cases} \tag{8}$$

where I_P is the $P \times P$ identity matrix.

Therefore, given $\boldsymbol{\Phi}$ and $\boldsymbol{y}$, our system aims to achieve the complete white space information $\boldsymbol{x}$. Then, as Fig. 3 shows, the central server transforms $\boldsymbol{x}$ into the indoor white space availability map and saves it in the database. If a user wants to use white spaces, he just needs to submit his location to the central server. The central server then returns the corresponding white space list at his location.

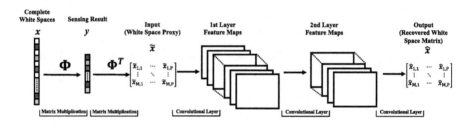

Fig. 4. The DCN architecture

3.2   DCN Model

FIWEX [6] models the white space reconstruction problem as a rank minimization problem and use convex optimization to solve it. We will show that this method is less accurate compared to our new method. Besides, it cannot be used in a time-agnostic context. Instead of traditional mathematical methods, we use a special DCN model to solve the white space information reconstruction problem.

We achieve the complete white space information $\boldsymbol{x}$ from the incomplete sensing results $\boldsymbol{y}$ by developing a special DCN model. The network structure is shown in Fig. 4. We have the training dataset which contains p training examples in the form of (sensing result, complete white space information), $i.e.$ $\mathcal{D}_{train} = \{(\boldsymbol{y}^{(1)}, \boldsymbol{x}^{(1)}), (\boldsymbol{y}^{(2)}, \boldsymbol{x}^{(2)}), ..., (\boldsymbol{y}^{(p)}, \boldsymbol{x}^{(p)})\}$. $\tilde{\boldsymbol{x}}$ is the white space information proxy ($\tilde{\boldsymbol{x}} = \boldsymbol{\Phi}^T \boldsymbol{y}$). So the training dataset is transformed into $\mathcal{D}_{train} = \{(\tilde{\boldsymbol{x}}^{(1)}, \boldsymbol{x}^{(1)}), (\tilde{\boldsymbol{x}}^{(2)}, \boldsymbol{x}^{(2)}), ..., (\tilde{\boldsymbol{x}}^{(p)}, \boldsymbol{x}^{(p)})\}$. Similarly, we can get the testing dataset

$\mathcal{D}_{test} = \{(\tilde{\boldsymbol{x}}^{(1)}, \boldsymbol{x}^{(1)}), (\tilde{\boldsymbol{x}}^{(2)}, \boldsymbol{x}^{(2)}), ..., (\tilde{\boldsymbol{x}}^{(q)}, \boldsymbol{x}^{(q)})\}$, which consists of q pairs of white space information proxy and the complete white space information.

We will show more details about our network architecture. Our network architecture consists of three convolutional layers. We do not adopt the downsampling max-pooling layer, which is for preserving the dimensionality of processing in the dimension of $\boldsymbol{x}$. As is described above, the white space information proxy $\tilde{\boldsymbol{x}}$ is a vector. To satisfy the input requirement of the convolutional layer, we reshape $\tilde{\boldsymbol{x}}$, and obtain a $M \times N$ matrix. In order to avoid confusion, $\tilde{\boldsymbol{x}}$ is denoted as the $M \times N$ matrix instead of a vector in the following parts. The first convolutional layer receives the white space information proxy $\tilde{\boldsymbol{x}}$ as input. The output of the $(i,j)_{th}$ element through the k_{th} filter is

$$(\boldsymbol{x}_{conv1})_{i,j}^k = \mathcal{T}(\text{ReLU}((\mathbf{W}_1^k \tilde{\boldsymbol{x}})_{i,j} + (\mathbf{b}_1^k)_{i,j})) \tag{9}$$

where $\text{ReLU}(\cdot)$ represents the Rectified Linear Units function. $\mathbf{W}_1^k$ is the weight of the k_{th} filter and $\mathbf{b}_1^k$ is the bias in the first convolutional layer. $\mathcal{T}(\cdot)$ is an important operation. It does the downsampling to make the output retain the same size as the raw input (*i.e.* $\tilde{\boldsymbol{x}}$) by neglecting the border added by zero-padding operation. The output of the second and third convolutional layer are similar to the first one. We use ℓ_1, ℓ_2, ℓ_3 to refer to the number of filters in three convolutional layers. Thus, we can get the set of parameters of the whole network, which need to be learned, denoted as

$$\Omega = \left\{ \{\mathbf{W}_1^k, \mathbf{b}_1^k\}_{k=1}^{\ell_1}, \{\mathbf{W}_2^k, \mathbf{b}_2^k\}_{k=1}^{\ell_2}, \{\mathbf{W}_3^k, \mathbf{b}_3^k\}_{k=1}^{\ell_3} \right\}. \tag{10}$$

We define the final output of the whole network as $\hat{\boldsymbol{x}} = f(\tilde{\boldsymbol{x}}, \Omega) \in \mathbb{R}^{M \times P}$, which is the reconstructed channel-location relative signal strength matrix. The entry in row i and column j of a channel-location relative signal strength matrix stores the relative signal strength of Channel j at Location i. $f(\cdot)$ is the nonlinear mapping function from the white space information proxy to the reconstructed white space information matrix, which represents the functionality of the whole network. The loss function is the mean squared error.

4 Unified Model

We have shown that TV spectrums have spectral and spatial correlations in Sect. 2. But in fact, the correlations are time-specific. Although they are stable at a specific time across different days [6], they are unstable in different times of a day. We will verify the insight in this section. Prior works such as [13] and [6] use the asynchronous measurement results to train models and reconstruct the complete white space information. However, the asynchronous measurement data are collected at a specific time of different days. Thus, the systems in these works are time-specific and cannot be used in our context of synchronous measurement which covers all the time of different days. In addition, these systems can't directly use the synchronous measurement data to get rid of the time restriction. Thus, we need a model which can adapt to the context. We call this kind of model time-agnostic or unified model.

4.1 Unstable Correlations

We first verify the unstable correlations. Similar to [6], we use matrix L and L_0 to represent the location dependence and use matrix C and C_0 to denote the channel dependence.

In Sect. 2, we do synchronous measurement at 22 locations and detect the signal strength of 45 channels. For the convenience of representation, we denote the complete white space information matrix as

$$X = \begin{bmatrix} x_{1,1} & x_{1,2} & x_{1,3} & \cdots & x_{1,45} \\ x_{2,1} & x_{2,2} & x_{2,3} & \cdots & x_{2,45} \\ \vdots & \vdots & \vdots & \ddots & \vdots \\ x_{22,1} & x_{22,2} & x_{22,3} & \cdots & x_{22,45} \end{bmatrix} \tag{11}$$

where $x_{i,j}$ is the relative signal strength of Channel j at Location i. Location dependence means

$$x_i \approx w_{i_0} x_0 + \sum_{k=1}^{K} w_{i_k} x_{i_k}, \tag{12}$$

which has been demonstrated in [6]. In this equation, x_0 is a vector (1×45), all the elements of which are 1. K is the number of the most correlated locations. The weights $w_{i_k} (k = 0, 1, ..., K)$ can be calculated through multivariate linear regression. Similarly, we can define and get the channel dependence (for channel dependence, we also use K to denote the number of the most correlated channels). As to the matrix L and L_0, we set $L(i, i) = 1$, $L(i, i_k) = -w_{i_k}$, $L_0(i, j) = w_{i0}$ for $k = 1, 2, ..., K$ and $j = 1, 2, ..., 45$. Using the similar way, we can get C and C_0. Just the same as [6], in order to keep the dependence in a specific time of a day, we choose $K = 1$ for location dependence and $K = 2$ for channel dependence. In [6], the value of $\|LX - L_0\|_F^2$ is used to decide whether the location dependence is stable, but it is limited to a specific time of different days. We adopt the similar way, but change the target time. We aim to decide whether the local dependence of different time in a day is stable. We divide the time of a day into 24 time slots, each of which represents one hour. Based on the measurement data of the first time slot, we achieve L and L_0. Then, we compare the value of $\|LX^{(1)} - L_0\|_F^2$ with the value of $\|LX^{(i)} - L_0\|_F^2 (i = 1, 2, 3 ..., 24)$. $X^{(i)}$ denote the complete white space information matrix in the i_{th} time slot. We define

$$STAT_L = \frac{\|LX^{(i)} - L_0\|_F^2}{\|LX^{(1)} - L_0\|_F^2}, i = 1, 2, ...24. \tag{13}$$

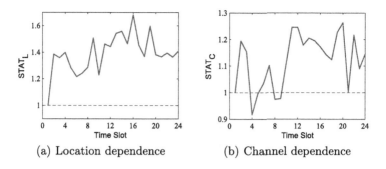

(a) Location dependence   (b) Channel dependence

Fig. 5. Instability of location and channel dependence

Similarly, channel dependence is on the value of $\|XC - C_0\|_F^2$. Accordingly, we define

$$STAT_C = \frac{\|X^{(i)}C - C_0\|_F^2}{\|PC^{(1)} - C_0\|_F^2}, i = 1, 2, ...24. \tag{14}$$

If $STAT_L$ is not always close to 1, then the location dependence is not stable. Likewise, $STAT_C$ deviating from 1 means that the channel dependence is not stable. As Fig. 5 shows, the values of $STAT_L$ and $STAT_C$ are not always close to 1, which means the location dependence and channel dependence are not stable. Furthermore, the dependence changes every hour. In this paper, we assume the dependence is stable within an hour. This is feasible because prior works [6,13] all performed well using the data collected in asynchronous measurement lasting more than one hour.

4.2   Build the Time-Agnostic Model

Since the spatial and spectral correlations are unstable, time-specific models such as [6,13], and our time-specific DCN model trained using the data collected in one time slot are less accurate if utilized to reconstruct the complete white space information in other time slots. A possible method to solve this problem is to train different time-specific DCN models for different time slots. But the training cost and run-time complexity are undesirable. Therefore, we need to train a time-agnostic DCN model, which can be used to accurately reconstruct the white space availability map for the whole day.

Our hypothesis is that the TV spectrums have complex general correlations in the features extracted from them, which can be captured by our DCN model. We get the insight because, in every time slot, the TV spectrums have specific channel and location linear correlation. Thus, combining all the linear correlations, TV spectrums are highly possible to have some complex general correlations. We take two steps to make our model time-agnostic.

First, We apply linear transformation to the input signal matrix to expose the intrinsic TV spectrum patterns. The transformation includes mean-centering and scaling. As a result, each input signal matrix to the DCN model has a zero mean and a variance of 1. Second, we use the mixture of measurement data in all the time slots as the input to train our DCN model. Compared to time-specific models, this minimizes the model training time and data requirements.

5   Performance Evaluation

In this section, we perform experiments to evaluate our system. We first evaluate the performance of our time-specific DCN model compared to that of WISER and FIWEX. Then, we scale our model to a time-agnostic (unified) DCN model. Just like the first step, we compare the time-agnostic DCN model with WISER and FIWEX.

5.1   Methodology

We evaluate our system using the data collected in Sect. 2. We divide the data into two parts: 10-day data as training data, 4-day data as testing data. Our DCN network has three convolutional layers. The first layer has 32 filters. Every filter has one channel with size 7×7. The number of filters in the second layer is 16. Each filter has 32 channels of size 7×7. The third layer has 1 filter, each having 16 channels, of which the size is 7×7. We use False Alarm Rate and White Space Loss rate as the metrics to evaluate our system. The definitions are as follows:

- *False Alarm Rate (FA Rate)*: the ratio between the number of channels that a system misidentifies as vacant and the total number of vacant channels that the system identifies.
- *White Space Loss Rate (WS Loss Rate)*: the ratio between the number of channels that a system misidentifies as occupied and the total number of actually vacant channels.

5.2   Performance of Time-Specific DCN Model

In this part, we compare the performance of the time-specific DCN model with FIWEX and WISER. In order to train the time-specific model, according to the 24 time slots, we divide the training dataset into 24 small training datasets, each containing 10-h data of the original training dataset. For example, the first training dataset has the data of the first hour every day. In total, the first training dataset has 10-h data. Corresponding testing datasets can be obtained using the same way. Each testing dataset has 4-h data. We train and evaluate the three systems (from 1 sensor to 22 sensors) using the 24 datasets, respectively. After that, we get 24 sets of FA Rate and WS Loss Rate. We average them and draw Fig. 6(a) and Fig. 6(b). Compared to FIWEX, our time-specific DCN model can identify 20.17% more indoor white space with 20.98% less FA rate. In addition, our time-specific DCN can identify 52.99% more indoor white space with 57.65% less FA Rate than WISER.

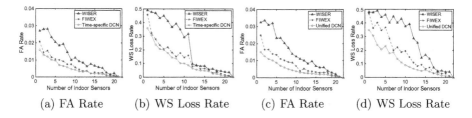

(a) FA Rate   (b) WS Loss Rate   (c) FA Rate   (d) WS Loss Rate

Fig. 6. Performance of our system

5.3   Performance of Time-Agnostic DCN Model

In this part, we compare the performance of the time-agnostic DCN model with
FIWEX and WISER. Instead of training 24 models in the previous part, now, we
train the three systems with the whole training dataset of 10 days and evaluate
them with the whole testing dataset of 4 days. The result is shown in Fig. 6(c) and
Fig. 6(d). The FA Rates of WISER and FIWEX are 1.40% and 0.75%. The WS
Loss Rates of WISER and FIWEX are 27.46% and 17.02%. We discover that the
performance of FIWEX is lower compared to training and testing in the time-
specific data. The reason for the performance degradation of FIWEX is that
FIWEX cannot capture the complex correlations of white spaces in the whole
day. It just assumes the white spaces have stable linear dependence of channels
and locations. Our time-agnostic model can identify 34.48% and 59.38% more
indoor white space than FIWEX and WISER. On the other hand, compared to
FIWEX, our time-agnostic DCN model has 36.27% less FA Rate. As to WISER,
the number is 65.99%.

6   Related Work

Nowadays, people have paid increasing attention to utilizing indoor white spaces
to alleviate spectrum shortage. At first, people analyzed TV white spaces based
on the TV tower registration information and signal propagation models [3,10].
After that, researchers focused on outdoor white spaces [1,9]. Then, in 2013,
Ying et al. [13] first explore white spaces indoors and proposed WISER. In
2015, Liu et al. [6] combines the location-channel linear correlations of white
spaces indoors with compressed sensing and proposed FIWEX, improving the
performance of identifying white space indoors.

DCN is a special kind of DNN model, most commonly applied to computer
vision. In [5], Hinton et al. used DCN to do ImageNet classification. DCN can
also be used to do image deconvolution [12]. In addition, DCN models can also
be adopted to solve compressed sensing problems [8].

7   Conclusion

In this paper, we performed indoor white space synchronous measurement and explored the volatility of white spaces. Then, we proposed a scalable DCN model to extract features from white space information, combine them and capture their correlations. Thus, we can utilize more correlations of indoor white spaces, apart from spatial and spectral correlations, to perform indoor white space exploration more accurately based on the measurement results. On the other hand, we prove the instability of the spatial and spectral correlations. Then, we scale our time-specific DCN model to a time-agnostic DCN model by extracting and utilizing the general, time-agnostic correlations among the extracted features. Our DCN model is able to identify more indoor white spaces with less FA Rate compared to the state-of-the-art system.

Acknowledgements. This work was supported in part by National Key R&D Program of China No. 2019YFB2102200, in part by China NSF grant No. 62025204, 62072303, 61972252, and 61972254, in part by Alibaba Group through Alibaba Innovation Research Program, and in part by Tencent Rhino Bird Key Research Project. The opinions, findings, conclusions, and recommendations expressed in this paper are those of the authors and do not necessarily reflect the views of the funding agencies or the government.

References

1. Chen, Z., Zhang, Y.: Providing spectrum information service using TV white space via distributed detection system. IEEE Trans. Veh. Technol. **68**(8), 7655–7667 (2019)
2. FCC: FCC adopts rules for unlicensed use of TV white spaces (2008). https://apps.fcc.gov/edocs_public/attachmatch/DOC-286566A1.pdf
3. Harrison, K., Mishra, S.M., Sahai, A.: How much white-space capacity is there? In: Proceedings of DySPAN, pp. 1–10. IEEE (2010)
4. Kasbekar, G.S., Sarkar, S.: Spectrum white space trade in cognitive radio networks. In: Proceedings of ITA, pp. 321–330. IEEE (2012)
5. Krizhevsky, A., Sutskever, I., Hinton, G.E.: ImageNet classification with deep convolutional neural networks. In: Proceedings of NIPS, pp. 1097–1105 (2012)
6. Liu, D., Wu, Z., Wu, F., Zhang, Y., Chen, G.: FIWEX: compressive sensing based cost-efficient indoor white space exploration. In: Proceedings of MobiHoc, pp. 17–26. ACM (2015)
7. Luo, Y., Gao, L., Huang, J.: HySIM: a hybrid spectrum and information market for TV white space networks. In: Proceedings of INFOCOM, pp. 900–908. IEEE (2015)
8. Mousavi, A., Baraniuk, R.G.: Learning to invert: signal recovery via deep convolutional networks. In: Proceedings of ICASSP, pp. 2272–2276. IEEE (2017)
9. Saeed, A., Harras, K.A., Zegura, E., Ammar, M.: Local and low-cost white space detection. In: Proceedings of ICDCS, pp. 503–516. IEEE (2017)
10. Van De Beek, J., Riihijarvi, J., Achtzehn, A., Mahonen, P.: TV white space in Europe. IEEE Trans. Mob. Comput. **11**(2), 178–188 (2012)

11. Xiao, H., Liu, D., Wu, F., Kong, L., Chen, G.: Corten: a real-time accurate indoor white space prediction mechanism. In: Proceedings of MASS, pp. 415–423. IEEE (2018)
12. Xu, L., Ren, J.S., Liu, C., Jia, J.: Deep convolutional neural network for image deconvolution. In: Proceedings of NIPS, pp. 1790–1798 (2014)
13. Ying, X., Zhang, J., Yan, L., Zhang, G., Chen, M., Chandra, R.: Exploring indoor white spaces in metropolises. In: Proceedings of MobiCom, pp. 255–266. ACM (2013)
14. Zhao, Q., Sadler, B.M.: A survey of dynamic spectrum access. IEEE Signal Process. Mag. **24**(3), 79–89 (2007)

Deep Learning-Based Power Control for Uplink Cognitive Radio Networks

Feng Liang[1], Anming Dong[2(✉)], Jiguo Yu[2,3], and You Zhou[4]

[1] School of Computer Science, Qufu Normal University, Rizhao 276826, China
[2] School of Computer Science and Technology, Qilu University of Technology
(Shandong Academy of Sciences), Jinan 250353, China
jiguoyu@sina.com
[3] Shandong Laboratory of Computer Networks, Jinan 250013, China
[4] Shandong HiCon New Media Institute Co., Ltd., Jinan 250013, Shandong, China

Abstract. In this paper, we study deep-learning-based power control methods for an underlay cognitive radio (CR) interference channel network, where the SUs are allowed to access the network on the promise of ensuring the quality of service (QoS) of PU. Aiming at boosting the throughput of the whole network, we consider a sum rate maximization power control problem subject to the rate and power constraints of all users. Due to the inter-user interference, the considered problem is nonconvex and thus NP-hard to solve. Different from traditional optimization techniques, we rely on the deep-learning (DL) method to find the solution adaptively. Specifically, we construct a multi-layer fully connected deep neural network (DNN) to deduce the transmit power of PU and SUs thorough self-learning. However, it is not straightforward to apply the classical DNN to solve the sum rate maximization problem. The challenges mainly originate from two aspects. On one hand, the lack of ground truth of the optimal power allocation makes it hard to train the DNN straightforwardly, and on the other hand, the QoS constraints of both PU and SUs in the optimization problem makes things even more complicated. To tackle those difficulties, we adopt unsupervised learning strategy after applying the barrier method to the formulated power control problem. Simulations demonstrate the effectiveness of the proposed DL-based power control method.

Keywords: Cognitive radio network · Sum rate · Deep learning

This work was supported in part by the National Key R&D Program of China under grant 2019YFB2102600, the National Natural Science Foundation of China (NSFC) under Grants 61701269, 61832012, 61771289 and 61672321, the Shandong Provincial Natural Science Foundation under Grant ZR2017BF012, the Key Research and Development Program of Shandong Province under Grants 2019JZZY010313 and 2019JZZY020124, the program for Youth Innovative Research Team in University of Shandong Province under grant 2019KJN010, the Pilot Project for Integrated Innovation of Science, Education and Industry of Qilu University of Technology (Shandong Academy of Sciences) under Grant 2020KJC-ZD02.

Z. Liu et al. (Eds.): WASA 2021, LNCS 12938, pp. 538–549, 2021.
https://doi.org/10.1007/978-3-030-86130-8_42

1   Introduction

With the emergence of traffic-intensive wireless applications, such as wearable devices, Internet of Things (IoT), virtual reality and cloud computing, the demand for higher user capacity and data rate will become more and more urgent for the future wireless communication systems, i.e., the beyond fifth generation (B5G) and the sixth generation (6G) wireless networks [9,20]. In order to satisfy these enhanced key performance indicators (KPIs), the ability to intelligently utilize resources marks the B5G and 6G [21]. As one of the most important resources for wireless communications, radio spectrum is characterized by its scarce nature. Just like all the previous generations, 6G will continuously pursue the improvement of spectral efficiency.

CR is a promising solution to improve the spectrum utilization for 6G. The underlying design principle of CR is to enable the licensed users share their licensed spectrum with the unlicensed users [21]. Based on the perceived wireless environment information, the equipments in cognitive radio network (CRN) can access the available spectrum dynamically and opportunistically.

The perception capability and reconfigurability are the essential features of CR [21], which are en-powered by machine learning (ML) techniques. Especially, as an important part of ML, DL has the advantages of powerful adaptivity and the ability of transfer learning [16]. The adaptivity enables it to quickly respond to environmental dynamics. Due to these advantages, DL enables the CRNs to automatically learn to adapt to the dynamic wireless environment with low computational complexity, and to improve the utility of the available resources.

There are many frontier research directions in CRN, for example,data aggregation [4], data collection [3], social activities [13] and so on. In this paper, we consider power control problems in the underlay CRNs. In an underlay CRN, the SUs get a chance to access the spectrum once the QoS of the PU is satisfied. Power control problem is generally NP-hard and thus difficult to deal with. Traditionally, the exhaustive search [12,14] and iterative optimization methods [5,6,18] have been investigated in literature by transforming the original non-convex problems as the corresponding approximated subproblems. However, the application of these methods in practical systems is hindered by the problems of performance, convergence and complexity, etc.

Due to the advantages of data-driven, DL have made achievements in many directions like Privacy protection [11]. DL techniques also have gained a lot of attention in the area of power control. Some interesting works have been proposed in literature. For example, paper [15] proposed a DL-based power control method for an interference channel network. Since the performance of DNN depends largely on how it is trained, the solutions obtained via the weighted minimum mean square error (WMMSE) method were constructed as the training ground truth for the DNN. It was shown that the DNN outperforms the WMMSE significantly in complexity, but takes the result of WMMSE as the upper bound. To solve the above problems, the paper [10] proposed a DL-based method that can find the global optimal solution through unsupervised learning and ensemble learning. Although the sum rate is maximized by the DNN scheme of [10], the users with weak channel conditions may be powered off. This is unacceptable in a CRN, especially for the primary users.

In this paper, we study power control methods based on DL for CRNs. Specifically, we formulate a sum rate maximization power control problem subject to QoS constraints for the PU and the SUs. The considered sum rate maximization problem is nonconvex and difficult to solve. In order to develop a DL-based solving method, we reformulate the original problem by transforming the QoS constraints as a part of the objective term using the barrier method. Based on this reformulated objective function, a DNN is then constructed leveraging the unsupervised learning strategy, i.e., the DNN adapts its parameters by minimizing the loss function constructed by the negative value of the barrier objective function. By applying such unsupervised learning strategy, the constructed DNN can output the optimized powers adaptively when inputing the channel state information. The effective of the proposed DL-based method is validated through simulations.

The rest of this paper is organized as follows. The system model and the considered problem are introduced in Sect. 2. A deep-learning-based power control method is proposed in Sect. 3. The simulations are carried out in Sect. 4. We finally conclusion the paper in Sect. 5.

2 System Model and Problem Formulation

2.1 System Model

We consider an uplink underlay spectrum sharing scenario in CRN shown in Fig. 1, which consists of a primary network (PN) and a secondary network (SN). There are totally K base stations in the CRN and each station serves one user. The PN is composed of a primary base station (PBS) and a PU, while the SN is composed of $K-1$ secondary base stations (SBSs) and the corresponding $K-1$ SUs. We assume that the PN and SN share the same narrowband spectrum and are synchronized. The SINR of the k-th user is written as

$$\text{SINR}_k \triangleq \frac{|h_{kk}|^2 p_k}{\sum_{j=1,j\neq k}^{K} |h_{kj}|^2 p_j + \sigma^2} \tag{1}$$

where $k = 1$ denotes the PU, $k = 2,\ldots,K$ denote the SUs, h_{kk} denotes the direct-link channel between the k-th user and the k-th BS, h_{kj} denotes the cross-link channel between the j-th user and the k-th BS, $p_k \triangleq \mathbb{E}[x_k^2]$ denotes the transmit power of k-th user, $n_k \sim \mathcal{CN}(0,\sigma^2)$ denotes the noise received by the k-th BS. Without loss of generality, we assume that the noises of all users follows the same distribution.

A block fading channel is assumed, i.e., the channel coefficients remain unchanged in one time slot but change independently from one time slot to another. In the considered underlay mode, the SUs are allowed to assess the spectrum only if the rate of PU is not less than a predefined threshold after they access the network.

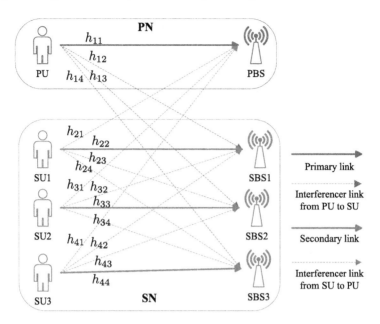

Fig. 1. System model.

2.2 Problem Formulation

In this paper, we aim at studying the DL-based power control method to maximize the sum rate of all users in the considered CRNs.

To this end, a straightforward power control optimization problem can be formulated to maximize the sum rate subject to per-transmitter power constraints, which is mathematically written as

$$\max_{p_k, \forall k} \quad \sum_{k=1}^{K} \log_2(1 + \text{SINR}_k) \tag{2a}$$

$$s.t.: \quad 0 \le p_k \le P_k^{\max}, \forall k = 1, 2, \ldots, K, \tag{2b}$$

where $P_k^{\max}$ denotes the power budget at the transmit of the k-th user.

It is noted that the problem (2) has been previously investigated in [10], where an ensemble deep learning method, which was named as *ensemble Power Control Network (ePCNet)*, was proposed to find the solution. Although the ePCNet can obtain a solution efficiently, the power allocated to the users with poor channel conditions will be zero. The result is unacceptable in a CRNs if the PU is shut down when its channel condition may be worse than that of the SUs, since the PU has the privilege to access the channel resource and the priority to transmit its information.

In this work, different from the simple sum rate maximization problem (2), we investigate a power control optimization problem that maximizes the sum rate subject to per-user QoS constraints. Mathematically, this QoS constrained power control problem is formulated as

$$\max_{p_k, \forall k} \quad \sum_{k=1}^{K} \log_2(1 + \text{SINR}_k) \tag{3a}$$

$$s.t.: \quad \log_2(1 + \text{SINR}_k) \geq R_k^{\min}, \tag{3b}$$

$$0 \leq p_k \leq P_k^{\max}, \forall k = 1, 2, \ldots, K, \tag{3c}$$

where $R_k^{\min} \geq 0$ is the predefined rate threshold of the k-th user.

Problem (3) is noncovex since both the objective and QoS constraint of all the users are nonconvex, which makes it NP-hard to obtain the global optimal solution [1,7,8].

Traditionally, the global optimization algorithms were developed in the literature to compute the solution. For example, the global optimization algorithms based on DC programming and branch and bound techniques were investigated in [7,17] and [19], etc. However, the computational complexity of these methods are generally prohibitively expensive, which limits their applications.

Different from the traditional algorithms that utilizes the convex optimization methods, we propose an DL-based method to solve the sum rate maximization problem for the considered CRNs in the following section.

3   Dynamic Spectrum Allocation Based on Deep Learning

In this section, we propose a DL-based methods to solve the sum rate maximization problems subject to the QoS constraint of the all users. Specifically, we first reformulate the original problem by transforming the rate constraint of the each user as a part of the objective term using the barrier method. We further construct a DNN which leverages the unsupervised learning strategy based on this reformulated objective function. By applying such unsupervised learning strategy, the constructed DNN can output the optimized powers adaptively when inputing the channel parameters.

3.1   Problem Reformulation

In order to develop a DL method to solve problem (3), we reformulate it as the following equivalent negative sum rate minimization problem

$$\min_{p_k, \forall k} \quad -\sum_{k=1}^{K} \log_2(1 + \text{SINR}_k) \tag{4a}$$

$$s.t.: \quad R_k^{\min} - \log_2(1 + \text{SINR}_k) \leq 0, \tag{4b}$$

$$0 \leq p_k \leq p_k^{\max}, \forall k = 1, 2, \ldots, K. \tag{4c}$$

We note that the inequality constraint (4b) brings new challenges to design DL scheme to solve the problem (4) since the DNN can not resolve the complex

Input layer   Hidden layers   Output layer

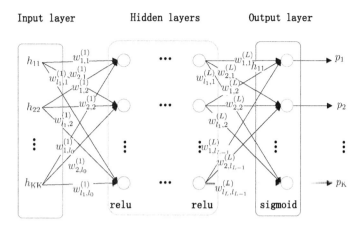

Fig. 2. Deep neural network structure.

rate constraints. In this work, we tackle this difficulty by making the inequality constraint (4b) as an implicit part of the objective using the barrier method [2]. Specifically, we approximately recast (4) as the following problem

$$\min_{p_k, \forall k} \quad -\sum_{k=1}^{K} \log_2(1 + \text{SINR}_k) - \hat{I}_k(R_k^{\min} - \log_2(1 + \text{SINR}_k))$$

$$s.t. : \quad 0 \le p_k \le P_k^{\max}, \forall k = 1, 2, \ldots, K. \tag{5}$$

where $\hat{I}_k(x) \triangleq -\frac{1}{t}\log(-x)$ denotes the differentiable Logarithmic barrier function, which is an approximation for the indicator function, the parameter $t > 0$ is used to set the accuracy of the approximation. Compared with the standard indicator function, the Logarithmic function is differentiable, which is convenient for constructing the loss function for the DL.

3.2   Network Design

The problem (5) is now an optimization problem with differential objective and the power constraints, which can be solved using a DNN. We adopt the full connected multiple layer nueral network as shown in Fig. 2. In specific, the DNN consists of one input layer with K^2 nodes, $L - 1$ hidden layers and an output layer with K nodes. To facilitate denoting, the layers are indexed from 0 to L. The activation functions of the hidden layers are set as $\text{ReLU}(\cdot)$(the rectified linear unit function), while the activation functions of the output layer is set as $\text{sig}(\cdot)$(the standard sigmoid function).

It is noted that the output of the Sigmoid function is within the range [0,1]. In order to output the powers ranging in $[0, P_k^{\max}, \forall k]$, we multiply the output of the sigmoid of the k-th user by a constant $P_k^{\max}$. Then the final power allocated to the k-th user is given by

$$p_k = P_k^{\max} c_{L,k}, \tag{6}$$

where $c_{L,k}$ denotes the k-th element of $\mathbf{c}_L$.

3.3   Training Method

In order to make the considered DNN structure work, it is necessary to design a training scheme. Recall that the considered problem is NP-hard, which implies that it is not easy to obtain the optimal training data. We note that although it is possible to obtain the global optimal solutions by the branch-and-bound methods (e.g., [7]), the computational complexity is prohibitive in practical systems. In fact, we expect to obtain a good solution via the DNN without too much computational complexity and human effort. To this end, we adopt the unsupervised learning scheme. In such training scheme, the DNN is fed with the channel state information $\{|h|_{kj}^2, \forall j, k \in 1, 2, \ldots, K\}$ and it outputs the final power allocation coefficients $\{c_{L,k}\}$ after an unsupervised learning process.

The loss function is the key of the unsupervised learning process. By reexamining the formulated problem (5), we define the loss function according to the objective function of (5), which is written as

$$\text{Loss}(\mathbf{p}) \triangleq -\sum_{k=1}^{K} \log_2(1 + \text{SINR}_k) - \hat{I}_k(R_k - \log_2(1 + \text{SINR}_k)). \tag{7}$$

Given such loss function, the coefficients of the DNN can be updated through gradient descent method, e.g., the stochastic gradient descent (SGD).

4   Simulation Results

In this section, we evaluate the performance of the proposed DL-based power control scheme via simulations. To compare the performance, several schemes presented in the literature are adopted in the experiments, including

1. *The DL scheme without QoS constraints*: Such a scheme is constructed by reducing the QoS constraints of all users.
2. *Time-division multiplexing (TDM)*: The TDM scheme is the classical interference avoidance scheme, in which the users take turns to access the channel resource. Since there is no interference, the sum rate is equivalent to the average achievable rate of all users, if the time slots are divided equally for all the users.
3. *Full power transmission*: Each user transmit under its maximal power budget. In this situation, the capacity is limited due to the strong interference.

$$\mathbf{H} = [h_{kj}] = \begin{bmatrix} 0.933 + 0.549j\ 0.663 + 0.194j\ 0.696 + 0.060j\ 0.502 + 0.027j \\ 0.581 + 0.113j\ 1.142 + 0.938j\ 1.115 + 0.577j\ 0.564 + 0.316j \\ 0.536 + 0.444j\ 0.785 + 0.779j\ 1.363 + 0.052j\ 0.422 + 0.217j \\ 0.743 + 0.062j\ 1.190 + 1.165j\ 0.934 + 0.085j\ 0.921 + 0.565j \end{bmatrix}$$

$$(8)$$

4. *Global optimal via brunch and bound (GOP-BB)*: The brunch and bound algorithm that was developed in [7] and [17] for solving the classical sum rate maximization problem. Such an algorithm can find the global optimal solution via exhausting search through partitioning the feasible spaces.

4.1 Simulation Conditions

In the experiments, the channel state information is generated following the complex Gaussian distribution with zero mean and unit variance, i.e., $h_{kj} \sim \mathcal{CN}(0,1), \forall k, j = 1, 2, \ldots, K$. The number of layers of the DNN is set as $L = 5$, with the numbers of neuron are set as $\{K^2, 100, 200, 200, K\}$ from layer 1 to 5. Without loss of generality, the noise power is normalized, i.e., $\sigma^2 = 1$. The proposed DL-based scheme is implemented in TensorFlow in our simulations.

We evaluate the proposed DL-based power control method for the CRNs with $K = 4$ and $K = 8$, respectively. For the network with $K = 4$, the randomly generated channel matrix that used to evaluate the performance of the proposed method is given by (8), which is listed on the top of the next page.

Given the channel matrix (8), if we remove all the interference links and just consider the direct links of the users, then each user achieves the maximum rate when each user is allocated with the maximum transmit power. For example, if the k-th user is accessing the channel, its transmit power is set as $p_k = P_k^{\max} = 100$ W, and all other users are set as $p_j = 0, \forall j \neq k$. The rates can be calculated as $\mathbf{r}_{\max}^{\text{TDM}} = \begin{bmatrix} 6.8852\ 7.7776\ 7.5467\ 6.8793 \end{bmatrix}$ bps/Hz. Such an interference avoiding scheme can be realized through TDM. When the time-slots of the TDM are allocated equally between all the users, the equivalent achievable rate vector is $\mathbf{r}^{\text{TDM}} = \frac{1}{4}\mathbf{r}_{\max}^{\text{TDM}}$ bps/Hz, and the average achievable sum rate is 7.2722 bps/Hz.

For the full power transmission scheme, all the users transmit with the maximum power simultaneously. It can be calculated that the achievable rates are $\mathbf{r}^{\text{FullPower}} = \begin{bmatrix} 0.9664\ 0.9468\ 0.9690\ 0.3522 \end{bmatrix}$ bps/Hz with the power allocation vector $\mathbf{p}^{\text{FullPower}} = \begin{bmatrix} 100\ 100\ 100\ 100 \end{bmatrix}$ W.

4.2 Convergence Performance

In Fig. 3(a), we demonstrate the convergence property of the DNN described by Fig. 2. In the simulations, the classical sum rate maximization problem is

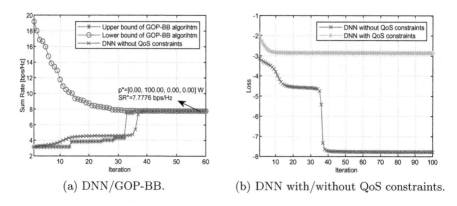

(a) DNN/GOP-BB.   (b) DNN with/without QoS constraints.

Fig. 3. Convergence performance for different methods when $K = 4$.

considered [10]. Since no rate constraint is applied to any user, the second term in the right hand side of the loss function (7) is removed. After training the DNN, the sum rate updating curve can be obtained by multiplying the loss curve with -1. Since the DNN may be sucked in one locally optimal solution at a specific training realization, we use the idea of ensemble learning to choose a better or even global solution, for there are multiple paralleled deep neural networks (i.e., Fig. 2), we choose the best solution among the outputs of the multiple DNNs.

As a comparison, we also plot the upper and lower bounds of the traditional GOP-BB algorithm [7], which is developed based on the branch and bound method together with linear programming. It can be observed that the DNN method converges to the global optimal sum rate $\text{SR}^* = 7.7776$ bps/Hz. The corresponding optimal power allocation outputted by the DNN is $\mathbf{p}^* = \begin{bmatrix} 0 & 100 & 0 & 0 \end{bmatrix}$ W. This means that only the strongest user (i.e., SU 1) is active and all other users are powered off, in order to maximize the sum rate of the whole network. In other words, the QoS of the PU cannot be guaranteed by the classical DNN-based sum rate maximization method, despite that the sum rate could be maximized from the perspective of the whole network.

Figure 3(b) shows the convergence property of the propose DL method in solving the QoS constrained problem (3), with the loss function is constructed by (7). Each user is set a minimum rate to ensuring a minimum requirement of QoS. In the simulations, we set these values as $R_1^{\min} = 0.5$, $R_2^{\min} = 0.4$, $R_3^{\min} = 0.3$, $R_4^{\min} = 0.2$. The parameter t in the Logarithmic barrier function in (5) is set as 2.0. The curve of the training loss of the DNN without the QoS constraints, i.e., the negative values of the corresponding sum rate shown in Fig. 3(a), is also plotted for performance comparison. It can be observed that the loss curve of the DNN with QoS constraints converges faster than the scheme without QoS constraints, but with higher loss values which means lower sum rate.

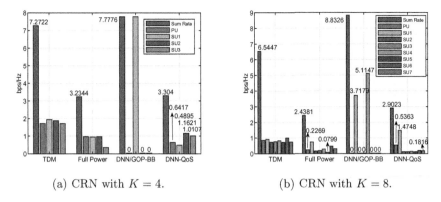

(a) CRN with $K = 4$.   (b) CRN with $K = 8$.

Fig. 4. Achievable rate comparison among users for different methods.

4.3 QoS Assurance Capability

As a trade-off, the sacrifice of sum rate in Fig. 3(b) pays for the QoS assurance of the users, especially the PU. This point is demonstrated in Fig. 4(a). For the TDM scheme, it achieves a rather high mean rate (7.2722 bps/Hz). However, the users in the TDM scheme have to alternatively access the channel, and they must be synchronized, which goes against the idea of CR. The full power scheme achieves the lowest sum rate, meanwhile consuming the largest energy. This is not economical. It is observed that DNN without the QoS constraints achieves the maximum sum rate, i.e., the same as that achieved by the GOP-BB scheme. However, the rate achieved by the PU is zero, which is unacceptable for the CRN. Finally, the DNN with QoS constraints (DNN-QoS) scheme achieves $\mathbf{p}^{\text{DNN-QoS}} = [27.1324\ 21.7725\ 41.8885\ 98.5712]$ W and $\mathbf{r}^{\text{DNN-QoS}} = [0.6417\ 0.4895\ 1.1621\ 1.0107]$ bps/Hz. It is shown that the rates achieved by all users are higher than its corresponding QoS thresholds. At the same time, it guarantees the QoS of all the users compared with the classical DNN scheme without the QoS constraints.

4.4 Generality and Expandability

In Fig. 4(b), we demonstrates the achieved rates of the proposed methods in a system with $K = 8$. Given a randomly generated channel matrix $\mathbf{H} \in \mathcal{C}^{8 \times 8}$, the maximum sum rate of the problem (2) can be obtained by the GOP-BB algorithm or the DNN methods by discarding the Logarithmic barriers.

In the simulations, the QoS threshold for the PU is set as $R_1^{\min} = 0.5$, and all the SUs are set as the same QoS value as $R_k^{\min} = 0.1, \forall k = 2, \ldots, K$. It is observed that the global optimal sum rate of the whole network achieved by the GOP -BB and DNN method is 8.8326 bps/Hz, under the power allocation $\mathbf{p}* = [0.0\ 100.0\ 0.0\ 0.0\ 100.0\ 0.0\ 0.0\ 0.0]$ W. The result shows that the PU is shut down, although these methods achieved the global optimal sum rate. This is not permitted in a CRN.

5   Conclusion

We investigated the sum rate maximization power control problem in CRNs subject to the QoS constraints of the users. After transforming the QoS constraints as part of the objective function through barrier method, we proposed a DL-based iAntelligent solving method based on DNN and the unsupervised learning strategy. Simulations demonstrate the effectiveness of the proposed DL-based power control method in guaranteeing the QoS of the PU when attempting to maximize the sum rate of the whole network.

References

1. Al-Shatri, H., Weber, T.: Achieving the maximum sum rate using DC programming in cellular networks. IEEE Trans. Signal Process. **60**(3), 1331–1341 (2011)
2. Boyd, S., Boyd, S.P., Vandenberghe, L.: Convex Optimization. Cambridge University Press, Cambridge (2004)
3. Cai, Z., Ji, S., He, J., Wei, L., Bourgeois, A.G.: Distributed and asynchronous data collection in cognitive radio networks with fairness consideration. IEEE Trans. Parallel Distrib. Syst. **25**(8), 2020–2029 (2014). https://doi.org/10.1109/TPDS.2013.75
4. Chen, Q., Cai, Z., Cheng, L., Gao, H.: Low-latency data aggregation scheduling for cognitive radio networks with non-predetermined structure. IEEE Trans. Mob. Comput. 1 (2020). https://doi.org/10.1109/TMC.2020.2979710
5. Dong, A., Zhang, H., Wu, D., Yuan, D.: QoS-constrained transceiver design and power splitting for downlink multiuser MIMO SWIPT systems. In: 2016 IEEE International Conference on Communications (ICC), pp. 1–6. IEEE (2016)
6. Dong, A., Zhang, H., Yuan, D., Zhou, X.: Interference alignment transceiver design by minimizing the maximum mean square error for MIMO interfering broadcast channel. IEEE Trans. Veh. Technol. **65**(8), 6024–6037 (2015)
7. Eriksson, K., Shi, S., Vucic, N., Schubert, M., Larsson, E.G.: Globally optimal resource allocation for achieving maximum weighted sum rate. In: 2010 IEEE Global Telecommunications Conference GLOBECOM 2010, pp. 1–6 (2010). https://doi.org/10.1109/GLOCOM.2010.5683826
8. Galindo-Serrano, A., Giupponi, L.: Distributed Q-learning for aggregated interference control in cognitive radio networks. IEEE Trans. Veh. Technol. **59**(4), 1823–1834 (2010). https://doi.org/10.1109/TVT.2010.2043124
9. Letaief, K.B., Chen, W., Shi, Y., Zhang, J., Zhang, Y.J.A.: The roadmap to 6G: AI empowered wireless networks. IEEE Commun. Mag. **57**(8), 84–90 (2019)
10. Liang, F., Shen, C., Yu, W., Wu, F.: Power control for interference management via ensembling deep neural networks. In: 2019 IEEE/CIC International Conference on Communications in China (ICCC), pp. 237–242 (2019). https://doi.org/10.1109/ICCChina.2019.8855869
11. Liang, Y., Cai, Z., Yu, J., Han, Q., Li, Y.: Deep learning based inference of private information using embedded sensors in smart devices. IEEE Netw. **32**(4), 8–14 (2018). https://doi.org/10.1109/MNET.2018.1700349
12. Liu, L., Zhang, R., Chua, K.: Achieving global optimality for weighted sum-rate maximization in the K-user gaussian interference channel with multiple antennas. IEEE Trans. Wireless Commun. **11**(5), 1933–1945 (2012). https://doi.org/10.1109/TWC.2012.031212.111585

13. Lu, J., Cai, Z., Wang, X., Zhang, L., Li, P., He, Z.: User social activity-based routing for cognitive radio networks. Pers. Ubiquit. Comput. **22**(3), 471–487 (2018). https://doi.org/10.1007/s00779-018-1114-9

14. Qian, L.P., Zhang, Y.J., Huang, J.: MAPEL: achieving global optimality for a non-convex wireless power control problem. IEEE Trans. Wireless Commun. **8**(3), 1553–1563 (2009). https://doi.org/10.1109/TWC.2009.080649

15. Sun, H., Chen, X., Shi, Q., Hong, M., Fu, X., Sidiropoulos, N.D.: Learning to optimize: training deep neural networks for interference management. IEEE Trans. Signal Process. **66**(20), 5438–5453 (2018). https://doi.org/10.1109/TSP.2018.2866382

16. Sun, Y., Peng, M., Zhou, Y., Huang, Y., Mao, S.: Application of machine learning in wireless networks: Key techniques and open issues. IEEE Commun. Surv. Tutor. **21**(4), 3072–3108 (2019)

17. Weeraddana, P.C., Codreanu, M., Latva-Aho, M., Ephremides, A.: Weighted sum-rate maximization for a set of interfering links via branch and bound. IEEE Trans. Signal Process. **59**(8), 3977–3996 (2011)

18. Zhao, N., et al.: Secure transmission via joint precoding optimization for downlink MISO NOMA. IEEE Trans. Veh. Technol. **68**(8), 7603–7615 (2019)

19. Zheng, L., Tan, C.W.: Maximizing sum rates in cognitive radio networks: Convex relaxation and global optimization algorithms. IEEE J. Sel. Areas Commun. **32**(3), 667–680 (2013)

20. Zheng, S., Chen, S., Qi, P., Zhou, H., Yang, X.: Spectrum sensing based on deep learning classification for cognitive radios. China Commun. **17**(2), 138–148 (2020)

21. Zhou, X., Sun, M., Li, G.Y., Fred Juang, B.: Intelligent wireless communications enabled by cognitive radio and machine learning. China Commun. **15**(12), 16–48 (2018)

MPDC: A Multi-channel Pipelined Data Collection MAC for Duty-Cycled Linear Sensor Networks

Fei Tong[1,2]($^{(\boxtimes)}$), Rucong Sui[1], Yujian Zhang[1], and Wan Tang[3]

[1] Southeast University, Nanjing 211189, Jiangsu, China
{ftong,suirucong,yjzhang}@seu.edu.cn
[2] Purple Mountain Laboratories, Nanjing 211111, Jiangsu, China
[3] South-Central University for Nationalities, Wuhan 430074, Hubei, China
tangwan@scuec.edu.cn

Abstract. The utilization of duty-cycling strategy in an energy-constrained linear sensor network (LSN) can save node energy. Nevertheless, it also results in the sleep latency issue. To solve it, existing work has proposed duty-cycling and pipelined-forwarding (DCPF) protocols. However, the contention and interference among the nodes maintaining the same sleep-wakeup schedule are unavoidable, especially for a network under bursty traffic. To this end, this paper proposes a novel multi-channel MAC for achieving pipelined data collection (MPDC) in a duty-cycled LSN. To eliminate contention and interference, the packet transmission paths in MPDC are allocated with different channels and the sleep-wakeup schedules for the paths in the same channel are mutually staggered. Through the extensive simulations in OPNET, the performance is shown superior to an existing DCPF protocol, in terms of packet delivery ratio, network throughput, packet delivery latency, and energy consumption efficiency.

Keywords: Duty-cycling · Data collection · MAC · Multi-channel

1 Introduction

The Internet of Things (IoT), as an indispensable part of people's daily life, has drawn plenty of attention from both academia and industry communities. Objects are connected together forming a network to realize the perception and control of

This work is supported in part by the National Natural Science Foundation of China under Grant 61971131, in part by the "Zhishan" Scholars Programs of Southeast University, in part by the Fundamental Research Funds for the Central Universities, in part by the Natural Science Foundation of Jiangsu Province of China under Grant BK20190346, in part by the Natural Science Foundation of Hubei Province of China under Grant 2020CFB629, and in part by the 2019 Industrial Internet Innovation and Development Project, Ministry of Industry and Information Technology (MIIT) under Grant 6709010003.

© Springer Nature Switzerland AG 2021
Z. Liu et al. (Eds.): WASA 2021, LNCS 12938, pp. 550–562, 2021.
https://doi.org/10.1007/978-3-030-86130-8_43

objects [7]. Wireless sensor network (WSN), consisting of a large number of wireless sensor nodes, is one of the most frequently-used branches in IoT. These sensor nodes have the capabilities of data detection, data collection and communication, greatly promoting the applications of IoT in the real world [1]. Because of these features, WSN can be deployed to monitor some remote and dangerous areas constantly [3].

The distribution of nodes varies depending on the topology of the region to be monitored. For example, when monitoring areas such as bridges, tunnels, gas, oil, and water pipelines, sensor nodes need to be deployed linearly, forming a linear sensor network (LSN) [13]. To complete data collection, a node needs to transmit its sensed data to the sink node located at one of the two ends of the network through a multi-hop transmission [5]. The sensor node in a transmission path can work as either a relay or a source node.

Since sensor nodes are usually battery-powered with a limited amount of energy, duty-cycling media access control (MAC) protocols were proposed [2,4,8]. The strategy of duty cycle allows nodes to sleep after completing data transmission, which not only saves energy, but also reduces interference and idle listening between nodes. However, this strategy leads to another well-known issue, called sleep latency. Specifically, supposing a node is ready to send data, it has to wait for its receiving node to enter the active state. As a result, the sending node may fail in forwarding data in time, if the receiving node fails to be active at the moment. Especially in multi-hop transmission, the delay will accumulate, which cannot meet the requirements of some scenarios requiring real-time monitoring. To cater for these scenarios, duty-cycling and pipelined-forwarding (DCPF) protocols [9–12] have been proposed to reduce packet queue waiting time. Pipelined forwarding is realized by staggering the sleep-wakeup schedules of the nodes along a data transmission path, so that a node can immediately forward data to the next-hop node after receiving it from the previous-hop node, forming the pipelined-forwarding feature. However, existing DCPF protocols usually make the nodes located the same communication hop distance (referred to as *grade*) to the sink node maintain the same schedule. If there are existing multiple packet transmission paths in the network, the concurrent transmissions in the same grades have to contend with each other and lead to interference, which becomes more serious if the network traffic load becomes heavier.

To alleviate the above issue, multi-channel communication in WSNs has attracted plenty of attention from researchers [6,16]. For example, a multi-channel data collection scheme was proposed in [16], where channels were allocated to disjoint tree topologies to achieve parallel transmissions. Although the transmission performance was improved through this way, the node energy consumption was not considered. To solve the delay efficient data aggregation scheduling problem in multi-channel asynchronous duty-cycled WSNs, the authors in [6] chose the forwarding nodes based on the fewest-children-first rule to benefit the link scheduling. Overall, compared to using a single channel, using multiple channels provides better performance. However, there is little work on combining duty-cycling and pipelined forwarding under multi-channel LSN scenarios.

To this end, this paper proposes a novel multi-channel MAC for achieving pipelined data collection (MPDC) in duty-cycled LSN. In MPDC, each packet transmission path is allocated with one channel. If the number of the packet transmission paths is smaller than or equal to that of channels, then each path occupies a different channel, and there is no contention or interference between paths. Otherwise, there are multiple paths in the same channel; then different from the existing DCPF protocols, in MPDC, the sleep-wakeup schedules of the nodes in the same grade are also mutually staggered, so that the concurrent transmissions between any two paths in the same channel will not interfere with each other. Therefore, the network contention and interference can be eliminated. MPDC has been implemented in OPNET. Its superior performance has been shown through the extensive simulations comparing with an existing DCPF protocol in terms of packet delivery ratio, network throughput, packet delivery latency, and energy consumption efficiency. As far as we are concerned, it is the first to achieve pipelined data collection for LSN by combining multi-channel and duty-cycling strategies to eliminate network contention and interference.

The rest of the paper is organized as follows. Preliminaries are shown in Sect. 2. MPDC is presented in detail in Sect. 3, followed by its performance evaluation in Sect. 4. Finally, the paper is summarized in Sect. 5.

2   Preliminaries

MPDC is a novel multi-channel, duty-cycling MAC designed for achieving pipelined data collection in LSN. Through multi-hop transmissions, sensed data are collected by a sink node located at one of the two ends of the linear region to be monitored. The packets encapsulating sensed data are generated by sensor nodes, which can also work as relay nodes. This section introduces some preliminaries for designing MPDC.

2.1   Grading

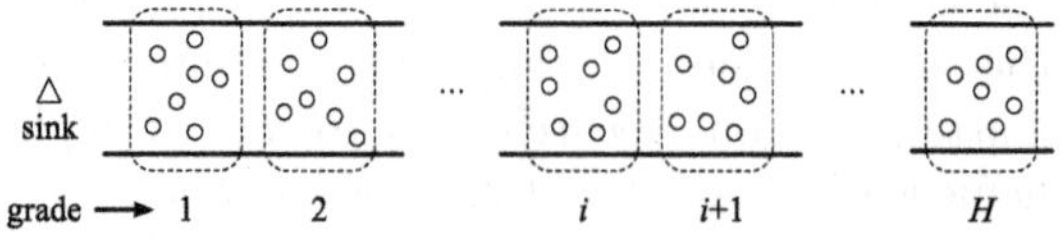

Fig. 1. Classification of nodes in LSN. The network is divided into H grades. Sensor nodes are denoted by circles. The sink node is denoted by a triangle.

Similar to the existing DCPF protocols, grading is also adopted by MPDC. Specifically, each node is classified into a grade according to its communication hop distance to the sink node. The grade of the sink node is zero. As shown in Fig. 1, the generated packets are forwarded successively from higher grade nodes to lower grade nodes, and finally received by the sink node. In MPDC, each grade area is viewed as either a network subarea or cluster, containing the same number of sensor or cluster head nodes, and each node is responsible for sensing or relaying one type of environment information, such as humidity, temperature, pressure, etc. Meanwhile, except for the last-hop transmission between grades one and zero, each node has a unique and different node in its adjacent lower grade as its next hop. Therefore, the whole network contains multiple parallel packet transmission paths as the network backbones to the sink node, the number of which is denoted by N.

2.2 Schedule Staggering in a Path

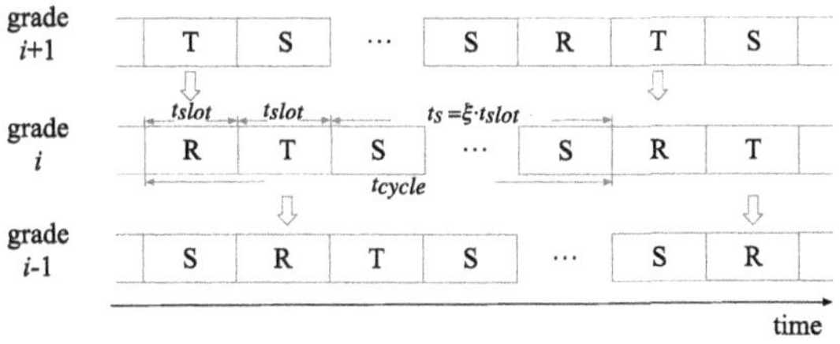

Fig. 2. Pipelined transmission along a packet transmission path.

To enable pipelined forwarding along a packet transmission path, the sleep-wakeup schedules of any two adjacent-grade nodes in the path are staggered. Specifically, the cycle of each node is divided into three states, including data receiving state **R**, data transmitting state **T**, and node sleeping state **S**. If a node in grade i ($i \geq 2$) is in the **R** state, it can receive data from a node in grade $(i + 1)$, which is in the **T** state. Then it can immediately enter its **T** state, and forward the received data to the node in grade $(i - 1)$, which is in the **R** state, thus forming a pipelined transmission mode, as shown in Fig. 2. Intuitively, **R** and **T** states have the same duration, referred to as a slot in this paper and denoted by t_{slot}. After completing the **R** and **T** states, each node enters the **S** state for ξ slots to save energy. So the sleep duration in one cycle is $t_S = \xi \cdot t_{slot}$, and the cycle duration is $t_{cycle} = t_S + 2 \cdot t_{slot}$. Following the same consideration commonly adopted in the current literature [10–12,15], this paper also considers that the interference range of the wireless communication in an open-space environment is about twice the transmission range. Then, to avoid the interference between any two concurrent transmissions along a packet transmission path, it is necessary to set ξ to at least two. For example, when two nodes, respectively, in grades $(i + 1)$ and i shown in Fig. 2 are communicating with each other, there is no interference from those nodes in grades $(i+2)$, $(i+3)$, $(i - 1)$ and $(i - 2)$, since they are all in the **S** state.

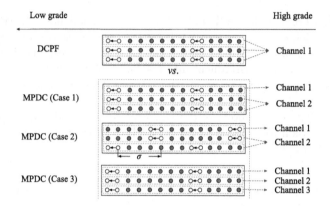

Fig. 3. An example illustrating the difference between MPDC and existing DCPF protocols. Three packet transmission paths (i.e., $N = 3$) are contained in the network with $\xi = 6$. Each three nodes located vertically are in the same grade. The nodes in white are in the **R** or **T** state, and those in black are in the **S** state. For MPDC, three cases are shown: in Case 1, there are totally two available channels, and there are two paths allocated with the same channel without schedule staggering between paths; in Case 2, it is under the same channel conditions as Case 1, but with schedule staggering between paths; in Case 3, each path is allocated with a distinctive channel.

2.3   Schedule Staggering Between Paths in the Same Channel

Existing DCPF protocols usually consider a single-channel communication and make those nodes in the same grade maintain the same sleep-wakeup schedule. Thus, those nodes may need to contend/interfere with each other in data transmission/reception, as the nodes of the same grade in an LSN are very likely to be located within the interference range of each other. Different from the existing work, MPDC adopts a multi-channel strategy. Take the network shown in Fig. 3 for example to illustrate the difference. The network contains three packet transmission paths, i.e., $N = 3$, and $\xi = 6$. Those nodes in white and black are in states **R/T** and **S**, respectively. The nodes located vertically are in the same grade, and for the existing DCPF working in a single channel, they need to contend with each other for data transmission, since they enter **T** simultaneously. Therefore, a contention window (CW) is adopted before the request-to-send (RTS)/clear-to-send (CTS) handshake for data transmission in [9,11,14], as shown in Fig. 4, with the duration of t_{slot} computed as follows:

$$t_{slot} = n_{cw} \cdot t_{cw} + t_{DIFS} + 3t_{SIFS} + t_{RTS} + t_{CTS} + t_{DATA} + t_{ACK}, \qquad (1)$$

where n_{cw} is the total number of mini-time slots contained in a CW, t_{cw} is the duration of each mini-time slot, t_{DIFS} is the duration of DCF Interframe Space, and t_{SIFS} is the duration of the Short Interframe Space (SIFS). t_{RTS}, t_{CTS}, t_{DATA} and t_{ACK} are the time durations that a one-hop transmission takes to transmit/receive an RTS, CTS, DATA and ACK packets, respectively. If the two nodes in the same grade choose the same number of mini-time slots before sending RTS, packet collision and loss will happen, which becomes even worse with a larger N.

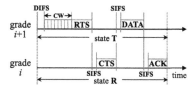

Fig. 4. RTS/CTS handshake with CW for data transmission.

By contrast, MPDC eliminates the aforementioned contention and collision by allocating one channel to each packet transmission path. If the number of available orthogonal channels is smaller than N, then the available channels are not enough, and there are multiple paths allocated with the same channel (see Case 1 and Case 2 shown in Fig. 3). Otherwise, each path is allocated with a different channel, and there is no contention or interference for the concurrent transmissions between paths (see Case 3 shown in Fig. 3). The sleep-wakeup schedules of the nodes in the same grade are also mutually staggered, so that the concurrent transmissions along a path or between any two paths allocated with the same channel will not contend or interfere with each other, either. For the latter case, also considering the relationship between interference and transmission range, to guarantee the success of any two adjacent concurrent transmissions in the same channel (no matter whether the two transmissions are in the same path or not), there exist at least two grades in between, corresponding to at least four hops between two adjacent transmitting nodes (denoted by σ, so $\sigma \geq 4$ hops), and the nodes in these grades are all in state **S**. Therefore, for the network shown in Fig. 3, if there are two paths allocated with the same channel, ξ needs to be set to at least six with $\sigma = 4$ in MPDC. Let N_{sc} denote the number of packet transmission paths allocated with the same channel. It is easy to find that N_{sc}, ξ, and σ should meet

$$\xi \geq \sigma \cdot N_{sc} - 2. \tag{2}$$

3 MPDC Design

To work with multiple channels, MPDC can either utilize a single or multiple sink node(s). For the former, the sink node is equipped with multiple antennas, the number of which is equal to that of the total available orthogonal channels, so that each antenna can work in a different channel at the same time. For the latter, each sink node is equipped with a single antenna and the sink number is equal to the available channel number, so each sink works in a different channel. In the initialization phase of the network, each sensor node will be classified into a grade, and select its next-hop node to formulate the routing table for data

Table 1. IM format

Fields	Descriptions
grade	The grade of the current sending node
duration	The time that the sending node has been in the **T** state when sending IM
source	Node ID or address of the current sending node
channel	The ID of the channel that the node is allocated with
order	The sending order of the message sent by the sink node

Algorithm 1. For the sink node to send the IM message

Require: raw IM, N, M, σ, t_{slot}
Ensure: updated IM
1: IM.$grade \leftarrow 0$;
2: IM.$duration \leftarrow 0$;
3: IM.$source \leftarrow$ sink ID;
4: IM.$channel \leftarrow 0$
5: **for** $n = 1$ to $\lceil \frac{N}{M} \rceil$ **do**
6:     IM.$order \leftarrow n$;
7:     Send IM out;
8:     Wait for $\sigma \cdot t_{slot}$ slots;
9: **end for**

---

transmission. Meanwhile, each packet transmission path will be allocated with a channel. Note that it is possible that there are existing multiple paths allocated with the same channel if the path number is larger than the channel number. Suppose there are totally M available orthogonal channels, the IDs of which are from 0 to $M - 1$. A common channel will be selected to carry out the network initialization process, and each node needs to maintain six attributes:

- $\mathcal{G}$: Node grade, initialized to -1;
- $\mathcal{S}$: Current state of the node, and $\mathcal{S} \in \{\mathbf{R}, \mathbf{T}, \mathbf{S}\}$;
- $\mathcal{T}$: Duration of the node in its current state;
- $\mathcal{N}$: Node address of the next hop of the node;
- $\mathcal{M}$: Node ID, assigned by the sink node, and $\mathcal{M} \in \mathbb{N} \cap [1, N]$ ($\mathbb{N}$ denotes the set of natural numbers in this paper);
- $\mathcal{C}$: Channel ID of the node.

Consider a network deployed with a single sink node equipped with multiple antennas. The sink node first needs to send a probe message to learn all its N neighbors within its one-hop communication range by receiving their reply messages. For the multi-sink case, a random sink node can be selected to do so. The receiving order of their reply messages will serve as the node IDs of the N neighbor nodes. Correspondingly, N packet transmission paths will be built in the initialization phase. These N paths will be divided into M groups, each of which is allocated with a different channel. The paths in the same group are allocated with the same channel. There are $N\%M$ groups, each of which contains $(N - N\%M)/M + 1$ paths, and $M - N\%M$ groups, each of which contains $(N - N\%M)/M$ paths. According to the aforementioned design, for the paths in the same group, the sleep-wakeup schedules of the nodes in the same grade need to be mutually staggered, so that the

---

Algorithm 2. For a one-hop neighbor of the sink node, node $\mathcal{M}$, to parse the received $\mathbb{IM}$

Require: received $\mathbb{IM}$, ξ, $\mathcal{M}$, M
Ensure: the five attributes of the node, i.e., $\langle \mathcal{G}, \mathcal{S}, \mathcal{T}, \mathcal{N}, \mathcal{C} \rangle$
1: **if** $(\mathbb{IM}.order - 1) \times M + 1 \leq \mathcal{M} \leq \mathbb{IM}.order \times M$ **then**
2:    $\mathcal{C} \leftarrow \mathcal{M}\%M$;
3:    $\mathcal{G} \leftarrow \mathbb{IM}.grade + 1$;
4:    $\mathcal{N} \leftarrow \mathbb{IM}.source$;
5:    Calculate δ according to (4);
6:    **if** $\delta < \xi \cdot t_{slot}$ **then**   ▷ Case (i)
7:        $\mathcal{S} \leftarrow \mathbf{S}$; $\mathcal{T} \leftarrow \delta$;
8:    **else if** $\delta < (\xi + 1) \cdot t_{slot}$ **then**   ▷ Case (ii)
9:        $\mathcal{S} \leftarrow \mathbf{R}$; $\mathcal{T} \leftarrow \delta - \xi \cdot t_{slot}$;
10:   **else**   ▷ Case (iii)
11:       $\mathcal{S} \leftarrow \mathbf{T}$; $\mathcal{T} \leftarrow \delta - (\xi + 1) \cdot t_{slot}$;
12:   **end if**
13: **else**
14:   Drop the received $\mathbb{IM}$;
15: **end if**

---

concurrent transmissions along a path or between any two paths allocated with the same channel will not contend or interfere with each other (note that, to achieve mutual staggering, the maximum number of paths in the same group should meet (2) given the settings of ξ and σ). To this end, every $\sigma \cdot t_{slot}$ slots, the sink node generates and sends an initialization message (denoted by $\mathbb{IM}$, and its format is shown in Table 1). The fields of the message, i.e., $\langle grade, duration, source, channel, order \rangle$, are set to $\langle 0, 0, \text{sink ID}, 0, n \rangle$, where n is set to one for the first message, and increases by one every time for sending the next message, until n increases to $\lceil \frac{N}{M} \rceil$. These messages are designated to the nodes whose IDs are smaller than or equal to $\mathbb{IM}.order \times M$ and larger than or equal to $(\mathbb{IM}.order - 1) \times M + 1$. The corresponding algorithm is summarized in Algorithm 1.

Suppose a one-hop neighbor of the sink node, node $\mathcal{M}$, receives a designated $\mathbb{IM}$, i.e., $\mathcal{M} \in [(\mathbb{IM}.order - 1) \times M + 1, \mathbb{IM}.order \times M]$. It will set its three attributes, $\langle \mathcal{G}, \mathcal{N}, \mathcal{C} \rangle$, to $\langle \mathbb{IM}.grade + 1, \mathbb{IM}.source, \mathcal{M}\%M \rangle$, establish a sleep-wakeup schedule by setting its other two attributes, $\langle \mathcal{S}, \mathcal{T} \rangle$, and rebroadcast $\mathbb{IM}$ in its $\mathbf{T}$ state after updating its fields. Especially, $\mathcal{S}$ and $\mathcal{T}$ are set according to the propagation delay of $\mathbb{IM}$, denoted by $t_{\mathbb{IM}}$, which is the difference between sending and receiving time of the message. When node $\mathcal{M}$ is receiving $\mathbb{IM}$, it might be in state $\mathbf{S}$, but may also be in state $\mathbf{R}$ or $\mathbf{T}$, totally three cases denoted by (i), (ii) and (iii), respectively. If $t_{\mathbb{IM}}$ is long enough so that

$$\mathcal{L} = \left\lfloor \frac{\mathbb{IM}.duration + t_{\mathbb{IM}}}{t_{\text{cycle}}} \right\rfloor \geq 1 , \tag{3}$$

then node $\mathcal{M}$ receives $\mathbb{IM}$ after one or even more cycles. To confine the settings of $\mathcal{S}$ and $\mathcal{T}$ in node $\mathcal{M}$ to the aforementioned three cases according to the schedule periodicity, we have

$$\delta = \mathbb{IM}.duration + t_{\mathbb{IM}} - \mathcal{L} \cdot t_{\text{cycle}}, \tag{4}$$

Algorithm 3. For a node more than one hop away from the sink node to parse the received $\mathbb{IM}$

Require: received $\mathbb{IM}$, ξ
Ensure: the five attributes of the node, i.e., $\langle \mathcal{G}, \mathcal{S}, \mathcal{T}, \mathcal{N}, \mathcal{C} \rangle$
1: **if** ($\mathcal{G} < 0$ **or** $\mathcal{G} > \mathbb{IM}.grade + 1$ **or** ($\mathcal{G} == \mathbb{IM}.grade + 1$ **and** The current $\mathbb{IM}$ reception has a higher level of RSSI than the previous)) **then**
2:     $\mathcal{C} \leftarrow \mathbb{IM}.channel$;
3:     Lines 3–12 in Algorithm 2;
4: **else**
5:     Drop the received $\mathbb{IM}$;
6: **end if**

Table 2. The parameters of simulation

Parameter	Value	Parameter	Value	Parameter	Value	Parameter	Value
t_{DIFS}	10 ms	t_{SIFS}	5 ms	t_{RTS}	11 ms	H	10
t_{CTS}	11 ms	t_{ACK}	11 ms	t_{DATA}	43 ms	N	3
n_{cw}	16	t_{cw}	1 ms	ξ	6	K	15

and the complete algorithm for node $\mathcal{M}$ to parse the received $\mathbb{IM}$ is shown in Algorithm 2. After carrying out the algorithm, node $\mathcal{M}$ enters state **R** after $(t_S - \mathcal{T})$ time in Case (i), or enters state **T** in Case (ii) or state **S** in Case (iii), both after $(t_{slot} - \mathcal{T})$ time. After then, node $\mathcal{M}$ has successfully joined the network. It will rebroadcast $\mathbb{IM}$ in its **T** state with the fields of the message, $\langle grade, duration, source, channel, order \rangle$, updated to $\langle \mathbb{IM}.grade + 1, t_{dur}, \mathcal{M}, \mathcal{C}, \mathbb{IM}.order \rangle$, in which t_{dur} is the duration that the node has resided for in state **T** right before rebroadcasting $\mathbb{IM}$.

For a node, denoted as $\mathcal{K}$, which is more than one hop away from the sink node and has yet to join the network, it will keep its radio on to join the network by parsing a received $\mathbb{IM}$. In order to guarantee that node $\mathcal{K}$ chooses a lower grade to join and receives $\mathbb{IM}$ from a link with better quality determined based on the Received Signal Strength Indicator (RSSI) [17], it sets its five attributes after receiving at least N $\mathbb{IM}$ messages. The corresponding algorithm for node $\mathcal{K}$ to parse the received $\mathbb{IM}$ is summarized in Algorithm 3, the main part of which is the same as Algorithm 2. After joining the network, node $\mathcal{K}$ also rebroadcasts $\mathbb{IM}$ in its **T** state with the five fields of the message updated to $\langle \mathbb{IM}.grade + 1, t_{dur}, \mathcal{K}, \mathcal{C}, \mathbb{IM}.order \rangle$, in which t_{dur} is the duration that node $\mathcal{K}$ has resided for in state **T** right before rebroadcasting $\mathbb{IM}$.

4   Performance Evaluation

For performance evaluation, MPDC has been implemented in OPNET, a well-known, industry-strength network simulator with high simulation fidelity. A state-of-the-art DCPF protocol [9] has also been implemented in OPNET for performance comparison. Consider an LSN which is divided into $H = 10$ grades. Each grade contains three sensor nodes, i.e., $N = 3$. Therefore, three packet

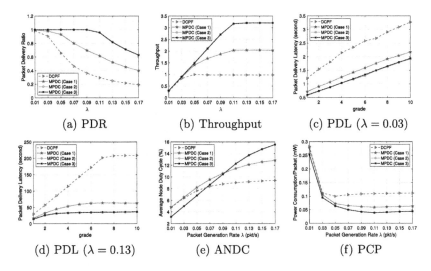

(a) PDR   (b) Throughput   (c) PDL ($\lambda = 0.03$)

(d) PDL ($\lambda = 0.13$)   (e) ANDC   (f) PCP

Fig. 5. Simulation results of MPDC, in comparison with DCPF.

transmission paths will be built in the network. The capacity of the first-in-first-out queue of each node is set to $K = 15$. Table 2 lists the simulation parameters. All sensor nodes are assumed to be able to generate packets independently following a Poisson process with a rate of λ packets/second. Packet retransmission is not considered in the network. Except for the sensor nodes in the highest grade, which are only sources, each sensor node also works as a relay node to forward data from higher-grade nodes.

For the comparison between MPDC and DCPF, four scenarios are investigated in this paper, including ① DCPF, ② MPDC (Case 1) in two available orthogonal channels without schedule staggering between paths, ③ MPDC (Case 2) in two available orthogonal channels with schedule staggering between paths, and ④ MPDC (Case 3) in three available orthogonal channels. The following five metrics of interest are chosen:

- **Packet Delivery Ratio (PDR)**: the ratio of the total number of packets that the sink node successfully receives to the total number of packets generated by all nodes.
- **Throughput**: the number of the data packets successfully received by the sink node per second.
- **Packet Delivery Latency (PDL)**: the average time taken by each data packet to be delivered from source nodes to the sink node.
- **Average Node Duty Cycle (ANDC)**: the ratio of the awake time of a node to the total simulation time. The lower the duty cycle, the less the energy consumption.
- **Power Consumption per Packet (PCP)**: the average amount of power totally consumed for the sink node to successfully receive one data packet. This metric indicates the energy consumption efficiency of the protocol.

For the four metrics, PDR, throughput, ANDC, and PCP, λ is increased from 0.01 to 0.17 by a step of 0.02. Based on the throughput results, $\lambda = 0.03$ and 0.13 are chosen to show PDL. The obtained results are shown in Fig. 5.

It can be found from Fig. 5a that, in all four scenarios, PDR decreases as λ increases. Because as more packets are generated in the network, there are also more packets dropped due to collision or overflow. Obviously, the PDR of MPDC (Case 1) is higher than that of the DCPF working in a single channel. However, there are still existing contention and interference in MPDC (Case 1). While for MPDC (Case 2), the sleep-wakeup schedules of the nodes in the two paths allocated with the same channel are completely staggered, so the contention and interference in the network can be eliminated, leading to a higher PDR. One can also find that both MPDC (Case 2) and MPDC (Case 3) achieve almost the same PDR. This is because in both two scenarios, there is no contention or interference, and the schedule staggering in scenario ③ does not change the network parameters shown in Table 2. Therefore, the two scenarios achieve almost the same network performance in terms of all the five metrics, as shown in Fig. 5. In other words, MPDC is quite adaptive to the number of available channels.

Due to the same reason, the throughput of MPDC (Case 2) is the same as that of MPDC (Case 3), as shown in Fig. 5b. For all four scenarios, when λ is smaller than their corresponding service rates, packets can be transmitted as fast as being injected into the network without causing queue overflow, and therefore, the throughput increases linearly as the traffic load increases. When λ exceeds the service rate, the throughput remains almost the same, since the network becomes saturated, and hence the network reaches its throughput limit. As shown in the figure, MPDC in scenarios ③ and ④ has the highest service rate and can achieve highest throughput as λ exceeds the service rate.

According to the results shown in Fig. 5b, two packet generation rates are chosen, including $\lambda = 0.03$ and 0.13 packets/second, corresponding to two cases: 1) λ in all four scenarios do not reach their service rates, and 2) it exceeds their service rates. The corresponding PDL results are shown in Fig. 5c and Fig. 5d, respectively. For all four scenarios, the PDL of the packets generated in the same grade increases as λ increases, as more and more packets are accumulated in nodes' queues. In addition, the PDL increases as grade increases, since the packets generated by the source nodes farther away from the sink node experience more packet transmitting and queueing processes. However, both of the above two kinds of increases in MPDC are much lower than those in DCPF. Especially, MPDC (Cases 2 and 3) shows lower PDL because of no contention or interference.

Figures 5e and 5f show ANDC and PCP versus λ, respectively. As shown in Fig. 5e, when λ is low, MPDC has a lower ANDC than DCPF, because in MPDC there is less contention or interference among nodes, so a node can utilize time more efficiently and thus have more time to sleep. On the other hand, as λ increases, MPDC still has a larger PDR than DCPF; while those nodes in DCPF can sleep more, since there are more packet collision and overflow in DCPF. Therefore, MPDC has a higher ANDC than DCPF, which means that each node in MPDC consumes more energy than DCPF. However, PCP in MPDC is always lower than DCPF as λ becomes larger, as shown in Fig. 5f, which means that MPDC outperforms DCPF with a higher energy efficiency.

5 Conclusion

This paper proposed MPDC, a novel multi-channel MAC for pipelined data collection in duty-cycled LSN. Unlike the existing DCPF protocols, MPDC eliminates the contention and interference among nodes by adopting the multi-channel and schedule staggering strategies. According to the extensive simulation results, MPDC significantly outperforms a state-of-the-art DCPF protocol in terms of packet delivery ratio, network throughput, packet delivery latency, and energy efficiency.

References

1. Abidoye, A.P., Obagbuwa, I.C.: Models for integrating wireless sensor networks into the Internet of Things. IET Wirel. Sens. Syst. **7**(3), 65–72 (2017)
2. Anubhama, R., Rajendran, T.: PRIB-MAC: a preamble-based receiver initiated MAC protocol for broadcast in wireless sensor networks. Sadhana **45**(1), 1–8 (2020). https://doi.org/10.1007/s12046-020-1322-7
3. Behera, T.M., Mohapatra, S.K., Samal, U.C., Khan, M.S., Daneshmand, M., Gandomi, A.H.: I-SEP: an improved routing protocol for heterogeneous WSN for IoT-based environmental monitoring. IEEE Internet Things J. **7**(1), 710–717 (2020)
4. Cheng, L., et al.: Adaptive forwarding with probabilistic delay guarantee in low-duty-cycle WSNs. IEEE Trans. Wireless Commun. **19**(7), 4775–4792 (2020)
5. Jawhar, I., Mohamed, N., Al-Jaroodi, J., Zhang, S.: A framework for using unmanned aerial vehicles for data collection in linear wireless sensor networks. J. Intell. Rob. Syst. **74**(1), 437–453 (2014)
6. Jiao, X., et al.: Delay efficient scheduling algorithms for data aggregation in multi-channel asynchronous duty-cycled WSNs. IEEE Trans. Commun. **67**(9), 6179–6192 (2019)
7. Shafique, K., Khawaja, B.A., Sabir, F., Qazi, S., Mustaqim, M.: Internet of things (IoT) for next-generation smart systems: a review of current challenges, future trends and prospects for emerging 5G-IoT scenarios. IEEE Access **8**, 23022–23040 (2020)
8. Shallahuddin, A.A., et al.: An enhanced adaptive duty cycle scheme for optimum data transmission in wireless sensor network. In: Kim, K.J., Kim, H.-Y. (eds.) Information Science and Applications. LNEE, vol. 621, pp. 33–40. Springer, Singapore (2020). https://doi.org/10.1007/978-981-15-1465-4_4
9. Singh, R., Rai, B.K., Bose, S.K.: Modeling and performance analysis for pipelined-forwarding MAC protocols for linear wireless sensor networks. IEEE Sens. J. **19**(15), 6539–6552 (2019)
10. Tong, F., Ni, M., Shu, L., Pan, J.: A Pipelined-forwarding, routing-integrated and effectively-identifying MAC for large-scale WSN. In: Proceedings of IEEE GLOBECOM, pp. 225–230 (2013)

11. Tong, F., Zhang, R., Pan, J.: One handshake can achieve more: an energy-efficient, practical pipelined data collection for duty-cycled sensor networks. IEEE Sens. J. **16**(9), 3308–3322 (2016)
12. Tong, F., He, S., Pan, J.: Modeling and analysis for data collection in duty-cycled linear sensor networks with pipelined-forwarding feature. IEEE Internet Things J. **6**(6), 9489–9502 (2019)
13. Varshney, S., Kumar, C., Swaroop, A.: Linear sensor networks: applications, issues and major research trends. In: International Conference on Computing, Communication Automation, pp. 446–451 (2015)
14. Villordo-Jimenez, I., Torres-Cruz, N., Carvalho, M.M., Menchaca-Mendez, R., Rivero-Angeles, M.E., Menchaca-Mendez, R.: A selective-awakening MAC protocol for energy-efficient data forwarding in linear sensor networks. Wirel. Commun. Mob. Comput. **2018**, 1–18 (2018)
15. Wadhwa, M., Kaur, K.: Interference and channel quality based channel assignment for cognitive radio networks. In: Arai, K., Kapoor, S., Bhatia, R. (eds.) SAI 2018. AISC, vol. 857, pp. 823–833. Springer, Cham (2019). https://doi.org/10.1007/978-3-030-01177-2_61
16. Wu, Y., Liu, K.S., Stankovic, J.A., He, T., Lin, S.: Efficient multichannel communications in wireless sensor networks. ACM Trans. Sens. Netw. **12**(1), 1–23 (2016)
17. Xu, K., Pu, L., Dai, J., Liu, Z., Meng, Z., Zhang, L.: ROR: an RSSI based OMNI-directional routing algorithm for geobroadcast in VANETs. In: Proceedings of IEEE VTC (spring), pp. 1–5 (2017)

Efficient Concurrent Transmission Scheme for Wireless Ad Hoc Networks: A Joint Optimization Approach

Zhigang Feng, Xiaoqin Song, and Lei Lei[✉]

College of Electronic and Information Engineering, Nanjing University
of Aeronautics and Astronautics, Nanjing 211106, China
{zgfeng,leilei}@nuaa.edu.cn

Abstract. In this paper, we focus on the joint optimization of scheduling and power control to achieve effective concurrent transmission. Under constraints, we describe the optimization problem as a scheduling problem based on power control. In order to solve the complexity problem, we have determined the best power control strategy in the large network area. Using the dual-link communication architecture, we decompose the optimization problem into two sub-problems, namely power control and link scheduling. By solving two sub-problems, we have determined the best link scheduling and power control mechanism suitable for the actual network environment. We realize efficient concurrent transmission based on the optimal solution obtained by joint optimization to effectively utilize network resources and improve energy efficiency. The simulation results prove the effectiveness of the scheme. Compared with existing solutions, the joint optimization solution has obvious advantages in terms of network throughput and energy consumption.

Keywords: Concurrent transmission · Power control · Link scheduling · Energy consumption · Dual-link structure

1 Introduction

The energy efficiency of wireless ad hoc networks has always been a very important issue [1, 2]. How to allocate network resources has become very important, such as how to allocate network resources in terms of routing, link scheduling, channel allocation and power control. Usually, different network resources will be coupled together, so we cannot independently determine the best performance, which requires joint optimization solutions. In addition, in order to meet the rapid growth of traffic demand, wireless ad hoc networks are being developed into increasingly complex structures. Therefore, large-scale joint optimization has become a challenging problem. This has prompted us to develop a more efficient joint optimization scheme, which regards the optimization variables as a combination of multiple resource allocation strategies such as channel allocation, transmission power control and link scheduling [3].

© Springer Nature Switzerland AG 2021
Z. Liu et al. (Eds.): WASA 2021, LNCS 12938, pp. 563–574, 2021.
https://doi.org/10.1007/978-3-030-86130-8_44

In [4], the Dinkelbach method is used to convert the energy efficiency problem into an equivalent subtractive form, which is solved by using the enhanced Lagrangian multiplier method. The author uses a two-layer iterative algorithm to combine power and bandwidth allocation to improve energy efficiency. However, the text always uses the maximum ratio for transmission, and some actual network information is not fully considered. In [5], the author first proposed the energy efficiency maximization problem, then converted it into a maximum matching problem and solved it by the Hungarian algorithm. The author finally motivates a resource allocation scheme based on stable matching, the focus is only on power control. In [6], the author studied the joint optimization of spectrum and energy efficiency in cognitive networks with power and sub-channel allocation, where the author proposed a problem transformation based on trade-off metric and used convex problem structure. The research work of [4, 5] and [6] basically focused on channel and power allocation. Improve system space utilization by controlling transmission power, thereby improving energy efficiency. In these studies, the virtualization of joint link scheduling has not been well studied, and there is still room for improvement in the overall performance of the network.

In [7], the author studies joint scheduling and radio configuration issues. However, it does not consider power control, but uses a fixed transmit power for information transmission. In [8], the author proposed an optimization scheme for joint scheduling and power control, assuming that the transmission power that can be achieved by the communication link is constant. This assumption does not fully consider the actual network information. In [9], the author proposed a two-step method. The method first uses a fixed transmit power to deal with the scheduling problem, and then optimizes the transmit power based on the completed scheduling scheme. However, such a decomposition will lead to suboptimal since scheduling and power control are indeed solved separately. In [7, 8] and [9] the author did not propose an effective joint optimization mechanism for link scheduling and power control. Therefore, we need to develop a more effective joint optimization program.

This paper proposes an optimization scheme for joint scheduling and power control. We obtain our objective function through analysis in a large-scale ideal network environment. Then introduce the actual network architecture to determine the optimal transmission power and target interference power in the actual network. In order to effectively utilize the network spectrum and energy, we have put forward the concept of master–slave transmission. Based on the optimal power value obtained by the proposed scheme, the main transmission reasonably schedules the most subordinate transmission link to achieve effective concurrent transmission.

The main contributions of this research are: (i) Under large-scale network conditions, we use constrained optimization to analyze the optimal scheduling and transmission power levels to obtain the network objective function. (ii) We introduce the actual network communication architecture to transform and solve the ideal conditions. Then we propose a joint optimization scheme based on link scheduling and power control. (iii) We verified the energy-saving effects of joint scheduling and power control through numerical calculations, and analyzed the impact of multi-dimensional network resource allocation on network energy efficiency.

The rest of this paper is structured as follows. Section 2 proposes the system model and formulates the model. Section 3 analyzes the joint optimization of scheduling and power control, and gives the optimal scheme of concurrent transmission. Section 4 gives the simulation results of the proposed scheme. Finally, Sect. 5 concludes the main remarks of this paper.

2   Problem Formulation

In the wireless Ad Hoc network MAC protocol based on the CSMA/CA mechanism,
    the carrier detection mechanism restricts all neighbor nodes within the transmission range of the receiving node from sending or receiving signals to ensure the successful transmission of data frames between the receiving/sending nodes. However, when the collision interference range of the receiving node is smaller than the transmission range of the CTS frame. In this case, outside the conflict interference range of the receiving node, the interference generated by the sending node within the transmission range of the CTS frame will not cause the receiving node to conflict. These sending nodes can correctly listen to the CTS frame that the receiving node responds, so this communication link can be scheduled through a scheduling scheme to initiate data transmission in parallel with the current sending node. If the MAC protocol can allow neighbor receiving/sending node pairs to initiate data transmission in parallel without destroying the SINR threshold required for the correct reception of other signals, the channel utilization rate and the total average network throughput will be greatly improved.

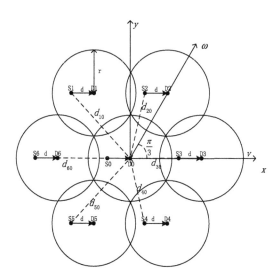

Fig. 1. The large-scale network area

We focus on single-hop transmission in a wireless Ad Hoc network. There are multiple communication nodes distributed in the network area. We give a large-scale network area, as shown in Fig. 1 (here we only draw the central link distribution, and the peripheral links are distributed in the same way). In this unlimited network area, the communication links are symmetrically distributed. Assuming that each communication link occupies a circular area with a radius of r in space, the distance between the sending node and the destination node of the communication link is d. It is required to find the most suitable scheduling set and transmission power to maximize the network data rate. Here we can convert to finding a suitable link space and transmission power to determine the basic capacity of the network, so as to determine the optimal scheduling and power control later. Because we assume an ideal symmetrical link, we only need to solve the problem around the central link. Finally, we can get a general solution model.

In Fig. 1, the signal power received by the destination node in the link is $cPd^{-\alpha}$, where P is the transmission power, c is a constant, α is the path loss index, and d is the distance of the link. As shown in Fig. 1, the presence of multiple links around the central link will interfere with its transmission. We use d_{i0} to represent the corresponding interference distance, where $i \in \{1, 2, 3, \ldots\}$ represents the distance between the sending node of the link i and the destination node of the central link. Through vector and coordinate conversion, we can get:

$$d_{i0} = \left[\left(\frac{3nr}{2} \right)^2 + \left(m\sqrt{3}r + \frac{n\sqrt{3}r}{2} - d \right)^2 \right]^{\frac{1}{2}} \tag{1}$$

Where $(m, n) \in \{\ldots,-1,0,1,\ldots\}^2$, $(m, n) \neq (0,0)$. For different link positions, the values of m and n are also different. We assume that the interference power is much greater than the background noise power. The SINR can be calculated as

$$SINR = \frac{cPd^{-\alpha}}{\sum_{i=0}^{\infty} cPd_{i0}^{-\alpha}} \tag{2}$$

The space which the scheduled link has occupied can be calculated as

$$S = \pi r^2 \tag{3}$$

Then we can get the total data rate per network (bit/s/Hz) which is given by

$$R = \frac{\log_2(1 + SINR)}{S} = \frac{\log_2(1 + SINR)}{\pi r^2} \tag{4}$$

Using (4), we can calculate the value of energy consumption per transmitted data bit (J/(bit/Hz)) which is give by

$$E = \frac{(2\xi_c + sP)/\pi r^2}{R} = \frac{2\xi_c + sP}{\log_2(1 + SINR)} \tag{5}$$

Where ξ_c is the power consumption of the circuit, and s is the reciprocal of the amplifier power efficiency. The power consumption when the node is receiving or idle is ξ_c, too. $2\xi_c + sP$ refers to the total power consumption of a scheduled communication link.

It can be derived from (1) and (2) that the ratio of the link area radius r to the link distance d determines the value of SINR. So we have G (r, d) = SINR. Based on the above analysis, we use energy consumption and SINR as constraints to maximize the network objective function, and we can get:

$$\max_{P,r} \frac{1}{d^2} \times \frac{\log_2(1 + G(r/d))}{\pi(r/d)^2} \tag{6}$$

$$s.t. \frac{2\xi_c + sP}{\log_2(1 + SINR)} \leq E_{l\,max}, SINR \geq SINR_{min} \tag{7}$$

Where E_{lmax} represents the maximum energy consumption per transmitted data bit constrained by link l. $SINR_{min}$ is the minimum SINR required by the destination node in a scheduled link when the information transmission is completed successfully. For formula (6), we use a solution method which called the Lagrangian multipliers method and Karush–Kuhn–Tucker (KKT) conditions to find the values of P and r.

3 Joint Optimization of Scheduling and Transmission Power Control

In the actual wireless Ad Hoc network, the position of the communication nodes are not always in an ideal symmetrical distribution state. The location of nodes will also change in the network over time. Therefore, we will introduce a dual-link communication network architecture based on Sect. 2. Use the actual network environment to further introduce our joint optimization program.

3.1 Power Analysis

In an actual wireless communication network, we consider a dual-link structure shown in Fig. 2. Two links are distributed randomly in the network area, and the distance between the sending and destination nodes will also change dynamically. Therefore, in actual wireless communication networks, there are great differences in the transmission power and interference power in the communication link. In order to make full use of network resources, we should use joint optimization to obtain the theoretically optimal transmission power and tolerable interference power. Based on the analysis of transmission power and interference power, the link scheduling scheme we designed can make the actual interference power as close as possible to our optimal solution. Therefore, the proposed mechanism can reasonably arrange link transmission according to the optimal solution, so that the scheduled link occupies a relatively small space. Then we can maximize the set of concurrent transmission links in the same network area.

In a network area, if the actual interference power which received by the destination node in the link is not greater than its target interference power, we can schedule more links. The constraints is

$$d_{lk} = \sqrt{d_{ss}^2 - 2d_{kk}d_{ss}\cos(\beta_k) + d_{kk}^2}$$

$$I_l = cP_k d_{lk}^{-\alpha} \leq I_l(*) \Rightarrow d_{lk} \geq \left(\frac{cP_k}{I_l(*)}\right)^{\frac{1}{\alpha}} \tag{8}$$

Where I_l and $I_l(*)$ are the actual interference power and the optimal target interference power of link l, respectively. d_{lk} is the interference distance between link l and link k in Fig. 2, d_{ss} is the distance between two sending nodes, $(l, k) \in \{(1, 2),(2,1)\}$ is the number of the link.

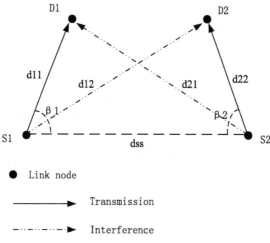

Fig. 2. The Dual-link structure

As shown in Fig. 2, the interference generated by link 1 to the receiving node of link 2 will also increase when we increase the transmission power of the sending node in link 1. In order to perform concurrent transmissions normally, we should increase the distance d_{12}. If we need to reduce the amount of interference from the sending node of one link to the receiving node of another link, we can also appropriately increase the distance between the receiving node of one link and the sending node of another link. For each link, we keep the product of the optimal transmission power and the target interference power at a constant value. As shown in Fig. 3, when the transmission power of link 1 is reduced, the interference caused by link 1 to link 2 will also be reduced. Then we can reduce the distance between link 2 and link 1. As shown in Fig. 3, when the transmission power of link 1 is gradually reduced from 25 to 6 mW, the optimal target interference power of link 2 will gradually increase. This change is consistent with our design to maintain a fixed value. By keeping a fixed value, we can ensure that the target interference power can be increased appropriately when the sending node of other links has a smaller transmission power. Then we can schedule another link that is closer to it, so that the actual interference power at the destination node is closer to the target interference power. Finally, we can schedule the most links in the same network area for concurrent transmission. This ensures effective spatial spectrum reuse. Therefore, combining (6) and (7), we can determine the optimal transmission power P_l (*) and target interference power I_l (*) for each link, that is

$$[P_l(*), I_l(*)] = \arg\max_{P_l, I_l} \frac{1}{d_{ll}^2} \times \frac{\log_2\left(1 + \frac{cP_l d_{ll}^{-\alpha}}{cP_k d_{lk}^{-\alpha}}\right)}{\pi \times \left[G^{-1}\left(\frac{cP_l d_{ll}^{-\alpha}}{cP_k d_{lk}^{-\alpha}}\right)\right]^2}$$

$$s.t. \ \frac{2\xi_c + sP_l}{\log_2\left(1 + \frac{cP_l d_{ll}^{-\alpha}}{I_l}\right)} \le E_{l\max}, P_l \times I_l = \rho, SINR \ge SINR_{\min} \qquad (9)$$

We obtain the optimal power value by maximizing the network objective function. The fixed value ρ is determined based on the feasible power range of the link in the network. We use the brute force search method for the solution of the transmission power P_l (*) and the target interference power I_l (*) in formula (8).

3.2 Link Scheduling Analysis

In order to schedule the most links to achieve concurrent transmission and make full use of network performance, the proposed solution needs to be scheduled based on some local network information. Therefore, we designed a Neighbor Node Table (NNT) for each node. NNT(i) stores information about nodes that are sending/receiving or will send/receive data around node i. For each neighbor node u of node i, the following information is stored in NNT(i): (i) The address of node u. (ii) Channel gain between node i and u.(iii) Target interference power of node u. (iv) The data transmission time and ACK transmission time between nodes u and v. Therefore, we designed a link scheduling scheme based on NNT and power control. According to NNT, we determine the master transmission and slave transmission links. The master transmission link schedules the slave transmission links that meet the requirements according to conditions such as power control. After the master transmission link schedules all the slave transmission links, all the links perform concurrent transmission. The proposed mechanism can effectively improve network performance.

Master–slave Concept

The nodes must exchange control messages before transmitting data to notify their neighboring nodes that they are about to send data. In order to better describe the concurrency relationship between adjacent link transmissions, we introduce two concepts: master transmission and slave transmission.

Master transmission: If the sending node and the destination node of the communication link are sending RTS and CTS frames respectively, there is no node that wants to send/receive data or is transmitting data in their adjacent communication links. We define this communication link as the master transmission link. This scheme only requires that when the sending node and the destination node of the master transmission link exchange control messages, their corresponding NNT is empty.

Slave transmission: If the sending node and the receiving node of a communication link are exchanging control messages, there are data transmission requests around them.

That is, at least one of the NNT of the sending node and the destination node is not empty. We define this link as the slave transmission link.

Optimal Scheduling Mechanism

When the transmission power of link l at slot t is not less than the optimal transmission power, the actual interference power at slot t is not greater than the target interference power, and the data rate at slot t is not greater than the maximum data rate required by link l, we schedule this link. We have

$$P_{lt} \geq P_l(*), I_{lt} \leq I_l(*), R_{lt} \leq R_{l\max} \tag{10}$$

Where P_{lt} represents the actual transmission power at the sending node of link l at slot t, and the interference generated by this link will not destroy the previously scheduled link. I_{lt} represents the interference power generated by the surrounding sending nodes that the link l suffered at the time slot t. R_{lt} represents the average data rate of link l at the time slot t. Our rules for scheduling link l are

$$[l, t] = \arg\max_{l,t} \left(\frac{P_l(*)}{P_{lt}} \times \frac{I_{lt}}{I_l(*)} \right)$$

$$s.t. P_{lt} \geq P_l(*), I_{lt} \leq I_l(*), R_{lt} \leq R_{l\max} \tag{11}$$

Where the ratio of transmission power and the ratio of interference power jointly determine the distance between the scheduled slave transmission link and the master transmission link in the space. The larger the ratio, the smaller the space occupied by the two links. That is, we can schedule more links in the same network area to achieve concurrent transmission. Therefore, in the process of scheduling links, the slave transmission link is scheduled based on maximizing the product of these two ratios.

After the master transmission link is determined, a slot is introduced before its data transmission. In this slot, the master transmission link calculates and schedules the slave transmission links capable of concurrent transmission according to the data information in the corresponding NNT. According to the given scheduling objective function (10), the master transmission link will sequentially schedule the surrounding slave transmission links that meet the requirements(We use brute force search to solve Eq. (11)). This round of scheduling will not end until all adjacent links of the master transmission are traversed. Until all the slave transmission links that meet the requirements are found, then concurrent transmission is performed. For the slave transmission links that not be scheduled in this round, the corresponding NNT will be updated in time. For a link that successfully performs data transmission, the corresponding sending node and receiving node can update the corresponding NNT in time after sending the DATA/ACK message. For nodes that do not perform data transmission, they will update their corresponding NNT after receiving DATA/ACK data from other nodes. After the first round of concurrent transmission is completed, a new round of scheduling will be started.

4   Simulation Results

In this section, we will use simulation results to verify our proposed joint scheduling and power control scheme. Consider a network area with multiple nodes, which are randomly distributed in the network area. The main simulation parameters are listed in Table 1. In order to simplify the digital representation, we set $E_{lmax} = \tau \times E_{lmin}$, where E_{lmin} represents the minimum average energy consumption per bit of data transmission. Figure 3 shows the relationship between the optimal power value after joint optimization and τ under different link distances. This is in line with what we described in Sect. 3, which is to keep the product of the transmission power and the target interference.

Table 1. Simulation parameters.

Parameter name	Numerical value
Bandwidth	2 MHz
The maximum transmission power P_{max}	100 mW
The minimum transmission power P_{min}	1 Mw
The maximum target interference power I_{max}	−45 dBm
The minimum target interference power I_{min}	−80 dBm
The maximum SINR	30 dB
The minimum SINR	6 dB
The maximum distance d_{max}	50 m
The signaling rate R	5 Mbps
The circuit power consumption ξ_c	1.25 W
The path-loss exponent α	3.5
S	10

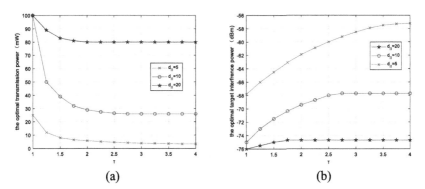

(a)   (b)

Fig. 3. The relationship between the optimal power value and τ under different link distances.

power at a constant value. We use indicators such as energy consumption and throughput to verify the performance of the proposed scheme. In order to verify the superiority of our proposed scheme, we compare the proposed scheme with the existing scheme. We use matlab to evaluate the mechanism of different schemes. The comparison schemes include:

1) The traditional DCF MAC of IEEE 802.11(802.11).
2) A scheme with an energy-saving mode and an optimized transmission power level based on the DCF MAC of IEEE 802.11 [10] (ES-DCF).

Figure 4 shows the throughput of different schemes under different network parameters. As shown in Fig. 4(a), considering the network traffic load. When the data rate is low, only a single link occupies the channel at the same time. Therefore, the throughput of all mechanisms is basically the same. As the data rate gradually increases, multiple transmissions will begin to compete for the shared channel. Although there are a large number of information transmission requests at this time, the 802.11 protocol can only perform the transmission of a single request at a time. So compared to the other two protocols, its throughput is lower. In addition, both our proposed scheme and the ES-DCF can achieve concurrent transmission. However, our proposed scheme adopts a joint optimization scheme combining scheduling and power control, and its performance is superior. In addition, our proposed scheme uses a variable power value for transmission in order to maximize the use of network resources. Therefore, we have added a group of transmission modes with maximum transmission power, namely $P_{\max}$ in Fig. 4(a) (ie, the transmission power of each link is fixed to be the same). Through comparison, it can be found that the method of using constrained optimization to obtain the best transmission power can better improve the network performance.

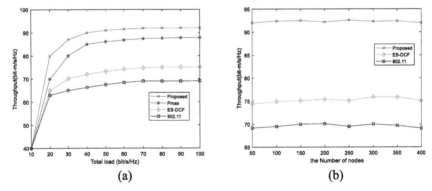

Fig. 4. Throughput comparison under different network parameters.

Considering the number of nodes in Fig. 4(b), there are a large number of transmission links in a large-scale network environment. At this time, the performance of various programs are basically in the best state. This is consistent with the optimal state in Fig. 4(a).Compared to other programs, the performance of our proposed scheme is also very superior. Figure 5 shows the energy consumption per bit of different schemes under different network parameters. Our proposed scheme takes power control and energy consumption constraints as constraints at the same time. Compared with the ES-DCF protocol, which simply considers energy consumption, the energy consumption of our proposed scheme is significantly lower. Since the traditional 802.11 protocol does not consider energy consumption constraints, its energy consumption is the highest.

In Fig. 5(b), both the proposed scheme and ES-DCF have energy constraints, so the energy consumption of these two schemes are in their own optimal state. However, the proposed scheme also jointly optimizes power control and link scheduling. Compared with ES-DCF, this scheme still has certain advantages in terms of energy consumption. In addition, as the network scale of the 802.11 protocol becomes larger and larger, its collision probability will increase sharply, and the number of retransmissions will also increase, and its energy consumption has been on an upward trend.

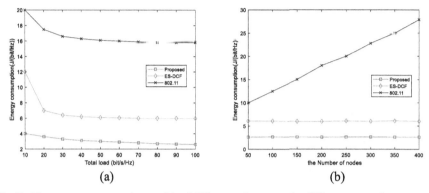

(a)   (b)

Fig. 5. The energy consumption per bit of different schemes under different network parameters

5   Conclusion

In this paper, we have achieved effective concurrent transmission in wireless Ad Hoc networks through joint scheduling and power control. Through the analysis of the large-scale idealized network environment, the optimization problem is proposed, and the Lagrangian multipliers method and Karush–Kuhn–Tucker (KKT) conditions are used to solve it. We introduce a dual-link communication architecture to analyze the actual network environment and analyze and solve the optimal power value. When we solve for the optimal power, we keep the product of the optimal transmission power and the target interference power at a constant value. Finally, we use the brute force search method to determine the transmission power and the target interference power. In the entire information transmission process, we use energy consumption, SINR and other conditions as constraints, and use constraint optimization to obtain the optimal power values of different links. Based on local network information, we define the concept of master–slave transmission. The master transmission link schedules the slave transmission links based on power control. The proposed scheduling mechanism can maximize the set of concurrent links to achieve the most effective concurrent transmission. The solution we put forward makes full use of network resources while making full use of energy. The proposed scheme not only maximizes the network spectrum, but also reduces energy consumption. The simulation results show that, compared with the existing schemes, the scheme proposed in this paper has great advantages in throughput and energy consumption.

574   Z. Feng et al.

Background. This work was supported in part by the National Natural Science Foundation of China (No. 61902182), the Natural Science Foundation of Jiangsu Province of China (No. BK20190409), the Aeronautical Science Foundation of China (No. 2016ZC52029), Qing Lan Project of Jiangsu Province of China, China Postdoctoral Science Foundation (No. 2019TQ0153), and the Foundation of CETC Key Laboratory of Aerospace Information Applications of China (No. SXX18629T022). The authors are with the College of Electronic and Information Engineering, Nanjing University of Aeronautics and Astronautics, Nanjing, 210,016, China.

References

1. Jaipriya, S., Malathy, S., Srinivasan, K., Priyanka, B., Charliene Karunya, L.: A framework for energy optimization in wireless sensor nodes at Ad-Hoc network. In: 2018 2nd International Conference on I-SMAC, pp. 419–422 (2018)
2. Sivabalan, S., Rathipriya, R.: Slot scheduling Mac using energy efficiency in ad hoc wireless networks. In: 2017 International Conference on Inventive Communication and Computational Technologies (ICICCT), Coimbatore, pp. 430–434 (2017)
3. Li, H., Cheng, Y., Zhou, C., Wan, P.: Multi-dimensional conflict graph based computing for optimal capacity in MR-MC wireless networks. In: Proceedings of IEEE International Conference Distribution Computing System, pp. 774–783 (2010)
4. Jiang, Y., et al.: Joint power and bandwidth allocation for energy-efficient heterogeneous cellular networks. IEEE Trans. Commun. **67**(9), 6168–6178 (2019)
5. Lu, L., He, D., Xingxing, Y., Li, G.Y.: Energy-efficient resource allocation for cognitive radio networks. In: Proceedings of IEEE Global Communication Conference, pp. 1026–1031 (2013)
6. Wang, S., Wang, C.: Joint optimization of spectrum and energy efficiency in cognitive radio networks. Digit. Commun. Netw. **1**(3), 161–170 (2015)
7. Anderson, E., Phillips, C., Sicker, D., Grunwald, D.: Optimization decomposition for scheduling and system configuration in wireless networks. IEEE/ACM Trans. Netw. **22**(1), 271–284 (2014)
8. Li, M., Li, P., Huang, X., Fang, Y., Glisic, S.: Energy consumption optimization for multihop cognitive cellular networks. IEEE Trans. Mobile Comput. **14**(2), 358–372 (2015)
9. Zhao, Y., Li, Y., Zhang, H., Ge, N., Lu, J.: Fundamental tradeoffs on energy-aware D2D communication underlaying cellular networks: a dynamic graph approach. IEEE J. Sel. Areas Commun. **34**(4), 864–882 (2016)
10. Kim, T.S., Lim, H., Hou, J.C.: Understanding and improving the spatial reuse in multihop wireless networks. IEEE Trans. Mobile Comput. **7**(10), 1200–1212 (2008)

Reinforcement Learning Based Sensor Encryption and Power Control for Low-Latency WBANs

Siyuan Hong[1], Xiaozhen Lu[1], Liang Xiao[1($\boxtimes$)], Guohang Niu[1], and Helin Yang[2]

[1] Department of Information and Communication Engineering, Xiamen University, Xiamen, China
lxiao@xmu.edu.cn
[2] School of Electrical and Electronic Engineering, Nanyang Technological University, Singapore, Singapore

Abstract. Healthcare sensing data in wireless body area networks are vulnerable to active eavesdropping that simultaneously performs sniffing and jamming attacks to raise the sensor transmit power and thus steal more data. In this paper, we propose a reinforcement learning based sensor encryption and power control scheme to resist active eavesdropping for low-latency wireless body area networks. This scheme enables the coordinator to jointly optimize the sensor encryption key size and the transmit power based on the sensing data priority, the jamming power and the channel states of the sensor. We design a safe exploration algorithm based on the Dyna architecture to avoid choosing the encryption and power control policies that result in data transmission failure or data leakage. A secure sensing data transmission game between the coordinator and the eavesdropper is formulated to analyze the performance bound of our proposed scheme in terms of the signal-to-interference-plus-noise ratio of sensor signals, the eavesdropping rate, the energy consumption and the transmission latency based on the Nash Equilibrium of the game. Simulation results show that this scheme significantly decreases the eavesdropping rate and the transmission latency, and saves the sensor energy compared with the benchmark against active eavesdropping.

Keywords: Wireless body area networks · Active eavesdropping · Encryption · Power control · Reinforcement learning · Game theory

1 Introduction

Healthcare sensors in wireless body area networks (WBANs) collect physiological data such as electrocardiograph data and send them to coordinators such as smart phones and smart watches for clinical diagnostics and health monitoring [1]. The data are threatened by eavesdroppers, especially the active eavesdroppers that send jamming signals to raise the sensor transmit power and thus aggravate the sensing data leakage [2]. Power allocation at the sensors determines

© Springer Nature Switzerland AG 2021
Z. Liu et al. (Eds.): WASA 2021, LNCS 12938, pp. 575–586, 2021.
https://doi.org/10.1007/978-3-030-86130-8_45

their battery life, the transmission performance and the amount of leakage data [3]. For example, the Lagrange dual decomposition based sensor power control scheme as proposed in [4] increases the secrecy rate against passive eavesdropping based on the perfect wiretap channel state under dynamic WBANs.

Encryption key size determines the data protection level against eavesdropping and the computational overhead that is especially important for sensors with restricted computational resources and bandwidth [5]. The standard WBAN encryption scheme SEAT that applies the Advanced Encryption Standard (AES) with the fixed key size for all the healthcare sensing data suffers from severe data leakage under active eavesdropping and costs too much computational resources and bandwidth for the sensors [6].

The senor encryption and power control policy determines the secrecy rate, the transmission latency and the sensor energy consumption. The sensor policy optimization depends on the wiretap channel state and the eavesdropping patterns [2,7], which cannot be accurately obtained by the coordinator in a dynamic WBAN. Reinforcement learning (RL) enables radio devices to optimize transmission policy via trial-and-error without being aware of the wiretap channel states [8]. For instance, the sensor power control scheme as proposed in [9] that applies the convolutional neural network based actor-critic algorithm to improve the secrecy rate against active eavesdropping suffers from high computational overhead for WBANs.

In this paper, we propose a low-latency RL based sensor encryption and power control scheme for WBANs against active eavesdropping. The scheme applies the elliptic curve Diffie-Hellman protocol to distribute the secret key and uses the AES to encrypt sensing data based on the secret key. The coordinator uses safe RL to choose the sensor encryption key and transmit power based on the current state that consists of the sensing data priority, the received jamming power and the sensor-coordinator channel state. A security criterion such as the signal-to-interference-plus-noise ratio (SINR) of the sensor signals received at the coordinator is used in the policy distribution formulation to avoid severe data leakage. We design a Dyna architecture to exploit both the real and simulated anti-eavesdropping transmission experiences to estimate the network and channel state transition probability and thus accelerate the learning speed.

We formulate a secure sensing data transmission game to investigate the interactions between the coordinator and the eavesdropper. In this game, the coordinator chooses the sensor encryption and power control policy to maximize its utility consisting of the eavesdropping rate, the data protection level and the transmission performance, while the active eavesdropper chooses the jamming power to decrease the coordinator utility with less jamming power. The Nash equilibrium (NE) of the game is analyzed to provide the performance bounds of the proposed scheme and discuss how the sensor-coordinator channel impacts on the eavesdropping rate, the SINR, the sensor energy consumption and the transmission latency. Simulation results based on electroencephalography (EEG) verify the efficacy of our proposed scheme compared with the benchmark SEAT in [6].

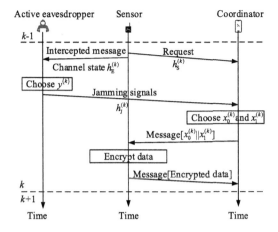

Fig. 1. Illustration of a WBAN system, where the sensor encrypts the sensing data with $x_0^{(k)}$ and sends it to the coordinator with power $x_1^{(k)}$ against an active eavesdropper.

The structure of this paper is organized as follows. We provide the system model in Sect. 2, followed by the RL based sensor encryption and power control scheme in Sect. 3. We analyze the performance bound of the proposed scheme in Sect. 4, provide the simulation results in Sect. 5 and draw the conclusion for this work in Sect. 6.

2   System Model

We consider a WBAN system as shown in Fig. 1, in which a sensor collects healthcare sensing data such as electrocardiogram data at sampling rate R and sends the data to the coordinator to provide healthcare applications such as heart rate monitoring. The sensing data priority denoted by $\chi^{(k)} \in \{1, 2, ..., K\}$ represents the emergency or importance of the healthcare information. For example, the seizure detection system in [10] uses a fixed 2 kHz sampling rate to generate the EEG data, reports the important data such as epileptic data with high priority and tolerates long latency for low priority data such as motor imagery data.

The shared secret key between the sensor and the coordinator is generated based on the elliptic curve Diffie-Hellman protocol. According to AES, Z kinds of encryption key are feasible to the sensor. The sensor uses the secret key with size $x_0^{(k)} \in \{V_z | 1 \leq z \leq Z\}$ to encrypt the sensing data.

According to [6], the sensor has N feasible transmit power levels with a power constraint P_S. The encrypted data is sent to the coordinator with the channel state $h_S^{(k)}$ and the sensor transmit power $x_1^{(k)} \in \{iP_S/N | 0 \leq i \leq N\}$. The coordinator estimates the SINR of the received sensor signals $\rho^{(k)}$, decrypts the sensing data and sends it to a remote medical server to provide the health monitoring [1].

A full-duplex active eavesdropper sniffs the WBAN to steal and sell the healthcare information for illegal profits. More specifically, the attacker sends jamming signals to induce the sensor to raise the transmit power for more data leakage [11]. As a powerful active eavesdropper, the smart eavesdropper even applies reinforcement learning to choose the jamming power $y^{(k)} \in \{jP_J/L | 0 \le j \le L\}$ from $L+1$ feasible jamming power with maximum value P_J. The attacker aims to steal more data from the WBAN with less jamming power. Let $h_E^{(k)}$ and $h_J^{(k)}$ denote the sensor-eavesdropper and eavesdropper-coordinator channel state, respectively.

3   RL Based Sensor Encryption and Power Control

We propose a reinforcement learning based WBAN encryption and power control scheme named LSET to choose the sensor encryption key x_0 and the transmit power x_1 against active eavesdropping without relying on the known wiretap channel states. This scheme estimates a state transition probability in the learning process to predict the next network and channel state and thus improves the learning efficiency. A safe architecture that uses the SINR of sensor signals as security criterion is designed to reduce explorations of the risky policies related to data leakage.

State: This scheme uses an energy detection method in [6] to evaluate the jamming power received by the coordinator p and applies channel estimation to evaluate the sensor-coordinator channel state h_S. The coordinator estimates the previous SINR of the sensor signals $\rho^{(k-1)}$ based on the bit error rate and evaluates the data priority χ to formulate the state as follows,

$$s^{(k)} = \left[\chi, p, h_S, \rho^{(k-1)} \right]. \tag{1}$$

The received jamming power, the SINR and the sensor-coordinator channel state are uniformly quantized into Ω_1, Ω_2 and Ω_3 levels, respectively, with the resulting state space denoted by $\boldsymbol{\Lambda}$.

Action: The action or the encryption and power control policy denoted by $\boldsymbol{x} = [x_i]_{0 \le i \le 1}$ is chosen based on the state $s^{(k)}$, the resulting Q-values denoted by $Q(s^{(k)}, \cdot)$ and the long-term risk level denoted by $E(s^{(k)}, \cdot)$. The action space of the coordinator denoted by $\boldsymbol{A}$ consists of $N+1$ feasible sensor transmit power and Z types of encryption key.

Policy Distribution: The scheme records the SINR and sets a security criterion ξ to avoid choosing risky actions that result in severe data leakage. More specifically, for $\forall a \in \boldsymbol{A}$, if the SINR under $(s^{(k)}, a)$ is lower than the criterion ξ, the risk level of $(s^{(k)}, a)$ equals to 1, and 0 otherwise. Let $\mathbf{I}(\cdot)$ be an indicator function with value 1 if the argument is true and 0 otherwise, and $\gamma \in [0, 1]$ denote the discount factor that represents the importance of the future risk levels. The long-term risk level $E(s^{(k)}, \boldsymbol{x})$ is updated based on the SINR of the future M time slots as follows,

$$E\left(s^{(k)}, \boldsymbol{x}\right) = \sum_{i=0}^{M} \gamma^i \mathbf{I}\left(\rho^{(k+i)} < \xi\right). \tag{2}$$

Algorithm 1. RL based sensor encryption and power control

1: **Initialize:** α, β, γ, D, M, Λ, $\mathbf{A}$, $\rho^{(0)}$, $\boldsymbol{Q} = 0$, $\boldsymbol{E} = 0$, $\Psi = 0$, $\Psi' = 0$, $\omega' = 0$, $\Phi = 0$ and $\omega = 0$

2: **for** $k = 1, 2, ...$ **do**

3:     Receive the request from the sensor

4:     Evaluate χ, p and h_S

5:     $s^{(k)} = \left[\chi, p, h_S, \rho^{(k-1)}\right]$

6:     Choose $\boldsymbol{x} = [x_i]_{0 \leq i \leq 1}$ via (3)

7:     Send $\boldsymbol{x}$ to the sensor

8:     Estimate l

9:     Receive the encrypted data from the sensor

10:    Estimate $\rho^{(k)}$, ι and τ

11:    Compute u via (4)

12:    Update $Q\left(s^{(k)}, \boldsymbol{x}\right)$ via the Bellman equation

13:    Update $E\left(s^{(k)}, \boldsymbol{x}\right)$ via (2)

14:    $\mathcal{P} \leftarrow \mathcal{P} \cup \left(s^{(k)}, \boldsymbol{x}\right)$

15:    $\Psi'\left(s^{(k)}, \boldsymbol{x}, s^{(k+1)}\right) \leftarrow \Psi'\left(s^{(k)}, \boldsymbol{x}, s^{(k+1)}\right) + 1$

16:    Update Ψ via (5)

17:    Compute $\Phi\left(s^{(k)}, \boldsymbol{x}, s^{(k+1)}\right)$ via (6)

18:    Obtain $\omega\left(s^{(k)}, \boldsymbol{x}\right)$ via (7)

19:    **for** $j = 1$ **to** D **do**

20:       Randomly select $\left(\bar{s}^{(j)}, \bar{\boldsymbol{x}}^{(j)}\right)$ from $\mathcal{P}$

21:       Obtain $\bar{s}^{(j+1)}$ via (6)

22:       Compute $\bar{u}^{(j)}$ via (4)

23:       Update $E\left(\bar{s}^{(j)}, \bar{\boldsymbol{x}}^{(j)}\right)$ via (2)

24:       Obtain $\omega\left(\bar{s}^{(j)}, \bar{\boldsymbol{x}}^{(j)}\right)$ via (7)

25:       Update $Q\left(\bar{s}^{(j)}, \bar{\boldsymbol{x}}^{(j)}\right)$ via the Bellman equation

26:    **end for**

27: **end for**

The sensor encryption and power control policy distribution depends on the Q-values and the long-term risk level that is given by

$$\Pr\left(\boldsymbol{x} = \boldsymbol{a}\right) = \frac{\exp\left(\frac{Q\left(s^{(k)}, \boldsymbol{a}\right)}{1 + E\left(s^{(k)}, \boldsymbol{a}\right)}\right)}{\sum_{\hat{\boldsymbol{x}} \in \mathbf{A}} \exp\left(\frac{Q\left(s^{(k)}, \hat{\boldsymbol{x}}\right)}{1 + E\left(s^{(k)}, \hat{\boldsymbol{x}}\right)}\right)}. \tag{3}$$

Based on the chosen $\boldsymbol{x}$, the coordinator sends the encryption key x_0 and the transmit power x_1 to the sensor.

Reward Function: The scheme estimates the data protection level l based on x_0 [5] and formulates the eavesdropping rate as $\log(1 + \kappa x_1 p)$ according to [12].

After receiving the encrypted data from the sensor, the coordinator measures the bit error rate to estimate the SINR $\rho^{(k)}$, and estimates the sensor energy consumption ι and the transmission latency τ.

The scheme aims to make a trade-off among the data protection level l, the eavesdropping rate, the SINR of sensor signals $\rho^{(k)}$, the sensor energy consumption ι and the transmission latency τ. Thus, the resulting utility is designed by

$$u = c_0 l - c_1 \log(1 + \kappa x_1 p) + c_2 \rho^{(k)} - c_3 \iota - \chi \tau, \tag{4}$$

where $[c_i]_{0 \leq i \leq 3}$ denotes the coefficient vector. According to the iterative Bellman equation in [13], the Q-values are updated based on the learning rate $\alpha \in [0, 1]$ and the discount factor $\beta \in [0, 1]$.

The anti-eavesdropping transmission experience $(s^{(k)}, x)$ is stored in a replay pool denoted by $\mathcal{P}$. By applying a Dyna architecture, the coordinator updates the counter of the next state Ψ' from $\mathcal{P}$ to calculate the occurrence count of the next state, denoted by Ψ, i.e.,

$$\Psi = \sum_{s' \in \Lambda} \Psi'\left(s^{(k)}, x, s'\right). \tag{5}$$

The state transition probability Φ from state-action $(s^{(k)}, x)$ to the next state $s^{(k+1)}$ is calculated by

$$\Phi\left(s^{(k)}, x, s^{(k+1)}\right) = \frac{\Psi'\left(s^{(k)}, x, s^{(k+1)}\right)}{\Psi}. \tag{6}$$

The reward record denoted by $\omega'\left(s^{(k)}, x, \Psi\right) = u$ is used to calculate the modeled reward given by

$$\omega\left(s^{(k)}, x\right) = \frac{1}{\Psi} \sum_{i=1}^{\Psi} \omega'\left(s^{(k)}, x, i\right). \tag{7}$$

The coordinator generates D simulated anti-eavesdropping transmission experiences to provide additional policy learning for faster optimization. In the j-th update, $(\bar{s}^{(j)}, \bar{x}^{(j)})$ is randomly chosen from $\mathcal{P}$ to calculate the simulated utility $\bar{u}^{(j)}$ and update the long-term risk level $E(\bar{s}^{(j)}, \bar{x}^{(j)})$ via (2), which is input to the Dyna architecture. By (6) and (7), the scheme obtains the next state $\bar{s}^{(j+1)}$ and the modeled utility $\omega(\bar{s}^{(j)}, \bar{x}^{(j)})$, which are used to update the Q-values according to the Bellman equation as summarized in Algorithm 1.

4   Performance Analysis

In the secure sensing data transmission game, the coordinator chooses the sensor encryption key $x_0 \in \{V_z | 1 \leq z \leq Z\}$ and the transmit power $x_1 \in [0, P_S]$ to maximize its utility in (4), while the active eavesdropper determines the jamming power $y \in [0, P_J]$ to degrade the coordinator utility with less jamming power. By deriving the NE of the game, we provide the performance bound of the proposed scheme.

According to [14], the eavesdropping rate in the WBAN system is modeled as

$$r = \log\left(1 + \frac{x_1 h_E}{\eta_E}\right), \tag{8}$$

where η_E denotes the receiver noise power at the eavesdropper. The SINR of sensor signals is given by

$$\rho = \frac{x_1 h_S}{\eta_C + y h_J}, \tag{9}$$

where η_C denotes the receiver noise power at the coordinator.

For simplicity, the data protection level l is assumed to be $\log x_0$, and the encryption latency is modeled with λx_0, where λ denotes the latency coefficient. We assume that the transmission latency mainly depends on the encryption latency λx_0. The sensor energy consumption ι includes the encryption energy consumption $b x_0$ and the transmission energy consumption $a x_1$, i.e., $\iota = a x_1 + b x_0$, where a and b are the energy coefficients. The sensor-coordinator, the sensor-eavesdropper and the eavesdropper-coordinator channel states are assumed to be static in the game.

Let

$$g(x_0) = c_0 \log x_0 - c_3 b x_0 - \chi \lambda x_0, \tag{10}$$

and

$$f(x_1) = \frac{c_2 x_1 h_S}{\eta_C + y h_J} - c_1 \log\left(1 + \frac{x_1 h_E}{\eta_E}\right) - c_3 a x_1. \tag{11}$$

By (4) and (8)–(11), the coordinator utility is given by

$$\hat{u} = g(x_0) + f(x_1). \tag{12}$$

The eavesdropper utility denoted by $\hat{u}_J$ deceases with the coordinator utility $\hat{u}$ and the jamming power, which is modeled as

$$\hat{u}_J = -\hat{u} - c_4 y, \tag{13}$$

where c_4 is the jamming energy coefficient.

Theorem 1. *The performance bound of LSET is given by*

$$r \geq \log\left(1 + \frac{P_S h_E}{\eta_E}\right) \tag{14}$$

$$\rho \leq \frac{P_S h_S}{\eta_C + P_J h_J} \tag{15}$$

$$\iota \geq a P_S + b V_1 \tag{16}$$

$$\tau \geq \lambda V_1 \tag{17}$$

$$\hat{u} \leq c_0 \log V_1 - c_1 \log\left(1 + \frac{P_S h_E}{\eta_E}\right) + \frac{c_2 P_S h_S}{\eta_C + P_J h_J} - c_3\left(a P_S + b V_1\right) - \chi \lambda V_1, \tag{18}$$

if

$$c_3 b + \chi\lambda > \max_{1 \leq z \leq Z} \left\{ \frac{\log V_z - \log V_1}{V_z - V_1} \right\} \tag{19}$$

$$c_2 h_S > \max \left\{ \frac{c_1 h_E (\eta_C + P_J h_J)}{(\eta_E + P_S h_E) \ln 2} + c_3 a (\eta_C + P_J h_J), \frac{c_4 (P_J h_J + \eta_C)^2}{P_S h_J} \right\}. \tag{20}$$

The corresponding encryption key and the transmit power are given by V_1 and P_S.

Proof. By (10), if (19) holds, $\forall x_0 \in \{V_z | 1 \leq z \leq Z\}$, we have

$$g(V_1) = c_0 \log V_1 - c_3 b V_1 - \chi\lambda V_1 \tag{21}$$
$$\geq c_0 \log x_0 - c_3 b x_0 - \chi\lambda x_0 = g(x_0). \tag{22}$$

By (11), if (20) holds, $\forall x_1 \in [0, P_S]$, we have

$$\frac{df(x_1)}{dx_1} = \frac{c_2 h_S}{\eta_C + P_J h_J} - \frac{c_1 h_E}{(\eta_E + x_1 h_E) \ln 2} - c_3 a > 0. \tag{23}$$

Thus, $\forall x_1 \in [0, P_S]$, we have

$$f(P_S) \geq f(x_1). \tag{24}$$

Hence, $\forall x_0 \in \{V_z | 1 \leq z \leq Z\}$ and $\forall x_1 \in [0, P_S]$, we have

$$\hat{u}\big((P_S, V_1), P_J\big)$$
$$= c_0 \log V_1 - c_1 \log \left(1 + \frac{P_S h_E}{\eta_E}\right) - c_3 a P_S - c_3 b V_1 + \frac{c_2 P_S h_S}{\eta_C + P_J h_J} - \chi\lambda V_1 \tag{25}$$
$$\geq c_0 \log x_0 - c_1 \log \left(1 + \frac{x_1 h_E}{\eta_E}\right) - c_3 a x_1 - c_3 b x_0 + \frac{c_2 x_1 h_S}{\eta_C + P_J h_J} - \chi\lambda x_0$$
$$= \hat{u}\big((x_0, x_1), P_J\big). \tag{26}$$

By (13), if (20) holds, $\forall y \in [0, P_J]$, we have

$$\frac{\partial \hat{u}_J\big((P_S, V_1), y\big)}{\partial y} = \frac{c_2 P_S h_S h_J}{(\eta_C + y h_J)^2} - c_4 > 0. \tag{27}$$

Hence, $\forall y \in [0, P_J]$, we have

$$\hat{u}_J\big((P_S, V_1), P_J\big) \geq \hat{u}_J\big((P_S, V_1), y\big). \tag{28}$$

By (25), (26) and (28), we have an NE given by $((P_S, V_1), P_J)$. Thus, by $\iota = a x_1 + b x_0$, $\tau = \lambda x_0$ and (8)–(12), we have (14)–(18).

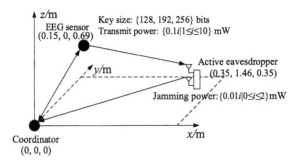

Fig. 2. Simulation topology based on EEG in a WBAN, in which the sensor sends the healthcare sensing data to the coordinator every time slot against an active eavesdropper.

Remark 1. The data is encrypted with the shortest key size if the encryption energy consumption b exceeds a bound based on the data priority χ and the encryption latency λ given by (19). As shown in (20), if the sensor-coordinator channel state h_S is larger than the bound that relies on the maximum transmit power P_S, the maximum jamming power P_J and the channel states of the eavesdropper, the sensor sends the encrypted data with its maximum power P_S. The resulting eavesdropping rate, SINR, energy consumption, transmission latency and coordinator utility are given by (14)–(18).

5 Simulation Results

Simulations were performed based on EEG to evaluate the performance of LSET and SEAT in a WBAN. The initial topology as shown in Fig. 2, in which the sensor located at (0.15, 0, 0.69) m collects sensing data with three priority. The sensor sampling rate 200 Hz according to [15], and the data is encrypted based on the AES with key size chosen from 128, 192 and 256 bits, respectively. According to [16], the corresponding encryption energy consumption and latency are (1.104 mJ, 1.09 s), (1.742 mJ, 1.72 s) and (2.603 mJ, 2.57 s), respectively. The encrypted message protected with Bose, Ray-Chaudhuri, Hocquenghem code is sent in each time slot that lasts 1 s to the coordinator located at (0, 0, 0) with power from 0.1 mW to 1 mW at 485.7 Kbps data rate according to [17].

The sensor-coordinator channel is assumed to change every time slot based on the log normal channel model with 3.11 path loss exponent and the shadowing that follows a zero-mean normal distribution with variance of 6 [18]. An active eavesdropper located at (0.35, 1.46, 0.35) m applies Q-learning to choose the jamming power from 0 to 0.02 mW with the goal of stealing more healthcare sensing data with less energy consumption. The receiver noise power of both the coordinator and the eavesdropper is −94 dBm. The security criterion is set as 9 dB to evaluate the risk level. The benchmark SEAT in [6] uses 192 bits encryption key and 0.5 mW sensor transmit power.

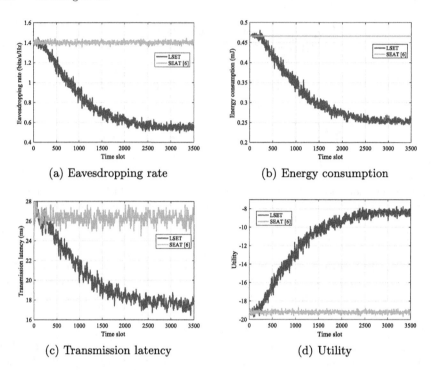

(a) Eavesdropping rate   (b) Energy consumption

(c) Transmission latency   (d) Utility

Fig. 3. Performance of the learning based sensor encryption and power control scheme in a WBAN against active eavesdropping.

As shown in Fig. 3, our proposed scheme decreases the eavesdropping rate, the sensor energy consumption and the transmission latency of the WBAN until reaching the optimal transmission policy at the 3500-th time slot. For example, LSET decreases the eavesdropping rate by 58.6% and the transmission latency by 34.7%, saves the sensor energy consumption by 44.6% and improves the coordinator utility by 56.4% after 3500 time slots. This scheme significantly outperforms SEAT in terms of 50.3% lower eavesdropping rate, 38.2% less energy consumption, 27.3% transmission latency reduction, and 46.2% utility improvement at the 1500-th time slot.

Figure 4 provides the average performance of LSET in the WBAN over 20 runs each lasting 3000 time slots, showing that our scheme efficiently protects the healthcare sensing data against eavesdropper. For instance, LSET has performance improvement with 98.6% lower eavesdropping rate, 13.1% less energy consumption, 12.1% lower transmission latency and 83.8% higher coordinator utility, as the sensor-eavesdropper distance changes from 1 m to 5 m. The performance of LSET exceeds SEAT under the variant sensor-eavesdropper distance scenario. For example, the performance gain over SEAT in terms of the eavesdropping rate increases from 37.8% to 59.1% as the eavesdropper moves from 1 m away to 3 m close to the sensor.

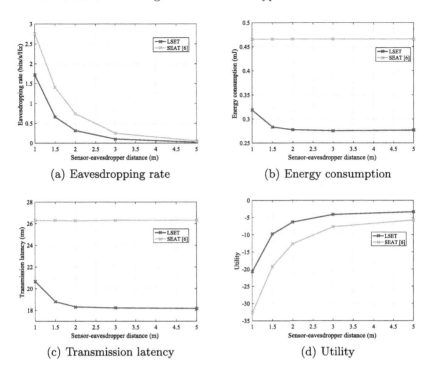

(a) Eavesdropping rate

(b) Energy consumption

(c) Transmission latency

(d) Utility

Fig. 4. Performance of the learning based sensor encryption and power control scheme in a WBAN against active eavesdropping.

6   Conclusion

In this paper, we proposed a low-latency sensor encryption and power control scheme, which jointly chooses the sensor encryption key and the transmit power to improve the coordinator utility. We formulated a secure sensing data transmission game between the coordinator and the active eavesdropper to provide the performance bound of the proposed RL based WBAN scheme. Simulation results based on EEG show that our proposed scheme outperforms the benchmark SEAT with 50.3% lower eavesdropping rate, 38.2% less sensor energy consumption and 27.3% lower transmission latency against an active eavesdropper 1.5 m away from the sensor.

Acknowledgment. This work was supported by the National Natural Science Foundation of China under Grant 61971366 and Grant 61731012, and in part by the Fundamental Research Funds for the central universities No. 20720200077.

References

1. He, D., Zeadally, S., Kumar, N., Lee, J.-H.: Anonymous authentication for wireless body area networks with provable security. IEEE Syst. J. **11**(4), 2590–2601 (2017)
2. Tang, X., Ren, P., Wang, Y., Han, Z.: Combating full-duplex active eavesdropper: a hierarchical game perspective. IEEE Trans. Commun. **65**(3), 1379–1395 (2017)
3. Osorio, D.P.M., Alves, H., Olivo, E.E.B.: On the secrecy performance and power allocation in relaying networks with untrusted relay in the partial secrecy regime. IEEE Trans. Inf. Forensics Secur. **1**(15), 2268–2281 (2019)
4. Zhang, H., Xing, H., Cheng, J., Nallanathan, A., Leung, V.C.M.: Secure resource allocation for OFDMA two-way relay wireless sensor networks without and with cooperative jamming. IEEE Trans. Ind. Informat. **12**(5), 1714–1725 (2016)
5. Hamamreh, J.M., Furqan, H.M., Arslan, H.: Classifications and applications of physical layer security techniques for confidentiality: a comprehensive survey. IEEE Commun. Surveys Tuts. **21**(2), 1773–1828 (2018)
6. IEEE Standard for Local and metropolitan area networks - Part 15.6: Wireless Body Area Networks, IEEE Std. 802.15.6-2012 (2012)
7. Dautov, R., Tsouri, G.R.: Securing while sampling in wireless body area networks with application to electrocardiography. IEEE J. Biomed. Health Inform. **20**(1), 135–142 (2016)
8. Xiao, L., Sheng, G., Liu, S., Dai, H., Peng, M., Song, J.: Deep reinforcement learning-enabled secure visible light communication against eavesdropping. IEEE Trans. Commun. **67**(10), 6994–7005 (2019)
9. Do, Q.V., Hoan, T., Koo, I.: Optimal power allocation for energy-efficient data transmission against full-duplex active eavesdroppers in wireless sensor networks. IEEE Sensors J. **9**(13), 5333–5346 (2019)
10. Sawan, M., Salam, M.T., Lan, J.L., et al.: Wireless recording systems: from non-invasive EEG-NIRS to invasive EEG devices. IEEE Trans. Biomed. Circuits Sys. **7**(2), 186–195 (2013)
11. Zhou, X., Maham, B., Hjorungnes, A.: Pilot contamination for active eavesdropping. IEEE Trans. Wireless Commun. **11**(3), 903–907 (2012)
12. Chorti, A., Perlaza, S.M., Han, Z., Poor, H.V.: On the resilience of wireless multiuser networks to passive and active eavesdroppers. IEEE J. Sel. Areas Commun. **31**(9), 1850–1863 (2013)
13. Min, M., et al.: Learning-based privacy-aware offloading for healthcare IoT with energy harvesting. IEEE Internet Things J. **6**(3), 4307–4316 (2019)
14. Moosavi, H., Bui, F.M.: Delay-aware optimization of physical layer security in multi-hop wireless body area networks. IEEE Trans. Inf. Forensics Secur. **11**(9), 1928–1939 (2016)
15. Bertrand, A.: Distributed signal processing for wireless EEG sensor networks. IEEE Trans. Neural Syst. Rehabil. Eng. **23**(6), 923–935 (2015)
16. Liu, Z., Huang, X., Hu, Z., Khan, M.K., Seo, H., Zhou, L.: On emerging family of elliptic curves to secure Internet of Things: ECC comes of age. IEEE Trans. Dependable Secure Comput. **14**(3), 237–248 (2017)
17. Zang, W., Zhang, S., Li, Y.: An accelerometer-assisted transmission power control solution for energy-efficient communications in WBAN. IEEE J. Sel. Areas Commun. **34**(12), 3427–3437 (2016)
18. Liu, Z., Liu, B., Chen, C.W.: Joint power-rate-slot resource allocation in energy harvesting-powered wireless body area networks. IEEE Trans. Veh. Technol. **67**(12), 12152–12164 (2018)

Modeling the Instantaneous Saturation Throughput of UAV Swarm Networks

Jie Wang, Lei Lei$^{(\boxtimes)}$, Shengsuo Cai, and Mengfan Yan

College of Electronic and Information Engineering, Nanjing University
of Aeronautics and Astronautics, Nanjing 211106, China
{wangjie199696,leilei,caishengsuo,mengfan.yan}@nuaa.edu.cn

Abstract. Unmanned Aerial Vehicle (UAV) swarm has been widely applied in border surveillance, public safety, transportation management and so on. Affected by the complex mission environment and rapidly changing network topology, the network performance decreases drastically especially when an unsuitable contention window size is selected in traditional media access control (MAC) protocol. In this work, we first introduce a node-counts-based UAV swarm MAC (NCU_MAC) protocol to dynamically adjust the contention window size according to the number of neighbor nodes. Next, a four- dimensional Markov Chain model is developed to model the media access process and evaluate the performance of NCU_MAC. The expressions of the collision, transmission probability and saturation throughput are obtained theoretically. Simulation results are presented to validate the effectiveness of the proposed model and show the saturation throughput of the swarm network in the process of cooperative movement.

Keywords: UAV swarm network · Saturation throughput · MAC protocol · Markov chain model

1 Introduction

Unmanned aerial vehicle (UAV) swarm is a type of swarm-robot system that can be remotely and autonomously controlled. It has been widely applied in border surveillance, public safety, and transportation management, etc. The unpredictable mission modes and complex environments also put forward higher requirements on the network, especially on MAC protocols. In addition to classical hidden terminal, exposed terminal and fairness problems, fluctuation in link quality poses new challenges to the design of MAC protocol.

One of the functions of MAC layer is to provide equal access opportunities for all nodes in the network. Bianchi first proposed a two-dimensional Markov model to analyze the traditional DCF protocol in IEEE 802.11 MAC layer [1]. Allocating wireless channel resources for each UAV in the network, MAC protocols [2] directly affect the overall performance of the network. In the literature, MAC protocols [3, 4] can be divided into two classes, i.e., scheduling and competitive ones. The traditional MAC protocol uses binary exponential backoff algorithm which incurs large discrepancies in the throughput achieved by the links sharing the UAV swarm network. Collision

© Springer Nature Switzerland AG 2021
Z. Liu et al. (Eds.): WASA 2021, LNCS 12938, pp. 587–599, 2021.
https://doi.org/10.1007/978-3-030-86130-8_46

manifests as a throughput distribution in which a few dominating links receive very high throughput and many starving links receive very low throughput. Due to the high mobility of UAVs, if the number of UAV is greater than the contention window owing to a fixed binary exponential backoff window [5], it is possible that multiple UAVs will choose the same back-off value, causing high collision and low throughput.

In response to the above deficiencies, we propose a four-dimensional Markov chain model to analyze the instantaneous saturation throughput. Firstly, a node-counts-based MAC protocol is proposed to dynamically adjust the backoff window size according to the current interference situation to improve the performance of traditional DCF protocol. Secondly, aiming at the problem of hidden and exposed terminals in multi-hop networks, we divide collision into instantaneous collision and continuous collision. Thirdly, by introducing "pseudo-state" into the Markov chain model, the instantaneous collision and continuous collision in the process of multi-hop data transmission are analyzed.

The remainder of this paper is organized as follows. Section 2 describes the node-counts-based MAC protocol for UAV swarm network. In Sect. 3, we introduce the four-dimensional Markov chain model in detail. Next, the simulation and analysis results are given in Sect. 4. Finally, Sect. 5 gives some conclusion remarks.

2   Node-Counts-Based MAC Protocol for UAV Swarm Network

In this section, we first briefly introduce the cooperation control of UAV swarm [6] with virtual potential field method. Next, the node-counts-based MAC protocol for high-speed UAV swarm network is described in detail.

The basic idea of virtual potential field method is to abstract the environment into a virtual potential field, and the intelligent individual moves under the influence of the forces in the virtual potential field [7]. As is shown in Fig. 1, the forces on an individual can be divided into three types: navigation force (NF), topology force (TF), obstacle avoidance force (OAF). Navigation force drives the UAV to reach the designated point which can be a temporary point in the path plan or the end point of the whole movement. Topology force not only plays a key role in maintaining the topology structure of the swarm, but also effectively avoids collision accidents between UAVs. The obstacle avoidance force hinders the movement of swarm. Compared with traditional geometric vector and model predictive control methods, virtual potential field method has the advantages of fast path planning and good real- time performance. It can plan a path that can quickly reach the destination for the swarm, and effectively avoid obstacles in the virtual potential field.

Traditional IEEE 802.11 DCF protocol was originally designed for single-hop networks, but its basic access mechanism has been widely used in various multi-hop environments. When traditional DCF protocol is applied to UAV swarm network, it will inevitably appear serious unfairness phenomenon among different links. So choosing a fixed contention window will obviously increase the collision probability.

In order to avoid the collision problem caused by too small contention window, we introduce a node-counts-based MAC (NCU_MAC) protocol to dynamically adjust the contention window value according to the current interference situation. In NCU_MAC,

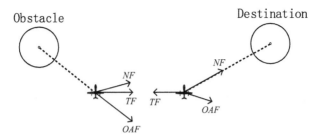

Fig. 1. Force principle of UAVs.

the UAV broadcasts its position to the neighbor nodes, so that each UAV knows the number of neighbor nodes within its detection range. Denote the number of UAVs in the network by N_0. The flowchart is as Fig. 2.

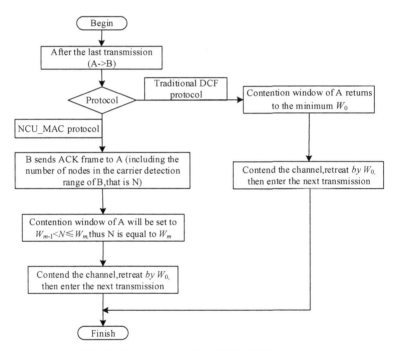

Fig. 2. The flowchart of the NCU_MAC protocol.

When the receiving UAV sends an ACK frame to the sending UAV, the number of UAVs N within the carrier detection range will be added to the frame header, where N ranges in $[0, N_0]$. The maximum contention window W_m is set to satisfy $N_0 \leq W_m$ to avoid multiple UAVs from selecting the same backoff window value and causing collision. After receiving ACK, the sending UAV will dynamically adjust the size of the contention window according to the number of received UAVs, instead of setting to the minimum value W_0 adopted in traditional mechanisms. The NCU_MAC protocol can dynamically adjust the size of the contention window according to the number of interfering UAVs, thus effectively improve the network performance.

In view of the above optimization of the traditional DCF protocol, the following will focus on modeling the throughput [8] of NCU_MAC in a multi-hop network. Since in a multi-hop network, nodes cannot monitor the state of all other nodes, the sending time of each node may overlap arbitrarily. This paper divides the network time into a series of fixed-length time slots, and establishes a four-dimensional (4D) Markov chain model based on fixed-length time slots.

3   Modeling the Saturation Throughput of NCU_MAC

In this section, we use the fixed-length time slot and "pseudo-state" to model and analyze the throughput of UAVs with a 4D Markov chain model. Next, we analyze different states of UAVs in the swarm from the backoff, transmission and suspend process respectively, and obtain the expressions of node collision, transmission probability and throughput.

3.1   Fixed-Length Time Slots

Variable-length time slots [9] has been widely used in the modeling of Markov chains in IEEE 802.11 DCF protocol. It is only suitable for single hop network where all nodes can view the same channel state. However, there are hidden terminals in a multi-hop network, which may cause collision. Fixed-length time slots can not only simplify the analysis of link states in multi-hop networks, but also avoid the influence of hidden terminals on the accuracy of network performance analysis. Therefore, this paper divides the network time into a series of fixed-length time slots of δ without considering the channel state. As is shown in Fig. 3, p_{c1} and p_{c2} are the collision probabilities in the first and the subsequent transmission slots, respectively.

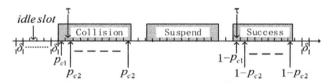

Fig. 3. Fixed-length time slot.

The single link throughput can be expressed as:

$$S(n) = \frac{\tau(n)p_s(n)E[P]}{\sigma} \qquad (1)$$

where $\tau(n)$ is the transmission probability that the node sends out a packet after an idle slot, $E[P]$ is the data successfully received in time δ, and $p_s(n)$ is the probability that the data packet of link n is successfully received.

3.2 Collision Probability

In Fig. 4, r_{tx} and r_{cs} represent the communication and carrier detection range of the sending UAV, respectively, and r_{co} represents the collision interference range of the receiving UAV. Suppose A sends data frame to B. The intersection of the carrier detection range of A and the collision interference range of B is termed the instantaneous collision area. The area outside the physical carrier detection range of A and within the collision interference range of B is the persistent collision area.

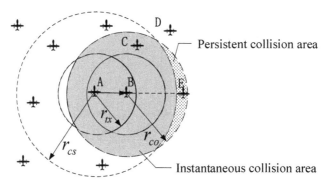

Fig. 4. Collision interference.

The collision probability is usually referred to the conditional packet loss probability. We assume that the collision probability in the first slot of transmission initiated by the sending node of link n is $p_{c1}(n)$, the collision probability in any other time slot during the transmission process is $p_{c2}(n)$. The sending process must take D time slots. Then the probability of the packet sent on link n being received successfully can be expressed as:

$$p_s(n) = (1 - p_{c1}(n))(1 - p_{c2}(n))^{D-1} \tag{2}$$

3.3 Four-Dimensional Markov Chain Model

Figure 5 shows the Markov chain model with fixed time slots, where the dotted ellipse below represents the suspend process. For any node n, its state at a certain moment can be expressed as $\{i, j, k, l\}$.

i has four values (0, 1, 2, 3), representing four different processes: backoff process, successful process, collision process, and suspend process.

l represents the number of slots left in the current procedure, and l is always equal to k during the backoff process.

j and k represent the backoff stage and the backoff counter, respectively. The backoff counter is decremented by one at the end of each backoff slot. If a packet transmission fails the backoff stage will increase. When the backoff counter reaches the retransmission limit, the current packet is discarded.

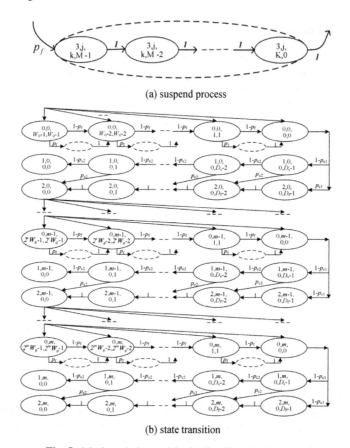

(a) suspend process

(b) state transition

Fig. 5. Markov chain model with fixed length time slot.

3.4 Backoff Process

Suppose $p(i, j, k, l)$ is the probability that a state of node at a certain moment is $\{i, j, k, l\}$. The size of the contention window size W_i can be expressed by the equations:

$$W_i = \begin{cases} 2^i W_0 & 0 \leq i \leq m' \\ W_{max} & m' < i \leq m \end{cases}$$

$$m' = \log_2 \frac{W_{max}}{W_0}$$

(3)

The backoff time is uniformly chosen in the range $[0, W_i - 1]$ at each transmission, which is an integer multiple of the fixed-length slot length δ. The node begins to transmit when the backoff counter reaches zero. Contention window of the node will be restored to the minimum value W_0, if the data is successfully received.

Based on Fig. 5, the state of backoff process can be obtained as follows:

$$p(0, j, k, k) = p(0, j, k + 1, k + 1) + \frac{(1 - p_s(n))p(0, j - 1, 0, 0)}{W_j} \quad 0 < k \leq W_j - 2, \ 0 < j \leq m$$

(4)

When k is equal to $W_j - 1$, $p(0, j, W_j - 1, W_j - 1) = \dfrac{(1 - p_s(n))p(0, j - 1, 0, 0)}{W_j}$

$$(5)$$

For any time slot, the probability $A(n)$ that node n is in the backoff process is the sum of the probabilities of all the backoff time slots, i.e.,

$$
\begin{aligned}
A(n) &= \sum_{j=0}^{m} \sum_{k=1}^{W_j-1} p(0, j, k, k) \\
&= \frac{p(0, 0, 0, 0)}{2} \frac{1 - (2(1 - p_s(n)))^{m+1}}{1 - 2(1 - p_s(n))} W_0 \\
&\quad - \frac{p(0, 0, 0, 0)}{2} \frac{1 - (1 - p_s(n))^{m+1}}{p_s(n)}
\end{aligned}
$$

$$(6)$$

3.5 Transmission Process

Transmission process includes successful transmission process and collision process.
    Successful transmission process:

$$
p(1, j, 0, l) = \begin{cases} p(0, j, 0, 0)(1 - p_{c1}(n)) & l = D - 1 \\ p(1, j, 0, l + 1)(1 - p_{c2}(n)) \ 0 \le l < D - 1 \end{cases}
$$

$$(7)$$

The first equation in (7) indicates that if no collision occurs when the node backoff counter reaches zero, the node will enter the successful transmission process. Therefore, the second means that the node does not encounter continuous collision in the subsequent time slots of the transmission process. In fact, in the assumption of perfect channel sensing by every node, collision may occur only when two (or more) packets are transmitted within the same slot time.
    Collision process:

$$
p(2, j, 0, k) = \begin{cases} p(0, j, 0, 0)p_{c1}(n) & k = D - 1 \\ p_{c2}(n) \sum_{l=k+1}^{D-1} p(1, j, 0, l) + p(2, j, 0, D - 1) \ 0 \le k < D - 1 \end{cases}
$$

$$(8)$$

Equation (8) indicates that node can enter the collision process with the probability of $p_{c1}(n)$ from the backoff process, or enter the collision process with the probability of $p_{c2}(n)$ from the successful sending process.

3.6 Suspend Process

We assume that node n is suspended with probability $p_f(n)$ in a backoff slot, and the duration of the suspend process is expected to be $M(n)$ time slots as shown in Fig. 5. In this section, we will refer to [10] to solve $p_f(n)$ and $M(n)$ by using a cyclic iterative method. It adopts the continuous time Markov model to calculate the proportion of the time that the node listens to the channel idle. To compute $p_f(n)$ and $M(n)$, we will resort to the continuous time Markov model. In the continuous time Markov model, the arrival rate of packets on each link is assumed to be a Poisson process with an average of $g(n)$, and the average length of packets is $1/u(n)$. The conditions of coexisting links in the network constitute each state of the continuous time Markov model, and the probability is

$$Q(B) = \left(\prod_{n \in B} \frac{g(n)}{\mu(n)} Q(\varphi) \right) \tag{9}$$

$Q(\varphi)$ means that no node is sending data.

In the fixed-length slot Markov chain, the probability of node n listening to the idle channel is $(1 - \tau(n))(1 - p_f(n))$. In the continuous time Markov model, this probability can be expressed as $e^{-G(n)\sigma}$, and then the suspend probability $p_f(n)$ can be expressed as

$$p_f(n) = 1 - \frac{e^{-G(n)\sigma}}{1 - \tau(n)} \tag{10}$$

$G(n)$ represents the total packet sending rate of node n and its neighbor nodes when node n can initiate transmission. $A(n)$ represents the probability that node n is listening for channel idle as follows:

$$A(n) = \sum_{H \subset N(n)} Q(H) = \frac{\sum\limits_{H \subset N(n)} \left(\prod\limits_{i \in H} \frac{g(i)}{u(i)} \right)}{\sum\limits_{all} \left(\prod\limits_{i \in H} \frac{g(i)}{u(i)} \right)} \tag{11}$$

If the channel is idle for a period equal to a distributed interframe space, the packet can be sent successfully only when there is no interference node sending data within the range of its persistent collision. Therefore, the throughput on the link of node n is

$$s(n) = A(n)g(n)(1 - p_{c2}(n)) \tag{12}$$

So far, we have established the relationship between continuous time Markov model and fixed-length time slot Markov chain through Eqs. (6) and (10). First, we preliminarily set $g(n)$ and $u(n)$, then $p_f(n)$ and $A(n)$ can be calculated by Eqs. (10) and (11). Substituting the calculated $A(n)$ into Eq. (6) $M(n)$ can be calculated. Given $p_f(n)$ and $M(n)$, the variables in the fixed-length time-slot Markov chain model can be solved. Then, the saturation throughput of the link of node n can be calculated by Eq. (1). Next, $g(n)$ is updated by Eq. (12), and other variables (such as $p_f(n)$, $\tau(n)$, $p_{c1}(n)$, $p_{c2}(n)$, $p_s(n)$, etc.) can be updated accordingly. These variables can again be used to calculate link saturation throughput according to Eq. (1). This cycle is repeated until the solution of the model tends to be stable.

4   Simulation Results

Our simulation is conducted in a 5000 m * 5000 m rectangle area with two circular obstacles locating at positions [2500, 2500] and [3500, 2500]. The total number of UAV nodes is 60, single-hop transmission range of UAV is 250 m, and the optimal distance between UAVs is 100 m.

In the initial state, UAVs are randomly distributed in the range of [0, 1000] in both horizontal and vertical coordinates, as shown in Fig. 6. Figure 6(b) gives the initial network topology of UAV swarm. The UAVs within the single-hop range are marked with dotted lines. The solid line represents the real transmission service at the current time, and the arrow direction represents the service transmission direction. For convenience, the index of sending UAV is used to represent the link sequence number. The UAV swarm moves from starting point to end point under the action of virtual potential field method introduced in Sect. 2. Each UAV will randomly select one UAV within its transmission range for data transmission periodically. The packet length is fixed at 256 bytes. Table 1 shows the values of some simulation parameters.

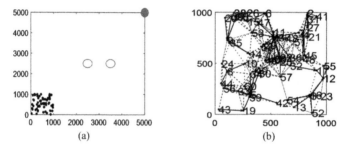

Fig. 6. Initial state of the UAV swarm: (a) movement scenario, (b) network topology.

Table 1. Parameter settings

Simulation time	320 S	SINR threshold	10 dB
Transmission rate	11 Mbps	Retransmission threshold	4
MAC layer head	224 bits	SIFS frame	10 μs
Physical layer head	92 bits	Length of the time slot	20 μs

We analyze the saturation throughput of UAV swarm throughout the whole movement cycle in Fig. 7. At two given moments, T = 125 s and T = 230 s, the results of collision and transmission probability are shown in Figs. 8 and 9. It can be observed that the simulation results coincide with theoretic values, which validates the accuracy of our proposed model.

Figure 7 shows a schematic diagram of the instantaneous saturation throughput of the UAV swarm based on the proposed Markov chain model. When T changes from 50 s to 140 s, due to the large density of swarm at this time, it leads to an increase in the collision probability and lower throughput. After T = 150 s, the swarm density decreases owing to passing the obstacles. Throughput is gradually increasing to reach the maximum. As the swarm reaches the destination, the density of the maximum. As the swarm reaches the destination, the density of the swarm increases again, resulting in a gradual decrease in throughput after T = 250 s. The topologies of swarm at 125 s and 230 s are shown in Fig. 7(a) and 7(b), respectively. The difference between the two cycles is that the obstacle avoidance force in the former has a relatively large effect on the swarm, thus leading to a significant increase in the overall density of UAVs.

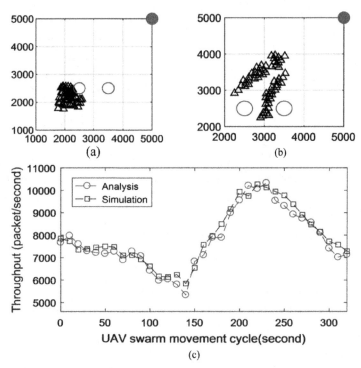

Fig. 7. Instantaneous saturation throughput: (a) topology at T = 125 s, (b) topology at T = 230 s, (c) throughput of UAV swarm over time.

As is shown in Fig. 8(a), the collision probability of links 35 and 40 being generally greater than other links. Because that when T = 125 s, links 35 and 40 are in the middle of the UAV swarm. There are more UAVs in the collision interference range, resulting in higher collision probability. Whereas, the increase of the collision probability decreases the transmission probability of the two links. Therefore, it can be seen from Fig. 8(b) that the transmission probability of links 35 and 40 is generally lower than that of other links. When T = 230 s, most of the UAVs have successfully passed the obstacles, and mainly affected by the navigation force and the topology force. As the effect of the obstacle avoidance force on the swarm gradually decreases, the effect of topology force is gradually increasing. It can be seen from Fig. 9(a) that link 43 and link 49 have relatively small collision probabilities. Because link 43 and link 49 are both at the edge of the swarm that the number of UAVs in the collision interference range is small. Therefore, transmission probability of links 43 and 49 are significantly higher than most other links, as shown in Fig. 9(b).

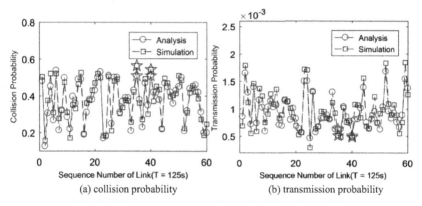

(a) collision probability   (b) transmission probability

Fig. 8. Collision and transmission probability at T = 125 s.

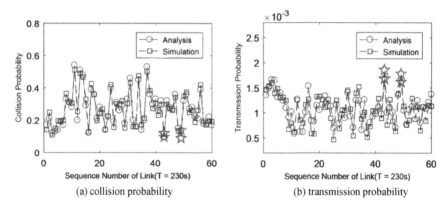

(a) collision probability   (b) transmission probability

Fig. 9. Collision and transmission probability at T = 230 s.

The reason why the collision probability in Fig. 8 is greater than that in Fig. 9 can be derived from Table 2. The obstacle avoidance force of the swarm are 1.3E + 7 and 2.7E + 6 respectively. The greater the obstacle avoidance force, the greater the collision probability. The obstacle avoidance force at two different moments verify the above results.

Table 2. Virtual force

Force (N)	T(S)	
	125	230
Navigation force	2.2E + 7	1.7E + 7
Topology force	10.5E + 6	6.6E + 6
Obstacle avoidance force	1.3E + 7	2.7E + 6

5   Conclusion

Aiming at the high-speed mobility and the rapid changes in network topology of UAVs, we present a modeling method to analyze the instantaneous saturation throughput. Using our proposed model, the collision, transmission probability and throughput of the nodes are calculated. The simulation results are consistent with the theoretic results, which shows the effectiveness of the four-dimensional Markov chain model established in this paper. At the same time, the NCU_MAC protocol we presented can effectively improve the network performance of the traditional MAC protocol in dynamic network environment. In our future work, we will focus on inducing linear programming, multi-objective optimization theory, convex optimization, and other theoretical methods to analyze the effect of complex swarm motion scenarios and further improve network performance.

Acknowledgments. This work was supported in part by the National Natural Science Foundation of China (No. 61902182), the Natural Science Foundation of Jiangsu Province of China (No. BK20190409), the Aeronautical Science Foundation of China (No. 2016ZC52029), Qing Lan Project of Jiangsu Province of China, China Postdoctoral Science Foundation (No. 2019TQ0153), and the Foundation of CETC Key Laboratory of Aerospace Information Applications of China (No. SXX18629T022). The authors are with the College of Electronic and Information Engineering, Nanjing University of Aeronautics and Astronautics, Nanjing, 210016, China.

References

1. Bianchi, G.: Performance analysis of the IEEE 802.11 distributed coordination function. IEEE J. Sel. Areas Commun. **18**(3), 535–547 (2000). https://doi.org/10.1109/49.840210
2. Brown, T.X., Argrow, B., Dixon, C., Doshi, S., Henkel, D.: Ad hoc UAV Ground Network (AUGNet). In: AIAA 3rd "Unmanned Unlimited" Technical Conference, Workshop and Exhibit, vol. 6321 (2004)
3. Ruan, Y., Zhang, Y., Li, Y., Zhang, R., Hang, R.: An adaptive channel division MAC protocol for high dynamic UAV networks. IEEE Sens. J. **20**(16), 9528–9539 (2020). https://doi.org/10.1109/JSEN.2020.2987525
4. Patibandla, S.T., Bakker, T., Klenke, R.H.: Initial evaluation of an IEEE 802.11s-based mobile ad-hoc network for collaborative unmanned aerial vehicles. In: [C]//2013 International Conference on Connected Vehicles and Expo (ICCVE), pp. 145–150. IEEE (2013)

5. Al-Hubaishi, M., Alahdal, T., Alsaqour, R., Berqia, A., Abdelhaq, M., Alsaqour, O.: Enhanced binary exponential backoff algorithm for fair channel access in the ieee 802.11 medium access control protocol. Int. J. Commun. Syst. **27**(12), 4166–4184 (2014)
6. Huang, D., Li, H., Li, X.: Formation of generic UAVs-USVs system under distributed model predictive control scheme. IEEE Trans. Circuits Syst. II Exp. Briefs **67**(12), 3123–3127 (2020). https://doi.org/10.1109/TCSII.2020.2983096
7. Di, W., Caihong, L., Na, G., Yong, S., Tengteng, G., Guoming, L.: Local path planning of mobile robot based on artificial potential field. In: 2020 39th Chinese Control Conference (CCC), Shenyang, China, pp. 3677–3682 (2020). https://doi.org/10.23919/CCC50068.2020.9189250
8. Felemban, E., Ekici, E.: Single hop IEEE 802.11 DCF analysis revisited: accurate modeling of channel access delay and throughput for saturated and unsaturated traffic cases. IEEE Trans. Wireless Commun. **10**(10), 3256–3266 (2011)
9. Tsertou, A., Laurenson, D.I.: Revisiting the hidden terminal problem in a CSMA/CA wireless network. IEEE Trans. Mob. Comput. **7**(7), 817–831 (2008)
10. Garetto, M., Salonidis, T., Knightly, E.W.: Modeling per-flow throughput and capturing starvation in CSMA multi-hop wireless networks. IEEE/ACM Trans. Netw. **16**(4), 864–877 (2008)

Learning-Based Aerial Charging Scheduling for UAV-Based Data Collection

Jia Yang, Kun Zhu$^{(\boxtimes)}$, Xiaojun Zhu, and Junhua Wang

Nanjing University of Aeronautics and Astronautics, Nanjing 211100, China
{yangjiacs305,zhukun,xzhu,jhua1207}@nuaa.edu.cn

Abstract. A major challenge to wide application of small size unmanned aerial vehicles (UAVs) is the limited working time. For recharging UAVs, ground-station based schemes had been proposed, for which contact charging by magnetic coupling and contactless charging by laser beam can be used. However, UAVs have to interrupt ongoing missions and cost extra time and energy on recharging. In this work, with the aim of charging UAVs without interrupting the mission, we propose the novel concept of charging UAVs aerially via wireless power transmission (WPT). In this case, the mission UAVs (MUAVs) can be recharged by the charging UAV (CUAV) while on the fly. Firstly, the feasibility of aerially wireless charging for small UAVs is verified. Then we consider the practical application of multiple MUAVs for collecting data from several points of interest (PoIs), where the MUAVs will be recharged by the CUAV. Accordingly, the issue of scheduling the CUAV's flying path and charging process to minimize the mission time arises. To this end, deep reinforcement learning based algorithms for scheduling CUAV recharging MUAVs is proposed. The CUAV explores and optimizes the scheduling strategies, thereby improving the working efficiency. Extensive evaluations and comparisons show the effectiveness of the proposed scheme.

Keywords: UAV scheduling · Wireless power transmission · Deep reinforcement learning

1 Introduction

In recent years, consumer-level small size unmanned aerial vehicles have been widely used due to the advantages of low cost, easy remote control, flexible deployment, and high mobility. Equipped with specific devices, various missions for many civil applications can be accomplished by UAVs, e.g., data collection [1], environment monitoring [2], area detection, data collection [3], communication, good delivery [4], etc.

A major challenge to wider application of small size UAVs is the limited battery capacity. Thus, the working scope and working time is limited. Expanding the battery capacity could significantly increase the weight and volume of the UAV, which may not be feasible for UAVs with size constraints. Replenishing energy for MUAVs during missions is another method.

© Springer Nature Switzerland AG 2021
Z. Liu et al. (Eds.): WASA 2021, LNCS 12938, pp. 600–611, 2021.
https://doi.org/10.1007/978-3-030-86130-8_47

For recharging UAVs during the mission, ground station based wireless charging schemes had been proposed. According to the techniques used, it can be divided into two types, i.e., contact charging and contactless charging. With contact charging, a UAV needs to land on the ground charging station, and can be charged through inductive coupling or magnetic resonance coupling [5,6]. Contactless charging is usually performed by laser beam [7]. The UAV hovering around a ground charging station can be charged by aligned laser beams. Though the working time of UAVs can be prolonged by existing ground charging stations solutions, several drawbacks still exist. Firstly, the ground stations need to be pre-deployed in certain fixed locations which is not flexible. Secondly, the MUAVs have to stop the ongoing missions and travel to the charging station for energy replenishing. Accordingly, extra energy will be consumed and mission completion time will be postponed.

In this work, similar to the concept of aerial refueling, with the aim of charging the UAVs without interrupting the mission, we propose the novel concept of aerially charging UAVs via wireless power transmission. In this case, a MUAV can be wirelessly recharged by a CUAV while on the fly. Several benefits can be achieved through aerially charging. Firstly, the use of charging UAVs instead of (or in complement with) ground charging stations could significantly increase the flexibility and lower the cost. Secondly, due to the advantages of wireless charging and the high mobility of UAV, the MUAVs can be charged whenever it is moving or hovering. The working efficiency can be significantly improved.

With aerially UAV charging, we consider a practical application in smart city where multiple MUAVs are used for collecting data from several points of interest (PoIs). CUAV aerially charging is used to recharge the MUAVs. The MUAVs collect data according to a mission plan which includes moving trajectories and connection time to each PoI. We assume that the energy of a MUAV is not sufficient to finish the mission. Traditionally, the UAVs will fly to a fixed ground charging station or platform for recharging. Instead, the CUAV is dispatched to replenish energy for the MUAVs. Accordingly, the issue of how to schedule the CUAV's charging plan to charge each MUAV on time. The problem is formulated as a Markov decision process, for which deep deterministic policy gradient (DDPG) [8] based algorithm is proposed. The CUAV continues to explore and optimize the scheduling strategies to minimize the entire mission completion time of MUAVs, thereby improving the working efficiency.

The main novelties and contributions can be summarized as follows:

- The novel concept of aerially charging small size battery-driven UAVs in wireless charging manner has been proposed, with which several benefits can be achieved. And the feasibility is verified.
- We investigate the problem of aerially charging scheduling for CUAV in a data collection scenario to minimize total mission time, for which a deep reinforcement learning based scheme is proposed.
- Comprehensive evaluations and comparisons are performed to demonstrate the effectiveness of our proposed method.

2   Feasibility Verification

In this paper, to charge the MUAVs by nearby CUAV during flying, both contact and contactless wireless charging are considered. In this section, feasible and effective recharging methods with the proposed charging scheme for MUAVs is verified.

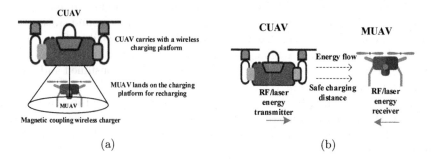

Fig. 1. CUAV wireless charging method: (a) Contact charging method, (b) Contactless charging method.

2.1   Contact Wireless Charging

Contact wireless charging means that the MUAV is charged by a wireless charging platform. Most of the existing contact wireless chargers are based on magnetic resonant coupling. Magnetic coupling allows loose alignment between charger and receiver [9]. However, coupling-based WPT techniques require a short charging distance.

The contact charging platform on the ground has been proposed for charging UAVs. A magnetic field based system was designed to provide enough power to charge UAV at a high efficiency in [10]. The unmanned ground vehicle with magnetic resonance coupling charging platform was dispatched for charging the UAVs on mission [11]. In our proposed charging scheme, the MUAV lands on the charging platform of CUAV for recharging (See Fig. 1(a)). The contact wireless charger can provide tens of Watts charging power. Contact aerial charging platform is a promising scheme for effectively charging small size UAVs.

2.2   Contactless Wireless Charging

Contactless wireless charging means that the CUAV can provide line-of-sight energy transmission for MUAVs in the air (See Fig. 1(b)). The CUAV provides charging power by energy transmitter and the MUAV receives power by receiver. Radio Frequency (RF) and laser can be used to transmit energy.

RF Wireless Charging. RF is a high-frequency AC electromagnetic wave with energy. The RF energy harvester can convert energy into direct current. The energy collected by the receiving antenna can extend the working time. The RF charging antenna arrays designed in [12] realized RF long-distance charging.

RF energy transmission is derived from the Friis transmission equation:

$$P_r = P_t \frac{G_t G_r \lambda^2}{(4\pi r)^2}. \tag{1}$$

where P_t represents the transmit power of the transmitting antenna and P_r is the power received by the receiving antenna. The antenna gain G is used to describe directionality of the antennas, which is proportional to the charging efficiency in specific directions. r is the distance between the two antennas, and λ is the wavelength of the electromagnetic wave. According to Eq. 1, when the charging distance is 0.5 m and the RF microwave signal frequency is 915 Mhz, the RF charging efficiency is 21.7%. The RF charging has better charging performance at longer charging distance than the Witricity in [13].

Laser Wireless Charging. Laser beams carry with high radiant energy. Because of its advantage of small divergence, there is little attenuation during the laser transmission in clear air. The charging system includes the laser transmitter and the photovoltaic-cell (PV-cell) as receiver. Distributed laser charging (DLC) system and laser wireless transmission efficiency were presented in [14]. The system can charge the portable devices and drones via DLC transmitters. In [7], the UAV was recharged by laser beam emitted from the grounded charging station while performing data collection missions.

Due to the harm of laser exposure and transmission loss (derive from long charging distance and air quality) of laser energy, short charging distance should be considered. In this case, we computed the charging efficiency by the numerical evaluation results in [14] and the parameters of a laser transmitter [15]. When charging the laser wavelength is 810 nm, the charging efficiency is 29%. The charging power is 116 W when the working power of laser transmitter is 400 W, which is sufficient for charging a MUAV.

3 Scenarios and System Model

3.1 Scenarios

In this paper, we consider the scenario that several MUAVs are dispatched to collect sensing data from multiple PoIs according to pre-scheduled travelling paths[1] and data collection sequence of PoIs (See Fig. 2). We assume that the MUAV's battery capacity is not sufficient. Accordingly, the MUAVs have to be recharged to avoid energy exhaustion during the mission.

---

[1] Note that the path planning and scheduling for MUAVs to collect data is not considered in this work.

The proposed CUAV based aerially wireless charging is considered to solve the energy shortage of MUAVs. With the advantages of wireless charging, the MUAV can be charged whenever it is flying to next PoI or hovering for data collection. The problem is how to schedule the CUAV to charge each MUAVs before energy exhaustion. In this case, the MUAVs don't have to interrupt their ongoing missions and the mission time of each MUAV will be shortened. Note that for comparison, we also consider the case with ground charging nodes. In these cases, the MUAVs have to travel to ground charging nodes, such as charging stations, fixed charging platforms or mobile charging vehicles. If its remaining energy is below the safety threshold, the MUAV has to get recharged at ground charging nodes, which would consume extra time and energy and accordingly lead to longer mission time. In this work, we consider that the MUAVs can be charged by CUAV during the working time by wireless charging. If a MUAV's energy is below the safety threshold, it will stop executing mission and wait to be charged.

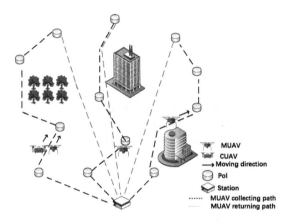

Fig. 2. Data collection scenario with CUAV

3.2   System Model

There are two types of UAVs in our scenario. The CUAV will be scheduled to charge the MUAVs. $M = \{M_i | i = 1, 2, ..., n\}$ is the set of MUAVs. The mission of each MUAV is to collect data according to a pre-planed path. The scenario is a 2D area with fixed border and there is a set of Blocks $B = \{B_i | i = 1, 2, ..., n\}$. $P = \{P_i | i = 1, 2, ..., n\}$ represents the set of PoIs where there exists data to be collected. The required data collection time of PoI P_i can be denoted as $Dt(P_i)$. The action of each MUAV is determined in advance. M_i^t denotes the action of MUAV M_i at time t. The action at timeslot t is moving in the direction (two-dimensional vector) of $\theta_{M_i}^t$ with velocity v or hovering at the position of PoI for data collection. The action of CUAV at timeslot t is denoted as C^t. The action of CUAV is moving in the direction of θ_{C^t} with velocity v or charging one MUAV.

The CUAV moves or hovers together with the target MUAV during the charging process. To simplify the scenario, the MUAV and CUAV moves with constant velocity v and constant moving distance l at each step. If the distance between CUAV and charging target is less than l, we can roughly think that the CUAV can reach the charging position at next step.

4   Problem Formulation

The problem is scheduling actions of the CUAV with the intension of charging MUAVs on time. The CUAV takes actions according to the current state. The total charging process of the CUAV can be model as a Markov decision process $M = (S, A, P, R, \gamma)$.

State Space. The state space S is a infinite state which includes the possible states during the charging process. The state at time t is S^t. The state includes the locations (2D coordinates) of UAVs, MUAV's remaining energy and working state. The working state includes charging state and moving state.

Action Space. The action of the CUAV at time t is represented by A^t. The action of CUAV contains the moving direction (2D vector) and the charging target.

Transition Probability. The state transition probability $P : S^t \times A^t \rightarrow S^{t+1}$ gives a probability distribution over states S^{t+1} at time $t + 1$ according to the state S^t and the CUAV's action A^t at time t.

Reward Function. The data collection mission completes when all the data is collected and the MUAVs return to the station. The mission completion time of MUAV M_i is T_i:

$$T_i = Tm_i + Tc_i + Tw_i, \tag{2}$$

where Tm denotes time spent on moving and Tc is the time spent on collecting data from PoIs. Tw is the waiting time for a MUAV below energy threshold to be recharged by a CUAV. T_i can be shortened if the missions have less interruption. The mission completion time of all MUAVs is shortened if the CUAV is scheduled by a good CUAV charging scheduling policy. The mission time of each MUAV may be different, so the purpose is to minimize the mean of all MUAVs' mission completion time:

$$\min \frac{\sum_{i=1}^{n} T_i}{n}. \tag{3}$$

The reward function $S^t \times A^t \rightarrow \mathbb{R}^{t+1}$ denotes the reward of the CUAV if it takes action C^t and its' state transforms from S^t to S^{t+1} at time t. In our problem, we aim to minimize the mission completion time. The actions of MUAVs are pre-planned. If the MUAVs can be charged by CUAV on time (keep energy state above a threshold), they will continue working without stopping. The reward function has to be defined to schedule the agent to choose charging target and moving direction correctly. The reward of CUAV at time t is designed as follows:

$$r^t = Rc^t + w_d D(i)^t + w_e Er_i^t - P_l - P_b. \tag{4}$$

606   J. Yang et al.

P_l denotes the punishment for CUAV if any MUAV's remaining energy is below the safety threshold E_{th}. P_b is the punishment if the CUAV flies out of the environments' boundary or hits a block. $D(i)^t$ is Euclidean distance between the CUAV and MUAV M_i and Er_i^t is remaining energy of M_i at time t which are used to encourage the CUAV to move close to a MUAV required to be recharged. w_d and w_e are weights to adjust the reward. Rc^t denotes CUAV's reward get from charging a MUAV at time t.

$$Rc^t = E^t \times Rc \times f_t, \tag{5}$$

where E^t is the charging capacity at time t. Rc and f_t are used to keep charging each MUAV fairly and prevent MUAVs interrupting ongoing mission because of lack of energy. $Er^t = \{Er_1^t, Er_2^t...Er_n^t\}$ denotes the remaining energy of MUAV at time t. $Em = \{Em_1, Em_2...Em_n\}$ is the estimated minimum required charging capacity for finishing its mission. $Ec^t = \{Ec_1^t, Ec_2^t...Ec_n^t\}$ is the energy charged by CUAV from time step 1 to t. Rc is a value decided by Er_i^t and Em_i of charging target M_i (it is smaller if Er_i^t is larger than Em_i). f_t is computed by Jain's fairness index [16], which is shown as follows:

$$f_t = w_f fc_t + (1 - w_f)fr_t, \tag{6}$$

$$fc_t = \frac{(\sum_{i=1}^n \min(\frac{Ec_i^t}{Em_i}, 1))^2}{n \times \sum_{i=1}^n \min(\frac{Ec_i^t}{Em_i}, 1)^2}, \tag{7}$$

$$fr_t = \frac{(\sum_{i=1}^n Er_i^t)^2}{n \times \sum_{i=1}^n Er_i^{t2}}. \tag{8}$$

f_t is used to encourage CUAV to charge MUAVs fairly. The fairness index is computed by remaining energy and charging requirement of each MUAV. It is closed to 1 if the CUAV charge the MUAVs fairly. The agent will get better reward if all MUAVs are fairly recharged.

Discount Factor. $\gamma \in [0, 1]$ is a discount factor which determines how much the future actions influence the instant reward. If it is close to 1, the future actions take more importance.

5 Reinforcement Learning Algorithm for CUAV Charging Scheduling

To effectively address the above CUAV charging scheduling problem, policy based learning scheme has been proposed. The policy of the CUAV is optimized to achieve better rewards from the environment. A CUAV scheduling algorithm based on Deep Deterministic Policy Gradient (DDPG) is proposed. Different from traditional DDPG algorithms, adaptive parameter space noise is used for better policy exploration instead of OU action noise.

5.1   Deep Deterministic Policy Gradient (DDPG)

Deep Deterministic Policy Gradient [8] introduce the neural network into the actor-critic approach. CUAV's observation includes the information of MUAVs, CUAV and blocks. Neural networks can approximate the Q function and action function easily. The actor $\mu(s|\theta^\mu)$ is a neural network that gives the CUAV actions according to its observation. The critic $Q(s, a|\theta^Q)$ is a approximated deep neural network that gives the estimated Q value of CUAV's action. Both of the actor and critic use a target network to train the parameter of neural network θ. The objective function is:

$$\nabla J_{\theta^\mu} = \mathbb{E}_{s \sim \rho^\beta}[\nabla_a Q(s, a|\theta^Q)|s = s_t, a = \mu(s_t)\nabla_{\theta^\mu}\mu(s|\theta^\mu)|s = s_t]. \qquad (9)$$

5.2   Adaptive Parameter Space Noise

Different form adding a noise to the action for policy exploration, parameters of actor network are perturbed by applying Gaussian noise. In our experiment, the parameter space noise has better performance while training. A time-varying scale σ_k is used for adapting the scale of the noise over time:

$$\sigma_{k+1} = \begin{cases} \alpha\sigma_k, & \text{if } d(\pi, \tilde{\pi}) < \delta \\ \frac{1}{\alpha}\sigma_k, & \text{otherwise,} \end{cases} \qquad (10)$$

where $d(\pi, \tilde{\pi})$ denotes the action distance between policy of actor and perturbed actor. α is used to rescale σ and δ is the threshold.

$$d(\pi, \tilde{\pi}) = \sqrt{\frac{1}{N}\sum_{i=1}^{N}\mathbb{E}_s[(\pi(s)_i - \tilde{\pi}(s)_i)^2,]}. \qquad (11)$$

where $\mathbb{E}$ is estimated by a sampled mini batch of experience from replay buffer. The algorithm of training CUAV is shown as follow:

6   Experiments and Analysis

6.1   Experiment Setting

In the experiment, we set the scenario area as a bounded 2D square and the position of the entities are denoted as a 2D coordinate. The CUAV and MUAVs take off from the UAV station. The MUAVs collect data from the PoIs according to the pre-planned collecting schedule and flying path. The data collection starts when the MUAV reaches the pre-planned collecting spot. The MUAV hovers over the spot (stop moving) and collects the data form the PoIs. The MUAV will travel to the next spot after all the data from current PoI is collected. The MUAVs' energy has to be replenished to avoid energy exhaustion during the mission. So, the algorithm has to schedule the CUAV to charge the MUAVs. We approximately consider that MUAV and CUAV has the same position when

---

Algorithm 1. DDPG with Adaptive Parameter Space Noise

Randomly initialize critic network Q and actor network $\mu(s|\theta^{\mu'})$
Initialize target network Q' and μ', set parameters of perturbed actor with the copy of actor's parameters
Initialize replay buffer R
for episode $= 1$ to M **do**
    Receive initial state s_1
    for step $t = 1$ to maximum episode length **do**
        Select action $a_t = \mu_\theta(s_t)$, the CUAV take actions a_t, and get the new state s_{t+1}
        Receive reward r_t, store (s_t, a_t, r_t, s_{t+1}) in replay buffer
        Sample a random minibatch of N samples (s_i, a_i, r_i, s_{i+1}) form reply buffer
        Compute $d(\pi, \widetilde{\pi})$ and σ, update perturbed actor parameters $\widetilde{\pi} \leftarrow \pi + \mathcal{N}(0, \sigma^2)$
        Set $y^i = r_i + \gamma Q'(s_{i+1}, \mu'(s_{i+1}|\theta^{\mu'}))$
        Update critic by minimizing the loss $L = \frac{1}{N} \sum_i (y^i - Q(s_i, ai|\theta^Q))^2$
        Update actor using the sampled policy gradient:
        $\nabla_{\theta^\mu} J \approx \frac{1}{N} \sum_i \nabla_a Q(s, a|\theta^Q)|_{s=s_i, a=\mu(s_i)} \nabla_{\theta^\mu} \mu(s|\theta^\mu)|_{s_i}$
        Update target networks for CUAV:
        $\theta^{Q'} \leftarrow \tau\theta^Q + (1-\tau)\theta^{Q'}, \theta^{\mu'} \leftarrow \tau\theta^\mu + (1-\tau)\theta^{\mu'}$
    end for
end for

MUAV is charged by a nearby CUAV. The MUAVs can be charged whenever it is flying to the next spot or hovering to collect data. After all the data have been collected, the UAVs have to return back to the UAV station. The UAVs cannot fly out of the boundary or hit the blocks.

The CUAV has to choose the charging target and travelling trajectory according current state in the environment. Since the moving and hovering of MUAVs add uncertainty of the environment, we simplify the problem as follows. If the MUAV's energy is below the safety threshold, it would stop executing mission. It will continue its mission after being charged by CUAV. The energy consumed by a MUAV at each step is a constant. The energy of CUAV is not considered and moves a fixed distance each step. The episode ends if all the MUAVs return the station or the steps exceed the maximum episode length. The actor and critic are neural networks with 2 fully-connected hidden layers. Each hidden layer has 64 neurons and output layer uses the softmax for outputting action probability distributions. More experiment parameters are shown in Table 1.

6.2 Experiment Analysis

The accumulated reward of training is shown in Fig. 3(a). The algorithm with parameter space noise has better performance. The completion steps are shown in Fig. 3(b). The maximum episode length is 100 steps. Note that the mission time of different MUAVs is different. The red line is the average mission completion time of all MUAVs and the blue line is the completion time of last mission. The mission completion time drops if better policy has been learnt. If the MUAVs are charged on time, the missions will not be delayed and the completion time

Table 1. Experiment parameters.

Symbol	Value	Explanation
α	0.01	Learning rate
γ	0.95	Discount factor
P_r	120 W	MUAV's charging power
P_m	80 W	MUAV's working power
E	50 Wh	MUAV's battery capacity
w_f	0.5	Weight in reward function

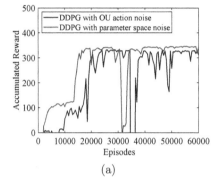
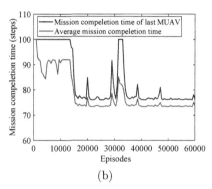

(a)   (b)

Fig. 3. Trainning results of (a) Accumulated reward, (b) Mission completion steps. (Color figure online)

would be reduced. The smaller steps spent on mission mean that there are fewer mission interruptions in the charging process.

The most prominent advantage of charging MUAVs by CUAV is that the MUAV can be charged when it is performing missions. Thus, the time spent on recharging at ground charging nodes can be saved. We compare our CUAV charging scheme with three other charging methods: flying back to UAV station and replace the battery, charging at a nearby fixed charging platform (2 fixed charging platforms) and charging by a mobile unmanned charging vehicle(the ground vehicles move close to the MUAVs and MUAVs take off for recharging). The charging platform and charging vehicle charge the MUAV by contact wireless charging. The comparison is shown in Fig. 4(a), mission completion time can be shortened if MUAVs are recharged by CUAV.

The CUAV charging mission and travelling trajectory are shown in Fig. 4(b). The red dotted line is the trajectory of CUAV during charging mission and the blue dotted lines are the trajectories of MUAVs during data collection missions. Arrows denote the moving directions of UAVs. The CUAV charges the MUAVs when it is moving closed to the MUAV. They have the same moving direction and similar trajectories while charging. The CUAV charges the MUAV1 at first. Then, the MUAV2 and MUAV3 are charged. The CUAV charges the MUAV2,

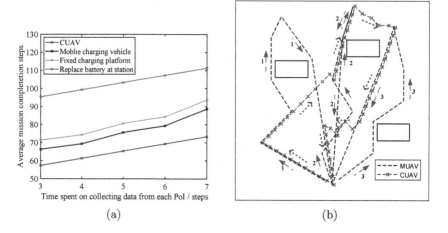

Fig. 4. (a) Comparison of 4 recharging methods, (b) Trajectory of UAVs. (Color figure online)

MUAV1 and returns to the UAV station in the end. None of the MUAVs stop working because of energy exhaustion during the mission process.

7   Conclusion

One of the challenges of UAV application is the endurance problem of UAV. In this work, we have proposed the novel idea of aerially charging MUAVs by the CUAV in wireless charging manner, which can achieve several benefits. Further, the feasibility is analyzed. Besides, we consider the practical application of multiple MUAVs for data collection. MUAVs can be recharged by CUAV during the data collection process. Then, we have investigated the problem of how to schedule the CUAVs' moving path and the charging process with the intention to minimize the mission time. Reinforcement learning based algorithm has been proposed to solve the charging scheduling problem. The results show that the mission can be completed faster than charging the MUAVs by traditional fixed ground charging nodes based solutions and mobile ground charging vehicles based solutions.

Acknowledgement. This work was supported by the National Natural Science Foundation of China (No. 62071230 and No. 61972199).

References

1. Liu, J., Wang, X., Bai, B., Dai, H.: Age-optimal trajectory planning for UAV-assisted data collection. In: IEEE INFOCOM 2018 - IEEE Conference on Computer Communications Workshops (INFOCOM WKSHPS), Honolulu, HI (2018)

2. Avola, D., Foresti, G.L., Martinel, N., Micheloni, C., Pannone, D., Piciarelli, C.: Aerial video surveillance system for small-scale UAV environment monitoring. In: 2017 14th IEEE International Conference on Advanced Video and Signal Based Surveillance (AVSS), Lecce (2017)
3. Zhang, B., Liu, C.H., Tang, J., Xu, Z., Ma, J., Wang, W.: Learning-based energy-efficient data collection by unmanned vehicles in smart cities. IEEE Trans. Industr. Inf. 14(4), 1666–1676 (2018)
4. Song, B.D., Park, K., Kim, J.: Persistent UAV delivery logistics: MILP formulation and efficient heuristic. Comput. Ind. Eng. 120, 418–428 (2018)
5. Han, Z., Zhu, X., Xu, L.: Scheduling rechargeable UAVs for long time barrier coverage. In: 2020 IEEE 26th International Conference on Parallel and Distributed Systems (ICPADS), pp. 282–289 (2020)
6. Junaid, A.B., Lee, Y., Kim, Y.: Design and implementation of autonomous wireless charging station for rotary-wing UAVs. Aerosp. Sci. Technol. 54, 253–266 (2016)
7. Chen, W., Zhao, S., Shi, Q., Zhang, R.: Resonant beam charging-powered UAV-assisted sensing data collection. IEEE Trans. Veh. Technol. 69(1), 1086–1090 (2020)
8. Lillicrap, T.P., et al.: Continuous control with deep reinforcement learning. arXiv preprint arXiv:1509.02971 (2015)
9. Lu, X., Wang, P., Niyato, D., Kim, D.I., Han, Z.: Wireless charging technologies: fundamentals, standards, and network applications. IEEE Commun. Surv. Tutor. 18(2), 1413–1452 (2016)
10. Ke, D., Liu, C., Jiang, C., Zhao, F.: Design of an effective wireless air charging system for electric unmanned aerial vehicles. In: 2017–43rd Annual Conference of the IEEE Industrial Electronics Society (IECON), Beijing (2017)
11. Yu, K., Budhiraja, A.K., Tokekar, P.: Algorithms for routing of unmanned aerial vehicles with mobile recharging stations. In: 2018 IEEE International Conference on Robotics and Automation (ICRA), Brisbane, QLD (2018)
12. Li, K., See, K., Koh, W., Zhang, J.: Design of 2.45 GHz microwave wireless power transfer system for battery charging applications. In: 2017 Progress in Electromagnetics Research Symposium - Fall (PIERS - FALL), Singapore (2017)
13. Ho, S.L., Wang, J., Fu, W.N., Sun, M.: A comparative study between novel witricity and traditional inductive magnetic coupling in wireless charging. IEEE Trans. Magn. 47(5), 1522–1525 (2011)
14. Zhang, Q., Fang, W., Liu, Q., Wu, J., Xia, P., Yang, L.: Distributed laser charging: a wireless power transfer approach. IEEE Internet Things J. 5(5), 3853–3864 (2018)
15. QCW Stacked Array with 'Fast Axis Collimation' QD-Q1yzz-BO/QD-Q1yzz-BSO/QD-Q1yzz-BSSO. https://www.laserdiodesource.com/files/pdfs/laserdiodesource_com/product-966/808nm_500W_stack_Quantel_Laser_Diodes-1416380890.pdf
16. Sediq, A.B., Gohary, R.H., Schoenen, R., Yanikomeroglu, H.: Optimal tradeoff between sum-rate efficiency and Jain's fairness index in resource allocation. IEEE Trans. Wireless Commun. 12(7), 3496–3509 (2013)
17. Plappert, M.: Parameter space noise for exploration. arXiv preprint arXiv:1706.01905 (2017)

Learning to Communicate for Mobile Sensing with Multi-agent Reinforcement Learning

Bolei Zhang[1(✉)], Junliang Liu[2], and Fu Xiao[1]

[1] School of Computer, Nanjing University of Posts and Telecommunications, Nanjing, China
{bolei.zhang,xiaof}@njupt.edu.cn
[2] JD.com, Beijing, China
liujunliang3@jd.com

Abstract. Mobile sensing has become a promising paradigm for monitoring the environmental state. When equipped with sensors, a group of unmanned vehicles can autonomously move around for distributed sensing. To maximize the sensing coverage, a critical challenge is to coordinate the decentralized vehicles for cooperation. In this work, we propose a novel algorithm Comm-Q, in which the vehicles can learn to communicate for cooperation via multi-agent reinforcement learning. At each step, the vehicles can broadcast a message to others, and condition on received aggregated message to update their sensing policies. The message is also learned via reinforcement learning. In addition, we decompose and reshape the reward function for more efficient policy training. Experimental results show that our algorithm is scalable and can converge very fast during training phase. It also outperforms other baselines significantly during execution. The results validate that communication message plays an important role to coordinate the behaviors of different vehicles.

Keywords: Mobile sensing · Reinforcement learning · Learning to communicate

1 Introduction

Recently, the ubiquitous adoption of unmanned (aerial) vehicles has greatly enabled the flexibility and convenience for sensing the environment. When equipped with sensors, the vehicles can autonomously move to different positions to collect wide area environmental data. As the battery capacity of the vehicles are often limited, there are typically charging stations so that the vehicles can regularly navigate back to recharge the batteries. Such mobile sensing paradigm has been adopted in a variety of disciplines such as air quality monitoring, intrusion detection, crowd counting, etc. [1,5,8].

Suppose there are a set of unmanned vehicles simultaneously moving in an area to sense the environment. A central problem is to efficiently coordinate their behaviors to maximize the sensing coverage. On one hand, the vehicles

Z. Liu et al. (Eds.): WASA 2021, LNCS 12938, pp. 612–623, 2021.
https://doi.org/10.1007/978-3-030-86130-8_48

need move to the hot POIs for higher benefit. On the other hand, different vehicles try to avoid coinciding in the same position with each other, otherwise the effort could be wasted. Extensive previous works have studied this problem. For example, Karaliopoulos et al. [7] modeled the user mobility as deterministic and use algorithms based on set cover for approximation solution. Zhou et al. [19] tried to assign the tasks jointly by planning routes for the UAVs. Liu et al. [9] proposed a multi-UAV mobile sensing framework based on MARL, and utilizes "centralized training decentralized execution" (CTDE) for cooperation.

Despite the efforts made over the last years, there are still several key challenges that are not fully addressed: First, as the vehicles only have local observation, they need to make decentralized decisions. Second, during mobile sensing, uncertain events could happen in the environment. Therefore, the vehicles should schedule their sensing plans in a model-free way. Most importantly, as the behaviors of different vehicles may interfere mutually, it is crucial to coordinate their behaviors for higher efficiency.

With the above challenges, in this paper, we propose a novel algorithm for mobile sensing based on multi-agent reinforcement learning (MARL), in which each mobile vehicle learns to maximize long-term cumulative team reward based only on local observations. With reinforcement learning (RL), the vehicles can learn the dynamics of the environment by exploration and exploitation. To coordinate the behaviors of different vehicles, we propose to use active communication among them. In particular, the communication protocol can also be learned via RL. The communication message does not directly impact the environment, but it can share the information among the mobile vehicles for efficient cooperation. In addition, we try to decompose and reshape the reward function, so that each agent can more easily update their policies. We implement and evaluate the sensing algorithm in a simulation environment. The results show that our algorithm can converge very fast during training phase. During execution, our algorithm can achieve the highest average step reward compared to other baselines. The results validate that communication plays an important role for promoting the cooperation between the agents.

2   Background

2.1   Mobile Sensing

Mobile sensing has become a promising paradigm recently mainly due to the emergence of unmanned vehicles. When equipped with sensors, the vehicles can autonomously move to different positions and monitor the environmental state. Moreover, there are typically charging stations distributed which can be used by the vehicles to recharge the battery. During sensing, multiple random events with different intensities could happen at each position. Sensing the positions with higher intensity will also gain higher reward. The aim is to maximize the coverage of sensing by planning the routes for the vehicles.

An illustration of the environment is presented in Fig. 1(a). As presented, the environment is represented as a grid space. There are 6 vehicles in the map to sense the environment with limited battery capacity. The battery capacity would continuously decrease during sensing. The vehicles should try to navigate to the charging stations (represented as blue circles) before running out of power. The grids with redder colors indicate higher intensity of the events. The intensities could also vary temporarily. Ideally, the mobile vehicles should move the grid with the redder color for higher reward. However, they also need to avoid coinciding with each other in case of repeated sensing.

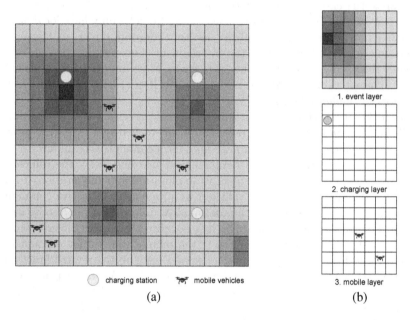

(a)   (b)

Fig. 1. a. An illustration of the mobile sensing environment; b. Different observation layers of the top mobile vehicle. (Color figure online)

2.2   Reinforcement Learning

Reinforcement Learning (RL) is one of the most successful approaches to AI, and has achieved great success in wide areas [12,14,17]. The problem of reinforcement learning can usually be modeled as a Markov Decision Process (MDP) $\langle S, A, T, R, \gamma \rangle$, where S is the state space, A is the action space, and $T : S \times A \rightarrow S$ is the transition model for generating the next state. $R : S \times A \rightarrow \mathbb{R}$ is the reward function. $\gamma \in [0, 1)$ is a discount factor. At each step t, when an agent observes the state $s_t \in S$ and executes an action $a_t \in A$, it will then be transitioned into a new state s_{t+1} and receives an immediate reward r_t. The goal of reinforcement learning is to find the optimal policy π^* to maximize the γ-discounted cumulative reward: $\pi^* = \arg\max_\pi \mathbb{E}[\sum_{t=0}^{T} \gamma^{T-t} r_t]$, where policy π is a function which maps the state s_t to a distribution of actions a_t.

Multi-agent Reinforcement Learning (MARL) generally models the environment as a Decentralized Partially Observable Markov Decision Processes (Dec-POMDP) [4,11]. Consider $I = (1, 2, ..., N)$ as the finite set of agents, $o_i \in \Omega$ as the local observation set of agent i. At each step t, each agent i chooses an action $a_i^t \in A$, forming a joint action $\mathbf{a}^t \in A^n$, and transition to the next state s_{t+1} according to the function $T(s_{t+1}|s_t, \mathbf{a}_t)$ with a vector of N rewards $r^{(t)} = (r_1^{(t)}, ..., r_N^{(t)})$. To optimize the policy of the agents in MARL, previous works mainly adopt a "centralized training, decentralized execution" (CTDE) [4,11, 13,16]: during training, global state information can be used to train the policy network; during execution, the agents can only condition on local observations. However, as the mobile vehicles could be owned by different entities, we address that the centralized training is not feasible in the mobile sensing paradigm. Recent works are considering learning to communicate for the distributed agents [2,3,6,10,15]. However, some of them still uses centralized training [6,10,15]. In other works, the messages are not fully utilized for communication.

3 System Model

In this paper, we consider a mobile sensing problem where a set of mobile vehicles $I = \{1, 2, ..., N\}$ cooperate to maximize the sensing coverage of the environment. Each of the vehicle is associated with a battery with capacity b_i^t. During sensing, the vehicle would consume one unit of the battery at each step. To avoid running out of power, the vehicle should regularly move to the charging station, in which the battery will be recharged for a fixed number of units.

For simplicity, we suppose the environment is a grid space A with m rows and n columns. Each grid (x, y) is associated with a sensing reward of A_{xy}^t at step t. In the grid space, each vehicle i can move at most one grid at each step if the capacity is above zero: $b_i^t \geq 0$. We will receive a reward of A_{xy}^t when the grid (x, y) is covered by at least one vehicle. Note that when multiple vehicles are at the same grid, the reward is still A_{xy}^t. Therefore, the vehicles should cooperate with each other to avoid coinciding in the same grid. Suppose the number of vehicles at each position (x, y) is n_{xy}^t at step t. The objective of the cooperative mobile sensing can be formulated as follows:

$$\max \sum_{t=0}^{\infty} \sum_{x,y} A_{xy}^t \mathbb{1}_{xy} \tag{1}$$
$$\text{s.t. } b_i^t \geq 0, \forall i \in I, \forall t \in \{0, 1, 2, ...\}$$

where the indicator function $\mathbb{1}_{xy}$ equals 1 when there are at least one vehicle at the grid at step t, i.e. $n_{xy}^t \geq 0$. The constraint in the objective means that the mobile vehicles could no longer move or sense when running out of battery. In the objective function, as the grid reward A_{xy}^t is time-varying with uncertainties, combination optimization based algorithms are no longer feasible. Accordingly, we use learning-based algorithm to find the optimal sensing policies.

4   The Environment

As the objective is to maximize the long-term cumulative reward by multiple vehicles, we model the problem as a Dec-POMDP. Now we formally describe the elements of the environment.

Agent. In mobile sensing, each vehicle acts as a decentralized agent. As the objective is shared among the vehicles, the agents should cooperate to maximize sensing coverage of the environment.

Observation. The observation radius of each agent is limited compared to the global grid space. We suppose the observation consists of three layers. Each layer is a 2-D matrix. The first layer is the event intensity in each grid. Sensing the grid with redder color will also gain higher reward. The second layer indicates the number of mobile vehicles in each grid. The third layer is the position of the charging stations. Figure 1(b) presents an illustration of the observation for one of the agents.

Action. As described above, the action of the mobile vehicles is discrete and consists of 5 actions: left, right, top, down, stay. In particular, we suppose the vehicle will stay at the previous grid if the mobile vehicle crosses over the border.

Reward. In this problem, the mobile vehicles cooperatively to maximize a shared reward r, which is the sensing coverage of the mobile vehicles at each step. In addition, due to the battery capacity constraint in Eq. 1, we relax the constraint by adding a large penalty c_{out} when the vehicle runs out of battery power. The vehicles will receive this penalty when the capacity is below zero: $b_i < 0, \forall i \in I$, i.e., $c(b_i^t) = c_{out}$ if $b_i^t < 0$. The reward can be formulated as:

$$r = \sum_{x,y} A_{xy}^t \mathbb{1}_{xy}^t - \sum_{i=1}^{N} c(b_i^t)$$

5   Learning to Communicate with MARL

As the mobile sensing problem requires multiple mobile vehicles to cooperate with each other, we propose a decentralized MARL algorithm for sequential sensing. Each of the mobile vehicles can work autonomously based on its own observation in a decentralized manner. In this section, we first introduce the method of learning to communicate among the mobile vehicles, which promotes the cooperation among the agents. Next, we will show how to reshape the reward for each agent to optimize the policy and present the algorithm.

5.1   Learning Communication

To promote the cooperation among the agents, previous works usually adopt the CTDE framework. However, we address that centralized training is not feasible in mobile sensing environment. Instead, we propose to use active communication among the agents. By communicating with others, the agents can share local observation and policy via message embedding. As the communication bandwidth is often limited, we adopt a RL framework to learn how to generate proper messages. An illustration of the procedure is presented in Fig. 2.

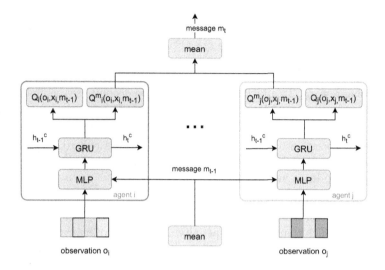

Fig. 2. The framework of learning to communicate between the mobile vehicles

As presented, at each step t, when taking action a_i^t, the agent i should condition on the mean of the message from the last step $m_{t-1} = \frac{1}{N}\sum_{i=1}^{N} m_i^{t-1}$. At the same time, each agent i also broadcasts a message m_i^t at each step. Note that the agent could not directly broadcast the action information through the message, since the message and action are mutually dependent. To optimize the action policy, we use DQN as the basic approach for each agent. Each agent learns to evaluate the action value based on the current observation and the aggregated message from last step: $Q_i(o_i, m^-, a_i)$. The Q-network with parameters θ_i can be updated by minimizing the following TD-error:

$$\mathcal{L}(\theta_i) = \mathbb{E}_{o_i, a_i, m^-, r, o_i'}[(y_i - Q_i(o_i, m^-, a_i; \theta_i))^2] \tag{2}$$

where $y_i = r + \gamma \max_{a_i'} Q_i(o_i', m, a_i'; \theta_i)$. Equivalently, for the communication channel, the agent also uses reinforcement learning to output the message. For the communication message, we assume that the message is discrete and also uses DQN for the optimal communication policy. The Q network is denoted as $Q_i^m(o_i, m^-, a_i; \theta_i^m)$ and can also be updated similarly by minimizing the TD-error.

By adopting this paradigm, the vehicles can communicate with each other and accordingly be more flexible for cooperation. On one hand, the agents can broadcast messages which encodes the agent current observation and policy to others. On the other hand, each agent can optimize the policy based on the message from other agents, which contains information from a wider scope.

5.2   The Algorithm

In addition to the communication protocol, we also propose to decompose and reshape the reward function to learn efficient sensing policy. Here, we introduce the methods and then present the details of the algorithm.

Reward Decomposition. As described above, the agents use the global reward r to update their state-action value Q_i, Q_i^m. Since this reward is shared among the agents, directly using the reward to update the policy has the problem of *credit assignment*: it can be difficult for the agents to infer their own contribution for the global reward. To alleviate this problem, we decompose the global reward into different local reward for each user. Each agent i owns a separated reward: $r_i = \frac{A_{l_i}}{n_{l_i}} - c(b_i)$ (We temporarily abbreviate the time indicator t), where l_i represents the position of i. By decomposing the global reward, each agent can own a reward function that is more related to its behaviors. Therefore, it is easier for the agents to learn an efficient sensing policy.

Reward Reshaping. Another major challenge is that the capacity penalty can be very sparse. The agent only receives this penalty when it runs out of battery power. Such sparsity of the penalty can be very difficult to learn efficient policy. In this work, we propose to reshape the penalty as into a smoother form. Formally, the new reward can be written as:

$$\hat{r}_i = \frac{A_{l_i}}{n_{l_i}} - \frac{c_{out}}{\alpha b_i + 1} \tag{3}$$

where α is a positive hyper-parameter coefficient. With the reshaped reward, the mobile agents will receive an increasing penalty when the battery capacity b_i decreases. The penalty will equal to c_{out} when running out of power: $b_i = 0$. By introducing this intrinsic item, the reward function can be smoother to guide the mobile agent to navigate back to the charging stations. Figure 3 presents the reward function curve w.r.t different values of α. The curve will become smoother with smaller values of α.

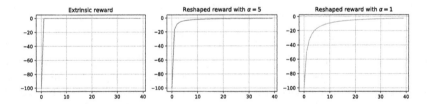

Fig. 3. The reward function w.r.t different values α

The Algorithm. Now we formally present the algorithm in Algorithm 1, denoted as Comm-Q. In this algorithm, we first initialize the parameters of the network Q_i and Q_i^m for each agent i. At each step, we first receive the broadcast message m^- from last step. The agents will then condition on the message to execute actions **a** and broadcast new messages **m**. The tuples will be stored into replay buffers. During training, we sample a mini-batch of tuples from the buffer and perform gradient back propagation to update the policy network and communication network.

Algorithm 1: Comm-Q learning

Initialize mobile agent network Q_i, Q_i^m for $i \in I$, mean message $m_0 \leftarrow 0$;
Receive initial observations $(o_1, o_2, ..., o_N)$;
for *step* $t = 1$ *to* ∞ **do**
    /* Execute the action and broadcast messages   */
    Get the mean message from last step $m^- = \frac{1}{N} \sum_{i=1}^{N} m_i^-$;
    for $i = 1$ *to* N **do**
        Sample and execute action $a_i \leftarrow \epsilon - \text{greedy}(Q_{\theta_i}(o_i, m^-, a_i))$;
        Sample and broadcast message $m_i \leftarrow \epsilon - \text{greedy}(Q_i^m(o_i, m^-, m_i))$;
    end
    /* Get reward and store in experience replay   */
    Get decomposed and reshaped reward $\hat{r}_i$ for $i \in I$;
    Store $\langle o_i, a_i, m^-, m, o_i', r_i \rangle$ in buffer $\mathcal{D}_i$ for $i \in I$;
    Set $o_i' = o_i$ for $i \in I$;
    /* Train the policy network and communication network   */
    for $i = 1$ *to* N **do**
        Sample K samples $(o_i, a_i, m^-, m, o_i', r_i)$ from $\mathcal{D}_i$;
        Set $y_i = r_i + \gamma \max_{a_i'} Q_i(o_i', m^-, a_i')$;
        Update policy network by minimizing:
        $\mathcal{L}(\theta_i) \leftarrow \frac{1}{K} \sum (y_i - Q_i(o_i, m^-, a_i))$
        Set $y_i^m = r_i + \gamma \max_{m_i'} Q_i^m(o_i', m^-, m_i')$;
        Update communication network by minimizing:
        $\mathcal{L}(\theta_i^m) \leftarrow \frac{1}{K} \sum (y_i^m - Q_i^m(o_i, m^-, m_i))$
    end
end

---

6 Evaluation

6.1 Experiment Setting

To validate the effectiveness of our algorithm, we manually construct a mobile sensing simulation environment. The discount factor γ is set as 0.95. The model is trained for $1,000,000$ steps and is evaluated by average step reward.

For each mobile vehicle, the battery capacity of each mobile vehicle is supposed to be 40 units. When reaching the mobile station, the vehicle will be recharged with 20 units at each time step. In the grid space, multiple random events are happening at different regions. We suppose the event will happen randomly and uniformly at different grid. When one event happens, the intensity of the center will first gradually increase to the peak value. Then it will decrease and fall to 0. The event intensity of the neighbor grid will also be incurred. But the intensity decreases with the distance to the event center. The message dimension is set as 4. The hyper-parameters are set as $\alpha = 5$ so that different costs are comparable. The penalty of running out of power is set as -100. Additionally, when the mobile vehicles run out of power, we randomly place the vehicle to one of the charging stations and restart the sensing.

We compare our algorithm with the following baselines. Note that both QMIX and VDN adopted centralized training framework, which is not applicable in practice. We only compare with them to validate the performance of our algorithm.

- Greedy: In the Greedy algorithm, each vehicle will greedily move to the grid with the highest event intensity at each step. We also force the agents to navigate back to the charging station in case of running out of power.
- IQL [18]: This algorithm uses independent Q-learning for each mobile agent. Each agent takes actions based only on local observations.
- VDN [16]: We compare with VDN in which a centralized critic is used. VDN assumes that the global reward is the sum of the reward from all the agents.
- QMIX [13]: The algorithm aims to minimize the summarized costs from all the mobile agents by using a mixing network to propagate gradient to all the agents. In QMIX, an underlying assumption is that the total return is monotone with the return of each agent.

In different RL-based algorithms, we use similar network structures with 2 layers of 3×3 convolution layer with 16 kernels. Each convolution layer is followed by a ReLU layer and a 2×2 max pooling layer. The output is first fed into a fully connected layer with 64 hidden dimensions. The hidden vector is then fed into a GRU layer and one fully connected layers to output the action values of Q_i and Q_i^m.

6.2   Performance Analysis

In the first experiment, we assume there are 6 mobile agents and 4 mobile stations, which are uniformly distributed in a grid with size 20×20. The observation range of each agent is 5, i.e., each agent can observer a grid of 11×11. The convergence of each algorithm is shown in Fig. 4(a). We run each algorithm for 3 times. The shaded area represents one standard deviation. As presented, our proposed Comm-Q achieves the best performance among the algorithms. Comm-Q can converge to around 100 after about $400,000$ steps. IQL can also achieve relatively high performance. However, since the vehicles cannot communicate with each other, they may easily coincide in the map. VDN and QMIX are cooperative algorithms where all the agents share the same reward. Their performances are poor mainly because the agents cannot infer individual contribution to the global reward. Comm-Q also has smaller variance compared to other algorithms, which makes the algorithm more robust in different scenarios.

After training, we fix the network parameters and compare the performance of different algorithms in the simulation environment. The result is shown in Fig. 4(b). In this figure, the purple part represents the battery penalty and the blue part represents the true reward function, which equals the sensing reward minus the battery penalty. As presented, our proposed method achieves the highest reward among the algorithms. In particular, the sensing reward outperforms other algorithms. This is because the vehicles in Comm-Q can avoid coinciding with each other through communication. The Greedy algorithm forces the agent to navigate back to the charging station, and accordingly incurs no battery penalty. However, it could deal with the dynamics of the environment and only has low sensing reward. IQL also performs well in charging, but the sensing reward can be quite limited. For the QMIX and VDN algorithms, their battery penalty can be very large. This is because the agents could hardly infer their contribution to the battery penalty.

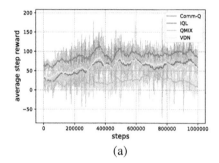
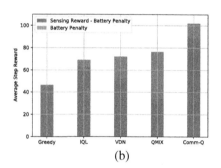

(a)   (b)

Fig. 4. a. The convergence of average step reward of different algorithms during training; b. The average step reward during execution for each algorithm. (Color figure online)

Next, we investigate the effect of the hyper-parameter α in shaping the battery penalty. We try different values of α and present the average step reward of Comm-Q in Fig. 5(a). In this figure, as the value of α increases, the battery penalty will become less smooth, and it would be harder for the vehicles to recharge. At the same time, they will explore the environment more and generate higher sensing reward. In the extreme case when $\alpha = 0$, the vehicle will always stay at the charging station to avoid losing power.

In the last experiment, we validate the scalability of Comm-Q. We increase the number of mobile vehicles as 128 and charging stations as 16. The grid space is now 80×80. As there are multiple agents, we assume that the agents are homogeneous and share the same network parameters. The agents can still behave differently with local observations. As QMIX and VDN take too much time, we only present the result of Comm-Q and IQL. As shown in Fig. 5(b), the Comm-Q algorithm can still achieve better performance. When there are more agents, they may become more easily to coincide. However, Comm-Q can still successfully coordinate the behaviors of the agents and achieve high performance.

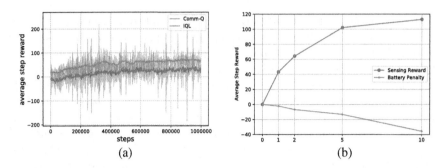

Fig. 5. a. The convergence of the algorithm; b. The convergence of average step reward of different algorithms during training.

7   Conclusion

This paper presents a novel algorithm for mobile sensing with charging stations. In this environment, the mobile vehicles should cooperate with each other to maximize the sensing coverage. Due to the vehicles make decentralized decisions, we propose to use active communication among them to promote cooperation. Specifically, the communication is learned based on Q-leaning algorithm. We also propose to decompose and reshape the reward function, so that the training efficiency can be greatly increased. Extensive evaluation shows that our algorithm can converge very fast during training. It also achieves the best performance during execution. In addition, the vehicles in our algorithm can successfully navigate back to the charging stations.

Acknowledgments. This research was funded by Natural Science Foundation of Jiangsu Province (No. BK20200752); The NUPTSF (No. NY220080).

References

1. Carnelli, P.E., Yeh, J., Sooriyabandara, M., Khan, A.: Parkus: a novel vehicle parking detection system. In: Twenty-Ninth IAAI Conference (2017)
2. Das, A., et al.: Tarmac: Targeted multi-agent communication. In: International Conference on Machine Learning, pp. 1538–1546. PMLR (2019)
3. Foerster, J., Assael, I.A., de Freitas, N., Whiteson, S.: Learning to communicate with deep multi agent reinforcement learning. Adv. Neural. Inf. Process. Syst. **29**, 2137–2145 (2016)
4. Foerster, J.N., Farquhar, G., Afouras, T., Nardelli, N., Whiteson, S.: Counterfactual multi-agent policy gradients. In: AAAI, pp. 2974–2982 (2018)
5. Guo, B., et al.: Mobile crowd sensing and computing: The review of an emerging human-powered sensing paradigm. ACM Comput. Surv. (CSUR) **48**(1), 1–31 (2015)
6. Jaques, N., et al.: Intrinsic social motivation via causal influence in multi-agent RL (2018)

7. Karaliopoulos, M., Telelis, O., Koutsopoulos, I.: User recruitment for mobile crowd-sensing over opportunistic networks. In: 2015 IEEE Conference on Computer Communications (INFOCOM), pp. 2254–2262. IEEE (2015)
8. Lane, N.D., Miluzzo, E., Lu, H., Peebles, D., Choudhury, T., Campbell, A.T.: A survey of mobile phone sensing. IEEE Commun. Mag. **48**(9), 140–150 (2010)
9. Liu, C.H., Ma, X., Gao, X., Tang, J.: Distributed energy-efficient multi-UAV navigation for long-term communication coverage by deep reinforcement learning. IEEE Trans. Mob. Comput. **19**(6), 1274–1285 (2019)
10. Lowe, R., Foerster, J., Boureau, Y.L., Pineau, J., Dauphin, Y.: On the pitfalls of measuring emergent communication. arXiv preprint arXiv:1903.05168 (2019)
11. Lowe, R., Wu, Y., Tamar, A., Harb, J., Abbeel, O.P., Mordatch, I.: Multi-agent actor-critic for mixed cooperative-competitive environments. Adv. Neural. Inf. Process. Syst. **30**, 6379–6390 (2017)
12. Mnih, V., et al.: Playing atari with deep reinforcement learning. arXiv preprint arXiv:1312.5602 (2013)
13. Rashid, T., Samvelyan, M., Schroeder, C., Farquhar, G., Foerster, J., Whiteson, S.: Qmix: monotonic value function factorisation for deep multi-agent reinforcement learning. In: International Conference on Machine Learning, pp. 4292–4301 (2018)
14. Silver, D., et al.: Mastering the game of go with deep neural networks and tree search. Nature **529**(7587), 484–489 (2016)
15. Sukhbaatar, S., Szlam, A., Fergus, R.: Learning multiagent communication with backpropagation. arXiv preprint arXiv:1605.07736 (2016)
16. Sunehag, P., et al.: Value-decomposition networks for cooperative multi-agent learning. arXiv preprint arXiv:1706.05296 (2017)
17. Sutton, R.S., Barto, A.G., et al.: Introduction to Reinforcement Learning, vol. 135. MIT Press, Cambridge (1998)
18. Tan, M.: Multi-agent reinforcement learning: independent vs. cooperative agents. In: ICML 1993 Proceedings of the Tenth International Conference on International Conference on Machine Learning, pp. 487–494 (1997)
19. Zhou, Z., et al.: When mobile crowd sensing meets UAV: energy-efficient task assignment and route planning. IEEE Trans. Commun. **66**(11), 5526–5538 (2018)

Enhancing Blackslist-Based Packet Filtration Using Blockchain in Wireless Sensor Networks

Wenjuan Li[1,2], Weizhi Meng[1,3], Yu Wang[1(✉)], and Jin Li[1]

[1] Institute of Artificial Intelligence and Blockchain,
Guangzhou University, Guangzhou, China
yuwang@gzhu.edu.cn
[2] Department of Computing, The Polytechnic University of Hong Kong,
Hung Hom, China
[3] Department of Applied Mathematics and Computer Science, Technical University
of Denmark, Kongens Lyngby, Denmark

Abstract. A wireless sensor network (WSN) consists of distributed sensors for monitoring network status and recording data, which is playing a major role in Internet of Things (IoT). This type of wireless network is driven by the availability of inexpensive and low-powered components. However, WSN is vulnerable to many kinds of attacks like Distributed Denial of Service (DDoS) due to its dispersed structure and unreliable transmission. In the literature, constructing a suitable distributed packet filter is a promising solution to help mitigate unwanted traffic. While how to ensure the integrity of exchanged data is a challenge as malicious internal node can share manipulated data to degrade the effectiveness of filtration. In this work, we design a blockchain-based blacklist packet filter with collaborative intrusion detection that can be deployed in WSNs. The blockchain technology is used to help build a robust blacklist for reducing unwanted traffic. In the evaluation, we investigate the performance of our filter with a real dataset and in a practical WSN environment. The results demonstrate that our proposed filter can enhance the robustness of blacklist generation.

Keywords: Wireless sensor network · Distributed denial-of-service attack · Blockchain technology · Network security · Packet filtration

1 Introduction

A wireless sensor network (WSN) is usually composed of distributed autonomous devices with sensors to monitor environmental conditions in a collaborated manner. It can be considered as the backbone of Internet of Things (IoT) environment, by transmitting data and offering access points for connection [31]. Each WSN node is typically equipped with a radio transceiver or some kind of wireless communication device, e.g., a small microcontroller [20]. WSN has been applied in many fields such as intelligent transportation [22], smart city [37], agriculture [39] and so on. The global industrial WSN market size was expected to reach 94.21 billion USD by the end of 2025 [1].

© Springer Nature Switzerland AG 2021
Z. Liu et al. (Eds.): WASA 2021, LNCS 12938, pp. 624–635, 2021.
https://doi.org/10.1007/978-3-030-86130-8_49

The relatively simple functioning makes WSNs easy to implement, but due to the unreliable transmission and the distributed structure, WSN is vulnerable to many attacks such as Sybil attack [25], spoofing attack, betrayal attack [34], and Distributed Denial of Service (DDoS) attacks [19]. For example, DDoS attacks can quickly consume the energy of WSN nodes and disrupt the normal functions provided by these sensor nodes [5, 10].

To mitigate these potential risks, intrusion detection system (IDS) is a basic and important security mechanism [17]. Basically, an IDS can be categorized as rule-based detection and anomaly-based detection. The former needs to make a signature matching between the current events and the signature database. The latter needs to build a normal profile and then to compare it with current profile. To fit the distributed network structure, distributed and collaborative intrusion detection has been deployed, which can enhance the detection performance by allowing different detection nodes exchanging required data and information [24, 34]. However, due to the resource constraint, many existing security solutions are unsuitable for WSNs. Thus, more lightweight intrusion detection is demanded for protecting WSNs.

Motivation and Contributions. In the literature, constructing an appropriate packet filter (deployed with a detector) is a promising solution for WSNs to reduce unwanted traffic. For instance, Meng et al. [33] introduced a trusted packet filter in a distributed environments, which can build a blacklist via trust management. However, cyber attackers may have a chance to share misleading information by compromising one or more internal nodes. It is a big challenge on how to secure the integrity of shared data.

For this issue, blockchain technology is a potential solution that can help build a shared and immutable ledger. In this work, we aim to design a blockchain-based blacklist packet filter based on some prior work [29, 32], which can reduce unwanted traffic under attacks. Our contributions can be summarized as follows.

- We introduce a blockchain-based blacklist packet filter, which consists of a blacklist packet filter, a monitor engine and a collaboration component. It can be integrated with collaborative intrusion detection and help refine traffic for WSN nodes. The blacklist generation is based on a weighted ratio-based statistical method.
- The use of blockchain aims to help establish a communication among different nodes without a trusted third party, as well as protect the integrity of shared data that would be used for building a robust blackslist.
- We evaluate the performance of our designed packet filter with a real dataset and in a real WSN under DDoS attack (external attack) and betrayal attack (insider attack). The experimental results demonstrate the effectiveness and robustness of our filter to reduce unwanted traffic in hostile conditions.

The remaining parts are structured as follows. We introduce the design of blockchain-based blacklist packet filter including its major components in Sect. 2. Section 3 investigates the performance of our packet filter under attacks and analyzes the experimental results. Section 4 introduces related research studies on intrusion detection in WSNs and packet filter construction. Section 5 concludes our work.

2   Our Approach

This section briefly introduces the background on blockchain technology and details our proposed blockchain-based blacklist packet filter.

2.1   Blockchain Background

With the popularity of bitcoin, blockchain technology has received much attention from both academia and industry. Such technology can be used for monitoring public health data, tracking donation, securing supply chains and more. The blockchain market surpassed 488 million USD in 2018 and was expected to climb to over 39 billion USD by 2025 [2].

Generally, blockchain can be considered as an open, distributed ledger that can record transactions among parties in a verifiable and efficient way. The blockchain structure contains a list of blocks with two major data items: a pointer that records the location information of next block, and data organized in an order. The first block, called Genesis block, is the first record in the blockchain. Each block includes a number of different transactions, previous block hash, timestamp and transaction root [35]. Due the benefits provided by blockchain, it has been applied in may fields, such as healthcare industry [7], intrusion detection [36], intelligent transportation [16] and more.

There are three main types of blockchain: a) *public blockchain* indicates that the data and access to the system is available to anyone like Ethereum [3], b) *private blockchain* indicates that the data and access is given by users from a specific organization or authorized users like Hyperledger [4], and c) *consortium blockchain* indicates the data and access is given by preliminary assigned users. To add a block to the chain, a consensus algorithm is often pre-agreed among all participants. If each node verifies the block and checks whether the information is correct, then the block is added to the chain.

2.2   Blockchain-Based Blacklist Packet Filter

Packet filtration is a promising solution to protect WSN nodes, while how to ensure the shared data is still a challenge on constructing an effective distributed packet filter. In this work, we focus on a type of blacklist packet filter from prior work [29,32,33] due to its lightweight computation. Motivated by the benefits of blockchain technology, we develop a blockchain-based blacklist packet filter that can be robust to data tempering. Figure 1 depicts the high-level structure of our proposed packet filter, including three major components: collaboration component, trust management component and blacklist packet filter.

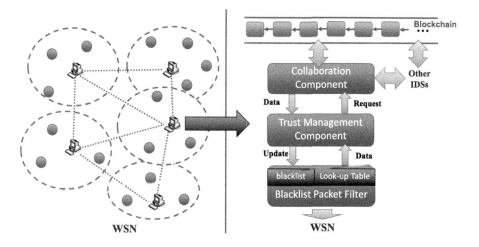

Fig. 1. The high-level review of blockchain structure.

– *Collaboration component.* This component is responsible for connecting with other IDS nodes and gathering the required information for computing the IP reputation and generating the blacklist. For the local IDS, the trust management component can send a request to this component and exchange the information with target nodes.
– *Trust management component.* This component is a key component with the purpose of generating the blacklist based on the collected information. It has to calculate the IP reputation and update the list regularly. In a CIDS environment, this component can request the data from target nodes.
– *Blacklist packet filter.* This component is mainly used to reduce traffic based on the IP reputation. It includes two parts: a blacklist and a look-up table. The former contains all blacklisted IP addresses (for unwanted packet reduction), and the latter indexes all IDS signatures by the blacklisted IP addresses (for process acceleration).

Filter Workflow. The incoming traffic should first reach the *blacklist packet filter.* If the IP address of the packet matches one in the blacklist, then the filter will further compare the payload of this packet with the signatures in its *look-up table* (contains all active IDS signatures).

– If a match is identified, then the blacklist packet filter can block this packet and generate an alert. Meanwhile, a short message will be sent to the monitor engine, reporting the IP address as malicious.
– On the other hand, if the payload of the packet does not match any signatures, then this packet will be sent to the internal network directly.

WSN with Collaborative Intrusion Detection. In such WSN, CIDSs are used to protect the security of sensor nodes. Similar to a cluster head, each CIDS manages the blacklist packet filter for several WSNs (as shown in Fig. 1). Each CIDS can exchange information with other nodes in order to collect required information for computing IP reputation and generating the blacklist.

Weighted Ratio-Based Blacklist Generation. The blacklist-based packet filter uses a weighted ratio-based method to compute the IP reputation as shown in Eq. (1), where i represents the total number of *good* packets, k represents the total number of *bad* packets and W is the weight value.

$$IP\ reputation = \frac{i}{\sum_1^k W \times k}\quad (i, k \in \mathbf{N}) \tag{1}$$

Blockchain Layer. To ensure the integrity of shared data, a consortium blockchain is used to identify malicious data provided by CIDS nodes. CIDS nodes would only accept the data/information that has been verified by chain nodes. Thus, the blockchain can be only expanded if the majority of nodes have agreed that the received data is trustful.

3   Evaluation

In this section, we conduct two experiments to investigate the performance of our proposed blacklist-based packet filter. The consortium blockchain was deployed in a mid-end computer with Intel(R) Core (TM)i6, CPU 2.5 GHz with 500 GB storage. There is a need for 2/3 nodes in the network to sign a block to be appended to the blockchain.

- *Experiment-1.* We use a real dataset captured from a honeynet environment (with five-day data) to explore the reduced time consumption between our filter and the original one.
- *Experiment-2.* We collaborated with an IT organization and investigate the filter performance under adversarial WSN scenarios with DDoS attack and betrayal attack.

To facilitate the comparison with previous work [29,32], we set the threshold as 1, the weight value as 10, and the update time was 5 s (which allows the blacklist packet filter to complete all required operations regarding blacklist generation and updating).

3.1   Experiment-1

We constructed a real dataset captured from a Honeynet project (https://www.honeynet.org/tag/hong-kong/) with the *base rate* [6] of around 0.003937. It consists of five-day incoming network traffic (denote as *DAY1*, *DAY2*, *DAY3*, *DAY4* and *DAY5*), with around 4–6 million packets each day [32]. The packets in the dataset were labeled as either *normal* or *attack* by means of expert knowledge.

Table 1. The reduced time consumption between the original blacklist packet filter and our proposed filter.

Week Day (Original Filter - normal)	DAY1	DAY2	DAY3	DAY4	DAY5
Reduction rate (%)	24.61	28.65	**30.42**	22.56	32.32
Week Day (Original Filter - attack)	DAY1	DAY2	DAY3	DAY4	DAY5
Reduction rate (%)	24.61	28.65	**26.56**	**17.83**	**26.37**
Week Day (Our Filter - attack)	DAY1	DAY2	DAY3	DAY4	DAY5
Reduction rate (%)	24.61	28.65	**30.42**	22.56	32.32

To explore the performance between the original filter and our proposed filter, we manipulated some false data in *DAY3*, *DAY4* and *DAY5* to influence the blacklist generation. Table 1 shows the reduced time consumption between the original filter and our proposed filter under normal and attack conditions. It is found that our proposed packet filter would not affect the performance of the original one (*DAY1* and *DAY2*), but can enhance its security under attack condition (from *DAY3* to *DAY5*). For example, due to the attack, the original filter had an obvious decrease of filtration rate from *DAY3* to *DAY5*, compared to the normal performance. By contrast, our proposed filter can be robust to such type of attack thanks to the usage of blockchain (i.e., malicious data would be rejected if major nodes does not accept it).

3.2 Experiment-2

To investigate the practical performance of our proposed filter, we worked with an IT organization (in Southern China) and conducted an experiment in a WSN environment with 35 CIDS nodes. We particularly launched two attacks: DDoS (flooding attack) and betrayal attack (where a trusted internal node becomes malicious), and observed the impact on both the network and our filter. The former aims to decrease the bandwidth while the latter aims to degrade the effectiveness of blacklist by sending false data.

The experiment was repeat three times and we adopted two metrics: average false positive rate (AFR) and average false negative rate (AFN), which are average values of false positives and false negatives.

Table 2. The average false positive rate (AFR) and average false negative rate (AFN) regarding the generation of blacklist.

Metric	Original filter	Our filter
AFP (%)	16.4	6.32
AFN (%)	18.6	7.83

Table 2 shows that under adversarial conditions, the original filter would suffer a high false rate of generating blacklist (with AFP 16.4% and AFN 18.6%).

Especially, the insider attack can cause a high false negative rate, so that the filter is ineffective in reducing unwanted traffic. In comparison, our proposed filter could reach an AFP of 6.32% and an AFN of 7.83%, demonstrating that our filter can enhance the security of blacklist generation. This is because the blockchain technology can help secure the integrity and authenticity of shared data. The malicious input would be rejected due to the consensus process among all CIDS nodes.

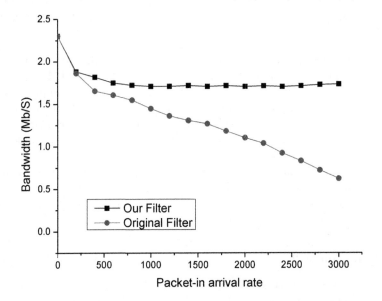

Fig. 2. The impact of flooding DDoS attacks on the network bandwidth between our filter and the original filter.

Figure 2 depicts the impact of flood DDoS attacks on the network bandwidth between the original filter and our filter, using the tool (https://www.netscantools.com/nstpro_packet_generator.html). It is observed that the bandwidth had a clear decrease under the original filter, i.e., the bandwidth decreased to below 1 when the packet-in arrival rate reached 2400 packets/s. In contrast, our filter could be robust against malicious input and protect the blacklist generation via the blockchain technology. Under our filter, the bandwidth could be maintained at around 1.7. The experimental results overall demonstrate the viability and effectiveness of our proposed filter.

3.3   Discussion

The use of blockchain in constructing a packet filter is not new in the literature. For instance, Kolokotronis et al. [21] proposed a collaborative trust-based packet filter, in which the trust calculation engine continuously updates the blacklist by collecting alerts from the detector and side information from the CIDS peers. However, they did not show any experimental results on the filter performance. In this work, we detail the design of our blockchain-based packet filter and analyze its performance with a real dataset and in a real WSN environment. Below are some open challenges that can be addressed in our future work.

- *Blockchain platform.* In our current work, we only use a demo blockchain system to realize our filter and explore its performance. In future work, we plan to consider a real blockchain platform such as Ethereum and Hyperledger and validate the performance.
- *Security threats and attacks.* In this work, we explore the filter performance under DDoS attack and betrayal attack. The results demonstrate the effectiveness of blockchain-based approach, while some other attacks could be considered in future, including advanced insider attacks such as fingerprinting attack [26].
- *Communication workload.* The blockchain can bring many benefits in protecting the data integrity, but it may also cause more delay and overhead during the consensus process (depending on the consensus algorithms). This is an important topic in our future studies.
- *Trust management in blacklist generation.* How to build trust is very important to generate a robust blacklist that can be used in the packet filter. In this work, we adopt a weighted ratio-based blacklist generation method, which can provide a false rate around 7–9% in the real WSN environment. In future, we plan to consider other trust management models (e.g., Bayesian model [31]) and investigate the filtration performance.

4 Related Work

This section introduces related research work regarding intrusion detection in WSNs and the construction of software or hardware-based packet filter.

4.1 Intrusion Detection in WSNs

To protect WSNs from security threats, intrusion detection has been widely studied. Chen et al. [12] focused on the security of WSNs and introduced a protocol to construct a trust framework model called ETSN. The trust value relies on different events of a sensor node in WSNs, and would be distributed based on the radio range of the sensor. Wang et al. [41] introduced IDMTM - Intrusion Detection Mechanism based on the Trust Model, which could help detect malicious nodes by collecting evidence from locally and the neighboring nodes. Dang et al. [13] introduced a Trusted Intrusion Detection System (TIDS) with double cluster heads and many cluster members for WSNs. There are a kind of monitoring nodes that are responsible for collecting the information and evaluating the credibility of cluster nodes. Han et al. [15] aimed to design a low-consumption IDS to detect malicious attacks for WSNs, based on game theory and an autoregressive model. It could consider energy consumption during detection process and select a balanced strategy between detection efficiency and cost. Bai et al. [9] presented a detection algorithm based on the changing rates of multiple attributes (CRMA), which can detect multiple attacks. The CRMA values could be calculated by minimizing the weighted deviation via convex optimization. If the deviation of Observed Change Rate exceeds the threshold, then an alarm can be made.

Trust management is an important solution to build a trust-based collaborative intrusion detection system (CIDS) for WSNs and distributed networks. For instance, Li et al. [24,25] designed a intrusion sensitivity-based CIDS and assigned the value via machine learning classifiers. The use of intrusion sensitivity can enhance the detection accuracy of malicious nodes. Ma et al. [27,28] proposed a Distributed Consensus based Trust Model (DCONST), which could detect multiple-mix-attacks and evaluate the trustworthiness of nodes by sharing certain information called cognition. More related work on WSN-related IDSs can refer to a survey [11].

4.2   Packet Filtration

Due to the computing resource and energy constrains, many existing security mechanisms are not suitable for WSNs. Thus, constructing a packet filter is a lightweight security solution to reduce malicious or unwanted traffic. Meng and Kwok [29,32] introduced a context-aware blacklist packet filter, which generated the blacklist using a weighted ratio-based approach. The results demonstrated that the filter could be effective to reduce the IDS burden in processing network packets without affecting the whole security level. Then they introduced a list packet filter using both whitelist and blacklist technique. Meng et al. [33] proposed a collaborative trust-based packet filter that could achieve robust trust computation and effectively reduce unwanted traffic. They defined a metric of overall IP confidence to represent the overall trustworthiness of an IP source. Trabelsi et al. [40] designed a hybrid mechanism based on both splay tree filters and pattern-matching algorithms to enhance IDS packet filtering, allowing early packet rejection or acceptance.

In addition to software-based packet filtration, many research focuses on hardware-assisted packet filtration. Sourdis et al. [38] selected only a small portion from each IDS rule to be matched in the pre-filtering step and then built a hardware-based pre-filtering solution with multiple processing engines. Leogrande et al. [23] pointed out that existing filtering expressions is too complex and introduced pFSA, which used finite state automata to ensure the optimal number of checks on the packets without sacrificing filtration time. Fiessler et al. [18] identified that complex rules requiring software-based processing may be interleaved at arbitrary positions and introduced HyPaFilter+, a hybrid classification system with an FPGA-based hardware matcher to reach a simple but effective hardware and software packet filtration. Durante et al. [14] introduced a formal model for networks including multiple cascaded firewalls, which can enable the transfer of a set of rules from a firewall to its downstream neighbors when the changes in the input traffic profile. The transformation algorithm can preserve the security integrity of the network while moving rules between cascaded firewalls, allowing tangible performance improvements in terms of packet processing rate for a given traffic profile.

While for distributed packet filtration, how to ensure the authenticity and integrity of shared data is a challenge, which motivates our work in designing a blockchain-based blacklist packet filter.

5   Conclusion

WSN is an important part of IoT environments, which can be used to monitor the environmental status and changes. While WSN is vulnerable to various attacks like DDoS attacks. To mitigate the unwanted traffic, this work proposes a blockchain-based blacklist packet filter. The use of blockchain technology is motivated by its capability of ensuring data integrity, and the use of blacklist is due to its wide adoption in practice. In the evaluation, we investigate the performance of our filter with a real dataset and in a practical WSN environment under DDoS attack and betrayal attack. It is found that, as compared with the original filter, our proposed filter can be more robust against malicious input and protect the blacklist generation process.

Acknowledgment. This work was partially supported by National Natural Science Foundation of China (No. 61802080 and 61802077), and Guangzhou University Research Project (No. RQ2020085 and RD2020076).

References

1. Wireless Sensor Network Market - Forecast (2021–2026). https://www.industryarc.com/Report/211/Wireless-Sensor-Network-Market-Research-Report.html. Accessed Feb 2021
2. Size of the blockchain technology market worldwide from 2018 to 2025. https://www.statista.com/statistics/647231/worldwide-blockchain-technology-market-size/. Accessed Mar 2021
3. Ethereum - open-source blockchain. https://ethereum.org/en/
4. Hyperledger, C.: Open Source Blockchain Technologies. https://www.hyperledger.org/
5. Abidoye, A.P., Obagbuwa, I.C.: DDoS attacks in WSNs: detection and countermeasures. IET Wirel. Sens. Syst. **8**(2), 52–59 (2018)
6. Axelsson, S.: The base-rate fallacy and the difficulty of intrusion detection. ACM Trans. Inf. Syst. Secur. **3**(3), 186–205 (2020)
7. De Aguiar, E.J., Facial, B.S., Krishnamachari, B., Ueyama, J.: A survey of blockchain-based strategies for healthcare. ACM Comput. Surv. **53**(2), 27:1–27:27 (2020)
8. Bannour, F., Souihi, S., Mellouk, A.: Adaptive distributed SDN controllers: application to content-centric delivery networks. Future Gener. Comput. Syst. **113**, 78–93 (2020)

9. Bai, H., Zhang, X., Liu, F.: Intrusion detection algorithm based on change rates of multiple attributes for WSN. Wirel. Commun. Mob. Comput. **2020**, 8898847:1–8898847:16 (2020)

10. Bhuyan, M.H., Azad, N.A., Meng, W., Jensen, C.D.: Analyzing the communication security between smartphones and IoT based on CORAS. In: Au, M.H., et al. (eds.) NSS 2018. LNCS, vol. 11058, pp. 251–265. Springer, Cham (2018). https://doi.org/10.1007/978-3-030-02744-5_19

11. Butun, I., Morgera, S.D., Sankar, R.: A survey of intrusion detection systems in wireless sensor networks. IEEE Commun. Surv. Tutorials **16**(1), 266–282 (2014)

12. Chen, H., Wu, H., Hu, J., Gao, C.: Event-based Trust Framework Model in Wireless Sensor Networks. In: Proceedings of the 2008 International Conference on Networking, Architecture, and Storage (NAS), pp. 359–364 (2008)

13. Dang, N., Liu, X., Yu, J., Zhang, X.: TIDS: trust intrusion detection system based on double cluster heads for WSNs. In: Biagioni, E.S., Zheng, Y., Cheng, S. (eds.) WASA 2019. LNCS, vol. 11604, pp. 67–83. Springer, Cham (2019). https://doi.org/10.1007/978-3-030-23597-0_6

14. Durante, L., Seno, L., Valenzano, A.: A formal model and technique to redistribute the packet filtering load in multiple firewall networks. IEEE Trans. Inf. Forensics Secur. **16**, 2637–2651 (2021)

15. Han, L., Zhou, M., Jia, W., Dalil, Z., Xu, X.: Intrusion detection model of wireless sensor networks based on game theory and an autoregressive model. Inf. Sci. **476**, 491–504 (2019)

16. Humayun, M., Jhanjhi, N.Z., Hamid, B., Ahmed, G.: Emerging smart logistics and transportation using IoT and blockchain. IEEE Internet Things Mag. **3**(2), 58–62 (2020)

17. Hutchison, K.: Wireless intrusion detection systems. SANS GSEC Whitepaper, pp. 1–18 (2005). http://www.sans.org/readingroom/whitepapers/wireless/wireless-intrusion-detection-systems1543

18. Fiessler, A., Lorenz, C., Hager, S., Scheuermann, B., Moore, A.W.: HyPaFilter+: enhanced hybrid packet filtering using hardware assisted classification and header space analysis. IEEE/ACM Trans. Netw. **25**(6), 3655–3669 (2017)

19. Kasim, O.: An efficient and robust deep learning based network anomaly detection against distributed denial of service attacks. Comput. Netw. **180**, 107390 (2020)

20. Khan, I., Belqasmi, F., Glitho, R.H., Crespi, N., Morrow, M., Polakos, P.: Wireless sensor network virtualization: a survey. IEEE Commun. Surv. Tutor. **18**(1), 553–576 (2016)

21. Kolokotronis, N., Brotsis, S., Germanos, G., Vassilakis, C., Shiaeles, S.: On blockchain architectures for trust-based collaborative intrusion detection. In: Proceedings of SERVICES, pp. 21–28 (2019)

22. Kong, F., Zhou, Y., Chen, G.: Multimedia data fusion method based on wireless sensor network in intelligent transportation system. Multim. Tools Appl. **79**(47), 35195–35207 (2020)

23. Leogrande, M., Risso, F., Ciminiera, L.: Modeling complex packet filters with finite state automata. IEEE/ACM Trans. Netw. **23**(1), 42–55 (2015)

24. Li, W., Meng, W., Kwok, L.-F.: Design of intrusion sensitivity-based trust management model for collaborative intrusion detection networks. In: Zhou, J., Gal-Oz, N., Zhang, J., Gudes, E. (eds.) IFIPTM 2014. IAICT, vol. 430, pp. 61–76. Springer, Heidelberg (2014). https://doi.org/10.1007/978-3-662-43813-8_5

25. Li, W., Meng, W.: Enhancing collaborative intrusion detection networks using intrusion sensitivity in detecting pollution attacks. Inf. Comput. Secur. **24**(3), 265–276 (2016)

26. Li, W., Meng, W., Kwok, L.F., Ip, H.H.S.: Developing advanced fingerprint attacks on challenge-based collaborative intrusion detection networks. Cluster Comput. **21**(1), 299–310 (2018)
27. Ma, Z., Liu, L., Meng, W.: DCONST: detection of multiple-mix-attack malicious nodes using consensus-based trust in IoT networks. In: Liu, J.K., Cui, H. (eds.) ACISP 2020. LNCS, vol. 12248, pp. 247–267. Springer, Cham (2020). https://doi.org/10.1007/978-3-030-55304-3_13
28. Ma, Z., Liu, L., Meng, W.: Towards multiple-mix-attack detection via consensus-based trust management in IoT networks. Comput. Secur. **96**, 101898 (2020)
29. Meng, Y., Kwok, L.F.: Adaptive context-aware packet filter scheme using statistic-based blacklist generation in network intrusion detection. In: Proceedings of the IAS, pp. 74–79 (2011)
30. Meng, Y., Kwok, L.: Enhancing list-based packet filter using IP verification mechanism against IP spoofing attack in network intrusion detection. In: Xu, L., Bertino, E., Mu, Y. (eds.) NSS 2012. LNCS, vol. 7645, pp. 1–14. Springer, Heidelberg (2012). https://doi.org/10.1007/978-3-642-34601-9_1
31. Meng, Y., Li, W., Kwok, L.: Evaluation of detecting malicious nodes using Bayesian model in wireless intrusion detection. In: Lopez, J., Huang, X., Sandhu, R. (eds.) NSS 2013. LNCS, vol. 7873, pp. 40–53. Springer, Heidelberg (2013). https://doi.org/10.1007/978-3-642-38631-2_4
32. Meng, Y., Kwok, L.F.: Adaptive blacklist-based packet filter with a statistic-based approach in network intrusion detection. J. Netw. Comput. Appl. **39**, 83–92 (2014)
33. Meng, W., Li, W., Kwok, L.F.: Towards effective trust-based packet filtering in collaborative network environments. IEEE Trans. Netw. Serv. Manage. **14**(1), 233–245 (2017)
34. Meng, W., Fei, F., Li, W., Au, M.H.: Evaluating challenge-based trust mechanism in medical smartphone networks: an empirical study. In: Proceedings of the 2017 IEEE Global Communications Conference (GLOBECOM), pp. 1–6 (2017)
35. Meng, W., et al.: Position paper on blockchain technology: smart contract and applications. In: Au, M.H., et al. (eds.) NSS 2018. LNCS, vol. 11058, pp. 474–483. Springer, Cham (2018). https://doi.org/10.1007/978-3-030-02744-5_35
36. Meng, W., Tischhauser, E.W., Wang, Q., Wang, Y., Han, J.: When intrusion detection meets blockchain technology: a review. IEEE Access **6**(1), 10179–10188 (2018)
37. Peixoto, J.P.J., Costa, D.G.: Wireless visual sensor networks for smart city applications: a relevance-based approach for multiple sinks mobility. Future Gener. Comput. Syst. **76**, 51–62 (2017)
38. Sourdis, I., Dimopoulos, V., Pnevmatikatos, D.N., Vassiliadis, S.: Packet pre-filtering for network intrusion detection. In: Proceedings of ANCS, pp. 183–192 (2006)
39. Thakur, D., Kumar, Y., Kumar, A., Singh, P.K.: Applicability of wireless sensor networks in precision agriculture: a review. Wirel. Pers. Commun. **107**(1), 471–512 (2019)
40. Trabelsi, Z., Zeidan, S., Masud, M.M.: Network packet filtering and deep packet inspection hybrid mechanism for IDS early packet matching. In: Proceedings of AINA, pp. 808–815 (2016)
41. Wang, F., Huang, C., Zhang, J., Rong, C.: IDMTM: a novel intrusion detection mechanism based on trust model for ad-hoc networks. In: Proceedings of the 22nd IEEE International Conference on Advanced Information Networking and Applications (AINA), p. 978C984 (2008)

Author Index

Li, Yufan   I-133
Li, Zhangtan   II-123
Li, Zhehao   I-416
Li, Zhengyu   III-192
Li, Zhi   I-240
Li, Zhiqiang   II-353
Li, Zhuo   III-274
Li, Zihao   II-186
Liang, Feng   II-538
Liang, Guangxian   III-282
Liang, Lin   III-200
Liang, Yuxiang   III-218
Liao, Zilan   I-441
Lin, Feng   I-511
Lin, Jingqiang   II-107, II-210
Lin, Junyu   II-160
Lin, Yaguang   I-364
Ling, Taiwei   II-262
Liu, Anqi   II-225
Liu, Baoxu   III-20
Liu, Bing   III-274
Liu, Chao   II-147
Liu, Chaoge   III-20
Liu, Chengsheng   III-291
Liu, Chunfeng   I-16
Liu, Chunhui   III-117
Liu, Dongjingdian   I-263
Liu, Hong   II-378, III-367
Liu, Jiahao   III-254
Liu, Jianqing   II-326
Liu, Jiawen   II-378, III-367
Liu, Jiaxi   III-450
Liu, Jing   III-512
Liu, Junliang   II-612
Liu, Kai   II-430
Liu, Liang   II-481, II-494, II-510
Liu, Linfeng   III-429
Liu, Ning   I-78
Liu, Qihe   III-172
Liu, Qixu   III-20
Liu, Shaofan   III-11
Liu, Shengli   III-479
Liu, Suhui   I-95
Liu, Wei   I-41
Liu, Wenrui   III-471
Liu, Xiang   II-417
Liu, Xiaojie   III-46
Liu, Xiaotong   III-209
Liu, Xiaowu   II-303
Liu, Xin   III-318

Liu, Xuan   II-135
Liu, Xue   II-314
Liu, Yangsu   II-277
Liu, Ye   I-41
Liu, Yihao   III-209
Liu, Yulei   II-510
Liu, Zewei   I-147
Liu, Zichun   III-390
Liu, Zouyu   III-553
Lu, Bingxian   I-65
Lu, Guangquan   I 203
Lu, Xian   III-310
Lu, Xiaomeng   III-582
Lu, Xiaozhen   II-575
Lu, Yang   III-11
Luan, He   III-471
Luo, Chuanwen   I-584
Luo, Lailong   I-301, III-86
Luo, Xiaoqing   III-56
Luo, Yixin   III-471
Luo, Zihui   II-481
Lv, Congdong   II-290
Lv, Pin   III-512, III-521
Lv, Qiujian   II-84
Lv, Zhiqiang   I-203, I-227, I-391, II-457

Ma, Dongchao   III-529
Ma, Li   III-529
Ma, Ming   III-108
Ma, Teng   III-244
Ma, Wenshuo   II-303
Ma, Ying   II-326
Ma, Zhenjie   I-29
Ma, Zhuo   III-244
Ma, Zuchao   II-494
Man, Yufei   I-597
Mei, Aoxue   I-376
Mei, Luoyu   I-494
Meng, Huixiao   I-429
Meng, Weizhi   II-186, II-624
Mi, Jiazhi   III-471
Mou, Wenhao   II-198

Nguyen, Camtu   I-275
Ning, Pan   I-523
Niu, Guohang   II-575
Niu, Qiang   III-441
Niu, Qun   I-78

Ouyang, Tao   I-535

Printed in the United States
by Baker & Taylor Publisher Services